Places Rated Retirement Guide

Finding the best places in America for retirement living

Richard Boyer & David Savageau

Rand McNally & Company

Chicago • New York • San Francisco

Acknowledgments

We have learned much from talking with the following demographers, all of whom have a special interest in the migration of retired people in America: Gladys Bowles, formerly of the U.S. Department of Agriculture, now a private consultant in Athens, Georgia; William Clifford of North Carolina State University, Raleigh; Glenn Fuguitt of the University of Wisconsin, Madison; Daniel Lichter of Pennsylvania State University, State College; and Stephen Tordella of the University of Wisconsin, Madison.

We also recognize our debt to the many people in government and with private organizations who kept our research out of blind alleys and pointed it in proper directions. Many of their publications are cited in this book.

Finally, special thanks are due Calvin L. Beale of the U.S. Department of Agriculture, an expert on the country's economic regions and their population trends, who shared with us in conversations and in correspondence his vast knowledge of an inexhaustible subject, the geography of America's small places.

Publisher's Note

Contents

Leisure Living: Making the most of local recreation 133

Putting It All Together: Finding your best retirement place 169

Retirement Place Finder 191

List of Tables and Maps 197

Introduction

When you retire, will you stay where you are? Most retired people do. But each year a growing number of people, in dropping their job responsibilities, pack up and move to sometimes distant places where they can live a life of their own choosing.

There are ample reasons for staying put. It certainly is easier to hang on to what you have. If you relocate, you might be able to take the philodendron and the oak blanket chest, but you can't necessarily take family and friends. Nor can you transport the familiarity born of launching children into the world, working at a job, and keeping a home in one town. You've known your neighbors for years, your doctor knows you, you've memorized the movie theater's phone number, and you know where to find a discount hardware store.

Besides, the climate is great, your neighborhood is safe, and there are plenty of cultural and recreational opportunities to take advantage of now that you've got the time. Your finances are limited now, but they're still secure, and the family home is bought and paid for. What you ultimately may want in retirement is R and R in familiar territory, not a new series of activities that requires high energy and risk on your part just to put down new roots.

If all this is true, you should stay put. But perhaps there is someplace in this country where you might thrive even more than you do now. And perhaps, too, it is a lack of objective information that keeps you where you are.

In 1981, the authors published *Places Rated Almanac: Your guide to finding the best places to live in America*, a book that provides tens of thousands of facts about 277 metropolitan areas throughout the country and is designed to meet the needs of a wide range of Americans—from college graduates looking for a job, to businesspeople being transferred to another state, to persons in midlife seeking a place to "start over."

The response to *Places Rated Almanac* has confirmed that people are indeed eager for reliable, practical information about places. *Places Rated Retirement Guide* is meant for those who are retired or are beginning to plan for retirement, and who may be weighing the pluses and minuses of moving or staying. It is a guide that offers a wealth of facts about 107 carefully chosen places, places that together have attracted a large number of the retirees who have made interstate moves since 1970. You won't find these facts in standard guidebooks or the puff-piece literature from highly publicized resort-retirement spots. Where, for instance, can you count on tougher driving examinations because of your age? Where do hurricanes have a history of repeatedly hitting? Where might you have trouble finding an apartment to rent?

But *Places Rated Retirement Guide* is more than a collection of interesting information about places because, like *Places Rated Almanac*, it also rates and ranks them. The 107 places are compared on the basis of six factors that greatly affect the quality of retirement life:

climate, housing, money matters, personal safety, health care, and leisure activities. *Places Rated Retirement Guide* might be considered a self-help book, but instead of describing stages, turning points, or transformations in later life, it gives you the facts you need to begin evaluating places nationwide; it may even help you decide whether to stay or go.

WHERE ARE THESE PLACES?

If you were suddenly asked, in a kind of geographical word-association test, to name five states that spring to mind when you hear the word "retirement," you might well say Arizona, California, Florida, New Mexico, and Texas. Each of these states has attracted so many retired people that several of their cities— Phoenix, San Diego, Fort Myers, Albuquerque, and McAllen, to name a few—have acquired the reputation of stereotypical retirement destinations.

But other states also belong in the geography of retirement. Arkansas ranks second after Florida in the portion of its population over 65, partly because thousands of retired Chicagoans, Iowans, and Nebraskans have moved to its Ozark counties. Oregon and Washington are also drawing Midwesterners, and retirees from southern California, too. In the wooded mountain counties of Georgia, North Carolina, and Virginia, many New Englanders, New Yorkers, and even disaffected Floridians are among the older population.

To determine where people over 65 are now moving, *Places Rated* consulted several demographers: Calvin L. Beale of the U.S. Department of Agriculture, a leading authority on American regional population trends; Gladys Bowles, a specialist on the migration of different age groups in America; Glenn Fuguitt of the University of Wisconsin and one of his former students, Daniel Lichter at Pennsylvania State University; and William Clifford of North Carolina State University; all of whom have studied the effect of retirement on the growth of American counties; and Stephen Tordella at the University of Wisconsin's Applied Population Laboratory, who recently completed a study using Medicare records and Census Bureau population counts.

Surprisingly, over the last 15 years fewer than 250 counties out of the country's more than 3,100 have attracted older people at a significant rate. Many, like Macomb County outside Detroit, are suburban enclaves in major metropolitan areas that are losing population. Others, like Wyoming's Johnson County, appear too isolated and sparsely settled for their gains in older population to indicate a trend.

Based on the demographic evidence and the advice of experts, *Places Rated* selected for comparison 107 places that reflect the expressed preferences of many mobile retirees. Although these places do not by any means include every desirable retirement destination, they do include many of the country's best and represent the kinds of places many people are choosing to

retire to. Care was taken to choose places outside the Sun Belt with much to offer retirees; many northern and mid-latitude locations are included, as well as year-round-golf spots. In all, 35 states are represented.

Thirty-four of the places—Austin, Boise, Miami, Ocala, San Antonio, and Tucson, to name a few—are each large enough to be called a Metropolitan Statistical Area, generally referred to in these pages as a "metro area." A metro area is defined by the U.S. Office of Management and Budget as an area having a central city of at least 50,000 population, or an urbanized area of at least 50,000 population located in a county or counties with a total population of 100,000 or more. For statistical purposes, a metro area's boundaries are those of the surrounding county or counties. Metropolitan Phoenix, for example, includes the Arizona capital plus Chandler, Scottsdale, Sun City, Tempe, and other places in suburban Maricopa County. A few metro areas in this book embrace more than one county. Metropolitan San Antonio, for example, includes heavily urbanized Bexar County, plus two suburban counties, Comal and Guadalupe.

Two thirds of the 107 retirement places, however, aren't metro areas. They are mainly rural counties and prime examples of the "countryside turnaround" that caused demographers some surprise in the late 1970s. After years of decline, these areas began growing again as people, especially retired people, moved in for low-cost, safe living in splendid natural surroundings. *Places Rated* included these non-metropolitan counties whenever the 1980 census revealed that relatively large numbers of older people had been moving there.

To make it easy to distinguish the metro areas from the more rural places in the listings, rankings, and Place Profiles throughout this book, capital letters are used for the metro areas (for example, COLORADO SPRINGS, CO) and capital and lowercase letters for non-metro places (Beaufort–Hilton Head, SC).

THE WAYS RETIREMENT PLACES ARE RATED

"Fiftieth in everything," Governor Rudy Perpich of Minnesota recently said of South Dakota, a neighboring state and competitor for industrial employers and the jobs they bring.

It may seem the utmost of brass to judge and rank American places from best to worst. Yet we all take part in the pastime, and we've been at it for quite a while. "There are plenty of Americans who regard Kansas as almost barbaric," noted H. L. Mencken in 1931, "just as there are other Americans who shudder whenever they think of Arkansas, Ohio, Indiana, Oklahoma, Texas, or California."

Mencken wrote these words in his *American Mercury* magazine to introduce his formula for "scientifically" measuring the progress of civilization in each of the American states. He mixed the numbers of Boy Scouts and *Atlantic Monthly* subscribers with those of lynchings and pellagra victims, added a dash of *Who's Who* listings and rates for divorce and murder, threw in figures for rainfall and gasoline consumption, and found that, hands down, Mississippi was the worst American state. Few were surprised by this finding since Mencken didn't like the rural South anyway. Massachusetts, a state he admired, came out best.

But Massachusetts got a demotion of sorts in 1978, when it was rated the worst state for retirement by Chase Econometrics Association, a well-known consulting firm. And the best state for retirement, according to the Chase forecasters? Utah.

You can forget how states stack up against each other when it comes to retirement. Springtime rain, a low cost of living, freedom from crime, and access to trout-filled water don't necessarily begin or end at major political boundaries.

Places Rated Retirement Guide, we believe, is more objective than Mencken and more useful than any system that limits its evaluations to states. There is a world of perceptible differences between the California areas of San Diego and Clear Lake; they can be more important in retirement than the differences between California and, say, South Carolina. This retirement guide is also more objective than the opinions that travelers may casually share in an airport bar or at a rest stop on the interstate highway. Each of the 107 places is rated by criteria that most persons planning for retirement deem highly important.

- Climate is rated on mildness; that is, where outdoor temperatures remain closest to 65 degrees Fahrenheit for the greatest percentage of time.
- Housing facilities are compared in terms of cost. We examine prices, taxes, and utility bills, and we note the buyer's choices from among single homes, condominiums, and mobile homes. We also look at rental costs.
- Economic matters are examined to see how far Social Security checks will go in each place. We also evaluate the part-time job market and the local outlook for economic growth.
- Personal safety is measured in terms of violent and property crimes per capita.
- Health care is evaluated on the basis of the supply of general health-care facilities and special options available.
- The chapter on leisure living compares recreational and cultural assets such as golf courses and libraries, orchestras and opera companies, inland lakes and national parks.

You may not agree with our rating system. If you like, you can devise your own system using the vast array of data presented. You may, for example, rule out all rural places, hot climates, and high taxes. You may give more weight to personal safety than to good fishing spots. For you, a place where fixed incomes go further might be more important than an abundance of physicians.

We have tried to put together the most up-to-date facts for all 107 retirement places. In most instances, our information is as fresh as 1983; in a few isolated cases, the most recent statistics predate 1980. Our sources, which we document throughout the book, are principally different branches of the federal government, but pertinent private sources have also been tapped. Bear in mind that the information in *Places Rated Retirement Guide* is somewhat perishable. An oil spill on the Gulf Coast can ruin a Texas barrier island's stretch of beach for years to come, just as a series of hurricanes may multiply a Florida condo's hazard-insurance payments beyond belief. With so much in life that is unpredictable, it's necessary to supplement *Places Rated Retirement Guide* with your own independent verification.

But for now you can be sure that you'll find mobile homes used by more people in Lake Havasu City–Kingman, Arizona, than on Cape Cod; public golf courses in greater supply in Myrtle Beach, South

Large and Small Retirement Places

Largest Metro Areas	1980 Population	Smallest Metro Areas	1980 Population
1. SAN DIEGO, CA	1,861,846	1. LAS CRUCES, NM	96,340
2. MIAMI, FL	1,625,979	2. STATE COLLEGE, PA	112,760
3. PHOENIX, AZ	1,508,030	3. CHARLOTTESVILLE, VA	113,568
4. SAN ANTONIO, TX	1,071,954	4. OCALA, FL	122,488
5. FORT LAUDERDALE –HOLLYWOOD, FL	1,014,043	5. OLYMPIA, WA	124,264

Largest Non-Metro Counties		Smallest Non-Metro Counties	
1. Toms River– Barnegat Bay, NJ	346,038	1. Rappahannock, VA	6,093
2. San Luis Obispo, CA	155,345	2. Bull Shoals, AR	11,334
3. Cape Cod, MA	147,925	3. Fredericksburg, TX	13,532
4. Myrtle Beach, SC	101,419	4. Rockport–Aransas Pass, TX	14,260
5. Rehoboth Bay– Indian River Bay, DE	98,004	5. Big Sandy, TN	14,901

Growth of 65-and-Over Population in the Retirement Places, 1970–80

Greatest Growth	Overall 65+ Increase*	Increase Due to 65+ In-migration†
1. Carson City, NV	237.47%	112.21%
2. Lake Havasu City–Kingman, AZ	217.81	116.86
3. MELBOURNE–TITUSVILLE–COCOA, FL	170.91	96.45
4. LAS VEGAS, NV	150.98	51.63
5. FORT MYERS–CAPE CORAL, FL	132.06	98.32
Least Growth		
1. Camden–Penobscot Bay, ME	13.84%	5.06%
2. Brattleboro, VT	16.82	0.00
3. ATLANTIC CITY–CAPE MAY, NJ	18.36	6.22
4. LEXINGTON–FAYETTE, KY	25.92	0.00
5. Rappahannock, VA	26.69	1.27

Source: U.S. Bureau of the Census.

*Includes both in-migration and "aging in place."

†Based on Census Survival Rate Method for determining in-migration.

Carolina, than in Phoenix; and more acres of inland water in Kalispell, Montana, than in Albuquerque.

FINDING YOUR WAY IN THE CHAPTERS

Each of *Places Rated Retirement Guide*'s chapters has four parts:

• The **introductory section** provides general information on a major retirement concern along with facts and figures to help you evaluate retirement places. We also describe the system we use to rate and rank the 107 places for that particular concern. A sample comparison analyzes why one place performs better than another in the ratings.

• **Places Rated:** This part ranks the 107 retirement places. They are listed first in their rank order, from best to worst, along with their *Places Rated* score. An alphabetical list of the places follows, with their individual rankings, so that you can quickly find the ranks of the ones you're interested in.

• **Place Profiles:** Arranged alphabetically by place, these capsule comparisons cover all the elements used to rate the retirement places, and usually provide additional data. Here you can see differences among the areas at a glance.

• **Et Cetera:** This section expands on topics mentioned in the introductory part and offers other information for retirement planning. The items range from lists of the worst places for ragweed pollen to essays on such subjects as state tax breaks for older persons and tips for buying supplemental health insurance.

The final chapter, "Putting It All Together," adds up the ranks to identify America's best all-round retirement places and discusses their good and bad points. We also weigh the pros and cons of city and countryside retirement living, and broadly characterize the regions where these 107 places are found.

A WORD ABOUT THE NAMES OF THE RETIREMENT PLACES

The 107 places examined in this guide are not towns, villages, cities, or national parks—they are counties. In the case of the 34 metropolitan areas, we used the official name assigned to them by the Office of Management and Budget.

For the non-metropolitan counties, however, a more flexible approach seemed warranted. Several counties described in this book have names that make them readily identifiable to most people. Maui County, Hawaii, is one such place; Rappahannock County, Virginia, is another. Other counties—such as Santa Fe in New Mexico, Bennington in Vermont, and San Luis Obispo on the southern California coast—have the same name as their well-known seats of government. In such instances, it seemed natural that the retirement place should be called by its county name.

But county names for the most part aren't as current in the popular mind as they once were. Marion County, Arkansas, is one of 17 counties in the United States honoring Francis Marion, the "Swamp Fox" of the Revolutionary War. The name may be meaningless to a Kansas City resident and only vaguely familiar to a citizen of Little Rock. Bull Shoals, the name of a huge water recreation area in the county, may be better known to both. So in our list of places, you'll find that Bull Shoals is the name given to the retirement place composing Marion County, Arkansas.

A similar case is Barnstable County, Massachusetts, which embraces all of Cape Cod from Buzzards Bay out U.S. 6 on the famous sandy spit of land to Provincetown. Long ago, the term Cape Cod elbowed Barnstable County aside in popular New England usage. Accordingly, Cape Cod is our name for the retirement place in Barnstable County.

Sometimes the name given a non-metropolitan retirement place is that of the principal population center(s); thus, New Mexico's Luna County becomes Deming, and Arizona's Mohave County becomes Lake Havasu City–Kingman. At other times, the name of a town may be paired with a well-known natural feature: Hamilton–Bitterroot Valley is our name for Ravalli County, Montana; likewise, New Hampshire's Carroll County becomes North Conway–White Mountains.

The list that follows gives the names of the 107 retirement places as they are used throughout the book (a reminder: names of metro areas are in capital letters) and shows their component counties. The Retirement Place Finder at the end of the book lists the names of selected towns and cities located within these counties.

The Places We Rate: 107 Retirement Places

Retirement Places and Component Counties	1980 Census Count	1970 Census Count	Population Increase, 1970–1980	Retirement Places and Component Counties	1980 Census Count	1970 Census Count	Population Increase, 1970–1980
ALBUQUERQUE, NM Bernalillo County	419,700	315,774	32.9%	**ATLANTIC CITY–CAPE MAY, NJ** Atlantic and Cape May counties	276,385	234,597	17.8
ASHEVILLE, NC Buncombe County	160,934	145,056	10.9	**AUSTIN, TX** Hays, Travis, and Williamson counties	536,688	360,463	48.9
Athens–Cedar Creek Lake, TX Henderson County	42,606	26,466	61.0				

Retirement Places and Component Counties	1980 Census Count	1970 Census Count	Population Increase, 1970–1980
Bar Harbor–Frenchman Bay, ME Hancock County	41,781	34,590	20.8
Beaufort–Hilton Head, SC Beaufort County	65,364	51,136	27.8
Bend, OR Deschutes County	62,142	30,442	104.1
Bennington, VT Bennington County	33,345	29,282	13.9
Benton–Kentucky Lake, KY Marshall County	25,637	20,381	25.8
Big Sandy, TN Benton County	14,901	12,126	22.9
Biloxi–Gulfport, MS Hancock, Harrison, and Stone counties	191,918	160,070	19.9
Boise City, ID Ada County	173,036	112,230	54.2
Branson–Lake Taneycomo, MO Taney County	20,467	13,023	57.2
Brattleboro, VT Windham County	36,933	33,476	10.3
Brevard, NC Transylvania County	23,417	19,713	18.8
Brunswick–Golden Isles, GA Glynn County	54,981	50,528	8.8
Bull Shoals, AR Marion County	11,334	7,000	61.9
Camden–Penobscot Bay, ME Knox County	32,941	29,013	13.5
Canton–Lake Tawakoni, TX Van Zandt County	31,426	22,155	41.8
Cape Cod, MA Barnstable County	147,925	96,656	53.0
Carson City, NV Carson City city and Douglas County	51,443	22,350	130.2
Cassville–Roaring River, MO Barry County	24,408	19,597	24.5
Charlottesville, VA Charlottesville city; Albemarle, Fluvanna, and Greene counties	113,568	89,529	26.9
Clarkesville–Mount Airy, GA Habersham County	25,020	20,691	20.9
Clear Lake, CA Lake County	36,366	19,548	86.0
Coeur d'Alene, ID Kootenai County	59,770	35,332	69.2
Colorado Springs, CO El Paso County	309,424	235,972	31.1
Cookeville, TN Putnam County	47,601	35,487	34.1
Crossville, TN Cumberland County	28,676	20,733	38.3
Daytona Beach, FL Volusia County	258,762	169,487	52.7
Delta, CO Delta County	21,225	15,286	38.9
Deming, NM Luna County	15,585	11,706	33.1
Eagle River, WI Vilas County	16,535	10,958	50.9
Easton–Chesapeake Bay, MD Talbot County	25,604	23,682	8.1
Fairhope–Gulf Shores, AL Baldwin County	78,440	59,382	32.1
Fort Collins, CO Larimer County	149,184	89,900	65.9
Fort Lauderdale–Hollywood, FL Broward County	1,014,043	620,100	63.5
Fort Myers–Cape Coral, FL Lee County	205,266	105,216	95.1
Fredericksburg, TX Gillespie County	13,532	10,553	28.2
Front Royal, VA Warren County	21,200	15,301	38.6
Gainesville–Lake Sidney Lanier, GA Hall County	75,649	59,405	27.3
Grand Junction, CO Mesa County	81,530	54,374	49.9
Hamilton–Bitterroot Valley, MT Ravalli County	22,493	14,409	56.1
Harrison, AR Boone County	26,067	19,073	36.7
Hendersonville, NC Henderson County	58,580	42,804	36.9
Hot Springs–Lake Ouachita, AR Garland County	69,916	54,131	29.2
Houghton Lake, MI Roscommon County	16,374	9,892	65.5
Kalispell, MT Flathead County	51,966	39,460	31.7
Keene, NH Cheshire County	62,116	52,364	18.6
Kerrville, TX Kerr County	28,780	19,454	47.9
Laconia–Lake Winnipesaukee, NH Belknap County	42,884	32,367	32.5
Lake Havasu City–Kingman, AZ Mohave County	55,693	25,857	115.4
Lakeland–Winter Haven, FL Polk County	321,652	228,515	40.8
Lake O' The Cherokees, OK Delaware County	23,946	17,767	34.8
Lancaster, PA Lancaster County	362,346	320,079	13.2
Las Cruces, NM Dona Ana County	96,340	69,773	38.1
Las Vegas, NV Clark County	461,816	273,288	69.0
Lexington–Fayette, KY Bourbon, Clark, Fayette, Jessamine, Scott, and Woodford counties	317,629	266,701	19.3
Lincoln City–Newport, OR Lincoln County	35,264	25,755	36.9
Maui, HI Maui County	70,847	46,156	53.5

Places Rated Retirement Guide

107 Retirement Places

MN

WI

Eagle River

Rhinelander

Petoskey-Straits of Mackinac

MI

Oscoda-Huron Shore

Houghton Lake

Traverse City-Grand Traverse Bay

ME

Bar Harbor-Frenchman Bay

Camden-Penobscot Bay

VT

North Conway-White Mountains

Laconia-Lake Winnipesaukee

Brattleboro

NH

Keene

Bennington

MA

CT

RI

Cape Cod

NY

Monticello-Liberty

NJ

Toms River-Barnegat Bay

ATLANTIC CITY-CAPE MAY

IA

PA

STATE COLLEGE

LANCASTER

IL

IN

OH

MO

Winchester

Front Royal

Rappahannock

WV

MD

DE

Rehoboth Bay-Indian River Bay

Ocean City-Assateague Island

Easton-Chesapeake Bay

CHARLOTTESVILLE

Cassville-Roaring River

LEXINGTON-FAYETTE

KY

VA

SPRINGFIELD

Table Rock Lake

Benton-Kentucky Lake

Paris

Cookeville

NC

ASHEVILLE

Lake O' The Cherokees

Branson-Lake Taneycomo

Big Sandy

Crossville

Hendersonville

Brevard

Mountain Home-Norfork Lake

Clarkesville-Mount Airy

Tahlequah-Lake Tenkiller

TN

Gainesville-Lake Sidney Lanier

Myrtle Beach

AR

Bull Shoals

Harrison

SC

Hot Springs-Lake Ouachita

AL

GA

Beaufort-Hilton Head

Canton-Lake Tawakoni

MS

Athens-Cedar Creek Lake

Brunswick-Golden Isles

LA

Fairhope-Gulf Shores

FL

BILOXI-GULFPORT

OCALA

DAYTONA BEACH

ORLANDO

MELBOURNE-TITUSVILLE-COCOA

LAKELAND-WINTER HAVEN

SARASOTA-BRADENTON

WEST PALM BEACH-BOCA RATON

FORT MYERS-CAPE CORAL

FORT LAUDERDALE-HOLLYWOOD

MIAMI

□ METROPOLITAN AREA

● Non-Metropolitan County

Retirement Places and Component Counties	1980 Census Count	1970 Census Count	Population Increase, 1970–1980	Retirement Places and Component Counties	1980 Census Count	1970 Census Count	Population Increase, 1970–1980
McALLEN–PHARR–EDINBURG, TX Hidalgo County	283,229	181,535	56.0	Rehoboth Bay–Indian River Bay, DE Sussex County	98,004	80,356	22.0
MEDFORD, OR Jackson County	132,456	94,533	40.1	RENO, NV Washoe County	193,623	121,068	59.9
MELBOURNE–TITUSVILLE–COCOA, FL Brevard County	272,959	230,006	18.7	Rhinelander, WI Oneida County	31,216	24,427	27.8
MIAMI, FL Dade County	1,625,979	1,267,792	28.3	Rockport–Aransas Pass, TX Aransas County	14,260	8,902	60.2
Missoula, MT Missoula County	76,016	58,263	30.5	Roswell, NM Chaves County	51,103	43,335	17.9
Monticello–Liberty, NY Sullivan County	65,155	52,580	23.9	St. George–Zion, UT Washington County	26,065	13,669	90.7
Mountain Home–Norfork Lake, AR Baxter County	27,409	15,319	78.9	SAN ANTONIO, TX Bexar, Comal, and Guadalupe counties	1,071,954	888,179	20.7
Myrtle Beach, SC Horry County	101,419	69,992	44.9	SAN DIEGO, CA San Diego County	1,861,846	1,357,854	37.1
Nevada City–Donner, CA Nevada County	51,645	26,346	96.0	San Luis Obispo, CA San Luis Obispo County	155,345	105,690	47.0
North Conway–White Mountains, NH Carroll County	27,931	18,548	50.6	Santa Fe, NM Santa Fe County	75,306	54,774	37.5
Oak Harbor, WA Island County	44,048	27,011	63.1	SANTA ROSA, CA Sonoma County	299,827	204,885	46.3
OCALA, FL Marion County	122,488	69,030	77.4	SARASOTA–BRADENTON, FL Manatee and Sarasota counties	350,693	217,528	61.2
Ocean City–Assateague Island, MD Worcester County	30,889	24,442	26.4	SPRINGFIELD, MO Christian and Greene counties	207,704	168,053	23.6
OLYMPIA, WA Thurston County	124,264	76,894	61.6	STATE COLLEGE, PA Centre County	112,760	99,267	13.6
ORLANDO, FL Orange, Osceola, and Seminole counties	700,699	453,270	54.6	Table Rock Lake, MO Stone County	15,587	9,921	57.1
Oscoda–Huron Shore, MI Iosco County	28,349	24,905	13.8	Tahlequah–Lake Tenkiller, OK Cherokee County	30,684	23,174	32.4
Paris, TN Henry County	28,656	23,749	20.7	Toms River–Barnegat Bay, NJ Ocean County	346,038	208,470	66.0
Petoskey–Straits of Mackinac, MI Emmet County	22,992	18,331	25.4	Traverse City–Grand Traverse Bay, MI Grand Traverse County	54,899	39,175	40.1
PHOENIX, AZ Maricopa County	1,508,030	971,228	55.3	TUCSON, AZ Pima County	531,263	351,667	51.1
Port Angeles–Strait of Juan de Fuca, WA Clallam County	51,648	34,770	48.5	Twain Harte–Yosemite, CA Tuolumne County	33,920	22,169	53.0
Prescott, AZ Yavapai County	68,145	37,005	84.2	WEST PALM BEACH–BOCA RATON, FL Palm Beach County	573,125	348,993	64.2
Rappahannock, VA Rappahannock County	6,093	5,199	17.2	Winchester, VA Winchester city and Frederick County	54,367	43,536	24.9
Red Bluff–Sacramento Valley, CA Tehama County	38,888	29,517	31.7	Yuma, AZ Yuma County	90,554	60,827	48.9

Source: U.S. Bureau of the Census.

Metro area names given above are those in use prior to June 30, 1983, when some of these designations were changed by the U.S. Office of Management and Budget.

Places
Rated
Retirement
Guide

Climate and Terrain:
Finding your place
in the sun

Climate and the day-to-day weather patterns it produces underlie all human pursuits. Climate affects our leisure activities, our pocketbooks, even our moods and health.

Patterns of recreation and leisure are largely molded by climate and terrain. Natives of San Antonio, Texas, which has 111 days per year of at least 90-degree heat, gather at backyard parties around the swimming pool. Bostonians look forward to summer weekends on cool Cape Cod. Residents of Colorado Springs can go hiking and skiing in the Rockies, while folks in Gainesville, Georgia, enjoy boating and fishing at Lake Sidney Lanier.

The economic impact of climate seems greater each year as bills for home heating and cooling increase with the rising costs of energy. Air conditioning, which makes the Sun Belt attractive year round, can be more expensive than home heating, leading cost-conscious retirees to consider moving to such mid-South states as Arkansas and North Carolina, where neither winter nor summer energy bills are costly.

Most of us believe that climate and weather profoundly affect our moods and emotions. Long, snowy winters that confine people indoors can have adverse emotional effects; many people become irritable when the weather gets so hot they cannot sleep. We are cheered by brisk, sunny weather but sobered by cloudy, rainy days or very cold temperatures. In addition, as a person grows older, the body becomes increasingly sensitive to weather changes and to extremes of heat and cold. Relative humidity, barometric pressure, and altitude are just a few factors related to climate or terrain that can influence your physical well-being. Some areas of the country are in fact better than others for sufferers of such maladies as asthma, arthritis, rheumatism, and heart problems, so an informed decision about where to relocate can make a real difference in the way you feel.

Most Americans are unaware of the enormous variety of climates they have to choose from, and the extreme range of weather conditions that comes with this wide choice. When asked where the mild climates are to be found, these people invariably answer that they're in the South, where the "good, warm" weather is. Not so. Many of America's best—and mildest—climates are found north of the Mason-Dixon line. Many of the most rugged and uncomfortable are found in the South. America has seven major climatic zones, and wide variation within each: We have northern maritime climates, subtropical marine climates, extremely mild Mediterranean climates, lowland desert climates, desert highland climates, southerly mountain climates, tropical "paradise" climates, rigorous northern continental climates, windward slope cli-

1

mates, leeward slope climates . . . You name it—we've probably got it.

This climatic variety allows a person considering a retirement move to choose a place that will allow the greatest personal comfort and the best use of leisure time. And most people would agree that these are two very precious commodities in the retirement years.

WHAT "MAKES" A CLIMATE?

Five factors have a major influence on the climate of a particular area: water, latitude, prevailing winds, elevation, and mountain ranges.

Water, especially in large bodies like oceans, has a moderating effect on temperatures. Water warms up slowly, holds much more heat than does land, and cools more slowly. Therefore, places near or surrounded by large bodies of water tend to be cooler in summer and warmer in winter than others far from water. Of all the 107 places presented in *Places Rated Retirement Guide*, San Diego, located on the Pacific Ocean and in the path of prevailing winds that have traveled thousands of miles across this large body of water, has the mildest climate. These prevailing ocean breezes give San Diego its extreme mildness. In fact, of

the five mildest retirement places in this book, all are located in the path of prevailing Pacific winds.

On the other hand, places in the middle of large land masses experience large swings of temperature. This is because land masses heat and cool quickly. Without the stabilizing effect of a large body of water, temperatures in these areas may rise and fall dramatically, both from day to day and from season to season. This type of climate—called continental—tends to become more rigorous as latitude (distance from the equator) increases. The closer to the poles we move, the more exaggerated the seasonal shifts become, because polar locations show the greatest seasonal variation in the amount and intensity of sunlight. In Fairbanks, Alaska, for example, the average "day" in December is only four hours long. But in late June, each day receives more than 18 hours of sun, and the heat is intense. Thus, places in the North and Far North can experience not only bitterly cold winters but broiling summers as well!

Comparing the mildest and least mild places in *Places Rated Retirement Guide* shows how the factor of water versus land mass works together with latitude to determine climatic mildness. The mildest place, San Diego, lies in a midsoutherly latitude on the shores of the world's largest body of water. San Diego's lowest average temperatures come in January, when the monthly mean dips to 55.2 degrees; August is the warmest month, with a mean temperature of 71.4 degrees. The least mild retirement place, Rhinelander, Wisconsin, lies in a much more northerly latitude and in the center of the North American land mass. There, the seasonal swings are much more pronounced, with monthly mean temperatures that range from a frigid 12.8 degrees in January to a warm 68.4 degrees in July.

The effect that prevailing winds have on climate is demonstrated by another pair of retirement places: Port Angeles–Strait of Juan de Fuca, Washington, and Bar Harbor–Frenchman Bay, Maine. Both of these places, located on major oceans, have marine climates; both have northerly locations. But Port Angeles ranks fourth among 107 retirement places in climatic mildness while Bar Harbor ranks 45th—even though Port Angeles, at about the same latitude as Newfoundland, is considerably farther north than Bar Harbor. Why is Port Angeles so much milder? The answer lies in the prevailing winds, which in North America blow from west to east. This is good for the West Coast, not so good for the East Coast. Places along the West Coast receive the full impact of winds that have moved thousands of miles over water, and thus enjoy much more of a maritime effect than places along the East Coast. And, thanks to the prevailing westerlies, cities many miles inland from the West Coast still receive some of the benefits of the Pacific. But inland cities in the East feel few consequences of the Atlantic save on those rare occasions when the prevailing wind direc-

---

The 8 Hottest Retirement Places

	90-Degree Days per Year	Relative Humidity
Athens–Cedar Creek Lake, TX	95	68%
AUSTIN, TX	101	67
Brunswick–Golden Isles, GA	75	75
FORT MYERS–CAPE CORAL, FL	106	76
Hot Springs–Lake Ouachita, AR	90	70
Kerrville, TX	101	63
ORLANDO, FL	104	74
Rockport–Aransas Pass, TX	77	80

Listed above are those retirement places described in the Place Profiles that combine 75 or more 90-degree days per year with an average relative humidity greater than 60 percent. Four places have more than 130 ninety-degree days per year—Las Vegas (131), Phoenix (164), Tucson (139), and Yuma (168)—but all of these have less than 40 percent relative humidity.

The 9 Coldest Retirement Places

	Zero Days per Year	Freezing Days per Year
Bennington, VT	17	166
Camden–Penobscot Bay, ME	11	152
FORT COLLINS, CO	15	175
Houghton Lake, MI	25	175
Kalispell, MT	17	191
Keene, NH	16	167
North Conway–White Mountains, NH	25	187
Oscoda–Huron Shore, MI	13	171
Rhinelander, WI	39	182

Listed above are those retirement places described in the Place Profiles that combine more than ten zero days per year with more than 150 freezing days.

tion *doesn't* prevail. (Unfortunately, this reversal of wind direction often brings a storm.)

Elevation, or height above sea level, has the same general effect as a higher latitude. Each 1,000 feet of elevation lowers the average temperature by 3.3 degrees Fahrenheit. Places that combine high altitudes with southerly latitudes tend to enjoy the mild, short winters of the South and the cooler nights and crisp falls of the North. Locations in the southern Appalachian Mountains in the East and the mountains of the Southwest have long been known for their mild four-season climates.

Mountain ranges help determine climate and weather by acting as giant barriers that deflect and channel winds and weather. The weather—and also climate—on one side of a mountain range is oftentimes radically different from that on the other. Because of this mountain ranges are natural dividing lines between climate zones.

AMERICA'S MAJOR CLIMATIC REGIONS

Mountain ranges delineate the seven major climatic regions of the continental United States. As explained above, the Pacific Coast is the mildest of these regions,

and the northern portion of the Great Interior is the most rigorous. The Intermountain Plateau (which is also called the Great Basin), lying between the Sierra Nevada range to the west and the Rocky Mountains to the east, is noted primarily for its dryness. Some of the best retirement climates—because of their variety and mildness—are found in the southern portion of this area. The southern half of the Appalachian Mountains region also offers climates that are both mild and variable.

Most Americans live in the large climatic zone called the Great Interior, Southern Plains, and Lowlands. This region, ironically, also happens to be the least desirable as far as mildness and human comfort are concerned. Those who live in its northern part are plagued by severe winters and hot, humid summers with very short springs and autumns. In the southern portion, winters are mild and springs and autumns are longer, but the "steam bath" summers are very uncomfortable and debilitating. The climate of the East Coast, called the Middle and North Atlantic Lowlands, is similar to that of the Great Interior, but milder and somewhat damper. Right on the coast, winters are milder and summers are noticeably cooler. There are some excellent retirement climates to be found in this

Climatic Regions of the United States

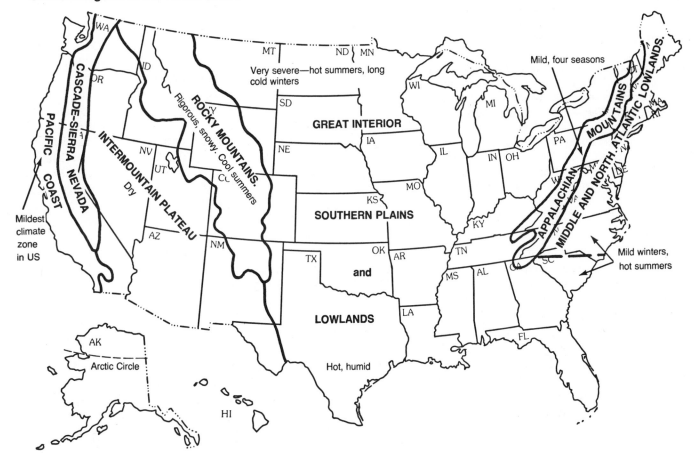

The 11 Rainiest Retirement Places

	Inches per Year		Inches per Year
Nevada City– Donner, CA	67.6	Hot Springs–Lake Ouachita, AR	55
Lincoln City– Newport, OR	63	FORT MYERS–CAPE CORAL, FL	54
MIAMI, FL	60	Gainesville–Lake Sidney Lanier, GA	53
BILOXI–GULFPORT, MS	59	OLYMPIA, WA	51
Clarkesville–Mount Airy, GA	58	ORLANDO, FL	51
Brunswick–Golden Isles, GA	55		

The 9 Snowiest Retirement Places

	Inches per Year		Inches per Year
Nevada City– Donner, CA	240	Kalispell, MT	67
North Conway–White Mountains, NH	98	Camden–Penobscot Bay, ME	60
Houghton Lake, MI	83	Keene, NH	60
Petoskey–Straits of Mackinac, MI	74	Bennington, VT	57
		Rhinelander, WI	56

Listed above are those retirement places described in the Place Profiles that average more than 50 inches of rain or more than 50 inches of snow per year.

Snowy (and Rainy) Nevada County

Nevada City–Donner, California, averages 240 inches of snow each winter, yet its climate is surprisingly mild (it ranks ninth among 107 retirement places). How can this be? Nevada County, perched on the western slope of the Sierra Nevada and with elevations ranging from 5,000 to 7,000 feet, receives a continual supply of moisture-laden winds from the Pacific. As these winds reach the mountains they ascend the slopes, dropping moisture as they climb. In the summertime this means rain—more than 67 inches per year. In the winter tremendous quantities of snow are released. Most people automatically equate large snowfalls with cold climates, but this is not always the case, as mild, alpine Nevada City–Donner proves. The climate is mild—but you'd better like snow, and lots of it.

region, especially in coastal locations.

The high-altitude regions that include the Rocky Mountains, the Cascades and Sierra Nevada, and the northern half of the Appalachian Mountains are resort areas because they all have cool, crisp, sunny summers with cold nights, and winters that provide plenty of snow for outdoor sports. Although not very mild, some of these places have excellent potential for retirees, depending on the health, weather sensitivity, and preferences of the individual.

Hawaii is the only state in the Union situated in the tropical zone. The islands experience very small seasonal temperature changes, their summer temperatures averaging only 4 to 8 degrees higher than those

in winter. The island chain is affected mostly by the moisture-laden trade winds from over the Pacific that have a modifying effect on the heat.

(Alaska, nearly one third of which lies north of the Arctic Circle, has a climate ranging from bitterly cold in the north to relatively mild in the southern regions. So rigorous is the climate there that none of the 107 retirement places considered by *Places Rated* is in Alaska.)

JUDGING CLIMATIC MILDNESS

More than any other climate-related variable, temperature most affects human comfort and our daily range of activities. Bioclimatologists—scientists who study the connection between weather and health—generally agree that an average temperature of 65 degrees Fahrenheit with 65 percent humidity is ideal for work, play, and general well-being. *Places Rated* uses 65 degrees Fahrenheit as a standard for mildness in the discussions that follow.

Most people prefer (or say they prefer) mild, sunny climates. Therefore *Places Rated* compares the 107 retirement places on the basis of climatic mildness, using a combination of temperature and humidity factors. "Mild," as we use the term, does not necessarily mean warm but simply refers to the absence of great variations or extremes of temperature. A mild climate is characterized by cool summers and warm winters, with long falls and springs. *Places Rated* defines the mildest climates as those whose mean temperatures remain closest to 65 degrees Fahrenheit for the greatest percentage of time. Any deviations from this mean are labeled negative indicators, and are scored as such. Each place's final score indicates its climatic mildness.

Nearly all climate and weather data presented in this chapter are from the National Oceanic and Atmospheric Administration (NOAA), the National Climatic Center, Asheville, North Carolina. The National Climatic Center houses the world's largest climate data bank, with the equivalent of 25 miles of shelf space devoted solely to worldwide climate and weather data and research.

Some figures are called 30-year normals—mean averages collected over three decades. Each ten years, the data for the new decade are added into the normal and the data for the earliest ten years are removed. Data are collected and averaged over this rather long time period to flatten out irregularities and weather extremes. Events such as the blizzards of 1978 and 1979, for example, or the record national heat wave of 1980, show little overall effect on a 30-year normal. Even the tremendously atypical weather experienced in 1982–83 on the West Coast won't significantly alter California's next 30-year normals. Other figures are the means of annual records kept for periods ranging from a few years to more than 100 years. Mean temperatures are the average of the highest and lowest readings during a given period. For example, to determine the mean temperature for a particular month, the mean maximum temperature (the average of the highest daily readings during the month) and the mean minimum temperature (the average of the lowest) are averaged.

Each place is given a base number of 1,000 points, from which points are subtracted according to the following indicators, based on yearly averages:

1. *Very hot and very cold months.* Ten points are subtracted for each month in which the mean temperature is above 70 degrees or below 32. An additional 10 points are subtracted, for a total of 20 points, if the mean temperature is above 80 degrees or below 20.
2. *Seasonal temperature variation.* The difference in degrees Fahrenheit between the summer mean maximum temperature and the winter mean minimum is subtracted from the base score.
3. *Heating- and cooling-degree days.* The total number of these days per year is divided by 50, and the result is subtracted from the score. The base temperature for arriving at heating- and cooling-degree days is 65 degrees. If, for example, the average temperature on a summer day is 66 degrees, 1 degree of cooling is necessary, which counts as 1 cooling-degree day. Similarly, if the average temperature on a particular winter day is 55 degrees, 10 degrees of heating are necessary, yielding 10 heating-degree days.
4. *Freezing days.* One point is subtracted for each day on which the average temperature is 32 degrees or below.
5. *Zero days.* Five additional points are subtracted for each day the temperature drops to zero or below.
6. *90-degree days.* Since relative humidity has a profound effect on "felt" heat and daily temperature range, points are subtracted in accordance with each location's mean relative humidity at noon in July, when high temperatures are most likely to occur. For each day with a high of at least 90 degrees, 4 points are subtracted if the place's July relative humidity is more than 60 percent, 3 points if relative humidity is 51 percent to 60 percent, 2 points if relative humidity is 41 percent to 50 percent, and 1 point if relative humidity is 40 percent or less.

Sample Comparison: San Diego, California, and Rhinelander, Wisconsin

The difference in mildness between San Diego's Mediterranean-style maritime climate and the rugged continental climate of Rhinelander, Wisconsin, is shown below, as we take you step by step through the *Places Rated* formula. (Specific data may be found in the Place Profiles later in this chapter.)

In the first category, very hot and very cold months, Rhinelander has no months in which the mean temperature exceeds 80 degrees, or even 70. However, it has two months in which the mean temperature is below freezing (at minus 10 points each) and three in which the mean is below 20 (at minus 20 points each). Therefore, in the first category, Rhinelander loses 80 points. San Diego has no months below 32 or 20 degrees, and only one month above 70. So in the category in which Rhinelander drops 80 points, San Diego loses but 10.

The difference between the winter daily mean low temperature and the summer daily mean high is

---

Heating- and Cooling-Degree Days

More than 60 years ago, America's gas utility industry devised a system for measuring climate mildness or severity, based on the deviation of outdoor temperature from 65 degrees Fahrenheit. Temperatures below 65 mean that homes must be heated and so result in heating-degree days; for instance, if the average temperature on a given day is 60 degrees, then that locality receives 5 heating-degree days. Five consecutive days of 60-degree weather result in 25 heating-degree days, and so on. Cooling-degree days measure temperatures over 65 in a similar manner. Generally, cooling-degree days are more expensive to homeowners than heating-degree days.

Total heating- and cooling-degree days are an excellent indication of a climate's severity or mildness. The lower the number, the milder the climate. Below is a brief table showing, in rough averages, how some parts of the United States compare with regard to total heating- and cooling-degree days.

	Heating-Degree Days	Cooling-Degree Days	Total
Southern California	1,500	750	2,250
Florida	500	3,500	4,000
Middle Atlantic States	4,500	1,000	5,500
Pacific Northwest	5,000	500	5,500
Northern Arizona, southern Nevada	4,000	2,000	6,000
Northern New England	7,500	500	8,000
Upper Midwest	8,000	500	8,500

subtracted from the base score. In San Diego it is only 31 degrees, but in Rhinelander it's 73.

Rhinelander has 9,400 heating- and cooling-degree days; San Diego has only 2,229. These numbers are divided by 50 and subtracted from each score. Rhinelander loses 188 points, San Diego only 44.

San Diego has no days on which the temperature drops below 32 degrees, so it loses no points for freezing days. Rhinelander has 182 of them, and drops a point for each.

San Diego has—obviously—no zero days either. But Rhinelander has 39, and must surrender 5 points for each, for a total of 195 points deducted.

San Diego, with its moisture-heavy sea winds, has a July noon mean humidity of more than 60 percent, so it loses the full 4 points for each of its three 90-degree days, or 12 points. Rhinelander has six 90-degree days and loses 4 points for each, too.

When the scores are tallied, San Diego's score is 903, which puts it easily in first place among our 107 retirement locales for climatic mildness. Rhinelander lost a total of 742 points, leaving it with a score of only 258, which puts it, and the nearby town of Eagle River, Wisconsin, bringing up the rear, tied for last place.

Nevertheless, even though San Diego is far milder, many people still prefer Rhinelander and Eagle River. They have long been famous as both resorts and retirement places, although most people who go there will admit that the summers are much better than the winters.

Climatic Mildness: The Winners and the Losers

If you glance at the tail end of the ranking list for climatic mildness, a lot of the places you see there might surprise you. Some of them you may have supposed were ideal as far as weather is concerned; instead, they receive very low marks.

Least Mild Retirement Places

Retirement Place	Places Rated Score
1. Eagle River, WI	258
1. Rhinelander, WI	258
3. Fort Myers–Cape Coral, FL	342
4. Lakeland–Winter Haven, FL	353
4. Orlando, FL	353

Egads! you're probably saying to yourself. What are all those places in Florida doing down here? Everyone knows that Florida is famous for its great weather!

There's no denying that Florida is usually terrific between November and March, when most places in the United States are reeling under blizzards and cold snaps. But what about Florida (or Texas) in August? The low scores that these locations receive are a direct result of the large numbers of 90-degree days they have—hot days that are also humid, which means that the nights are uncomfortably warm, too. Orlando, for example, has 104 days in which the temperature hits 90 degrees or higher.

So as you examine the ranking list, you'll notice that toward the lower end, places in the hot South are bedfellows of places in the cold North: both rigorous, but for opposite reasons. Those places near the top of the list tend to be in the middle latitudes in coastal or mountain locations, or else in the path of those mild Pacific breezes.

Places Rated: Retirement Places Ranked for Climatic Mildness

Six criteria are used to determine a score for climatic mildness, according to the formula described above: (1) very hot and very cold months, (2) seasonal temperature variation, (3) heating- and cooling-degree days, (4) freezing days, (5) zero days, and (6) 90-degree days. Places that receive tie scores are given the same rank and are listed in alphabetical order.

The Place Profiles that follow the alphabetical listing describe only 60 weather stations, for reasons of space, but they cover a broad range of climatic conditions. The places described in the profiles are identified by an asterisk (*) in the lists below.

Retirement Places from Best to Worst

Places Rated Rank	Places Rated Score	Places Rated Rank	Places Rated Score	Places Rated Rank	Places Rated Score
1. San Diego, CA*	903	11. Olympia, WA*	726	21. Lexington–Fayette, KY*	635
2. Lincoln City–Newport, OR*	865	12. Asheville, NC	694	22. Miami, FL*	630
3. San Luis Obispo, CA	861	13. Cape Cod, MA*	686	23. Beaufort–Hilton Head, SC*	627
4. Port Angeles–Strait of Juan de Fuca, WA*	835	14. Clarkesville–Mount Airy, GA*	680	24. Charlottesville, VA*	618
5. Oak Harbor, WA	807	15. Red Bluff–Sacramento Valley, CA*	677	25. Easton–Chesapeake Bay, MD	616
6. Maui, HI*	786	16. Albuquerque, NM*	659	26. Atlantic City–Cape May, NJ*	615
7. Hendersonville, NC*	735	17. Myrtle Beach, SC*	654	26. Santa Fe, NM*	615
8. Santa Rosa, CA*	732	17. Rappahannock, VA	654	26. Toms River–Barnegat Bay, NJ	615
9. Nevada City–Donner, CA*	731	19. Cookeville, TN	649		
10. Brevard, NC	730	19. Crossville, TN	649		

Places Rated Rank	Places Rated Score
29. Gainesville–Lake Sidney Lanier, GA*	613
29. Ocean City–Assateague Island, MD	613
31. Roswell, NM*	612
32. MEDFORD, OR*	611
32. Prescott, AZ	611
34. Front Royal, VA	605
34. Winchester, VA*	605
36. Twain Harte–Yosemite, CA	598
37. BOISE CITY, ID*	592
38. TUCSON, AZ*	589
39. Coeur d'Alene, ID*	585
40. BILOXI–GULFPORT, MS*	584
41. Deming, NM	578
41. Rehoboth Bay–Indian River Bay, DE	578
43. STATE COLLEGE, PA*	575
44. FORT LAUDERDALE–HOLLYWOOD, FL	572
45. Bar Harbor–Frenchman Bay, ME	567
46. Bend, OR*	564
46. Lake O' The Cherokees, OK	564
46. Tahlequah–Lake Tenkiller, OK	564
49. LANCASTER, PA*	559
50. DAYTONA BEACH, FL	556
50. Lake Havasu City–Kingman, AZ	556
50. LAS VEGAS, NV*	556
50. MELBOURNE–TITUSVILLE–COCOA, FL	556
54. PHOENIX, AZ*	555

Places Rated Rank	Places Rated Score
55. St. George–Zion, UT*	554
56. Yuma, AZ*	553
57. LAS CRUCES, NM*	552
58. SPRINGFIELD, MO*	544
59. Harrison, AR	543
60. Carson City, NV	535
60. RENO, NV*	535
62. Branson–Lake Taneycomo, MO	533
62. Cassville–Roaring River, MO	533
62. Table Rock Lake, MO	533
65. Camden–Penobscot Bay, ME*	532
66. Clear Lake, CA*	530
67. COLORADO SPRINGS, CO*	526
68. Monticello–Liberty, NY	509
68. WEST PALM BEACH–BOCA RATON, FL	509
70. Benton–Kentucky Lake, KY*	508
71. Big Sandy, TN	504
71. Paris, TN	504
73. Bull Shoals, AR*	501
73. Delta, CO	501
73. Grand Junction, CO*	501
73. Mountain Home–Norfork Lake, AR	501
73. Traverse City–Grand Traverse Bay, MI	501
78. FORT COLLINS, CO*	490
79. Brunswick–Golden Isles, GA*	486
80. Oscoda–Huron Shore, MI*	484
81. Hamilton–Bitterroot Valley, MT	479
82. Bennington, VT*	476

Places Rated Rank	Places Rated Score
82. Brattleboro, VT	476
84. Missoula, MT	474
85. Petoskey–Straits of Mackinac, MI*	472
86. Athens–Cedar Creek Lake, TX*	471
86. Canton–Lake Tawakoni, TX	471
88. Keene, NH*	461
89. Hot Springs–Lake Ouachita, AR*	460
90. Rockport–Aransas Pass, TX*	454
91. Fairhope–Gulf Shores, AL	442
92. AUSTIN, TX*	435
93. Kalispell, MT*	406
94. SARASOTA–BRADENTON, FL	401
95. SAN ANTONIO, TX	398
96. Fredericksburg, TX	392
96. Kerrville, TX*	392
98. Laconia–Lake Winnipesaukee, NH	389
98. North Conway–White Mountains, NH*	389
100. McALLEN–PHARR–EDINBURG, TX	386
101. Houghton Lake, MI*	385
102. OCALA, FL	371
103. LAKELAND–WINTER HAVEN, FL	353
103. ORLANDO, FL*	353
105. FORT MYERS–CAPE CORAL, FL*	342
106. Eagle River, WI	258
106. Rhinelander, WI*	258

Retirement Places Listed Alphabetically

Retirement Place	Places Rated Rank
ALBUQUERQUE, NM*	16
ASHEVILLE, NC	12
Athens–Cedar Creek Lake, TX*	86
ATLANTIC CITY–CAPE MAY, NJ*	26
AUSTIN, TX*	92
Bar Harbor–Frenchman Bay, ME	45
Beaufort–Hilton Head, SC*	23
Bend, OR*	46
Bennington, VT*	82
Benton–Kentucky Lake, KY*	70
Big Sandy, TN	71
BILOXI–GULFPORT, MS*	40
BOISE CITY, ID*	37
Branson–Lake Taneycomo, MO	62
Brattleboro, VT	82
Brevard, NC	10
Brunswick–Golden Isles, GA*	79
Bull Shoals, AR*	73
Camden–Penobscot Bay, ME*	65
Canton–Lake Tawakoni, TX	86
Cape Cod, MA*	13
Carson City, NV	60
Cassville–Roaring River, MO	62

Retirement Place	Places Rated Rank
CHARLOTTESVILLE, VA*	24
Clarkesville–Mount Airy, GA*	14
Clear Lake, CA*	66
Coeur d'Alene, ID*	39
COLORADO SPRINGS, CO*	67
Cookeville, TN	19
Crossville, TN	19
DAYTONA BEACH, FL	50
Delta, CO	73
Deming, NM	41
Eagle River, WI	106
Easton–Chesapeake Bay, MD	25
Fairhope–Gulf Shores, AL	91
FORT COLLINS, CO*	78
FORT LAUDERDALE–HOLLYWOOD, FL	44
FORT MYERS–CAPE CORAL, FL*	105
Fredericksburg, TX	96
Front Royal, VA	34
Gainesville–Lake Sidney Lanier, GA*	29
Grand Junction, CO*	73
Hamilton–Bitterroot Valley, MT	81
Harrison, AR	59

Retirement Place	Places Rated Rank
Hendersonville, NC*	7
Hot Springs–Lake Ouachita, AR*	89
Houghton Lake, MI*	101
Kalispell, MT*	93
Keene, NH*	88
Kerrville, TX*	97
Laconia–Lake Winnipesaukee, NH	98
Lake Havasu City–Kingman, AZ	50
LAKELAND–WINTER HAVEN, FL	103
Lake O' The Cherokees, OK	46
LANCASTER, PA*	49
LAS CRUCES, NM*	57
LAS VEGAS, NV*	50
LEXINGTON–FAYETTE, KY*	21
Lincoln City–Newport, OR*	2
Maui, HI*	6
McALLEN–PHARR–EDINBURG, TX	100
MEDFORD, OR*	32
MELBOURNE–TITUSVILLE–COCOA, FL	50
MIAMI, FL*	22
Missoula, MT	84
Monticello–Liberty, NY	68
Mountain Home–Norfork Lake, AR	73

Retirement Place	Places Rated Rank	Retirement Place	Places Rated Rank	Retirement Place	Places Rated Rank
Myrtle Beach, SC*	17	Prescott, AZ	32	SARASOTA–BRADENTON, FL	94
Nevada City–Donner, CA*	9	Rappahannock, VA	17	SPRINGFIELD, MO*	58
		Red Bluff–Sacramento Valley, CA*	15	STATE COLLEGE, PA*	43
North Conway–White Mountains, NH*	98	Rehoboth Bay–Indian River Bay, DE	41	Table Rock Lake, MO	62
Oak Harbor, WA*	5			Tahlequah–Lake Tenkiller, OK	46
OCALA, FL	102	RENO, NV*	60		
Ocean City–Assateague Island, MD	29	Rhinelander, WI*	106	Toms River–Barnegat Bay, NJ	26
OLYMPIA, WA*	11	Rockport–Aransas Pass, TX*	90	Traverse City–Grand Traverse Bay, MI	73
		Roswell, NM*	31		
ORLANDO, FL*	103	St. George–Zion, UT*	55	TUCSON, AZ*	38
Oscoda–Huron Shore, MI*	80			Twain Harte–Yosemite, CA	36
Paris, TN	71	SAN ANTONIO, TX	95	WEST PALM BEACH–BOCA RATON, FL	68
Petoskey–Straits of Mackinac, MI*	85	SAN DIEGO, CA*	1		
PHOENIX, AZ*	54	San Luis Obispo, CA	3		
		Santa Fe, NM*	26	Winchester, VA*	34
Port Angeles–Strait of Juan de Fuca, WA*	4	SANTA ROSA, CA*	8	Yuma, AZ*	56

Place Profiles: Climate and Terrain of 60 Selected Weather Stations

The pages that follow are brief profiles of 60 weather stations. The locations represent more than half the places examined in *Places Rated Retirement Guide* and have been carefully selected to cover all the climates that you might encounter should you choose any of the 107 retirement places, or even nearby locations.

The information presented in each profile is taken from extensive government data tables. Some of the narrative summaries describing the climate and terrain of each place are condensations of those that appear in the NOAA publication *Local Climatological Data*. For the smaller towns and rural locations presented in this book, it was necessary to refer to substation reports that do not appear in any current NOAA publication. For a few places—Beaufort–Hilton Head, South Carolina, for example—monthly temperature averages had to be garnered from a variety of sources describing resort areas for the general public. In these instances, the figures available were not carried out to the nearest tenth of a degree, and they are shown as whole numbers in the profiles below.

The narrative summaries provide brief descriptions of each location and point out important or distinctive features of the climate and the local terrain. When terrain is described in the profiles, it is usually in connection with the effect—if any—it has on the climate in the immediate area. But few people would deny that terrain is an important element in its own right; to many it's as important as climate. Some people prefer mountains or seacoast, others rolling plains or forest. Rather than attempt to judge, rate, or score terrain, *Places Rated* simply describes it briefly and lets you decide. Remember, the *Places Rated* score a place receives has nothing to do with its terrain. Some places with good climates have terrain that many people would consider dull, uninviting, or even ugly.

The table of average temperatures on the right-hand side of each profile is a detailed and extremely useful set of data, from which you can get a clear idea of the temperature ranges, averages, and extremes of each place. For example, if you want to know how hot it gets in Albuquerque in July, simply look at the table in Albuquerque's profile. There you'll see that in July the daily high temperatures (which usually occur in midafternoon) average 92.2 degrees. That sounds hot, and it is. But note that the average low, or minimum, temperature for the same month is only 65.2 degrees. The minimum temperature generally occurs in the early hours of the morning. Therefore, even a quick glance at these temperatures tells us that Albuquerque in the summertime has hot days and rather cool nights, with a mean temperature of less than 80 degrees (78.7). This is in keeping with Albuquerque's dry, desert location and altitude of around 5,000 feet.

About 500 miles to the southeast lies Austin, Texas. Austin's July maximum average is about 3 degrees higher than Albuquerque's, and its minimum temperature is almost 9 degrees higher; the mean for the month is in the mid-80s (84.6). It's easy to see that Austin is hotter in summer than is Albuquerque. Some reasons for this are its lower elevation (only 570 feet), more southerly location, and nearness to the Gulf of Mexico, which results in its having greater relative humidity (67 percent, versus only 43 percent for Albuquerque). Since *Places Rated* downgrades hot weather as much as cold, it's not surprising that Albuquerque receives a higher score and rank (16th) for climatic mildness than does Austin (ranked 92nd).

Rounding out the weather picture of each locale are data such as wind speed, amount of snow and rain, and number of clear and cloudy days, storms, and very hot and cold days. To derive the greatest benefit from these assorted indicators, compare two or more places. Which has more snow? More rain? More 90-degree days? Comparing two places you're interested in may lead to your deciding which to visit first. It can be extremely enlightening to compare a place you've never visited with a place you know.

A unique visual device in each profile is the circular graph showing the length of each season. These graphs are prepared from a formula developed by *Places Rated* and reflect the theory that seasonal change should be defined and measured by weather conditions, human activities, and growth or dormancy of plant life rather than by the calendar. In *Places Rated Retirement Guide*, the seasons are defined as follows: Summer begins when the mean monthly temperature rises above 60 degrees Fahrenheit; summer ends when

it falls below 60. Winter begins when the average daily low falls below 32 degrees and ends when it rises above this mark. The remaining portions of the year constitute fall and spring. In the seasonal graphs, winter is shown by the black segments, spring and fall appear as gray, and summer is white.

If you glance at several graphs you will see that the length of a season can vary tremendously. For instance, winter is represented by a tiny sliver in places like Hot Springs, Arkansas, and a semicircle in a rugged place like Kalispell, Montana. You will also notice that some places do not have four separate seasons. Places along the South Atlantic and Gulf shores, for example, usually have two seasons: spring and summer. Some, like Miami, have only one—perpetual summer.

ALBUQUERQUE, NM

Terrain: Rests in the Rio Grande Valley 55 miles southwest of Santa Fe, and surrounded by mountains, most of them to the east. These mountainous areas receive more precipitation than does the city proper. With an annual rainfall of 8 inches, only the most hardy desert flora can grow. However, successful farming—primarily fruit and produce—is carried out in the valley by irrigation.
Climate: Arid continental. No muggy days. Half the moisture falls between July and September in the form of brief but severe thunderstorms. Long drizzles are unknown. These storms do not greatly interfere with outdoor activities and have a moderating effect on the heat. The hottest month is July, with temperatures reaching 90° F almost constantly. However, the low humidity and cool nights make the heat much less felt.

Pluses: Sunny and dry, with mild winters.

Minuses: Dust storms.

Places Rated Score: 659   **Places Rated Rank: 16**

Elevation: 5,314 feet

Relative Humidity: 43%
Wind Speed: 9 mph

Seasonal Change

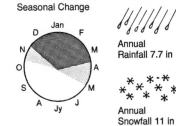

Annual Rainfall 7.7 in

Annual Snowfall 11 in

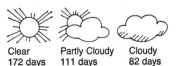

Clear 172 days   Partly Cloudy 111 days   Cloudy 82 days

Precipitation Days: 59   Storm Days: 43

	Daily High	Daily Low	Monthly Mean
	Average Temperatures		
January	46.9	23.5	35.2
February	52.6	27.4	40.0
March	59.2	32.3	45.8
April	70.1	41.4	55.8
May	79.9	50.7	65.3
June	89.5	59.7	74.6
July	92.2	65.2	78.7
August	89.7	63.4	76.6
September	83.4	56.7	70.1
October	71.7	44.7	58.2
November	57.1	31.8	44.5
December	47.5	24.9	36.2

Zero-Degree Days: 1
Freezing Days: 123
90-Degree Days: 61
Heating- and Cooling-Degree Days: 5,608

Athens–Cedar Creek Lake, TX

Terrain: Athens, seat of Henderson County, is located in the pine and post oak area of East Texas, about 70 air miles southeast of Dallas. The surrounding rolling to hilly terrain drains to the Neches River on the east and the Trinity River on the west. Cedar Creek Reservoir, 5 miles northwest, is one of the most popular recreation areas in the state. Nestled among the post oaks and pines, the lakes offer innumerable campsites, excellent fishing, swimming, and boating.
Climate: Humid subtropical, with hot summers. Rainfall is about 39 inches annually, evenly distributed. July and August, though, are somewhat dry. Winters are mild, with temperatures almost always rising above freezing in the daytime. No zero temperatures on record. Spring and fall are the best seasons, and are long. There are sufficient changes to make the weather interesting. The growing season is long (260 days); flowers bloom as late as December, as early as March.

Pluses: Mild winters, lovely springs and falls.

Minuses: Hot, humid summers.

Places Rated Score: 471   **Places Rated Rank: 86**

Elevation: 490 feet

Relative Humidity: 68%
Wind Speed: 10.8 mph

Seasonal Change

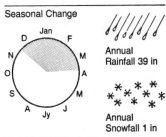

Annual Rainfall 39 in

Annual Snowfall 1 in

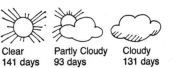

Clear 141 days   Partly Cloudy 93 days   Cloudy 131 days

Precipitation Days: 55   Storm Days: 52

	Daily High	Daily Low	Monthly Mean
	Average Temperatures		
January	58.0	36.4	47.2
February	63.0	40.5	51.8
March	69.0	45.7	57.4
April	78.7	56.4	67.6
May	84.8	63.4	74.1
June	90.7	68.8	79.8
July	96.1	72.4	84.3
August	96.0	71.1	83.6
September	89.9	66.3	78.1
October	80.6	56.3	68.5
November	69.9	46.7	58.3
December	61.5	39.7	50.6

Zero-Degree Days: 0
Freezing Days: 33
90-Degree Days: 95
Heating- and Cooling-Degree Days: 4,055

ATLANTIC CITY–CAPE MAY, NJ

Terrain: Located on a sand island south of Absecon Inlet on the southeast coast of New Jersey. Surrounding terrain, composed of tidal marshes and beach sand, is flat and lies slightly above sea level.

Climate: Continental, but the moderating influence of the Atlantic Ocean is apparent throughout the year. Summers are relatively cooler, winters warmer than those of other places at the same latitude. During the warm season, sea breezes in the late morning and afternoon prevent excessive heat. On occasion, sea breezes may lower the temperature between 15 degrees and 20 degrees within a half hour. Temperatures of 90° F or higher are recorded about a dozen times a year here. Fall is long, lasting until almost mid-November. On the other hand, warming is somewhat delayed in the spring. Ocean temperatures range from an average near 37° F in winter to 72° F in August. Precipitation is moderate and well distributed throughout the year, but great variation is seen from year to year in precipitation during the late summer and early fall (August, September, and October).

Pluses: Moderate temperatures.

Minuses: Late springs.

Places Rated Score: 615

Places Rated Rank: 26

Elevation: 10 feet

Relative Humidity: 73%
Wind Speed: 10.7 mph

Seasonal Change

Annual Rainfall 46 in

Annual Snowfall 16 in

Clear 96 days
Partly Cloudy 108 days
Cloudy 161 days

Precipitation Days: 112   Storm Days: 25

Average Temperatures			
	Daily High	Daily Low	Monthly Mean
January	41.4	24.0	32.7
February	42.9	24.9	33.9
March	50.7	31.5	41.1
April	62.3	41.0	51.7
May	72.4	50.7	61.6
June	80.8	59.7	70.3
July	84.7	65.4	75.1
August	83.0	63.8	73.4
September	77.3	56.8	67.1
October	67.5	45.9	56.7
November	55.9	36.1	46.0
December	44.2	26.0	35.1

Zero-Degree Days: 1
Freezing Days: 15
90-Degree Days: 16
Heating- and Cooling-Degree Days: 5,810

AUSTIN, TX

Terrain: Located on the Colorado River where it crosses the Balcones Escarpment that separates the Texas Hill Country from the Blackland Prairies of East Texas. Elevations within the city limits vary from 400 feet to 900 feet above sea level. Native trees include cedar, oak, walnut, mesquite, and pecan.

Climate: Subtropical. Although summers are hot, the nights are a bit cooler, with temperatures usually dropping into the 70s. Winters are mild, with below-freezing temperatures on fewer than 25 days; strong "northers" may bring cold spells, but these rarely last more than a few days. Precipitation is well distributed, but heaviest in late spring, with a secondary rainfall "peak" in September. With summer come heavy thunderstorms; in winter, the rain tends to be slow and steady. Snowfall (1 inch per year) is inconsequential. Prevailing winds are southerly. Destructive weather infrequent. Freeze-free season: 270 days. Average date of last freeze: March 3. First freeze: November 28.

Pluses: Mild winters.

Minuses: Hot.

Places Rated Score: 435

Places Rated Rank: 92

Elevation: 570 feet

Relative Humidity: 67%
Wind Speed: 9.4 mph

Seasonal Change

Annual Rainfall 33 in

Annual Snowfall 1 in

Clear 115 days
Partly Cloudy 116 days
Cloudy 134 days

Precipitation Days: 82   Storm Days: 41

Average Temperatures			
	Daily High	Daily Low	Monthly Mean
January	60.0	39.3	49.7
February	63.8	42.8	53.3
March	70.7	48.2	59.5
April	79.0	58.2	68.6
May	85.2	65.1	75.2
June	91.7	71.4	81.6
July	95.4	73.7	84.6
August	95.9	73.5	84.7
September	89.4	68.4	78.9
October	81.3	58.9	70.1
November	70.2	48.0	59.1
December	63.0	41.6	52.3

Zero-Degree Days: 0
Freezing Days: 23
90-Degree Days: 101
Heating- and Cooling-Degree Days: 4,645

Beaufort–Hilton Head, SC

Terrain: This area comprises a group of islands in the southern tip of the state. The land is low and flat with elevations mostly under 25 feet. There are dozens of islands of various shapes and sizes, and on them are fresh and saltwater streams, inlets, rivers, and sounds. Most of the islands (except Hilton Head and Port Royal) contain much swampy area. The best beaches are found on Hilton Head, Fripps, and Hunting islands.

Climate: The island group is just on the edge of the balmy subtropical climate enjoyed by Florida and the Caribbean islands. The surrounding water produces a maritime climate, with mild winters, hot summers, and temperatures that shift slowly. The inland Appalachian Mountains block much cold air from the northern interior, and the Gulf Stream moderates the climate considerably.

Pluses: Mild, yet with more seasonal change than places to the south.

Minuses: Summers can be uncomfortably hot and humid.

Places Rated Score: 627

Places Rated Rank: 23

Elevation: 25 feet

Relative Humidity: 75%
Wind Speed: 7.2 mph

Seasonal Change

Annual Rainfall 49 in

Annual Snowfall 0 in

Clear 102 days
Partly Cloudy 112 days
Cloudy 151 days

Precipitation Days: 115   Storm Days: 77

Average Temperatures			
	Daily High	Daily Low	Monthly Mean
January	59	38	49
February	61	42	52
March	67	46	57
April	76	55	66
May	82	62	72
June	86	68	77
July	89	71	80
August	89	71	80
September	84	67	76
October	77	57	67
November	69	47	58
December	61	39	58

Zero-Degree Days: 0
Freezing Days: 31
90-Degree Days: 39
Heating- and Cooling-Degree Days: 3,227

Bend, OR

Terrain: Located along the western border of the Great Basin, near the center of the state. The Cascade foothills rise immediately west of the city and terrace upwards to crests of 10,000 feet about 10 miles away. The rolling plateau extends south and east from Bend into California, Nevada, and Idaho. To the north, the plateau is cut by canyons and drainage streams that feed into the Columbia River.

Climate: Bend has primarily the continental climate of the Great Basin. The mountains moderate the more extreme temperatures of summer. Precipitation is generally light (12 inches of rain annually as opposed to 60 inches to 100 inches on the coast!) because the high Cascades block the moisture-laden Pacific winds. Moderate days and cool nights characterize the climate here. Even in July the temperature may drop to freezing one night. There is, on the average, only one day per year with rainfall of an inch or more.

Pluses: Scenic terrain. Dry and mild, with cool nights.

Minuses: Large temperature shifts. Too dry for some.

Places Rated Score: 564   **Places Rated Rank: 46**

Elevation: 3,599 feet

Relative Humidity: 70%
Wind Speed: 7 mph

Seasonal Change

Annual Rainfall 12 in

Annual Snowfall 36 in

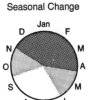

Clear 123 days | Partly Cloudy 92 days | Cloudy 150 days

Precipitation Days: 33   Storm Days: 8

Average Temperatures			
	Daily High	Daily Low	Monthly Mean
January	39.7	20.0	29.9
February	45.1	23.9	34.5
March	50.0	25.0	37.5
April	58.7	29.1	43.9
May	65.3	34.5	49.9
June	71.9	39.6	55.8
July	82.0	44.0	63.0
August	80.0	42.8	61.4
September	74.0	37.6	55.8
October	63.2	31.7	47.5
November	49.8	26.6	38.2
December	42.9	24.0	33.5

Zero-Degree Days: 3
Freezing Days: 190
90-Degree Days: 11
Heating- and Cooling-Degree Days: 7,375

Bennington, VT

Terrain: This historic city is nestled in the valley of the Walloomsac River, which is a part of the Hudson River drainage system. At 700 feet, it is surrounded by mountains. Mount Anthony (2,300 feet) is nearby to the southwest. A ridge of the Green Mountains, at a similar altitude, lies a few miles to the east. The terrain is more open to the west, though many hills rise to 1,000 feet between Bennington and the Hudson.

Climate: The surrounding mountains tend to modify the local climate, especially those to the east, which block some effects of the coastal storms, called "northeasters," which pass along the Atlantic Coast (125 miles distant). There are large differences of temperature, both daily and annually. Winters are cold and snowy, which accounts for the region's many fine ski resorts. Summers are very comfortable, with daytime temperatures in the 70s and low 80s and nighttime temperatures in the 50s.

Pluses: Beautiful summers. Scenic terrain. Great winter skiing.

Minuses: Winters long and fairly rigorous.

Places Rated Score: 476   **Places Rated Rank: 82**

Elevation: 670 feet

Relative Humidity: 70%
Wind Speed: 8.8 mph

Seasonal Change

Annual Rainfall 37 in

Annual Snowfall 57 in

Clear 57 days | Partly Cloudy 102 days | Cloudy 206 days

Precipitation Days: 88   Storm Days: 25

Average Temperatures			
	Daily High	Daily Low	Monthly Mean
January	31.3	10.9	21.1
February	34.7	13.5	24.1
March	42.5	22.6	32.6
April	57.7	33.8	45.8
May	70.3	42.7	56.5
June	78.2	51.8	65.0
July	82.2	56.0	69.1
August	79.6	54.2	66.9
September	72.5	47.3	59.9
October	62.3	37.5	49.9
November	49.1	29.7	39.4
December	35.2	16.9	26.1

Zero-Degree Days: 17
Freezing Days: 166
90-Degree Days: 8
Heating- and Cooling-Degree Days: 7,400

Benton–Kentucky Lake, KY

Terrain: This hilly, heavily wooded area covers several hundred square miles in western Kentucky, and is known as the Two Rivers Breaks area. Elevations vary from 350 feet to 600 feet. Lakes Barkley and Kentucky were formed by damming the Tennessee and Cumberland rivers. The thin finger of land between them is called Land Between the Lakes Recreation Area. The entire area, both in Kentucky and Tennessee, is famous for fishing.

Climate: Temperate, with moderately cold winters and warm, humid summers. Precipitation is ample and well-distributed throughout the year. Most days, even those in winter, are suitable for outdoor activity, with temperatures in winter reaching 50° F or more 11 to 16 days per month. Spring and fall are the most comfortable seasons, with fall being remarkably free from storms or cold. There are about 52 thunderstorms per year. The sunniest months are September and October; the cloudiest is January.

Pluses: Milder than many locations farther north. Scenic.

Minuses: Fairly damp. Summers can be uncomfortable.

Places Rated Score: 508   **Places Rated Rank: 70**

Elevation: 450 feet

Relative Humidity: 70%
Wind Speed: 8 mph

Seasonal Change

Annual Rainfall 49 in

Annual Snowfall 8 in

Clear 102 days | Partly Cloudy 108 days | Cloudy 155 days

Precipitation Days: 76   Storm Days: 53

Average Temperatures			
	Daily High	Daily Low	Monthly Mean
January	48	27	38
February	52	29	40
March	60	35	48
April	72	45	58
May	80	53	67
June	88	61	75
July	91	65	78
August	91	64	77
September	85	56	70
October	75	45	60
November	60	34	47
December	50	28	39

Zero-Degree Days: 1
Freezing Days: 87
90-Degree Days: 67
Heating- and Cooling-Degree Days: 4,754

BILOXI–GULFPORT, MS

Terrain: In speaking of the Mississippi Gulf Coast, one usually thinks of the thickly settled area stretching from St. Louis Bay at Pass Christian to Biloxi Bay and Ocean Springs. This area is climatologically homogeneous, and a summary of any town (in this case, Biloxi) is applicable to the others. The terrain is flat, consisting of low-lying delta floodplains sloping down to sand beaches and rather shallow harbors and bays.

Climate: The Gulf waters have a modifying effect on the local climate that is not felt further inland. Temperatures of 90° F or higher occur only half as often in Biloxi as they do in Hattiesburg, 60 miles north. However, there is no such reverse effect on cold air moving down from the north in winter. Rainfall is plentiful, and heaviest in July, with March and September following close behind. Damage from hurricanes and tropical storms can occur six to seven times a year.

Pluses: Warm, mild beach climate.

Minuses: Winters relatively chilly. Hurricane threat.

Places Rated Score: 584   **Places Rated Rank: 40**

Elevation: 15 feet

Relative Humidity: 77%
Wind Speed: 9.1 mph

Seasonal Change

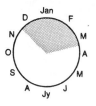

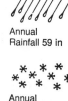

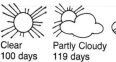
Annual Rainfall 59 in

Annual Snowfall 0 in

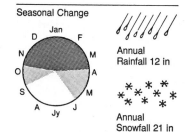

Clear 100 days
Partly Cloudy 119 days
Cloudy 146 days

Precipitation Days: 75   Storm Days: 94

Average Temperatures			
	Daily High	Daily Low	Monthly Mean
January	61.7	45.5	53.6
February	63.6	47.2	55.4
March	68.2	52.0	60.1
April	75.0	59.6	67.3
May	82.4	67.2	74.8
June	87.9	73.2	80.6
July	89.3	74.5	81.9
August	89.6	74.2	81.9
September	85.9	70.3	78.1
October	79.1	60.7	69.9
November	68.8	50.4	59.6
December	62.6	46.2	54.4

Zero-Degree Days: 0
Freezing Days: 11
90-Degree Days: 52
Heating- and Cooling-Degree Days: 3,652

BOISE CITY, ID

Terrain: Cradled in the valley of the Boise River about 8 miles below the mouth of a mountain canyon, where this valley widens. The Boise Mountains rise to a height of 5,000 feet to 6,000 feet within 8 miles. Their slopes are partially mantled with sagebrush and chaparral, changing to stands of fir, spruce, and pine trees higher up.

Climate: Almost a typical upland continental climate in summer but one tempered by periods of cloudy or stormy and mild weather during the course of almost every winter. The cause of this modification in the winter months is the flow of warm, moist Pacific air from the west, called Chinook winds. While this air is considerably modified by the time it reaches Boise, its effect is nonetheless felt. Summer hot spells rarely last longer than a few days, but temperatures may reach 100° F each year. However, due to the low humidity, the average 5:00 PM temperature in July is a comfortable 62° F. In general, the climate is dry and temperate, with enough variation to be stimulating.

Pluses: Mild. Low humidity.

Minuses: Stormy winters.

Places Rated Score: 592   **Places Rated Rank: 37**

Elevation: 2,868 feet

Relative Humidity: 57%
Wind Speed: 9 mph

Seasonal Change

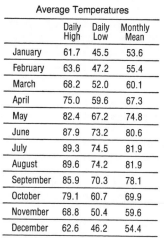

Annual Rainfall 12 in

Annual Snowfall 21 in

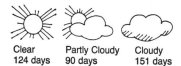

Clear 124 days
Partly Cloudy 90 days
Cloudy 151 days

Precipitation Days: 91   Storm Days: 15

Average Temperatures			
	Daily High	Daily Low	Monthly Mean
January	36.5	21.4	29.0
February	43.8	27.2	35.5
March	51.6	30.5	41.1
April	61.4	36.5	49.0
May	70.6	44.1	57.4
June	78.3	51.2	64.8
July	90.5	58.5	74.5
August	87.6	56.7	72.2
September	77.6	48.5	63.1
October	64.7	39.4	52.1
November	48.9	30.7	39.8
December	39.1	25.0	32.1

Zero-Degree Days: 2
Freezing Days: 124
90-Degree Days: 43
Heating- and Cooling-Degree Days: 6,547

Brunswick–Golden Isles, GA

Terrain: The city of Brunswick, and neighboring St. Simons Island, which lies across the intracoastal waterway, are located on Georgia's southeast coast. Land surface is flat, and elevation averages from 10 feet to 15 feet. Much of the surrounding area is marshland. Fine beaches are plentiful. The low terrain and low latitude East Coast location of the area make it vulnerable to occasional tropical storms, though their full force is felt only infrequently.

Climate: The area enjoys mild and relatively short winters due to the moderating effect of coastal waters. There are only 11 days below freezing in the average winter, and no zero days. Summers are warm and humid, but very high temperatures are rare. Heat waves are usually interrupted by thundershowers, and even in the summer the nights are usually pleasant. Most of the annual 53 inches of rain falls in the summer and early autumn.

Pluses: Warm, mild climate with little temperature change.

Minuses: Can be hot and humid, with frequent rain.

Places Rated Score: 486   **Places Rated Rank: 79**

Elevation: 13 feet

Relative Humidity: 75%
Wind Speed: 8 mph

Seasonal Change

Jan

Annual Rainfall 55 in

Annual Snowfall 0 in

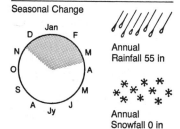

Clear 99 days
Partly Cloudy 113 days
Cloudy 153 days

Precipitation Days: 74   Storm Days: 72

Average Temperatures			
	Daily High	Daily Low	Monthly Mean
January	64.6	43.6	54.1
February	66.5	45.2	55.9
March	71.8	50.6	61.2
April	79.1	58.5	68.8
May	85.6	65.2	75.4
June	89.9	71.1	80.5
July	91.6	73.0	82.3
August	91.1	73.1	82.1
September	86.9	70.2	78.6
October	79.9	61.4	70.7
November	72.2	51.3	61.8
December	65.4	44.5	55.0

Zero-Degree Days: 0
Freezing Days: 11
90-Degree Days: 75
Heating- and Cooling-Degree Days: 3,225

Bull Shoals, AR

Terrain: Bull Shoals Dam and the White River lakes (Beaver, Table Rock, Bull Shoals, and Norfork) are located in the Arkansas–Missouri Ozark Mountain country. These lakes are really reservoirs, with a water surface area of 290 square miles. Elevations in the area vary from 500 feet to 1,400 feet. The most rugged terrain is near Beaver Dam. Gently rolling hills surround Lake Norfork. The country is rugged and wooded, with farms small and scattered. This area is one of the most famous fishing spots in the country. In addition, the woods are full of game such as deer, turkey, duck, and quail.

Climate: Primarily modified continental, with warm summers and mild winters. Each year it can vary from warm and humid maritime to cold and dry continental, but it is relatively free from climatic extremes.

Pluses: Scenic. Great recreational opportunities. Mild winters.

Minuses: Some winter cold snaps and summer heat waves. Subject to ice and sleet.

Places Rated Score: 501

Places Rated Rank: 73

Elevation: 900 feet

Relative Humidity: 67%
Wind Speed: 11 mph

Seasonal Change

Annual Rainfall 42 in

Annual Snowfall 7.6 in

Clear 119 days   Partly Cloudy 96 days   Cloudy 150 days

Precipitation Days: 68   Storm Days: 81

Average Temperatures			
	Daily High	Daily Low	Monthly Mean
January	49.6	27.1	38.3
February	53.4	29.9	41.7
March	61.0	36.2	48.6
April	72.1	46.7	59.4
May	79.4	55.0	67.2
June	88.0	63.4	75.7
July	92.2	67.1	79.7
August	91.9	65.9	78.9
September	85.9	58.1	72.0
October	75.8	46.9	61.3
November	61.0	35.4	48.2
December	51.6	29.3	40.5

Zero-Degree Days: 0
Freezing Days: 88
90-Degree Days: 69
Heating- and Cooling-Degree Days: 4,961

Camden–Penobscot Bay, ME

Terrain: Penobscot Bay lies at the mouth of the Penobscot River in the middle of Maine's seacoast. Although low-lying, the coastal terrain is very rugged and rocky in most places, allowing for hundreds of bays, islands, peninsulas, and harbors. Just to the northeast of Penobscot Bay lies the smaller Frenchman Bay, containing Mount Desert Island and Acadia National Park. Vegetation consists of evergreen coniferous trees, maple, birch, and scrub oak, and many marshes and ponds with cranberry bogs. Fruit orchards, truck farming, and fishing are the predominant coastal industries.

Climate: The Atlantic Ocean has a considerable modifying effect on the local climate, resulting in cool summers and winters that are very mild for so northerly a location. Though fall is generally mild, spring comes late and the weather isn't really warm until July.

Pluses: Cool summers. Winters relatively mild.

Minuses: Long winters. Cold, damp springs.

Places Rated Score: 532

Places Rated Rank: 65

Elevation: 49 feet

Relative Humidity: 79%
Wind Speed: 8.7 mph

Seasonal Change

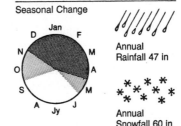

Annual Rainfall 47 in

Annual Snowfall 60 in

Clear 106 days   Partly Cloudy 98 days   Cloudy 161 days

Precipitation Days: 85   Storm Days: 21

Average Temperatures			
	Daily High	Daily Low	Monthly Mean
January	32.4	13.7	23.1
February	34.0	14.4	24.2
March	41.2	23.5	32.4
April	52.1	32.8	42.5
May	62.7	41.6	52.2
June	71.9	50.3	61.1
July	77.6	55.9	66.8
August	76.5	54.6	65.6
September	69.3	47.9	58.6
October	59.6	39.0	49.3
November	48.0	30.8	39.4
December	36.0	18.4	27.2

Zero-Degree Days: 11
Freezing Days: 152
90-Degree Days: 4
Heating- and Cooling-Degree Days: 7,551

Cape Cod, MA

Terrain: Cape Cod is a crooked spit of land that juts out into the Atlantic Ocean from the southeastern corner of Massachusetts, stretching roughly 80 miles from the Cape Cod Canal (at Buzzards Bay) to its tip at Provincetown. The western end of the cape is higher and hillier than the eastern, or "outer cape," which is almost flat and treeless. The sandy soil, arranged in rolling hills and dunes, supports scrub oak and pine trees, while dune grasses and low trees grow on the outer cape.

Climate: Mild, cool, and maritime, with cool summers and cold, wet winters that are seldom severe. Summer temperatures are usually ideal for outdoor recreation. Both zero and 90° F days are very rare.

Pluses: Mild four-season climate, with long and pleasant falls.

Minuses: Winters wet and sleety. Summers can be damp and foggy.

Places Rated Score: 686

Places Rated Rank: 13

Elevation: 35 feet

Relative Humidity: 78%
Wind Speed: 13 mph

Seasonal Change

Annual Rainfall 43 in

Annual Snowfall 24 in

Clear 97 days   Partly Cloudy 114 days   Cloudy 154 days

Precipitation Days: 79   Storm Days: 14

Average Temperatures			
	Daily High	Daily Low	Monthly Mean
January	38.2	22.5	30.4
February	38.7	22.7	30.7
March	44.3	28.9	36.6
April	53.4	36.9	45.2
May	63.7	46.3	55.0
June	72.7	55.9	64.3
July	78.6	62.1	70.4
August	77.7	61.2	69.5
September	71.5	54.7	63.1
October	62.7	45.5	54.1
November	52.8	36.7	44.8
December	41.8	25.6	33.7

Zero-Degree Days: 1
Freezing Days: 115
90-Degree Days: 2
Heating- and Cooling-Degree Days: 6,000

CHARLOTTESVILLE, VA

Terrain: Located in the center of Albemarle County, which is on the Central Piedmont Plateau. The Blue Ridge Mountains are on the western edge of the county. These and several smaller ranges make the topography vary from rolling to quite steep. Elevations range from 300 feet to 800 feet, with some points in the Blue Ridge as high as 3,200 feet.

Climate: Modified continental, with mild winters and warm, humid summers. The mountains produce various steering and blocking effects on storms and air masses. Chesapeake Bay to the east further modifies the climate, making it warmer in winter, cooler in summer. Precipitation is well distributed throughout the year, with the maximum in July, the minimum in January. Tornadoes and violent storms are rare, but severe thunderstorms occur each year. Growing season: 211 days.

Pluses: Scenic mountain terrain. Mild four-season climate.

Minuses: Summers can be hot and rainy.

Places Rated Score: 618　　　**Places Rated Rank: 24**

Elevation: 870 feet

Relative Humidity: 70%
Wind Speed: 8.3 mph

Seasonal Change

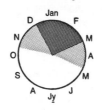

Annual Rainfall 44 in

Annual Snowfall 23 in

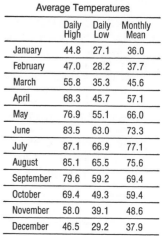

Clear 102 days　　Partly Cloudy 114 days　　Cloudy 149 days

Precipitation Days: 116　Storm Days: 45

Average Temperatures			
	Daily High	Daily Low	Monthly Mean
January	44.8	27.1	36.0
February	47.0	28.2	37.7
March	55.8	35.3	45.6
April	68.3	45.7	57.1
May	76.9	55.1	66.0
June	83.5	63.0	73.3
July	87.1	66.9	77.1
August	85.1	65.5	75.6
September	79.6	59.2	69.4
October	69.4	49.3	59.4
November	58.0	39.1	48.6
December	46.5	29.2	37.9

Zero-Degree Days: 0
Freezing Days: 87
90-Degree Days: 35
Heating- and Cooling-Degree Days: 5,019

Clarkesville–Mount Airy, GA

Terrain: Located in Habersham County in the Mountain and Intermountain Plateau Province of northeast Georgia. The terrain of the county is hilly to mountainous, with elevations averaging 1,500 feet. To the north, within Habersham County, some of the mountains rise above 3,000 feet.

Climate: Nearby mountains, and higher mountains farther north, have a marked influence. Summer heat is tempered by the higher elevations. The contrast of valley and hill exposures results in wide variations in winter low temperatures. Generally, places halfway up the mountain slopes remain warmer during winter nights than do places on the valley floor. Summers are quite pleasant, with warm days and cool nights. Winters are cold but not severe. Spring is changeable and sometimes stormy. Fall is clear and sunny, with chilly nights.

Pluses: Ideal mountain climate, with cool nights year round.

Minuses: Large daily temperature shifts. Stormy springs.

Places Rated Score: 680　　　**Places Rated Rank: 14**

Elevation: 1,470 feet

Relative Humidity: 70%
Wind Speed: 6.8 mph

Seasonal Change

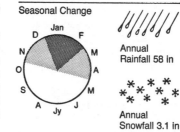

Annual Rainfall 58 in

Annual Snowfall 3.1 in

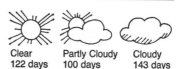

Clear 122 days　　Partly Cloudy 100 days　　Cloudy 143 days

Precipitation Days: 86　Storm Days: 70

Average Temperatures			
	Daily High	Daily Low	Monthly Mean
January	51.6	31.2	41.4
February	54.3	32.3	43.3
March	61.2	37.8	49.5
April	71.9	46.9	59.4
May	78.8	54.1	66.5
June	84.3	61.3	72.8
July	86.4	64.3	75.4
August	86.1	63.9	75.0
September	80.0	58.4	69.2
October	71.6	47.7	59.7
November	60.9	37.7	49.3
December	52.2	31.5	41.9

Zero-Degree Days: 0
Freezing Days: 73
90-Degree Days: 26
Heating- and Cooling-Degree Days: 4,198

Clear Lake, CA

Terrain: Clear Lake (and the nearby city of Lakeport) is located at an elevation of 1,347 feet in one of California's major recreational and agricultural areas. The rounded mountains of the Coast Range surround the lake on all sides, reaching heights of 3,000 feet to 4,000 feet. A broad valley extends from the lake southward, and the smaller Scott's Valley is directly northwest. Clear Lake is about 40 miles due east of the coast and Point Arena.

Climate: Winters here are cool and wet, and summers are warm and dry. The Pacific remains the dominant climatic influence, but it is modified by the lake's high, mountainous location. There are marked seasonal differences here, and greater temperature extremes than at coastal locations. About 60% of the 29 inches of rain annually falls in the winter months. Summers can be hot, but nights are cool.

Pluses: Scenic setting. Mild, warm climate with seasonal variations.

Minuses: A bit hot and dry.

Places Rated Score: 530　　　**Places Rated Rank: 66**

Elevation: 1,347 feet

Relative Humidity: 68%
Wind Speed: 7.4 mph

Seasonal Change

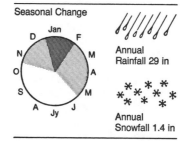

Annual Rainfall 29 in

Annual Snowfall 1.4 in

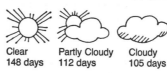

Clear 148 days　　Partly Cloudy 112 days　　Cloudy 105 days

Precipitation Days: 50　Storm Days: 9

Average Temperatures			
	Daily High	Daily Low	Monthly Mean
January	51.8	32.2	42.0
February	57.0	34.2	45.6
March	61.7	35.3	48.5
April	69.4	38.8	54.1
May	76.8	42.9	59.9
June	84.1	47.8	66.0
July	93.5	52.2	72.9
August	91.7	50.3	71.0
September	87.9	47.8	67.9
October	75.5	42.0	58.8
November	62.2	36.0	49.1
December	54.3	33.3	43.8

Zero-Degree Days: 0
Freezing Days: 74
90-Degree Days: 74
Heating- and Cooling-Degree Days: 5,104

Coeur d'Alene, ID

Terrain: The city lies north of Coeur d'Alene Lake, which is about 30 miles long and 2 miles wide. To the east and southwest the city is sheltered by forested hills or low mountains. To the north and northwest lies Rathrum Prairie. The Coeur d'Alene, St. Joe, and St. Maries rivers drain the heavily forested mountains between the lake and the Bitterroot Mountains, which form the boundary between Idaho and Montana. Within a 10-mile radius of the city, quite a few mountain peaks rise over 4,000 feet.

Climate: Can be generally described as temperate, with dry summers and rainy winters. Though seasonal variation is large, it is less so than most other locations this far north. Rain is heaviest from autumn to early spring. Sunshine records haven't been kept here, but for nearby (and similar) Spokane, they reveal sun 20% of the time in January, 81% in July.

Pluses: Dry, warm summers. **Minuses:** Long, rainy winters.

Places Rated Score: 585 **Places Rated Rank: 39**

Elevation: 2,158 feet

Relative Humidity: 64%
Wind Speed: 8 mph

Seasonal Change

Annual Rainfall 26 in

Annual Snowfall 50 in

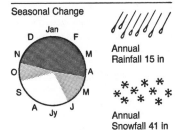

Clear 85 days   Partly Cloudy 89 days   Cloudy 191 days

Precipitation Days: 73   Storm Days: 14

Average Temperatures			
	Daily High	Daily Low	Monthly Mean
January	34.2	21.0	27.6
February	41.1	24.7	32.9
March	47.8	27.0	37.4
April	59.3	33.5	46.4
May	69.7	41.0	55.4
June	75.8	47.4	61.6
July	86.4	51.5	69.0
August	84.8	50.2	67.5
September	75.9	44.4	60.2
October	60.2	37.4	48.8
November	44.3	30.2	37.3
December	36.9	26.0	31.5

Zero-Degree Days: 4
Freezing Days: 141
90-Degree Days: 29
Heating- and Cooling-Degree Days: 7,500

COLORADO SPRINGS, CO

Terrain: At an elevation of more than 6,000 feet, Colorado Springs is located in relatively flat semiarid country on the eastern slope of the Rocky Mountains. Immediately to the west, the mountains rise abruptly to heights ranging from 10,000 feet to 14,000 feet. To the east lies the gently undulating prairie land of eastern Colorado. The land slopes upward to the north, reaching an average height of 8,000 feet within 20 miles, at the top of Palmer Lake Divide.

Climate: The terrain of the area, particularly its wide range of elevations, helps to give Colorado Springs the pleasant "plains and mountain" mixture of climate that has established it as a desirable place to live. Precipitation is generally light, with 80% of it falling between April 1 and September 30. Heavy downpours accompany summer thunderstorms. Temperatures are on the mild side for a city in this latitude and at this elevation.

Pluses: Dry. Sunny. Variable. **Minuses:** Long winters.

Places Rated Score: 526 **Places Rated Rank: 67**

Elevation: 6,170 feet

Relative Humidity: 49%
Wind Speed: 10.4 mph

Seasonal Change

Annual Rainfall 16 in

Annual Snowfall 40 in

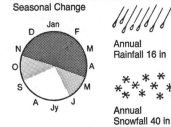

Clear 130 days   Partly Cloudy 119 days   Cloudy 116 days

Precipitation Days: 87   Storm Days: 59

Average Temperatures			
	Daily High	Daily Low	Monthly Mean
January	41.0	16.1	28.6
February	43.6	18.9	31.3
March	47.7	22.8	35.3
April	59.2	33.1	46.2
May	68.4	42.6	55.5
June	78.1	51.1	64.6
July	84.4	57.0	70.7
August	82.4	55.8	69.1
September	74.9	46.9	60.9
October	64.2	36.8	50.5
November	49.8	25.1	37.5
December	43.1	18.9	31.0

Zero-Degree Days: 7
Freezing Days: 162
90-Degree Days: 15
Heating- and Cooling-Degree Days: 6,934

FORT COLLINS, CO

Terrain: Located on the eastern slope of the Rocky Mountains between Denver and Cheyenne, Wyoming, Fort Collins lies in some of the most spectacular mountain terrain in the country. Steep cliffs (some nearly vertical), high waterfalls, and forested mountain slopes cut by swift rivers are all found to the west. Within 30 miles to the east, the landscape settles into grassland prairies of the Great Plains.

Climate: Near the center of the continent, Fort Collins is removed from any major source of airborne moisture; it is further shielded from rainfall by the high Rockies to the west. In wintertime, cold air masses from Canada may bring temperatures well below zero at night. In summer, hot, dry air from the desert to the southwest brings with it daytime temperatures of 90° F. However, felt heat is low because of dryness.

Pluses: Semirigorous four-
season climate. Spec-
tacular terrain.

Minuses: Cold winters. Hot,
dry summers.

Places Rated Score: 490 **Places Rated Rank: 78**

Elevation: 5,004 feet

Relative Humidity: 60%
Wind Speed: 9 mph

Seasonal Change

Annual Rainfall 15 in

Annual Snowfall 41 in

Clear 118 days   Partly Cloudy 128 days   Cloudy 119 days

Precipitation Days: 37   Storm Days: 50

Average Temperatures			
	Daily High	Daily Low	Monthly Mean
January	40.3	11.9	26.1
February	42.5	14.6	28.6
March	49.7	22.2	36.0
April	60.1	32.1	46.1
May	68.0	40.8	54.4
June	78.4	48.9	63.7
July	84.4	54.4	69.4
August	83.2	52.7	68.0
September	75.6	43.8	59.7
October	64.3	32.8	48.6
November	51.1	21.6	36.4
December	42.3	14.3	28.3

Zero-Degree Days: 15
Freezing Days: 175
90-Degree Days: 17
Heating- and Cooling-Degree Days: 7,052

Fort Myers–Cape Coral, FL

Terrain: Located on the south bank of the Caloosahatchee River, about 15 miles from the Gulf of Mexico, Fort Myers lies at roughly the middle of the southern half of Florida's west coast. The land all around is low and flat. To the east and south, much of it is swampy.

Climate: Subtropical, with the extremes of summer and winter tempered by the marine influence of the Gulf. The annual average temperature is 74° F, with a mean fluctuation between summer and winter average temperatures of only 20 degrees. Occasional winter cold snaps can bring the temperature down into the 30s, but only rarely does it fall below freezing. In nearby farmlands, frost occurs on the average of twice a year. Fort Myers has one of America's stormiest locations, with thundershowers occurring two out of every three days during the summer.

Pluses: Warm and mild, with gradual temperature shifts.

Minuses: Thundershowers. Hot and muggy.

Places Rated Score: 342   **Places Rated Rank: 105**

Elevation: 15 feet

Relative Humidity: 76%
Wind Speed: 8.2 mph

Seasonal Change

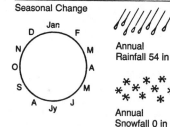

Annual Rainfall 54 in

Annual Snowfall 0 in

Clear
103 days

Partly Cloudy
161 days

Cloudy
101 days

Precipitation Days: 112   Storm Days: 93

Average Temperatures			
	Daily High	Daily Low	Monthly Mean
January	74.7	52.3	63.5
February	76.0	53.3	64.7
March	79.7	57.3	68.5
April	84.8	61.8	73.3
May	89.0	66.4	77.7
June	90.5	71.7	81.1
July	91.1	73.8	82.5
August	91.5	74.1	82.8
September	89.8	73.4	81.6
October	85.3	67.5	76.4
November	79.9	58.8	69.4
December	75.9	53.6	64.8

Zero-Degree Days: 0
Freezing Days: 1
90-Degree Days: 106
Heating- and Cooling-Degree Days: 4,168

Gainesville–Lake Sidney Lanier, GA

Terrain: Gainesville is located in central Hall County, where the Piedmont Plateau Province joins the foothills of the Blue Ridge Mountains. The soil is sandy clay loam and the terrain is rolling to hilly. Elevation in Gainesville is around 1,200 feet, but varies considerably over the county. The city is on the eastern shore of Lake Sidney Lanier, a huge reservoir noted for its fishing, recreational facilities, and beauty.

Climate: Due to its elevation and proximity to the higher elevation of the mountains to the north and northwest, Gainesville has a comparatively mild summer climate. Some hot days can be expected, but fewer than half the days in summer reach 90° F, and summer nights are almost always comfortable. Winters are not severe, though cold weather can be expected. There is usually snow every year, but accumulations are rare.

Pluses: Mild yet variable, with seasonal changes.

Minuses: Rainy. Tornado danger. Can be hot.

Places Rated Score: 613   **Places Rated Rank: 29**

Elevation: 1,170 feet

Relative Humidity: 67%
Wind Speed: 9.1 mph

Seasonal Change

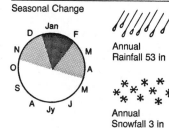

Annual Rainfall 53 in

Annual Snowfall 3 in

Clear
112 days

Partly Cloudy
105 days

Cloudy
148 days

Precipitation Days: 84   Storm Days: 70

Average Temperatures			
	Daily High	Daily Low	Monthly Mean
January	52.6	32.7	42.7
February	56.1	34.1	45.1
March	63.4	39.5	51.5
April	73.3	47.6	60.5
May	81.3	55.8	68.6
June	86.8	63.7	75.3
July	88.4	66.6	77.5
August	88.4	66.1	77.3
September	82.6	60.4	71.5
October	73.3	49.0	61.2
November	62.1	39.1	50.6
December	53.1	33.0	43.1

Zero-Degree Days: 0
Freezing Days: 63
90-Degree Days: 48
Heating- and Cooling-Degree Days: 4,260

Grand Junction, CO

Terrain: Situated in a large mountain valley at the junction of the Colorado and Gunnison rivers, Grand Junction lies on the western slope of the Rocky Mountains. The city's climate is marked by wide seasonal temperature changes, but thanks to the protection of the surrounding mountains, sudden and severe weather changes are infrequent. Elevations on the valley floor average about 4,600 feet above sea level, with mountains on all sides reaching as high as 12,000 feet.

Climate: The interior location, coupled with the ring of high mountains, results in low rainfall, and agriculture depends heavily on irrigation, derived from mountain streams and runoff. Winter snows are frequent but light, and do not remain long. In the summer, relative humidity is very low, making the region as dry as parts of Arizona. Sunny days predominate in all seasons.

Pluses: Four-season climate milder than others in comparable latitudes.

Minuses: Low rainfall. Some hot weather.

Places Rated Score: 501   **Places Rated Rank: 73**

Elevation: 4,843 feet

Relative Humidity: 47%
Wind Speed: 8.1 mph

Seasonal Change

Annual Rainfall 8.4 in

Annual Snowfall 27 in

Clear
139 days

Partly Cloudy
107 days

Cloudy
119 days

Precipitation Days: 70   Storm Days: 33

Average Temperatures			
	Daily High	Daily Low	Monthly Mean
January	36.7	16.5	26.6
February	44.0	23.2	33.6
March	52.8	29.6	41.2
April	64.6	38.8	51.7
May	75.8	48.5	62.2
June	85.9	56.6	71.3
July	93.1	64.2	78.7
August	89.1	61.6	75.4
September	81.3	53.0	67.2
October	67.9	41.9	54.9
November	50.9	28.6	39.8
December	39.4	19.6	29.5

Zero-Degree Days: 7
Freezing Days: 137
90-Degree Days: 66
Heating- and Cooling-Degree Days: 6,745

Hendersonville, NC

Terrain: Hendersonville (and Hendersonville County, 358 square miles), is located in the mountainous southwestern part of the state, just above the South Carolina border. The relief is mostly broken, mountainous, and rugged, with some very steep slopes and high waterfalls. There is a large intermountain valley, with rolling to strongly rolling mountain meadows. This valley averages 2,100 feet to 2,400 feet in elevation, whereas the county averages 2,400 feet to 5,200 feet. The cool climate favors the growth of pasture grasses, potatoes, apples and tree fruits, cabbage, and late truck crops.

Climate: Mildly continental, with considerable differences in temperature between winter and summer. It is mild and pleasant from late spring to late fall, and summer nights are always cool, even following hot afternoons. Hendersonville and the cities surrounding it (Asheville, Brevard, Tryon, and Highlands) have long been famous as recreational and health resorts.

Pluses: Ideal mild four-season climate.

Minuses: Pronounced temperature shifts possible.

Places Rated Score: 735   **Places Rated Rank: 7**

Elevation: 2,153 feet

Relative Humidity: 77%
Wind Speed: 7 mph

Seasonal Change

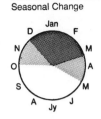

Annual
Rainfall 50 in

Annual
Snowfall 8.6 in

Clear
110 days

Partly Cloudy
103 days

Cloudy
152 days

Precipitation Days: 132   Storm Days: 47

Average Temperatures			
	Daily High	Daily Low	Monthly Mean
January	48.4	27.3	39.2
February	50.6	28.2	40.3
March	58.3	33.5	47.6
April	69.4	42.4	54.8
May	76.8	50.6	63.0
June	82.5	58.7	70.0
July	84.3	62.6	72.8
August	83.8	61.8	72.2
September	78.0	55.4	67.3
October	69.1	44.5	56.5
November	58.2	34.3	46.6
December	49.3	28.1	39.6

Zero-Degree Days: 0
Freezing Days: 80
90-Degree days: 8
Heating- and Cooling-Degree Days: 4,682

Hot Springs–Lake Ouachita, AR

Terrain: This region, famous for its fishing and thermal springs, is located in Garland County in south-central Arkansas. The city of Hot Springs is adjacent to Hot Springs National Park and is in the eastern part of the Ouachita Mountain system. It is near the boundary between the highland (Ozark) and delta regions of the state.

Climate: The irregular topography, with elevations varying from 400 feet to 1,000 feet, has considerable effect on the microclimate of the area, particularly with regard to temperature extremes, ground fog, and precipitation. The climate is generally mild, and favors outdoor activities almost year round. However, the area is subject to storms, flash floods, and extreme heat and cold. Winter temperatures fall below freezing only half the time. Summers are warm and long, springs changeable. The freeze-free growing period is long: 225 days.

Pluses: Long, warm summers. Mild winters.

Minuses: Hot, muggy spells in summer.

Places Rated Score: 460   **Places Rated Rank: 89**

Elevation: 630 feet

Relative Humidity: 70%
Wind Speed: 8.1 mph

Seasonal Change

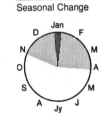

Annual
Rainfall 55 in

Annual
Snowfall 3 in

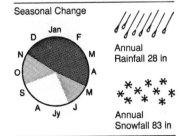

Clear
119 days

Partly Cloudy
101 days

Cloudy
145 days

Precipitation Days: 72   Storm Days: 79

Average Temperatures			
	Daily High	Daily Low	Monthly Mean
January	54.0	34.5	44.3
February	58.6	36.9	47.8
March	66.1	42.5	54.3
April	76.1	51.7	63.9
May	82.5	58.9	70.7
June	91.0	67.7	79.4
July	94.5	71.1	82.8
August	95.3	70.5	82.9
September	88.7	64.1	76.4
October	78.3	53.7	66.0
November	63.1	41.7	52.4
December	54.6	35.5	45.1

Zero-Degree Days: 0
Freezing Days: 47
90-Degree Days: 90
Heating- and Cooling-Degree days: 4,659

Houghton Lake, MI

Terrain: This resort area is located in north-central Lower Michigan. Houghton Lake, the largest inland lake in the state, lies within Michigan's central plateau, which is 1,000 feet above sea level. The land around the lake is level to rolling, gradually dropping off toward the east and, more rapidly, to the south; to the north are hills and ridges 100 feet to 300 feet higher. However, the region's thick woods and abundant streams and lakes make it a natural tourist and recreation area.

Climate: The daily and seasonal temperature range is greater here than along Michigan's shorelines, where the modifying effects of the various Great Lakes can be felt. Rainfall is heaviest in the summer, with 60% of it falling between April and September. Winters here are cold and snowy, though not as snowy as those in locations to the north and west. Cloudiness is greatest in late fall and winter. The growing season is only 90 days.

Pluses: Excellent fishing, hunting, water sports.

Minuses: Long, cold winters. Cloudy.

Places Rated Score: 385   **Places Rated Rank: 101**

Elevation: 1,149 feet

Relative Humidity: 70%
Wind Speed: 8.9 mph

Seasonal Change

Annual
Rainfall 28 in

Annual
Snowfall 83 in

Clear
70 days

Partly Cloudy
98 days

Cloudy
197 days

Precipitation Days: 144   Storm Days: 36

Average Temperatures			
	Daily High	Daily Low	Monthly Mean
January	25.8	9.0	17.4
February	28.0	8.3	18.2
March	36.9	16.4	26.7
April	53.2	30.5	41.9
May	65.2	40.3	52.8
June	75.2	50.0	62.6
July	78.8	53.6	66.2
August	77.0	52.6	64.8
September	68.2	45.7	57.0
October	58.0	37.2	47.6
November	41.7	27.1	34.4
December	29.6	15.5	22.6

Zero-Degree Days: 25
Freezing Days: 175
90-Degree Days: 2
Heating- and Cooling-Degree Days: 8,928

Kalispell, MT

Terrain: Kalispell, the seat of Flathead County, is located 8 miles northwest of the north end of Flathead Lake, in the valley of the same name. The climate of Flathead Valley differs from that found east of the Continental Divide (40 miles east of Kalispell), largely because of the high mountains to the east, which block cold air from Alberta in the wintertime. These rise 4,500 feet above the valley floor, and assure frequent and beneficial rains by cooling the moist ocean air arriving from the west. In addition to Flathead, the valley contains four smaller lakes and numerous streams and sloughs.

Climate: There is more precipitation on the eastern side of the valley than the western. In winter, the eastern portion receives 68 inches of snow, the western only 49 inches. Kalispell is windy, with intense winds often reaching 30 mph to 40 mph. Winter is cold; summers are pleasant and dry.

Pluses: Beautiful, rugged northern mountain country.

Minuses: Can be cold, cloudy, windy.

Places Rated Score: 406   **Places Rated Rank: 93**

Elevation: 2,965 feet

Relative Humidity: 67%
Wind Speed: 6.7 mph

Seasonal Change

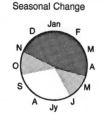

Annual Rainfall 16 in

Annual Snowfall 67 in

Clear 71 days   Partly Cloudy 81 days   Cloudy 213 days

Precipitation Days: 131   Storm Days: 23

	Daily High	Daily Low	Monthly Mean
January	27.1	11.0	19.1
February	34.1	15.9	25.0
March	40.7	20.3	30.5
April	53.5	30.4	42.0
May	63.6	38.1	50.9
June	70.0	44.0	57.0
July	80.8	47.8	64.3
August	79.1	45.9	62.5
September	68.0	38.6	53.3
October	54.4	30.5	42.5
November	38.7	22.7	30.7
December	30.8	16.6	23.7

Average Temperatures

Zero-Degree Days: 17
Freezing Days: 191
90-Degree Days: 15
Heating- and Cooling-Degree Days: 8,671

Keene, NH

Terrain: Located in southwestern New Hampshire, in the relatively flat Ashuelot River Valley, which is about 2 miles wide near the city. The valley is about 500 feet above sea level and is surrounded by hills. Peaks of 1,300 feet to 1,500 feet are within 5 miles of Keene. High peaks of the White Mountains lie 80 miles north northwest, while the main ridge of the Green Mountains lies 40 miles west.

Climate: Semirigorous continental, characterized by changeable weather, large annual and daily temperature ranges, and great differences between the same seasons in different years. In common with most of New England, there is no "rainy" or "dry" season, but rather, abundant rainfall year round. Summers are delightful but short, winters moderately cold and fairly long, and springs and falls pleasant, changeable, and brief.

Pluses: Fine four-season climate, a bit on the rugged side.

Minuses: Brief summers.

Places Rated Score: 461   **Places Rated Rank: 88**

Elevation: 490 feet

Relative Humidity: 70%
Wind Speed: 10.4 mph

Seasonal Change

Annual Rainfall 41 in

Annual Snowfall 60 in

Clear 90 days   Partly Cloudy 109 days   Cloudy 166 days

Precipitation Days: 83   Storm Days: 24

	Daily High	Daily Low	Monthly Mean
January	32.9	12.6	22.8
February	35.3	13.1	24.2
March	43.6	22.2	32.9
April	57.6	32.6	45.1
May	70.5	42.2	56.4
June	78.4	51.8	65.1
July	83.0	56.6	69.8
August	80.9	54.6	67.8
September	73.2	47.5	60.4
October	62.8	36.8	49.8
November	48.6	28.4	38.5
December	35.4	16.7	26.1

Average Temperatures

Zero-Degree Days: 16
Freezing Days: 167
90-Degree Days: 11
Heating- and Cooling-Degree Days: 7,958

Kerrville, TX

Terrain: Kerr County lies across the hills, valleys, and uplands of the rolling Hill Country of southwest Texas, at the edge of the Edwards Plateau. The western part of the county is on a rolling plain covered with cedars and live oak trees. The eastern part breaks into the deep valleys of the Guadalupe River and its tributaries. Kerr County is an outstanding tourist resort area for hunting deer, turkey, and other game.

Climate: Mainly continental in character, especially in the winter, with wide swings of temperature both daily and seasonally. Rainfall tapers off from east to west rather sharply, from annual totals of 32 inches in the east to only 24 inches in the west. Winter precipitation is mostly slow, steady, light rain. Summer months are dry and hot. Falls are pleasant but can be stormy due to "northers" and Gulf storms moving north.

Pluses: Minimal winter. Warm.

Minuses: Summers can be hot.

Places Rated Score: 392   **Places Rated Rank: 96**

Elevation: 1,650 feet

Relative Humidity: 63%
Wind Speed: 9.3 mph

Seasonal Change

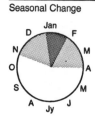

Annual Rainfall 32 in

Annual Snowfall 1.1 in

Clear 116 days   Partly Cloudy 114 days   Cloudy 135 days

Precipitation Days: 50   Storm Days: 51

	Daily High	Daily Low	Monthly Mean
January	60.5	33.2	46.9
February	63.7	36.5	50.1
March	70.8	41.5	56.2
April	77.6	50.4	64.0
May	83.6	59.1	71.4
June	90.4	66.2	78.3
July	93.6	67.8	80.7
August	94.6	67.1	80.9
September	88.6	61.8	75.2
October	80.2	52.0	66.1
November	67.8	40.4	54.1
December	62.5	33.9	48.2

Average Temperatures

Zero-Degree Days: 0
Freezing Days: 60
90-Degree days: 101
Heating- and Cooling-Degree Days: 5,650

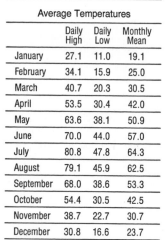

LANCASTER, PA

Terrain: Situated in the heart of Pennsylvania Dutch country in the southeastern part of the state, Lancaster lies about 100 miles northwest of the Atlantic and 30 miles southeast of the Blue Ridge Mountains. All around the city, the rich farmland—flat to gently rolling—is extensively cultivated.

Climate: Because of its proximity to the ocean and the protection afforded by the mountains of central Pennsylvania, Lancaster enjoys a comparatively moderate climate. Conditions range from relatively mild in winter to warm and humid in summer, with weather changes every few days throughout the year. Cold air outbreaks in winter can result in zero or near zero temperatures, but these are rare. Hot spells occur each summer, during which afternoons are uncomfortable. However, nights are generally cooler—in the 70s—and the heat spells don't last more than a few days.

Pluses: Mild four-season climate.

Minuses: Humid, can be muggy.

Places Rated Score: 559

Places Rated Rank: 49

Elevation: 255 feet

Relative Humidity: 70%
Wind Speed: 7.7 mph

Seasonal Change

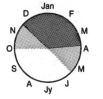

Annual Rainfall 43 in

Annual Snowfall 24 in

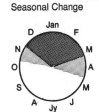

Clear 86 days   Partly Cloudy 107 days   Cloudy 172 days

Precipitation Days: 77   Storm Days: 46

Average Temperatures			
	Daily High	Daily Low	Monthly Mean
January	40.6	22.5	31.6
February	42.7	22.2	32.5
March	52.0	28.9	40.6
April	65.1	38.2	51.6
May	75.8	48.6	62.2
June	82.8	57.6	70.3
July	86.7	62.0	74.4
August	84.2	60.5	72.4
September	77.6	53.1	65.4
October	66.5	41.6	54.0
November	54.0	32.1	43.1
December	42.1	23.6	32.8

Zero-Degree Days: 2
Freezing Days: 135
90-Degree Days: 27
Heating- and Cooling-Degree Days: 5,982

LAS CRUCES, NM

Terrain: The seat of Dona Ana County, Las Cruces is located in the Rio Grande River Valley, about 25 miles north of the Texas border. The wide, level valley runs northwest to southeast through this area, with rolling desert bordering it to the southwest and west. About 12 miles to the east the Organ Mountains, with peaks above 8,500 feet, form a rugged backdrop for the city. The northwest portion of the valley narrows, and is bordered by low hills and buttes.

Climate: Arid continental, characterized by low rainfall, moderately warm summers, and mild, pleasant winters. The rainfall, at 8 inches per year, is light. But since almost all of it falls during the summer growing months, considerable forage is available on nearby grazing lands. The rain falls in brief showers; drizzles are unknown. Summers are hot, but the nights are cool. Winters tend to be mild and sunny.

Pluses: Warm and sunny, even in winter.

Minuses: Summer afternoons can be hot and dusty.

Places Rated Score: 552

Places Rated Rank: 57

Elevation: 3,881 feet

Relative Humidity: 50%
Wind Speed: 9.5 mph

Seasonal Change

Annual Rainfall 8 in

Annual Snowfall 2.5 in

Clear 194 days   Partly Cloudy 99 days   Cloudy 72 days

Precipitation Days: 21   Storm Days: 58

Average Temperatures			
	Daily High	Daily Low	Monthly Mean
January	56.3	25.2	40.9
February	62.2	27.7	44.9
March	26.5	33.7	51.1
April	77.1	41.2	59.3
May	85.4	49.3	67.3
June	94.1	59.0	76.6
July	93.9	65.2	79.5
August	91.7	63.8	77.8
September	87.0	56.0	71.5
October	77.9	44.0	61.0
November	65.3	30.0	47.7
December	58.2	25.9	42.0

Zero-Degree Days: 0
Freezing Days: 111
90-Degree Days: 101
Heating- and Cooling-Degree Days: 5,848

LAS VEGAS, NV

Terrain: Situated near the center of a broad desert valley surrounded by mountains ranging from 2,000 feet to 10,000 feet higher than the valley's floor. These mountains act as effective barriers to moisture-laden storms moving eastward from the Pacific Ocean, so that Las Vegas sees very few overcast or rainy days.

Climate: Summers are typical of a desert climate—low humidity with maximum temperatures in the 100-degree levels. Nearby mountains contribute to relatively cool nights, with minimums between 70° F and 75° F. Springs and falls are ideal: Outdoor activities are rarely interrupted by adverse weather conditions. Winters, too, are mild, with daytime averages of 60° F, clear skies, and warm sunshine.

Pluses: Mild year-round climate with especially pleasant springs and falls.

Minuses: High winds, though infrequent, bring dust and sand.

Places Rated Score: 556

Places Rated Rank: 50

Elevation: 2,180 feet

Relative Humidity: 29%
Wind Speed: 9 mph

Seasonal Change

Annual Rainfall 4 in

Annual Snowfall 1.5 in

Clear 216 days   Partly Cloudy 84 days   Cloudy 65 days

Precipitation Days: 24   Storm Days: 15

Average Temperatures			
	Daily High	Daily Low	Monthly Mean
January	55.7	32.6	44.2
February	61.3	36.9	49.1
March	67.8	41.7	54.8
April	77.5	50.0	63.8
May	87.5	59.0	73.3
June	97.2	67.4	82.3
July	103.9	75.3	89.6
August	101.5	73.3	87.4
September	94.8	65.4	80.1
October	81.0	53.1	67.1
November	65.7	40.8	53.3
December	56.7	33.7	45.2

Zero-Degree Days: 0
Freezing Days: 41
90-Degree Days: 131
Heating- and Cooling-Degree Days: 5,547

LEXINGTON–FAYETTE, KY

Terrain: Located in the heart of the Kentucky Bluegrass region on a gently rolling plateau with varying elevations of 900 feet to 1,050 feet. The surrounding country is noted for its beauty, fertile soil, excellent grass, stock farms, and burley tobacco. There are no bodies of water nearby that are large enough to have an effect on climate.

Climate: Decidedly continental, temperate, but subject to sudden large but brief changes in temperature. Precipitation is evenly distributed throughout the winter, spring, and summer, with an average of 12 inches falling in each of these seasons. Snowfall is variable, but the ground does not retain snow for more than a few days at a time. The months of September and October are the most pleasant of the year; they have the least precipitation, the most clear days, and generally comfortable temperatures.

Pluses: Temperate four-season climate with pleasant falls.

Minuses: Large diurnal temperature range.

Places Rated Score: 635

Places Rated Rank: 21

Elevation: 989 feet

Relative Humidity: 70%
Wind Speed: 9.7 mph

Seasonal Change

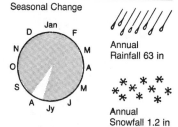

Annual Rainfall 50 in

Annual Snowfall 16 in

Clear 95 days | Partly Cloudy 102 days | Cloudy 168 days

Precipitation Days: 130 Storm Days: 47

Average Temperatures			
	Daily High	Daily Low	Monthly Mean
January	41.3	24.5	32.9
February	44.3	26.2	35.3
March	53.4	33.7	43.6
April	66.0	44.6	55.3
May	75.5	53.8	64.7
June	83.5	62.5	73.0
July	86.4	65.9	76.2
August	85.5	64.4	75.0
September	79.6	57.6	68.6
October	68.8	46.8	57.8
November	53.9	35.3	44.6
December	43.7	27.2	35.5

Zero-Degree Days: 2
Freezing Days: 97
90-Degree Days: 16
Heating- and Cooling-Degree Days: 5,926

Lincoln City–Newport, OR

Terrain: These places lie directly on the Pacific Coast, with marine climates typical of Oregon's coastal area. Although this climate summary describes Newport, it is applicable to Lincoln City, 25 miles north. Just to the east of Newport's city limits, the foothills of the Coast Range begin their fairly steep ascent to ridges which are 2,000 feet to 3,000 feet high 12 miles east of the city. Though part of the city sits at the water's edge, a considerable portion of it is built on level bench land about 150 feet above sea level.

Climate: Newport receives warm, moist air from the Pacific. Accordingly, summers are mild and pleasant. In the winter, the air releases its moisture over the cold landmass, resulting in frequent clouds and rain from November through March. Some 70% of the annual rainfall occurs during these winter months. Very high and very low temperatures are almost nonexistent.

Pluses: Very mild maritime climate, with cool summers, mild winters.

Minuses: Cloudy, wet winters with little sun or snow.

Places Rated Score: 865

Places Rated Rank: 2

Elevation: 136 ft

Relative Humidity: 82%
Wind Speed: 7.6 mph

Seasonal Change

Annual Rainfall 63 in

Annual Snowfall 1.2 in

Clear 75 days | Partly Cloudy 80 days | Cloudy 210 days

Precipitation Days: 122 Storm Days: 3

Average Temperatures			
	Daily High	Daily Low	Monthly Mean
January	49.8	38.5	44.2
February	51.4	39.1	45.3
March	53.2	39.7	46.5
April	56.1	42.0	49.1
May	59.3	45.5	52.4
June	62.1	49.0	55.6
July	64.3	50.8	57.6
August	64.6	50.9	57.8
September	64.5	49.0	56.8
October	61.0	46.4	53.7
November	55.5	42.4	49.0
December	51.1	39.8	45.5

Zero-Degree Days: 0
Freezing Days: 17
90-Degree Days: 0
Heating- and Cooling-Degree Days: 4,624

Maui, HI

Terrain: The most centrally located of Hawaii's major islands, Maui lies between Oahu and the Big Island of Hawaii. The island is mountainous, with the peaks of west Maui rising to almost 6,000 feet, and those to the southeast rising to over 10,000 feet (Mount Haleakala).

Climate: The outstanding features of Maui's climate are the equable temperatures from day to day and season to season; the marked variation in rainfall on the island from season to season and place to place; the persistence of winds from the northeast quadrant; and the rarity of severe storms. For a visitor from the mainland, the steady, mild temperature is probably the biggest surprise. The normal temperature range between the warmest month (August) and the coldest (February) is only eight degrees! At Kahului, where these data were recorded, the average mean humidity is fairly high (72%) and rainfall is low, averaging under 30 inches.

Pluses: Very mild maritime climate.

Minuses: Monotonous.

Places Rated Score: 786

Places Rated Rank: 6

Elevation: 103 feet

Relative Humidity: 76%
Wind Speed: 6.4 mph

Seasonal Change

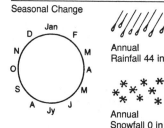

Annual Rainfall 44 in

Annual Snowfall 0 in

Clear 124 days | Partly Cloudy 149 days | Cloudy 92 days

Precipitation Days: 202 Storm Days: 8

Average Temperatures			
	Daily High	Daily Low	Monthly Mean
January	77.9	64.4	71.2
February	77.9	64.4	71.2
March	77.9	65.4	71.7
April	79.2	67.3	73.3
May	81.4	69.5	75.5
June	83.3	71.7	77.5
July	84.0	72.7	78.4
August	84.6	73.6	79.1
September	84.8	72.8	78.8
October	83.3	71.3	77.3
November	80.8	69.6	75.2
December	78.2	66.8	72.5

Zero-Degree Days: 0
Freezing Days: 0
90-Degree Days: 0
Heating- and Cooling-Degree days: 3,719

MEDFORD, OR

Terrain: Located in a mountain valley formed by the famous Rogue River and one of its tributaries, Bear Creek. Most of the valley ranges in elevation from 1,300 feet to 1,400 feet above sea level. The valley's outlet to the ocean 80 miles west is the narrow canyon of the Rogue.
Climate: Moderate, with marked seasonal characteristics. Late fall, winter, and early spring are cloudy, damp, and cool. The remainder of the year is warm, dry, and sunny. The rain shadow afforded by the Siskiyous and the Coast Range results in relatively light rainfall, most of which falls in the wintertime. Snowfalls are very light and seldom remain on the ground more than 24 hours. Winters are mild, with the temperatures just dipping below freezing during December and January. Summer days can reach 90° F, but nights are cool. The climate is ideal for truck and fruit farming, and the area is dotted with orchards.

Pluses: Very mild four-season climate. Sunny summers.

Minuses: Half the year is damp and cloudy.

Places Rated Score: 611   **Places Rated Rank: 32**

Elevation: 1,298 feet

Relative Humidity: 67%
Wind Speed: 4.8 mph

Seasonal Change

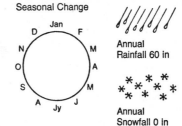

Annual Rainfall 21 in

Annual Snowfall 8 in

Clear 117 days   Partly Cloudy 79 days   Cloudy 169 days

Precipitation Days: 101   Storm Days: 9

Average Temperatures			
	Daily High	Daily Low	Monthly Mean
January	44.2	29.0	36.6
February	51.8	30.7	41.3
March	56.7	32.8	44.8
April	63.8	36.6	50.2
May	71.7	42.8	57.3
June	79.4	49.1	64.3
July	89.5	53.8	71.7
August	87.8	52.9	70.4
September	82.1	46.7	64.4
October	67.4	39.4	53.4
November	52.7	34.2	43.5
December	44.2	31.1	37.7

Zero-Degree Days: 0
Freezing Days: 90
90-Degree Days: 54
Heating- and Cooling-Degree Days: 5,492

MIAMI, FL

Terrain: Located on the lower east coast of Florida. To the east lies Biscayne Bay, and east of it Miami Beach. The surrounding countryside is level and sparsely wooded.
Climate: Essentially subtropical marine, characterized by a long, warm summer with abundant rainfall and a mild, dry winter. The Atlantic Ocean greatly influences the city's small range of daily temperature and the rapid warming of colder air masses that pass to the east of the state. During the early morning hours, more rainfall occurs at Miami Beach than at the airport (9 miles inland), while during the afternoon the reverse is true. Even more striking is the difference in the annual number of days over 90° F: at Miami Beach, 15 days; at the airport, 60. Freezing temperatures occur occasionally in surrounding farming districts but almost never near the ocean. For the first time in Miami's history, traces of snow were reported in 1977. Tropical hurricanes affect the area and are the most frequent in September and October.

Pluses: Single-season, subtropical marine climate.

Minuses: Hurricanes. Frequent thunderstorms.

Places Rated Score: 630   **Places Rated Rank: 22**

Elevation: 12 feet

Relative Humidity: 75%
Wind Speed: 9.1 mph

Seasonal Change

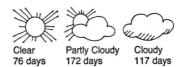

Annual Rainfall 60 in

Annual Snowfall 0 in

Clear 76 days   Partly Cloudy 172 days   Cloudy 117 days

Precipitation Days: 129   Storm Days: 75

Average Temperatures			
	Daily High	Daily Low	Monthly Mean
January	75.6	58.7	67.2
February	76.6	59.0	67.8
March	79.5	63.0	71.3
April	82.7	67.3	75.0
May	85.3	70.7	78.0
June	88.0	73.9	81.0
July	89.1	75.5	82.3
August	89.9	75.8	82.9
September	88.3	75.0	81.7
October	84.6	71.0	77.8
November	79.9	64.5	72.2
December	76.6	60.0	68.3

Zero-Degree Days: 0
Freezing Days: 0
90-Degree Days: 31
Heating- and Cooling-Degree Days: 4,244

Myrtle Beach, SC

Terrain: Located in the center of the long coastal area known as the Grand Strand, which extends for 43 miles and has a populated area only a few blocks wide. The land is low and swampy inland, and the entire area is quite flat, with no elevations greater than 50 feet above sea level. There are many more trees and wooded areas than are usually found in a beach area. The beaches themselves are of white sand, and the water is quite clean, as there are no harbors, shipping, or major industries nearby. Also, no rivers or streams empty into the sea for a distance of almost 30 miles.
Climate: Mild winters and warm summers are the rule. The ocean has a pronounced modifying effect on temperatures, and the Blue Ridge Mountains inland block much cold air from the interior. Some tropical storms reach the area every few years.

Pluses: Warm, mild, steady.

Minuses: Can be hot and muggy. Tropical storms.

Places Rated Score: 654   **Places Rated Rank: 17**

Elevation: 25 feet

Relative Humidity: 75%
Wind Speed: 8.8 mph

Seasonal Change

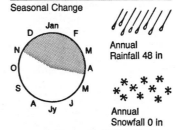

Annual Rainfall 48 in

Annual Snowfall 0 in

Clear 102 days   Partly Cloudy 110 days   Cloudy 153 days

Precipitation Days: 112   Storm Days: 76

Average Temperatures			
	Daily High	Daily Low	Monthly Mean
January	57	35	46
February	59	36	48
March	64	42	54
April	73	52	62
May	80	61	70
June	84	67	76
July	88	70	79
August	89	70	79
September	83	65	74
October	75	53	65
November	68	44	55
December	58	35	47

Zero-Degree Days: 0
Freezing Days: 54
90-Degree Days: 28
Heating- and Cooling-Degree Days: 3,803

Nevada City–Donner, CA

Terrain: Located on the western slope of the Sierra Nevada. The climate is primarily that of a mountainous region, in this instance modified by the proximity of the Sacramento Valley to the west. The temperature and snowfall can vary greatly from one town to the next in Nevada County, due to the high peaks and ridges of the Sierra Nevada, which serve to block air masses from the coast and the Great Basin, and to channel warm, moist air to high elevations where the moisture is extracted in the form of rain or snow.

Climate: The average annual temperature for the area is about 50° F, with the mean wintertime low being around 29° F and the mean high temperature in the summertime about 76° F. The temperature range during the year is great, with occasional lows at zero and highs in the low 90s. Though the climate is generally mild during most of the year, blizzard conditions and very deep snows (245 inches at Blue Canyon) may prevail during the winter.

Pluses: Spectacular scenery. Pleasant summers and falls.

Minuses: High elevations have blizzard conditions in winter.

Places Rated Score: 731   **Places Rated Rank: 9**

Elevation: 5,280 feet

Relative Humidity: 51%
Wind Speed: 8 mph

Seasonal Change

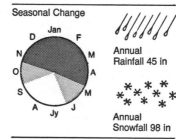

Annual Rainfall 67.6 in

Annual Snowfall 240 in

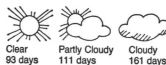

Clear 175 days   Partly Cloudy 64 days   Cloudy 126 days

Precipitation Days: 89   Storm Days: 12

Average Temperatures			
	Daily High	Daily Low	Monthly Mean
January	42.9	29.8	36.4
February	44.2	30.5	37.4
March	45.0	30.9	38.0
April	51.7	36.1	43.9
May	59.8	42.7	51.3
June	67.8	50.4	59.1
July	77.5	58.7	68.1
August	76.4	57.1	66.8
September	72.7	53.1	62.9
October	62.6	45.3	54.0
November	51.7	37.3	44.5
December	45.6	32.6	39.1

Zero-Degree Days: 0
Freezing Days: 100
90-Degree Days: 1
Heating- and Cooling-Degree Days: 6,006

North Conway–White Mountains, NH

Terrain: North Conway, long famous as a recreation and resort area for both winter and summer sports and summer recreation, lies nestled in the White Mountains. About 20 miles south is Lake Winnipesaukee, the state's largest, noted for year-round recreation and fine fishing. From the lake to the ski resorts around North Conway, the terrain rises dramatically from elevations of about 2,000 feet to more than 6,000 feet in the Presidential Range. The area is generally rugged, scenic, and heavily forested. Interspersed between ranges and peaks are broad valleys suitable for dairy and truck farming.

Climate: Semirigorous continental, with delightful summers that aren't too hot. Summer nights are cool, and the days usually sunny. Falls are pleasant, and famous throughout the region for the bright colors of the foliage. Winters are long, snowy, and sometimes very cold for periods of several days to a week. Springs changeable.

Pluses: Scenic. Pleasant summers.

Minuses: Winters are long and snowy.

Places Rated Score: 389   **Places Rated Rank: 98**

Elevation: 720 feet

Relative Humidity: 80%
Wind Speed: 6.8 mph

Seasonal Change

Annual Rainfall 45 in

Annual Snowfall 98 in

Clear 93 days   Partly Cloudy 111 days   Cloudy 161 days

Precipitation Days: 90   Storm Days: 46

Average Temperatures			
	Daily High	Daily Low	Monthly Mean
January	29.5	8.3	18.9
February	32.5	9.9	21.2
March	41.1	19.3	30.2
April	53.9	29.9	41.9
May	65.6	39.8	52.7
June	76.0	48.7	62.4
July	80.5	53.4	67.0
August	78.7	51.5	65.1
September	70.7	44.7	57.7
October	61.4	35.0	48.2
November	45.4	26.9	36.2
December	32.2	12.7	22.5

Zero-Degree Days: 25
Freezing Days: 187
90-Degree Days: 7
Heating- and Cooling-Degree Days: 8,241

Olympia, WA

Terrain: The capital of the state of Washington, Olympia lies at the southernmost end of Puget Sound, some 60 miles south southwest of Seattle. The Olympic Peninsula, with its fine remnants of the Pacific Northwest rain forests, active glaciers, and alpine meadows, lies to the northwest. The city and vicinity are quite well protected by the Coast Range from the strong south and southwest winds accompanying many Pacific storms during the fall and winter.

Climate: Characterized by warm, generally dry summers and wet, mild winters. Fall rains begin in October and continue with few interruptions until spring. During the rainy season there is little variation in temperature, with days in the 40s and 50s and nights in the 30s, and constant cloud cover. The summer highs are between 60° F and 80° F, with up to 20 days without rain. The summer is marked by clear skies at night and frequent morning fog.

Pluses: Mild winters, dry summers.

Minuses: Cloudy, damp.

Places Rated Score: 726   **Places Rated Rank: 11**

Elevation: 195 feet

Relative Humidity: 71%
Wind Speed: 6.7 mph

Seasonal Change

Annual Rainfall 51 in

Annual Snowfall 19 in

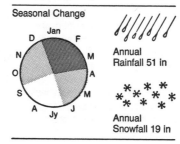

Clear 49 days   Partly Cloudy 88 days   Cloudy 228 days

Precipitation Days: 163   Storm Days: 5

Average Temperatures			
	Daily High	Daily Low	Monthly Mean
January	44.0	30.4	37.2
February	49.0	32.4	41.0
March	53.6	32.8	43.2
April	59.9	36.5	48.2
May	67.2	40.8	54.0
June	71.9	45.9	58.9
July	78.4	48.7	63.6
August	77.2	48.4	62.8
September	72.1	45.0	58.6
October	61.2	40.0	50.6
November	51.3	35.2	43.3
December	45.8	33.1	39.5

Zero-Degree Days: 0
Freezing Days: 89
90-Degree Days: 6
Heating- and Cooling-Degree Days: 5,631

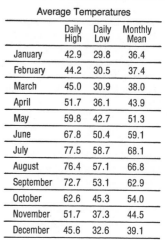

ORLANDO, FL

Terrain: Located in the central section of the Florida peninsula, almost surrounded by lakes. Countryside is flat, with no natural barriers to exterior weather systems.

Climate: Because of the surrounding water, relative humidity remains high the year round, hovering near 90% at night and dipping to 50% in the afternoon. The rainy season extends from June through September: Afternoon thundershowers occur daily. Rain is light during the winter; snow and sleet are rare. Winter temperatures may drop to freezing at night, but days are usually pleasant, with brilliant sunshine.

Pluses: Warm and steady.

Minuses: Humid year round. Hot summers with daily thundershowers.

Elevation: 106 feet

Relative Humidity: 74%
Wind Speed: 8.7 mph

Seasonal Change

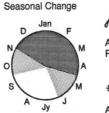

Annual Rainfall 51 in

Annual Snowfall 0 in

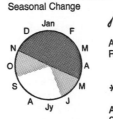

Clear 94 days   Partly Cloudy 148 days   Cloudy 123 days

Precipitation Days: 116   Storm Days: 81

Average Temperatures		
	Daily High	Daily Low	Monthly Mean
January	70.5	50.0	60.3
February	71.8	51.2	61.5
March	76.0	55.7	65.9
April	81.5	61.1	71.3
May	86.7	66.1	76.4
June	89.3	71.1	80.2
July	89.8	72.9	81.4
August	90.0	73.5	81.8
September	87.9	72.3	80.1
October	82.5	66.0	74.3
November	76.2	56.9	66.6
December	71.5	51.5	61.5

Zero-Degree Days: 0
Freezing Days: 2
90-Degree Days: 104
Heating- and Cooling-Degree Days: 3,959

Places Rated Score: 353   **Places Rated Rank: 103**

Oscoda–Huron Shore, MI

Terrain: Located on the shore of Lake Huron at the northern edge of Saginaw Bay. The land is level and the soil is sandy. Most of the surrounding area is heavily forested with conifers, maple, oak, and birch.

Climate: Definitely influenced by the lake, especially when the winds are from the south or east. As in other parts of Michigan's Lower Peninsula, the climate is also modified by the westerly winds that have passed over Lake Michigan, picking up warmth and moisture in winter and being cooled in summer. The wettest month is June; the driest is February. Cloudiness is most pronounced in late fall and early winter. Winter comes early (in mid-to-late October) and does not cease until late April or early May. Thick ice extends over all the inland lakes during most of this period and oftentimes does not melt away until late May. Summers are delightful but rather short.

Pluses: Ideal summer weather, with warm days and cool nights.

Minuses: Winters are long and cold.

Elevation: 590 feet

Relative Humidity: 75%
Wind Speed: 7.6 mph

Seasonal Change

Annual Rainfall 29 in

Annual Snowfall 41 in

Clear 68 days   Partly Cloudy 108 days   Cloudy 189 days

Precipitation Days: 65   Storm Days: 39

Average Temperatures		
	Daily High	Daily Low	Monthly Mean
January	30.1	14.1	22.2
February	31.3	13.2	22.3
March	38.6	20.5	29.6
April	52.0	31.1	41.6
May	63.9	41.0	52.5
June	74.9	51.2	63.1
July	80.6	56.0	68.3
August	78.8	55.0	66.9
September	70.3	47.7	59.0
October	59.4	38.5	49.0
November	44.3	29.1	36.7
December	33.7	19.9	26.7

Zero-Degree Days: 13
Freezing Days: 171
90-Degree Days: 6
Heating- and Cooling-Degree Days: 7,473

Places Rated Score: 484   **Places Rated Rank: 80**

Petoskey–Straits of Mackinac, MI

Terrain: The Straits of Mackinac are located in the northernmost part of Lower Michigan, where the waters of Lake Michigan meet those of Lake Huron. The land north of the straits forms Michigan's Upper Peninsula. The town of Petoskey is located some 30 miles south of the straits, on the south shore of Little Traverse Bay on the Lake Michigan shore. The terrain is generally level or gently undulating, with sandy and gravelly soils. The region abounds with lakes ideal for fishing and summer recreation.

Climate: Though rigorous because of its interior and northerly location, the climate is modified by the presence of the lakes on either side. Consequently, summertime temperatures average at least 5 degrees cooler than locations in the southern part of the state. However, winters are quite severe, with cold spells that may last for a week and snowfall that averages almost 75 inches.

Pluses: Pleasant summers with cool nights. Crisp falls.

Minuses: Long, cold, snowy winters.

Elevation: 586 feet

Relative Humidity: 75%
Wind Speed: 8 mph

Seasonal Change

Annual Rainfall 27 in

Annual Snowfall 74 in

Clear 68 days   Partly Cloudy 88 days   Cloudy 209 days

Precipitation Days: 67   Storm Days: 33

Average Temperatures		
	Daily High	Daily Low	Monthly Mean
January	28.2	12.7	20.5
February	29.5	10.7	20.1
March	36.8	18.3	27.6
April	50.7	30.2	40.5
May	64.0	39.8	51.9
June	74.1	50.1	62.1
July	80.4	56.5	68.5
August	78.1	55.6	66.9
September	69.2	48.6	58.9
October	58.4	39.5	49.0
November	43.1	29.3	36.2
December	32.1	19.4	25.8

Zero-Degree Days: 14
Freezing Days: 147
90-Degree Days: 9
Heating- and Cooling-Degree Days: 8,394

Places Rated Score: 472   **Places Rated Rank: 85**

PHOENIX, AZ

Terrain: Located in the center of the Salt River Valley, on a broad, oval, nearly flat plain. To the south, west, and north are nearby mountain ranges, and 35 miles to the east are the famous Superstition Mountains, which rise to an elevation of 5,000 feet.

Climate: Typical desert, with low annual rainfall and low humidity. Daytime temperatures are high throughout the summer. Winters are mild, but nighttime temperatures frequently drop below freezing during December, January, and February. The valley floor is generally free of wind except during the thunderstorm season in July and August, when local gusts flow from the east. The majority of days are clear and sunny, except for July and August; then, considerable afternoon cloudiness builds up over nearby mountains.

Pluses: Dry, two-season desert climate.

Minuses: Hot summers.

Places Rated Score: 555   **Places Rated Rank: 54**

Elevation: 1,107 feet

Relative Humidity: 36%
Wind Speed: 6.2 mph

Seasonal Change

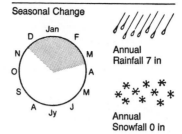

Annual Rainfall 7 in

Annual Snowfall 0 in

Clear 214 days   Partly Cloudy 81 days   Cloudy 70 days

Precipitation Days: 34   Storm Days: 23

Average Temperatures			
	Daily High	Daily Low	Monthly Mean
January	64.8	37.6	51.2
February	69.3	40.8	55.1
March	74.5	44.8	59.7
April	83.6	51.8	67.7
May	92.9	59.6	76.3
June	101.5	67.7	84.6
July	104.8	77.5	91.2
August	102.2	76.0	89.1
September	98.4	69.1	83.8
October	87.6	56.8	72.2
November	74.7	44.8	59.8
December	66.4	38.5	52.5

Zero-Degree Days: 0
Freezing Days: 32
90-Degree Days: 164
Heating- and Cooling-Degree Days: 5,060

Port Angeles–Strait of Juan de Fuca, WA

Terrain: Located in the northeastern section of the Olympic Peninsula between the Strait of Juan de Fuca and the Olympic Mountains, which begin rising near the southern edge of the city and reach elevations of 6,000 feet within 15 miles. There are several glaciers on Mount Olympus, at 7,965 feet the highest point in the Olympic Range.

Climate: Predominantly marine, with cool summers, mild winters, moist air, and small daily temperature variation. Summers are cool and rather dry. The average summertime temperature is 65° F to 70° F during the day and about 55° F at night. The temperature seldom exceeds 75° F. The water temperature of the strait is 44° F in winter and 52° F in summer, which is an indication of the temperature stability of the climate. In winter, the daily temperatures are in the 40s in the daytime, dropping to the 30s at night. Like most other places in this region, the area is often foggy and cloudy.

Pluses: Cool, mild, maritime climate.

Minuses: Beach and sunbathing weather very scarce.

Places Rated Score: 835   **Places Rated Rank: 4**

Elevation: 99 feet

Relative Humidity: 80%
Wind Speed: 6.4 mph

Seasonal Change

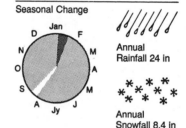

Annual Rainfall 24 in

Annual Snowfall 8.4 in

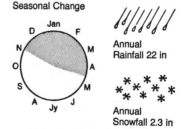

Clear 47 days   Partly Cloudy 72 days   Cloudy 246 days

Precipitation Days: 64   Storm Days: 8

Average Temperatures			
	Daily High	Daily Low	Monthly Mean
January	43.2	33.0	38.1
February	45.9	34.4	40.2
March	48.9	36.4	42.7
April	54.2	40.1	47.2
May	59.4	44.3	51.9
June	62.7	48.5	55.6
July	66.3	50.9	58.6
August	66.5	51.0	58.8
September	63.6	48.5	56.1
October	56.5	43.5	50.0
November	49.1	38.2	43.7
December	46.1	36.0	41.1

Zero-Degree Days: 0
Freezing Days: 40
90-Degree Days: 0
Heating- and Cooling-Degree Days: 4,529

Red Bluff–Sacramento Valley, CA

Terrain: Located at the northern end of the Sacramento Valley, which is the northern half of the great Central Valley of California. Mountains surround the city on three sides, forming a huge horseshoe: The Coast Range is located 30 miles west, the Sierra Nevada system 40 miles east, and the Cascade Range about 50 miles north northeast. The western part of the valley floor is mostly rolling hills with scrub oak trees. The Sacramento River flows in a north-south direction through the eastern portion of the valley, through fertile orchards and grain lands.

Climate: Precipitation is confined mostly to rain during the winter and spring months. Snowfall is infrequent and light. In the hot months (June through September), temperatures often exceed 100° F, but nighttime temperatures are almost always comfortable. The summer and fall are nearly cloudless, and the resulting warm days are ideal for fruit drying.

Pluses: Warm, dry, sunny.

Minuses: Hot summer days.

Places Rated Score: 677   **Places Rated Rank: 15**

Elevation: 342 feet

Relative Humidity: 53%
Wind Speed: 8.7 mph

Seasonal Change

Annual Rainfall 22 in

Annual Snowfall 2.3 in

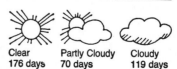

Clear 176 days   Partly Cloudy 70 days   Cloudy 119 days

Precipitation Days: 70   Storm Days: 10

Average Temperatures			
	Daily High	Daily Low	Monthly Mean
January	53.6	36.7	45.2
February	59.5	40.4	50.0
March	63.8	42.5	53.2
April	71.6	47.3	59.5
May	80.6	54.2	67.4
June	89.3	61.7	75.5
July	98.0	66.6	82.3
August	95.7	64.1	79.9
September	90.6	60.0	75.3
October	78.3	51.7	65.0
November	64.0	43.3	53.7
December	54.7	38.1	46.4

Zero-Degree Days: 0
Freezing Days: 21
90-Degree Days: 99
Heating- and Cooling-Degree Days: 4,592

Reno, NV

Terrain: Located at the west edge of Truckee Meadows in a semiarid plateau lying in the lee of the Sierra Nevada. To the west, this range rises to elevations of 9,000 feet to 10,000 feet, and hills to the east reach 6,000 feet to 7,000 feet in height. The Truckee River, flowing from the Sierra Nevada eastward through Reno, drains into Pyramid Lake to the northeast.

Climate: Sunshine is abundant throughout the year. Temperatures are mild, but the daily range may exceed 45° F. Even when afternoons reach the upper 90s, a light jacket is needed shortly after sunset. Nights with a minimum temperature over 60° F are rare. Afternoon temperatures are moderate, and only about ten days a year fail to reach a level above freezing. Humidity is very low during the summer months and moderately low during winter.

Pluses: Mild, sunny climate in alpine setting.

Minuses: Considerable daily temperature variation. Little precipitation.

Places Rated Score: 535

Places Rated Rank: 60

Elevation: 4,400 feet

Relative Humidity: 50%
Wind Speed: 6.3 mph

Seasonal Change

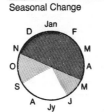

Annual Rainfall 7 in

Annual Snowfall 27 in

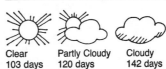

Clear 165 days Partly Cloudy 90 days Cloudy 110 days

Precipitation Days: 49 Storm Days: 13

Average Temperatures			
	Daily High	Daily Low	Monthly Mean
January	45.4	18.3	31.9
February	51.1	23.0	37.1
March	56.0	24.6	40.3
April	64.0	29.6	46.8
May	72.2	37.0	54.6
June	80.4	42.5	61.5
July	91.1	47.4	69.3
August	89.0	44.8	66.9
September	81.8	38.6	60.2
October	70.0	30.5	50.3
November	56.3	23.9	40.1
December	46.4	19.6	33.0

Zero-Degree Days: 3
Freezing Days: 189
90-Degree Days: 52
Heating- and Cooling-Degree Days: 6,351

Rhinelander, WI

Terrain: Rhinelander, seat of Oneida County, is located on the Wisconsin River in the northern part of the state. The area was once part of a great white pine forest, but it is now covered with second growth. Within a 12-mile radius of the city there are 232 lakes. The area is known for its fishing, particularly for smallmouth bass, walleye, and muskie.

Climate: Continental, and largely determined by the movement and interaction of large air masses. Winters are long and cold, while summers are warm and pleasant, with cool nights. Weather changes can be expected every few days in winter and spring. Spring and fall are short, with rapid transition from winter to summer and vice versa. The average number of thunderstorms per year is 30. With a mean of 39 days when the temperature falls below zero, this should be considered a rigorous climate.

Pluses: Warm, pleasant summers.

Minuses: Long, cold winters.

Places Rated Score: 258

Places Rated Rank: 106

Elevation: 1,560 feet

Relative Humidity: 75%
Wind Speed: 10.2 mph

Seasonal Change

Annual Rainfall 31 in

Annual Snowfall 56 in

Clear 89 days Partly Cloudy 102 days Cloudy 174 days

Precipitation Days: 66 Storm Days: 30

Average Temperatures			
	Daily High	Daily Low	Monthly Mean
January	22.5	3.0	12.8
February	26.1	3.7	14.9
March	35.7	14.5	25.1
April	52.6	29.6	41.1
May	66.5	42.0	54.3
June	75.3	52.1	63.7
July	79.9	56.9	68.4
August	77.6	54.4	66.0
September	68.2	46.1	57.2
October	56.7	36.6	46.7
November	38.3	23.5	30.9
December	26.2	10.1	18.2

Zero-Degree Days: 39
Freezing Days: 182
90-Degree Days: 6
Heating- and Cooling-Degree Days: 9,400

Rockport–Aransas Pass, TX

Terrain: Aransas County is a flat coastal plain, with many bays and inlets. Elevations range from sea level to 50 feet. The sandy loam and coastal clay soils are dotted with mesquite and live oak. About 90% of the agricultural income is derived from livestock, chiefly beef cattle. For recreation, many fishing, hunting, and camping facilities are available, including Goose Island State Park.

Climate: Humid subtropical, with warm summers. Also, the prevailing southeasterly winds off the Gulf provide a climate that is predominantly maritime. Winters are pleasantly mild, with freezing temperatures occurring at night, and only about 10 times per year. Summers are warm and humid, but the heat is moderated somewhat by Gulf breezes. Spring and fall are the most pleasant months, with moderate temperatures and changeable weather.

Pluses: Mild, warm, maritime climate, with little daily change.

Minuses: Hot and muggy in summer. Monotonous.

Places Rated Score: 454

Places Rated Rank: 90

Elevation: 15 feet

Relative Humidity: 80%
Wind Speed: 12 mph

Seasonal Change

Annual Rainfall 37 in

Annual Snowfall 0 in

Clear 103 days Partly Cloudy 120 days Cloudy 142 days

Precipitation Days: 49 Storm Days: 37

Average Temperatures			
	Daily High	Daily Low	Monthly Mean
January	64.5	45.3	54.9
February	67.9	49.1	58.5
March	72.9	54.5	63.7
April	78.8	63.3	71.1
May	84.0	69.4	76.7
June	89.1	74.9	82.0
July	91.5	75.9	83.7
August	91.8	75.0	83.4
September	88.6	71.8	80.2
October	82.6	63.6	73.1
November	74.3	54.7	64.5
December	67.6	47.9	57.8

Zero-Degree Days: 0
Freezing Days: 10
90-Degree Days: 77
Heating- and Cooling-Degree Days: 3,542

Roswell, NM

Terrain: Located in a valley in southern New Mexico amid higher land masses that modify air masses, especially the cold outbreaks in winter.

Climate: Conforms to the basic trend of four seasons. Summers are warm and dry. Half of the annual precipitation falls then. In the fall, frosty nights alternate with warm days of extremely low humidity. Winter is the season of least precipitation and is characterized by subfreezing temperatures at night followed by considerable warming in the day. The wind speed is in excess of 25 mph on some 60 days a year, usually between February and May.

Pluses: Low humidity year round. Long summers. Abundance of clear days.

Minuses: Cold nights. High winds.

Elevation: 3,669 feet

Relative Humidity: 48%
Wind Speed: 9 mph

Seasonal Change

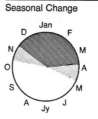

Annual Rainfall 11 in

Annual Snowfall 11 in

Clear 176 days   Partly Cloudy 111 days   Cloudy 78 days

Precipitation Days: 47   Storm Days: 31

Average Temperatures			
	Daily High	Daily Low	Monthly Mean
January	55.4	20.8	38.1
February	60.9	24.8	42.9
March	67.7	30.9	49.3
April	78.2	41.2	59.7
May	86.4	50.5	68.5
June	94.2	59.8	77.0
July	94.7	63.7	79.2
August	93.4	62.3	77.9
September	86.5	54.3	70.4
October	77.0	42.2	59.6
November	64.8	29.0	46.9
December	56.8	21.8	39.3

Zero-Degree Days: 0
Freezing Days: 94
90-Degree Days: 75
Heating- and Cooling-Degree Days: 5,257

Places Rated Score: 612   **Places Rated Rank: 31**

St. George–Zion, UT

Terrain: St. George, at an elevation of 2,700 feet, is located 2 miles north of the junction of the Virgin and Santa Clara rivers in the fairly broad Virgin River Valley of southwestern Utah. Fifteen miles north the Pine Valley Mountains rise to over 10,000 feet. The same distance west are the Beaver Dam Mountains, rising to 7,000 feet. To the east and south is principally high plateau land. Nearby Zion National Park is noted for its spectacular canyons and rock formations.

Climate: Semiarid (steppe) type, with the most striking features being bright sunshine, small annual precipitation, dryness and purity of air, and large daily variations in temperature. Summers are characterized by hot, dry weather, with temperatures over 100° F occurring frequently during July and August. However, the low humidity makes these high temperatures somewhat bearable. Winters are short and mild, with the Rocky Mountains blocking cold air masses from the north and east.

Pluses: Very sunny, dry, and warm.

Minuses: Can be very hot and dry in summer.

Elevation: 2,880 feet

Relative Humidity: 40%
Wind Speed: 8.7 mph

Seasonal Change

Annual Rainfall 8 in

Annual Snowfall 3.5 in

Clear 153 days   Partly Cloudy 103 days   Cloudy 109 days

Precipitation Days: 24   Storm Days: 48

Average Temperatures			
	Daily High	Daily Low	Monthly Mean
January	53.1	25.7	39.2
February	56.9	30.5	44.5
March	65.1	36.0	51.8
April	74.5	43.6	60.5
May	83.0	50.8	68.3
June	95.0	58.2	76.6
July	101.4	66.0	83.7
August	95.8	62.8	82.1
September	93.6	55.8	74.7
October	80.4	42.4	62.1
November	64.7	30.3	48.0
December	55.0	27.0	40.8

Zero-Degree Days: 0
Freezing Days: 95
90-Degree Days: 117
Heating- and Cooling-Degree Days: 4,950

Places Rated Score: 554   **Places Rated Rank: 55**

SAN DIEGO, CA

Terrain: Located on San Diego Bay in the southwest corner of California near the Mexican border. Coastal location backed by coastal foothills and mountains to the east.

Climate: One of the mildest in North America. Typically marine, sometimes called Mediterranean. No freezing days and an average of only three 90-degree days each year. Abundant sunshine, mild sea breezes. Two seasons: A dry, mild summer, and a spring that is cooler with some rain. Storms are practically unknown, though there is considerable fog along the coast, and many low clouds appear in early morning and evening during the summer.

Pluses: One of the best climates for sun and mildness.

Minuses: "Paradise" climate lacking variety and seasonal contrasts.

Elevation: 28 feet

Relative Humidity: 68%
Wind Speed: 6.7 mph

Seasonal Change

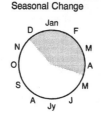

Annual Rainfall 9 in

Annual Snowfall 0 in

Clear 150 days   Partly Cloudy 117 days   Cloudy 98 days

Precipitation Days: 41   Storm Days: 3

Average Temperatures			
	Daily High	Daily Low	Monthly Mean
January	64.6	45.8	55.2
February	65.6	47.8	56.7
March	66.0	50.1	58.1
April	67.6	53.8	60.7
May	69.4	57.2	63.3
June	71.1	59.9	65.5
July	75.3	63.9	69.6
August	77.3	65.4	71.4
September	76.5	63.2	69.9
October	73.8	58.4	66.1
November	70.1	51.5	60.8
December	66.1	55.4	62.9

Zero-Degree Days: 0
Freezing Days: 0
90-Degree Days: 3
Heating- and Cooling-Degree Days: 2,229

Places Rated Score: 903   **Places Rated Rank: 1**

Santa Fe, NM

Terrain: This historic city, the capital of New Mexico and seat of Santa Fe County, sits in the Rio Grande Valley in the north central section of the state. It is situated amid the rolling foothills of the Sangre de Cristo Mountains, which rise to peaks of 10,000 feet. Westward the terrain slopes downward to the Rio Grande River, some 20 miles away. The high mountains to the east protect the city from much of the cold air of winter.The city's historic legacy, cultural facilities, and fine climate have long attracted tourists and retired people.
Climate: Semiarid continental, with cool and pleasant summers. Days are in the 80s, but nights in the 50s. Long cloudy periods are unknown. Winters are crisp, clear, and sunny, with considerable daytime warming.

Pluses: Beautiful scenery. Mild, sunny, four-season climate.

Minuses: Wide temperature range and high altitude may present health problems for some persons.

Places Rated Score: 615

Places Rated Rank: 26

Elevation: 7,200 feet

Relative Humidity: 50%
Wind Speed: 9 mph

Seasonal Change

Annual Rainfall 14 in

Annual Snowfall 32 in

Clear 172 days Partly Cloudy 110 days Cloudy 83 days

Precipitation Days: 37   Storm Days: 54

Average Temperatures			
	Daily High	Daily Low	Monthly Mean
January	41.0	19.3	29.9
February	44.9	22.5	33.7
March	51.6	26.8	39.2
April	61.7	34.5	48.0
May	70.7	42.9	56.6
June	81.4	52.1	66.4
July	84.3	56.7	70.4
August	82.2	55.0	68.6
September	76.5	49.1	62.9
October	65.2	38.7	52.0
November	51.5	26.5	39.0
December	43.3	21.2	32.0

Zero-Degree Days: 1
Freezing Days: 152
90-Degree Days: 7
Heating- and Cooling-Degree Days: 6,809

SANTA ROSA, CA

Terrain: Located in the east-central portion of the Petaluma–Santa Rosa–Russian River Valley, which extends northwestward from San Pablo Bay, about 45 miles from the Golden Gate. This valley lies parallel to the Pacific Coast, with only low hills (300 feet to 500 feet) between it and the ocean 25 miles southwest. Higher hills rise to the east of the city, with greater elevations about 10 miles farther east, in the foothills of the Coast Range.
Climate: The nearness of the ocean and the surrounding topography join with the prevailing westerly circulation in producing a predominantly southerly air flow year round. However, the city is sufficiently inland so that its climate is more varied than San Francisco's. Summers are warmer, winters cooler, and there is more daily temperature shift, less fog and drizzle.

Pluses: Mild, yet sunnier and warmer than coastal locations. Ideal retirement climate.

Minuses: Some hot weather.

Places Rated Score: 732

Places Rated Rank: 8

Elevation: 167 feet

Relative Humidity: 70%
Wind Speed: 7 mph

Seasonal Change

Annual Rainfall 30 in

Annual Snowfall 0 in

Clear 176 days Partly Cloudy 109 days Cloudy 80 days

Precipitation Days: 47   Storm Days: 4

Average Temperatures			
	Daily High	Daily Low	Monthly Mean
January	57.1	35.7	46.4
February	62.3	37.9	50.1
March	66.6	39.5	53.1
April	70.1	40.1	55.1
May	75.0	44.6	59.8
June	80.2	49.2	64.1
July	83.6	48.8	66.4
August	83.4	48.8	66.1
September	83.3	47.7	65.5
October	77.7	44.3	61.0
November	67.7	39.2	53.5
December	58.4	37.0	47.7

Zero-Degree Days: 0
Freezing Days: 43
90-Degree Days: 33
Heating- and Cooling-Degree Days: 3,900

SPRINGFIELD, MO

Terrain: Located on very gently rolling tableland, almost atop the crest of the Missouri Ozark Mountain Plateau. The average elevation of the city proper is just over 1,300 feet above sea level.
Climate: As a result of this advantageous position, the city and surrounding countryside enjoy what is described as a plateau climate. The area enjoys the mild and changeable climate often associated with high places in southerly latitudes, with warmer winters and cooler summers than other parts of the state at lower elevations. The city sits astride two major drainage systems: the Missouri River system to the north, and the White-Mississippi system to the south.

Pluses: Mild. Changeable.

Minuses: Short springs and falls.

Places Rated Score: 544

Places Rated Rank: 58

Elevation: 1,270 feet

Relative Humidity: 70%
Wind Speed: 11.2 mph

Seasonal Change

Annual Rainfall 40 in

Annual Snowfall 15 in

Clear 117 days Partly Cloudy 99 days Cloudy 149 days

Precipitation Days: 107   Storm Days: 58

Average Temperatures			
	Daily High	Daily Low	Monthly Mean
January	43.2	22.6	32.9
February	47.5	26.5	37.0
March	55.1	32.8	44.0
April	68.0	45.0	56.5
May	76.1	54.0	65.1
June	84.2	62.9	73.6
July	89.0	66.5	77.8
August	88.9	65.2	77.1
September	81.2	57.3	69.3
October	71.1	46.8	59.0
November	56.4	34.5	45.5
December	45.7	26.3	36.0

Zero-Degree Days: 3
Freezing Days: 105
90-Degree Days: 40
Heating- and Cooling-Degree Days: 5,952

STATE COLLEGE, PA

Terrain: Located in Centre County, the geographic center of the state of Pennsylvania. The orientation of the ridges and valleys of the Appalachian Mountains is northeast to southwest. Elevations within Centre County vary from 977 feet to 2,400 feet. The largest valley in the area is Nittany Valley, much of which is under cultivation. The surrounding higher elevations are covered with second-growth forests.
Climate: A composite of the relatively dry midwestern continental climate and the more humid climate characteristic of the eastern seaboard. Prevailing westerly winds carry weather disturbances from the interior of the country into the area; coastal storms occasionally affect the local weather as they move toward the northeast, but generally, the Atlantic is too distant to have a noticeable effect on the climate. Winters are cold and relatively dry, with thick cloud cover. Summer and fall are the most pleasant seasons of the year.

Pluses: Nice falls, summers.

Minuses: Humid. Lots of cloudy days.

Places Rated Score: 575

Places Rated Rank: 43

Elevation: 1,200 feet

Relative Humidity: 67%
Wind Speed: 7.8 mph

Seasonal Change

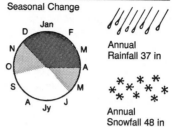

Annual Rainfall 37 in

Annual Snowfall 48 in

Clear 66 days
Partly Cloudy 114 days
Cloudy 185 days

Precipitation Days: 122 Storm Days: 35

Average Temperatures			
	Daily High	Daily Low	Monthly Mean
January	34.2	19.8	27.0
February	36.1	20.2	28.2
March	45.4	27.7	36.5
April	59.2	38.9	49.1
May	70.2	48.8	59.3
June	78.7	57.3	68.0
July	82.6	61.1	71.9
August	80.7	59.1	69.9
September	73.5	52.0	62.8
October	62.9	42.5	52.7
November	48.7	33.2	41.0
December	36.3	22.9	29.6

Zero-Degree Days: 4
Freezing Days: 132
90-Degree Days: 8
Heating- and Cooling-Degree Days: 6,797

TUCSON, AZ

Terrain: Lies at the foot of the Catalina Mountains in a flat to gently rolling valley floor in southern Arizona.
Climate: Desert, characterized by a long, hot season beginning in April and ending in October. Temperature maxima above 90° F are the rule during this period; and on 41 days each year, on the average, the temperature reaches 100° F. These high temperatures are modified by low humidity, reducing discomfort. Tucson lies in the zone receiving more sunshine than any other in the United States. Clear skies or very thin, high clouds permit intense surface heating during the day and active radiational cooling at night, a process enhanced by the characteristic atmospheric dryness.

Pluses: Clear. Warm. Dry.

Minuses: Intense summer heat.

Places Rated Score: 589

Places Rated Rank: 38

Elevation: 2,555 feet

Relative Humidity: 38%
Wind Speed: 8.2 mph

Seasonal Change

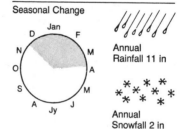

Annual Rainfall 11 in

Annual Snowfall 2 in

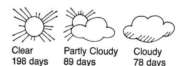

Clear 198 days
Partly Cloudy 89 days
Cloudy 78 days

Precipitation Days: 50 Storm Days: 40

Average Temperatures			
	Daily High	Daily Low	Monthly Mean
January	63.5	38.2	50.9
February	67.0	39.9	53.5
March	71.5	43.6	57.6
April	80.7	50.3	65.5
May	89.6	57.5	73.6
June	97.9	66.2	82.1
July	98.3	74.2	86.3
August	95.3	72.3	83.8
September	93.1	67.1	80.1
October	83.8	56.4	70.1
November	72.2	44.8	58.5
December	64.8	39.1	52.0

Zero-Degree Days: 0
Freezing Days: 21
90-Degree Days: 139
Heating- and Cooling-Degree Days: 4,566

Winchester, VA

Terrain: Located in central Frederick County, which is at the northern tip of the Shenandoah Valley and shares a common border with West Virginia on the north and west. The western part of the county is in the Allegheny Mountains, with Little North Mountain dividing it into two essentially different agricultural regions: Warmer-weather truck and farm crops to the east and more rugged, cold-weather farming and pasture to the west. The terrain varies from rolling–hilly to rugged in the mountains. Elevations range from 600 feet to 1,800 feet in the county.
Climate: Modified continental, with mild winters and warm, humid summers. The mountains produce various steering, blocking, and modifying effects on storms and air masses. High elevations near the city promote the downward flow of cool mountain air tempering otherwise hot summer nights. All seasons are pleasant, except that summer (especially July) can be hot.

Pluses: Scenic. Mild.

Minuses: Can be hot and humid.

Places Rated Score: 605

Places Rated Rank: 34

Elevation: 760 feet

Relative Humidity: 70%
Wind Speed: 8.3 mph

Seasonal Change

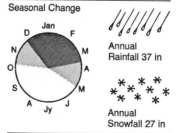

Annual Rainfall 37 in

Annual Snowfall 27 in

Clear 99 days
Partly Cloudy 103 days
Cloudy 163 days

Precipitation Days: 115 Storm Days: 47

Average Temperatures			
	Daily High	Daily Low	Monthly Mean
January	42.5	24.8	33.7
February	45.0	25.8	35.5
March	54.2	32.6	43.4
April	66.8	42.8	54.8
May	76.1	52.2	64.2
June	83.5	60.3	71.9
July	87.0	64.3	75.7
August	85.6	62.6	74.2
September	79.0	55.9	67.5
October	68.5	45.7	57.2
November	55.5	36.2	45.9
December	43.8	26.8	35.4

Zero-Degree Days: 0
Freezing Days: 103
90-Degree Days: 30
Heating- and Cooling-Degree Days: 5,504

Yuma, AZ

Terrain: Yuma is located in the extreme southwest corner of Arizona, near the California and Mexican borders. The land is typical desert-steppe, with dry, sandy, and dusty soil, scant vegetation, and craggy buttes and mountains that take their characteristic texture from wind erosion rather than water erosion. The various mountain ranges that surround Yuma are perhaps the dominant geologic features. They include the Trigo, Chocolate, Castle Dome, Mohawk, and Gila ranges.

Climate: Yuma's climate is definitely a desert product. Home heating is necessary from late October to mid-April. However, outdoor activities can be conducted comfortably during this period from 10:00 AM to 5:00 PM. It is very dry, with many places in the world receiving more rain in a year than has fallen in Yuma in the past 90 years. Yuma is officially the sunniest place in America.

Pluses: America's sunniest spot.

Minuses: Hot, dry, dusty.

Places Rated Score: 553

Places Rated Rank: 56

Elevation: 194 feet

Relative Humidity: 37%
Wind Speed: 7.8 mph

Seasonal Change

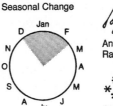

Annual Rainfall 2.7 in

Annual Snowfall 0 in

Clear 246 days   Partly Cloudy 68 days   Cloudy 51 days

Precipitation Days: 16   Storm Days: 7

Average Temperatures			
	Daily High	Daily Low	Monthly Mean
January	67.4	43.3	55.4
February	72.6	46.1	59.4
March	77.6	50.2	63.9
April	85.6	56.7	71.2
May	93.4	63.9	78.7
June	100.8	70.8	85.8
July	106.0	81.4	93.7
August	104.4	81.2	92.8
September	100.3	73.9	87.1
October	89.8	62.0	75.9
November	76.5	50.5	63.5
December	68.2	44.4	56.3

Zero-Degree Days: 0
Freezing Days: 2
90-Degree Days: 168
Heating- and Cooling-Degree Days: 5,205

Et Cetera

CLIMATE AND HEALTH

People have long noticed the relationship between climate and physical well-being. Some of the earliest spas were those of the ancient Romans. Such places as Pompeii and the island of Capri were warm and pleasant even in the middle of winter, and their natural hot springs—fed by seawater flowing over heated rock near active volcanoes—provided relief from aching joints and muscles.

Not much has changed since the days of ancient Rome. While air conditioning has made comfortable living possible in hot, steamy climes, many places in Europe and America have become popular because of their pleasant, healthful climates. For example, the arid desert regions of America's Southwest—particularly the states of Arizona, New Mexico, and Utah—have long been famous for providing relief from respiratory allergies and diseases. Those who have tuberculosis, emphysema, or asthma generally improve in the warm, dry air that is relatively free from airborne pollens, mold spores, excessive moisture, and other irritants. Similarly, the high mountain country of the southern Appalachians has been known during the last hundred years as a region where invalids (particularly people with tuberculosis) could recover their health amid beautiful scenery.

A classic work in the field of bioclimatology is H. E. Landsberg's *Weather and Health* (1969). This book explains in detail some of the relationships that have been observed between climate/weather and the aggravation of, or relief from, various physical afflictions. Drawing on this and other works, *Places Rated* describes some basic weather phenomena and explains how they can affect the way you feel.

Stages of Weather Progression

The weather changes that initiate responses in the body have been carefully studied by meteorologists and classified into six basic stages, which make up the clear-stormy-clear weather cycle that repeats itself constantly all over the globe. The stages in the cycle have been successfully linked to some of the joys and tragedies of human existence.

The Six Stages of Weather Progression

Stage 1. Cool, high-pressure air, with few clouds and moderate winds, followed by . . .

Stage 2. Perfectly clear, dry air, high pressure, and little wind, which leads to . . .

Stage 3. Considerable warming, steady or slightly falling pressure, and some high clouds, until . . .

Stage 4. The warm, moist air gets into the lower layers; pressure falls, clouds thicken, precipitation is common, and the wind picks up speed; then . . .

Stage 5. An abrupt change takes place: showery precipitation is accompanied by cold, gusty winds, rapidly rising pressure, and falling humidity as the moisture in the air is released.

Stage 6. Gradually, the pressure rises still further and the clouds diminish; temperatures reach low levels and the humidity continues to drop, leading back to . . .

Stage 1. Cool, high-pressure air. . . .

Of course, these phases aren't equally long, either in any given sequence or in the course of a year. During winter, all six stages may follow each other within three days, while in the summer two weeks may pass before the cycle is completed.

Obviously, the "beautiful weather" stages 1 and 2 stimulate the body very little. They make few demands on us that cannot be met by adequate clothing and housing. In contrast, weather stages 4 and 5 are often violent; they stir us up, both mentally and physically.

That weather phases affect the human body is beyond question; the records of hospital births and deaths prove it. For example, in the case of human pregnancy, in far more cases than statistical accident would permit, labor begins on days that are in weather stage 3. Coronary thrombosis—"heart attack"—shows a strong peak of frequency in weather stages 3 and 4, and a definite low in stages 1 and 6. Bleeding ulcers and migraine attacks peak in stage 4, too.

Weather events may affect our moods and behavior as well. There is a strong correlation between weather stage 3 and suicide, behavior problems in schoolchildren, and street riots. A study in Poland over a five-year period (1966–70) showed that accident rates in factory workers doubled during cyclonic weather conditions (stages 3 and 4: periods of falling pressure, rising temperatures and humidity, which signal the onset of stormy weather) and returned to normal low levels in fair weather. And animals as well as humans are affected. Dogcatchers are invariably busiest during stages 3, 4, and 5 because dogs become restless, stray from their homes, and wander through the streets.

The Three Determinants of Human Comfort

As the six weather stages suggest, everyday human comfort is influenced by three basic climatic factors:

humidity, temperature, and barometric pressure.

Humidity. Humidity, or the amount of moisture in the air, is closely related to air temperature in determining the comfort level of the atmosphere. Much of the discomfort and nervous tension experienced at the approach of stormy weather (weather stage 4), for example, is the result of rising temperatures and humidity. These atmospheric conditions are also responsible at least in part for the behavioral problems and medical emergencies described previously.

Extremely high levels of atmospheric moisture, such as those experienced most of the time in the Pacific Northwest and around the Gulf of Mexico and southern Atlantic Coast, aren't usually the cause of direct discomfort except in persons suffering from certain types of arthritis or rheumatism. But even in these cases, the mild temperatures found in these maritime locations usually do much to offset discomfort. In fact, the stability of the barometric pressure (which means small or gradual shifts in the air pressure) in these areas makes them ideal for people with muscle and joint pain.

But damp air coupled with low temperatures can be uncomfortable. Most people who've experienced damp winters, especially in places with high winds, complain that the cold, wet wind seems to go right through them. And the harmful effect of cold, damp air on pulmonary diseases, particularly tuberculosis, has long been known. With this in mind, it's wise to consider carefully before moving to the northerly coastal locations on the Eastern Seaboard—Cape Cod and the coast of Maine, for example—where these conditions will be common during the winter months.

Perhaps the most noticeable drawback to very moist air is the wide variety of organisms it supports. Bacteria, and the spores of fungi and molds, thrive in moist air but are almost absent in dry air. If the air is moist and also warm, the problem is multiplied. Therefore, people prone to bacterial skin infections, fungal infections such as athlete's foot, or mold aller-

Temperature, Humidity, and Apparent Temperature

Apparent Temperature

Air Temperature (°F)	0	5	10	15	20	25	30	35	40	45	50	55	60	65	70	75	80	85	90	95	100
110	99	102	105	108	112	117	123	130	137	143	150										
105	95	97	100	102	105	109	113	118	123	129	135	142	149								
100	91	93	95	97	99	101	104	107	110	115	120	126	132	138	144						
95	87	88	90	91	93	94	96	98	101	104	107	110	114	119	124	130	136				
90	83	84	85	86	87	88	90	91	93	95	96	98	100	102	106	109	113	117	122		
85	78	79	80	81	82	83	84	85	86	87	88	89	90	91	93	95	97	99	102	105	108
80	73	74	75	76	77	77	78	79	79	80	81	81	82	83	85	86	86	87	88	89	91
75	69	69	70	71	72	72	73	73	74	74	75	75	76	76	77	77	78	78	79	79	80
70	64	64	65	65	66	66	67	67	68	68	69	69	70	70	70	70	71	71	71	71	72

Relative Humidity (%)

Locate the air temperature at the left and the relative humidity along the bottom. The intersection of the horizontal row of figures opposite the temperature with the vertical row of figures above the relative humidity is the apparent temperature. For example, an air temperature of 85 degrees feels like 89 degrees at 55 percent relative humidity; but when the humidity is 90 percent, 85 degrees feels like 102.

Apparent Temperatures (July)

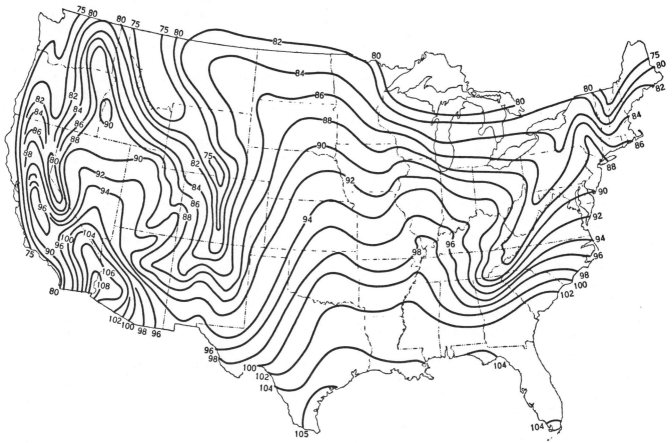

Source: National Oceanic and Atmospheric Administration, National Climatic Center, Asheville, North Carolina.

gies should carefully check out places with high humidities before moving there.

On the other end of the spectrum, very dry air produces effects on our bodies that are perceptible almost immediately and can cause discomfort within a day. When the relative humidity falls below 50 percent, most of us experience dry nasal passages and perhaps a dry, tickling throat. In the dry areas of the Southwest, where the humidity can drop to 20 percent or less, many people experience nosebleeds, flaking skin, and a constant sore throat.

Temperature. Many bioclimatologists maintain that the human body (or most human bodies) is most comfortable and productive at "65–65," meaning an air temperature of 65 degrees with 65 percent humidity. High relative humidity intensifies the felt effect of high temperatures (see the table "Temperature, Humidity, and Apparent Temperature") because it impairs the evaporative cooling effect of sweating. At apparent temperatures as low as 80 to 90 degrees Fahrenheit, a person may begin to suffer symptoms of heat stress. The degree of heat stress experienced will vary depending on age, health, and body characteristics; generally speaking, infants, young children, and older

people are most likely to be affected by high temperature/humidity combinations. In the summer of 1980, record heat waves often accompanied by high humidity swept the Southwest, leaving hundreds dead.

The map "Apparent Temperatures (July)" shows how felt temperatures vary across the country. The places in America where the highest temperatures are constantly recorded are mostly in the desert areas of the Great Basin (the southern half of the plateau between the Sierra Nevada to the west and the Rocky Mountains to the east), the great interior valley of California, and parts of the High Plains regions of New Mexico, Oklahoma, and Texas. However, these areas are generally dry, so the effects of the high temperatures on the human body are not particularly noticeable or damaging. This is particularly true of the locations west of eastern New Mexico.

America's southeastern quadrant (which includes those states that border on the Gulf of Mexico and the southern half of the Atlantic Coast) has temperatures that are less spectacularly high but humidity that can be very oppressive. Most people would find a 90-degree day in Mobile or Orlando far more uncomfortable than they would the same temperature in Las Vegas or Yuma, Arizona.

What about cold temperatures? In the past, most retirement-aged people have shunned cold weather in favor of the hot and sunny "beach" climates of the Sun Belt. More recently, however, they're discovering the benefits of seasonal change and some cold weather, particularly around the holiday season. Therefore, *Places Rated Retirement Guide* includes many retirement places that have cold weather. Some of these—most notably in Michigan, Wisconsin, and Montana—have winters that can be rigorous and are not for the faint of heart.

Cold weather can have an adverse effect on persons with heart or circulatory ailments. According to Landsberg, these diseases follow a seasonal pattern, with a peak of deaths occurring in January and February. The cooling of the extremities can place greater stress on the heart as it tries to maintain a safe body temperature; breathing very cold air can tax the heart-lung system, and some persons who have hardening of the coronary arteries may get chest pains when outdoors in a cold wind. Cold weather can also increase blood pressure, with adverse consequences for those with circulatory problems. Although extremely cold (polar) weather inhibits the survival of respiratory germs, these microbes thrive in a damp, cloudy, cool climate, and contribute to high incidences of influenza, bronchitis, and colds.

As the body ages, its circulatory system loses effectiveness. Add to this another natural consequence of aging—the decreased rate of the metabolic system (which keeps the body warm)—and you have partially explained older people's need for higher household temperatures. Therefore, the expense of heating costs in a cool climate may offset the appeal of seasonal changes and winter weather.

But despite the dangers of extremes of heat or cold, sudden wide shifts of temperature in either direction constitute the gravest threat to human health. When the weather and especially the temperature change suddenly and dramatically, the rates of cardiac arrest, respiratory distress, stroke, and other medical emergencies skyrocket. This is true mostly in the older population.

Sudden atmospheric cooling can bring on attacks of asthma, bronchitis, and stroke. Heart attacks and other associated symptoms are also more frequent following these periods of rapid cooling. Often these are produced by changing air masses during autumn, particularly by the passage of a cold frontal system following a quickly falling barometer.

A sudden rise in the temperature may precipitate its own assortment of medical emergencies, among them heat stroke, heart attack, and stroke. It has been found that during a heat wave, the nighttime maximum temperatures are far more significant than the daytime maxima. This is because the body recuperates

during the night. A hot night prevents the body from reestablishing its thermal equilibrium and tends to lessen the amount of sleep people get, thus increasing fatigue. Hospital employees call these sudden temperature shifts, which cause so much discomfort and harm, especially to older people, ambulance weather. It's a term that proves to be accurate, if unseemly. A study of the New York City heat wave of July 1966 revealed that the death rate more than doubled during the period of record temperatures. The number of deaths from flu and pneumonia rose 315 percent, from strokes more than 176 percent, from heart attacks 161 percent, and from cancer 128 percent.

Barometric pressure. Even though most people may be unaware of the source of their discomfort, barometric pressure—and wide and rapid fluctuations in it—is an extremely powerful influence on human performance, comfort, and health. Pressure changes are felt even more keenly by older persons, whose bodies are generally more sensitive to change. As previously stated, the rapid fall of pressure that signals the arrival of storms and advancing cold fronts can trigger episodes of asthma, heart disease, stroke, and pain in joints. People with rheumatism or arthritis may be suffering unduly if they live in places where the pressure changes are continual and rapid. The map "Pressure Changes from Day to Day (February)" shows the regions with greatest and least pressure change during the average day in February, when joint pain and other discomforts reach their peak.

As the map shows, the northern and eastern sections of the country experience the greatest variance, averaging a barometric change of .20 inches to .25 inches from one day to the next. (In summer, when pressure changes are relatively small, the average change in these regions is approximately .10 inches.) States in the southern latitudes, particularly Florida and southern California, show the least change, only about .10 inches in February (and less than .05 inches in summer). Of course, these figures are averages, and along the Gulf and Atlantic coasts, large and rapid pressure changes are caused on occasion by hurricanes.

The map, and the phenomenon it depicts, explains perhaps more than any other single reason why so many older people have chosen to move to Florida and the Gulf Coast. Additionally, due to the stabilizing and modifying effect that large bodies of water have on temperature and pressure, weather conditions by seacoasts are steadier than those of most inland, desert, or mountain locations.

Although the climates found in Florida and other Gulf states are not as mild or pleasant as they are advertised to be, there is no denying that the semitropical climate—hot, humid, monotonous, and even depressing as it might be to some—is just about perfect for people with severe rheumatoid joint pain or those who cannot tolerate sudden changes in the weather.

Where to Go to Find Relief

Here is a breakdown of disorders that can be helped to some extent by climatic change. Following each are places to avoid and those to seek, at least for a trial period.

People with heart conditions should definitely avoid extreme heat and cold, rapid temperature variations, and extreme and sudden pressure changes. This seems to rule out most interior regions as well as northerly ones, even those on coastal locations. Recommended are places that have warm, mild, and steady weather. Mountains and high altitude should be avoided on two counts: less oxygen and strain caused by steep grades. Best bets are southerly coastal locations where sea-level, oxygen-rich air, and stable pressures and temperatures predominate most of the year. Look from the mid-Atlantic Shore southward around Florida, along the Gulf, and on the southern half of the Pacific coastline.

Emphysema brings a completely different set of problems and solutions. In general, excessive dampness coupled with cool or cold weather is harmful. This eliminates all northerly locations, particularly those on both coasts and around the Great Lakes. Southerly coastal locations would be better, but the air is perhaps still too damp. Seek out warm, sunny, dry climates such as those found in Arizona, New Mexico, Utah, Nevada, and the interior valleys of California. Remember, though, that high elevations should be avoided.

Asthma is a complex disorder that isn't totally understood yet. While it is believed to be an autoimmune disorder similar to allergies, it may be precipitated or worsened by different things in different individuals. Your wisest course is to consult medical specialists first to determine, if possible, the specific causes of your attacks. (If airborne allergens seem to be primarily responsible, consult the tables in the chapter "Health and Health Care.") Asthmatics seem to do best in pollen-free, dry, warm air. This is found in greatest abundance in the Southwest. Because desert air can be dusty, moderate altitude may be beneficial.

Tuberculosis, a disease recently considered under control and fast disappearing, is on the rise again. It generally strikes people who have weakened resistance to infection, making older people more susceptible than the rest of the population. Treatment is multifaceted, but an area that is mild, dry, sunny, and has clear air helps a great deal. Mountain locations have always been popular and can provide relief if the altitude is not excessive. Because dampness isn't recommended, the dry, sunny places in the southern mountains of the West are preferable to locations in the southern Appalachians, though these are also good. Ocean breezes are thought to be beneficial, too, and may be better for people who cannot tolerate the slightly more rugged climate of the interior mountains. Hawaii or the coast of southern California would be ideal.

For people with rheumatic pains, and discomfort in amputated limbs (called phantom pains because the limb is absent) or in old scar tissue, the warm and

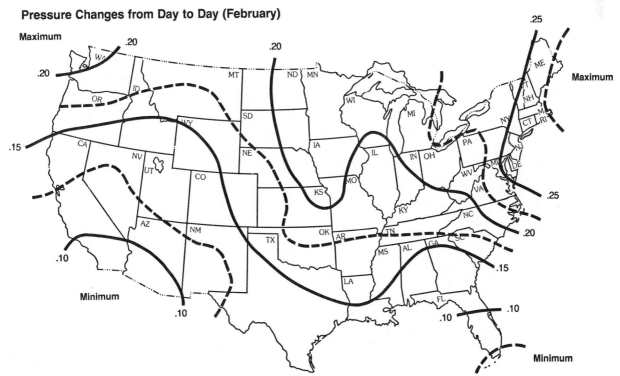

Pressure Changes from Day to Day (February)

Source: National Oceanic and Atmospheric Administration, National Climatic Center, Asheville, North Carolina.

steady climates of the subtropics are perfect. Here the surrounding water keeps temperatures and pressures from shifting quickly, and the prevailing warmth is soothing. It would be hard to miss with any seafront location from Myrtle Beach, South Carolina, south to the Florida Keys, around and up the west coast of the Florida peninsula, westward along the Gulf and down to Rockport–Aransas Pass, Texas, or points even farther south. Southern California and Hawaii, of course, should not be overlooked.

So is *Places Rated* saying that people should avoid the northern country altogether? No! Let's not forget those retirees (and others) who are in robust health, or who have no weather-sensitive ailment. And let's not disregard the many people who tire of an endless procession of sunny days and clear skies. Finally, let's consider the effect of an extremely mild climate on the large number of Americans who have spent most of their lives in the northern half of the country and several hundred miles from either coast. To a great many born and raised amid four distinct seasons, each with its own special significance and nostalgia, the monotony of a one- or two-season climate can lead to boredom and depression. After all, people seem to thrive on change and challenge. And while you might not be ready to take on a place like Kalispell, Montana, it would be wise to explore the variable and stimulating climates of the northern coasts, the Great Lakes, or the mountains of the East or West.

And Finally, Some Caveats

Any person considering moving to a different climate to alleviate certain ailments should seek expert counsel. *Places Rated* talked with Bill Hodge of the National Climatic Center in Asheville, North Carolina, for his views. Over the years, Hodge has been closely associated with climate and health studies at the center, and he was a leading spokesman at the Climate and Health Workshop in Research Triangle Park, North Carolina.

Bill Hodge's observations and responses to *Places*

The 7 Sunniest Retirement Places   . . . and the 6 Cloudiest

	Clear Days per Year		Cloudy Days per Year
Yuma, AZ	246	Port Angeles–Strait of Juan de Fuca, WA	246
LAS VEGAS, NV	216	OLYMPIA, WA	228
PHOENIX, AZ	214	Kalispell, MT	213
TUCSON, AZ	198	Lincoln City–Newport, OR	210
LAS CRUCES, NM	194	Petoskey–Straits of Mackinac, MI	209
Roswell, NM	176	Bennington, VT	206
SANTA ROSA, CA	176		

Listed above are those retirement places described in the Place Profiles that have more than 175 clear days per year or more than 200 cloudy days. Yuma is the sunniest place in America for which data are recorded.

The 9 Dampest Retirement Places   . . . and the 9 Driest

	Relative Humidity		Relative Humidity
Lincoln City–Newport, OR	82%	LAS VEGAS, NV	29%
North Conway–White Mountains, NH	80	PHOENIX, AZ	36
Port Angeles–Strait of Juan de Fuca, WA	80	Yuma, AZ	37
Rockport–Aransas Pass, TX	80	TUCSON, AZ	38
Camden–Penobscot Bay, ME	79	St. George–Zion, UT	40
Cape Cod, MA	78	ALBUQUERQUE, NM	43
BILOXI–GULFPORT, MS	77	Grand Junction, CO	47
Hendersonville, NC	77	Roswell, NM	48
Maui, HI	76	COLORADO SPRINGS, CO	49

Listed above are those retirement places described in the Place Profiles with an average relative humidity greater than 75 percent or less than 50 percent.

Rated's questions contained a few surprises. While confirming that some regions of America are better than others for certain maladies, he stressed the fact that individual sensitivities show such variation that general recommendations for health moves should be made—and followed—only with caution.

Hodge stated that "we know that many cases of bronchial asthma are triggered by cold fronts and humid air. Therefore, it's been an almost standard recommendation over the years for people with this condition to move to the sunny Southwest. And, to be sure, many asthmatics have moved to places like Arizona and found relief. But . . . many others have moved there only to find their problem worsening. Why, when Arizona has warm, dry air and sunshine? Well, the Southwest also has pollen and dust, which can aggravate asthma. Therefore it's often a trade-off between two types of irritation." The answer? Before you move, said Hodge, take up residence in your chosen destination for at least several weeks, and during different seasons of the year. This way you'll get a good idea of how your body will react to the various weather conditions and allergens.

Bill Hodge, like so many others, suffers from a mild sinus condition. He's noticed over the years that his condition takes a decided change for the worse during the approach of cold fronts from the North. Why? He's not sure but suspects it has to do with more than just temperature change. One suspicion is that ions, or charged air particles, may be the culprits. In any case, it's certainly more than possible that the same irritant in the cold fronts that affects his sinuses is what triggers attacks in asthmatics, too. "But maybe it's not ions at all," Hodge said, "but simply pollen. The worst region in the country for allergenic pollen is the agricultural Midwest. Perhaps those cold fronts coming down here from the North bring a lot of pollen with them. Who knows?"

Where, then, should you move? Remember first and foremost Hodge's cautionary words: Don't buy property and take off without several trial periods of residence in your dream location. This is good advice for anyone, but particularly for persons with health complaints. You may discover that an existing medical condition is aggravated, not improved, in your new place. Or you might even see the emergence of a new problem brought on by the new location. Remember always that individual human bodies, with their unique quirks, tolerances, and sensitivities, are far more important determinants of acclimatization than are even the most well-founded generalizations.

LIFE AT THE TOP

Many places at high elevations have long been regarded as healthful and desirable, but high altitude carries risks for some people. Many mountain resort areas, like those found in the southern Appalachians, got their start as health retreats for people suffering from tuberculosis. The clear mountain air was thought to be beneficial for the lungs. While most mountain air is clear and relatively free from pollutants, it is also less dense and contains less oxygen. If you suffer from asthma, emphysema, or anemia, you should consult local physicians before moving to any place more than 2,000 feet above sea level. Even if all indications point to a positive reaction on your part, it would be wise to take up residence for several months at least before making a permanent move.

For those who can tolerate high altitudes, the advantages of such locations are well known. Because atmospheric temperature decreases with increasing elevation (about 3.3 degrees Fahrenheit per 1,000 feet), places at high elevations in southerly locales (such as Santa Fe, New Mexico; or Asheville, Hendersonville, and Brevard, North Carolina) enjoy the long summers and mild winters typical of the South, and also the cool summer nights, crisp falls, and absence of mugginess usually associated with more northerly areas.

Since altitude puts a certain amount of stress on the body's circulatory system and lungs, becoming acclimated to high places makes us healthier. Our lung capacity increases, our hearts grow stronger, and the number and proportion of red blood cells increase.

In the United States, the highest town with an official post office is Climax, Colorado. At 11,350 feet, Climax is perhaps beyond the comfort range of most people, particularly those of retirement age. Up there, a three-minute egg takes seven minutes to boil, corn on the cob needs to be on the fire 45 minutes, and home-brewed beer matures in half the expected time. Yet many of the 1,500 residents love it. The incidence of infection is amazingly low, and insects are practically unknown. In the East, the highest town of any size is Highlands, North Carolina, near the Great Smoky Mountains. Though less than half as high up as Climax, Highlands and the neighboring towns offer the cool, clear air and invigorating climate that have long drawn people to the mountains.

The table below shows the states with the greatest and the least mean elevation; it also identifies the highest and lowest points in each state.

Mean and Extreme Elevations

Highest States	Mean Elevation in Feet	Highest Place (Elevation)	Lowest Place (Elevation)
1. Colorado	6,800	Mount Elbert (14,494)	Arkansas River (3,350)
2. Wyoming	6,700	Gannett Peak (13,804)	Belle Fourche River (3,100)
3. Utah	6,100	Kings Peak (13,528)	Beaverdam Creek (2,000)
4. New Mexico	5,700	Wheeler Peak (13,161)	Red Bluff Reservoir (2,817)
5. Nevada	5,500	Boundary Peak (13,143)	Colorado River (470)
6. Idaho	5,000	Borah Peak (12,662)	Snake River (710)
7. Arizona	4,100	Humphreys Peak (12,633)	Colorado River (70)
8. Montana	3,400	Granite Peak (12,799)	Kootenai River (1,800)
9. Oregon	3,300	Mount Hood (11,235)	Pacific Ocean (sea level)
10. Hawaii	3,030	Mauna Kea (13,796)	Pacific Ocean (sea level)

Lowest States			
1. Delaware	60	Ebright Road (442)	Atlantic Ocean (sea level)
2. Florida	100	Sec. 30, T. 6 N, R. 20 W (345)	Atlantic Ocean (sea level)
2. Louisiana	100	Driskill Mountain (555)	New Orleans (−5)
4. Rhode Island	200	Jerimoth Hill (812)	Atlantic Ocean (sea level)
5. New Jersey	250	High Point (1,803)	Atlantic Ocean (sea level)
6. Mississippi	300	Woodall Mountain (806)	Gulf of Mexico (sea level)
7. Maryland	350	Backbone Mountain (3,360)	Atlantic Ocean (sea level)
7. South Carolina	350	Sassafras Mountain (3,560)	Atlantic Ocean (sea level)
9. Alabama	500	Cheaha Mountain (2,407)	Gulf of Mexico (sea level)
9. Connecticut	500	Mount Frissell (2,380)	Atlantic Ocean (sea level)
9. Massachusetts	500	Mount Greylock (3,491)	Atlantic Ocean (sea level)

Source: U.S. Geological Survey, Elevations and Distances, 1975.

NATURE ON THE RAMPAGE

We're all familiar—even if only through television or newspapers—with the awesome destruction that nature can unleash. Perhaps no sight in recent memory was more dramatic than the eruption of Mount St. Helens in 1980, with an initial blast equivalent to that of 10 million tons of TNT, which blew off the topmost 1,300 feet of the mountain. Volcanic eruptions can wipe out lives and property in an instant. Fortunately, however, volcanoes usually give warning of impending activity, as did Mount St. Helens. Even more fortunately, the places where volcanic activity is a potential hazard are very few. A number of violent natural events are much more common and widespread, and although they may be less cataclysmic than a full-blown volcanic eruption, they can cause great damage and present life-threatening conditions. Many of these natural hazards follow definite geographic patterns within the United States, and some retirement places are at much greater risk than others.

The Sun Belt Is Also a Storm Belt

Many if not most severe storms occur in the southern half of the nation. For this reason, you might say that the Sun Belt is also a storm belt.

Thunderstorms and Lightning. Thunderstorms are common and don't usually cause death. But lightning kills 200 Americans a year. It remains the most common and frequent natural danger. At any given moment there are about 2,000 thunderstorms in progress around the globe; in the time it takes you to read this paragraph, lightning will have struck the earth 700 times.

Florida, the Sunshine State, is actually the country's stormiest state, with three times as much thunder and lightning as any other. California, on the other hand, is one of the three most storm-free states (the other two are Oregon and Washington). In a typical year, coastal California towns will average between two and five thunderstorm episodes. Most American towns average between 35 and 50. Fort Myers, Florida, averages 128. (A thunderstorm episode represents the presence of a single storm cell; a place like Fort Myers can register four or five episodes in a single day.)

The Place Profiles earlier in this chapter tell how many thunderstorm days each place can expect in an average year. The southeastern quadrant of our country generally receives more rain and thunderstorms than the rest, although the thunderstorms of the Great Plains are awesome spectacles.

Tornadoes. While they are not nearly as large or long-lived as hurricanes and release much less total force, tornadoes have more destructive and killing power concentrated in a small area than any other storm known. For absolute ferocity and wind speed, a tornado has no rival.

The hallmark of this vicious inland storm is the huge, snakelike funnel cloud that sweeps and bounces along the ground, destroying buildings, sweeping up cars, trains, livestock, and trees, and sucking them up hundreds of feet into the whirling vortex. Wind speeds close to 300 miles per hour have been recorded.

Although no one can tell for certain just where a particular tornado might touch down, their season, origin, and direction of travel are fairly predictable. Tornado season reaches its peak in late spring and early summer, and most storms originate in the central and southern Great Plains, in the states of Oklahoma, Texas, Arkansas, Kansas, and Missouri. After forming in the intense heat and rising air of the plains, these storms proceed toward the northeast at speeds averaging 25 to 40 miles per hour. Most tornadoes do not last very long or travel very far. Half of all tornadoes reported travel less than five miles on the ground; a few have been tracked for more than 200 miles.

Of our retirement places, the lake locations in Oklahoma, any location in Texas or Arkansas, and even the locations in Kentucky and Tennessee have a high potential for tornado damage and danger (see map). Nearly one third of all tornadoes ever reported in the United States have occurred within the boundaries of Kansas, Oklahoma, and Texas.

Hurricanes. Giant tropical cyclonic storms that originate at sea, hurricanes are unmatched for sheer power over a very large area. Hurricanes last for days, measure hundreds of miles across, and release tremendous energy in the form of high winds, torrential rains, lightning, and tidal surges. They occur in late summer and fall, and strike the Gulf states and southern segments of the Atlantic Coast primarily, though they will also strike locations farther north (see map). Like thunderstorms, hurricanes are much less frequent, and less severe, on the Pacific Coast.

Hurricanes usually originate in the tropical waters of the Atlantic Ocean. They occur toward summer's end because it takes that long for the water temperature and evaporation rate to rise sufficiently to begin the cyclonic, counterclockwise rotation of a wind system around a low-pressure system. When the wind velocities are less than 39 miles per hour, this cyclone is called a tropical depression; when wind velocities are between 39 and 74 miles per hour, the cyclone is called a tropical storm. And when the winds reach 74 miles per hour, the storm becomes a hurricane.

Often the greatest danger and destruction from hurricanes aren't due to the winds but to the tidal surges that sweep ashore with seas 15 or more feet higher than normal high tides. Although Florida and the southern coasts are most vulnerable to hurricanes, locations as far north as Cape Cod and the coast of Maine are by no means immune.

Earthquake Hazard

California and the states of the Pacific Northwest may be relatively free of the thunderstorms, tornadoes, and hurricanes that buffet other parts of the country. But

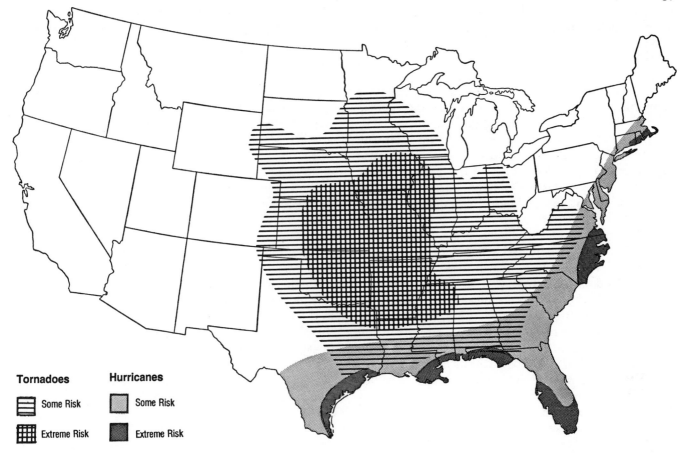

Tornadoes

Some Risk

Extreme Risk

Hurricanes

Some Risk

Extreme Risk

Earthquake Hazard Zones

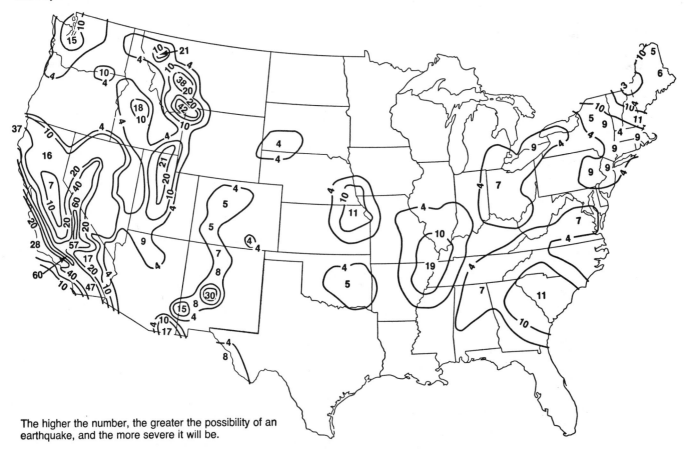

The higher the number, the greater the possibility of an earthquake, and the more severe it will be.

Source: U.S. Geological Survey Open-File Report 76-416, 1976.

these states are in the area of the country most prone to earthquake damage. A glance at the map "Earthquake Hazard Zones," which predicts not only the probability of earthquakes but their severity as well, confirms this.

All retirement places in California, Nevada, and Utah have the potential for substantial earthquake damage. Some locations in Oregon (such as Bend, Medford, and Lincoln City–Newport) are relatively safe, but the Puget Sound area of Washington has experienced two major shocks in the past 35 years, both causing considerable damage. Portions of Montana and Idaho also are very vulnerable to earthquakes.

Other pockets of earthquake risk might surprise you. Albuquerque is situated in a danger area, and so is Deming, New Mexico. The resorts of the South Carolina and Georgia coasts sit in the middle of a quake-sensitive zone that was the site of the strongest quake ever measured east of the Mississippi (it happened in Charleston, South Carolina, in 1886). The entire New England region shares a danger roughly comparable to this area; Boston has suffered a severe quake and remains earthquake-prone today. A series of quakes occurred in southeastern Missouri in 1811–12, changing the course of the Mississippi River and creating a major lake. There is still some risk in this area, which includes the retirement places in western Kentucky and Tennessee and part of the Ozarks.

Conclusion: When It Comes to Natural Hazards, You Just Can't Win

After studying the maps for a while, you may come to the dismal conclusion that you cannot win: Where one natural disaster area stops, another begins. Some areas, like the coasts of South Carolina and Georgia, appear to contain a "triple threat" combination of earthquake, tornado, and hurricane possibilities.

Studying the map more closely, you might begin to detect retirement areas that seem safer than others. One "safe" area appears to be the Pacific Northwest, with the exception of the significant earthquake risk around Puget Sound. Much of Arizona, Utah, and New Mexico also seems relatively free from disaster risk. The southern Appalachians, despite a moderate earthquake risk, do not experience many storms, due to the protection of the mountains. But some parts of the region are very flood-prone. And moderate earthquake risk seems almost unavoidable anywhere but the frigid North Central Plains or the steamy, tornado-ridden flatlands of Texas and the Gulf States.

So, as with most things in life, when it comes to avoiding natural disasters, you can only pay your money and take your chances.

Housing:
Affording it in retirement

"It's like a sex drive," Martin Mayer quoted a well-known housing economist in his book *The Builders*, "—to own my own home on my own piece of land." It may well be. And it may well be true that people can't get too much housing, as brokers and contractors tell themselves when they want to endow their professions with recession-proof respectability.

But when you retire, even though the drive to own your own address and the land surrounding it is undiminished, you may find that you've finally got too much housing indeed. This phenomenon is called overhousing, and it comes on when children grow up, leave home, and scatter like tumbleweeds in the wind. The signs are unmistakable. Rooms are furnished but closed off, the creakings and settlings you used to hear at night when everything was quiet you now hear all the time, and the bills for property taxes, insurance, and upkeep on the old ark are still high and still being paid.

Overhousing isn't the exclusive province of "empty nesters," however. If you're planning to travel during your retirement, an unoccupied house and a yard running to weeds may give you cause for worry at a time when you're trying to enjoy yourself. Moreover, your home is now your biggest asset; more than seven of every ten retired persons in this country own their home, and 85 percent of these people have paid off their mortgage. Might your home's market value,

which has appreciated over the years, be put to better use? Perhaps now is the time to take advantage of the once-in-a-lifetime $125,000 capital-gains exclusion for people over 55 who sell their homes.

Consider your options. You can:

- Stay at your present address. Five out of six retired people in this country do, according to the latest census statistics on geographic mobility.
- Stay close to town but sell or rent your home and move to another address, perhaps an apartment, condominium, or smaller house. One in ten retired people take this route.
- Move out of town to another part of the state and buy or rent other housing. One retired person in 25 does this.
- Move out of state and either buy or rent housing there. For every 29 retired people, one of them takes this course.

MAJOR HOUSING CHOICES

If your response to the burdens of overhousing is to move, you may want to scale down your housing needs as you look for another address. And if you're thinking of moving to a retirement place hundreds of miles distant, you'll undoubtedly need to know what housing prices and choices you'll encounter there.

Single Houses

Cape Cods and Cape Anns, American and Dutch colonials, California bungalows and Puget Sounds, garrison houses and catslides, desert adobes, plantation cottages, mountain A-frames and cabins of peeled pine log, Greek revivals, Victorians, suburban split-levels, glass solaria and earth berms—there are several thousand possible combinations of building styles, interior layouts, and story configurations in the National Association of Realtors classification system. Single houses are still the major option simply because there are so many of them (57 million in the United States) and because so many of them are for sale.

You can buy single houses in local neighborhoods of retirement places, or you can buy a single house in a retirement village or planned community. Most planned communities offer a wide range of services and facilities, such as recreational centers, club meeting rooms, and swimming pools. Some, like Sun City in the Phoenix metro area, are large enough to include shopping centers, medical centers, and golf courses.

If you look past architecture to the inside of a typical house, the features that come up most frequently on the Census Bureau's Annual Housing Survey form a composite house that was built in 1964, has a single-level layout with five rooms—three bedrooms, one bath, a complete kitchen—no basement, and an insulated attic and storm windows to conserve the heat from its gas-fired, warm-air furnace. This house is kept cool during hot spells by a central air-conditioning unit. It is on city water and sewerage lines. But the percentage of single homes among all housing units varies from retirement place to place.

Single Houses in the Retirement Places

Most Single Houses	As % of All Units	Fewest Single Houses	As % of All Units
1. Harrison, AR	91%	1. Ocean City–Assateague Island, MD	54%
2. Rappahannock, VA	90	2. Fort Lauderdale–Hollywood, FL	55
3. Crossville, TN	87	2. Maui, HI	55
3. Houghton Lake, MI	87	4. Lake Havasu City–Kingman, AZ	56
5. Canton–Lake Tawakoni, TX	86	4. Miami, FL	56
6. Cape Cod, MA	85	4. Yuma, AZ	56
6. Cassville–Roaring River, MO	85	7. Carson City, NV	59
6. Fredericksburg, TX	85	8. Clear Lake, CA	60
6. Hot Springs–Lake Ouachita, AR	85	8. Fort Myers–Cape Coral, FL	60
6. Toms River–Barnegat Bay, NJ	85	8. Las Vegas, NV	60

Source: U.S. Bureau of the Census, *1980 Census of Population and Housing.*

The national average for single houses as a percentage of all housing units is 71%.

Condominiums

The fact that the number of residential condominiums in the United States grew from zero in 1960 to more than two and a half million today is ample testimony to their appeal. In most Florida metro areas, and in such resorts as Beaufort–Hilton Head, South Carolina, and Maui, condominiums make up the majority of the residential market. Developers aware of demographics know that the two biggest condo-buying groups are young couples making a first-time home purchase, and retired couples who have unloaded their oversize house for a smaller, easily maintained unit with ready-made recreational activities and neighbors of a similar age.

"Condominium" was little more than a Latin word in the United States in 1960, when a new law was imported from Puerto Rico that made it possible for a person to own a legally described cube of air space in a residential development in which the land beneath the unit, its exterior walls and roof, the streets, parking spaces, landscaping, lights, walkways, and other facilities were owned in common with the rest of the development's residents.

The word is still misunderstood. For some, it connotes a style of architecture, typically high-rise in form, pale in color, most frequently seen beside a sandy beach. For others, it means a life-style, sharing a sauna, pool, recreation room, and even meals. The best definition, from the Uniform Condominium Act (1980), is "real estate, portions of which are designated for separate ownership and the remainder of which is designated for common ownership solely by the owners of those portions."

Condominiums in the Retirement Places

Most Condominiums	As % of All Units
1. Maui, HI	32%
2. West Palm Beach–Boca Raton, FL	30
3. Ocean City–Assateague Island, MD	29
4. Fort Lauderdale–Hollywood, FL	28
5. Beaufort–Hilton Head, SC	17
6. Sarasota–Bradenton, FL	15
7. Fort Myers–Cape Coral, FL	14
8. Miami, FL	13
9. Reno, NV	9
10. San Diego, CA	8

Source: U.S. Bureau of the Census, *1980 Census of Population and Housing.*

The national average for condominiums as a percentage of all housing units is 3%.

Twelve retirement places have no condominiums: Benton–Kentucky Lake, KY; Big Sandy, TN; Canton–Lake Tawakoni, TX; Clarkesville–Mount Airy, GA; Delta, CO; Deming, NM; Fredericksburg, TX; Hamilton–Bitterroot Valley, MT; Harrison, AR; Paris, TN; Rappahannock, VA; and Red Bluff–Sacramento Valley, CA.

Mobile Homes

According to a recent National Family Opinion Survey, one third of the buyers of new mobile homes are persons over 55. Can they be on to something?

When many defense workers were housed in trailers during World War II, living in a 300-square-foot sheet-metal box with ersatz cooking facilities and no plumbing acquired a tacky reputation. Today's mobile homes—or "manufactured housing," as the industry trade association is pressing us to call them—only faintly resemble the trailers of the early forties.

Mobile homes now are at least 14 feet wide. Seventy-foot-long Double Wides can enclose three bedrooms, two baths, a living room, dining room, kitchen, and closets. New mobile homes are usually sold complete; appliances, furniture, draperies, lamps, and carpeting are all included in the purchase price, as are the built-in plumbing, heating, air conditioning, and electrical systems. You can order a mobile home with a sunken living room, sunken bathtub, wet bar, flueless fireplace, trash-masher, dishwasher, and built-in cabinets and counters. Outside, owners often landscape the surroundings with grass, trees, and flower gardens, and embellish their homes with carports, porches, sheds, patios, and shake roofs that make them barely distinguishable from a conventional house.

Perhaps the industry is correct in preferring the label "manufactured housing"; the only time the mobile home is actually mobile is when it leaves the factory and is towed by a truck in one or more sections to a concrete foundation, whether on the owner's acreage or at one of 24,000 trailer parks in the country. When it arrives, the wheels, axle, and towing tongue are removed, and all that still resembles a trailer is the I-beamed chassis, which quickly becomes hidden structural reinforcement once the unit is winched onto the foundation and plumbed. After that, the mobile home becomes more or less permanent; no more than 2 percent of them are ever moved again.

They are decidedly part of the Sun Belt housing mix. Last year, one quarter of all new mobile homes were trucked to just two states: Florida and Texas. Another quarter went to California, Georgia, Louisiana, North Carolina, and Oklahoma.

You will search in vain for mobile-home lots and park developments in Hawaii, Cape Cod, and other resort areas where the astronomically high cost of residential land offsets any economic benefits of owning a mobile home. Nor will you find large numbers of mobile homes in metro areas. Among the rapidly growing rural retirement places, however, mobile homes are a major housing choice.

The Ground Factor

There are many factors at play in determining the different prices for housing around the country. Such things as the age of the structure, its maintenance and repair, turnover in the neighborhood, and local zoning laws are a few. But whatever the factors, they all are of secondary importance to basic supply and demand.

Cut off a slice of a tract development in suburban Boise City, Idaho, and drop it on the outskirts of Los Angeles, and you can see supply and demand at work. The transplanted homes will double in market value, not because they are roomier or better built, but because of the more intense competition for housing in southern California. You can find well-cared-for three-bedroom ranches in Boise City for less than $50,000 and dumpy stucco boxes in the South Bay area of Los Angeles for a quarter of a million. The location of the site, more than any other factor, is the best single determinant of a home's price.

Based on Federal Housing Authority measurements, the value of the land on which a typical existing home is built represents 22 percent of the price of the home if it were to be sold immediately. This figure can vary considerably depending on where in the country this typical house is located. In Hawaii, the true cost of the site is more than half the price of the house; in California, it's 35 percent. Elsewhere, in Michigan or Indiana, for example, it's only 14 percent and 15 percent respectively.

Land Costs as Percent of House Prices

Highest		Lowest	
1. Hawaii	51%	1. Michigan	14%
2. California	35	2. Indiana	15
3. Oregon	30	3. Georgia	16
4. Florida	27	3. South Dakota	16
5. Washington	26	5. Arkansas	17

Source: Federal Housing Authority, *Property Characteristics, 1-Family Homes, by States,* 1982.

The national average for land costs as percentage of house prices is 22%.

Mobile Homes in the Retirement Places

Most Mobile Homes	As % of All Units	Fewest Mobile Homes	As % of All Units
1. Lake Havasu City–Kingman, AZ	34%	1. Maui, HI	0%
2. Clear Lake, CA	30	1. Cape Cod, MA	0
3. Yuma, AZ	28	3. Rappahannock, VA	1
4. Athens–Cedar Creek Lake, TX	23	4. ATLANTIC CITY–CAPE MAY, NJ	2
5. Branson–Lake Taneycomo, MO	21	4. MIAMI, FL	2
5. Deming, NM	21	6. SAN ANTONIO, TX	3
5. Ocala, FL	21	6. Toms River–Barnegat Bay, NJ	3
8. Rehoboth Bay–Indian River Bay, DE	19	8. AUSTIN, TX	4
9. Bend, OR	18	8. COLORADO SPRINGS, CO	4
10. Lake O' The Cherokees, OK	17	8. LEXINGTON–FAYETTE, KY	4

Source: U.S. Bureau of the Census, *1980 Census of Population and Housing.*

The national average for mobile homes as a percentage of all housing units is 5%.

TYPICAL HOUSING PRICES

If you sell your present home, you'll undoubtedly realize enough cash to buy another home, perhaps a smaller one. Or you might opt for a mobile home or condo. You might even choose to rent, investing the cash from the sale of your old home to provide you with income in your retirement.

Of course, if you decide to buy, what you buy and where you buy it will have a great effect on the price you pay. On the national average, prices are lowest for mobile homes, rise for single houses, and peak for condominiums.

It takes the average contractor several months to build a typical three-bedroom suburban ranch. Mobile homes take 80 to 100 hours. In 1982, when the average cost of building a conventional home was around $45 per square foot, the cost of manufacturing a mobile home was $20 per square foot. The reason is simple. Of the total cost of a conventional home, more than half is labor. Labor costs in a mobile home amount to 11 percent.

In addition to a low purchase price ($20,500, according to the Department of Commerce), mobile homes also have lower maintenance costs. On the other hand, you have to put the unit somewhere; this means either buying acreage or finding a mobile-home park with space to rent.

In 1983, according to the National Association of Realtors, an existing single house in the United States carried a price tag of $85,500, an increase of only 13 percent since 1980. In the West, house prices were up 16 percent in these three years; they were up by 20 percent in the South; and in the slower-growing North Central and northeastern regions, they had risen by only 7.6 percent and 10.8 percent respectively. That's a far cry from what buyers and sellers saw during the 1970s, when prices shot up an average of 178 percent nationwide.

Among the more than 3,000 counties in the United States, the one with the highest-priced housing is Pitkin County, Colorado, where Aspen is located. There, cantilevered, cathedral-beamed, glass-faced condominiums dominate the market. In other resort areas where condominiums make up a large part of the residential mix, average prices for all housing tend to be high as well.

In spite of their advertised affordability to first-time home buyers, condominiums currently average more than $90,000 across the country.

The following prices come from the *1980 Census of Population and Housing* and are boosted by regional inflation factors reported by the National Association of Realtors to reflect realistic 1983 market values. These prices are the average of what all owners in an area would take for their homes if they were to sell immediately, and they represent the average market values of all owner-occupied housing units: single houses, condos, and mobile homes. It's not surprising that Maui—where 32 percent of the housing mix is condos and none is mobile homes—has the highest prices, while Houghton Lake, Michigan—with only 1 percent of its housing condos and 87 percent houses—has the lowest.

Typical Housing Prices

Highest		Lowest	
1. Maui, HI	$149,000	1. Houghton Lake, MI	$35,600
2. SAN DIEGO, CA	121,600	2. Cassville–	
3. SANTA ROSA, CA	114,500	Roaring River, MO	36,300
4. RENO, NV	106,300	3. Oscoda–Huron	
5. Nevada City–		Shore, MI	37,100
Donner, CA	100,000	4. McALLEN–PHARR–	
		EDINBURG, TX	37,400
		5. Canton–Lake	
		Tawakoni, TX	38,000

Source: U.S. Bureau of the Census, *1980 Census of Population and Housing,* and the National Association of Realtors, 1983.

PROPERTY-TAX "SHOPPING"

Being overhoused doesn't only mean finding yourself with a surplus of livable space. You can be *financially* overhoused, too, especially when you pay property taxes on a house that has increased in value with income that has abruptly become fixed.

Just because you're getting older doesn't mean the tax assessor will take notice and graciously lower your home's tax bill. Property-tax relief, in the states that grant it to older people, only comes after specific low-income tests. The only place in this country where all people over 65 can completely forget their property taxes is Alaska (a state, incidentally, with the lowest proportion of people over 65). Why not "shop" for favorable property taxes the way corporations do when they plan a move?

In the late 1970s, homeowners protesting confiscatory property taxes in California and Massachusetts likened them to a ransom families were forced to pay to keep their homes from the local assessing jurisdiction. Using that analogy today, New Yorkers buy their homes back from the tax assessor every 36 years, since the statewide average real-estate tax rate on the house's full value is 2.75 percent. In Louisiana, on the other hand, the "ransom" period is 357 years because of an extremely low average rate of 0.28 percent.

Although states don't set tax rates (that is done by individual assessors in counties, cities, towns, and districts within the state), a statewide average property-tax rate on a home's fair market value is useful for comparing tax burdens among states and among regions of the country, too. The difference in the following figures, which are from FHA records of average rates in the 50 states on a home's full value, indicates a wide range in property-tax burdens.

Average Property-Tax Rates

Highest	Tax Rate	"Ransom" Period
1. New York	2.75%	36 yrs
2. Michigan	2.74	37
3. New Jersey	2.53	40
4. Massachusetts	2.43	41
5. Nebraska	2.31	43
Lowest		
1. Louisiana	0.28%	357 yrs
2. Hawaii	0.36	278
3. West Virginia	0.37	270
4. Alabama	0.38	263
5. Wyoming	0.47	213

Source: Advisory Commission on Intergovernmental Relations, *Significant Features of Fiscal Federalism, 1983.*

The national average is 1.25% for the tax rate and 80 years for the "ransom" period.

These statewide average property-tax rates are also useful in estimating local property-tax bills. The following estimated tax bills are derived from the 1983 average price of housing within 107 retirement places, taxed at the particular state's average rate on the full value of the house.

House Property-Tax Bills

Highest		Lowest	
1. ATLANTIC CITY–CAPE MAY, NJ	$1,700	1. Fairhope–Gulf Shores, AL	$183
2. Cape Cod, MA	1,645	2. Lake O' The Cherokees, OK	358
3. Traverse City–Grand Traverse Bay, MI	1,520	3. Tahlequah–Lake Tenkiller, OK	361
4. Toms River–Barnegat Bay, NJ	1,474	4. Yuma, AZ	387
5. Petoskey–Straits of Mackinac, MI	1,408	5. SPRINGFIELD, MO	417

Source: U.S. Bureau of the Census, 1980 Census of Population and Housing, and Advisory Commission on Intergovernmental Relations, Significant Features of Fiscal Federalism, 1983.

The national average for house property-tax bills is $757.

WHAT DIFFERENCE DOES AGE MAKE?

"They don't build them the way they used to," you'd say if you were to watch a building crew putting up cheap-jack houses just off an exit from an urban beltway.

No, they don't. Remember the ten-foot ceilings in homes built before World War II? The standard height is eight feet now. Formal stairways with well-turned balusters and natural-finished rails aren't needed—most new homes are built on a single level. Milled oak molding is hard to come by; party walls are three-eighths inch gypsum board nailed to studs rather than the old "mud jobs" of plaster on lath; solid six-panel doors have lost out to hollow flush doors of hemlock veneer.

On the other hand, radiators have disappeared into the walls; copper and polyvinyl chloride have replaced galvanized iron plumbing; tube-and-knob wiring has given way to safer electrical circuitry; pressure-treated wood has eliminated termite and dry-rot risks; and the problem of cellar flooding arises less often because there just aren't many cellars being excavated.

One useful indicator of the quality of an area's housing stock is the percent of units built before 1940. Although the age of a housing unit isn't always an index of dilapidation, it can be a sign of functional obsolescence and looming maintenance headaches. Retrofitting storm windows, repainting clapboards every three years, and "snaking" clogged sewer drains can mean both dollars and difficulties.

Old and New Retirement Places

Newest	Housing Units Built Before 1940	Oldest	Housing Units Built Before 1940
1. FORT LAUDERDALE–HOLLYWOOD, FL	2%	1. Camden–Penobscot Bay, ME	61%
1. LAS VEGAS, NV	2	2. Bar Harbor–Frenchman Bay, ME	52
3. Lake Havasu City–Kingman, AZ	3	3. Brattleboro, VT	48
3. MELBOURNE–TITUSVILLE–COCOA, FL	3	4. Bennington, VT	47
5. Carson City, NV	4	5. Keene, NH	46
5. FORT MYERS–CAPE CORAL, FL	4	6. Rappahannock, VA	44
5. PHOENIX, AZ	4	7. Laconia–Lake Winnipesaukee, NH	43
5. SARASOTA–BRADENTON, FL	4	8. STATE COLLEGE, PA	41
9. Beaufort–Hilton Head, SC	5	9. Easton–Chesapeake Bay, MD	40
9. Rockport–Aransas Pass, TX	5	10. North Conway–White Mountains, NH	38

Source: U.S. Bureau of the Census, 1980 Census of Population and Housing.

HOME ENERGY REQUIREMENTS

After mortgage interest rates, fuel and electricity for the home have been the fastest-rising items on the monthly Consumer Price Index since 1967. What was once a minor and predictable expense, averaging less

The Filtering Theory of Prices

Most Americans live in homes that were built years ago and were bought, lived in, and sold by a succession of owners. Nearly half of all homeowners over 65, for example, live in homes built before World War II. We all confirm the "filtering theory" of housing, which states that houses filter down from high-income first owners to middle-income subsequent owners and finally to lower-income owners. Or, to put it another way, many high-income families live in newer homes and most lower-income households occupy older homes.

So what else is new?

Just that when real-estate sections of The Old House Journal, Yankee, Sunset, and other regional magazines show country homes a hundred years old on the market for hundreds of thousands of dollars,

you're looking at a big exception to filtering theory.

There are certain retirement places where older homes command, in the words of the local real-estate broker, "an arm and a leg and a quart of rubies." A prime example, on Maryland's Eastern Shore, is Easton-Chesapeake Bay, where four out of ten of the rambling homes were built before World War II and where a typical house costs $83,600. Many of the older Georgian mansions close to the bay are never sold, only inherited. Two other retirement places where filtering theory has been knocked into a cocked hat are Charlottesville, Virginia, and Santa Rosa, California.

Nevertheless, the theory holds true for most of the country and for most of our retirement places, too. The older the housing, the lower the price.

than one percent of a household's budget 15 years ago, now may amount to more than the cost of medical care or clothing.

There is a good deal of difference between the household utility bills in Maine's Bar Harbor–Frenchman Bay and those of Oak Harbor, Washington. The dollar differences between these two retirement places and others around the country can be explained by three factors: climate, the form of energy used to maintain comfortable temperatures in the house, and the source of this energy.

Counting the Hours

It's facetiously said that the Texas Gulf Coast, from South Padre Island north to the petrochemical town of Port Arthur, is a place where air conditioning, like food and water, is a necessity without which all mankind becomes delirious, withers, and dies. There, a meteorologist measuring humidity with a psychrometer whenever the temperature climbs over 80 degrees Fahrenheit will count nearly 2,500 hours every year when the psychrometer's bulb stays wet from moist air. New Delhi has similar numbers, and so does Kinshasa, capital of Zaire. It's the equivalent of more than 200 days per year that have uncomfortable, sweaty 12-hour periods of high humidity.

In southwestern retirement destinations like Las Vegas, Phoenix, and Tucson, the days are considerably less humid, but the number of hours there when it's more than 80 degrees Fahrenheit outside is even greater than the number found on the Texas Gulf Coast. These hours were first measured by Defense Department building engineers in the late 1940s for a worldwide inventory of air and naval bases, supply depots, and weather stations. The old Defense Department numbers were adopted by the American Society of Heating, Refrigeration, and Air Conditioning Engineers (ASHRAE) for designing cooling systems for buildings. Not only are they useful for gauging how hot a given place is over time, they are also good indicators of how often your home's air conditioner may be humming.

Counting the Days

In 1915, Eugene P. Milener, an engineer with the Gas Company of Baltimore, made a discovery for which he received little recognition outside of his industry: the amount of natural gas needed to keep buildings warm can be accurately predicted for every degree that the outdoor temperature falls below 65 degrees Fahrenheit. To this day, natural-gas utilities use this measurement, called a degree day, to determine consumption patterns among their customers.

A heating-degree day is the number of degrees the daily average temperature is below 65. Heating your home is not usually necessary when the temperature outdoors is more than 65, but furnaces are fired up

---

Air-Conditioning Needs: The Top 10 Hot-Weather Retirement Places

Retirement Place	Over 80° F per Year
1. Yuma, AZ	3,148 hrs
2. PHOENIX, AZ	2,845
3. Rockport–Aransas Pass, TX	2,531
4. McALLEN–PHARR–EDINBURG, TX	2,527
5. TUCSON, AZ	2,445
6. MIAMI, FL	2,388
7. WEST PALM BEACH–BOCA RATON, FL	2,387
8. LAS VEGAS, NV	2,360
9. AUSTIN, TX	2,243
10. MELBOURNE–TITUSVILLE–COCOA, FL	2,113

Heating Needs: The Top 10 Cold-Weather Retirement Places

Retirement Place	Degree Days
1. Petoskey–Straits of Mackinac, MI	8,964
2. Rhinelander, WI	8,657
2. Traverse City–Grand Traverse Bay, MI	8,657
4. Eagle River, WI	8,656
5. Oscoda–Huron Shore, MI	8,073
6. Kalispell, MT	8,055
7. Bennington, VT	8,037
7. Brattleboro, VT	8,037
9. Hamilton–Bitterroot Valley, MT	7,873
9. Missoula, MT	7,873

Source: American Society of Heating, Refrigeration, and Air Conditioning Engineers, *Standards.*

---

when the outdoor temperature falls below that mark. Thus, a heating-degree day indicates the number of degrees of heating required to keep a house at 65. If, for example, the temperature on a winter day is 35, that day has 30 heating-degree days, meaning that 30 degrees of heating are necessary.

The average for annual heating-degree days (total heating-degree days over one year) in the United States is 4,671, ranging among *Places Rated* retirement places from 0 in Maui to 8,964 in Michigan's Petoskey–Straits of Mackinac area. Not only is the number of annual degree days an indicator of how cold it gets in a given place over time, it also is a good predictor of how often you'll need to run a home's heating system to keep the indoors comfortable.

Household Energy Geography

Where were you in 1950? If you lived in any county east of the Mississippi (except in New England and Florida), you may remember the coal trucks rumbling along their delivery routes through urban residential neighborhoods. At three dollars a ton, black anthracite was the dominant home heating fuel then. Natural gas, the major choice today, was just starting to burn its blue flame in new refrigerators, stoves, clothes dryers, and in furnaces in newly built homes. Electric-power utilities were beginning to push total electric homes.

Today, coal has virtually disappeared from the

home energy scene. Even though coal stoves have made a comeback, the number of homes burning coal declined by more than one million over the past decade. The major options, from most expensive to least, are electric power, bottled gas, residual fuel oil, and piped-in natural gas. And, in some retirement places, there's wood.

Electricity. Census takers who had asked Americans every ten years whether their home was wired for electricity stopped asking that question in 1960. Like telephones, running water, and leak-proof roofs, this basic household amenity is now taken for granted.

In 1950, the only place where you'd find a majority of total electric homes was the small desert town of Las Vegas, seat of Nevada's Clark County. The power here was the cheapest in the country, simply because it was generated by falling water at the new Boulder Canyon hydroelectric project some 25 miles east. It still is cheap, relative to nuclear- or fossil fuel–generated power that homeowners pay for elsewhere in the country. So is the power that heats and lights homes in the Puget Sound area, the Oregon Cascades, and the Kentucky and Tennessee lakes region, places that also get their power from major hydroelectric projects.

Although most American homes are heated with natural gas, electricity is gaining fast. Between 1970 and 1980, the number of total electric homes increased by more than 200 percent. The reason: It costs much less to wire a new house for electric resistance heat than it does to install a gas or oil furnace with pipes and sheet-metal hot-air conduits. The Department of Energy surveys average annual household consumption and price, and the following are its figures for 1983:

- Average Home Consumption: 17,287 kilowatt-hours per year
- Average Bill: $1,186 per year
- Cost per Million Btus: $20.09

Bottled Gas. Bottled, or liquefied petroleum (LP), gas is derived from petroleum and sold in compressed or liquid form. Like residual fuel oil, it requires on-site storage tanks. Unlike piped-in natural gas and electricity, it offers the advantage of an on-hand supply in case of interrupted service. In rural retirement spots, particularly in the Missouri Ozarks and the area around Oklahoma's Lake O' The Cherokees, it is the fuel of choice for heat and even for running air conditioners and refrigerators.

Most mobile homes from New England to the desert Southwest are also heated by bottled gas. While this fuel today is more expensive than piped-in natural gas, in the future it may be cheaper given the dramatic price increases in natural gas that experts anticipate. Below are 1983 statistics from the National LP Gas Association, and the Department of Energy, which monitors average household prices and consumption:

- Average Home Consumption: 1,145 gallons per year
- Average Bill: $933 per year
- Cost per Million Btus: $8.88

Oil. Though today its price is dropping because of the current worldwide oil glut, #2 heating oil, until the end of 1980, was the only item on the Consumer Price Index to sextuple in cost since 1967 (it has since been surpassed by mortgage interest costs). This explains why the number of homes heated with fuel oil declined by almost two million since 1970. You won't find the price varying greatly by location. But you will find this distillate of imported crude to be the most common heating fuel in New England and Mid-Atlantic retirement places, and in the retirement places of western North Carolina and northern Michigan. The Department of Energy, which tracks consumption, supply, and prices, gives these figures for 1983:

- Average Home Consumption: 1,043 gallons per year
- Average Bill: $1,237 per year
- Cost per Million Btus: $8.53

Natural Gas. The heating fuel in three out of four houses in the country is a by-product of oil drilling that for many years flamed at the wellhead for lack of a market. A fossil fuel, natural gas has been a relatively cheap source for heat—mainly because the federal government has regulated its interstate price. It is slowly being deregulated and is quickly becoming expensive; some experts predict its price will equal that of fuel oil in five years.

It has never been cheap to homeowners at the end of the continental transmission lines that originate in Louisiana and Texas gas fields, however. This explains why natural gas is not the fuel choice in New England or Middle Atlantic homes, where oil is the least expensive of fuels; or in the Pacific Northwest, where hydroelectric power is the least expensive. The Department of Energy, which monitors current price and home-use patterns, and the American Gas Association are the sources of the following 1983 figures:

- Average Home Consumption: 13,100 cubic feet per year
- Average Bill: $724 per year
- Cost per Million Btus: $5.53

Wood. An ancient proverb about wood states that it is the only fuel that warms you twice, first when you cut and stack it, and second when you burn it in your stove or fireplace. From Rocky Mountain piñon to hickory and ash from Ozark forests, it is the primary heating fuel in 2.6 million homes (an increase of 1.8 million since 1970). Among the *Places Rated* retirement places, more than a third of the homes in Rappahannock, Virginia; Hamilton–Bitterroot Valley, Montana; and Twain Harte–Yosemite, California, are heated with wood because it is cheap and available right outside a householder's door.

Nationally, the cost of a cord of good seasoned hardwood varies a great deal. You can pay up to $300 in Manhattan, or, with a little work and permission, you can gather fallen timber in local state forests for nothing. The U.S. Forest Service has established energy content for various kinds of wood; prices and consumption come from an informal 1983 *Places Rated* survey of wood-stove manufacturers:

- Average Home Consumption: 3.75 cords (hardwood) per year
- Average Bill: $468 per year
- Cost per Million Btus: $5.34 (hardwood)

Keeping It All Going

Energy for utilities—home heating and cooling, lighting, and running appliances—costs $1,447 down in the Gulf Coast retirement place of Biloxi–Gulfport, Mississippi; $1,173 up in Traverse City–Grand Traverse Bay, Michigan; and only $382 out in Coeur d'Alene, Idaho. Why such great differences?

Although the cost of heating a house with natural gas is much lower in Biloxi–Gulfport than in Traverse City–Grand Traverse Bay ($316 versus $602 a year), the kilowatt-hours of electric power used just to keep that Gulf Coast home cool in the summer far surpass the total number of kilowatt-hours used by the northern Michigan home year round. And Coeur d'Alene? Homes there are all-electric, and get their bills from the Washington Water Power Company, the distributor of inexpensive, hydro-generated power.

If you'd like to escape heating and air-conditioning bills, move to any of the four Hawaiian islands that make up Maui County. But don't count on being entirely free of utility costs. While Maui has no heated homes, and air conditioning isn't necessary, you'll still pay $1,161 to keep water hot, food cool, and lamps lit.

JUDGING HOMEOWNING COSTS

Are homes more affordable in Tucson than Phoenix? When it comes to paying property taxes, would you be better off choosing the western slope of the Colorado Rockies over the High Sierra of California? Might a move to Florida in February haunt you in July when you realize just how much air conditioning costs?

To help you answer these questions, *Places Rated* tallies the three biggest dollar expenses of homeownership: utility bills, property taxes, and mortgage payments. The total of these three equals the amount you can expect to pay each year for the basics of homeownership. It also represents each retirement place's score. If you're thinking of renting rather than buying, the score for homeowning is also useful for judging relative rental costs in retirement places.

Property taxes and mortgage payments are based on the average market value of owner-occupied housing units within each retirement place, as reported by the *1980 Census of Population and Housing*. These were owners' estimates of what their home, condominium, or mobile home would be worth if they decided to sell immediately. To show realistic 1983 prices, *Places Rated* updated these estimates with regional inflation factors reported by the National Association of Realtors.

Each area starts with a base score of zero. Points are added according to the following indicators:

1. *Utility bills.* The utility bills are estimated for a housing unit that uses natural gas for space heating, water heating, and cooking, since this fuel is not only available everywhere but is the most frequently chosen in most of the 107 retirement places. Also included in a place's utility bill are the costs of electricity for lighting, running appliances, and air conditioning, based on the local average number of kilowatt-hours of power consumed by residential customers as reported by the Department of Energy. In counties where total electric homes predominate, utility bills are estimates of annual residential all-electric costs, also from the Department of Energy.

Housing Winners and Losers

Least Expensive Retirement Places	Places Rated Score	Most Expensive Retirement Places	Places Rated Score
1. Cassville–Roaring River, MO	$4,466	1. Maui, HI	$13,426
2. Bull Shoals, AR	4,647	2. SAN DIEGO, CA	12,839
3. Canton–Lake Tawakoni, TX	4,674	3. SANTA ROSA, CA	11,818
4. Big Sandy, TN	4,716	4. RENO, NV	11,309
5. Lake O' The Cherokees, OK	4,740	5. Carson City, NV	10,794
6. Clarkesville–Mount Airy, GA	4,758	6. Nevada City–Donner, CA	10,415
7. Paris, TN	4,765	7. San Luis Obispo, CA	10,401

The fact that the seven most expensive retirement places for housing are all in the West shouldn't surprise you if you've followed newspaper accounts of the land boom that's been going on there since 1975. Although high market values don't always indicate desirable housing, they do indicate the pitch of local supply and demand in desirable places. On the other hand, the high prices for homes is one major reason that certain demographers and economists predict a deceleration in the Pacific region's population growth by the end of the 1980s.

The top seven retirement places for inexpensive housing aren't nationally known but are all located near regional vacation areas in the country's interior. Could it be that these places, in their own way, might be part of a new, minor land boom during the 1980s? Certainly, the rate at which retired persons are migrating to them would indicate so.

2. *Property taxes.* Property taxes are calculated by multiplying the average market value of a housing unit by a state's average effective tax rate for residential property. For example, the property-tax bill in Myrtle Beach, South Carolina, of $501 on a home valued at $59,700 in 1983 is derived from South Carolina's effective tax rate of 0.84 percent.

3. *Mortgage payments.* Annual mortgage payments are based on a 12 percent, 25-year mortgage on the average market value of local housing units, after making a one-third down payment.

Sample Comparison: Cassville–Roaring River, Missouri, and Maui, Hawaii

If a home's price tag depended entirely on supply and demand, there would seem to be little competition for shelter in Barry County, Missouri. With an average 1983 market value of $36,300, housing here is more affordable than in most retirement places. Cassville–Roaring River is more new than old. Four out of ten homes in the area have been built since 1970 (another three out of ten predate World War II). Most are single homes occupied by their owners. There are no condos to speak of, nor rental apartments, but there are many mobile homes, usually located on private acreage rather than in a trailer park. The average utility bill in Cassville–Roaring River is $1,062, property taxes $344

(estimated from Missouri's statewide effective rate of 0.95 percent), and mortgage payments $3,060, totaling $4,466 per year, the lowest basic homeowning costs of any of the *Places Rated* retirement places.

Thousands of miles to the west of Cassville–Roaring River, the four Pacific islands that make up Maui County, Hawaii, have the highest basic homeowner costs of the 107 places. The average 1983 market value of a Maui home is $149,000. It is likely to be a high-rise condo, likely to have been built within the last decade, and likely to be rented rather than owned by the people living in it. In Maui, there is a greater percentage of year-round housing units that are condos than anywhere else in the *Places Rated* retirement universe. Owing to the distance from stateside manufacturers, plus the astronomical cost of land, there are no mobile homes. Also, unlike the freehold tenure common to most of the United States mainland, homes here tend to be built on ground leased for 99 years.

Even though homes in Maui County are neither air conditioned nor heated, the monthly bills from Maui Electric, Ltd., for lighting, cooking, and running appliances total $1,161 a year. With Hawaii's exceptionally low effective property-tax rate of 0.36 percent, however, the estimated annual tax bill on this $149,000 dwelling comes to only $536. But mortgage payments amount to $11,729. Add them all together and you get a total homeowner cost of $13,426 a year.

Places Rated: Retirement Places Ranked for Homeowning Costs

Three criteria are used to rank the 107 retirement places for basic costs of owning a home over one year: (1) annual average utility bill, (2) annual average property taxes, and (3) annual average mortgage payment. The sum of these three items represents the score for each retirement place. Places that receive tie scores are given the same rank and are listed in alphabetical order.

Retirement Places from Least to Most Expensive

Places Rated Rank	Places Rated Score	Places Rated Rank	Places Rated Score	Places Rated Rank	Places Rated Score
1. Cassville–Roaring River, MO	$4,466	12. Hot Springs–Lake Ouachita, AR	$5,134	23. Mountain Home–Norfork Lake, AR	$5,487
2. Bull Shoals, AR	4,647	13. Deming, NM	5,137	24. Bar Harbor–Frenchman Bay, ME	5,492
3. Canton–Lake Tawakoni, TX	4,674	14. Crossville, TN	5,139	25. Athens–Cedar Creek Lake, TX	5,498
4. Big Sandy, TN	4,716	15. Houghton Lake, MI	5,143		
5. Lake O' The Cherokees, OK	4,740	16. SPRINGFIELD, MO	5,179	26. Cookeville, TN	5,705
6. Clarkesville–Mount Airy, GA	4,758	17. Fairhope–Gulf Shores, AL	5,237	27. ASHEVILLE, NC	5,901
7. Paris, TN	4,765	17. Harrison, AR	5,237	28. LAKELAND–WINTER HAVEN, FL	5,986
8. Tahlequah–Lake Tenkiller, OK	4,938	19. Branson–Lake Taneycomo, MO	5,269	29. BILOXI–GULFPORT, MS	5,991
9. McALLEN–PHARR–EDINBURG, TX	4,950	20. Oscoda–Huron Shore, MI	5,317	30. Brevard, NC	6,074
10. Roswell, NM	4,965	21. Benton–Kentucky Lake, KY	5,324		
11. Camden–Penobscot Bay, ME	5,015	22. Table Rock Lake, MO	5,339	31. OCALA, FL	6,088

Places Rated Rank	Places Rated Score	Places Rated Rank	Places Rated Score	Places Rated Rank	Places Rated Score
32. Gainesville–Lake Sidney Lanier, GA	$6,136	58. Laconia–Lake Winnipesaukee, NH	$6,767	83. AUSTIN, TX	$7,998
33. LAS CRUCES, NM	6,137	59. Red Bluff–Sacramento Valley, CA	6,824	84. FORT MYERS–CAPE CORAL, FL	8,001
34. Brattleboro, VT	6,211	60. LANCASTER, PA	6,843	85. Toms River–Barnegat Bay, NJ	8,008
35. Delta, CO	6,215	61. Winchester, VA	6,891	86. Bend, OR	8,054
36. Monticello–Liberty, NY	6,225	62. Petoskey–Straits of Mackinac, MI	6,910	87. TUCSON, AZ	8,253
37. Rhinelander, WI	6,294	63. ORLANDO, FL	6,963	88. Oak Harbor, WA	8,490
38. Keene, NH	6,298	64. Port Angeles–Strait of Juan de Fuca, WA	7,068	89. PHOENIX, AZ	8,659
39. Hamilton–Bitterroot Valley, MT	6,360	65. North Conway–White Mountains, NH	7,075	90. FORT COLLINS, CO	8,725
40. Front Royal, VA	6,373	66. LEXINGTON–FAYETTE, KY	7,127	91. Cape Cod, MA	8,832
40. Rappahannock, VA	6,373	67. Prescott, AZ	7,197	92. Beaufort–Hilton Head, SC	8,920
42. Rehoboth Bay–Indian River Bay, DE	6,404	68. Rockport–Aransas Pass, TX	7,224	93. ATLANTIC CITY–CAPE MAY, NJ	8,940
43. Fredericksburg, TX	6,405	69. OLYMPIA, WA	7,297	94. Twain Harte–Yosemite, CA	8,974
44. Brunswick–Golden Isles, GA	6,409	70. Traverse City–Grand Traverse Bay, MI	7,367	95. MIAMI, FL	9,029
45. Myrtle Beach, SC	6,423	71. BOISE CITY, ID	7,387	96. WEST PALM BEACH–BOCA RATON, FL	9,258
46. Yuma, AZ	6,447	72. COLORADO SPRINGS, CO	7,571	97. Santa Fe, NM	9,285
47. DAYTONA BEACH, FL	6,455	73. Missoula, MT	7,578	98. FORT LAUDERDALE–HOLLYWOOD, FL	9,313
48. Kalispell, MT	6,473	74. St. George–Zion, UT	7,597	99. Easton–Chesapeake Bay, MD	9,460
49. SAN ANTONIO, TX	6,515	75. MELBOURNE–TITUSVILLE–COCOA, FL	7,664	100. LAS VEGAS, NV	9,628
50. Hendersonville, NC	6,543	76. Lincoln City–Newport, OR	7,744	101. San Luis Obispo, CA	10,401
51. STATE COLLEGE, PA	6,550	77. ALBUQUERQUE, NM	7,818	102. Nevada City–Donner, CA	10,415
52. Bennington, VT	6,576	78. CHARLOTTESVILLE, VA	7,822	103. Carson City, NV	10,794
53. Ocean City–Assateague Island, MD	6,590	79. Grand Junction, CO	7,867	104. RENO, NV	11,309
54. Coeur d'Alene, ID	6,666	80. SARASOTA–BRADENTON, FL	7,969	105. SANTA ROSA, CA	11,818
55. Eagle River, WI	6,684	81. MEDFORD, OR	7,980	106. SAN DIEGO, CA	12,839
56. Kerrville, TX	6,714	82. Clear Lake, CA	7,990	107. Maui, HI	13,426
57. Lake Havasu City–Kingman, AZ	6,755				

Retirement Places Listed Alphabetically

Retirement Place	Places Rated Rank	Retirement Place	Places Rated Rank	Retirement Place	Places Rated Rank
ALBUQUERQUE, NM	77	CHARLOTTESVILLE, VA	78	Harrison, AR	17
ASHEVILLE, NC	27	Clarkesville–Mount Airy, GA	6		
Athens–Cedar Creek Lake, TX	25			Hendersonville, NC	50
ATLANTIC CITY–CAPE MAY, NJ	93	Clear Lake, CA	82	Hot Springs–Lake Ouachita, AR	12
AUSTIN, TX	83	Coeur d'Alene, ID	54	Houghton Lake, MI	15
		COLORADO SPRINGS, CO	72	Kalispell, MT	48
Bar Harbor–Frenchman Bay, ME	24	Cookeville, TN	26	Keene, NH	38
Beaufort–Hilton Head, SC	92	Crossville, TN	14		
Bend, OR	86			Kerrville, TX	56
Bennington, VT	52	DAYTONA BEACH, FL	47	Laconia–Lake Winnipesaukee, NH	58
Benton–Kentucky Lake, KY	21	Delta, CO	35	Lake Havasu City–Kingman, AZ	57
		Deming, NM	13	LAKELAND–WINTER HAVEN, FL	28
Big Sandy, TN	4	Eagle River, WI	55	Lake O' The Cherokees, OK	5
BILOXI–GULFPORT, MS	29	Easton–Chesapeake Bay, MD	99		
BOISE CITY, ID	71			LANCASTER, PA	60
Branson–Lake Taneycomo, MO	19	Fairhope–Gulf Shores, AL	17	LAS CRUCES, NM	33
Brattleboro, VT	34	FORT COLLINS, CO	90	LAS VEGAS, NV	100
		FORT LAUDERDALE–HOLLYWOOD, FL	98	LEXINGTON–FAYETTE, KY	66
Brevard, NC	30	FORT MYERS–CAPE CORAL, FL	84	Lincoln City–Newport, OR	76
Brunswick–Golden Isles, GA	44	Fredericksburg, TX	43		
Bull Shoals, AR	2			Maui, HI	107
Camden–Penobscot Bay, ME	11	Front Royal, VA	40	McALLEN–PHARR–EDINBURG, TX	9
Canton–Lake Tawakoni, TX	3	Gainesville–Lake Sidney Lanier, GA	32	MEDFORD, OR	81
		Grand Junction, CO	79	MELBOURNE–TITUSVILLE–COCOA, FL	75
Cape Cod, MA	91	Hamilton–Bitterroot Valley, MT	39	MIAMI, FL	95
Carson City, NV	103				
Cassville–Roaring River, MO	1			Missoula, MT	73

Retirement Place	Places Rated Rank	Retirement Place	Places Rated Rank	Retirement Place	Places Rated Rank
Monticello–Liberty, NY	36	Port Angeles–Strait of Juan de Fuca, WA	64	SANTA ROSA, CA	105
Mountain Home–Norfork Lake, AR	23	Prescott, AZ	67	SARASOTA–BRADENTON, FL	80
Myrtle Beach, SC	45	Rappahannock, VA	40	SPRINGFIELD, MO	16
Nevada City–Donner, CA	102	Red Bluff–Sacramento Valley, CA	59	STATE COLLEGE, PA	51
North Conway–White Mountains, NH	65	Rehoboth Bay–Indian River Bay, DE	42	Table Rock Lake, MO	22
Oak Harbor, WA	88			Tahlequah–Lake Tenkiller, OK	8
OCALA, FL	31	RENO, NV	104	Toms River–Barnegat Bay, NJ	85
Ocean City–Assateague Island, MD	53	Rhinelander, WI	37	Traverse City–Grand Traverse Bay, MI	70
OLYMPIA, WA	69	Rockport–Aransas Pass, TX	68	TUCSON, AZ	87
		Roswell, NM	10	Twain Harte–Yosemite, CA	94
ORLANDO, FL	63	St. George–Zion, UT	74	WEST PALM BEACH–BOCA RATON, FL	96
Oscoda–Huron Shore, MI	20				
Paris, TN	7	SAN ANTONIO, TX	49		
Petoskey–Straits of Mackinac, MI	62	SAN DIEGO, CA	106	Winchester, VA	62
		San Luis Obispo, CA	101	Yuma, AZ	47
PHOENIX, AZ	89	Santa Fe, NM	97		

Place Profiles: Housing Features of 107 Retirement Places

The following pages summarize housing features for each retirement place, dividing them into the categories of Typical Housing, Choices, Energy Requirements, and Annual Costs.

In the first category, Typical Housing, information on the average prices for all owner-occupied housing units (houses, condominiums, and mobile homes) comes from the *1980 Census of Population and Housing* and is adjusted for inflation with 1983 data from the National Association of Realtors. Property taxes are based on statewide average residential rates taken from the 1983 issue of *Significant Features of Fiscal Federalism*, a publication of the Advisory Commission on Intergovernmental Relations. The percent of housing units built before 1940 also comes from the *1980 Census of Population and Housing*.

Data in the second category, Choices (the mix of single homes, condos, and mobile homes in each retirement place), are derived from the *1980 Census of Population and Housing*. All percent figures are rounded

and do not add up to 100; the balance represents multi-unit buildings, usually apartments.

The heating season, listed under Energy Requirements, is given in terms of heating-degree days per year. Air conditioning is defined as the normal number of hours per year when the outside temperature climbs over 80 degrees Fahrenheit. The figures for each retirement place are from the Department of Defense manual *Engineering Weather Data* and from ASHRAE's *Standards*.

The dollar amount given for mortgage and taxes is the annual sum of property taxes and mortgage payments. Utilities, too, are annual dollar amounts. Typical bills for residential natural gas by state are in *Gas Facts*, a 1982 report from the American Gas Association. The Department of Energy's 1982 publication *Typical Electric Bills* details electricity consumption and costs for each retirement place. To reflect realistic 1983 costs, data are adjusted for inflation by the Bureau of Labor's Consumer Price Index for January 1983.

ALBUQUERQUE, NM
Typical Housing
Price: $68,900
Property Taxes: $785
Built Before 1940: 7%
Choices
70% houses, 2% condos, 6% mobile homes
Energy Requirements
Heating Season: 4,389 degree days
Major Source: Natural gas/Electricity
Air Conditioning: 1,130 hours
Annual Costs
Mortgage and Taxes: $6,542

Utilities: $1,276
Places Rated Score: $7,818
Places Rated Rank: 77

ASHEVILLE, NC
Typical Housing
Price: $49,300
Property Taxes: $520
Built Before 1940: 23%
Choices
77% houses, 1% condos, 11% mobile homes
Energy Requirements
Heating Season: 4,072 degree days

Major Source: Total electric
Air Conditioning: 610 hours
Annual Costs
Mortgage and Taxes: $4,717
Utilities: $1,184
Places Rated Score: $5,901
Places Rated Rank: 27

Athens–Cedar Creek Lake, TX
Typical Housing
Price: $46,100
Property Taxes: $774
Built Before 1940: 10%

Choices
72% houses, 1% condos, 23% mobile homes
Energy Requirements
Heating Season: 2,272 degree days
Major Source: Natural gas/Electricity
Air Conditioning: 1,855 hours
Annual Costs
Mortgage and Taxes: $4,661
Utilities: $837
Places Rated Score: $5,498
Places Rated Rank: 25

ATLANTIC CITY–CAPE MAY, NJ
Typical Housing
Price: $67,200
Property Taxes; $1,700
Built Before 1940: 28%
Choices
69% houses, 4% condos, 2% mobile homes
Energy Requirements
Heating Season: 4,870 degree days
Major Source: Oil/Electricity
Air Conditioning: 473 hours
Annual Costs
Mortgage and Taxes: $7,320
Utilities: $1,620
Places Rated Score: $8,940
Places Rated Rank: 93

AUSTIN, TX
Typical Housing
Price: $68,300
Property Taxes: $1,147
Built Before 1940: 9%
Choices
69% houses, 2% condos, 4% mobile homes
Energy Requirements
Heating Season: 1,713 degree days
Major Source: Natural gas/Electricity
Air Conditioning: 2,243 hours
Annual Costs
Mortgage and Taxes: $6,900
Utilities: $1,098
Places Rated Score: $7,998
Places Rated Rank: 83

Bar Harbor–Frenchman Bay, ME
Typical Housing
Price: $44,100
Property Taxes: $626
Built Before 1940: 52%
Choices
78% houses, 1% condos, 9% mobile homes
Energy Requirements
Heating Season: 7,643 degree days
Major Source: Oil/Electricity
Air Conditioning: 137 hours
Annual Costs
Mortgage and Taxes: $4,341
Utilities: $1,151
Places Rated Score: $5,492
Places Rated Rank: 24

Beaufort–Hilton Head, SC
Typical Housing
Price: $86,000
Property Taxes: $722
Built Before 1940: 5%
Choices
64% houses, 17% condos, 15% mobile homes
Energy Requirements
Heating Season: 1,769 degree days
Major Source: Total electric
Air Conditioning: 1,393 hours
Annual Costs
Mortgage and Taxes: $7,968
Utilities: $952
Places Rated Score: $8,920
Places Rated Rank: 92

Bend, OR
Typical Housing
Price: $72,800
Property Taxes: $1,135
Built Before 1940: 12%
Choices
69% houses, 1% condos, 18% mobile homes
Energy Requirements
Heating Season: 4,122 degree days
Major Source: Total electric
Air Conditioning: 375 hours
Annual Costs
Mortgage and Taxes: $7,271
Utilities: $783
Places Rated Score: $8,054
Places Rated Rank: 86

Bennington, VT
Typical Housing
Price: $46,900
Property Taxes: $749
Built Before 1940: 47%
Choices
71% houses, 1% condos, 8% mobile homes
Energy Requirements
Heating Season: 8,037 degree days
Major Source: Oil/Electricity
Air Conditioning: 335 hours
Annual Costs
Mortgage and Taxes: $5,110
Utilities: $1,466
Places Rated Score: $6,576
Places Rated Rank: 52

Benton–Kentucky Lake, KY
Typical Housing
Price: $45,700
Property Taxes: $520
Built Before 1940: 12%
Choices
83% houses, 12% mobile homes
Energy Requirements
Heating Season: 4,279 degree days
Major Source: Total electric
Air Conditioning: 1,160 hours
Annual Costs
Mortgage and Taxes: $4,370

Utilities: $954
Places Rated Score: $5,324
Places Rated Rank: 21

Big Sandy, TN
Typical Housing
Price: $38,700
Property Taxes: $549
Built Before 1940: 12%
Choices
81% houses, 15% mobile homes
Energy Requirements
Heating Season: 3,513 degree days
Major Source: Total electric
Air Conditioning: 1,160 hours
Annual Costs
Mortgage and Taxes: $3,812
Utilities: $904
Places Rated Score: $4,716
Places Rated Rank: 4

BILOXI–GULFPORT, MS
Typical Housing
Price: $49,000
Property Taxes: $421
Built Before 1940: 11%
Choices
77% houses, 1% condos, 7% mobile homes
Energy Requirements
Heating Season: 1,600 degree days
Major Source: Natural gas/Electricity
Air Conditioning: 2,052 hours
Annual Costs
Mortgage and Taxes: $4,544
Utilities: $1,447
Places Rated Score: $5,991
Places Rated Rank: 29

BOISE CITY, ID
Typical Housing
Price: $71,100
Property Taxes: $668
Built Before 1940: 13%
Choices
82% houses, 2% condos, 8% mobile homes
Energy Requirements
Heating Season: 5,890 degree days
Major Source: Natural gas/Electricity
Air Conditioning: 674 hours
Annual Costs
Mortgage and Taxes: $6,656
Utilities: $731
Places Rated Score: $7,387
Places Rated Rank: 71

Branson–Lake Taneycomo, MO
Typical Housing
Price: $44,900
Property Taxes: $426
Built Before 1940: 11%
Choices
73% houses, 1% condos, 21% mobile homes
Energy Requirements
Heating Season: 4,693 degree days
Major Source: Bottled gas/Electricity
Air Conditioning: 1,058 hours

Annual Costs
Mortgage and Taxes: $4,207
Utilities: $1,062
Places Rated Score: $5,269
Places Rated Rank: 19

Brattleboro, VT
Typical Housing
Price: $43,500
Property Taxes: $696
Built Before 1940: 48%
Choices
67% houses, 1% condos, 7% mobile homes
Energy Requirements
Heating Season: 8,037 degree days
Major Source: Oil/Electricity
Air Conditioning: 335 hours
Annual Costs
Mortgage and Taxes: $4,745
Utilities: $1,466
Places Rated Score: $6,211
Places Rated Rank: 34

Brevard, NC
Typical Housing
Price: $52,500
Property Taxes: $561
Built Before 1940: 14%
Choices
81% houses, 3% condos, 12% mobile homes
Energy Requirements
Heating Season: 4,072 degree days
Major Source: Total electric
Air Conditioning: 610 hours
Annual Costs
Mortgage and Taxes: $4,984
Utilities: $1,090
Places Rated Score: $6,074
Places Rated Rank: 30

Brunswick–Golden Isles, GA
Typical Housing
Price: $55,900
Property Taxes: $676
Built Before 1940: 13%
Choices
78% houses, 2% condos, 9% mobile homes
Energy Requirements
Heating Season: 1,268 degree days
Major Source: Natural gas/Electricity
Air Conditioning: 1,361 hours
Annual Costs
Mortgage and Taxes: $5,381
Utilities: $1,028
Places Rated Score: $6,409
Places Rated Rank: 44

Bull Shoals, AR
Typical Housing
Price: $39,400
Property Taxes: $559
Built Before 1940: 13%
Choices
83% houses, 1% condos, 10% mobile homes

Energy Requirements
Heating Season: 3,537 degree days
Major Source: Wood/Electricity
Air Conditioning: 1,207 hours
Annual Costs
Mortgage and Taxes: $3,878
Utilities: $769
Places Rated Score: $4,647
Places Rated Rank: 2

Camden–Penobscot Bay, ME
Typical Housing
Price: $45,900
Property Taxes: $651
Built Before 1940: 61%
Choices
75% houses, 1% condos, 6% mobile homes
Energy Requirements
Heating Season: 7,681 degree days
Major Source: Oil/Electricity
Air Conditioning: 236 hours
Annual Costs
Mortgage and Taxes: $3,864
Utilities: $1,151
Places Rated Score: $5,015
Places Rated Rank: 11

Canton–Lake Tawakoni, TX
Typical Housing
Price: $38,000
Property Taxes: $638
Built Before 1940: 14%
Choices
86% houses, 10% mobile homes
Energy Requirements
Heating Season: 2,272 degree days
Major Source: Natural gas/Electricity
Air Conditioning: 1,855 hours
Annual Costs
Mortgage and Taxes: $3,837
Utilities: $837
Places Rated Score: $4,674
Places Rated Rank: 3

Cape Cod, MA
Typical Housing
Price: $67,700
Property Taxes: $1,645
Built Before 1940: 19%
Choices
85% houses, 3% condos
Energy Requirements
Heating Season: 6,102 degree days
Major Source: Oil/Electricity
Air Conditioning: 164 hours
Annual Costs
Mortgage and Taxes: $7,345
Utilities: $1,487
Places Rated Score: $8,832
Places Rated Rank: 91

Carson City, NV
Typical Housing
Price: $112,300
Property Taxes: $1,268
Built Before 1940: 4%

Choices
59% houses, 7% condos, 16% mobile homes
Energy Requirements
Heating Season: 5,813 degree days
Major Source: Natural gas/Electricity
Air Conditioning: 574 hours
Annual Costs
Mortgage and Taxes: $9,643
Utilities: $1,151
Places Rated Score: $10,794
Places Rated Rank: 103

Cassville–Roaring River, MO
Typical Housing
Price: $36,300
Property Taxes: $344
Built Before 1940: 32%
Choices
85% houses, 10% mobile homes
Energy Requirements
Heating Season: 4,693 degree days
Major Source: Natural gas/Electricity
Air Conditioning: 1,058 hours
Annual Costs
Mortgage and Taxes: $3,404
Utilities: $1,062
Places Rated Score: $4,466
Places Rated Rank: 1

CHARLOTTESVILLE, VA
Typical Housing
Price: $70,400
Property Taxes: $668
Built Before 1940: 21%
Choices
73% houses, 1% condos, 5% mobile homes
Energy Requirements
Heating Season: 4,223 degree days
Major Source: Natural gas/Electricity
Air Conditioning: 826 hours
Annual Costs
Mortgage and Taxes: $6,598
Utilities: $1,224
Places Rated Score: $7,822
Places Rated Rank: 78

Clarkesville–Mount Airy, GA
Typical Housing
Price: $38,700
Property Taxes: $468
Built Before 1940: 18%
Choices
80% houses, 15% mobile homes
Energy Requirements
Heating Season: 4,102 degree days
Major Source: Bottled gas/Electricity
Air Conditioning: 1,011 hours
Annual Costs
Mortgage and Taxes: $3,730
Utilities: $1,028
Places Rated Score: $4,758
Places Rated Rank: 6

Clear Lake, CA
Typical Housing
Price: $74,000

Property Taxes: $769
Built Before 1940: 10%
Choices
  60% houses, 1% condos, 30% mobile
  homes
Energy Requirements
  Heating Season: 2,460 degree days
  Major Source: Total electric
  Air Conditioning: 1,200 hours
Annual Costs
  Mortgage and Taxes: $7,006
  Utilities: $984
Places Rated Score: $7,990
Places Rated Rank: 82

Coeur d'Alene, ID
Typical Housing
  Price: $67,100
  Property Taxes: $630
  Built Before 1940: 16%
Choices
  73% houses, 1% condos, 13% mobile
  homes
Energy Requirements
  Heating Season: 6,852 degree days
  Major Source: Total electric
  Air Conditioning: 363 hours
Annual Costs
  Mortgage and Taxes: $6,284
  Utilities: $382
Places Rated Score: $6,666
Places Rated Rank: 54

COLORADO SPRINGS, CO
Typical Housing
  Price: $71,800
  Property Taxes: $725
  Built Before 1940: 13%
Choices
  71% houses, 3% condos, 4% mobile
  homes
Energy Requirements
  Heating Season: 6,254 degree days
  Major Source: Natural gas/Electricity
  Air Conditioning: 508 hours
Annual Costs
  Mortgage and Taxes: $6,773
  Utilities: $798
Places Rated Score: $7,571
Places Rated Rank: 72

Cookeville, TN
Typical Housing
  Price: $49,700
  Property Taxes: $705
  Built Before 1940: 12%
Choices
  77% houses, 1% condos, 9% mobile
  homes
Energy Requirements
  Heating Season: 3,590 degree days
  Major Source: Total electric
  Air Conditioning: 1,094 hours
Annual Costs
  Mortgage and Taxes: $4,895
  Utilities: $810
Places Rated Score: $5,705
Places Rated Rank: 26

Crossville, TN
Typical Housing
  Price: $43,000
  Property Taxes: $610
  Built Before 1940: 13%
Choices
  87% houses, 2% condos, 8% mobile
  homes
Energy Requirements
  Heating Season: 3,590 degree days
  Major Source: Total electric
  Air Conditioning: 1,150 hours
Annual Costs
  Mortgage and Taxes: $4,229
  Utilities: $910
Places Rated Score: $5,139
Places Rated Rank: 14

DAYTONA BEACH, FL
Typical Housing
  Price: $54,100
  Property Taxes: $497
  Built Before 1940: 9%
Choices
  69% houses, 6% condos, 11% mobile
  homes
Energy Requirements
  Heating Season: 868 degree days
  Major Source: Total electric
  Air Conditioning: 1,597 hours
Annual Costs
  Mortgage and Taxes: $5,058
  Utilities: $1,397
Places Rated Score: $6,455
Places Rated Rank: 47

Delta, CO
Typical Housing
  Price: $54,700
  Property Taxes: $552
  Built Before 1940: 37%
Choices
  76% houses, 14% mobile homes
Energy Requirements
  Heating Season: 6,065 degree days
  Major Source: Natural gas/Electricity
  Air Conditioning: 988 hours
Annual Costs
  Mortgage and Taxes: $5,162
  Utilities: $1,053
Places Rated Score: $6,215
Places Rated Rank: 35

Deming, NM
Typical Housing
  Price: $40,400
  Property Taxes: $460
  Built Before 1940: 15%
Choices
  65% houses, 21% mobile homes
Energy Requirements
  Heating Season: 3,019 degree days
  Major Source: Natural gas/Electricity
  Air Conditioning: 1,848 hours
Annual Costs
  Mortgage and Taxes: $3,861
  Utilities: $1,276
Places Rated Score: $5,137
Places Rated Rank: 13

Eagle River, WI
Typical Housing
  Price: $54,700
  Property Taxes: $957
  Built Before 1940: 23%
Choices
  78% houses, 1% condos, 5% mobile
  homes
Energy Requirements
  Heating Season: 8,656 degree days
  Major Source: Oil/Electricity
  Air Conditioning: 436 hours
Annual Costs
  Mortgage and Taxes: $5,568
  Utilities: $1,116
Places Rated Score: $6,684
Places Rated Rank: 55

Easton–Chesapeake Bay, MD
Typical Housing
  Price: $83,600
  Property Taxes: $1,045
  Built Before 1940: 40%
Choices
  84% houses, 1% condos, 4% mobile
  homes
Energy Requirements
  Heating Season: 4,245 degree days
  Major Source: Oil/Electricity
  Air Conditioning: 635 hours
Annual Costs
  Mortgage and Taxes: $8,086
  Utilities: $1,374
Places Rated Score: $9,460
Places Rated Rank: 99

Fairhope–Gulf Shores, AL
Typical Housing
  Price: $48,100
  Property Taxes: $183
  Built Before 1940: 6%
Choices
  80% houses, 1% condos, 13% mobile
  homes
Energy Requirements
  Heating Season: 1,529 degree days
  Major Source: Natural gas/Electricity
  Air Conditioning: 1,844 hours
Annual Costs
  Mortgage and Taxes: $4,235
  Utilities: $1,002
Places Rated Score: $5,237
Places Rated Rank: 17

FORT COLLINS, CO
Typical Housing
  Price: $71,900
  Property Taxes: $726
  Built Before 1940: 14%
Choices
  73% houses, 4% condos, 8% mobile
  homes
Energy Requirements
  Heating Season: 6,450 degree days
  Major Source: Natural gas/Electricity
  Air Conditioning: 647 hours
Annual Costs
  Mortgage and Taxes: $7,698
  Utilities: $1,027

Places Rated Score: $8,725
Places Rated Rank: 90

FORT LAUDERDALE–HOLLYWOOD, FL
Typical Housing
Price: $85,700
Property Taxes: $788
Built Before 1940: 2%
Choices
55% houses, 28% condos, 5% mobile homes
Energy Requirements
Heating Season: 248 degree days
Major Source: Total electric
Air Conditioning: 2,052 hours
Annual Costs
Mortgage and Taxes: $8,010
Utilities: $1,303
Places Rated Score: $9,313
Places Rated Rank: 98

FORT MYERS–CAPE CORAL, FL
Typical Housing
Price: $71,900
Property Taxes: $661
Built Before 1940: 4%
Choices
60% houses, 14% condos, 17% mobile homes
Energy Requirements
Heating Season: 405 degree days
Major Source: Total electric
Air Conditioning: 1,863 hours
Annual Costs
Mortgage and Taxes: $6,716
Utilities: $1,285
Places Rated Score: $8,001
Places Rated Rank: 84

Fredericksburg, TX
Typical Housing
Price: $55,400
Property Taxes: $930
Built Before 1940: 32%
Choices
85% houses, 8% mobile homes
Energy Requirements
Heating Season: 2,107 degree days
Major Source: Natural gas/Electricity
Air Conditioning: 1,715 hours
Annual Costs
Mortgage and Taxes: $5,598
Utilities: $807
Places Rated Score: $6,405
Places Rated Rank: 43

Front Royal, VA
Typical Housing
Price: $53,800
Property Taxes: $747
Built Before 1940: 22%
Choices
81% houses, 1% condos, 5% mobile homes
Energy Requirements
Heating Season: 4,784 degree days
Major Source: Oil/Electricity
Air Conditioning: 679 hours
Annual Costs
Mortgage and Taxes: $5,277

Utilities: $1,096
Places Rated Score: $6,373
Places Rated Rank: 40

Gainesville–Lake Sidney Lanier, GA
Typical Housing
Price: $53,000
Property Taxes: $641
Built Before 1940: 14%
Choices
77% houses, 1% condos, 13% mobile homes
Energy Requirements
Heating Season: 3,239 degree days
Major Source: Natural gas/Electricity
Air Conditioning: 1,077 hours
Annual Costs
Mortgage and Taxes: $5,108
Utilities: $1,028
Places Rated Score: $6,136
Places Rated Rank: 32

Grand Junction, CO
Typical Housing
Price: $71,900
Property Taxes: $726
Built Before 1940: 18%
Choices
70% houses, 2% condos, 12% mobile homes
Energy Requirements
Heating Season: 5,613 degree days
Major Source: Natural gas/Electricity
Air Conditioning: 988 hours
Annual Costs
Mortgage and Taxes: $6,781
Utilities: $1,086
Places Rated Score: $7,867
Places Rated Rank: 79

Hamilton–Bitterroot Valley, MT
Typical Housing
Price: $58,800
Property Taxes: $635
Built Before 1940: 29%
Choices
75% houses, 13% mobile homes
Energy Requirements
Heating Season: 7,873 degree days
Major Source: Natural gas/Electricity
Air Conditioning: 303 hours
Annual Costs
Mortgage and Taxes: $5,592
Utilities: $768
Places Rated Score: $6,360
Places Rated Rank: 39

Harrison, AR
Typical Housing
Price: $45,400
Property Taxes: $644
Built Before 1940: 18%
Choices
91% houses, 8% mobile homes
Energy Requirements
Heating Season: 3,537 degree days
Major Source: Natural gas/Electricity
Air Conditioning: 1,207 hours

Annual Costs
Mortgage and Taxes: $4,468
Utilities: $769
Places Rated Score: $5,237
Places Rated Rank: 17

Hendersonville, NC
Typical Housing
Price: $57,400
Property Taxes: $614
Built Before 1940: 16%
Choices
77% houses, 1% condos, 13% mobile homes
Energy Requirements
Heating Season: 4,072 degree days
Major Source: Total electric
Air Conditioning: 610 hours
Annual Costs
Mortgage and Taxes: $5,453
Utilities: $1,090
Places Rated Score: $6,543
Places Rated Rank: 50

Hot Springs–Lake Ouachita, AR
Typical Housing
Price: $50,800
Property Taxes: $721
Built Before 1940: 20%
Choices
85% houses, 4% condos, 10% mobile homes
Energy Requirements
Heating Season: 2,982 degree days
Major Source: Natural gas/Electricity
Air Conditioning: 1,559 hours
Annual Costs
Mortgage and Taxes: $4,495
Utilities: $639
Places Rated Score: $5,134
Places Rated Rank: 12

Houghton Lake, MI
Typical Housing
Price: $35,600
Property Taxes: $975
Built Before 1940: 10%
Choices
87% houses, 1% condos, 8% mobile homes
Energy Requirements
Heating Season: 7,151 degree days
Major Source: Oil/Electricity
Air Conditioning: 218 hours
Annual Costs
Mortgage and Taxes: $3,970
Utilities: $1,173
Places Rated Score: $5,143
Places Rated Rank: 15

Kalispell, MT
Typical Housing
Price: $60,900
Property Taxes: $657
Built Before 1940: 23%
Choices
70% houses, 1% condos, 16% mobile homes

Energy Requirements
Heating Season: 8,055 degree days
Major Source: Natural gas/Electricity
Air Conditioning: 26 hours
Annual Costs
Mortgage and Taxes: $5,785
Utilities: $688
Places Rated Score: $6,473
Places Rated Rank: 48

Keene, NH
Typical Housing
Price: $49,200
Property Taxes: $851
Built Before 1940: 46%
Choices
70% houses, 1% condos, 7% mobile
homes
Energy Requirements
Heating Season: 7,458 degree days
Major Source: Oil/Electricity
Air Conditioning: 335 hours
Annual Costs
Mortgage and Taxes: $4,992
Utilities: $1,306
Places Rated Score: $6,298
Places Rated Rank: 38

Kerrville, TX
Typical Housing
Price: $57,900
Property Taxes: $972
Built Before 1940: 16%
Choices
72% houses, 1% condos, 14% mobile
homes
Energy Requirements
Heating Season: 2,107 degree days
Major Source: Natural gas/Electricity
Air Conditioning: 1,715 hours
Annual Costs
Mortgage and Taxes: $5,851
Utilities: $863
Places Rated Score: $6,714
Places Rated Rank: 56

Laconia–Lake Winnipesaukee, NH
Typical Housing
Price: $53,800
Property Taxes: $930
Built Before 1940: 43%
Choices
67% houses, 3% condos, 8% mobile
homes
Energy Requirements
Heating Season: 7,612 degree days
Major Source: Oil/Electricity
Air Conditioning: 398 hours
Annual Costs
Mortgage and Taxes: $5,461
Utilities: $1,306
Places Rated Score: $6,767
Places Rated Rank: 58

Lake Havasu City–Kingman, AZ
Typical Housing
Price: $61,700
Property Taxes: $456
Built Before 1940: 3%

Choices
56% houses, 2% condos, 34% mobile
homes
Energy Requirements
Heating Season: 3,375 degree days
Major Source: Natural gas/Electricity
Air Conditioning: 1,662 hours
Annual Costs
Mortgage and Taxes: $5,653
Utilities: $1,102
Places Rated Score: $6,755
Places Rated Rank: 57

Lakeland–Winter Haven, FL
Typical Housing
Price: $50,000
Property Taxes: $460
Built Before 1940: 12%
Choices
72% houses, 2% condos, 16% mobile
homes
Energy Requirements
Heating Season: 649 degree days
Major Source: Total electric
Air Conditioning: 1,759 hours
Annual Costs
Mortgage and Taxes: $4,673
Utilities: $1,313
Places Rated Score: $5,986
Places Rated Rank: 28

Lake O' The Cherokees, OK
Typical Housing
Price: $43,700
Property Taxes: $358
Built Before 1940: 15%
Choices
79% houses, 1% condos, 17% mobile
homes
Energy Requirements
Heating Season: 3,584 degree days
Major Source: Bottled gas/Electricity
Air Conditioning: 1,399 hours
Annual Costs
Mortgage and Taxes: $4,036
Utilities: $704
Places Rated Score: $4,740
Places Rated Rank: 5

Lancaster, PA
Typical Housing
Price: $56,100
Property Taxes: $841
Built Before 1940: 30%
Choices
77% houses, 1% condos, 5% mobile
homes
Energy Requirements
Heating Season: 5,482 degree days
Major Source: Oil/Electricity
Air Conditioning: 654 hours
Annual Costs
Mortgage and Taxes: $5,563
Utilities: $1,280
Places Rated Score: $6,843
Places Rated Rank: 60

Las Cruces, NM
Typical Housing
Price: $53,400

Property Taxes: $608
Built Before 1940: 11%
Choices
65% houses, 1% condos, 16% mobile
homes
Energy Requirements
Heating Season: 3,201 degree days
Major Source: Natural gas/Electricity
Air Conditioning: 1,848 hours
Annual Costs
Mortgage and Taxes: $5,104
Utilities: $1,033
Places Rated Score: $6,137
Places Rated Rank: 33

Las Vegas, NV
Typical Housing
Price: $86,000
Property Taxes: $971
Built Before 1940: 2%
Choices
60% houses, 5% condos, 11% mobile
homes
Energy Requirements
Heating Season: 2,425 degree days
Major Source: Total electric
Air Conditioning: 2,360 hours
Annual Costs
Mortgage and Taxes: $8,215
Utilities: $1,413
Places Rated Score: $9,628
Places Rated Rank: 100

Lexington–Fayette, KY
Typical Housing
Price: $64,500
Property Taxes: $735
Built Before 1940: 21%
Choices
69% houses, 2% condos, 4% mobile
homes
Energy Requirements
Heating Season: 4,979 degree days
Major Source: Natural gas/Electricity
Air Conditioning: 954 hours
Annual Costs
Mortgage and Taxes: $6,171
Utilities: $956
Places Rated Score: $7,127
Places Rated Rank: 66

Lincoln City–Newport, OR
Typical Housing
Price: $69,700
Property Taxes: $1,087
Built Before 1940: 17%
Choices
70% houses, 3% condos, 14% mobile
homes
Energy Requirements
Heating Season: 4,574 degree days
Major Source: Total electric
Air Conditioning: 296 hours
Annual Costs
Mortgage and Taxes: $6,958
Utilities: $786
Places Rated Score: $7,744
Places Rated Rank: 76

Maui, HI
Typical Housing
Price: $149,000
Property Taxes: $536
Built Before 1940: 13%
Choices
55% houses, 32% condos
Energy Requirements
Heating Season: 0 degree days
Major Source: Total electric
Air Conditioning: 576 hours
Annual Costs
Mortgage and Taxes: $12,265
Utilities: $1,161
Places Rated Score: $13,426
Places Rated Rank: 107

McALLEN–PHARR–EDINBURG, TX
Typical Housing
Price: $37,400
Property Taxes: $628
Built Before 1940: 9%
Choices
72% houses, 1% condos, 9% mobile homes
Energy Requirements
Heating Season: 617 degree days
Major Source: Natural gas/Electricity
Air Conditioning: 2,527 hours
Annual Costs
Mortgage and Taxes: $3,778
Utilities: $1,172
Places Rated Score: $4,950
Places Rated Rank: 9

MEDFORD, OR
Typical Housing
Price: $72,100
Property Taxes: $1,124
Built Before 1940: 14%
Choices
73% houses, 1% condos, 12% mobile homes
Energy Requirements
Heating Season: 4,547 degree days
Major Source: Total electric
Air Conditioning: 630 hours
Annual Costs
Mortgage and Taxes: $7,197
Utilities: $783
Places Rated Score: $7,980
Places Rated Rank: 81

MELBOURNE–TITUSVILLE–COCOA, FL
Typical Housing
Price: $67,100
Property Taxes: $617
Built Before 1940: 3%
Choices
70% houses, 7% condos, 11% mobile homes
Energy Requirements
Heating Season: 345 degree days
Major Source: Total electric
Air Conditioning: 2,113 hours
Annual Costs
Mortgage and Taxes: $6,271
Utilities: $1,393
Places Rated Score: $7,664
Places Rated Rank: 75

MIAMI, FL
Typical Housing
Price: $81,100
Property Taxes: $746
Built Before 1940: 7%
Choices
56% houses, 13% condos, 2% mobile homes
Energy Requirements
Heating Season: 178 degree days
Major Source: Total electric
Air Conditioning: 2,388 hours
Annual Costs
Mortgage and Taxes: $7,575
Utilities: $1,454
Places Rated Score: $9,029
Places Rated Rank: 95

Missoula, MT
Typical Housing
Price: $71,700
Property Taxes: $774
Built Before 1940: 19%
Choices
66% houses, 1% condos, 11% mobile homes
Energy Requirements
Heating Season: 7,873 degree days
Major Source: Natural gas/Electricity
Air Conditioning: 303 hours
Annual Costs
Mortgage and Taxes: $6,810
Utilities: $768
Places Rated Score: $7,578
Places Rated Rank: 73

Monticello–Liberty, NY
Typical Housing
Price: $44,700
Property Taxes: $1,229
Built Before 1940: 33%
Choices
71% houses, 1% condos, 9% mobile homes
Energy Requirements
Heating Season: 6,556 degree days
Major Source: Oil/Electricity
Air Conditioning: 623 hours
Annual Costs
Mortgage and Taxes: $4,997
Utilities: $1,228
Places Rated Score: $6,225
Places Rated Rank: 36

Mountain Home–Norfork Lake, AR
Typical Housing
Price: $47,900
Property Taxes: $680
Built Before 1940: 7%
Choices
82% houses, 2% condos, 12% mobile homes
Energy Requirements
Heating Season: 3,537 degree days
Major Source: Total electric
Air Conditioning: 1,207 hours

Annual Costs
Mortgage and Taxes: $4,718
Utilities: $769
Places Rated Score: $5,487
Places Rated Rank: 23

Myrtle Beach, SC
Typical Housing
Price: $59,700
Property Taxes: $501
Built Before 1940: 10%
Choices
70% houses, 4% condos, 15% mobile homes
Energy Requirements
Heating Season: 2,023 degree days
Major Source: Total electric
Air Conditioning: 1,204 hours
Annual Costs
Mortgage and Taxes: $5,533
Utilities: $890
Places Rated Score: $6,423
Places Rated Rank: 45

Nevada City–Donner, CA
Typical Housing
Price: $100,000
Property Taxes: $1,040
Built Before 1940: 16%
Choices
77% houses, 2% condos, 10% mobile homes
Energy Requirements
Heating Season: 6,036 degree days
Major Source: Total electric
Air Conditioning: 647 hours
Annual Costs
Mortgage and Taxes: $9,470
Utilities: $945
Places Rated Score: $10,415
Places Rated Rank: 102

North Conway–White Mountains, NH
Typical Housing
Price: $56,800
Property Taxes: $982
Built Before 1940: 38%
Choices
81% houses, 3% condos, 8% mobile homes
Energy Requirements
Heating Season: 7,612 degree days
Major Source: Oil/Electricity
Air Conditioning: 398 hours
Annual Costs
Mortgage and Taxes: $5,769
Utilities: $1,306
Places Rated Score: $7,075
Places Rated Rank: 65

Oak Harbor, WA
Typical Housing
Price: $85,000
Property Taxes: $807
Built Before 1940: 9%
Choices
78% houses, 1% condos, 10% mobile homes

Energy Requirements
 Heating Season: 4,438 degree days
 Major Source: Total electric
 Air Conditioning: 41 hours
Annual Costs
 Mortgage and Taxes: $7,970
 Utilities: $520
Places Rated Score: $8,490
Places Rated Rank: 88

OCALA, FL
Typical Housing
 Price: $49,500
 Property Taxes: $455
 Built Before 1940: 7%
Choices
 71% houses, 2% condos, 21% mobile
 homes
Energy Requirements
 Heating Season: 530 degree days
 Major Source: Total electric
 Air Conditioning: 1,824 hours
Annual Costs
 Mortgage and Taxes: $4,625
 Utilities: $1,463
Places Rated Score: $6,088
Places Rated Rank: 31

Ocean City–Assateague Island, MD
Typical Housing
 Price: $54,000
 Property Taxes: $675
 Built Before 1940: 21%
Choices
 54% houses, 29% condos, 6% mobile
 homes
Energy Requirements
 Heating Season: 4,303 degree days
 Major Source: Oil/Electricity
 Air Conditioning: 461 hours
Annual Costs
 Mortgage and Taxes: $5,223
 Utilities: $1,367
Places Rated Score: $6,590
Places Rated Rank: 53

OLYMPIA, WA
Typical Housing
 Price: $72,200
 Property Taxes: $685
 Built Before 1940: 13%
Choices
 72% houses, 1% condos, 11% mobile
 homes
Energy Requirements
 Heating Season: 5,501 degree days
 Major Source: Total electric
 Air Conditioning: 117 hours
Annual Costs
 Mortgage and Taxes: $6,768
 Utilities: $529
Places Rated Score: $7,297
Places Rated Rank: 69

ORLANDO, FL
Typical Housing
 Price: $63,400
 Property Taxes: $583
 Built Before 1940: 6%

Choices
 75% houses, 4% condos, 7% mobile
 homes
Energy Requirements
 Heating Season: 650 degree days
 Major Source: Total electric
 Air Conditioning: 1,609 hours
Annual Costs
 Mortgage and Taxes: $5,920
 Utilities: $1,043
Places Rated Score: $6,963
Places Rated Rank: 63

Oscoda–Huron Shore, MI
Typical Housing
 Price: $37,100
 Property Taxes: $1,016
 Built Before 1940: 14%
Choices
 81% houses, 1% condos, 8% mobile
 homes
Energy Requirements
 Heating Season: 8,073 degree days
 Major Source: Oil/Electricity
 Air Conditioning: 219 hours
Annual Costs
 Mortgage and Taxes: $4,144
 Utilities: $1,173
Places Rated Score: $5,317
Places Rated Rank: 20

Paris, TN
Typical Housing
 Price: $40,300
 Property Taxes: $572
 Built Before 1940: 12%
Choices
 81% houses, 11% mobile homes
Energy Requirements
 Heating Season: 3,513 degree days
 Major Source: Total electric
 Air Conditioning: 1,160 hours
Annual Costs
 Mortgage and Taxes: $3,969
 Utilities: $796
Places Rated Score: $4,765
Places Rated Rank: 7

Petoskey–Straits of Mackinac, MI
Typical Housing
 Price: $51,400
 Property Taxes: $1,408
 Built Before 1940: 37%
Choices
 76% houses, 2% condos, 8% mobile
 homes
Energy Requirements
 Heating Season: 8,964 degree days
 Major Source: Oil/Electricity
 Air Conditioning: 301 hours
Annual Costs
 Mortgage and Taxes: $5,737
 Utilities: $1,173
Places Rated Score: $6,910
Places Rated Rank: 62

PHOENIX, AZ
Typical Housing
 Price: $76,600

Property Taxes: $566
 Built Before 1940: 4%
Choices
 72% houses, 7% condos, 8% mobile
 homes
Energy Requirements
 Heating Season: 1,492 degree days
 Major Source: Natural gas/Electricity
 Air Conditioning: 2,845 hours
Annual Costs
 Mortgage and Taxes: $7,021
 Utilities: $1,638
Places Rated Score: $8,659
Places Rated Rank: 89

Port Angeles–Strait of Juan de Fuca, WA
Typical Housing
 Price: $72,100
 Property Taxes: $684
 Built Before 1940: 17%
Choices
 74% houses, 1% condos, 14% mobile
 homes
Energy Requirements
 Heating Season: 5,850 degree days
 Major Source: Total electric
 Air Conditioning: 0 hours
Annual Costs
 Mortgage and Taxes: $6,756
 Utilities: $312
Places Rated Score: $7,068
Places Rated Rank: 64

Prescott, AZ
Typical Housing
 Price: $66,700
 Property Taxes: $493
 Built Before 1940: 14%
Choices
 72% houses, 2% condos, 17% mobile
 homes
Energy Requirements
 Heating Season: 4,533 degree days
 Major Source: Natural gas/Electricity
 Air Conditioning: 925 hours
Annual Costs
 Mortgage and Taxes: $6,116
 Utilities: $1,081
Places Rated Score: $7,197
Places Rated Rank: 67

Rappahannock, VA
Typical Housing
 Price: $53,500
 Property Taxes: $743
 Built Before 1940: 44%
Choices
 90% houses, 1% mobile homes
Energy Requirements
 Heating Season: 4,784 degree days
 Major Source: Oil/Electricity
 Air Conditioning: 679 hours
Annual Costs
 Mortgage and Taxes: $5,253
 Utilities: $1,120
Places Rated Score: $6,373
Places Rated Rank: 40

Red Bluff–Sacramento Valley, CA
Typical Housing
Price: $61,700
Property Taxes: $641
Built Before 1940: 16%
Choices
68% houses, 18% mobile homes
Energy Requirements
Heating Season: 2,546 degree days
Major Source: Natural gas/Electricity
Air Conditioning: 1,540 hours
Annual Costs
Mortgage and Taxes: $5,840
Utilities: $984
Places Rated Score: $6,824
Places Rated Rank: 59

Rehoboth Bay–Indian River Bay, DE
Typical Housing
Price: $53,400
Property Taxes: $421
Built Before 1940: 23%
Choices
71% houses, 5% condos, 19% mobile homes
Energy Requirements
Heating Season: 4,303 degree days
Major Source: Oil/Electricity
Air Conditioning: 456 hours
Annual Costs
Mortgage and Taxes: $4,915
Utilities: $1,489
Places Rated Score: $6,404
Places Rated Rank: 42

Reno, NV
Typical Housing
Price: $106,300
Property Taxes: $1,201
Built Before 1940: 8%
Choices
61% houses, 9% condos, 10% mobile homes
Energy Requirements
Heating Season: 6,036 degree days
Major Source: Natural gas/Electricity
Air Conditioning: 647 hours
Annual Costs
Mortgage and Taxes: $10,158
Utilities: $1,151
Places Rated Score: $11,309
Places Rated Rank: 104

Rhinelander, WI
Typical Housing
Price: $50,900
Property Taxes: $890
Built Before 1940: 27%
Choices
75% houses, 1% condos, 10% mobile homes
Energy Requirements
Heating Season: 8,657 degree days
Major Source: Oil/Electricity
Air Conditioning: 436 hours
Annual Costs
Mortgage and Taxes: $5,178

Utilities: $1,116
Places Rated Score: $6,294
Places Rated Rank: 37

Rockport–Aransas Pass, TX
Typical Housing
Price: $56,600
Property Taxes: $950
Built Before 1940: 5%
Choices
76% houses, 4% condos, 16% mobile homes
Energy Requirements
Heating Season: 1,011 degree days
Major Source: Natural gas/Electricity
Air Conditioning: 2,531 hours
Annual Costs
Mortgage and Taxes: $5,716
Utilities: $1,508
Places Rated Score: $7,224
Places Rated Rank: 68

Roswell, NM
Typical Housing
Price: $42,100
Property Taxes: $479
Built Before 1940: 14%
Choices
82% houses, 1% condos, 6% mobile homes
Energy Requirements
Heating Season: 3,424 degree days
Major Source: Natural gas/Electricity
Air Conditioning: 1,617 hours
Annual Costs
Mortgage and Taxes: $4,024
Utilities: $941
Places Rated Score: $4,965
Places Rated Rank: 10

St. George–Zion, UT
Typical Housing
Price: $74,200
Property Taxes: $764
Built Before 1940: 15%
Choices
72% houses, 6% condos, 13% mobile homes
Energy Requirements
Heating Season: 3,756 degree days
Major Source: Total electric
Air Conditioning: 789 hours
Annual Costs
Mortgage and Taxes: $7,011
Utilities: $586
Places Rated Score: $7,597
Places Rated Rank: 74

San Antonio, TX
Typical Housing
Price: $50,300
Property Taxes: $845
Built Before 1940: 13%
Choices
78% houses, 1% condos, 3% mobile homes
Energy Requirements
Heating Season: 1,579 degree days
Major Source: Natural gas/Electricity

Air Conditioning: 2,004 hours
Annual Costs
Mortgage and Taxes: $5,080
Utilities: $1,435
Places Rated Score: $6,515
Places Rated Rank: 49

San Diego, CA
Typical Housing
Price: $121,600
Property Taxes: $1,264
Built Before 1940: 9%
Choices
70% houses, 8% condos, 5% mobile homes
Energy Requirements
Heating Season: 1,574 degree days
Major Source: Natural gas/Electricity
Air Conditioning: 130 hours
Annual Costs
Mortgage and Taxes: $11,504
Utilities: $1,335
Places Rated Score: $12,839
Places Rated Rank: 106

San Luis Obispo, CA
Typical Housing
Price: $99,500
Property Taxes: $1,034
Built Before 1940: 12%
Choices
70% houses, 2% condos, 11% mobile homes
Energy Requirements
Heating Season: 2,382 degree days
Major Source: Natural gas/Electricity
Air Conditioning: 329 hours
Annual Costs
Mortgage and Taxes: $9,417
Utilities: $984
Places Rated Score: $10,401
Places Rated Rank: 101

Santa Fe, NM
Typical Housing
Price: $83,700
Property Taxes: $954
Built Before 1940: 16%
Choices
69% houses, 3% condos, 10% mobile homes
Energy Requirements
Heating Season: 6,123 degree days
Major Source: Natural gas/Electricity
Air Conditioning: 686 hours
Annual Costs
Mortgage and Taxes: $8,009
Utilities: $1,276
Places Rated Score: $9,285
Places Rated Rank: 97

Santa Rosa, CA
Typical Housing
Price: $114,500
Property Taxes: $1,190
Built Before 1940: 15%
Choices
78% houses, 3% condos, 7% mobile homes

Energy Requirements
  Heating Season: 2,860 degree days
  Major Source: Natural gas/Electricity
  Air Conditioning: 205 hours
Annual Costs
  Mortgage and Taxes: $10,834
  Utilities: $984
Places Rated Score: $11,818
Places Rated Rank: 105

SARASOTA–BRADENTON, FL
Typical Housing
  Price: $70,400
  Property Taxes: $647
  Built Before 1940: 4%
Choices
  65% houses, 15% condos, 16% mobile
  homes
Energy Requirements
  Heating Season: 674 degree days
  Major Source: Total electric
  Air Conditioning: 1,786 hours
Annual Costs
  Mortgage and Taxes: $6,576
  Utilities: $1,393
Places Rated Score: $7,969
Places Rated Rank: 80

SPRINGFIELD, MO
Typical Housing
  Price: $43,900
  Property Taxes: $417
  Built Before 1940: 21%
Choices
  80% houses, 1% condos, 5% mobile
  homes
Energy Requirements
  Heating Season: 4,693
  Major Source: Natural gas/Electricity
  Air Conditioning: 964 hours
Annual Costs
  Mortgage and Taxes: $4,117
  Utilities: $1,062
Places Rated Score: $5,179
Places Rated Rank: 16

STATE COLLEGE, PA
Typical Housing
  Price: $54,400
  Property Taxes: $816
  Built Before 1940: 41%
Choices
  70% houses, 1% condos, 7% mobile
  homes
Energy Requirements
  Heating Season: 6,297 degree days
  Major Source: Oil/Electricity
  Air Conditioning: 351 hours
Annual Costs
  Mortgage and Taxes: $5,399
  Utilities: $1,151
Places Rated Score: $6,550
Places Rated Rank: 51

TABLE ROCK LAKE, MO
Typical Housing
  Price: $45,600
  Property Taxes: $433

Built Before 1940: 17%
Choices
  83% houses, 1% condos, 14% mobile
  homes
Energy Requirements
  Heating Season: 4,693 degree days
  Major Source: Bottled gas/Electricity
  Air Conditioning: 1,058 hours
Annual Costs
  Mortgage and Taxes: $4,277
  Utilities: $1,062
Places Rated Score: $5,339
Places Rated Rank: 22

Tahlequah–Lake Tenkiller, OK
Typical Housing
  Price: $44,100
  Property Taxes: $361
  Built Before 1940: 12%
Choices
  78% houses, 1% condos, 17% mobile
  homes
Energy Requirements
  Heating Season: 3,584 degree days
  Major Source: Natural gas/Electricity
  Air Conditioning: 1,399 hours
Annual Costs
  Mortgage and Taxes: $4,077
  Utilities: $861
Places Rated Score: $4,938
Places Rated Rank: 8

Toms River–Barnegat Bay, NJ
Typical Housing
  Price: $58,300
  Property Taxes: $1,474
  Built Before 1940: 9%
Choices
  85% houses, 8% condos, 3% mobile
  homes
Energy Requirements
  Heating Season: 5,272 degree days
  Major Source: Oil/Electricity
  Air Conditioning: 447 hours
Annual Costs
  Mortgage and Taxes: $6,388
  Utilities: $1,620
Places Rated Score: $8,008
Places Rated Rank: 85

Traverse City–Grand Traverse Bay, MI
Typical Housing
  Price: $55,500
  Property Taxes: $1,520
  Built Before 1940: 25%
Choices
  77% houses, 1% condos, 10% mobile
  homes
Energy Requirements
  Heating Season: 8,657 degree days
  Major Source: Natural gas/Electricity
  Air Conditioning: 308 hours
Annual Costs
  Mortgage and Taxes: $6,194
  Utilities: $1,173
Places Rated Score: $7,367
Places Rated Rank: 70

TUCSON, AZ
Typical Housing
  Price: $74,200
  Property Taxes: $549
  Built Before 1940: 6%
Choices
  71% houses, 4% condos, 11% mobile
  homes
Energy Requirements
  Heating Season: 1,776 degree days
  Major Source: Natural gas/Electricity
  Air Conditioning: 2,445 hours
Annual Costs
  Mortgage and Taxes: $6,801
  Utilities: $1,452
Places Rated Score: $8,253
Places Rated Rank: 87

Twain Harte–Yosemite, CA
Typical Housing
  Price: $84,400
  Property Taxes: $877
  Built Before 1940: 13%
Choices
  76% houses, 1% condos, 15% mobile
  homes
Energy Requirements
  Heating Season: 6,036 degree days
  Major Source: Wood/Electricity
  Air Conditioning: 647 hours
Annual Costs
  Mortgage and Taxes: $7,990
  Utilities: $984
Places Rated Score: $8,974
Places Rated Rank: 94

WEST PALM BEACH–BOCA RATON, FL
Typical Housing
  Price: $83,100
  Property Taxes: $764
  Built Before 1940: 5%
Choices
  62% houses, 30% condos, 5% mobile
  homes
Energy Requirements
  Heating Season: 248 degree days
  Major Source: Total electric
  Air Conditioning: 2,387 hours
Annual Costs
  Mortgage and Taxes: $7,766
  Utilities: $1,492
Places Rated Score: $9,258
Places Rated Rank: 96

Winchester, VA
Typical Housing
  Price: $58,800
  Property Taxes: $817
  Built Before 1940: 27%
Choices
  80% houses, 1% condos, 7% mobile
  homes
Energy Requirements
  Heating Season: 4,784 degree days
  Major Source: Oil/Electricity
  Air Conditioning: 679 hours
Annual Costs
  Mortgage and Taxes: $5,771

Utilities: $1,120
Places Rated Score: $6,891
Places Rated Rank: 61

Yuma, AZ
Typical Housing
  Price: $52,400

Property Taxes: $387
Built Before 1940: 6%
Choices
  56% houses, 2% condos, 28% mobile
  homes
Energy Requirements
  Heating Season: 951 degree days

Major Source: Total electric
Air Conditioning: 3,148 hours
Annual Costs
  Mortgage and Taxes: $4,805
  Utilities: $1,642
Places Rated Score: $6,447
Places Rated Rank: 46

Et Cetera

YOUR $125,000 DECISION

According to federal income-tax law, your house is a capital asset, and if you sell it at a profit, that profit may be taxable in the year in which you sell. A loss on the sale, however, isn't deductible.

There are two important exceptions to this rule that can help you put off the payment of taxes or eliminate them altogether: the "rollover" available to sellers of any age, and the one-time exclusion, which can be taken advantage of only by sellers 55 and over.

The Rollover. If you sell your house at a profit, the tax on the profit may be postponed if, within two years from the date you sell, you buy another house and pay as much or more than the sale price of your old house. This time limit works forward and backward: You can buy the new house as long as 24 months before or 24 months after you sell your old house. If you anticipate retiring, this rule allows you to buy a vacation home up to two years before you sell your principal residence and claim the rollover when you move into the vacation home for full-time living.

If the price of your new home is less than the sale price of your old one, part of the profit will be taxable during the year. The profit will also be taxable during the year in which you sold in the event that you don't buy a new principal residence but instead rent an apartment or house.

The rollover can be used over and over again until the day you sell your home and don't buy another. When that happens, the taxes are due on all the accumulated profits realized in all your principal residences sold over prior years. That is an ideal time to claim the one-time exclusion.

The Exclusion. If either you or your spouse are 55 by the day you sell your home at a profit, and you've owned and used the home as your principal residence for at least three of the five years ending on the day the property is sold, you can elect to exclude up to $125,000 of profit from tax altogether ($62,500 for married persons filing separately).

The exclusion can be claimed only once, so don't use it to shelter a paltry gain if you anticipate an even larger gain later on. Also, the once-in-a-lifetime feature of the exclusion can be an important one when a person marries, divorces, or remarries.

HOME-EQUITY CONVERSION: LIVING "ON THE HOUSE"

When it comes to real estate, you may have several good things going for you. If you're over 65, you're more likely to own a home than younger people; like other homeowners, you're likely to possess an asset that has appreciated dramatically since 1970. Some economists put the total value of homes owned by people over 65 in the United States at more than $600 billion.

Home-equity conversion, or reverse-equity plans, are designed to help older house-rich and cash-poor homeowners unlock the value of their home and convert it into additional retirement income, without being forced to move or to repay the loan from monthly income. Some plans involve actual transfer of title to the property; others do not. Some provide income for only a specified period, whereas others provide income for life.

Deciding which plan is best for your own personal circumstances takes careful thought; interested homeowners should seek the advice of a knowledgeable attorney for help in weighing the benefits and liabilities of specific local plans. The following are three major variations:

A Reverse Appreciation Mortgage (RAM) is a loan paid out in monthly installments to the homeowner by a lender, thereby creating a debt (hence the word "mortgage") that increases each month. The house must be free of any mortgage or lien, since the amount of the loan is determined by the price the home would fetch if the property were put up for sale. The loan comes due at the end of the term or when the owner dies or decides to sell the property. The RAM is repaid out of money from the sale of the house or from other resources.

The Rental Scene

According to a 1981 annual housing survey conducted by the Census Bureau, 20 percent of homeowners over 65 who move start out renting in their new location, apparently taking some time to look around for a good buy before purchasing a home or a condo. The list below, which gives monthly median rents in the 107 retirement places, might be helpful if you decide to do the same.

A quick glance at these rents and the housing prices in the Place Profiles will reveal a strong correlation between the two. Maui, for example, has the most expensive homes of all the retirement places ($149,000) as well as the highest rent ($452). And retirement places in Missouri, Tennessee, and Texas that have some of the lowest housing prices in *Places Rated*'s universe also offer some of the lowest rents.

Retirement Place	Monthly Median Rent	Retirement Place	Monthly Median Rent	Retirement Place	Monthly Median Rent	Retirement Place	Monthly Median Rent
ALBUQUERQUE, NM	$292	Coeur d'Alene, ID	$307	Lake O' The Cherokees, OK	$203	Port Angeles– Strait of Juan de Fuca, WA	$297
ASHEVILLE, NC	248	COLORADO SPRINGS, CO	282	LANCASTER, PA	287	Prescott, AZ	279
Athens–Cedar Creek Lake, TX	219	Cookeville, TN	236	LAS CRUCES, NM	252	Rappahannock, VA	243
ATLANTIC CITY– CAPE MAY, NJ	341	Crossville, TN	209	LAS VEGAS, NV	377	Red Bluff– Sacramento Valley, CA	262
AUSTIN, TX	330	DAYTONA BEACH, FL	302	LEXINGTON– FAYETTE, KY	286	
		Delta, CO	261	Lincoln City– Newport, OR	292	Rehoboth Bay–Indian River Bay, DE	264
Bar Harbor– Frenchman Bay, ME	269	Deming, NM	213	Maui, HI	452	RENO, NV	437
		Eagle River, WI	267	McALLEN–PHARR– EDINBURG, TX	212	Rhinelander, WI	274
Beaufort–Hilton Head, SC	327	Easton–Chesapeake Bay, MD	292	MEDFORD, OR	317	Rockport–Aransas Pass, TX	291
Bend, OR	351			MELBOURNE– TITUSVILLE–COCOA, FL	325	Roswell, NM	246
Bennington, VT	286	Fairhope–Gulf Shores, AL	279			St. George–Zion, UT	287
Benton–Kentucky Lake, KY	244	FORT COLLINS, CO	326	MIAMI, FL	341	SAN ANTONIO, TX	325
		FORT LAUDERDALE– HOLLYWOOD, FL	391			SAN DIEGO, CA	352
Big Sandy, TN	218	FORT MYERS– CAPE CORAL, FL	348	Missoula, MT	286	San Luis Obispo, CA	350
BILOXI–GULFPORT, MS	261	Fredericksburg, TX	258	Monticello–Liberty, NY	279	Santa Fe, NM	313
BOISE CITY, ID	326			Mountain Home– Norfork Lake, AR	263	SANTA ROSA, CA	362
Branson–Lake Taneycomo, MO	237	Front Royal, VA	258	Myrtle Beach, SC	277	
Brattleboro, VT	279	Gainesville–Lake Sidney Lanier, GA	257	Nevada City– Donner, CA	357	SARASOTA– BRADENTON, FL	338
		Grand Junction, CO	322			SPRINGFIELD, MO	256
Brevard, NC	239	Hamilton–Bitterroot Valley, MT	236	North Conway–White Mountains, NH	292	STATE COLLEGE, PA	313
Brunswick–Golden Isles, GA	258	Harrison, AR	229	Oak Harbor, WA	301	Table Rock Lake, MO	217
Bull Shoals, AR	228			OCALA, FL	271	Tahlequah– Lake Tenkiller, OK	213
Camden–Penobscot Bay, ME	279	Hendersonville, NC	256	Ocean City– Assateague Island, MD	262	
Canton–Lake Tawakoni, TX	214	Hot Springs–Lake Ouachita, AR	219	OLYMPIA, WA	325	Toms River– Barnegat Bay, NJ	373
		Houghton Lake, MI	247			Traverse City–Grand Traverse Bay, MI	342
Cape Cod, MA	365	Kalispell, MT	271	ORLANDO, FL	320	TUCSON, AZ	308
Carson City, NV	256	Keene, NH	309	Oscoda–Huron Shore, MI	251	Twain Harte– Yosemite, CA	313
Cassville–Roaring River, MO	198	Kerrville, TX	283	Paris, TN	208	WEST PALM BEACH– BOCA RATON, FL	350
CHARLOTTESVILLE, VA	351	Laconia–Lake Winnipesaukee, NH	288	Petoskey–Straits of Mackinac, MI	289	
Clarkesville–Mount Airy, GA	204	Lake Havasu City– Kingman, AZ	346	PHOENIX, AZ	361	Winchester, VA	282
Clear Lake, CA	303	LAKELAND–WINTER HAVEN, FL	274			Yuma, AZ	293

Source: U.S. Bureau of the Census, *1980 Census of Population and Housing*; figures adjusted for inflation with 1983 Consumer Price Index estimates.

A sale-leaseback arrangement permits you to stay in your home for the rest of your life as long as you're physically able. You sell your house to an investor, who leases the property back to you at a fixed rent for as long as you can or want to live in the house. You receive a down payment and a monthly mortgage payment from the investor, who is responsible for taxes, maintenance, and insurance on the property. The investor takes full possession of the property when you choose to move out of the house or in the event of your death.

Deferred payment loans are home-improvement

loans offered most often by city governments or neighborhood housing-service agencies. They are generally open to all ages and charge low or no interest. The loan comes due when the owner dies or sells the property. In either case, the deferred loan is then paid out of cash from the sale of the house or at the estate settlement.

For several publications relating to home-equity conversion, including the *Home Equity* newsletter, contact the National Center for Home Equity Conversion, 110 East Main Street, Room 1010, Madison, WI 53703 (608-256-2111).

ARE MOBILE HOMES INVESTMENTS?

Whether real-estate salespeople tout detached houses, condos, townhouses, or sited mobile homes, they've all learned the five factors that influence price tags: quality of original construction, the neighborhood's turnover rate, supply and demand for housing, current upkeep, and location.

With these factors at work in the housing market, mobile homes, like automobiles, tend to go down in value as they get older. According to a 1979 study from the American Institute of Real Estate Appraisers, the typical mobile home sited in a typical park depreciates 10 percent the first year and between 5 and 6 percent each year thereafter.

But this isn't the case in all parts of the country. In seven states, all but two of them in the West, mobile homes have appreciated from between 4 and 7 percent annually, according to a 1980 survey from the Foremost Insurance Company. These states are Alaska, Arizona, California, Florida, New Jersey, Oregon, and Washington. In the central states, values are keeping pace with new home costs. In the eastern third of the country, however, mobile homes still tend to decline in value from the moment they are first winched onto a permanent pad.

Do mobile homes make good investments?

Yes, if you want to live in Florida, New Jersey, Arizona, or the Pacific Coast states but can't afford to buy a house or a condominium in the competitive real-estate markets there. While the appreciation in mobile homes lags behind that of conventional houses, you still have a good chance to make money when you sell.

Perhaps, if you have your sights set on a destination in the Rocky Mountain states, the Ozarks, northern Michigan, or Texas but can't afford conventional housing. Search carefully for a well-managed park near popular resorts or natural outdoor endowments.

No, if you're headed for the southeastern states, Pennsylvania, New York, or New England and have enough money to buy conventional housing. Mobile homes here have a history of depreciating when prices for existing site-built homes have gone up.

LEGAL PROTECTION FOR RENTERS, CONDO BUYERS, AND MOBILE-HOME OWNERS

Older people who move from one state to another are no more immune than others from varying laws that affect them if they rent, buy a condominium, or buy a mobile home and rent space in a mobile-home park. If you're aware of the law, you might avoid potentially expensive surprises.

Renters' Rights

Seventeen states have enacted landlord-tenant laws based on the Uniform Residential Landlord and Tenant Act (1972), a piece of model legislation drawn up by the National Conference of Commissioners on Uniform State Laws. These states are Alaska, Arizona, Connecticut, Florida, Hawaii, Iowa, Kansas, Kentucky, Michigan, Montana, Nebraska, New Mexico, Oklahoma, Oregon, Tennessee, Virginia, and Washington.

This landlord-tenant act defines rights and obligations of both parties to a lease on an apartment or house, and it also specifies the way disputes can be resolved. Among its provisions are:

- If your dispute with a landlord leads you to complain to the local housing board, join a tenants' group, or bring suit against the landlord, your landlord may not retaliate by cutting services, raising your rent, or evicting you.
- If the landlord doesn't make needed repairs, and the cost of the repairs is no more than $100 or half the rent, whichever is greater, you may make repairs and deduct the expense from your monthly rent.
- After you vacate the apartment or house, any money you've deposited as security must be returned. If there are any deductions from the deposit for damages or other reasons, these deductions must be itemized.
- If the landlord does not live up to the terms of the lease, you may recover damages in small claims court.

Protection for Condo Buyers

As the condominium form of ownership swept the country in the 1960s and 1970s, many states realized consumers had little protection at the point of purchase. Eight states have enacted comprehensive statutes to deal with condominium ownership based on the Uniform Condominium Act (1980) drawn up by the National Conference of Commissioners on Uniform State Laws. These states are Maine, Minnesota, Missouri, New Mexico, Pennsylvania, South Carolina, Virginia, and West Virginia.

The act covers owners' associations, developers'

activities, eminent domain, separate titles and taxation, and safeguards for condominium buyers. Among its provisions are:

- The developer must provide you with a Public Offering Statement, accurately and fully disclosing a schedule for completion of all construction, the total number of condominium units, the bylaws of the owners' association, copies of any contracts or leases that you must sign, a current balance sheet and projected one-year budget for the owners' association, and a statement of the monthly common assessments you'll have to pay.
- After signing a purchase agreement, you still have 15 days to "cool off," after which you can either cancel the agreement without penalty or accept conveyance of the property.

- If you buy a condominium without first being given the Public Offering Statement, you are entitled to receive from the developer an amount equal to ten percent of the sales price of the unit you bought.
- The developer and real-estate agent must guarantee that the unit you are buying is free from defective materials, is built according to sound engineering and construction standards, and conforms to local codes.

Rights for Mobile-Home Owners

In most states, a mobile-home park owner can evict you for any reason. You aren't protected by landlord-tenant laws as you would be if you were renting an apartment. The park owner owns the property, rarely gives leases, and can demand sharp rent increases and a variety of costly fees once you've spent money siting your mobile home in the park. You may be forced to sell at a loss if the park owner tells you to move and no other park has space for your home.

Six states have passed "just cause" laws to protect mobile-home owners from being arbitrarily evicted from mobile-home parks, according to a survey by the American Mobilhome Association. Just causes for eviction include nonpayment of rent, being tried and convicted of a crime, violation of reasonable park rules, or conversion of park land to other uses. The states are California, Colorado, Florida, Oregon, Utah, and Washington.

PROPERTY-TAX RELIEF FOR OLDER HOMEOWNERS

When you shop for low property taxes around the country, adopt a circumspect attitude when you hear of places that give retired people additional property-tax relief. Are any of these benefits, by themselves, worth a move?

Read on.

Exemptions

Exemptions are specific dollar amounts deducted by local assessors when they compute your bill. In Hawaii, for example, homeowners over 60 get an exemption of $24,000; when they turn 70, the exemption increases to $30,000. Older homeowners in Texas receive a $15,000 exemption. According to the Washington, D.C.–based Advisory Commission on Intergovernmental Relations, ten states currently allow special exemptions to older homeowners without any income qualifications: Alabama, Alaska, Georgia, Hawaii, Illinois, Kentucky, Mississippi, South Carolina, Texas, and West Virginia.

Do the exemptions in these states translate into much hard cash? Except in Alaska—where you can forget property taxes once you turn 65—not really. Based on statewide average property-tax rates, you'll

---

Condo Complaints

There are negative sides to living in a condo. Many of the complaints reported by the Urban Land Institute ten years ago in an extensive survey of condominium residents are being voiced today. Among them are:

- living cheek by jowl with unfamiliar neighbors
- noisy children and undesirable neighbors
- pets
- parking problems
- poor association management
- ticky-tacky construction
- dishonest salespeople
- renters in other units
- thin party walls
- long, single-blueprinted rows of houses

If you are thinking of condominium living in your retirement, you might do well to anticipate these common complaints and use them as a guide to judging condominium developments. Ask pertinent questions of the association and the broker. What are the restrictions on pets? Children? How well are they enforced? Does each unit have an assigned parking space? Are there rules in the association's bylaws limiting the number of rental units? What is the average tenure of the unit owners? Of the renters? Are any units set aside for time shares? Is their number restricted?

Bear in mind that, as a retired person, you are one of the two major targets of condominium marketing. The other is the young person or family buying their first home. Both groups want lower costs, freedom from house and yard maintenance in a ready-made environment, social life, and recreation facilities, all with the tax advantages of ownership. There isn't any reason the two groups can't live together harmoniously in the same development. In well-managed condominiums they often do. But in other developments, the mix can prove unhappy. There may well be advantages in sticking with your own kind.

Taxing the Home: Statewide Averages

If your home's latest property-tax bill seems higher than it has ever been, take comfort. The rate at which your home is being taxed is actually going *down*.

Over the past decade, when prices of existing homes have risen dramatically, nationwide property-tax rates have declined from nearly 2 percent of these values to less than 1.25 percent, and the trend is continuing downward.

Although there isn't a single privately owned house in the United States that is immune from property taxes (except those in Alaska owned by persons over 65), homeowners in certain states (like Louisiana, where the statewide average property-tax rate is 0.28 percent) shoulder less of a burden than do homeowners in other states (such as New York, which has an average tax rate of 2.75 percent).

Property Tax on a $100,000 Home by State

State	Average Effective Rate	Annual Bill	State	Average Effective Rate	Annual Bill	State	Average Effective Rate	Annual Bill
Alabama	0.38%	$ 380	Louisiana	0.28%	$ 280	Ohio	1.07%	$1,070
Alaska	1.35	1,350	Maine	1.42	1,420			
Arizona	0.74	740	Maryland	1.25	1,250	Oklahoma	0.82	820
Arkansas	1.42	1,420				Oregon	1.56	1,560
California	1.04	1,040	Massachusetts	2.43	2,430	Pennsylvania	1.50	1,500
			Michigan	2.74	2,740	Rhode Island	1.93	1,930
Colorado	1.01	1,010	Minnesota	0.79	790	South Carolina	0.84	840
Connecticut	1.53	1,530	Mississippi	0.86	860			
Delaware	0.79	790	Missouri	0.95	950	South Dakota	1.69	1,690
Florida	0.92	920				Tennessee	1.42	1,420
Georgia	1.21	1,210	Montana	1.08	1,080	Texas	1.68	1,680
			Nebraska	2.31	2,310	Utah	1.03	1,030
Hawaii	0.36	360	Nevada	1.13	1,130	Vermont	1.60	1,600
Idaho	0.94	940	New Hampshire	1.73	1,730			
Illinois	1.47	1,470	New Jersey	2.53	2,530	Virginia	1.39	1,390
Indiana	1.13	1,130				Washington	0.95	950
Iowa	1.75	1,750	New Mexico	1.14	1,140	West Virginia	0.37	370
			New York	2.75	2,750	Wisconsin	1.75	1,750
Kansas	0.93	930	North Carolina	1.07	1,070	Wyoming	0.47	470
Kentucky	1.14	1,140	North Dakota	1.01	1,010			

Source: Advisory Commission on Intergovernmental Relations, *Significant Features of Fiscal Federalism,* 1983.

save $28 in Alabama, $121 in Georgia, $86 in Hawaii ($108 if you're over 70), $66 in Illinois, $74 in Kentucky, $43 in Mississippi, $126 in South Carolina, $252 in Texas, and $37 in West Virginia.

The bottom line? Property-tax exemptions can be an extra benefit in retirement, but if you're planning a move, you'd do well to put other considerations such as energy costs and house prices first.

Deferrals

Nine states that don't allow property-tax exemptions to older homeowners unless they qualify for low-income status do allow persons over 65 (62 in California) to legally postpone payment of all or part of their property taxes. According to a survey by the National Conference of State Legislatures, these states are California, Colorado, Florida, Massachusetts, Oregon, Texas, Utah, Virginia, and Washington. Texas and Georgia allow both exemptions and postponements.

The program is actually a debt, or lien, on the home, secured by its sale value. The tax-deferral loan comes due when the home is sold, given away, or when the owner dies.

HOME FEATURES: WHERE YOU SEE THEM, WHERE YOU GET THEM

Several years ago, the National Association of Realtors set out to classify the housing market in the United States. Researchers identified 90 different architectural styles, from California bungalow through mobile home to Victorian. They also found eight types of interior layouts, from single- and bilevel to multilevel and high-rise. There were 720 possible kinds of houses under this classification system.

But the housing market doesn't exist in the same way the stock market, meat market, or automobile market does. Instead, there are many housing markets typically defined by the age of the structure, its design, and especially its location within the neighborhood and the country. Income of buyers as well as their tastes further define the market.

In Rockport–Aransas Pass, Texas, there is no market for houses with full basements; in Asheville, North Carolina, the demand for houses with carports is nonexistent. Formica kitchen counters sell in Hot Springs–Lake Ouachita, Arkansas, but in San Luis Obispo, California, the counters had better be ceramic tile. Breezeways are included in the descriptive brochures of new home developments in Myrtle Beach, South Carolina, but the word is unknown in Kalispell, Montana.

Each year, the Federal Housing Authority reports on the characteristics of single-family homes whose mortgages it insures. What follows is a geography of these features.

Construction and Exterior. In frame construction, the wood frame supports the floors and roof; in masonry construction, the exterior masonry wall serves as the support. Masonry construction in brick or stone has virtually disappeared in new houses. Concrete-block masonry construction, however, is a common technique in Arizona (40 percent of new houses have it) and Florida (85 percent), where the exterior is either spray-painted or stuccoed. Everywhere else, the majority of new houses are of frame construction.

Aluminum siding is the preferred exterior in Maryland and Ohio; wood is the choice in Georgia and Washington. Exteriors of brick or stucco are preferred in California, Louisiana, Nevada, Oklahoma, South Carolina, and Texas.

Stories. The use of the word "story" to refer to flights of buildings may have originated with tiers of stained-glass or painted windows that used to describe a special event. The common definition today is the space between the floor and the ceiling, roof, or the floor above, in the case of a multistory home. It has nothing to do with the height of a house; a house that appears from the outside to be two stories may actually be a single-story with a cathedral ceiling. More than 85 percent of new houses have only one story. Older homes with more than one story predominate in Connecticut, Maine, Maryland, Massachusetts, New Jersey, New York, Pennsylvania, and Wisconsin.

Basements. The basement is an area of full-story height below the first floor that is not meant for year-round living. Only 15 percent of new houses have basements, for they have become too expensive to excavate. In six states, however, two out of three new houses come with some kind of basement, reflecting a pattern of locating the furnace below grade and a preference for extra living space. These states are Illinois, Iowa, Michigan, Minnesota, New York, and Pennsylvania.

The majority of new houses have no basements at all: They either have a crawl space (an unfinished accessible space below the first floor that is usually less than full-story height) or are simply resting on a concrete slab poured on the ground. In the United States, crawl spaces are preferred only in the Pacific Northwest and in the Carolinas. Concrete-slab footings support almost all new houses in the Sun Belt states of Arizona, Arkansas, Georgia, Louisiana, Mississippi, Oklahoma, and Texas.

Bathrooms. Bathrooms are either full (a tub or shower stall, a sink, and a toilet) or half (just a sink and a toilet). All new houses have at least one full bathroom. You'll find the majority of new homes with both a full bathroom and a half-bathroom only in Alabama, Arkansas, Georgia, Louisiana, Maryland, Mississippi, New Jersey, Oklahoma, South Carolina, and Tennessee.

Garages and Carports. Garages, as everyone knows, are completely enclosed shelters for automobiles; carports are roofed shelters that aren't completely enclosed. Six out of ten houses, new and old, have garages; one in ten have only carports. Only in Arizona, Hawaii, Louisiana, and Mississippi is this pattern reversed.

Fireplaces. Flueless, imitation fireplaces, like dinettes and rumpus rooms, are memories of the 1950s. Nearly half of new American homes now have a working fireplace and chimney. Homes with two fireplaces can be found more frequently in the northern timber states of Idaho, Minnesota, Montana, Oregon, and Washington, and also in North Carolina and Pennsylvania.

Swimming Pools. You won't find new tract houses anywhere with in-ground swimming pools. An expensive option, the swimming pool doesn't interest most home buyers. Among older homes, less than 2 percent have them. You're most likely to find them in Arizona, California, Nevada, and surprisingly, Maine and New York.

Enclosed Porches. A porch is a covered addition or recessed space at the entrance of a home. Main Street lookouts, they have disappeared from new home markets. You'll find enclosed porches on 8 percent of older homes in this country. In Connecticut, Iowa, Maine, Massachusetts, New Jersey, and New York, more than 20 percent of older homes have them.

Money Matters:
Making retirement income go further

For Americans, money might well be the root of all mobility.

For centuries, our ancestors redistributed themselves, more in search of better opportunities than elbow room. In the 1700s, they jostled each other in steerage during the long ocean passage to the New World. In the early 1800s, they climbed aboard creaking wagons in Pennsylvania to make the dangerous, one-way trip to the Northwest Territories, where farmland was opening up. In this century they bundled their things together in western Oklahoma and trucked away from dust-bowl farms for fertile, sunny California.

We are still at it, for similar reasons. A 1981 Census Bureau survey found that most people who quit one state for another were tracking down a better job (or *any* job, period), being transferred by their employer, or fleeing high taxes and other day-to-day living costs. By now, everyone knows that the South and the West have been the most frequent destinations during the 1970s; if the latest Census Bureau forecasts are correct, the migration to the sun will continue into the twenty-first century.

But retired people don't always behave like others when it comes to finding a better place to live in America. In 1981, demographers at the University of Wisconsin looked carefully at why people over 65 had moved to different states over the previous three decades. They found to no one's surprise that this group was less subject to the ups and downs of business cycles than younger groups, and that they were attracted to places offering benefits that had more to do with quality of life than economics.

Because of a variety of payments that regularly arrive in their mail—interest, dividends, annuities, private pensions, civil service and military benefits, Social Security payments—retirees don't have to stay rooted in the place where they've lived and worked for so many years. And it is likely, too, that keeping up with the Joneses isn't any longer the big motivator it may have been in the years before 60.

Perhaps the only economic impulse behind relocating after you've tied up your job responsibilities is a quest for a lower cost of living during retirement. Choosing the right place may make the difference between living precariously and living comfortably, between paying high taxes and paying no taxes at all, and between landing a part-time job (if you want and need one) and searching in vain in the face of stiff competition.

MONEY IN RETIREMENT: GETTING IT AND SPENDING IT

Can you afford to retire? And can you afford to retire where you now live?

Lack of enough money to retire on causes many people to cling to unsatisfying jobs; for others who do retire, it can crimp plans for travel or for year-round living in a warm, sunny place where the bass fishing is good. It can indefinitely defer the dreams of a small part-time business or the book you may want to write. And it can work hardships on your family.

A practical approach for deciding whether you can afford to retire is to take stock of your sources of income and how you spend it, and then look at how your own circumstances stack up against those of the average retired person in the United States.

For Americans, there isn't one source of retirement income but many. Along with Social Security, there are a multitude of annuities, Individual Retirement Accounts (IRAs) and Keogh Plans, various government-employee plans (federal civil service, military, state, and local), and thousands of private pension plans, each of which has different rules for age of eligibility, years of service required, amounts to be paid, and how spouses are covered.

For a couple over 65, the main sources—from most dollars to least—are Social Security benefits, earnings, private pensions, and asset income.

Social Security

Social Security benefits are tax-free money paid by the federal government each month to retired workers who contributed to the system during their working years. Social Security was never meant to be the only source of retirement income, however. Rather, it was to provide a base, the slack theoretically being taken up by money from private pensions, savings, investments, and earnings.

According to the current formula, single workers who pulled down minimum wages before retiring will receive Social Security checks of slightly more than half of final pre-retirement earnings, while those at the

maximum wage level will receive less than one third. In 1983, the maximum monthly benefit was $726 for a single worker and $1,093 for a couple. The average amount mailed each month to a retired couple was $695, or $8,340 a year.

No one knows why, back in 1935, the new Social Security Administration fixed on 65 as the age for full retirement benefits. "We just picked it out of a hat," the administration's first director later said. Your Social Security checks will be reduced if you retire before age 65. Currently, there's a permanent reduction of five ninths of 1 percent for each month that payments are received before you are 65. If you retire at 62, for example, your monthly checks will be 20 percent less than what they would have been if you had waited until 65.

More workers today opt for early retirement and reduced checks rather than collecting full benefits at age 65. If you decide to stick with your job after you turn 65, benefits will be increased by one fourth of 1 percent for each month (3 percent a year) that retirement is delayed past 65.

Earnings

As you plot your financial course you may find that you'll need or want to work in retirement. The options can run from an eight-hour-a-day, 50-week-per-year new career to a part-time or seasonal job.

Though savings, investment, and pension income don't affect the amount of your Social Security check, there is a ceiling on how much you can earn and still receive full Social Security benefits. In 1983 workers under 65 were permitted to earn up to $4,920 without losing benefits; those between 65 and 70 could earn $6,600 without penalty. If your income exceeds the ceiling, benefits will be reduced by one dollar for every two dollars of earnings over the ceiling.

In this country, more than one third of couples over 65 count wages, salaries, or money from self-employment among their income sources. In 1980 the median amount was $5,990 per year.

Private Pensions

Only half of all workers in the private sector are covered by employer pension plans. And only half of those ever see the money because of vesting requirements. Unlike the Social Security system, which is contributed to by workers no matter how many different jobs they hold, private pensions are the equivalent of a corporate loyalty test—at least for the standard 10-year period required before an employee can be considered vested and share in a pension fund. Unlike Social Security, too, most private pension plans do not have a cost-of-living escalator clause.

In 1980, the median amount of income from a private pension was $2,980 for couples over 65 who were eligible for payments. While that amount isn't exactly paltry, neither is it generous. Only seven out of

Where the Money Comes From	
Of every 100 retired couples in the United States . . .	**depend on regular income from:**
91	Social Security
75	interest payments
33	private pensions
31	wages and salaries
20	dividends
14	rents and royalties
10	state and local employee pensions
6	federal civil service pensions
6	self-employment
2	estates and trusts
2	military pensions
2	railroad employee pensions

Source: Social Security Bulletin, January 1983.

Living Moderately or Well in 25 Places: What It Costs a Retired Couple

Place	Living Moderately	Living Well
Anchorage, AK	$13,435	$19,115
Atlanta, GA	10,340	15,129
Baltimore, MD	10,921	16,141
Boston, MA	12,972	20,018
Buffalo, NY	11,687	17,117
Chicago, IL	10,942	16,315
Cincinnati, OH	10,907	15,760
Cleveland, OH	11,409	16,664
Dallas, TX	10,614	16,202
Denver, CO	10,444	15,656
Detroit, MI	11,295	17,308
Honolulu, HI	12,661	18,305
Houston, TX	10,861	16,545
Kansas City, MO	10,842	16,386
Los Angeles, CA	10,662	16,300
Milwaukee, WI	11,597	17,049
Minneapolis–St. Paul, MN	10,997	16,122
New York, NY	12,643	18,886
Philadelphia, PA	11,580	17,142
Pittsburgh, PA	11,425	16,371
St. Louis, MO	10,983	16,041
San Diego, CA	10,235	15,209
San Francisco–Oakland, CA	11,374	16,766
Seattle, WA	11,813	16,943
Washington, D.C.	11,952	17,614

Source: U.S. Bureau of Labor Statistics, News Bulletin, July 1982.

Figures have been adjusted by regional consumer price indexes to reflect 1983 costs.

100 retired people who collect a private pension rely on it for at least half their income, according to a recent study from the Social Security Administration.

Assets

Dividends from blue-chip stock investments you may have made over the years; rents from real estate you may own; royalties from your invention, song, or best-selling book; and interest from IRAs, Keogh Plans, certificates of deposit, and passbook savings accounts are different kinds of asset income.

Like private pensions and earnings from wages, salaries, and self-employment, asset income supplements Social Security benefits for a more comfortable retirement. Three quarters of couples over 65 count on money from this source. In 1980, the median amount was $1,700 per year.

HOUSEHOLD INCOMES

Do incomes indicate living costs? For the most part, yes.

According to recent studies from the Bureau of Labor Statistics, two thirds of the difference in personal incomes between, say, San Diego and Asheville, North Carolina, reflects their different costs of living; the other third reflects their different employers and worker skills and prevailing wages.

Since the Consumer Price Index (which measures the cost of living through the prices of goods and services) doesn't cover all of our retirement places, Places Rated Retirement Guide uses personal income as an indicator of local costs of living.

Scraping By on $22,072 a Year

When it comes to a statistic like per capita income in a given place, we know the textbook definition: It's the total of all the wages, salaries, interest, dividends, alimony, and pensions divided by the number of people living there. But we also know that a corporate vice-president pulling down $100,000 a year plus five pensioners receiving benefits of $10,000 apiece doesn't really add up to six people earning an average of $25,000 a year. Nonetheless, whether we're talking of social phenomena, following the stock market, or arguing baseball, we can seldom sidestep averages.

To estimate the income for a typical two-person household, Places Rated starts with figures from the 1983 "County and Metropolitan Area Personal Incomes" survey by the U.S. Bureau of Economic Analysis. These per capita incomes were multiplied by two to estimate the income of a household composed of two people. The national average amount is $22,072 per year. Among retirement places, incomes range from $27,939 in Reno to $10,806 in Lake O' The Cherokees, Oklahoma.

Is the amount of money a typical two-person household brings in per year really helpful in estimating living costs for a retired couple? It is if you consider to what extent Social Security checks can replace the income of that two-person household.

Local Social Security "Replacement Rates"

You're not going to live comfortably on monthly Social Security checks alone; these payments by themselves were never intended to completely support you and your spouse in retirement. If you are a $35,000-a-year employee retiring at 65 with maximum earnings in "covered employment" (a job in which wages are deducted for Social Security) each year since 1955, for example, you can expect a monthly check of $726. That's only $8,712 a year. If you have a dependent spouse over 65, this amount is boosted by $367, for a combined benefit of $1,093 per month, or $13,116 per year. Even though Social Security payments do increase with the cost of living, the money comes way short of replacing the dollars you were pulling down at work.

One useful indicator of how far your Social Security benefits will go is to consider the rate at which Social Security replaces average personal incomes around the country. Throughout 1983, the benefits for a typical retired couple were $8,340. In Alaska, that won't replace a great deal of the high average personal income for which the nation's largest state is noted. Nor will it replace much of the income a typical New Yorker, Bostonian, or Chicagoan is accustomed to.

In certain retirement places in Texas, New Mexico, and the Carolinas, however, Social Security checks go a lot further in replacing local average personal incomes. Small wonder that, over the last three decades, retired people who moved tended to quit richer areas with high personal incomes and even higher living costs for "poorer" places with low personal incomes. They were looking for spots where fixed Social Security and pension benefits could be stretched; in short, where living costs were lower.

Average Household Income, 1983

Highest	Income	Social Security Replacement Rate
1. RENO, NV	$27,939	29.85%
2. WEST PALM BEACH–BOCA RATON, FL	27,468	30.36
3. FORT LAUDERDALE–HOLLYWOOD, FL	25,339	32.91
4. Carson City, NV	24,977	33.39
5. Easton–Chesapeake Bay, MD	24,726	33.73

Lowest		
1. Lake O' The Cherokees, OK	$10,806	77.18%
2. MCALLEN–PHARR– EDINBURG, TX	10,993	75.87
3. Crossville, TN	12,254	68.06
4. Tahlequah–Lake Tenkiller, OK	13,321	62.61
5. Clarkesville–Mount Airy, GA	13,749	60.66

Source: U.S. Department of Commerce, Bureau of Economic Analysis, "County and Metropolitan Area Personal Incomes," *Survey of Current Business,* May 1983.

The national average for income before taxes for a two-person household is $22,072; the national average Social Security replacement rate is 37.78%.

RETIRING WON'T GET YOU OUT OF PAYING TAXES

According to the Washington, D.C.–based Tax Foundation, Americans spend two hours and 44 minutes of every eight-hour day working to make enough money just to pay taxes. Looking at it another way, in a calendar year, May 15 marks the mythical Tax Freedom Day on which we stop contributing our entire paychecks to federal, state, and local tax collectors and finally start pocketing money for ourselves for the rest of the year.

In retirement, even though you've chucked the tie and briefcase and bid good-bye to the commuting hassles that go with full-time working, you won't be completely immune from paying taxes, in spite of the many tax breaks coming along when you turn 65.

Although your tax bracket may be lower after you retire, federal income taxes will still hit you with the same impact whether you surface in San Diego, Santa Fe, or San Antonio. But state and local taxes can differ tremendously.

To determine the relative tax bite in retirement areas, *Places Rated* focuses on the two most common levies: state income taxes and state sales taxes.

Based on the average two-person household in-

come in a retirement place, state income taxes are calculated for a couple filing jointly using state tax rates from the latest *State Tax Handbook* published by Commerce Clearing House. Standard personal exemptions are claimed. Double personal exemptions, which are available in most states for people over 65, are not included since most people retire before they reach 65. And because Social Security retirement benefits can begin only after a person reaches 62, and dollar amounts can vary a great deal between retired persons, we haven't included Social Security income exemptions in our tax-bite calculations. What you have, then, are representative tax bites without any exemptions other than the standard ones available to the majority of taxpayers.

The dollar amount spent throughout the year in the store on local sales taxes is also based on the retirement place's average income for a couple, using Internal Revenue Service tables of estimated state sales taxes paid at that income level.

As a percentage of household income, state income and sales taxes take the biggest bite from incomes in California, Minnesota, Oregon, New York, and Wisconsin. In Connecticut, Florida, New Hampshire, and Texas, the bite is smallest.

The Bite State Taxes Take from Household Income

Biggest Bites		Smallest Bites	
1. Lincoln City–Newport, OR	7.94%	1. Keene, NH	0%
2. MEDFORD, OR	7.75	1. Laconia–Lake Winnipesaukee, NH	0
3. Maui, HI	7.73	1. North Conway–White Mountains, NH	0
4. Rhinelander, WI	7.71	4. Kerrville, TX	0.66
5. Bend, OR	7.70	5. AUSTIN, TX	0.67
		5. Fredericksburg, TX	0.67

PART-TIME JOBS

There are three good reasons for including a part-time job in your retirement plans along with pursuits like golf and gardening. First, a paycheck helps many a retired household hang on to a more comfortable life-style. Second, a job provides psychic rewards in the form of human contact and some challenge; work can simply keep your mind and body from turning to mush. Third, although Social Security checks are reduced if you earn more than $6,600 a year (if you're 70 or older, you can earn as much extra income as you like and still collect full benefits), they need not be if you limit the amount you earn by working only part-time.

When Harris pollsters recently asked retired people whether they wanted to work in retirement, half answered yes. Why, then, are nearly four out of five people over 65 neither working nor looking for work? Poor health is one reason. Lack of interest in working, compared to the attractions of travel, hobbies, or simple rest and relaxation is another. But the biggest reason is the difficulty of finding any kind of job at all.

Let's face it—your age can be a handicap when convincing new employers that you can cut it. But changing attitudes among employers are helping to improve job prospects for older people. There is also the Age Discrimination in Employment Act, which protects anyone between 40 and 70 from being passed over in hiring or being involuntarily retired solely on the basis of age.

Forget manufacturing as a possible place to start your job hunt. Unless you are a master machinist, an accomplished numerical control programmer, or have certification in a specialized area of production, there are simply too many other willing workers looking for the same opportunity. Forget construction, too. Unless you have a class-A license for operating a D-9 bulldozer, or a master carpenter's ticket, construction jobs tend to go to younger people.

If you're going to compete with younger workers in the job marketplace, consider focusing on part-time jobs. You have a big advantage that you may have overlooked: Many younger part-time workers want a full-time job but are working part-time because that's all they can find. Employers know this and anticipate turnover when the local economy begins to expand. You, on the other hand, want only a part-time job on a permanent basis, a big plus to many employers.

What kinds of employers use part-timers? There are ten that account for most of the short-schedule, temporary, or seasonal work in this country:

- Every retail-trade establishment
- Real estate
- Business services
- Personal services
- Repair services
- Entertainment and recreation services
- Churches
- Nonprofit membership organizations
- U.S. Postal Service
- Door-to-door sales

What Are the Odds?

Consider the odds of tracking down a part-time job. What kind of competition will you encounter when hunting for a good position? Are there crowds of would-be part-time workers everywhere, or is the competition more favorable in, say, Fort Lauderdale–Hollywood than Myrtle Beach, South Carolina, or Santa Fe?

To help you find an answer, *Places Rated* compares the number of people in their sixties in each retirement area with two groups of likely part-time job-seekers: college-age workers (persons between 17 and 21) and women aged 38 to 57, who may be reentering the workplace after their children are grown.

Based on this comparison in each retirement place, the part-time job opportunities are:

Good if the number of college-age persons and the number of women between 38 and 57 is less than three and one-half times the number of people in their 60s.

Average if the number of college-age persons and the number of women between 38 and 57 is between three and one-half and four and one-half times the number of people in their 60s.

Poor if the number of college-age persons and women between 38 and 57 is more than four and one-half times the number of people in their 60s.

When it comes to determining the strength of the competition, one fact stands out in retirement places: College towns, for all their lively cultural and social attractions, aren't ideal grounds for retired people to hunt for a job. Among retirement places in this book, the competition is particularly stiff in Las Cruces, New Mexico; Austin, Texas; and State College, Pennsylvania, each of which is dominated by a major university. Indeed, one reason Massachusetts was rated the worst state in which to retire by the forecasting firm of Chase Econometrics Association in 1978 was because the Bay State's ratio of college students to retired people was the highest of any of the 50 states.

Competition for Part-Time Work

Stiffest Odds*		Most Favorable Odds*	
1. Las Cruces, NM	6.50 to 1	1. Clear Lake, CA	1.87 to 1
2. Colorado Springs, CO	6.42	2. Mountain Home–Norfork Lake, AR	1.98
3. McAllen–Pharr–Edinburg, TX	6.25	3. Sarasota–Bradenton, FL	2.00
4. Austin, TX	5.96	4. Fort Myers–Cape Coral, FL	2.10
5. State College, PA	5.76	5. Houghton Lake, MI	2.14

Source: U.S. Bureau of the Census, *1980 Census of Population and Housing.*

The national average is 4.49 to 1.

*Odds given represent the ratio of college-age people and women aged 38 to 57 to the number of people in their 60s.

LOCAL INCOME AND JOB GROWTH IN THE 1980s

Simply determining who and how numerous your competitors are for part-time work isn't all you'll need to know if you plan to return to work. You've also got to learn what parts of the country will see expanding opportunities.

In 1929, the average personal income in the United States was a little over $700 per capita (versus $11,000 now). There was no Social Security. Nor could most people count on a private pension from their employer. Indeed, most older persons worked until they could no longer hold a job; then they fell back on family or savings, or went into the poorhouse.

Back then, a typical house could be bought for less than $3,000 and heated with natural gas for $15 a year

Unemployment Threat

One of the few things you'll find economists agreeing on is that local manufacturing and construction industries are more harshly hit during business slumps than such service-sector businesses as banking, recreation, health, and education.

In 1974, for example, the Florida resort and retirement areas of Fort Lauderdale–Hollywood, Miami, Orlando, and West Palm Beach–Boca Raton, as well as Phoenix, Arizona, each experienced high unemployment increases.

What did these places have in common? A large number of workers employed in the construction trades who had been attracted to the vacation- and retirement-home building boom there in the early 1970s, a boom that went bust in mid-decade.

Elsewhere in 1974, one out of every three cities in the country experienced increases in its unemployment rates that were greater than the national average. Each of these areas had a heavier-than-usual concentration of people who punched time clocks, whether in automobile plants in the Great Lakes states, in Pacific Northwest lumber mills, in factories that put out iron and steel in the Ohio Valley, or in petrochemical refineries in the Gulf South.

It hasn't been any different in the past few years, during what some economists call the triple-dip slump of 1980, 1981–82, and 1983. Every section of the country has its share of hard times, but the stories that come out of what might be called muscle-bound economies—places with the largest numbers of workers who make the goods that industry and consumers buy in confident times—have been the saddest.

In contrast to the number of overheated boomtowns (which we may never see again, at least not on the scale of Houston in 1980, for example) there are a great many more places where the factories are fewer, where the pace is not quite as fast, and where a large number of white-collar workers commute to downtown or suburban jobs with financial, real-estate, and insurance firms. Others find their work at colleges and universities, at big medical centers in the area, or at local resorts. The employment mix in these areas is said to be more balanced, with most of the weight going increasingly toward the service sector.

Finally, there are the places that are at the opposite extreme from the "rust bowl" cities of the industrial Great Lakes, not because they are thriving, but because manufacturing jobs play almost no part in their existence. These have nearly pure service-based economies (referred to sometimes as taking-in-each-other's-laundry economies) characterized by people employed almost exclusively in retail trade, government, health, finance, education, and recreation.

Even though in retirement you may have little to fear from being without a full-time job, local unemployment may still hurt you in unforeseen ways. By increasing the competition for available work, high unemployment can drastically limit your chances of finding a part-time job, should you ever want one. Joblessness, too, plays a part in growing rates of property crime. And it also boosts the cost of local social services.

Just as retirement places can be rated for the mildness of their climates and their supply of local public golf links, so also can they be rated for how vulnerable they are to high unemployment during a bad business cycle. It can be said that the cyclical threat of unemployment in a retirement place is:

High

- if the number of factory workers is more than 35 percent
- or if the number of construction workers is more than 12 percent
- or if together they number more than 40 percent *of total area employment*

Moderate

- if the number of factory workers is between 21 percent and 35 percent
- or if the number of construction workers is between 6 percent and 12 percent
- or if together they number between 25 percent and 40 percent *of total area employment*

Low

- if the number of factory workers is less than 21 percent
- or if the number of construction workers is less than 6 percent
- or if together they number less than 25 percent *of total area employment*

Among *Places Rated*'s 107 retirement places, the threat of unemployment is high in 23, moderate in 38, and low in 46.

Cyclical Threat of Unemployment

Highest (Muscle-Bound Economies)	Goods-Producing Workers
1. Rappahannock, VA	65.23%
2. Clarkesville–Mount Airy, GA	65.21
3. Benton–Kentucky Lake, KY	61.81
4. Paris, TN	59.47
5. Mountain Home–Norfork Lake, AR	58.44

Lowest (Taking-in-Each-Other's-Laundry Economies)	Workers in Service Sectors
1. Monticello–Liberty, NY	89.49%
2. LAS VEGAS, NV	89.29
3. Cape Cod, MA	85.92
4. Clear Lake, CA	85.25
5. RENO, NV	85.16

Source: U.S. Department of Commerce, County Business Patterns, 1983.

In those days, too, personal income in the richest of the country's regions, the Mideast, was nearly three times the personal income in the country's poorest, the Southeast.

The gap between regions has since narrowed considerably, for several reasons. There is more industrial employment in the historically low-income regions where, once upon a time, jobs were mainly found in the mines and on the farm. Moreover, the regional differences in wage rates have diminished; you're no longer going to find a good carpenter, electrician, or plumber in Mississippi who will work at a fraction of Northeast or West Coast scale.

So much have regional dollar advantages shrunk that personal income in the Far West, now the richest region, is only 32 percent higher than personal income in the Southeast (still the country's poorest region). Fifty years ago it was 248 percent greater. At this rate, one might want to live long enough just to see incomes in the regions even out, perhaps by the turn of the twenty-first century.

If you had the choice, all other things being equal, where would you rather live? A place like Fort Lauderdale–Hollywood, on Florida's Atlantic Coast, where personal incomes are high but income growth is slowing? Or a place like Crossville, in the Cumberland country of Tennessee, where people have low incomes but income growth is rapid?

Historically, Americans have moved from rich regions where the benefits of high incomes are made empty by even higher costs of living to low-income regions where low costs of living more than make up for the liabilities of low incomes. In a game of catch-up spread over the next several decades, incomes in poorer places like Crossville are predicted to grow faster than incomes in richer places like Fort Lauderdale–Hollywood. Retired people can benefit from this scenario.

Why? Simply because low but rapidly rising incomes indicate not only current low costs of living. They also are a sign of future prosperity, the benefits of which can range from safer real-estate investments to assured funding of municipal services.

Personal Income Growth in the 1980s

Most Rapid		Least Rapid	
1. LEXINGTON–FAYETTE, KY	31.69%	1. CHARLOTTESVILLE, VA	9.00%
2. Crossville, TN	28.60	2. COLORADO SPRINGS, CO	12.14
3. Cookeville, TN	28.39	3. Twain Harte–Yosemite, CA	16.93
4. Benton–Kentucky Lake, KY	28.21	4. Carson City, NV	17.67
5. BILOXI–GULFPORT, MS	28.11	4. RENO, NV	17.67

Source: U.S. Department of Commerce, Bureau of Economic Analysis, *OBERS Regional Projections*, 1981.

The national average for income growth is projected to be 23.07%.

Certain industries, such as retail trade, are predicted to offer much better opportunities for employment over the next ten years than others, such as private

household help, taking tickets at the local drive-in, or cutting hair. Knowing what these industries are and having a realistic grasp of how your qualifications fit will help narrow your choices. Recognizing, too, that there are certain areas of the country that will grow more quickly in job opportunities during the years between now and 1990 completes the picture.

According to Commerce Department economists, the parts of our economy that offer the best chances for a job through the end of the decade are finance, insurance, and real estate; retail trade; and services, particularly health and recreation, hotels, campgrounds, and other resort lodging.

But where in this country are you likely to find a job in the 1980s? According to the same Commerce Department economists, half of the country's eight economic regions will have job "growth advantages"; that is, their growth will be faster than that of the nation as a whole. The major reason for this is that manufacturing and service industries are likely to move to these regions to take advantage of lower wage rates, taxes, energy costs, land costs, and a milder climate. The four regions, in order of how greatly they are predicted to outdistance the rest of the country in the rate of job growth by 1990, and along with their estimated growth percentages, are the Rocky Mountain states (Colorado, Idaho, Montana, Utah, and Wyoming): 172 percent; the Southwest (Arizona, New Mexico, Oklahoma, and Texas): 148 percent; the Far West (Alaska, California, Hawaii, Nevada, Oregon, and Washington): 131 percent; and the Southeast (Alabama, Arkansas, Florida, Georgia, Kentucky, Louisiana, Mississippi, North Carolina, South Carolina, Tennessee, Virginia, and West Virginia): 127 percent.

Job Growth in the 1980s

Most Rapid		Least Rapid	
1. Carson City, NV	32.91%	1. Bennington, VT	3.14%
1. RENO, NV	32.91	2. Coeur d'Alene, ID	4.63
3. LAS VEGAS, NV	31.78	3. LANCASTER, PA	5.58
3. St. George–Zion, UT	31.78	4. Monticello–Liberty, NY	5.95
5. FORT COLLINS, CO	24.17	5. STATE COLLEGE, PA	6.30

Source: U.S. Department of Commerce, Bureau of Economic Analysis, *OBERS Regional Projections*, 1981.

The national average for job growth is projected to be 12.04%.

JUDGING RETIREMENT MONEY MATTERS

If your annual income from Social Security benefits, a private pension, and interest and dividends from investments you've made over the years comes to $20,000, will it stretch farther in Cape Cod; Charlottesville, Virginia; or Coeur d'Alene, Idaho? What about state and local taxes in those three retirement places? Are they less favorable than those in Florida or Texas?

Of all the retirement places, which ones are prone to high unemployment during business slumps, and which ones are projected to expand the most in jobs and personal income over the next few years? These two circumstances might seem of minor importance in retirement, now that you're supposed to be immune to the ups and downs of business cycles. Local joblessness and slow economic growth can hurt you, however. Tracking down part-time work might prove fruitless. Quality health, transportation, and recreation services provided by municipalities during flush times might be cut in times of fiscal crisis. And the threat of property crime, which rises with unemployment, might keep you indoors.

To help answer questions about the economic scene in the 107 retirement places, *Places Rated Retirement Guide* compares four factors in each place: the proportion of average income for a two-person household that will be replaced by Social Security benefits, state and local income and sales tax bite, the future for income growth, and prospects for job expansion.

Each retirement place starts with a base score of zero. Points are added or subtracted according to four indicators:

1. *Social Security replacement rate.* The U.S. average annual Social Security benefits for a retired couple ($8,340) are divided by the estimated average income for a two-person household. This replacement rate, expressed as a percentage, is multiplied by 100 and added to the base score of zero.
2. *Effective tax bite.* The tax bite, or the percentage of household income eaten up by local sales and income taxes, is multiplied by 100 and subtracted from the total.
3. *Income growth for the 1980s.* The percentage by which personal income is projected to grow from now to 1990 is multiplied by 100 and added to the total score.
4. *Job growth for the 1980s.* The percentage of local job growth projected from now to 1990 is multiplied by 100 and added to the total score.

Sample Comparison: McAllen–Pharr–Edinburg, Texas, and Easton–Chesapeake Bay, Maryland

The two retirement places used in this comparison to illustrate extremes in money matters for retired couples are, not surprisingly, from parts of the country that also represent economic opposites: McAllen–Pharr–Edinburg, on the banks of the Rio Grande in historically poor southernmost Texas, and the affluent Easton–Chesapeake Bay area on Maryland's Eastern Shore, a place attracting many ex-urbanites from Baltimore and Washington, D.C.

Financially, people do quite well in Talbot County,

Maryland, where Easton is the seat of local government. The place ranks near the top in per capita personal income, not only in the Old Line State but in the nation. A retired couple here, however, may not do nearly so well as elsewhere. The $8,340 in annual Social Security benefits that they can count on for 1983 will replace only a third of the estimated $24,726 that a typical two-person household gets by on in Talbot County. This replacement rate, 33.73 percent to be exact, when multiplied by 100 yields 3,373 points to be added to the base score. The impact of state sales and income taxes on household earnings, as in much of the country's northeastern quadrant, is not lightly felt. The tax bite of 5.23 percent when multiplied by 100 results in 523 points to be subtracted from the total. Personal income is estimated to grow 22.97 percent by 1990, yielding 2,297 points. The prospects for job growth are not as rosy here as they are elsewhere. Economists project an expansion of only 8.54 percent by 1990 for the Baltimore economic area, which includes Easton–Chesapeake Bay, translating into 854 points. When these two growth projections are combined, they total 3,151 points, which are added to the score. Easton–Chesapeake Bay's money matters score, then, is 6,001, the lowest of the 107 retirement places. It owes its poor economic showing to two factors: a low Social Security replacement rate and lackluster prospects for job expansion over the rest of this decade.

The winter resort of McAllen–Pharr–Edinburg, lined with palms, bougainvillea, poinsettias, and citrus trees, ranks low in estimated income for a two-person household. This fact may suggest poverty to some, but to others it means extremely low costs of living. Not for nothing has the number of retirement-age people doubled here since 1970. Average Social Security benefits will replace 75.87 percent of a two-person household's income, adding 7,587 points to McAllen–Pharr–Edinburg's score. The Texas tax bite is notoriously forgiving; there are no levies on personal incomes nor any on interest and dividends. Everyone pays sales taxes, but these eat up only .83 percent of household incomes, mainly because groceries and medicine are exempted from an already low tax rate. That's a negative indicator of only 83 points to be subtracted from the score. Personal income growth to the end of this decade is projected to be 24.04 percent, which converts to 2,404 points, and job growth is anticipated to reach 16.01 percent, which converts to 1,601 points. Together these two indicators equal 4,005 points, giving McAllen–Pharr–Edinburg a final score of 11,509, best among the retirement places for money matters.

Places Rated: Retirement Places Ranked for Personal Money Matters

Places Rated Retirement Guide chooses four criteria to rank the retirement places for financial matters: (1) average income for a two-person household and the extent that average 1983 Social Security benefits for a retired couple ($8,340) can replace that income, (2) effective local income and sales tax bite, (3) projected rate of income growth for the rest of the 1980s, and (4) projected rate of job growth for the rest of the 1980s. Places that receive tie scores are given the same rank and are listed in alphabetical order.

Retirement Places from Best to Worst

Places Rated Rank	Places Rated Score	Places Rated Rank	Places Rated Score	Places Rated Rank	Places Rated Score
1. McAllen–Pharr–Edinburg, TX	11,509	39. Red Bluff–Sacramento Valley, CA	8,291	74. Rappahannock, VA	7,495
2. Lake O' The Cherokees, OK	11,393	40. Brevard, NC	8,243	75. Olympia, WA	7,445
3. Crossville, TN	11,313				
4. St. George–Zion, UT	10,428	41. Mountain Home–Norfork Lake, AR	8,210	76. Sarasota–Bradenton, FL	7,437
5. Tahlequah–Lake Tenkiller, OK	10,116	42. State College, PA	8,157	77. Petoskey–Straits of Mackinac, MI	7,414
		43. Bar Harbor–Frenchman Bay, ME	8,152	78. Missoula, MT	7,399
6. Cookeville, TN	10,085	44. San Antonio, TX	8,098	79. Fort Lauderdale–Hollywood, FL	7,360
7. Big Sandy, TN	10,038	45. Prescott, AZ	8,087	80. North Conway–White Mountains, NH	7,359
8. Bull Shoals, AR	9,913				
9. Athens–Cedar Creek Lake, TX	9,802	46. Roswell, NM	8,080	81. Springfield, MO	7,350
10. Paris, TN	9,761	47. Camden–Penobscot Bay, ME	8,078	82. Nevada City–Donner, CA	7,330
		48. Bend, OR	8,067	83. San Luis Obispo, CA	7,243
11. Delta, CO	9,634	49. Hot Springs–Lake Ouachita, AR	8,063	84. Laconia–Lake Winnipesaukee, NH	7,184
12. Las Cruces, NM	9,560	50. Austin, TX	8,058	85. Rhinelander, WI	7,183
13. Clarkesville–Mount Airy, GA	9,541				
14. Yuma, AZ	9,519	51. Medford, OR	8,040	86. Ocean City–Assateague Island, MD	7,181
15. Biloxi–Gulfport, MS	9,472	52. Orlando, FL	7,993	87. Monticello–Liberty, NY	7,137
		53. Albuquerque, NM	7,989	88. Toms River–Barnegat Bay, NJ	7,130
16. Canton–Lake Tawakoni, TX	9,440	54. Reno, NV	7,957	89. West Palm Beach–Boca Raton, FL	7,107
17. Benton–Kentucky Lake, KY	9,252	55. Oak Harbor, WA	7,953	90. Winchester, VA	7,098
18. Deming, NM	9,223				
19. Myrtle Beach, SC	9,126	56. Gainesville–Lake Sidney Lanier, GA	7,933	91. Bennington, VT	7,070
20. Ocala, FL	8,917	57. Asheville, NC	7,926	92. Colorado Springs, CO	7,064
		58. Melbourne–Titusville–Cocoa, FL	7,869	93. Boise City, ID	7,043
21. Lake Havasu City–Kingman, AZ	8,770	59. Fort Myers–Cape Coral, FL	7,857	93. Twain Harte–Yosemite, CA	7,043
22. Table Rock Lake, MO	8,762	60. Branson–Lake Taneycomo, MO	7,824	95. Rehoboth Bay–Indian River Bay, DE	7,022
23. Harrison, AR	8,558				
24. Fairhope–Gulf Shores, AL	8,463	61. Clear Lake, CA	7,807	96. Brunswick–Golden Isles, GA	7,020
25. Cassville–Roaring River, MO	8,456	62. Tucson, AZ	7,771	97. Keene, NH	7,008
		63. Miami, FL	7,768	98. Santa Rosa, CA	6,977
26. Rockport–Aransas Pass, TX	8,442	64. Fredericksburg, TX	7,761	99. Traverse City–Grand Traverse Bay, MI	6,943
27. Hamilton–Bitterroot Valley, MT	8,436	65. Port Angeles–Strait of Juan de Fuca, WA	7,684	100. Maui, HI	6,921
28. Las Vegas, NV	8,423				
29. Daytona Beach, FL	8,417	66. Lincoln City–Newport, OR	7,672	101. Lancaster, PA	6,857
30. Grand Junction, CO	8,360	67. Beaufort–Hilton Head, SC	7,661	102. Coeur d'Alene, ID	6,584
		68. Kerrville, TX	7,658	103. San Diego, CA	6,502
31. Houghton Lake, MI	8,349	69. Brattleboro, VT	7,621	104. Atlantic City–Cape May, NJ	6,419
32. Santa Fe, NM	8,339	69. Hendersonville, NC	7,621	105. Cape Cod, MA	6,109
33. Eagle River, WI	8,335				
33. Lakeland–Winter Haven, FL	8,335	71. Kalispell, MT	7,615	106. Charlottesville, VA	6,070
35. Fort Collins, CO	8,333	72. Front Royal, VA	7,586	107. Easton–Chesapeake Bay, MD	6,001
36. Lexington–Fayette, KY	8,323	73. Phoenix, AZ	7,578		
37. Carson City, NV	8,306				
38. Oscoda–Huron Shore, MI	8,299				

Retirement Places Listed Alphabetically

Retirement Place	Places Rated Rank	Retirement Place	Places Rated Rank	Retirement Place	Places Rated Rank
Albuquerque, NM	53	Bar Harbor–Frenchman Bay, ME	43	Big Sandy, TN	7
Asheville, NC	57	Beaufort–Hilton Head, SC	67	Biloxi–Gulfport, MS	15
Athens–Cedar Creek Lake, TX	9	Bend, OR	48	Boise City, ID	93
Atlantic City–Cape May, NJ	104	Bennington, VT	91	Branson–Lake Taneycomo, MO	60
Austin, TX	50	Benton–Kentucky Lake, KY	17	Brattleboro, VT	69

Retirement Place	Places Rated Rank
Brevard, NC	40
Brunswick–Golden Isles, GA	96
Bull Shoals, AR	8
Camden–Penobscot Bay, ME	47
Canton–Lake Tawakoni, TX	16
Cape Cod, MA	105
Carson City, NV	37
Cassville–Roaring River, MO	25
CHARLOTTESVILLE, VA	106
Clarkesville–Mount Airy, GA	13
Clear Lake, CA	61
Coeur d'Alene, ID	102
COLORADO SPRINGS, CO	92
Cookeville, TN	6
Crossville, TN	3
DAYTONA BEACH, FL	29
Delta, CO	11
Deming, NM	18
Eagle River, WI	33
Easton–Chesapeake Bay, MD	107
Fairhope–Gulf Shores, AL	24
FORT COLLINS, CO	35
FORT LAUDERDALE–HOLLYWOOD, FL	79
FORT MYERS–CAPE CORAL, FL	59
Fredericksburg, TX	64
Front Royal, VA	72
Gainesville–Lake Sidney Lanier, GA	56
Grand Junction, CO	30
Hamilton–Bitterroot Valley, MT	27
Harrison, AR	23
Hendersonville, NC	69

Retirement Place	Places Rated Rank
Hot Springs–Lake Ouachita, AR	49
Houghton Lake, MI	31
Kalispell, MT	71
Keene, NH	97
Kerrville, TX	68
Laconia–Lake Winnipesaukee, NH	84
Lake Havasu City–Kingman, AZ	21
LAKELAND–WINTER HAVEN, FL	33
Lake O' The Cherokees, OK	2
LANCASTER, PA	101
LAS CRUCES, NM	12
LAS VEGAS, NV	28
LEXINGTON–FAYETTE, KY	36
Lincoln City–Newport, OR	66
Maui, HI	100
McALLEN–PHARR–EDINBURG, TX	1
MEDFORD, OR	51
MELBOURNE–TITUSVILLE–COCOA, FL	58
MIAMI, FL	63
Missoula, MT	78
Monticello–Liberty, NY	87
Mountain Home–Norfork Lake, AR	41
Myrtle Beach, SC	19
Nevada City–Donner, CA	82
North Conway–White Mountains, NH	80
Oak Harbor, WA	55
OCALA, FL	20
Ocean City–Assateague Island, MD	86
OLYMPIA, WA	75
ORLANDO, FL	52
Oscoda–Huron Shore, MI	38

Retirement Place	Places Rated Rank
Paris, TN	10
Petoskey–Straits of Mackinac, MI	77
PHOENIX, AZ	73
Port Angeles–Strait of Juan de Fuca, WA	65
Prescott, AZ	45
Rappahannock, VA	74
Red Bluff–Sacramento Valley, CA	39
Rehoboth Bay–Indian River Bay, DE	95
RENO, NV	54
Rhinelander, WI	85
Rockport–Aransas Pass, TX	26
Roswell, NM	46
St. George–Zion, UT	4
SAN ANTONIO, TX	44
SAN DIEGO, CA	103
San Luis Obispo, CA	83
Santa Fe, NM	32
SANTA ROSA, CA	98
SARASOTA–BRADENTON, FL	76
SPRINGFIELD, MO	81
STATE COLLEGE, PA	42
Table Rock Lake, MO	22
Tahlequah–Lake Tenkiller, OK	5
Toms River–Barnegat Bay, NJ	88
Traverse City–Grand Traverse Bay, MI	99
TUCSON, AZ	62
Twain Harte–Yosemite, CA	93
WEST PALM BEACH–BOCA RATON, FL	89
Winchester, VA	90
Yuma, AZ	14

Place Profiles: Money Matters in 107 Retirement Places

The following profiles highlight certain economic features in the retirement places. These include the indicators that were used to rank the places—estimated average income for a two-person household, tax bite, income growth, and job growth—along with information on the level of competition for part-time jobs you may encounter there, and the place's potential for unemployment during a recession.

The information comes from these sources: American Association of Retired Persons, *Your Retirement State Tax Guide,* 1983; Commerce Clearing House, *State Tax Handbook,* 1983; Internal Revenue Service, *Your Individual Income Tax,* 1983; U.S. Bureau of the Census, *1980 Census of Population and Housing;* and U.S. Department of Commerce, Bureau of Economic Analysis, *OBERS Regional Projections,* 1981, "County and Metropolitan Area Personal Income," *Survey of Current Business,* 1983, and *County Business Patterns, 1981,* 1983.

ALBUQUERQUE, NM
Household Money Matters
  Income: $20,097
  Taxes: $597
  Tax Bite: 2.97%
Local Jobs
  Part-Time Opportunities: Poor
  Unemployment Threat: Low
Growth During the 1980s
  Income: 24.92%
  Jobs: 16.44%
Places Rated Score: 7,989
Places Rated Rank: 53

ASHEVILLE, NC
Household Money Matters
  Income: $18,220
  Taxes: $1,096
  Tax Bite: 6.02%
Local Jobs
  Part-Time Opportunities: Average
  Unemployment Threat: High
Growth During the 1980s
  Income: 27.04%
  Jobs: 12.47%
Places Rated Score: 7,926
Places Rated Rank: 57

Athens-Cedar Creek Lake, TX
Household Money Matters
  Income: $14,806
  Taxes: $113
  Tax Bite: .76%
Local Jobs
  Part-Time Opportunities: Good
  Unemployment Threat: High
Growth During the 1980s
  Income: 23.31%
  Jobs: 19.14%
Places Rated Score: 9,802
Places Rated Rank: 9

ATLANTIC CITY-CAPE MAY, NJ
Household Money Matters
Income: $23,525
Taxes: $593
Tax Bite: 2.52%
Local Jobs
Part-Time Opportunities: Average
Unemployment Threat: Low
Growth During the 1980s
Income: 23.18%
Jobs: 8.08%
Places Rated Score: 6,419
Places Rated Rank: 104

AUSTIN, TX
Household Money Matters
Income: $21,146
Taxes: $142
Tax Bite: .67%
Local Jobs
Part-Time Opportunities: Poor
Unemployment Threat: Moderate
Growth During the 1980s
Income: 23.67%
Jobs: 18.14%
Places Rated Score: 8,058
Places Rated Rank: 50

Bar Harbor–Frenchman Bay, ME
Household Money Matters
Income: $17,494
Taxes: $612
Tax Bite: 3.50%
Local Jobs
Part-Time Opportunities: Average
Unemployment Threat: Moderate
Growth During the 1980s
Income: 25.15%
Jobs: 12.20%
Places Rated Score: 8,152
Places Rated Rank: 43

Beaufort–Hilton Head, SC
Household Money Matters
Income: $18,251
Taxes: $754
Tax Bite: 4.13%
Local Jobs
Part-Time Opportunities: Average
Unemployment Threat: Low
Growth During the 1980s
Income: 24.86%
Jobs: 10.18%
Places Rated Score: 7,661
Places Rated Rank: 67

Bend, OR
Household Money Matters
Income: $17,690
Taxes: $1,362
Tax Bite: 7.70%
Local Jobs
Part-Time Opportunities: Average
Unemployment Threat: Moderate
Growth During the 1980s
Income: 20.76%
Jobs: 20.46%
Places Rated Score: 8,067
Places Rated Rank: 48

Bennington, VT
Household Money Matters
Income: $17,799
Taxes: $577
Tax Bite: 3.24%
Local Jobs
Part-Time Opportunities: Poor
Unemployment Threat: High
Growth During the 1980s
Income: 21.16%
Jobs: 3.14%
Places Rated Score: 7,070
Places Rated Rank: 91

Benton–Kentucky Lake, KY
Household Money Matters
Income: $15,299
Taxes: $872
Tax Bite: 5.70%
Local Jobs
Part-Time Opportunities: Average
Unemployment Threat: High
Growth During the 1980s
Income: 28.21%
Jobs: 15.50%
Places Rated Score: 9,252
Places Rated Rank: 17

Big Sandy, TN
Household Money Matters
Income: $14,231
Taxes: $207
Tax Bite: 1.45%
Local Jobs
Part-Time Opportunities: Average
Unemployment Threat: High
Growth During the 1980s
Income: 27.58%
Jobs: 15.65%
Places Rated Score: 10,038
Places Rated Rank: 7

BILOXI-GULFPORT, MS
Household Money Matters
Income: $15,731
Taxes: $453
Tax Bite: 2.88%
Local Jobs
Part-Time Opportunities: Poor
Unemployment Threat: Low
Growth During the 1980s
Income: 28.11%
Jobs: 16.47%
Places Rated Score: 9,472
Places Rated Rank: 15

BOISE CITY, ID
Household Money Matters
Income: $21,601
Taxes: $1,321
Tax Bite: 6.12%
Local Jobs
Part-Time Opportunities: Poor
Unemployment Threat: Moderate
Growth During the 1980s
Income: 22.11%
Jobs: 15.83%
Places Rated Score: 7,043
Places Rated Rank: 93

Branson–Lake Taneycomo, MO
Household Money Matters
Income: $16,773
Taxes: $786
Tax Bite: 4.69%
Local Jobs
Part-Time Opportunities: Good
Unemployment Threat: Low
Growth During the 1980s
Income: 24.64%
Jobs: 8.57%
Places Rated Score: 7,824
Places Rated Rank: 60

Brattleboro, VT
Household Money Matters
Income: $17,354
Taxes: $553
Tax Bite: 3.19%
Local Jobs
Part-Time Opportunities: Average
Unemployment Threat: Moderate
Growth During the 1980s
Income: 19.90%
Jobs: 8.70%
Places Rated Score: 7,621
Places Rated Rank: 69

Brevard, NC
Household Money Matters
Income: $16,947
Taxes: $1,066
Tax Bite: 6.29%
Local Jobs
Part-Time Opportunities: Average
Unemployment Threat: High
Growth During the 1980s
Income: 27.04%
Jobs: 12.47%
Places Rated Score: 8,243
Places Rated Rank: 40

Brunswick–Golden Isles, GA
Household Money Matters
Income: $19,897
Taxes: $903
Tax Bite: 4.54%
Local Jobs
Part-Time Opportunities: Poor
Unemployment Threat: Moderate
Growth During the 1980s
Income: 22.64%
Jobs: 10.18%
Places Rated Score: 7,020
Places Rated Rank: 96

Bull Shoals, AR
Household Money Matters
Income: $12,966
Taxes: $497
Tax Bite: 3.83%
Local Jobs
Part-Time Opportunities: Good
Unemployment Threat: High
Growth During the 1980s
Income: 26.44%
Jobs: 12.20%
Places Rated Score: 9,913
Places Rated Rank: 8

Camden–Penobscot Bay, ME
Household Money Matters
Income: $18,027
Taxes: $670
Tax Bite: 3.72%
Local Jobs
Part-Time Opportunities: Average
Unemployment Threat: Moderate
Growth During the 1980s
Income: 24.90%
Jobs: 13.34%
Places Rated Score: 8,078
Places Rated Rank: 47

Canton–Lake Tawakoni, TX
Household Money Matters
Income: $16,269
Taxes: $123
Tax Bite: .76%
Local Jobs
Part-Time Opportunities: Average
Unemployment Threat: Moderate
Growth During the 1980s
Income: 23.79%
Jobs: 20.11%
Places Rated Score: 9,440
Places Rated Rank: 16

Cape Cod, MA
Household Money Matters
Income: $23,431
Taxes: $1,155
Tax Bite: 4.93%
Local Jobs
Part-Time Opportunities: Good
Unemployment Threat: Low
Growth During the 1980s
Income: 22.72%
Jobs: 7.71%
Places Rated Score: 6,109
Places Rated Rank: 105

Carson City, NV
Household Money Matters
Income: $24,977
Taxes: $228
Tax Bite: .91%
Local Jobs
Part-Time Opportunities: Average
Unemployment Threat: Low
Growth During the 1980s
Income: 17.67%
Jobs: 32.91%
Places Rated Score: 8,306
Places Rated Rank: 37

Cassville–Roaring River, MO
Household Money Matters
Income: $14,943
Taxes: $667
Tax Bite: 4.46%
Local Jobs
Part-Time Opportunities: Average
Unemployment Threat: High
Growth During the 1980s
Income: 24.64%
Jobs: 8.57%
Places Rated Score: 8,456
Places Rated Rank: 25

CHARLOTTESVILLE, VA
Household Money Matters
Income: $19,397
Taxes: $1,015
Tax Bite: 5.23%
Local Jobs
Part-Time Opportunities: Poor
Unemployment Threat: Moderate
Growth During the 1980s
Income: 9.00%
Jobs: 13.93%
Places Rated Score: 6,070
Places Rated Rank: 106

Clarkesville-Mount Airy, GA
Household Money Matters
Income: $13,749
Taxes: $503
Tax Bite: 3.66%
Local Jobs
Part-Time Opportunities: Poor
Unemployment Threat: High
Growth During the 1980s
Income: 25.82%
Jobs: 12.59%
Places Rated Score: 9,541
Places Rated Rank: 13

Clear Lake, CA
Household Money Matters
Income: $18,280
Taxes: $636
Tax Bite: 3.48%
Local Jobs
Part-Time Opportunities: Good
Unemployment Threat: Low
Growth During the 1980s
Income: 21.79%
Jobs: 14.14%
Places Rated Score: 7,807
Places Rated Rank: 61

Coeur d'Alene, ID
Household Money Matters
Income: $17,953
Taxes: $1,031
Tax Bite: 5.74%
Local Jobs
Part-Time Opportunities: Poor
Unemployment Threat: Moderate
Growth During the 1980s
Income: 20.50%
Jobs: 4.63%
Places Rated Score: 6,584
Places Rated Rank: 102

COLORADO SPRINGS, CO
Household Money Matters
Income: $19,308
Taxes: $1,006
Tax Bite: 5.21%
Local Jobs
Part-Time Opportunities: Poor
Unemployment Threat: Low
Growth During the 1980s
Income: 12.14%
Jobs: 20.52%
Places Rated Score: 7,064
Places Rated Rank: 92

Cookeville, TN
Household Money Matters
Income: $14,617
Taxes: $207
Tax Bite: 1.42%
Local Jobs
Part-Time Opportunities: Poor
Unemployment Threat: High
Growth During the 1980s
Income: 28.39%
Jobs: 16.82%
Places Rated Score: 10,085
Places Rated Rank: 6

Crossville, TN
Household Money Matters
Income: $12,254
Taxes: $191
Tax Bite: 1.56%
Local Jobs
Part-Time Opportunities: Average
Unemployment Threat: High
Growth During the 1980s
Income: 28.60%
Jobs: 18.03%
Places Rated Score: 11,313
Places Rated Rank: 3

DAYTONA BEACH, FL
Household Money Matters
Income: $18,592
Taxes: $175
Tax Bite: .94%
Local Jobs
Part-Time Opportunities: Good
Unemployment Threat: Low
Growth During the 1980s
Income: 22.28%
Jobs: 17.97%
Places Rated Score: 8,417
Places Rated Rank: 29

Delta, CO
Household Money Matters
Income: $15,740
Taxes: $700
Tax Bite: 4.45%
Local Jobs
Part-Time Opportunities: Average
Unemployment Threat: Low
Growth During the 1980s
Income: 24.33%
Jobs: 23.47%
Places Rated Score: 9,634
Places Rated Rank: 11

Deming, NM
Household Money Matters
Income: $14,960
Taxes: $384
Tax Bite: 2.57%
Local Jobs
Part-Time Opportunities: Average
Unemployment Threat: Low
Growth During the 1980s
Income: 23.63%
Jobs: 15.42%
Places Rated Score: 9,223
Places Rated Rank: 18

Eagle River, WI
Household Money Matters
  Income: $14,718
  Taxes: $1,017
  Tax Bite: 6.91%
Local Jobs
  Part-Time Opportunities: Good
  Unemployment Threat: Low
Growth During the 1980s
  Income: 22.89%
  Jobs: 10.70%
Places Rated Score: 8,335
Places Rated Rank: 33

Easton–Chesapeake Bay, MD
Household Money Matters
  Income: $24,726
  Taxes: $1,294
  Tax Bite: 5.23%
Local Jobs
  Part-Time Opportunities: Average
  Unemployment Threat: Moderate
Growth During the 1980s
  Income: 22.97%
  Jobs: 8.54%
Places Rated Score: 6,001
Places Rated Rank: 107

Fairhope–Gulf Shores, AL
Household Money Matters
  Income: $15,681
  Taxes: $728
  Tax Bite: 4.64%
Local Jobs
  Part-Time Opportunities: Average
  Unemployment Threat: Moderate
Growth During the 1980s
  Income: 28.83%
  Jobs: 13.79%
Places Rated Score: 8,463
Places Rated Rank: 24

FORT COLLINS, CO
Household Money Matters
  Income: $19,741
  Taxes: $1,041
  Tax Bite: 5.27%
Local Jobs
  Part-Time Opportunities: Poor
  Unemployment Threat: Moderate
Growth During the 1980s
  Income: 22.18%
  Jobs: 24.17%
Places Rated Score: 8,333
Places Rated Rank: 35

FORT LAUDERDALE-HOLLYWOOD, FL
Household Money Matters
  Income: $25,339
  Taxes: $213
  Tax Bite: .84%
Local Jobs
  Part-Time Opportunities: Good
  Unemployment Threat: Low
Growth During the 1980s
  Income: 22.77%
  Jobs: 18.76%
Places Rated Score: 7,360
Places Rated Rank: 79

FORT MYERS–CAPE CORAL, FL
Household Money Matters
  Income: $21,428
  Taxes: $188
  Tax Bite: .88%
Local Jobs
  Part-Time Opportunities: Good
  Unemployment Threat: Low
Growth During the 1980s
  Income: 22.19%
  Jobs: 18.34%
Places Rated Score: 7,857
Places Rated Rank: 59

Fredericksburg, TX
Household Money Matters
  Income: $21,059
  Taxes: $142
  Tax Bite: .67%
Local Jobs
  Part-Time Opportunities: Good
  Unemployment Threat: Moderate
Growth During the 1980s
  Income: 22.63%
  Jobs: 16.05%
Places Rated Score: 7,761
Places Rated Rank: 64

Front Royal, VA
Household Money Matters
  Income: $17,112
  Taxes: $873
  Tax Bite: 5.10%
Local Jobs
  Part-Time Opportunities: Average
  Unemployment Threat: High
Growth During the 1980s
  Income: 23.11%
  Jobs: 9.11%
Places Rated Score: 7,586
Places Rated Rank: 72

Gainesville–Lake Sidney Lanier, GA
Household Money Matters
  Income: $18,394
  Taxes: $813
  Tax Bite: 4.42%
Local Jobs
  Part-Time Opportunities: Poor
  Unemployment Threat: High
Growth During the 1980s
  Income: 25.82%
  Jobs: 12.59%
Places Rated Score: 7,933
Places Rated Rank: 56

Grand Junction, CO
Household Money Matters
  Income: $20,253
  Taxes: $1,090
  Tax Bite: 5.38%
Local Jobs
  Part-Time Opportunities: Poor
  Unemployment Threat: Low
Growth During the 1980s
  Income: 24.33%
  Jobs: 23.47%
Places Rated Score: 8,360
Places Rated Rank: 30

Hamilton-Bitterroot Valley, MT
Household Money Matters
  Income: $15,561
  Taxes: $731
  Tax Bite: 4.70%
Local Jobs
  Part-Time Opportunities: Average
  Unemployment Threat: Moderate
Growth During the 1980s
  Income: 24.45%
  Jobs: 11.01%
Places Rated Score: 8,436
Places Rated Rank: 27

Harrison, AR
Household Money Matters
  Income: $16,304
  Taxes: $687
  Tax Bite: 4.21%
Local Jobs
  Part-Time Opportunities: Average
  Unemployment Threat: Moderate
Growth During the 1980s
  Income: 26.44%
  Jobs: 12.20%
Places Rated Score: 8,558
Places Rated Rank: 23

Hendersonville, NC
Household Money Matters
  Income: $19,495
  Taxes: $1,186
  Tax Bite: 6.08%
Local Jobs
  Part-Time Opportunities: Average
  Unemployment Threat: High
Growth During the 1980s
  Income: 27.04%
  Jobs: 12.47%
Places Rated Score: 7,621
Places Rated Rank: 69

Hot Springs–Lake Ouachita, AR
Household Money Matters
  Income: $18,385
  Taxes: $821
  Tax Bite: 4.47%
Local Jobs
  Part-Time Opportunities: Good
  Unemployment Threat: Moderate
Growth During the 1980s
  Income: 27.17%
  Jobs: 12.57%
Places Rated Score: 8,063
Places Rated Rank: 49

Houghton Lake, MI
Household Money Matters
  Income: $15,155
  Taxes: $769
  Tax Bite: 5.07%
Local Jobs
  Part-Time Opportunities: Good
  Unemployment Threat: Low
Growth During the 1980s
  Income: 22.29%
  Jobs: 11.24%
Places Rated Score: 8,349
Places Rated Rank: 31

Kalispell, MT
Household Money Matters
Income: $18,180
Taxes: $941
Tax Bite: 5.18%
Local Jobs
Part-Time Opportunities: Poor
Unemployment Threat: Moderate
Growth During the 1980s
Income: 24.45%
Jobs: 11.01%
Places Rated Score: 7,615
Places Rated Rank: 71

Keene, NH
Household Money Matters
Income: $20,106
Taxes: None
Tax Bite: 0%
Local Jobs
Part-Time Opportunities: Average
Unemployment Threat: High
Growth During the 1980s
Income: 19.90%
Jobs: 8.70%
Places Rated Score: 7,008
Places Rated Rank: 97

Kerrville, TX
Household Money Matters
Income: $21,627
Taxes: $142
Tax Bite: .66%
Local Jobs
Part-Time Opportunities: Good
Unemployment Threat: Low
Growth During the 1980s
Income: 22.63%
Jobs: 16.05%
Places Rated Score: 7,658
Places Rated Rank: 68

Laconia–Lake Winnipesaukee, NH
Household Money Matters
Income: $20,138
Taxes: None
Tax Bite: 0%
Local Jobs
Part-Time Opportunities: Average
Unemployment Threat: High
Growth During the 1980s
Income: 22.72%
Jobs: 7.71%
Places Rated Score: 7,184
Places Rated Rank: 84

Lake Havasu City–Kingman, AZ
Household Money Matters
Income: $17,236
Taxes: $746
Tax Bite: 4.33%
Local Jobs
Part-Time Opportunities: Good
Unemployment Threat: Moderate
Growth During the 1980s
Income: 23.65%
Jobs: 19.99%
Places Rated Score: 8,770
Places Rated Rank: 21

LAKELAND–WINTER HAVEN, FL
Household Money Matters
Income: $19,067
Taxes: $175
Tax Bite: .92%
Local Jobs
Part-Time Opportunities: Average
Unemployment Threat: Moderate
Growth During the 1980s
Income: 22.19%
Jobs: 18.34%
Places Rated Score: 8,335
Places Rated Rank: 33

Lake O' The Cherokees, OK
Household Money Matters
Income: $10,806
Taxes: $204
Tax Bite: 1.89%
Local Jobs
Part-Time Opportunities: Good
Unemployment Threat: Low
Growth During the 1980s
Income: 26.44%
Jobs: 12.20%
Places Rated Score: 11,393
Places Rated Rank: 2

LANCASTER, PA
Household Money Matters
Income: $20,544
Taxes: $369
Tax Bite: 1.80%
Local Jobs
Part-Time Opportunities: Poor
Unemployment Threat: High
Growth During the 1980s
Income: 24.19%
Jobs: 5.58%
Places Rated Score: 6,857
Places Rated Rank: 101

LAS CRUCES, NM
Household Money Matters
Income: $14,111
Taxes: $360
Tax Bite: 2.55%
Local Jobs
Part-Time Opportunities: Poor
Unemployment Threat: Low
Growth During the 1980s
Income: 23.63%
Jobs: 15.42%
Places Rated Score: 9,560
Places Rated Rank: 12

LAS VEGAS, NV
Household Money Matters
Income: $24,044
Taxes: $228
Tax Bite: .95%
Local Jobs
Part-Time Opportunities: Poor
Unemployment Threat: Low
Growth During the 1980s
Income: 18.71%
Jobs: 31.78%
Places Rated Score: 8,423
Places Rated Rank: 28

LEXINGTON–FAYETTE, KY
Household Money Matters
Income: $20,453
Taxes: $1,276
Tax Bite: 6.24%
Local Jobs
Part-Time Opportunities: Poor
Unemployment Threat: Moderate
Growth During the 1980s
Income: 31.69%
Jobs: 17.00%
Places Rated Score: 8,323
Places Rated Rank: 36

Lincoln City–Newport, OR
Household Money Matters
Income: $19,201
Taxes: $1,525
Tax Bite: 7.94%
Local Jobs
Part-Time Opportunities: Good
Unemployment Threat: Moderate
Growth During the 1980s
Income: 20.76%
Jobs: 20.46%
Places Rated Score: 7,672
Places Rated Rank: 66

Maui, HI
Household Money Matters
Income: $20,045
Taxes: $1,549
Tax Bite: 7.73%
Local Jobs
Part-Time Opportunities: Average
Unemployment Threat: Low
Growth During the 1980s
Income: 19.87%
Jobs: 15.46%
Places Rated Score: 6,921
Places Rated Rank: 100

McALLEN-PHARR-EDINBURG, TX
Household Money Matters
Income: $10,993
Taxes: $91
Tax Bite: .83%
Local Jobs
Part-Time Opportunities: Poor
Unemployment Threat: Low
Growth During the 1980s
Income: 24.04%
Jobs: 16.01%
Places Rated Score: 11,509
Places Rated Rank: 1

MEDFORD, OR
Household Money Matters
Income: $17,982
Taxes: $1,393
Tax Bite: 7.75%
Local Jobs
Part-Time Opportunities: Average
Unemployment Threat: Low
Growth During the 1980s
Income: 21.00%
Jobs: 20.54%
Places Rated Score: 8,040
Places Rated Rank: 51

MELBOURNE-TITUSVILLE-COCOA, FL
Household Money Matters
Income: $21,206
Taxes: $188
Tax Bite: .89%
Local Jobs
Part-Time Opportunities: Average
Unemployment Threat: Moderate
Growth During the 1980s
Income: 22.28%
Jobs: 17.97%
Places Rated Score: 7,869
Places Rated Rank: 58

MIAMI, FL
Household Money Matters
Income: $22,515
Taxes: $201
Tax Bite: .89%
Local Jobs
Part-Time Opportunities: Average
Unemployment Threat: Low
Growth During the 1980s
Income: 22.77%
Jobs: 18.76%
Places Rated Score: 7,768
Places Rated Rank: 63

Missoula, MT
Household Money Matters
Income: $19,011
Taxes: $1,015
Tax Bite: 5.34%
Local Jobs
Part-Time Opportunities: Poor
Unemployment Threat: Low
Growth During the 1980s
Income: 24.45%
Jobs: 11.01%
Places Rated Score: 7,399
Places Rated Rank: 78

Monticello-Liberty, NY
Household Money Matters
Income: $17,057
Taxes: $836
Tax Bite: 4.90%
Local Jobs
Part-Time Opportunities: Average
Unemployment Threat: Low
Growth During the 1980s
Income: 21.43%
Jobs: 5.95%
Places Rated Score: 7,137
Places Rated Rank: 87

Mountain Home-Norfork Lake, AR
Household Money Matters
Income: $17,453
Taxes: $756
Tax Bite: 4.33%
Local Jobs
Part-Time Opportunities: Good
Unemployment Threat: High
Growth During the 1980s
Income: 26.44%
Jobs: 12.20%
Places Rated Score: 8,210
Places Rated Rank: 41

Myrtle Beach, SC
Household Money Matters
Income: $15,274
Taxes: $519
Tax Bite: 3.40%
Local Jobs
Part-Time Opportunities: Poor
Unemployment Threat: Moderate
Growth During the 1980s
Income: 26.67%
Jobs: 13.39%
Places Rated Score: 9,126
Places Rated Rank: 19

Nevada City–Donner, CA
Household Money Matters
Income: $18,067
Taxes: $627
Tax Bite: 3.47%
Local Jobs
Part-Time Opportunities: Good
Unemployment Threat: Low
Growth During the 1980s
Income: 18.01%
Jobs: 12.60%
Places Rated Score: 7,330
Places Rated Rank: 82

North Conway–White Mountains, NH
Household Money Matters
Income: $19,323
Taxes: None
Tax Bite: 0%
Local Jobs
Part-Time Opportunities: Average
Unemployment Threat: Low
Growth During the 1980s
Income: 22.72%
Jobs: 7.71%
Places Rated Score: 7,359
Places Rated Rank: 80

Oak Harbor, WA
Household Money Matters
Income: $20,229
Taxes: $301
Tax Bite: 1.49%
Local Jobs
Part-Time Opportunities: Average
Unemployment Threat: Low
Growth During the 1980s
Income: 21.94%
Jobs: 17.85%
Places Rated Score: 7,953
Places Rated Rank: 55

OCALA, FL
Household Money Matters
Income: $16,235
Taxes: $162
Tax Bite: 1.00%
Local Jobs
Part-Time Opportunities: Good
Unemployment Threat: Moderate
Growth During the 1980s
Income: 22.64%
Jobs: 16.51%
Places Rated Score: 8,917
Places Rated Rank: 20

Ocean City–Assateague Island, MD
Household Money Matters
Income: $18,238
Taxes: $990
Tax Bite: 5.43%
Local Jobs
Part-Time Opportunities: Average
Unemployment Threat: Moderate
Growth During the 1980s
Income: 22.97%
Jobs: 8.54%
Places Rated Score: 7,181
Places Rated Rank: 86

OLYMPIA, WA
Household Money Matters
Income: $23,148
Taxes: $318
Tax Bite: 1.37%
Local Jobs
Part-Time Opportunities: Poor
Unemployment Threat: Low
Growth During the 1980s
Income: 21.94%
Jobs: 17.85%
Places Rated Score: 7,445
Places Rated Rank: 75

ORLANDO, FL
Household Money Matters
Income: $20,548
Taxes: $188
Tax Bite: .91%
Local Jobs
Part-Time Opportunities: Poor
Unemployment Threat: Low
Growth During the 1980s
Income: 22.28%
Jobs: 17.97%
Places Rated Score: 7,993
Places Rated Rank: 52

Oscoda–Huron Shore, MI
Household Money Matters
Income: $15,293
Taxes: $776
Tax Bite: 5.07%
Local Jobs
Part-Time Opportunities: Average
Unemployment Threat: Moderate
Growth During the 1980s
Income: 22.29%
Jobs: 11.24%
Places Rated Score: 8,299
Places Rated Rank: 38

Paris, TN
Household Money Matters
Income: $14,956
Taxes: $207
Tax Bite: 1.38%
Local Jobs
Part-Time Opportunities: Average
Unemployment Threat: High
Growth During the 1980s
Income: 27.58%
Jobs: 15.65%
Places Rated Score: 9,761
Places Rated Rank: 10

Petoskey–Straits of Mackinac, MI
Household Money Matters
　Income: $18,584
　Taxes: $965
　Tax Bite: 5.19%
Local Jobs
　Part-Time Opportunities: Average
　Unemployment Threat: Low
Growth During the 1980s
　Income: 22.64%
　Jobs: 11.81%
Places Rated Score: 7,414
Places Rated Rank: 77

PHOENIX, AZ
Household Money Matters
　Income: $22,252
　Taxes: $1,188
　Tax Bite: 5.34%
Local Jobs
　Part-Time Opportunities: Average
　Unemployment Threat: Moderate
Growth During the 1980s
　Income: 23.65%
　Jobs: 19.99%
Places Rated Score: 7,578
Places Rated Rank: 73

Port Angeles–Strait of Juan de Fuca, WA
Household Money Matters
　Income: $21,697
　Taxes: $301
　Tax Bite: 1.39%
Local Jobs
　Part-Time Opportunities: Average
　Unemployment Threat: Moderate
Growth During the 1980s
　Income: 21.94%
　Jobs: 17.85%
Places Rated Score: 7,684
Places Rated Rank: 65

Prescott, AZ
Household Money Matters
　Income: $19,807
　Taxes: $966
　Tax Bite: 4.88%
Local Jobs
　Part-Time Opportunities: Good
　Unemployment Threat: Moderate
Growth During the 1980s
　Income: 23.65%
　Jobs: 19.99%
Places Rated Score: 8,087
Places Rated Rank: 45

Rappahannock, VA
Household Money Matters
　Income: $17,434
　Taxes: $891
　Tax Bite: 5.11%
Local Jobs
　Part-Time Opportunities: Average
　Unemployment Threat: High
Growth During the 1980s
　Income: 23.11%
　Jobs: 9.11%
Places Rated Score: 7,495
Places Rated Rank: 74

Red Bluff-Sacramento Valley, CA
Household Money Matters
　Income: $17,051
　Taxes: $571
　Tax Bite: 3.35%
Local Jobs
　Part-Time Opportunities: Average
　Unemployment Threat: Moderate
Growth During the 1980s
　Income: 18.56%
　Jobs: 12.46%
Places Rated Score: 8,291
Places Rated Rank: 39

Rehoboth Bay–Indian River Bay, DE
Household Money Matters
　Income: $18,511
　Taxes: $1,128
　Tax Bite: 6.09%
Local Jobs
　Part-Time Opportunities: Average
　Unemployment Threat: High
Growth During the 1980s
　Income: 23.18%
　Jobs: 8.08%
Places Rated Score: 7,022
Places Rated Rank: 95

RENO, NV
Household Money Matters
　Income: $27,939
　Taxes: $241
　Tax Bite: .86%
Local Jobs
　Part-Time Opportunities: Average
　Unemployment Threat: Low
Growth During the 1980s
　Income: 17.67%
　Jobs: 32.91%
Places Rated Score: 7,957
Places Rated Rank: 54

Rhinelander, WI
Household Money Matters
　Income: $18,151
　Taxes: $1,400
　Tax Bite: 7.71%
Local Jobs
　Part-Time Opportunities: Average
　Unemployment Threat: Moderate
Growth During the 1980s
　Income: 22.89%
　Jobs: 10.70%
Places Rated Score: 7,183
Places Rated Rank: 85

Rockport–Aransas Pass, TX
Household Money Matters
　Income: $16,995
　Taxes: $123
　Tax Bite: .72%
Local Jobs
　Part-Time Opportunities: Good
　Unemployment Threat: Low
Growth During the 1980s
　Income: 22.10%
　Jobs: 14.96%
Places Rated Score: 8,442
Places Rated Rank: 26

Roswell, NM
Household Money Matters
　Income: $18,704
　Taxes: $532
　Tax Bite: 2.84%
Local Jobs
　Part-Time Opportunities: Average
　Unemployment Threat: Low
Growth During the 1980s
　Income: 23.63%
　Jobs: 15.42%
Places Rated Score: 8,080
Places Rated Rank: 46

St. George–Zion, UT
Household Money Matters
　Income: $13,781
　Taxes: $928
　Tax Bite: 6.73%
Local Jobs
　Part-Time Opportunities: Average
　Unemployment Threat: Low
Growth During the 1980s
　Income: 18.71%
　Jobs: 31.78%
Places Rated Score: 10,428
Places Rated Rank: 4

SAN ANTONIO, TX
Household Money Matters
　Income: $19,398
　Taxes: $133
　Tax Bite: .69%
Local Jobs
　Part-Time Opportunities: Average
　Unemployment Threat: Moderate
Growth During the 1980s
　Income: 22.63%
　Jobs: 16.05%
Places Rated Score: 8,098
Places Rated Rank: 44

SAN DIEGO, CA
Household Money Matters
　Income: $22,767
　Taxes: $870
　Tax Bite: 3.82%
Local Jobs
　Part-Time Opportunities: Poor
　Unemployment Threat: Low
Growth During the 1980s
　Income: 19.93%
　Jobs: 12.28%
Places Rated Score: 6,502
Places Rated Rank: 103

San Luis Obispo, CA
Household Money Matters
　Income: $20,065
　Taxes: $723
　Tax Bite: 3.60%
Local Jobs
　Part-Time Opportunities: Average
　Unemployment Threat: Low
Growth During the 1980s
　Income: 19.86%
　Jobs: 14.61%
Places Rated Score: 7,243
Places Rated Rank: 83

Santa Fe, NM
Household Money Matters
  Income: $18,587
  Taxes: $528
  Tax Bite: 2.84%
Local Jobs
  Part-Time Opportunities: Poor
  Unemployment Threat: Low
Growth During the 1980s
  Income: 24.92%
  Jobs: 16.44%
Places Rated Score: 8,339
Places Rated Rank: 32

SANTA ROSA, CA
Household Money Matters
  Income: $22,162
  Taxes: $840
  Tax Bite: 3.79%
Local Jobs
  Part-Time Opportunities: Average
  Unemployment Threat: Moderate
Growth During the 1980s
  Income: 21.79%
  Jobs: 14.14%
Places Rated Score: 6,977
Places Rated Rank: 98

SARASOTA–BRADENTON, FL
Household Money Matters
  Income: $24,017
  Taxes: $213
  Tax Bite: .89%
Local Jobs
  Part-Time Opportunities: Good
  Unemployment Threat: Moderate
Growth During the 1980s
  Income: 22.19%
  Jobs: 18.34%
Places Rated Score: 7,437
Places Rated Rank: 76

SPRINGFIELD, MO
Household Money Matters
  Income: $18,470
  Taxes: $897
  Tax Bite: 4.86%
Local Jobs
  Part-Time Opportunities: Poor
  Unemployment Threat: Moderate
Growth During the 1980s
  Income: 24.64%
  Jobs: 8.57%
Places Rated Score: 7,350
Places Rated Rank: 81

STATE COLLEGE, PA
Household Money Matters
  Income: $16,021
  Taxes: $301
  Tax Bite: 1.88%
Local Jobs
  Part-Time Opportunities: Poor
  Unemployment Threat: Moderate
Growth During the 1980s
  Income: 25.09%
  Jobs: 6.30%
Places Rated Score: 8,157
Places Rated Rank: 42

Table Rock Lake, MO
Household Money Matters
  Income: $14,187
  Taxes: $621
  Tax Bite: 4.38%
Local Jobs
  Part-Time Opportunities: Good
  Unemployment Threat: High
Growth During the 1980s
  Income: 24.64%
  Jobs: 8.57%
Places Rated Score: 8,762
Places Rated Rank: 22

Tahlequah–Lake Tenkiller, OK
Household Money Matters
  Income: $13,321
  Taxes: $318
  Tax Bite: 2.39%
Local Jobs
  Part-Time Opportunities: Poor
  Unemployment Threat: Low
Growth During the 1980s
  Income: 25.35%
  Jobs: 15.59%
Places Rated Score: 10,116
Places Rated Rank: 5

Toms River–Barnegat Bay, NJ
Household Money Matters
  Income: $19,616
  Taxes: $487
  Tax Bite: 2.48%
Local Jobs
  Part-Time Opportunities: Good
  Unemployment Threat: Low
Growth During the 1980s
  Income: 23.18%
  Jobs: 8.08%
Places Rated Score: 7,130
Places Rated Rank: 88

Traverse City-Grand Traverse Bay, MI
Household Money Matters
  Income: $20,743
  Taxes: $1,085
  Tax Bite: 5.23%
Local Jobs
  Part-Time Opportunities: Poor
  Unemployment Threat: Low
Growth During the 1980s
  Income: 22.64%
  Jobs: 11.81%
Places Rated Score: 6,943
Places Rated Rank: 99

TUCSON, AZ
Household Money Matters
  Income: $20,025
  Taxes: $996
  Tax Bite: 4.97%
Local Jobs
  Part-Time Opportunities: Average
  Unemployment Threat: Low
Growth During the 1980s
  Income: 23.09%
  Jobs: 17.94%
Places Rated Score: 7,771
Places Rated Rank: 62

Twain Harte–Yosemite, CA
Household Money Matters
  Income: $18,548
  Taxes: $647
  Tax Bite: 3.49%
Local Jobs
  Part-Time Opportunities: Average
  Unemployment Threat: Low
Growth During the 1980s
  Income: 16.93%
  Jobs: 12.03%
Places Rated Score: 7,043
Places Rated Rank: 93

WEST PALM BEACH-BOCA RATON, FL
Household Money Matters
  Income: $27,468
  Taxes: $225
  Tax Bite: .82%
Local Jobs
  Part-Time Opportunities: Good
  Unemployment Threat: Moderate
Growth During the 1980s
  Income: 22.77%
  Jobs: 18.76%
Places Rated Score: 7,107
Places Rated Rank: 89

Winchester, VA
Household Money Matters
  Income: $18,964
  Taxes: $990
  Tax Bite: 5.22%
Local Jobs
  Part-Time Opportunities: Poor
  Unemployment Threat: High
Growth During the 1980s
  Income: 23.11%
  Jobs: 9.11%
Places Rated Score: 7,098
Places Rated Rank: 90

Yuma, AZ
Household Money Matters
  Income: $15,083
  Taxes: $564
  Tax Bite: 3.74%
Local Jobs
  Part-Time Opportunities: Average
  Unemployment Threat: Low
Growth During the 1980s
  Income: 23.65%
  Jobs: 19.99%
Places Rated Score: 9,519
Places Rated Rank: 14

Et Cetera

YOUR RETIREMENT STATE TAX GUIDE

Question: Where in America can you find rock-bottom property taxes, no personal income tax on any of your retirement income, no sales tax on the basics you'll need like food and medicine, no inheritance taxes for your heirs to pay, and a minimum of nickel-and-dime fees for licensing a car or for taking out a fishing license?

Answer: Dream on. To fit the requirements for an ideal retirement tax haven, this place would have to have the low property taxes of Louisiana, Alaska's forgiveness of taxes on personal income, the absence of retail sales taxes as in Oregon, Nevada's lack of estate taxes, and Wisconsin's omission of niggling license fees. Unfortunately, you just can't find all these wonderful tax breaks together in one state.

When you retire, federal taxes on private pensions and any income you may have from investments will take the same bite whether you live in Anchorage, Atlanta, or Altoona, but state taxes can differ dramatically around the country. Sales taxes, excise taxes, license taxes, income taxes, property taxes, inheritance taxes, and gift taxes are just some of the forms state taxes can take. Depending on where you want to live, you may encounter all of them or only a few.

Property Taxes. Taxes on land and the buildings on it—whether they are homes, farms, industrial plants, or commercial buildings—are the biggest source of cash for local governments. They are imposed not by states but by the 13,516 cities, townships, counties, school districts, sanitary districts, hospital districts, and other special districts in the nation. All the states do is specify the maximum rate on the market value of the property, or a percentage of it, as the legal standard for local assessors to follow. The local assessor determines the value to be taxed. If you think the valuation is too high, you have a limited right of appeal.

You can't escape property taxes in any state except Alaska (you must be over 65 to take advantage of that break), but you can find dramatically low rates in certain parts of the country. Nationally, the average bills on homes amount to 1.25 percent of their market value, while the average bills in Alabama, Hawaii, Louisiana, and West Virginia are based on less than half that rate. In addition, 17 states allow specific exemptions on property valuation for retired homeowners.

Sales Taxes. Sometimes called retail taxes or consumption taxes, sales taxes are collected at the store level on the purchase of goods. After property taxes, they account for the largest source of revenue for state and local governments.

Among the states, the average sales tax is 4 percent. If you're living in Connecticut, you're paying the nation's highest state rate, 7.5 percent. But the highest rate paid by anyone in the country is the 8.5 percent levied on purchases of retail goods in New York City, a rate created in 1975 to help the Big Apple pay its debts.

Five states—Alaska, Delaware, Montana, New Hampshire, and Oregon—collect no sales taxes at all. To a retired couple, this could mean $200 a year in avoided costs. But you can avoid almost that much in states where such basics as food, medicine, and clothes are excluded from any sales tax. In Vermont, the last state to impose a sales tax, you receive an income-tax credit; that is, a reduction of income taxes owed for any sales tax you paid in the state during the year.

Personal Income Taxes. When paying federal income taxes began in 1914, two states—Mississippi and Wisconsin—were already collecting income taxes on their own. It was only during the 1920s and 1930s that the majority of states began to raise cash by tapping personal incomes. Today, 40 states impose the tax; two (New Hampshire and Tennessee) apply it only to income from interest and dividends; one (Connecticut) applies it only to income from capital gains and dividends; and seven (Alaska, Florida, Nevada, South Dakota, Texas, Washington, and Wyoming) don't tax incomes at all.

Taxing the Necessities*

You'll pay sales tax on groceries in . . .

Alabama	Michigan	South Carolina
Arizona	Mississippi	South Dakota
Arkansas	Missouri	Tennessee
Georgia	Nebraska	Utah
Hawaii	New Mexico	Virginia
Idaho	North Carolina	Wyoming
Kansas	Oklahoma	

And sales tax on medicine in . . .

Arizona	Michigan	Utah
Arkansas	Mississippi	Vermont
Georgia	Missouri	Virginia
Hawaii	New Mexico	

But NO sales tax on clothes in . . .

Massachusetts	New Hampshire
Minnesota	Rhode Island

And NO sales tax, period, in . . .

Alaska	New Hampshire
Delaware	Oregon
Montana	

You cannot take medical deductions on state income-tax returns in . . .

Illinois	Ohio
Indiana	Pennsylvania
Michigan	

Source: American Association of Retired Persons, *State Tax Guide,* 1982.

*This refers to all taxpayers, not only those of retirement age.

Estate and Inheritance Taxes. Death duties, as they are called sometimes, are taxes imposed when any kind of real property is transferred at death. They are imposed on the dead person's estate under the Federal Estate Tax, and in most states they take the form of inheritance taxes on the beneficiaries of the estate.

The philosophy underlying estate and inheritance taxes is that heirs should be required to pay a tax on additions to their wealth that they receive as an inheritance. To make the laws stick, however, gift taxes are also levied. Otherwise, property could be passed on tax-free by the owner in anticipation of death. Even though death and gift taxes are minor sources of revenue, several states—California, Connecticut, Iowa, New Jersey, and Pennsylvania—take greater pains to tap this source than the others.

License Taxes. These usually are enacted as flat fees for regulating a certain kind of privilege. For example, you'll pay a license tax on the family car for the right to use it on public highways; you'll buy a fishing license for the privilege of trolling for bass at the lake maintained by the state; you'll need a retail license to serve beer and wine at the roadhouse you've just bought. Together, these license taxes and fees make up a small part of a state's revenues. Of all the states, Wyoming gets the most money per capita out of its taxes on driving a car, and New York—surprisingly—the least. Alaska's taxes on hunting and fishing privileges are the steepest in the country, Indiana's the lightest. If you're going to open a bar in West Virginia, you can expect to shell out the highest license fees in the nation, whereas in Hawaii, Nevada, Wisconsin, and Wyoming, you'd pay nothing.

Excise Taxes. In most states, when you return from an errand having bought a tankful of gas for the family car, a bottle of gin, and a pack of cigarettes, you've also just paid excise taxes.

Excise taxes are related to sales taxes but are different in that they are levied only on specific items. Gasoline at the pump, for example, is taxed in every state at a higher rate than the local sales-tax rate (excise taxes on gasoline are heaviest in Wyoming, lightest in Texas). Tobacco and alcohol, too, are big targets for excise taxes, usually at rates that suggest social disapproval. In fact, taxes on cigarettes and liquor are popularly called sin taxes.

STATE PROFILES: DIRECT TAXES AND TAX BREAKS IN RETIREMENT

The difference between the states of Alabama and New York is more than one between the green and rural South and the grimy and glittery megalopolitan Northeast. In the three biggest state and local direct taxes—personal income, retail sales, and residential property—New Yorkers shoulder more in tax dollars per capita than do citizens in any other state, and their burden is three times that of Alabama citizens, whose tax burden is the least in the Union.

To help you compare the states' taxes, *Places Rated* totals up the personal income, retail sales, and residential property tax dollars that each state collects per capita. Against the U.S. average per capita collections from these sources, each state's taxes can be expressed as a percentage. New York's direct taxes, for example, are 164 percent of the U.S. average; Alabama's are 55 percent. In the category Retirement Tax Breaks, *Places Rated* examines specific tax breaks for retired persons in each state.

ALABAMA   Tax Burden: 55% of U.S. average
After Mississippi, Alabama is the poorest state in the country in taxable resources. The state's per capita take from personal income, sales, and property taxes is the lowest in the 50 states. On the other hand, like many other Sun Belt states, the Cotton State makes up much of this deficiency with heavy sin taxes on alcohol and tobacco.

Retirement Tax Breaks: The first $8,000 of military retirement income is exempt; Social Security, Railroad Retirement, and federal civil service pensions are entirely exempt.

Pluses: Along with Louisiana and West Virginia, Alabama imposes the lowest property taxes in the country, with complete exemptions for homeowners over 65 whose taxable income is less than $7,500.

Minuses: High sales tax (5%); only prescriptions are exempted.

ALASKA   Tax Burden: 76% of U.S. average
This state holds so many fiscal records that it's in a class by itself. It is the richest state in tax dollars per capita, but 90% of these dollars come not from residents but from North Slope oil and gas levies. The state's notorious tax on personal incomes has recently been repealed, and there is no statewide sales tax (cities and boroughs, however, may impose local rates of 1% to 5%).

Retirement Tax Breaks: No income tax.

Pluses: Persons over 65 are exempted from any residential property tax, regardless of gross income; there is no inheritance tax or statewide sales tax.

Minuses: Residential property-tax collections from homeowners under 65 years of age rank seventh nationally in per capita dollars.

ARIZONA   Tax Burden: 122% of U.S. average
Without question, the Grand Canyon State overuses its sales tax. It was the second state in the country to adopt a sales tax (Mississippi was first), doing so in 1933, and currently its collections per capita from that source rank fourth in the country. Property taxes are the highest of the four southwestern states and rank 15th among all 50 states in per capita dollars levied. In contrast, the state ranks 34th in personal income taxes.

Retirement Tax Breaks: Double personal exemptions for persons over 65. Up to $2,500 in federal civil service benefits are exempt, as are all benefits from

Arizona's public-employee and teacher-retirement systems.

Pluses: No inheritance taxes, low estate taxes (40th in the country in per capita collections).

Minuses: High residential property tax collections that are not significantly lessened for retired people; no sales-tax exemptions for food or medicine.

ARKANSAS   Tax Burden: 57% of U.S. average
Perhaps there's another meaning to Arkansas' nickname, Land of Opportunity. The state levies the least amount of taxes per capita from all sources—including severance and excise taxes as well as the three major direct taxes—of any state in the country. Can there be a connection between this fact and the rapid growth of certain retirement spots within the state? Among the 45 states that tax retail sales, Arkansas ranks 36th in per capita collections; among the 43 states with personal income taxes, the state ranks 35th. Arkansas does impose high taxes on alcohol and tobacco.

Retirement Tax Breaks: Arkansas exempts the first $6,000 of benefits from federal civil service, state, or local government retirement plans and military retirement pay.

Pluses: Low (3%) statewide sales tax; no inheritance taxes.

Minuses: The effective property-tax rate here is nearly twice what it is in the neighboring states of Louisiana, Oklahoma, Mississippi, and Missouri; sales tax is charged on groceries, medicine, and clothing.

CALIFORNIA   Tax Burden: 112% of U.S. average
This state's taxable wealth ranks fifth in the country. After the state's voters approved Proposition 13 in late 1978, California's residential property taxes plunged. The state now ranks 33rd in per capita property-tax collections. Offsetting that are the highest per capita receipts from inheritance and estate taxes, the sixth highest sales-tax collections, and the 11th highest income-tax collections.

Retirement Tax Breaks: None.

Pluses: People over 62 may postpone property-tax payments until the sale of the home or death of the owner.

Minuses: Extremely high inheritance taxes; very high income taxes with no breaks for retired people.

COLORADO   Tax Burden: 118% of U.S. average
Since the 1960s the Silver State's economy has rapidly shifted from agriculture and mining to service and high-technology manufacturing. This state was the first to impose a gasoline sales tax (1919) but today its excise taxes on motor fuel, as well as on tobacco and liquor, rank near the bottom (48th) in per capita dollars. But retail sales taxes and estate taxes are high.

Retirement Tax Breaks: Double personal exemptions for persons over 65; an exclusion of up to $20,000 in pension and annuity income that is taxable on federal income-tax returns.

Pluses: Low excise taxes; food and medicine are exempted from the sales tax.

Minuses: High sales-tax rate (7%), ranking ninth of the 50 states in per capita collections.

CONNECTICUT   Tax Burden: 103% of U.S. average
Connecticut is well-off in the amount of taxable wealth within its borders, and the Constitution State's effort to mine that wealth in the form of tax revenues ranks 13th in the country. There is no tax on earned incomes, but capital gains and dividends are taxed at 7%. Four overused taxes here are the property tax, the excise tax, inheritance taxes, and the sales tax.

Retirement Tax Breaks: Retirement benefits from any source are not taxed.

Pluses: People over 65 who sell their homes at a profit are exempt from the capital-gains tax (the house must have been their principal residence for five of the last eight years).

Minuses: High property taxes (sixth in per capita collections); highest statewide sales-tax rate (7.5%), with key exemptions on groceries and medicine.

DELAWARE   Tax Burden: 85% of U.S. average
Delaware's taxes on corporation income and license fees rank first in the country. Although the Diamond State has no sales taxes, and its per capita property taxes are the lowest in the northeastern quarter of the United States, it compensates for these breaks by having the highest per capita personal income-tax collections in the country.

Retirement Tax Breaks: A $2,000 exclusion of pension benefits from private plans; retired couples over 60 also qualify for an additional $4,000 if their adjusted gross income doesn't exceed $20,000.

Pluses: No sales tax; a very low property tax.

Minuses: High taxes on personal incomes and inheritances.

FLORIDA   Tax Burden: 71% of U.S. average
This is the archetypical retirement state, and its tax effort shows it. Ranking 20th in potential revenue per capita, the Sunshine State limps in at 36th in actual tax dollars. This state was also the last to adopt a death tax (1931).

Retirement Tax Breaks: No income tax of any kind.

Pluses: A low property-tax rate substantially relieved by an exemption of $25,000 on the home's assessed value for owners over 65. The catch: You must be a permanent resident of the state for at least five years. There is no inheritance tax in Florida, though estate taxes amount to the maximum allowable for federal estate purposes.

Minuses: High sales taxes (5%), relieved by exemptions for groceries, medicine, and apartment rent.

GEORGIA   Tax Burden: 82% of U.S. average
Georgia is well-off in terms of potential taxes but poor when it comes to actually levying them. This can be regarded as good news for individual taxpayers. Two

overused taxes (by U.S. standards) are the taxes on sales and personal income; two underused taxes are property and estate taxes.

Retirement Tax Breaks: Each person over 65 gets a personal exemption of $700, in addition to Georgia's standard exemption of $1,500. Teacher retirement benefits, from Georgia and other states, are entirely exempt. Finally, the first $2,000 in taxable pension benefits from other sources are exempt.

Pluses: Modest property-tax rates relieved by an exemption of $4,000 for persons over 65.

Minuses: Georgia's collections on sales tax rank 20th nationally, and there are no exemptions for food, clothing, or medicine.

HAWAII   Tax Burden: 147% of U.S. average

In 1901, well before any state on the mainland, the Hawaiian Islands began taxing personal income. This tax continues to be the Aloha State's most overused levy. Two other taxes—the retail sales tax and excise taxes on gasoline, tobacco, and liquor—are also high by mainland standards.

Retirement Tax Breaks: Double personal exemption for persons over 65; pensions from any public retirement system and federal retirement annuities are entirely exempt.

Pluses: Second-lowest effective property-tax rate in the country; homeowners over 60 get a $24,000 exemption from property valuation, which increases to $30,000 for homeowners over 70.

Minuses: Aside from the double personal exemption and exemption for any government retirement pensions, retired persons in Hawaii are taxed on the same basis as any other resident. Income taxes are sixth in the country in per capita collections. Sales tax, which is charged on food, medicine, and clothing, ranks first in the country in per capita dollars.

IDAHO   Tax Burden: 82% of U.S. average

The Gem State's per capita tax collections from all possible sources are the lowest in the Pacific Northwest. There's very little that is exceptional about Idaho's taxes (except perhaps to residents of New York or Massachusetts); the state occupies the low to middle ground in its per capita revenues from sales (41st), personal income (22nd), and property (30th).

Retirement Tax Breaks: Idaho keeps benefit exemptions in the family, so to speak. Teachers from outside the state do not qualify for exclusion of benefits on their income-tax forms. Idaho does exclude the first $8,500 in taxable pensions for single taxpayers and $12,741 for married taxpayers drawing benefits from civil service and military plans.

Pluses: Modest property taxes, although unrelieved by any significant exemptions for retired people. Low (3%) statewide sales tax.

Minuses: An inheritance tax; groceries not exempted from the sales tax.

Comparing Tax Burdens: The States Ranked from Lowest to Highest

State and Rank	Tax Burden per Capita	Percent of U.S. Average	State and Rank	Tax Burden per Capita	Percent of U.S. Average
1. Alabama	$362.66	55.48%	26. Maine	$579.17	88.61%
2. Arkansas	374.74	57.33	27. Indiana	589.12	90.13
3. Oklahoma	415.71	63.60	28. Pennsylvania	595.64	91.13
4. Tennessee	430.72	65.90	29. Vermont	599.42	91.71
5. New Hampshire	435.99	66.70	30. Kansas	613.92	93.93
6. Texas	437.73	66.97	31. Utah	636.81	97.43
7. Mississippi	444.26	67.97	32. Nebraska	661.82	101.25
8. Kentucky	444.34	67.98	33. Oregon	663.44	101.50
9. South Carolina	447.65	68.49	34. Iowa	671.29	102.70
10. Louisiana	447.86	68.52	35. Connecticut	674.04	103.12
11. West Virginia	449.03	68.70	36. Rhode Island	675.55	103.36
12. North Carolina	458.93	70.21	37. Washington	688.06	105.27
13. Florida	465.42	71.21	38. California	734.23	112.33
14. New Mexico	487.69	74.61	39. Illinois	737.22	112.79
15. North Dakota	494.75	75.69	40. Colorado	769.78	117.77
16. Alaska	494.95	75.72	40. Minnesota	769.78	117.77
17. Virginia	518.64	79.35	42. New Jersey	772.27	118.15
18. Missouri	519.94	79.55	43. Maryland	777.81	119.00
19. South Dakota	535.85	81.98	44. Michigan	780.77	119.45
20. Georgia	536.42	82.07	45. Arizona	796.25	121.82
21. Idaho	539.07	82.47	46. Wisconsin	809.43	123.84
22. Ohio	552.64	84.55	47. Wyoming	844.09	129.14
23. Delaware	553.89	84.74	48. Massachusetts	953.19	145.83
24. Nevada	569.33	87.10	49. Hawaii	959.07	146.73
25. Montana	571.67	87.46	50. New York	1,072.28	164.05

Source: Advisory Commission on Intergovernmental Relations, 1983.

ILLINOIS   Tax Burden: 113% of U.S. average

This state has a broad range of tax breaks for retired people. The irony is that even with these breaks, taxes remain high compared with those in other states. The three worst offenders here are sales, excise, and property taxes.

Retirement Tax Breaks: All pensions, whether government or private, are exempted entirely from Illinois personal income tax. Keogh and Individual Retirement Account distributions also are completely exempt.

Pluses: Persons over 65 get a $4,500 exemption on the value of their homes when local assessors determine property taxes; food and medicine are taxed at one third of the state rate for retail sales; inheritance tax was recently abolished.

Minuses: Illinois sales tax collections are the country's 15th highest per capita, in spite of the reduced rate on groceries and medicine. Property taxes, even after the exemption for people over 65, remain 14th highest per capita in the country.

INDIANA   Tax Burden: 90% of U.S. average

This state fits most people's idea of Middle America, and in fact Indiana's per capita collections of income taxes, property taxes, and estate taxes tend to place it in the middle rank among the 50 states.

Retirement Tax Breaks: Double personal exemption for everyone over 65; military benefits, Social Security, and Railroad Retirement pensions entirely exempt.

Pluses: Modest property-tax collections (32nd per capita nationally); food and medicine are exempt from the state's 4% sales tax.

Minuses: No significant property-tax breaks, without income qualifiers, for retired people.

IOWA   Tax Burden: 103% of U.S. average

The Hawkeye State was the first (1921) to spot tobacco as a weed worthy of a tax. Like its neighbor Minnesota, Iowa overuses the personal income tax and underuses the retail sales tax. Property taxes here rank 17th in the nation in per capita dollars collected.

Retirement Tax Breaks: Iowa gives the same tax breaks to retired people as the federal government does, but exempts the benefits of Iowa public employees. Up to $8,184 of benefits from federal civil service are also excluded, but the exemption is reduced by each dollar of Social Security payments.

Pluses: A low (3%) statewide sales tax, coupled with exemptions for food and medicine.

Minuses: Stiff inheritance taxes (fourth in the country); high property taxes with no significant exemptions for retired homeowners.

KANSAS   Tax Burden: 94% of U.S. average

Kansas imposes direct taxes that rank between 20th and 29th in the country. It may surprise you to learn that the Sunflower State ranks 12th in potential tax wealth but only 26th in the pains it actually takes to collect the money.

Retirement Tax Breaks: Kansas ranks 29th in collection of personal income tax per capita. Federal income taxes are completely deductible, as are Social Security, Railroad Retirement, self-employment taxes, federal civil service, and Kansas public-employee benefits. The first $2,000 of military retirement income for people over 65 is also exempt.

Pluses: Low (3%) sales taxes, further reduced by exemptions on medicine and disability appliances.

Minuses: No property-tax breaks for retired people; stiff inheritance taxes.

KENTUCKY   Tax Burden: 68% of U.S. average

In spite of the many Cadillacs and large new homes you see in Kentucky's coal counties, the state ranks only 41st in potential tax revenues. The Bluegrass State's collections of property taxes, after Alabama's and Louisiana's, are the country's lowest. This contrasts with the state's rank of 17th for revenue from personal income taxes.

Retirement Tax Breaks: None, except for Kentucky public employees and teachers.

Pluses: Modest property taxes, reduced substantially by an exemption of $12,900 on the homes of people over 65. Groceries, prescription medicines, and public utilities are exempted from the 5% sales tax.

Minuses: High personal income taxes and inheritance taxes.

LOUISIANA   Tax Burden: 69% of U.S. average

The Pelican State is rich in taxable wealth from oil and natural gas production. This wealth does take some of the tax pressure off average citizens, even though Louisiana doesn't heavily tax mineral production the way Alaska does. The tax burdens of retired people are light here. The only overused tax is the sales tax; indeed, Louisiana ranks seventh in the nation in per capita revenues from this source.

Retirement Tax Breaks: A deduction of $12,000 is allowed married couples; if both are over 65, an additional deduction of $12,000 is given against any taxable retirement income, thereby effectively eliminating income taxes for most retired couples.

Pluses: Louisiana has the lowest effective property-tax rate of any state in America.

Minuses: High sales-tax rate (6%), relieved by exemptions on groceries, medicine, and disability appliances.

MAINE   Tax Burden: 89% of U.S. average

The Pine Tree State is the poorest of all the states in the country's northeastern quarter and ranks only 46th in the nation in per capita taxable wealth. In spite of this liability, the state taps all possible sources for cash. Maine is said to get the most revenue from the least resources.

Retirement Tax Breaks: None.

Pluses: Groceries and medicine are exempt from sales tax.

Minuses: No significant property-tax relief for retired homeowners; high (16th nationally) estate taxes.

MARYLAND   Tax Burden: 119% of U.S. average

The Old Line State ranks second only to Delaware in amount of income tax per capita collected each year. On the other hand, revenue from sales, excise, property, and estate taxes is ranked middling.

Retirement Tax Breaks: Double personal exemptions for people over 65; up to $8,700 in pensions, annuities, or endowments may be excluded from taxable income. However, these exclusions must be reduced by the amount of Social Security and Railroad Retirement benefits received.

Pluses: Food, medicine, and disability appliances are exempt from Maryland's 5% sales tax.

Minuses: No significant property-tax breaks for retired homeowners.

MASSACHUSETTS   Tax Burden: 146% of U.S. average

Taxachusetts, a name pinned on the Bay State during the 1970s, still applies. In spite of the 1980 approval by voters of Proposition 2½ (a measure to reduce property taxes), the state's per capita take on property taxes still ranks first in the country. Another overused tax here is the personal income tax.

Retirement Tax Breaks: Pensions, annuities, and endowments from Massachusetts and from federal programs are exempt.

Pluses: State sales tax (5%) exempts food, clothing, and medicine..

Minuses: Dividends and interest taxed at double the rate of earned income; no significant property-tax breaks for retired persons; high estate taxes (seventh in the country in per capita collections).

MICHIGAN   Tax Burden: 119% of U.S. average

Because of huge unemployment obligations in this state, the tax situation is bleak. Michigan is middling in taxable wealth. In per capita dollars, its two heaviest taxes are income tax (tenth in the United States) and property tax (ninth).

Retirement Tax Breaks: Double personal exemptions for persons over 65; pensions from military, federal civil service, state, local, and private systems are exempt up to a maximum of $7,500 for a single taxpayer ($10,000 if filing jointly).

Pluses: Modest inheritance and estate taxes (32nd in the country in revenues).

Minuses: Food, medicine, and clothing are not exempt from Michigan's 4% sales tax. Despite modest breaks for people over 65, income and property taxes remain high compared with those of other states.

MINNESOTA   Tax Burden: 118% of U.S. average

Not only is Minnesota's tax on personal income the highest in the Midwest, it is also notoriously high among all 50 states: fifth in per capita dollars collected. Two other overused taxes in the Gopher State are property taxes, and excise taxes on gasoline, tobacco, and alcohol.

Retirement Tax Breaks: Minnesota excludes from income tax up to $11,000 in pension income from any source. If your gross income is more than $17,000, the exclusion is reduced by the amount over $17,000.

Pluses: Food, clothing, and medicine are exempted from the 5% sales tax.

Minuses: High income taxes with no significant relief for retired people.

MISSISSIPPI   Tax Burden: 68% of U.S. average

In 1900, this state was the poorest in the country; in 1932, it became the first state to adopt a tax on retail sales. Today, Mississippi remains the poorest of the 50 states in potential tax revenue. Its 51-year-old sales tax, however, is its major single source of revenue.

Retirement Tax Breaks: Married couples over 65 filing jointly get a personal exemption of $12,500 on taxable income; additional exemptions include up to $5,000 of federal civil service, military, and private pension benefits.

Pluses: Low property taxes are made even lower by an exemption of $5,000 on assessed valuation for homeowners over 65.

Minuses: Thirteenth highest per capita sales taxes collected in the country, with no exemptions on food, medicine, or clothing.

MISSOURI   Tax Burden: 80% of U.S. average

When it comes to per capita taxable wealth, Missouri ranks 33rd in the country. And it takes a moderate approach to tapping revenue from residents; none of its taxes are exceptionally high or low.

Retirement Tax Breaks: Public-employee benefits from any state including Missouri are entirely exempt. All other income (except Social Security) is taxed without consideration to age or work status.

Pluses: Low property taxes (37th nationally in per capita receipts) and estate taxes.

Minuses: Local sales taxes unrelieved by exemptions; no significant property-tax breaks for retirees.

MONTANA   Tax Burden: 87% of U.S. average

This state is the ninth wealthiest in the country in potential tax revenue. Actual taxes levied is another thing, however. Montana ranks a middle-of-the-road 22nd in total collections per capita. Two overused taxes are the income tax and property tax.

Retirement Tax Breaks: Double personal exemption for people over 65; Montana public-employee benefits entirely exempt; federal civil service and military benefits also exempt up to $3,600.

Pluses: No sales tax.

Minuses: Property-tax collections per capita rank eighth; income-tax collections rank 15th.

NEBRASKA   Tax Burden: 101% of U.S. average

The Cornhusker State, like so many other states in America's midsection, has moderate taxable wealth (29th) and makes a moderate effort to tap that wealth (24th). The most overused tax is the property tax (11th in the country in per capita dollars).

Retirement Tax Breaks: None. Nebraska claims a flat 17% of your federal income-tax liability.

Do Retired Newcomers Help Local Economies?

The Winthrop Rockefeller Foundation, based in Little Rock, Arkansas, stirred up a hot controversy when it pointed out in a recent economic report that attracting retired people from outside of Arkansas wasn't a priority because retired people "contribute little to the state's economic base." An argument offered to support that claim is the fact that, in spite of increases in Social Security and private-pension benefits during the 1970s, "graying" populations usually demand more from government health, welfare, and transportation services than they return in taxes.

Of all the states, only Florida has a greater proportion of people over 65 than Arkansas. A significant number of Arkansas's older residents, particularly in the rural Ozark counties along its northern border, are newcomers from Illinois, Iowa, and Nebraska. Many Mountain Home–Norfork Lake, Harrison, and Bull Shoals natives compare the hard Depression and postwar years with the 1970s and 1980s, and credit the relative good times to retired people who immigrated from the North. "Our banks here have deposits ten times higher than the national average," a local chamber of commerce official told the *Dallas Morning News*. "And our economy here is recession-proof. These people get their regular retirement income regardless of what the economy is doing," he said.

The view that retired newcomers are a boon to an area's economy isn't confined to Arkansas. In Florida, state government economists are well aware that the "mailbox economy" of Social Security, private pension, annuity, interest, and dividend checks goes directly to retailers, doctors, accountants, and other service professionals, as well as local banks and public utilities. Florida may not be completely immune to economic slumps, but neither does the state suffer as harshly as states with younger populations.

Can it be that states might start competing for retired persons to stabilize the local economy much the same way as they skirmish for high-technology industry? Perhaps. "We recognize the value of having what is a fairly affluent elderly population," the *Wall Street Journal* quoted Florida's planning and budget director. "We're happy to see anyone come here who has the resources to take care of themselves."

Pluses: Sales tax exempts medicine; each citizen also gets a $28 food tax credit.

Minuses: High property taxes without any significant tax breaks for retired people.

NEVADA   Tax Burden: 87% of U.S. average

It's said that gambling is Nevada's biggest man-made tax resource, and that if it weren't for the tables and slots in Reno and Las Vegas, the local citizenry would be shelling out money in the form of income taxes and higher property taxes.

Retirement Tax Breaks: No income tax.

Pluses: Nevada is the only state with no inheritance or estate taxes.

Minuses: In spite of exemptions on food and medicine, Nevada's high sales tax (5.75%) results in the eighth highest per capita receipts in the nation.

NEW HAMPSHIRE   Tax Burden: 67% of U.S. average

Southern New Hampshire has been filling up with Boston commuters for a good reason. Compared with Massachusetts (and any other New England or Middle Atlantic state), the Granite State is a tax haven. There is no sales tax here, nor are there taxes on earned income. On the other hand, property and excise taxes are high, a pattern typical throughout New England.

Retirement Tax Breaks: Residents pay no tax on income. There is a 5% tax on interest and dividend income, relieved by a $2,400 exemption for each person over 65 ($4,800 for couples filing jointly).

Pluses: No sales tax.

Minuses: Property taxes per capita rank fifth highest in the country, with modest relief to people over 65 with gross incomes less than $12,000 if married or $10,000 if single.

NEW JERSEY   Tax Burden: 118% of U.S. average

This state was the last to adopt the income tax, doing so in 1976 mainly to tap the earnings of New York City and Philadelphia commuters. The effective property-tax rate here is third highest of the 50 states.

Retirement Tax Breaks: Double personal exemptions for persons 65 and over; persons 62 and over with Social Security benefits are entitled to exclude up to $7,500 in benefits received from any other public or private pension programs. Or, if their income in wages, salaries, or business and partnership profits does not exceed $3,000 and they do not have any other benefits besides Social Security, they can take the same deduction.

Pluses: New Jersey rebates $240 each year to homeowners over 65 from their property taxes. An additional deduction of $250 is allowed homeowners over 65 if their annual income exclusive of Social Security or federal or railroad pensions isn't more than $10,000. Food, clothing, and prescription drugs are exempted from New Jersey's 5% sales tax.

Minuses: Collections from estate and inheritance taxes are fifth highest per capita in the country.

NEW MEXICO   Tax Burden: 75% of U.S. average

The Land of Enchantment has attracted many retired people over the past two decades, and one of the reasons is its relatively small effort to tax property, incomes, and estates. Nationally, the state ranks 17th in taxable wealth but only 27th in the pains it takes to tap that wealth for revenue.

Retirement Tax Breaks: Each taxpayer over 65 may deduct $6,000 from taxable income. Standard deductions are $1,000 additional for each taxpayer ($2,000 for married couples). Furthermore, up to $3,000 from federal, military, and state employee benefits are deductible. If you're over 65, however, you have to reduce your $6,000 exemption by the amount of benefits that you deduct.

Pluses: Low property taxes are further relieved by a $2,000 exemption for veterans; no inheritance taxes.

Minuses: High local sales taxes (fifth in the nation in per capita collections) with no exemptions.

NEW YORK   Tax Burden: 164% of U.S. average

The Empire State collects more direct taxes from its residents than any other state. (Alaska collects more per capita revenue, but the lion's share is paid by oil and gas producers at North Slope fields.) There are three glaringly overused taxes here: personal income (third highest in per capita dollars collected), property (again, third highest), and sales (12th highest).

Retirement Tax Breaks: New York public-employee pensions, and other pensions excludable from federal gross income, are exempt up to $20,000 for persons 60 and over.

Pluses: Groceries, medicine, and disability appliances are exempted from sales tax.

Minuses: New York City's sales tax is the highest in the country (8.5 percent); no significant tax breaks on earned income, interest and dividends, business profits, or residential property for retired people.

NORTH CAROLINA   Tax Burden: 70% of U.S. average

Like South Carolina, the Tar Heel State has no abundance of taxable resources and therefore doesn't make a strenuous effort to extract money from its citizens. Two overused taxes, however, are income (16th highest per capita in the country) and excise (in 1969, North Carolina became the last state in the country to tax cigarettes).

Retirement Tax Breaks: Three thousand dollars of federal civil service or military retirement benefits are exempted. Retired public employees and teachers are exempted from taxes on their benefits.

Pluses: A homeowner over 65 gets an exemption of $8,500 from property-tax valuation if total income is less than $9,000.

Minuses: A sales tax of 4% on everything but medicine and disability appliances.

NORTH DAKOTA   Tax Burden: 76% of U.S. average

The popular conception of the Flickertail State is that it is out of the mainstream, and that the state and its windblown prairie deserve each other. Actually, this agrarian state ranks 14th in taxable wealth per capita, ahead of such industrial states as Michigan and Connecticut. Unlike those two states, however, North Dakota still keeps to the agrarian tradition and doesn't exhaust its taxable wealth for revenue.

Retirement Tax Breaks: Benefits of military people over 60, police officers, fire fighters, and federal civil service employees are exempt up to $5,000, less Social Security.

Pluses: No inheritance tax, low 3% sales taxes reduced even further by exemptions on groceries and medicine.

Minuses: Modest property taxes carry no significant exemptions for retired people.

OHIO   Tax Burden: 85% of U.S. average

The Buckeye State ranks exactly in the middle—25th —of the states in taxable wealth and ranks second lowest in the northeast quadrant of the country (after New Hampshire) in the amount of revenue it extracts from its citizens.

Retirement Tax Breaks: All taxpayers receiving retirement benefits, annuities, or distributions from any retirement plan may exclude $4,000 from their state return. In addition, people over 65 get a $25 credit against tax.

Pluses: Modest property-tax concessions to households with either spouse over 65; food and medicine exempted from sales tax.

Minuses: High (6%) sales tax.

OKLAHOMA   Tax Burden: 64% of U.S. average

In the Sooner State, you won't pay taxes on gasoline, cigarettes, beer, automobiles, mobile homes, or farm tractors. In contrast to Arkansas, its neighbor to the east, Oklahoma could be the sixth richest state in tax revenues in the country if it really wanted to. But apparently it doesn't; nearly all of its taxes are underused, particularly severance taxes on oil and gas and excise taxes on tobacco and liquor.

Retirement Tax Breaks: The first $4,000 of federal civil service benefits, the first $1,500 of military retirement benefits, and only Oklahoma public-employee and teacher benefits are exempt from state income tax.

Pluses: Oklahoma's effective property-tax rate is 42nd in the country.

Minuses: Food, clothing, over-the-counter medicine, and disability appliances aren't exempt from the sales tax; Oklahoma's per capita take from inheritance and estate taxes ranks 17th in the country.

OREGON   Tax Burden: 102% of U.S. average

This state has no sales tax, and it ranks last in its efforts to tax alcohol, tobacco, and gasoline. As for its tax burdens, Oregon has extremely high income and estate taxes (it was the first state to adopt the gift tax). Furthermore, the state ranks 13th in per capita property tax collections.

Retirement Tax Breaks: Military and federal benefits are excluded up to $3,400; however, if your household income is $25,000 or more, you get no deduction. All benefits from Oregon's public-employee retirement programs are exempt.

Pluses: No sales tax; property-tax deferrals are available to homeowners over 62.

Minuses: Oregon's property taxes are the highest taxes west of the Rocky Mountains; its income-tax collections rank fourth per capita in the country, highest of any state west of the Mississippi.

PENNSYLVANIA   Tax Burden: 91% of U.S. average

For a relatively poor state (35th in potential tax revenues) the Keystone State resembles others in the northeastern portion of the country in leaving no possible tax untried. Two greatly overused taxes here are personal income tax and the inheritance tax.

Retirement Tax Breaks: Income in the form of pensions and annuities is exempt. Interest and dividend income is taxable, with no personal exemptions.

Pluses: Groceries and medicine are exempt from sales tax.

Minuses: High (6%) sales-tax rate; extremely high inheritance tax (third in the country in per capita receipts).

RHODE ISLAND   Tax Burden: 103% of U.S. average

After Maine, Rhode Island is the poorest state in the Northeast (43rd in potential tax wealth). Yet the state ranks 18th in the per capita amount of revenue it extracts from all sources. Of those sources, the biggest are residential property, personal income, and estate taxes.

Retirement Tax Breaks: None; Rhode Island claims a flat 22% of the taxpayer's federal income-tax liability.

Pluses: High (6%) sales tax relieved by exemptions for food, clothing, and medicine.

Minuses: High estate taxes (6th in per capita collections in the country); extremely high property taxes with no significant breaks for retired people.

SOUTH CAROLINA   Tax Burden: 68% of U.S. average

For all of South Carolina's industrial growth, particularly in the textile industry and in high technology, the state ranks 48th in taxable wealth (higher than only Mississippi and Alabama). Two taxes that the Palmetto State tends to overuse are income taxes (26th in per capita collections) and general sales taxes (27th).

Retirement Tax Breaks: Married couples over 65 get a double exemption of $3,200 if they file jointly. All pension income for people over 65 is exempted up to $1,200.

Pluses: The first $15,000 of assessed valuation of homes is exempt from property taxes for people over 65 who have lived in South Carolina at least one year.

Minuses: There is a 4% sales tax on everything but fuel and medicine.

SOUTH DAKOTA   Tax Burden: 82% of U.S. average

All else being equal, demographers say, South Dakota will continue to decline in population. This state is a contrast to North Dakota, its neighbor. It is poorer in taxable wealth yet doesn't make up for this deficiency by imposing an income tax.

Retirement Tax Breaks: There is no income tax of any kind in South Dakota.

Pluses: Excise taxes on tobacco and liquor are light (39th nationally in per capita receipts).

Minuses: High sales taxes (19th nationally in per capita collections) with only one exemption: medicine. High property taxes (18th in the country in per capita collections) without any significant exemptions for retired people; high inheritance taxes (15th nationally in per capita collections).

TENNESSEE   Tax Burden: 66% of U.S. average

The Volunteer State adopted the sales tax somewhat late (1947); today retail sales and special taxes on liquor, tobacco, and gasoline are the state's major source of cash. Like other states in the country's southern quarter, Tennessee isn't tax-rich by any standard, nor does it take pains to tap citizens beyond their capacity to pay.

Retirement Tax Breaks: No tax on earned income or income from public and private pensions.

Pluses: Medicine and disability appliances exempted from sales tax.

Minuses: High sales taxes (up to 6.75% in some counties); income from interest and dividends taxed at 6%.

TEXAS   Tax Burden: 67% of U.S. average

Texas is so wealthy in taxable resources that if it were to levy average U.S. taxes on oil, gas, personal income, property, and retail sales it could collect another $6 billion a year in revenue. As it stands, the Lone Star State ranks only 45th in its effort to tap citizens on the big three direct taxes; indeed, there is really no tax that can be regarded as overused here.

Retirement Tax Breaks: There is no income tax in Texas.

Pluses: People over 65 get a $10,000 exemption on their homes from property taxes; furthermore, property taxes cannot increase from the first year of qualification for people over 65; and food and medicine are exempt from sales tax.

Minuses: None.

UTAH   Tax Burden: 97% of U.S. average

There are few tax breaks for retired people in Utah worth writing home about. The state is poor in taxable resources (39th) but manages to extract enough tax dollars to push it into the middle rank of tax collections.

Retirement Tax Breaks: If you're under 65 and retired, pensions and annuities from qualified federal or state plans are deductible up to $4,800; if you're over 65, they are deductible up to $6,000.

Pluses: Modest property taxes, low estate taxes.

Minuses: High (5%) sales taxes unrelieved by any exemptions.

VERMONT   Tax Burden: 92% of U.S. average

The Green Mountain State was the last state in the Union to adopt a sales tax (1969). Much of its revenue comes from property taxes, which it charges the owners of vacation homes and Vermonters with equal rapacity. In fact, its property-tax collections are the tenth highest per capita in the country. Another tax Vermont overuses is the personal income tax.

Retirement Tax Breaks: No significant income-tax breaks. Vermont claims a flat 24% of taxpayer's federal income-tax liability.

Pluses: Vermont's effort to raise revenue through its 4% sales tax rate ranks 46th in the country.

Minuses: No significant tax breaks are offered to retired people.

VIRGINIA Tax Burden: 79% of U.S. average

For all its industrial growth since World War II, the Old Dominion remains relatively poor. Its most overused tax is the one on personal income, which denies a tax haven to Washington, D.C., commuters. Another overused tax is the "sin" excise tax on tobacco, liquor, and gasoline.

Retirement Tax Breaks: Persons over 65 are given a $400 personal exemption on taxable income in addition to Virginia's $600 standard exemption. Everyone over 62 qualifies for a 5% credit. Credits are computed on the difference between what you receive in Social Security benefits and what the maximum benefits are. Also, the credit is reduced by twice the amount of adjusted gross income over $12,000. Result: a negligible break.

Pluses: A modest property tax (35th in the country in per capita collections), with some provision for exemptions and deferrals for people over 65 if household income doesn't exceed $18,000.

Minuses: Most retirement income is subject to a relatively high personal income tax. Groceries and medicine are not exempt from the sales tax.

WASHINGTON Tax Burden: 105% of U.S. average

Washington's sales tax is high (it ranks second in the nation in per capita collections), but this levy that residents encounter every day is partially offset at year's end by the absence of a tax on personal incomes. In addition to the overused sales tax, the Evergreen State's other heavily used taxes are the excise taxes on liquor, tobacco, and gasoline.

Retirement Tax Breaks: No income tax in the state of Washington.

Pluses: Washington voters repealed the inheritance tax effective January 1, 1982.

Minuses: After Hawaii, Washington's sales tax is the highest in collected revenue per capita in the country. Food is not exempt from this tax.

WEST VIRGINIA Tax Burden: 69% of U.S. average

West Virginia is no longer as poor as many people think, ranking 32nd in taxable wealth. The overused sales tax is offset by low taxes on personal income and residential property.

Retirement Tax Breaks: The benefits of firemen and policemen from any state (not just West Virginia) and of ex–military people are not taxed. Up to $8,000 of any other retirement income excluded from your federal income tax is also excluded here once you're 65.

Pluses: West Virginia's effective property-tax rate, after Louisiana's and Hawaii's, is the lowest in the country; in addition, homeowners over 65 get an exemption of $20,000 on residential property valuation.

Minuses: A 5% sales tax, relieved somewhat by exemptions on medicine and disability appliances.

WISCONSIN Tax Burden: 124% of U.S. average

Like its neighbor Minnesota, the Badger State has a tax package with an onerous reputation. Wisconsin's potential tax wealth ranks 30th in the country, yet its actual tax revenues push it up to ninth in the category of collections. The state taps every possible source for revenue, and it overuses three taxes: personal income, inheritance and estate, and property.

Retirement Tax Breaks: Wisconsin public-employee and teacher benefits are exempt.

Pluses: The 5% sales tax exempts food, medicine, and disability appliances.

Minuses: No significant property- or income-tax breaks for retired people.

WYOMING Tax Burden: 129% of U.S. average

Few people realize that, after Alaska, this state is the richest in the country in potential tax wealth per capita. Three features of Wyoming's fiscal scene are its absence of a state income tax, its extremely high property taxes (fourth in the country in per capita collections), and the highest taxes for using an automobile (license, registration, and motor fuel) in the country.

Retirement Tax Breaks: Wyoming has no personal income tax.

Pluses: A 3% state sales tax exempting medicine and disability appliances.

Minuses: No property-tax concessions for retired persons; inheritance tax coupled with an estate tax.

CHANGES IN THE SOCIAL SECURITY PROGRAM

The Social Security legislation enacted by Congress in March 1983 will make the following changes in the program:

- Require Social Security beneficiaries to include one half of their annual Social Security benefit amount in taxable income if that half increases their adjusted gross income to more than $25,000 for individuals and $32,000 for married couples filing joint returns. Nontaxable income is to be added in with adjusted gross income only for the purpose of determining whether to tax half of the Social Security benefit. Taxes will begin with 1984 income.
- Postpone payment of the 1983 cost-of-living adjustment to January 1984, and pay all future cost-of-living adjustments each January.
- Gradually raise the age at which full retirement benefits are paid from 65, beginning in

the year 2000, until it reaches age 67, in 2027. The age at which reduced retirement benefits are paid will stay at 62.

- Improve incentives for older workers to delay retirement in two ways: By increasing the delayed retirement credit in Social Security benefits from 3 percent to 8 percent for each year of delay in retirement prior to age 70 (the credit would rise gradually between 1990 and 2007) and by lowering the rate at which Social Security benefits are decreased for earnings above the limit ($6,600) from $1 for every $2 to $1 for every $3, beginning in 1990.
- Bring new federal employees hired on or after January 1, 1984, and all current members of Congress, the vice-president, and the president under Social Security.
- Bring all employees of nonprofit organizations under Social Security beginning January 1, 1984, and immediately prevent any more state and local governments from withdrawing their employees from Social Security.

Source: Senate Special Committee on Aging, *Special Reports*, March 1983.

OVERCOMING THE "OVERQUALIFIED" OBJECTION

While job discrimination on the basis of age is against the law, you might still be a victim of what labor economists call "statistical discrimination," which happens when an employer assumes three things about an older person applying for a job:

- You want more money because you have more experience.
- Your fringe coverage—life insurance, health insurance, and pension benefits—will cost more than fringes for younger applicants.
- Your prospects for staying with a job and justifying the employer's investment in on-the-job training are less than those of a younger worker.

All of these factors fall under the catch-all word "overqualification"; it's the word most frequently used by an employer when turning down older people who've applied for a job.

Anyone who has worked 20, 30, or 40 years is overqualified by standard definition. Too often, older workers nod agreement, thank the employer for his time, and hit the pavement for more job-hunting.

Why not ask the employer what he means by being overqualified? If you'll go to work at the going rate, plus bring experience and maturity to the job, won't that mean that the cost of your productivity will be less than or equal to a younger worker's? If you're already covered by Medicare and Social Security, won't the employer avoid the cost of health insurance and a

pension plan if you're hired? If the average tenure of younger workers in certain jobs is less than the shelf life of hamburger or yogurt, mightn't you make a better bet for longevity?

SHOULD YOU RAID YOUR SAVINGS?

How long would your savings last if you dipped into it for regular income? Suppose you have a $20,000 savings account with a local savings and loan association earning the standard 5.5 percent interest, compounded quarterly. You could withdraw $136 each month for the next 20 years before your nest egg would be reduced to zero. Or you could take out $92 from the account each month for as long as you want and the $20,000 balance of your savings account would remain intact.

Whether you should raid your savings depends on how much you want to leave your heirs, how well insured you are against medical and other emergencies, how prudently you make other investments, and the vagaries of inflation. Drawing from your savings isn't wrong; after all, it's your money. Some retired persons, however, spend too much of their savings too soon. Others never touch their savings; to their regret, they learn too late that they could easily have afforded more comforts in their retirement.

Drawing on a Savings Account

Starting with savings of . . .	. . . you can withdraw this much each month for the stated number of years, reducing the savings account to zero				OR, you can withdraw this much each month and leave original amount intact
	10 years	**15 years**	**20 years**	**25 years**	
$10,000	$ 107	$ 81	$ 68	$ 61	$ 46
15,000	161	121	102	91	69
20,000	215	162	136	121	92
25,000	269	202	170	152	115
30,000	322	243	204	182	138
40,000	430	323	272	243	184
50,000	537	404	340	304	230
60,000	645	485	408	364	276
80,000	859	647	544	486	368
100,000	1,074	808	680	607	468

Source: Action for Independent Maturity, *Guide to Planning Your Retirement Finances*, 1982.

Figures are based on a standard savings and loan interest rate of 5.5% per year compounded quarterly.

DO-IT-YOURSELF PENSIONING

Before 1982, Individual Retirement Accounts (IRAs) were available only to workers who weren't covered by a pension plan at work. But for tax year 1982 and afterward, any worker can establish an IRA, even if he or she is already covered by a pension plan.

You can invest the lesser of $2,000 or 100 percent of your work income in an IRA. If you have a nonworking spouse, you can establish a "spousal" account with a maximum investment of $2,250 for the two of you. If

How an IRA Grows

The table below shows how an IRA will earn money at differing rates of interest based on a contribution of $2,000 a year.

The column titled "Age" gives the age at which the investor begins making contributions to the account.

For example, if at age 50 you start depositing $2,000 each year to an 11 percent IRA, by the time you turn 65 you will have deposited $30,000, which would be worth $82,001 and would give you a monthly payment of $825.

Age	Total Deposit at Age 65	8%		11%		14%	
		Value at Age 65	Approximate Monthly Payment at Age 65	Value at Age 65	Approximate Monthly Payment at Age 65	Value at Age 65	Approximate Monthly Payment at Age 65
20	$90,000	$961,713	$7,753	$2,845,142	$28,656	$8,958,466	$109,642
25	80,000	632,554	5,099	1,621,049	16,327	4,398,527	53,833
30	70,000	413,125	3,330	920,124	9,267	2,155,727	26,383
35	60,000	266,845	2,151	518,769	5,225	1,052,610	12,882
40	50,000	169,330	1,365	288,950	2,910	510,043	6,242
45	40,000	104,323	841	157,354	1,584	243,182	2,976
50	30,000	60,986	491	82,001	825	111,927	1,369
55	20,000	32,097	258	38,853	391	47,369	579
60	10,000	12,836	103	14,147	142	15,617	191

Source: Bell Federal Savings and Loan Association.

both husband and wife work, each can invest up to $2,000, making it possible for a working couple to put away as much as $4,000 a year.

The amount you invest each year is tax deductible. And the earnings on your IRA are not taxed until you withdraw your money from the account. Unless you become totally disabled, you will have to pay a 10 percent penalty plus any taxes due if you withdraw your money before you reach age 59½. The idea behind an IRA is to not withdraw money until you're retired and in a lower tax bracket. Anyone eligible for an IRA should certainly investigate its advantages. By age 65, the effect of having set aside a maximum of $2,000 each year can be dramatic.

You can put your money into a wide variety of investment plans, from money-market funds and high-tech growth stocks, to pork bellies and propane futures. Banks, savings and loan associations, credit unions, money market and mutual funds, stockbrokers, and life insurance companies administer the plans. Some plans have more administrative costs than others; some allow higher interest rates. Each invests your money in a different way. Once you have an IRA with one institution, you can switch your account to another institution to take advantage of changing economic conditions.

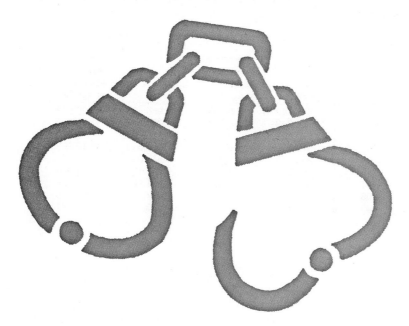

Crime:
Where the safe places are

Does an individual's vulnerability to crime differ from place to place? You bet it does! In the 107 retirement places compared in *Places Rated Retirement Guide*, the variety is enormous. Some places are so safe you couldn't pay someone to assault you; others, by comparison, seem just plain dangerous.

If you decide to retire in Bull Shoals, Arkansas, for example, your odds of encountering any violent crime (murder, rape, assault, or robbery) in a year's residence are about one in 11,111. On the other hand, should you decide to move to Miami, the odds of your encountering violent crime in a year are one in 56. Considering the vast difference in these odds, we could say that Miami is almost 200 times more violent than Bull Shoals.

Some general national trends in crime have been fairly constant throughout the past decade:

- Crime is highest in the big cities and in the South, lowest in rural areas, in the West North Central region of the country, and in most of New England.
- All crimes except robbery are most frequent during July and August.
- Criminal behavior is closely related to the economic status, age, race, and sex of given populations.

- A large number of police per capita is usually an indication of a high-crime area rather than an area where crime is being prevented.
- Robbery, burglary, and larceny are more prevalent in big cities than elsewhere, and the overwhelming majority of these crimes are committed by people with criminal records.
- Two of the most serious violent crimes, murder and aggravated assault, are often committed by people without criminal records, probably because they are usually unpremeditated crimes of passion. Furthermore, there is less difference between urban and rural crime rates for these two felonies than for others.

MAJOR FACTORS LINKED WITH CRIME

What causes crime, and what can be done about it? The FBI has identified several basic factors that are linked with local crime rates:

Population density, as well as the overall size of the area's population. This factor does not appear to affect crime rate directly until population density becomes very high. Thus the high crime rate of a metropolitan area like Miami will be partially attributable to pockets of overcrowding, which can spawn violence. (In fact, of the 107 retirement places compared in this book, seven of the ten rated most dangerous are metro areas, while only one of the ten rated safest—Las Cruces, New Mexico—is a metro area.)

Composition of the population, especially in regard to age and sex. Populations with a high percentage of males between 15 and 25 will almost always have higher crime rates than comparably sized cities with a low percentage of this group.

Economic status of the population, including job availability. High unemployment, especially when coupled with a large percentage of the population that is unskilled, poor, and uneducated, will result in unacceptably high crime. In addition, given similar sets of circumstances, rich people tend to be arrested less frequently than poor people, especially on suspicion. Once arrested, they are convicted with less frequency. This is especially true in regard to property crimes and crimes committed by juveniles.

Cultural conditions of the population, such as educational level and recreational and religious behavior.

Transience. The single most effective weapon against crime—and the factor preventing crime from becoming a problem in the first place—has been found to be the close-knit neighborhood community. Populations that are unstable due to large numbers of people continually moving in and out are almost always high in crime. A highly urbanized area with its population in flux and with little individual commitment to the area's well-being will suffer greater incidence of crime than a more rural setting with little population turnover.

Climate, which has a marked relationship with criminal behavior. As mentioned in the chapter on climate, crimes increase dramatically during certain weather phases. Crime, especially violent crime, tends to be more frequent in warm climates than cold ones. All crimes except robbery occur most frequently in hot months (July and August) and least frequently in cold ones (January and February). Robbery, the exception, is highest in December, perhaps because during the holiday season pedestrians carrying large amounts of cash and stores doing brisk business make tempting targets.

Other factors the FBI has found to be related to crime rates include strength or weakness of the police force; the policies and attitudes of prosecuting officials, judges, juries, and parole boards; and the attitudes of the community toward crime and its tendency to report crime.

One common myth about crime and crime prevention is that the safety of a community rises or falls in direct proportion to the size and strength of the local police force. Not so. Police definitely help to fight crime, but most of what police do is after the fact. They respond to complaints or tips; they search for offend-

Are Older Persons Really More Vulnerable to Crime?

Many people believe that older Americans are especially vulnerable to crime and that they are the preferred targets of criminals. Yet data gathered by the National Crime Survey over the years 1973–80 show that younger persons (especially those between 12 and 34) are the most often victimized. The rates of crime against those over 65 are lower than for any other age group.

The graph shows the victimization rates for all major crimes except murder. Note that the over-65 age group generally averages less than half the rate suffered by the 12–64 age group. In fact, the only group of offenses in which older Americans suffer greater rates than the rest of the population is that of purse-snatching and pocket-picking.

So if you are an older American, you needn't worry about being singled out as a target of crime, because in fact the statistics say you are much less likely than most to be a victim.

Victimization Rates, 1973–80

Age 65 and Over   Age 12–64

Household Larceny
Personal Larceny Without Contact
Household Burglary
Motor Vehicle Theft
Simple Assault
Aggravated Assault
Robbery
Purse-Snatching / Pocket-Picking
Rape

0   20   40   60   80   100   120   140
Rate per 1,000 persons or households

Source: U.S. Department of Justice, "Crimes Against the Elderly," 1981.

Crime in the Retirement Places: Bigger is Almost Never Better

If you study the list of crime rates for the various retirement places (given in the Place Profiles later in this chapter), one factor more than any other will become immediately obvious: Whether you're considering property crimes or crimes of violence, the larger urbanized areas suffer far greater levels of crime than the smaller, more rural places.

For example, of the 17 retirement places with a total property crime rate of 7,000 or more (well above the national average of 5,223), all but four are metropolitan areas. And Las Cruces, New Mexico, is the only metro area among the 17 retirement places registering a property crime total under 2,500, or less than half the national average.

Property Crime in the Retirement Places

Safest Retirement Places	Property Crime Rate	Most Dangerous Retirement Places	Property Crime Rate
1. Clarkesville-Mount Airy, GA	218	1. ATLANTIC CITY–CAPE MAY, NJ	9,734
2. Bull Shoals, AR	519	2. Ocean City–Assateague Island, MD	9,334
3. LAS CRUCES, NM	761	3. LAS VEGAS, NV	9,112
4. Cassville-Roaring River, MO	1,042	4. MIAMI, FL	9,029
5. Rappahannock, VA	1,075	5. WEST PALM BEACH–BOCA RATON, FL	8,579

Source: FBI, *Uniform Crime Reports*, 1981, 1982, and "Crimes by County," unpublished document, 1981.

The property crime rate is the sum of rates for burglary, larceny-theft, and motor vehicle theft.

Metro areas lead the list when it comes to violent crimes, too. Only four non-metro areas are among the 14 retirement places suffering a violent crime rate of 700 or more (the national average is 577.4). And again, Las Cruces stands as the only metro area among 17 retirement places with a violent crime rate under 100.

Violent Crime in the Retirement Places

Safest Retirement Places	Violent Crime Rate	Most Dangerous Retirement Places	Violent Crime Rate
1. Bull Shoals, AR	9.0*	1. MIAMI, FL	1,791.9
2. Eagle River, WI	12.0*	2. LAS VEGAS, NV	1,185.7
3. Clarkesville-Mount Airy, GA	16.0*	3. WEST PALM BEACH–BOCA RATON, FL	1,182.1
4. Big Sandy, TN	46.7*	4. ORLANDO, FL	993.7
5. Mountain Home-Norfork Lake, AR	47.7*	5. Beaufort–Hilton Head, SC	971.4

Source: FBI, *Uniform Crime Reports*, 1981, 1982, and "Crimes by County," unpublished document, 1981.

*These places had no murders in the year for which data were collected.

The violent crime rate is the sum of rates for murder, forcible rape robbery, and aggravated assault.

ers; they apprehend criminals and bring them to trial. But they have very little control when it comes to crime prevention.

In a now famous experiment conducted in Kansas City in the early 1970s, three sections of the city were selected to test the effect of police strength on crime rates. In one area, the number of police and frequency of patrols were doubled; in the second neighborhood (the control neighborhood), the police force maintained its usual strength; in the third section, patrols were halted altogether, and the police entered the neighborhood only in response to calls from residents. All three areas were carefully monitored for a year. When the current crime rates were compared with each section's history of crime, there was practically no difference in crime rates during the experiment in any of the three sections.

What can we infer from these results? Are police unnecessary? Hardly. But the experiment does seem to support the contention that a place's crime rate primarily reflects the nature of its citizenry rather than the size or strength of its police force.

The crime rate of an area indicates more than how safe an individual may be there; along with rates of alcoholism, divorce, and suicide, it is one of four social indicators often cited by sociologists that help provide a rough gauge of a place's social solidarity. Areas with high crime rates tend to have a weak social fabric characterized by transience, poverty, and little sense of community. Low-crime areas, whether rich or poor, are generally characterized by some degree of community spirit and, above all, a willingness on the part of residents to watch out for each other's welfare.

KEEPING TRACK OF CRIME

Each year, more than 15,000 police departments voluntarily submit their arrest data for various crimes to the FBI's Uniform Crime Reporting Program. Seven of these crimes, because of their seriousness, frequency, and likelihood of being reported to police, were chosen to serve as an index for determining trends in crime across the country. They compose the FBI Crime Index offenses and are reported on yearly in the FBI *Uniform Crime Reports:*

Violent Crimes	Property Crimes
murder	burglary
forcible rape	larceny-theft
robbery	motor vehicle theft
aggravated assault	

The FBI distinguishes between violent crimes (those offenses that involve bodily injury or threat of injury) and property crimes (those involving theft of property). Robbery differs from burglary and larceny-theft in that it is a theft or attempted theft by violence or threat of violence. Burglary is defined by the FBI as the unlawful entry of a building to commit a felony or theft, and larceny-theft as the theft of property from the possession of another. This includes purse-snatching, pocket-picking, shoplifting, bicycle theft, and theft from motor vehicles. (Arson was designated an FBI Index offense in 1978 and collection of data was begun during 1979; however, summary tabulations on this property crime are still spotty.) Property crimes are considered less serious than violent crimes and occur far more frequently, accounting for about 90 percent of all crimes recorded by the FBI.

It's important to distinguish between *incidence* of crime and crime *rate*. The actual number of *occurrences* of a crime in a year represents its incidence. Naturally, the bigger the place in terms of population, the greater the incidence of crime tends to be. The only way to determine relative safety is to examine the crime *rate*, which is the incidence of a crime per year per 100,000 people.

If we were to ask ourselves, for example, whether San Diego is "safer" than Albuquerque, we could be misled if we considered only the incidence of crime in the two places. San Diego had 6,594 reports of either murder, rape, assault, or robbery in 1981. That's a lot of violent crime. Albuquerque, on the other hand, reported only 2,985 incidents of violent crime in the same period. Does this mean Albuquerque is less violent than San Diego? Not necessarily. San Diego has almost two million inhabitants, Albuquerque

Crime in the Retirement Places

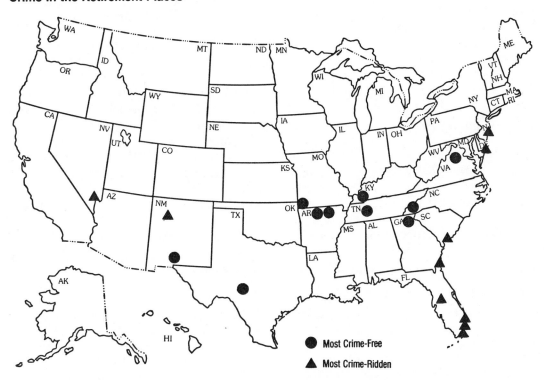

● Most Crime-Free

▲ Most Crime-Ridden

Most Crime-Free Retirement Places	Places Rated Score	Most Crime-Ridden Retirement Places	Places Rated Score
1. Clarkesville–Mount Airy, GA	38	1. MIAMI, FL	2,696
2. Bull Shoals, AR	61	2. LAS VEGAS, NV	2,097
3. LAS CRUCES, NM	163	3. WEST PALM BEACH– BOCA RATON, FL	2,040
4. Rappahannock, VA	173	4. ORLANDO, FL	1,804
5. Big Sandy, TN	175	5. ATLANTIC CITY–CAPE MAY, NJ	1,782
6. Cassville–Roaring River, MO	193	6. FORT LAUDERDALE– HOLLYWOOD, FL	1,756
7. Mountain Home– Norfork Lake, AR	197	7. Brunswick–Golden Isles, GA	1,634
8. Fredericksburg, TX	221	8. Beaufort–Hilton Head, SC	1,574
9. Brevard, NC	243	9. ALBUQUERQUE, NM	1,557
10. Benton–Kentucky Lake, KY	260	10. Ocean City–Assateague Island, MD	1,554

The *Places Rated* score is the sum of the violent crime rate and one tenth the property crime rate.

fewer than half a million. The violent crime *rates* of the two places tell their true relative safety: San Diego has a rate of 627, whereas Albuquerque has one of 847. So which is the safer city? San Diego, although its violent crime rate is nothing to brag about.

The basic shortcoming of the FBI's *Uniform Crime Reports* is its failure to adequately differentiate between violent crimes and the far more numerous but less serious property crimes. In the *Uniform Crime Reports* the two kinds of crime weigh equally in the final Crime Index total. According to this statistical method, stealing hubcaps is counted as heavily as first-degree murder. Obviously, this can be misleading, so in rating retirement places *Places Rated* weighs violent crimes and property crimes differently, to allow a more realistic estimate of relative danger levels.

Many crimes, of course, including many petty thefts and rapes, are never reported to the police, and this affects the Crime Index. And police departments, in turn, often underreport to the FBI to protect or improve their images. In all, it is estimated that fewer than half of all crimes committed are reported to the FBI.

JUDGING SAFETY FROM CRIME

The formula used to rate the 107 retirement places for safety is simple: *Places Rated Retirement Guide* uses the FBI *Uniform Crime Reports* data for violent and property crimes, but since we consider property crimes much less serious than crimes against people, we give them one tenth the weight of violent crimes. Each metro area starts with a base score of zero, and points are assigned according to these indicators:

1. *Violent crime rate.* The rates for all violent crimes—murder, forcible rape, robbery, and aggravated assault—as reported by the FBI are totaled.
2. *Property crime rate.* The FBI rates for burglary, larceny-theft, and motor vehicle theft are added together and the result divided by 10.

The sum of a place's violent crime rate and one tenth its property crime rate, rounded off, represents the score (the higher the score, the more dangerous the place). Each place's rates for specific crimes are given in the Place Profiles later in this chapter.

Sample Comparison: Fort Myers–Cape Coral, Florida, and Front Royal, Virginia

According to the FBI *Uniform Crime Reports*, Fort Myers–Cape Coral, a medium-sized metro area on Florida's southwest coast, and Front Royal, Virginia, a small but relatively industrial town near the gateway to Shenandoah National Park, both have crime rates below the national average: Fort Myers–Cape Coral's FBI Crime Index total for the crimes being considered by *Places Rated* is 5,030 and Front Royal's is 4,389. These figures, representing the incidence of crime per 100,000 population, mean that a person living in either place has about a 5 percent chance of being a victim of crime.

But is Front Royal almost as dangerous to live in as

County Crime Rates Can Be Misleading

We are all aware that in any town, crime will usually be more prevalent in some neighborhoods than in others. So it should be in no way surprising that within the retirement places described in this book, crime rates may vary dramatically from one spot to another.

Obviously, recording and analyzing crime statistics neighborhood by neighborhood would be unwieldy and unrealistic for a guide to retirement places. The crime rates recorded by the FBI for both metropolitan areas and rural counties are based on county boundaries; in the case of metro areas made up of more than one county, the crime rates are averages of the several counties. So even though a retirement place may end up with a crime score locating it among the dangerous places, some parts of it may be virtually crime-free.

An example can be found in the non-metropolitan retirement place of Beaufort–Hilton Head, South Carolina. With a *Places Rated* crime score of 1,574 and a rank of 100 out of 107, there is no doubt that Beaufort County is one of the most crime-ridden and violent places presented here. But despite this poor

social indicator, most of the people with retirement homes (or vacation condos) on Hilton Head Island will tell you they love the place. They probably will not dwell on the fact that less than five miles across Port Royal Sound lies the Marine Corps training base of Parris Island.

What's wrong with military bases? Nothing per se, but in almost all cases they are associated with high crime rates—most especially aggravated assault. In the case of Beaufort-Hilton Head, the rate for aggravated assault is 822, almost three times the national average. Considering the job that may be expected of these soldiers someday, perhaps the high assault rate in military towns is a sign that the young men are taking their calling seriously. However, there is little doubt that those civilians who live around the base— retired people or others—aren't too keen on the violence associated with it.

How safe is Beaufort–Hilton Head? There, as elsewhere, it depends on which part of the county you live in.

Fort Myers–Cape Coral? The *Places Rated* formula says no. A closer look shows that Fort Myers–Cape Coral has a violent crime rate of 500.9 and a property crime rate of 4,530. To arrive at the *Places Rated* score for crime, its violent crime rate (rounded off) is added to one tenth its property crime rate (501 + 453), resulting in a *Places Rated* crime score of 954. Front Royal, by contrast, has a violent crime rate of 149.3, less than one third that of Fort Myers–Cape Coral. When this is added to one tenth Front Royal's property crime rate of 4,249, the Virginia community receives a *Places Rated* score of 574.

By this formula, Front Royal is only about 60 percent as dangerous as Fort Myers–Cape Coral and ranks 34th among the retirement places in safety from crime, while the Florida metro area ranks 71st.

Places Rated: Retirement Places Ranked for Safety from Crime

In ranking the 107 retirement places for relative safety, *Places Rated* uses two criteria: (1) violent crime rate and (2) property crime rate divided by 10. The sum of these rates, rounded off, is the retirement place's score. The higher the score, the more dangerous the place. Places that receive tie scores are given the same rank and are listed in alphabetical order.

Scores in parentheses have been calculated using statewide averages from the FBI for violent and property crime since data on these places were unavailable.

Retirement Places from Safest to Most Dangerous

Places Rated Rank	Places Rated Score	Places Rated Rank	Places Rated Score	Places Rated Rank	Places Rated Score
1. Clarkesville–Mount Airy, GA	38	31. Bar Harbor–Frenchman Bay, ME	526	58. San Luis Obispo, CA	813
2. Bull Shoals, AR	61	32. ASHEVILLE, NC	556	59. Grand Junction, CO	816
3. LAS CRUCES, NM	163	33. Rhinelander, WI	559	60. CHARLOTTESVILLE, VA	822
4. Rappahannock, VA	173	34. Front Royal, VA	574		
5. Big Sandy, TN	175	35. Hot Springs–Lake Ouachita, AR	594	61. Rockport–Aransas Pass, TX	836
6. Cassville–Roaring River, MO	193	36. Paris, TN	600	62. Toms River–Barnegat Bay, NJ	840
7. Mountain Home–Norfork Lake, AR	197	37. Bennington, VT	(622)	63. Easton–Chesapeake Bay, MD	849
8. Fredericksburg, TX	221	37. Brattleboro, VT	(622)	64. OLYMPIA, WA	850
9. Brevard, NC	243	39. Fairhope–Gulf Shores, AL	625	65. Tahlequah–Lake Tenkiller, OK	(867)
10. Benton–Kentucky Lake, KY	260	40. Prescott, AZ	638		
11. Harrison, AR	303			66. Twain Harte–Yosemite, CA	874
12. Canton–Lake Tawakoni, TX	318	41. Branson–Lake Taneycomo, MO	(639)	67. Rehoboth Bay–Indian River Bay, DE	879
13. Oak Harbor, WA	329	41. Table Rock Lake, MO	(639)	68. Lincoln City–Newport, OR	901
14. Hamilton–Bitterroot Valley, MT	338	43. Petoskey–Straits of Mackinac, MI	650	69. Coeur d'Alene, ID	903
15. Lake O' The Cherokees, OK	350	44. Traverse City–Grand Traverse Bay, MI	652	70. SANTA ROSA, CA	908
16. Eagle River, WI	359	45. Delta, CO	660	71. FORT MYERS–CAPE CORAL, FL	954
17. Crossville, TN	365	46. Winchester, VA	676	72. SPRINGFIELD, MO	955
18. Athens–Cedar Creek Lake, TX	395	47. Oscoda–Huron Shore, MI	704	73. Red Bluff–Sacramento Valley, CA	967
19. Cookeville, TN	400	48. Laconia–Lake Winnipesaukee, NH	736	74. BOISE CITY, ID	987
20. St. George–Zion, UT	404	48. Missoula, MT	736	75. LEXINGTON–FAYETTE, KY	1,011
21. Kerrville, TX	410	50. Bend, OR	755	76. Deming, NM	1,050
22. LANCASTER, PA	417	51. McALLEN–PHARR–EDINBURG, TX	759	77. SARASOTA–BRADENTON, FL	1,056
23. Keene, NH	439	52. Nevada City–Donner, CA	782	78. AUSTIN, TX	1,063
24. Hendersonville, NC	463	53. MEDFORD, OR	786	79. Cape Cod, MA	1,083
25. Kalispell, MT	490	54. FORT COLLINS, CO	796	80. SAN ANTONIO, TX	1,090
26. Port Angeles–Strait of Juan de Fuca, WA	494	55. Monticello–Liberty, NY	800	81. Houghton Lake, MI	1,104
27. STATE COLLEGE, PA	507	56. Gainesville–Lake Sidney Lanier, GA	811	82. Maui, HI	1,115
28. Camden–Penobscot Bay, ME	515	57. Roswell, NM	812	83. BILOXI–GULFPORT, MS	1,116
29. Carson City, NV	516			84. Lake Havasu City–Kingman, AZ	1,121
30. North Conway–White Mountains, NH	519			85. COLORADO SPRINGS, CO	1,175

Places Rated Rank	Places Rated Score
86. MELBOURNE–TITUSVILLE–COCOA, FL	1,195
86. Yuma, AZ	1,195
88. Myrtle Beach, SC	1,204
89. SAN DIEGO, CA	1,210
90. RENO, NV	1,278
91. Santa Fe, NM	1,381
92. PHOENIX, AZ	1,416
93. OCALA, FL	1,428

Places Rated Rank	Places Rated Score
94. TUCSON, AZ	1,451
95. Clear Lake, CA	1,500
95. LAKELAND–WINTER HAVEN, FL	1,500
97. DAYTONA BEACH, FL	1,522
98. Ocean City–Assateague Island, MD	1,554
99. ALBUQUERQUE, NM	1,557
100. Beaufort–Hilton Head, SC	1,574

Places Rated Rank	Places Rated Score
101. Brunswick–Golden Isles, GA	1,634
102. FORT LAUDERDALE–HOLLYWOOD, FL	1,756
103. ATLANTIC CITY–CAPE MAY, NJ	1,782
104. ORLANDO, FL	1,804
105. WEST PALM BEACH–BOCA RATON, FL	2,040
106. LAS VEGAS, NV	2,097
107. MIAMI, FL	2,696

Retirement Places Listed Alphabetically

Retirement Place	Places Rated Rank
ALBUQUERQUE, NM	99
ASHEVILLE, NC	32
Athens–Cedar Creek Lake, TX	18
ATLANTIC CITY–CAPE MAY, NJ	103
AUSTIN, TX	78
Bar Harbor–Frenchman Bay, ME	31
Beaufort–Hilton Head, SC	100
Bend, OR	50
Bennington, VT	37
Benton–Kentucky Lake, KY	10
Big Sandy, TN	5
BILOXI–GULFPORT, MS	83
BOISE CITY, ID	74
Branson–Lake Taneycomo, MO	41
Brattleboro, VT	38
Brevard, NC	9
Brunswick–Golden Isles, GA	101
Bull Shoals, AR	2
Camden–Penobscot Bay, ME	28
Canton–Lake Tawakoni, TX	12
Cape Cod, MA	79
Carson City, NV	29
Cassville–Roaring River, MO	6
CHARLOTTESVILLE, VA	60
Clarkesville–Mount Airy, GA	1
Clear Lake, CA	95
Coeur d'Alene, ID	69
COLORADO SPRINGS, CO	85
Cookeville, TN	19
Crossville, TN	17
DAYTONA BEACH, FL	97
Delta, CO	45
Deming, NM	76
Eagle River, WI	16
Easton–Chesapeake Bay, MD	63
Fairhope–Gulf Shores, AL	39
FORT COLLINS, CO	54
FORT LAUDERDALE–HOLLYWOOD, FL	102

Retirement Place	Places Rated Rank
FORT MYERS–CAPE CORAL, FL	71
Fredericksburg, TX	8
Front Royal, VA	34
Gainesville–Lake Sidney Lanier, GA	56
Grand Junction, CO	59
Hamilton–Bitterroot Valley, MT	14
Harrison, AR	11
Hendersonville, NC	24
Hot Springs–Lake Ouachita, AR	35
Houghton Lake, MI	81
Kalispell, MT	25
Keene, NH	23
Kerrville, TX	21
Laconia–Lake Winnipesaukee, NH	48
Lake Havasu City–Kingman, AZ	84
LAKELAND–WINTER HAVEN, FL	95
Lake O' The Cherokees, OK	15
LANCASTER, PA	22
LAS CRUCES, NM	3
LAS VEGAS, NV	106
LEXINGTON–FAYETTE, KY	75
Lincoln City–Newport, OR	68
Maui, HI	82
McALLEN–PHARR–EDINBURG, TX	51
MEDFORD, OR	53
MELBOURNE–TITUSVILLE–COCOA, FL	86
MIAMI, FL	107
Missoula, MT	48
Monticello–Liberty, NY	55
Mountain Home–Norfork Lake, AR	7
Myrtle Beach, SC	88
Nevada City–Donner, CA	52
North Conway–White Mountains, NH	30
Oak Harbor, WA	13
OCALA, FL	93

Retirement Place	Places Rated Rank
Ocean City–Assateague Island, MD	98
OLYMPIA, WA	64
ORLANDO, FL	104
Oscoda–Huron Shore, MI	47
Paris, TN	36
Petoskey–Straits of Mackinac, MI	43
PHOENIX, AZ	92
Port Angeles–Strait of Juan de Fuca, WA	26
Prescott, AZ	40
Rappahannock, VA	4
Red Bluff–Sacramento Valley, CA	73
Rehoboth Bay–Indian River Bay, DE	67
RENO, NV	90
Rhinelander, WI	33
Rockport–Aransas Pass, TX	61
Roswell, NM	57
St. George–Zion, UT	20
SAN ANTONIO, TX	80
SAN DIEGO, CA	89
San Luis Obispo, CA	58
Santa Fe, NM	91
SANTA ROSA, CA	70
SARASOTA–BRADENTON, FL	77
SPRINGFIELD, MO	72
STATE COLLEGE, PA	27
Table Rock Lake, MO	41
Tahlequah–Lake Tenkiller, OK	65
Toms River–Barnegat Bay, NJ	62
Traverse City–Grand Traverse Bay, MI	44
TUCSON, AZ	94
Twain Harte–Yosemite, CA	66
WEST PALM BEACH–BOCA RATON, FL	105
Winchester, VA	46
Yuma, AZ	86

Place Profiles: Crime Rates in 107 Retirement Places

The following charts detail each retirement place's rates for seven FBI Crime Index offenses: murder, forcible rape, robbery, aggravated assault, burglary, larceny-theft, and motor vehicle theft. These offenses are divided into violent and property crimes and a total rate for each of the categories is also given.

All figures for metropolitan areas and the larger counties are based upon the 1982 FBI *Uniform Crime Reports*. Another FBI source, "Crimes by County," was used to determine crime rates in most of the rural areas

described in this book. Since "Crimes by County" lists only incidence of crime and not crime rate (incidence per 100,000 population), the rates for these smaller counties were computed by the authors. Because two different sets of data were used for these profiles, some crime rate figures (for robbery and aggravated assault) were rounded off. The figures for some places are enclosed in parentheses and represent statewide averages for crime rates from the FBI. Data for these retirement places were unavailable.

	Violent Crime Rates					Property Crime Rates				Places Rated Score	Places Rated Rank
	Murder	Forcible Rape	Robbery	Aggravated Assault	Total	Burglary	Larceny-Theft	Motor Vehicle Theft	Total		
U.S. National Average	9.8	35.6	251	281	577.4	1,632	3,122	469	5,223	1,099.7	—
ALBUQUERQUE, NM	13.5	58.3	268	507	846.8	2,369	4,314	418	7,101	1,557	99
ASHEVILLE, NC	7.8	13.9	53	165	239.7	840	2,110	210	3,160	556	32
Athens–Cedar Creek Lake, TX	6.9	13.8	9	95	124.7	1,045	1,545	113	2,703	395	18
ATLANTIC CITY–CAPE MAY, NJ	10.0	59.8	382	357	808.8	2,382	6,620	732	9,734	1,782	103
AUSTIN, TX	8.8	58.2	142	183	392.0	1,842	4,511	354	6,707	1,063	78
Bar Harbor–Frenchman Bay, ME	2.4	11.9	10	109	133.3	1,434	2,386	109	3,929	526	31
Beaufort–Hilton Head, SC	6.1	59.3	84	822	971.4	2,074	3,653	295	6,022	1,574	100
Bend, OR	6.4	19.1	38	98	161.5	1,297	4,344	286	5,927	755	50
Bennington, VT	(4.3)	(33.0)	(28)	(63)	(128.3)	(1,560)	(3,080)	(293)	(4,933)	(622)	37
Benton–Kentucky Lake, KY	0	7.8	4	66	77.8	656	1,040	128	1,824	260	10
Big Sandy, TN	0	6.7	7	33	46.7	594	667	20	1,281	175	5
BILOXI–GULFPORT, MS	14.6	49.2	144	355	562.8	1,860	3,310	357	5,527	1,116	83
BOISE CITY, ID	4.0	38.1	72	315	429.1	1,803	3,551	229	5,583	987	74
Branson–Lake Taneycomo, MO	(10.4)	(23.2)	(82)	(115)	(230.6)	(915)	(2,922)	(244)	(4,081)	(639)	41
Brattleboro, VT	(4.3)	(33.0)	(28)	(63)	(128.3)	(1,560)	(3,080)	(293)	(4,933)	(622)	37
Brevard, NC	4.2	0	8	63	75.2	573	1,019	88	1,680	243	9
Brunswick–Golden Isles, GA	9.7	75.1	259	567	910.8	2,743	4,101	390	7,234	1,634	101
Bull Shoals, AR	0	0	0	9	9.0	273	211	35	519	61	2
Camden–Penobscot Bay, ME	0	12.0	36	75	123.0	1,036	2,735	148	3,919	515	28
Canton–Lake Tawakoni, TX	3.1	9.2	12	95	119.3	785	1,069	135	1,989	318	12
Cape Cod, MA	1.3	21.5	54	349	425.8	2,711	3,496	365	6,572	1,083	79
Carson City, NV	3.7	14.7	101	114	233.4	800	1,802	224	2,826	516	29
Cassville–Roaring River, MO	5.0	0	5	79	89.0	481	536	25	1,042	193	6
CHARLOTTESVILLE, VA	15.6	18.2	64	169	266.8	853	4,502	193	5,548	822	60
Clarkesville–Mount Airy, GA	0	0	12	4	16.0	51	148	19	218	38	1
Clear Lake, CA	10.7	37.3	56	830	934.0	2,535	2,879	243	5,657	1,500	95
Coeur d'Alene, ID	1.6	27.9	46	337	412.5	1,414	3,245	241	4,900	903	69
COLORADO SPRINGS, CO	6.7	58.7	185	289	539.4	2,117	3,930	312	6,359	1,175	85
Cookeville, TN	0	8.4	23	74	105.4	1,156	1,606	185	2,947	400	19
Crossville, TN	3.5	10.5	21	115	150.0	1,024	968	157	2,149	365	17
DAYTONA BEACH, FL	11.7	58.9	222	465	757.6	2,501	4,787	352	7,640	1,522	97
Delta, CO	0	9.6	43	240	292.6	1,092	2,343	230	3,665	660	45
Deming, NM	6.2	31.2	87	337	461.4	1,983	3,592	306	5,881	1,050	76
Eagle River, WI	0	0	6	6	12.0	1,171	2,102	197	3,470	359	16

	Violent Crime Rates					Property Crime Rates				Places Rated Score	Places Rated Rank
	Murder	Forcible Rape	Robbery	Aggravated Assault	Total	Burglary	Larceny-Theft	Motor Vehicle Theft	Total		
U.S. National Average	9.8	35.6	251	281	577.4	1,632	3,122	469	5,223	1,099.7	—
Easton–Chesapeake Bay, MD	0	19.3	73	374	466.3	1,038	2,620	170	3,828	849	63
Fairhope–Gulf Shores, AL	7.6	17.7	57	225	307.3	1,119	1,864	191	3,174	625	39
Fort Collins, CO	4.6	30.9	21	185	241.5	1,302	4,035	204	5,541	796	54
Fort Lauderdale–Hollywood, FL	16.1	51.3	445	442	954.4	2,744	4,633	643	8,020	1,756	102
Fort Myers–Cape Coral, FL	11.5	36.4	174	279	500.9	1,510	2,778	242	4,530	954	71
Fredericksburg, TX	0	21.4	14	29	64.4	421	1,020	121	1,562	221	8
Front Royal, VA	0	23.3	23	103	149.3	1,264	2,831	154	4,249	574	34
Gainesville–Lake Sidney Lanier, GA	21.2	25.1	74	235	355.3	1,384	2,858	319	4,561	811	56
Grand Junction, Co	3.6	34.6	61	185	284.2	1,273	3,718	328	5,319	816	59
Hamilton–Bitterroot Valley, MT	0	4.4	4	128	136.4	392	1,549	70	2,011	338	14
Harrison, AR	0	7.7	4	42	53.7	598	1,777	116	2,491	303	11
Hendersonville, NC	8.5	10.1	24	174	216.6	992	1,286	186	2,464	463	24
Hot Springs–Lake Ouachita, AR	7.0	8.3	73	323	411.3	40	1,636	151	1,827	594	35
Houghton Lake, MI	0	73.7	43	154	270.7	3,441	4,454	442	8,337	1,104	81
Kalispell, MT	3.8	38.3	2	140	184.1	723	2,157	178	3,058	490	25
Keene, NH	3.2	12.7	27	73	115.9	768	2,298	160	3,226	439	23
Kerrville, TX	3.3	9.9	23	96	132.2	1,044	1,644	86	2,774	410	21
Laconia–Lake Winnipesaukee, NH	0	14.8	22	104	140.8	1,855	3,847	245	5,947	736	48
Lake Havasu City–Kingman, AZ	8.8	7.0	79	453	547.8	1,488	3,822	425	5,735	1,121	84
Lakeland–Winter Haven, FL	11.7	52.0	135	691	889.7	1,845	3,965	296	6,106	1,500	95
Lake O' The Cherokees, OK	4.2	16.7	38	63	121.9	988	1,172	125	2,285	350	15
Lancaster, PA	1.7	7.4	46	72	127.1	835	1,889	170	2,894	417	22
Las Cruces, NM	3.1	18.7	17	48	86.8	301	395	65	761	163	3
Las Vegas, NV	23.6	78.1	653	431	1,185.7	3,446	4,936	730	9,112	2,097	106
Lexington–Fayette, KY	6.6	36.6	156	226	425.2	1,657	3,837	363	5,857	1,011	75
Lincoln City–Newport, OR	5.6	30.7	59	246	341.3	1,879	3,387	332	5,598	901	68
Maui, HI	2.8	45.6	64	146	258.4	2,376	5,824	361	8,561	1,115	82
McAllen–Pharr–Edinburg, TX	10.3	14.4	38	223	285.7	1,677	2,741	314	4,732	759	51
Medford, OR	2.3	17.3	66	146	231.6	1,459	3,861	224	5,544	786	53
Melbourne–Titusville–Cocoa, FL	4.5	36.2	115	418	573.7	2,003	3,882	323	6,208	1,195	86
Miami, FL	34.5	68.4	863	826	1,791.9	2,926	5,227	876	9,029	2,696	107
Missoula, MT	5.4	40.4	5	167	217.8	941	3,929	315	5,185	736	48
Monticello–Liberty, NY	6.1	24.5	67	250	347.6	2,568	1,759	198	4,525	800	55
Mountain Home–Norfork Lake, AR	0	3.7	4	40	47.7	617	825	55	1,497	197	7
Myrtle Beach, SC	7.7	34.5	95	484	621.2	1,922	3,866	43	5,831	1,204	88
Nevada City–Donner, CA	11.3	37.6	49	269	366.9	1,382	2,520	250	4,152	782	52
North Conway–White Mountains, NH	10.6	24.8	7	57	99.4	1,379	2,634	184	4,197	519	30
Oak Harbor, WA	0	2.2	16	55	73.2	772	1,790	95	2,557	329	13
Ocala, FL	8.7	49.1	163	501	721.8	2,458	4,294	313	7,065	1,428	93
Ocean City–Assateague Island, MD	9.7	58.4	110	442	620.1	3,013	5,912	409	9,334	1,554	98
Olympia, WA	10.2	37.7	53	176	276.9	1,757	3,747	223	5,727	850	64
Orlando, FL	10.8	66.9	311	605	993.7	3,055	4,657	395	8,107	1,804	104
Oscoda–Huron Shore, MI	10.6	17.7	25	202	255.3	1,380	2,965	145	4,490	704	47
Paris, TN	0	24.2	48	176	248.2	1,239	2,094	190	3,523	600	36

	Violent Crime Rates					Property Crime Rates					Places Rated Score	Places Rated Rank
	Murder	Forcible Rape	Robbery	Aggravated Assault	Total	Burglary	Larceny-Theft	Motor Vehicle Theft	Total		
U.S. National Average	9.8	35.6	251	281	577.4	1,632	3,122	469	5,223	1,099.7	—
Petoskey–Straits of Mackinac, MI	0	8.8	40	136	184.8	1,389	3,011	251	4,651	650	43
PHOENIX, AZ	9.2	41.6	224	359	633.8	2,296	5,044	484	7,824	1,416	92
Port Angeles–Strait of Juan de Fuca, WA	2.0	8.1	18	69	97.1	962	2,862	146	3,970	494	26
Prescott, AZ	8.5	11.4	38	195	252.9	1,120	2,480	246	3,846	638	40
Rappahannock, VA	0	16.3	0	49	65.3	798	277	0	1,075	173	4
Red Bluff–Sacramento Valley, CA	7.5	30.0	68	336	441.5	1,280	3,708	261	5,249	967	73
Rehoboth Bay–Indian River Bay, DE	7.1	24.5	45	331	407.6	1,315	3,200	199	4,714	879	67
RENO, NV	9.8	67.9	247	250	574.7	2,111	4,431	490	7,032	1,278	90
Rhinelander, WI	0	26.7	7	57	90.7	1,498	2,979	207	4,684	559	33
Rockport–Aransas Pass, TX	0	40.4	54	390	484.4	1,204	2,045	269	3,518	836	61
Roswell, NM	5.7	30.6	46	264	346.3	1,221	3,269	170	4,660	812	57
St. George–Zion, UT	0	7.4	19	67	93.4	511	2,409	189	3,109	404	20
SAN ANTONIO, TX	18.8	40.3	177	245	481.1	2,161	3,442	489	6,092	1,090	80
SAN DIEGO, CA	8.4	51.6	279	288	627.0	1,923	3,267	637	5,827	1,210	89
San Luis Obispo, CA	3.1	43.4	60	261	367.5	1,428	2,779	248	4,455	813	58
Santa Fe, NM	5.3	29.3	84	733	851.6	1,141	3,857	292	5,290	1,381	91
SANTA ROSA, CA	6.0	40.3	99	219	364.3	1,706	3,420	310	5,436	908	70
SARASOTA–BRADENTON, FL	5.1	51.1	125	302	483.2	1,884	3,615	232	5,731	1,056	77
SPRINGFIELD, MO	5.3	21.2	66	148	240.5	2,304	4,588	251	7,143	955	72
STATE COLLEGE, PA	.9	10.6	31	94	136.5	787	3,058	124	3,969	507	27
Table Rock Lake, MO	(10.4)	(23.2)	(82)	(115)	(230.6)	(915)	(2,922)	(244)	(4,081)	(639)	41
Tahlequah–Lake Tenkiller, OK	(9.0)	(35.2)	(115)	(267)	(426.2)	(1,589)	(2,404)	(418)	(4,411)	(867).	65
Toms River–Barnegat Bay, NJ	2.6	19.6	89	165	276.2	1,742	3,628	274	5,644	840	62
Traverse City–Grand Traverse Bay, MI	0	25.7	29	103	157.7	1,245	3,530	167	4,942	652	44
Tucson, AZ	6.9	44.6	189	398	638.5	2,473	5,231	419	8,123	1,451	94
Twain Harte–Yosemite, CA	0	37.3	29	414	480.3	1,413	2,352	172	3,937	874	66
WEST PALM BEACH–BOCA RATON, FL	12.1	61.0	318	791	1,182.1	2,718	5,320	541	8,579	2,040	105
Winchester, VA	7.8	9.7	56	114	187.5	1,145	3,537	205	4,887	676	46
Yuma, AZ	3.2	41.2	120	403	567.4	1,684	4,244	352	6,280	1,195	86

Et Cetera

REGIONAL PATTERNS OF CRIME

Certain areas of the country are more prone to certain crimes than others, and although rates for individual offenses will vary from place to place and from year to year, regional patterns have shown little change in the past two decades. For example, the murder rate is traditionally highest in the South, usually about twice as high as that in the North Central states. Rape is highest in the western states (especially Alaska) and has been for some time. Rape is lowest in the Northeast and the West North Central states. Armed robbery, always a crime of big cities, is highest in the Middle Atlantic states, lowest in the North Central and East South Central regions. Assault rates are highest in the West and South and lowest in the West North Central area.

Among the safer areas of the country are the Ozark region of southern Missouri and northern Arkansas, and the Southern Appalachian Highland region, which encompasses Clarkesville–Mount Airy, Georgia; Brevard, North Carolina; and Rappahannock, Virginia. That Camden–Penobscot Bay, Maine, ranks among the safest retirement places should come as no great surprise to those who study crime and its geographic patterns, since Maine, like the other two northern New England states (Vermont and New Hampshire), has traditionally had very low rates for all crimes. Benton–Kentucky Lake, Kentucky, enjoys the generally favorable social indicators found in much of the Mid-South region.

The distribution of the dangerous places follows traditional patterns of high crime rates that any criminologist would recognize immediately. For example, many of the country's most dangerous places are located on the East Coast from New Jersey southward. What's the reason for this? For one thing, all of these coastal areas have shown tremendous growth rates over the past 30 years. New people moving into an area disrupt neighborhoods and social patterns. Florida especially has had explosive increases in population —including many displaced Caribbean islanders—and

now suffers from the instability and crime that such growth can spawn.

But there are other reasons as well. Professional criminals gravitate to places where the living is easy and the pickings bountiful; they don't stay in the declining industrial towns of the North but head South to warm weather and popular resorts and tourist towns. This is one reason Las Vegas and Miami have been plagued by high crime for decades.

Finally, most of the dangerous places are hot much of the year. Knowing what we do about climate's influence on crime, it is not terribly surprising that large cities in the steamy South have traditionally been among America's most crime-ridden and violent. Thus, retirees leaving places like Cedar Rapids, Iowa; Lansing, Michigan; Madison, Wisconsin; Schenectady, New York; or Lincoln, Nebraska, to make their new homes in places like West Palm Beach, Orlando, Phoenix, or Las Vegas may be in for a rude shock as far as personal safety is concerned.

Regional Crime Rates

Region	Violent Crime Rates				Property Crime Rates		
	Murder	Forcible Rape	Robbery	Aggravated Assault	Burglary	Larceny-Theft	Motor Vehicle Theft
U.S. National Average	9.8	35.6	250.6	281	1,632	3,122	469
Northeast: Maine, New Hampshire, Vermont, Massachusetts, Rhode Island, Connecticut	4.0	23.4	204.6	240	1,584	2,760	729
Mid-Atlantic: New York, New Jersey, Pennsylvania	9.3	28.5	453.7	265	1,631	2,708	627
East North Central: Ohio, Indiana, Illinois, Michigan, Wisconsin	8.2	30.8	200.5	219	1,394	3,118	454
West North Central: Minnesota, Iowa, Missouri, North Dakota, South Dakota, Nebraska, Kansas	5.2	23.8	118.3	170	1,278	2,947	273
South Atlantic: District of Columbia, Delaware, Maryland, Virginia, West Virginia, North Carolina, South Carolina, Georgia, Florida	12.2	38.8	246.1	370	1,698	3,299	330
East South Central: Kentucky, Tennessee, Alabama, Mississippi	10.5	28.4	126.5	213	1,285	2,207	270
West South Central: Arkansas, Louisiana, Oklahoma, Texas	14.8	42.0	174.1	286	1,684	2,872	475
Mountain: Montana, Idaho, Wyoming, Colorado, New Mexico, Arizona, Utah, Nevada	7.8	39.1	150.4	313	1,756	4,043	373
Pacific: Washington, Oregon, California, Alaska, Hawaii	11.0	54.1	326.9	364	2,144	3,898	593

Source: FBI, *Crime in the United States*, 1982.

Regions are those defined by the FBI. Figures are crime rates (incidence per 100,000 population) for 1981.

Violent Crime in the States

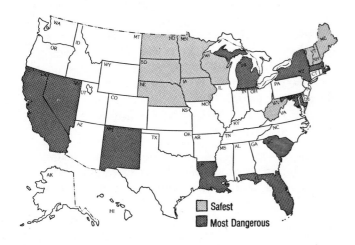

☐ Safest

■ Most Dangerous

Safest States	Violent Crime Rate	Most Dangerous States	Violent Crime Rate
1. North Dakota	67.9	1. New York	1,069.4
2. South Dakota	105.1	2. Florida	965.0
3. Vermont	127.9	3. Nevada	896.4
4. New Hampshire	147.2	4. Maryland	887.1
5. West Virginia	175.0	5. California	863.4
6. Nebraska	181.3	6. New Mexico	671.5
7. Wisconsin	187.7	7. Michigan	642.4
8. Maine	195.5	8. South Carolina	640.9
9. Iowa	203.6	9. Louisiana	637.7
10. Minnesota	228.2	10. Massachusetts	632.5

Source: FBI, *Crime in the United States,* 1982.

Property Crime in the States

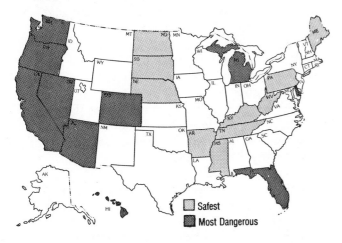

☐ Safest

■ Most Dangerous

Safest States	Property Crime Rate	Most Dangerous States	Property Crime Rate
1. West Virginia	2,443	1. Nevada	7,695
2. South Dakota	2,908	2. Florida	7,068
3. North Dakota	2,924	3. Arizona	7,038
4. Mississippi	3,233	4. Colorado	6,822
5. Kentucky	3,242	5. California	6,728
6. Pennsylvania	3,312	6. Oregon	6,558
7. Arkansas	3,486	7. Hawai	6,295
8. Tennessee	3,899	8. Washington	6,294
9. Nebraska	3,996	9. Michigan	6,212
10. Maine	4,048	10. Delaware	6,180

Source: FBI, *Crime in the United States,* 1982.

States Ranked for Safety from Crime, from Safest to Most Dangerous

State and Places Rated Rank	Places Rated Score	Violent Crime Rate (Rank)	Property Crime Rate (Rank)
1. North Dakota	360	67.9 (1)	2,924 (3)
2. South Dakota	396	105.1 (2)	2,908 (2)
3. West Virginia	419	175.0 (5)	2,443 (1)
4. New Hampshire	565	147.2 (4)	4,175 (12)
5. Nebraska	581	181.3 (6)	3,996 (9)
6. Maine	600	195.5 (8)	4,048 (10)
7. Kentucky	613	289.0 (14)	3,242 (5)
8. Vermont	621	127.9 (3)	4,933 (27)
9. Mississippi	628	305.0 (16)	3,233 (4)
10. Wisconsin	646	187.7 (7)	4,579 (21)
11. Iowa	655	203.6 (9)	4,512 (20)
12. Arkansas	659	310.7 (17)	3,486 (7)
13. Minnesota	679	228.2 (10)	4,507 (19)
14. Pennsylvania	703	372.1 (21)	3,312 (6)
15. Idaho	708	282.8 (13)	4,248 (14)
16. Montana	729	252.6 (12)	4,765 (25)
17. Virginia	757	322.0 (18)	4,350 (15)
18. Indiana	761	341.7 (19)	4,198 (13)
19. Tennessee	802	412.0 (22)	3,899 (8)
20. Utah	844	298.5 (15)	5,451 (34)
21. North Carolina	845	436.6 (25)	4,084 (11)
22. Oklahoma	868	426.6 (23)	4,410 (16)
23. Kansas	873	369.8 (20)	5,035 (29)
24. Hawaii	877	247.9 (11)	6,295 (44)
25. Illinois	894	443.9 (27)	4,506 (18)
26. Wyoming	900	429.8 (24)	4,702 (24)
27. Alabama	913	470.5 (30)	4,428 (17)
28. Rhode Island	983	442.1 (26)	5,410 (33)
29. Connecticut	987	448.4 (29)	5,390 (32)
30. Ohio	991	496.3 (32)	4,951 (28)
31. Missouri	1,021	540.3 (36)	4,811 (26)
32. Georgia	1,056	548.0 (37)	5,081 (30)
33. Washington	1,077	447.3 (28)	6,294 (43)
34. Texas	1,084	532.1 (34)	5,518 (35)
35. Louisiana	1,101	637.7 (42)	4,630 (22)
36. South Carolina	1,109	640.9 (43)	4,679 (23)
37. Delaware	1,127	509.2 (33)	6,180 (41)
38. Oregon	1,134	478.7 (31)	6,558 (45)
39. Massachusetts	1,153	632.5 (41)	5,207 (31)
40. New Jersey	1,191	631.0 (40)	5,599 (37)
41. Alaska	1,213	615.2 (39)	5,980 (40)
42. Colorado	1,214	532.2 (35)	6,822 (47)
43. New Mexico	1,224	671.5 (45)	5,529 (36)
44. Michigan	1,264	642.4 (44)	6,212 (42)
45. Arizona	1,280	575.8 (38)	7,038 (48)
46. Maryland	1,454	887.1 (47)	5,671 (38)
47. California	1,536	863.4 (46)	6,728 (46)
48. New York	1,653	1,069.4 (50)	5,836 (39)
49. Nevada	1,666	896.4 (48)	7,695 (50)
50. Florida	1,672	965.0 (49)	7,068 (49)

Source: FBI, *Crime in the United States,* 1982.

The *Places Rated* score is the sum of the violent crime rate and one tenth the property crime rate.

CRIME ON THE DECLINE

And you thought crime was still on the rise?

According to the U.S. Justice Department's Bureau of Justice Statistics, there were 4.1 percent fewer victims of crime in 1982 than the previous year, one of the biggest declines in the last decade. The number of Americans who were victimized by crime in 1982 was 39.8 million, compared with 41.5 million in 1981.

Lower rates of burglary and larceny were largely responsible for the overall drop: Household burglary was down 10 percent and household larceny 5 percent. Although rape fell 1.4 percent, personal robbery 3 percent, and assault 1 percent, the bureau said these figures did not represent a significant change over the last two years.

The bureau's report is based on Census Bureau interviews in about 58,000 households comprising some 132,000 individuals, and it includes crimes that were not reported to the police. Only about one of three crimes and about one of two violent crimes is reported to the police, the bureau estimated.

The decline in crime reported by the bureau mirrors the data collected by the FBI, which indicated a 3 percent drop in the number of serious crimes reported to police in 1982. The FBI also reported a decline of about 3 percent in such violent crimes as murder, robbery, rape, and aggravated assault for 1982, while the rates of property crimes of burglary, larceny, theft, and motor vehicle theft fell 4 percent.

Among the explanations offered by the Bureau of Justice Statistics for the overall decline in crime were a population with a smaller percentage of crime-prone younger people; longer sentences being handed down by many courts, which may act as a deterrent; and a record number of criminals now in prison who are temporarily unable to commit crimes.

DON'T BE A VICTIM OF STREET CRIME

Most older people's fear of crime is out of proportion to the likelihood of their being victimized. As was pointed out in the introductory section of this chapter, people age 65 and over are actually the victims of most crimes less than half as frequently as the general population. The only major crime category in which older Americans suffer greater rates than the rest of the population is "personal larceny with contact," a term that covers mugging, purse-snatching, and pocket-picking. Thugs like to select older victims on the assumption that they will offer less resistance and will be slow to give chase.

What can people do to protect themselves from these street crimes? The precautions vary with the crime. Muggers look for isolated pedestrians in deserted areas. Alleys, unlighted parking lots, dimly lit parking garages, or dark streets are where they like to strike. Avoid these places—at least when you're walking alone—and you greatly reduce your risk of being mugged. Retirement communities and neighborhoods that encourage street activities and community gatherings discourage muggers because people go out together rather than alone.

But just as crowds and activity discourage muggers, they encourage pickpockets. These thieves like crowded, busy locations and careless people. And purse-snatchers, most of whom are teenagers, often select older victims. To make it harder for these criminals to make you their next victim, here are some basic defense strategies:

- Never carry a wallet in your back pocket. Even an amateur pickpocket can manage to lift it and escape before you even realize what's happening.
- Don't dangle your handbag at your side or leave it unattended on store counters while you shop or in your shopping cart at the supermarket. In fact, if you can avoid it, *don't carry a purse at all*. Instead, tuck money and credit cards in an inside pocket. If you can sew, make a small hidden cloth pocket inside your coat for valuables.
- Avoid flashing your cash around. This is a signal to potential robbers, especially if you present an image of one who is not strong or fast. They might follow you to a spot where it's easy to rob you.
- Arrange your schedule so you don't have to walk alone on dark, deserted streets. Stay clear of shrubbery and parked cars, which are convenient hiding places for criminals. Try to have at least one friend accompany you when you must go out on night errands.
- Don't wait alone at bus or subway stops. Whenever possible, walk up to the next stop where other people are waiting.
- Don't enter dark parking lots or dimly lit underground parking garages alone. Even if you're in a hurry, wait until others arrive and walk close to them. The same holds true of elevators: Don't enter one alone or with a stranger—wait until a group arrives.
- Unless you are specially trained and licensed, forget carrying a lethal weapon; an attacker may only use it against you.
- Arrange for direct deposit of Social Security benefits, paychecks, and dividends to your bank account. This will reduce the risk of theft from your mailbox and the risk of the checks being stolen from you as you take them to the bank.

According to the U.S. Department of Justice, this all boils down to three commonsense rules:

- **Be aware** of situations in which street crimes can occur.
- **Be alert** at all times, even in your own neighborhood.

• **Be accompanied** by a friend or group whenever possible, especially in high-risk neighborhoods or at night.

If you do become a victim of a street crime, do not resist or attempt to overpower your attacker. To do so might enrage or frighten him into severely injuring you. Sit down—even on the sidewalk—so you won't be thrown or knocked down. If you are in an isolated area, screaming for help may frighten or anger a mugger. Many police officials suggest that you always carry some cash with you so that your assailant will not harm you simply out of frustration. If you are in a relatively busy area, making noise may attract help and scare the criminal away. Yell or use a whistle or alarm device that you can carry in your pocket. What about carrying a small container of Mace? It is illegal without a permit in many cities. In any case, it may only infuriate your assailant. Questions about this or any other protection device should be referred to local police.

THE GREAT LAND SCAM

Every year interstate real-estate operators ring up more than $4 billion in land sales. During the 1970s, one of the unfortunate results of this extremely lucrative business was to leave a million Americans with real estate they didn't want and couldn't sell. Many of these unwitting buyers who found themselves holding title to swampland or desert were retired people looking for a spot to put up a vacation home or permanent residence.

Purchasing out-of-state land is always risky, especially if the buyer does not visit the property for an on-site inspection. Even if you do see the homesite before buying, it may be very difficult to be sure the developer will actually follow through on promised amenities. The beautifully illustrated brochure and booklets will describe golf courses, landscaped parks, swimming pools, clubhouses, and marinas, but any promise not clearly outlined in the sales contract is not enforceable. What you consider to be a sound retirement investment may turn out to be no more of a sure thing than the prospects at the two-dollar window at the track.

"You can always resell your lot if you change your mind," the salesperson will tell you. "In fact, the developer will buy it back from you." What is not revealed is that the price you are paying for the lot has already been inflated to nearly twice its real value to cover the advertising and other initial sales costs. Where do you suppose the money comes from for the fancy literature, the gourmet dinners fed to prospective buyers, the free trips often proffered to hot prospects who want to see what they're buying? Right out of that earnest money you're about to write a check for, that's where! So even if you do successfully resell your lot, you may take a heavy loss on the transaction.

A Land Buyer's Rights

Recent federal legislation designed to protect the buyer from unscrupulous brokers and developers applies to subdivided land sold or advertised in more than one state. Here are some of the provisions:

• The buyer has seven calendar days in which to back out of any sales agreement. A legal or legitimate reason is not necessary for the cancellation.
• Any buyer who fails to receive a property report before signing a purchase agreement may cancel the agreement up to two years from the time of signing.
• Buyers who do not receive a warranty deed within 180 days of signing a purchase agreement may, in most cases, cancel the agreement.
• Buyers who legally revoke their contracts are entitled to a refund.
• For a period of not more than three years after signing the purchase contract, the buyer may sue the seller if he: sells property without giving the property report to the buyer before he signs the contract; sells any property when the property report contains any false fact or omits a material fact; provides or distributes promotional material that is inconsistent with material in the property report.

Here are some important things to check on before signing any land-purchase agreement:

• Where will your lot be in relation to other homes, public buildings, and stores?
• Has there been an analysis of soil and subsoil by qualified experts to be sure it is suitable for building?
• If the lot has ocean or lake frontage, might there be serious erosion problems in the future? What about flooding? This is a distinct possibility if your lot is lower than those around you and drainage is not properly controlled.
• Do actual measurements of the lot conform to the legal description?

The Office of Interstate Land Sales Registration (OILSR) publishes a free booklet called "Before Buying Land, Get the Facts." Send for it and do a little homework on real-estate investment before making any commitment. Their address is Room 4108, 451 Seventh Street, S.W., Washington, D.C., 20411.

Always be on guard if sales tactics appear excessively high-pressured. It's your right to know everything possible about the property you are considering buying, so if your salesperson is less than forthright in answering your questions, you'd probably better back away.

Get everything in writing—the refund policy, financing terms, community amenities to be built, and the timetable for building them. Most important of all, be sure the developer delivers a property report to you. If you have any difficulty obtaining this report from the seller, send $2.50 to OILSR and they will furnish one.

If you do visit the site of a proposed new development in which you are considering an investment, do a little detective work while you're there. Visit other realtors, the county tax assessor's office, perhaps the local newspaper, and ask some questions. Do area residents believe that everything is on the up-and-up and that prices set on the property are fair? Has anyone heard of any pending lawsuits or shady dealings?

Finally, if the deal looks good and there is nothing to indicate any sort of fraud, be sure to get a detailed financial statement from the developer and check out his reputation for integrity and the soundness of his financial backing. Not all losses on land deals are the result of outright dishonesty—sometimes the developer simply goes broke! This can be even more disastrous for the buyer than outright chicanery, since there may be even less possibility of recouping one's losses.

CON MEN AND CONSUMER FRAUD

P. T. Barnum is credited with the wise but cynical comment that there is "a sucker born every minute and two [con men] to take advantage of him." He was speaking from bitter experience; twice in his lifetime he was the victim of swindlers.

Why do people continue to fall for ancient con games? Basically, because the proposals sound too good to pass up and because the people who present them appear to be sincere and honest individuals.

Older people, who are likely to have sizable bank accounts, are favorite targets of these unscrupulous folks. It's hard to believe that people can still be taken in by the thousand-year-old scam known as the "pigeon drop," in which a "mark" is persuaded to ante up some of his or her own money in order to be cut in on an imaginary find of a small fortune. A similar game involves persuading a victim that he can help bank examiners and the FBI catch an embezzler by withdrawing some of his funds and turning them over to the supposed law enforcement officer.

Despite the fact that these scams have been around for centuries and have been exposed time after time, victims continue to be bilked out of literally tens of billions of dollars every year. Consumer fraud, too, nets billions for its perpetrators. Here are some common examples:

Home repair frauds are perpetrated by crooks working in tandem. One poses as a building inspector who "discovers" serious violations and the need for immediate repairs, for example, to a homeowner's furnace.

Don't Forget to Lock Your Plane

If you're planning to use your private airplane a lot near your retirement home, be forewarned: Three popular retirement states led the nation in aircraft thefts during 1982.

Nationwide some 600 airplanes were stolen last year; thefts in Florida accounted for 27 percent of the total, trailed by 16 percent in California and 14 percent in Texas. Intelligence officers of the Drug Enforcement Administration (DEA) linked many of the Florida thefts with illegal drug traffic.

Apparently, owners of airplanes should observe the same basic precautions law enforcement officials urge upon automobile owners. "Most of the aircraft were parked and tied down near runways," said a spokesperson for the DEA, "but left unlocked by careless owners. All the thieves had to do was hot-wire the ignition."

Shortly afterward the accomplice arrives, pretending to be a repairman who can perform the needed work at low cost. Typically, little or nothing is done to the furnace, but the victim gets a bill for several hundred dollars.

Con men playing the *home improvement* game may show up late in the day, offering to perform some service, such as installing insulation, at half price. They claim they have just finished a job in the neighborhood and have material left over, which accounts for the good deal they can give you. You have to make up your mind on the spot and shell out the money immediately. The job probably never gets finished, and the materials used are worth even less than the bargain price you paid.

Another fraud aimed primarily at older people is the *work at home* scheme, offering extra income to people who can knit baby booties at home, assemble fishing tackle in their basement, or make costume jewelry in their living room. Some such ventures are honest, but most are not. Beware especially of ads that require an initial investment in materials you'll need to make products the advertising company claims it will sell for you. In most cases your "small initial investment" is never earned back.

There are door-to-door sales swindles, charity frauds, and mail frauds, with new angles being dreamed up all the time. Here are some things to keep in mind to avoid being conned:

- Be suspicious of high-pressure sales tactics aimed at quickly parting you from your money. If a salesman or repairman is reluctant to give you time to think things over, don't deal with him.
- Beware of any person or organization that insists on payment in cash rather than by check or money order.

- If you're in doubt about the legitimacy of any person or deal, say you want time to check the situation out with local officials or the Better Business Bureau. Legitimate operators will not object to this; crooked ones will disappear.
- Whenever possible, deal with local people and institutions whose good reputation is known to you. If you are in a new location, act slowly and ask around before committing yourself to anything.

SECURITY FACTORS IN A RETIREMENT COMPLEX

If you are considering retiring in a community of any sort—high-rise apartment or condominium, trailer park, townhouse complex, housing tract, or enclosed dwelling with adjoining courtyards and interior patios—you should examine four basic security factors: opportunity for surveillance, differentiation of space and territory, access control, and supportive siting and clustering.

Opportunity for Surveillance. How well both residents and police patrols can watch what is going on is determined almost totally by the design of the building complex. The ability to survey, supervise, and question strangers will depend on how each residence is designed and on its relationship to neighboring dwellings. How close elevator doors are to apartment entrances, the number of apartments opening onto each landing, the location and proximity of parking lots and open spaces, the layout of streets and walkways, the evenness and intensity of both exterior and interior lighting—all of these factors affect ease of surveillance.

All entryways and walkways should be clearly visible to residents and police at any time of day or night. This means that the landscaping surrounding them should be level and free from obstacles and heavy foliage. Walkways should be evenly illuminated at night with lamps that are not so bright as to cause light "tunnels."

Housing units built in clusters in which residents know their neighbors generally encourage watchfulness. In large buildings, if only a few apartments open onto a common landing or hallway, the same sort of neighborly concern is promoted.

Differentiation of Space and Territory. This is another important aspect of building design. The most dangerous places within large buildings have been found to be interior public areas with no definite territorial boundaries. Areas seemingly belonging to no one are, in effect, open to everyone. When places are definitely marked off, an intruder will be more obvious, and owners and neighbors will be alerted to potential danger more quickly.

Access Control. Obviously, the quality of locks, doors, doorframes, and windows affects how easily your residence can be entered. Yet many builders give little attention to these details. Still less may be given to entrances, a surprising fact when you consider that the design and layout of entrances are crucial elements in security, since they define territory and boundaries to residents, visitors, and intruders.

Entrances and exits to a complex should be limited in number, and entrance routes should pass near activity areas so that those who come and go can be observed by many people. An increasingly popular type of retirement community designed for metro areas high in crime (like many found in Florida, for example) consists of an enclosed complex of either condominium townhouses or cluster homes surrounded by a wall or secure fence and connected by courtyards and terraces. The entrance in these developments is usually a single gate guarded by a watchman who probably has closed-circuit television and elaborate communications systems.

Siting and Clustering. The placement of buildings on the grounds and their relationship to each other affect ease of access. In complexes where the design allows anyone to wander at will between dwellings or through courtyards, the opportunity for crime increases. When residences are clustered so that entrances face each other and access is limited, strangers are less likely to wander through and are more apt to be questioned if they do. The practice of clustering units together, then, limits access naturally and unobtrusively, while at the same time providing a setting for the casual social contacts between neighbors that promote security.

Beware the Armed Camp. Despite the obvious feeling of security that walls, fences, guard posts, and television scanners provide for retirees in a community setting, too heavy a concentration of these precautions should be a warning flag to the potential resident. Security measures piled on top of one another, like excessive numbers of police with attack dogs, are an indicator of unacceptably high crime in the area. If, upon inspecting your "model community," you sense an inordinate preoccupation with security, it's wise to make local inquiries about crime or simply eliminate the community from consideration altogether.

Health and Health Care:
Chief concerns for a fulfilling retirement

As America's retirement-aged population becomes an ever larger segment of the total population, ideas and attitudes about this special time of life are undergoing major changes. Retirement, once viewed as the final and sedentary stage of life, is now considered by most people to be an active period of work, leisure, continuing education, and compelling interests.

Many of our hopes for a "good" retirement are predicated on good health. Health is important at any age, and retirees often put good health ahead of sound finances when asked to rank retirement concerns. Even persons currently in good health—wisely— sometimes plan for health problems they may have in the future when making retirement decisions.

The chapter "Climate and Terrain" deals with many of the biometeorological factors that can affect the way people feel. This chapter touches upon more conventional kinds of health-related information, of special interest to the older segments of the population, and also surveys the health-care facilities available in the 107 retirement places.

SOME MISCONCEPTIONS ABOUT AGING AND HEALTH

"Retirement is supposed to be a fulfilling period, but by the time you reach age 65 you really don't have many years left to enjoy yourself—after all, the average life expectancy is only a little over 70."

The fact is that scientists who specialize in research on aging think the average life span could be well over 100 years. It's important to remember that life expectancies are based on total populations and include all those who die in infancy or in youth. For example, a person born in 1979 had an average life expectancy of 73.7 years *at birth*. But the longer that person survives, the longer the total life expectancy: Persons who had reached age 65 in 1979, for example, could expect an average of an additional 16.6 years, pushing their life span to more than 80 years. In effect, the statistics say, the longer you have lived, the longer you will live.

"Who wants to live forever, anyway? Aging invariably leads to physical and mental decline, including an end to your sexual life."

There are some physical changes to experience as part of aging. Some of the visible signs of aging are graying hair, loss of hair (though this can happen in relative youth), wrinkled or sagging skin, diminution of strength and endurance, onset of dental problems, or twitching, throbbing muscles that formerly never acknowledged fatigue. But these visible signs are not life-threatening, and many can be dealt with successfully by such means as exercise, diet, cosmetics, or even face-lifts.

Aging and frailty or dissipation of strengths need not necessarily go hand in hand. More often cultural expectation is the culprit. All older people do not become biologically incapable of physical accomplishments or sexual relations; rather, factors other than age may have a greater effect than is realized and can cause problems. Bodily organs and systems fail at different rates and for different reasons. Excessive alcohol consumption, for example, damages the liver and is thought by some authorities to affect sexual function. Being chronically overweight places stress on the heart. Lack of exercise affects circulation in a harmful way. And many stresses of everyday life can contribute to failing capabilities.

Some people fear that senility or loss of mental capacity is also an inevitable result of aging. But the fact is that most mental problems result from illness or brain damage and not from aging itself. Older people use mental-health services at about half the rate of the general population, and true senility affects only a small percentage of elderly.

"There's nothing I can do about my health—and besides, I'm headed for a nursing home in any case."

Your life-style has tremendous influence on your health. Your physician will tell you that a few good habits will do a great deal to help you avoid unnecessary illnesses and keep you feeling fit:

- Moderate, regular exercise
- Proper nutrition and weight control
- No smoking and moderate consumption of alcohol
- Adequate sleep
- Regular medical care, including periodic checkups and needed immunizations

A study conducted at the California Department of Health and Human Population Laboratory found that such healthful habits could increase the average life span in men by 11 years and in women by seven years.

As to ending up in a nursing home, less than 5 percent of America's over-65 population is likely to spend time in a nursing home. It should be remembered that in any case some persons in every age group are ill and need round-the-clock care. According to the National Opinion Research Center, fully 60 percent of people over age 65 who are not in institutions say they are in good or excellent health; of the general U.S. population, by contrast, 74 percent rate their health as good or excellent.

MAJOR HEALTH CONCERNS

The outlook for a healthy retirement for older Americans has never been better. Life expectancy is on the rise and, in fact, the decline in death rates has been particularly evident in the upper age groups: The annual death rate for women 85 and older fell by nearly one third between 1950 and 1978, and that of men dropped by about 20 percent. Most older Americans are in reasonably good health; 80 percent of them live independently without any assistance; another 15 percent require only limited assistance.

Yet retirement-aged people are susceptible both to a wide variety of ailments that strike most people and to certain conditions that single out members of the older segment of the population.

America's Leading Killers

The odds are that the average American will die of heart disease, which causes 38.2 percent of all deaths each year in the United States. The term "heart disease" encompasses many different maladies—including disease of the valves, membrane infections, degeneration of tissue, enlargement of the heart, irregularities of the heart's rhythm—but they all interfere with the main function of the heart, which is to distribute blood throughout the body. The death rate from heart disease is falling, but it is still the nation's number-one killer. Actuaries estimate that a 65-year-old could expect to live 11.4 years longer than at present if heart disease were eliminated.

Cancer is next, claiming 20.9 percent of total annual deaths. Unlike heart disease, cancer has been on the rise, causing about 4 percent more deaths now than it did ten years ago. Stroke is the third leading killer, causing about 8.6 percent of all deaths each year.

The top three killers—heart disease, cancer, and stroke—have also traditionally been the most common causes of death among the older population. According to the National Center for Health Statistics, these three accounted for more than three quarters of all deaths of people 65 and over in 1978. Heart disease was the number-one cause of death from age 45 on, its incidence increasing from 30.9 percent of deaths at ages 45–54 to 48.2 percent of deaths at 85 and over.

Life Expectancy in the United States

Age in Years*	White Male	White Female	Black Male	Black Female	Average for Everyone	Total Average Life Expectancy for Everyone
At birth	70.6	78.2	64.0	72.7	73.7	73.7
10	61.8	69.3	56.0	64.5	65.0	75.0
20	52.3	59.5	46.4	54.8	55.4	75.4
30	43.2	49.8	37.9	45.3	46.1	76.1
40	33.9	40.2	29.6	36.2	36.8	76.8
45	29.4	35.6	25.8	31.9	32.2	77.2
50	25.1	31.0	22.1	27.8	27.9	77.9
55	21.2	26.7	18.8	24.0	23.9	78.9
60	17.5	22.6	15.3	20.4	20.0	80.0
65	14.2	18.7	13.3	17.2	16.6	81.6
70	11.3	15.0	10.7	13.9	13.4	83.4
75	8.8	11.7	8.6	11.5	10.6	85.6
80	6.9	9.0	7.8	10.7	8.4	88.4
85 and over	5.5	7.0	6.8	9.2	6.7	91.7+

Source: U.S. Bureau of the Census, *Statistical Abstract of the United States; 1982–83, 1982.*

*Figures are for age in 1979.

The Top 10 Killers

These ten causes accounted for 85 percent of all deaths in 1980, with heart disease, cancer, and stroke accounting for 68 percent of all deaths.

Cause of Death	Estimated Rate per 100,000 People
Heart diseases	336.0
Malignant neoplasms	183.9
Cerebrovascular diseases	75.1
Accidents	46.7
Chronic obstructive pulmonary conditions	24.7
Influenza and pneumonia	24.1
Diabetes mellitus	15.4
Chronic liver conditions and cirrhosis of the liver	13.5
Atherosclerosis	13.0
Suicide	11.9

Source: National Center for Health Statistics, *Monthly Vital Statistics Report, Advanced Data: Final Mortality*, 1980, 1983.

Cancer was the second most common cause of death in the 45-and-over population but, in contrast to heart disease, declined as a percentage of total deaths with advancing age: 30.2 percent of those between 45 and 54 died of cancer in 1978, while only 18 percent of those between 75 and 84 did. Stroke was the second most prevalent cause of death in the 85-and-over age group, claiming 15.5 percent of all mortalities.

The most common causes of death in people over 45 after heart disease, cancer, and stroke were influenza and pneumonia, cirrhosis of the liver, diabetes, and arteriosclerosis. In the under-45 age group, accidents ranked first as a cause of death, whereas for those 65 and older accidents were only the seventh leading cause. Similarly, suicide was common in younger age groups but accounted for less than 4 percent of all deaths for persons over 65.

Other Health Problems

Not all the ailments of retirement-aged people are as deadly as they are annoying or painful. Such conditions as arthritis and diabetes, which can affect mobility and the degree to which people can care for themselves, commonly plague those in the older age groups. According to a 1979 survey by the National Center for Health Statistics, more than 80 percent of older Americans have at least one chronic condition, and multiple conditions are common.

In 1979 the most frequently reported chronic condition in the 65-and-over age group was arthritis, cited by 44 percent of the population surveyed. A blanket term for more than 100 diseases of the joint, "arthritis" can mean gout, rheumatoid arthritis, or the osteoarthritis that affects the majority of those of retirement age in some form or another, usually stiffness and swelling in the joints. More than 31 million people in the United States suffer from arthritis.

The chronic conditions reported most frequently after arthritis in 1979 were hypertension, at 39 percent; hearing impairment, 28 percent; heart conditions, 27 percent; visual impairments, 12 percent; and diabetes, 8 percent.

Despite the prevalence of chronic conditions among the older population, most of these persons reported in the 1979 survey that their disabilities did not prevent them from functioning normally. Of the 80 percent of Americans 65 and over who reported having a chronic condition, fewer than one in six said they could no longer carry on regular activities because of their ailments, and only one in five reported being limited in daily activities.

A HEALTH-CARE INVENTORY

For many people, the availability of a variety of health-care facilities could be an important part of their decision about where to live in retirement. *Places Rated Retirement Guide* does not attempt to judge the relative quality of medical care from location to location, but it does survey both general health-care facilities and those of special interest to an older population. The Place Profiles later in this chapter provide a complete listing of the principal health-care services in each of the 107 retirement places.

Health-care facilities are generally found in greatest abundance in large metropolitan areas, especially those with universities. This does not mean that a person cannot receive excellent medical care in a rural area of a poor state, or, conversely, experience medical care that is bad enough to be life-threatening in even the best of hospitals. The quality of medical care most people receive depends on a number of variables, including blind chance and human error.

Basic Health-Care Institutions

The backbone of any community's health-care program is in its physicians and such basic institutions as hospitals. The supply of physicians is an important indicator of the quality of health care. (And because physicians tend to be well educated and well paid, one could even argue that where they choose to live and practice might be an indicator of a place's desirability.) There is a national average of 160–170 physicians for each 100,000 people in America. Rural areas tend to have fewer than this, metro areas many more.

Physicians per Capita

Retirement Places with the Most	Physicians per 100,000 Residents	Retirement Places with the Fewest	Physicians per 100,000 Residents
1. CHARLOTTESVILLE, VA	501	1. Deming, NM	28
2. Winchester, VA	387	2. Canton–Lake Tawakoni, TX	33
3. Petoskey–Straits of Mackinac, MI	325	3. Lake O' The Cherokees, OK	35
4. Easton–Chesapeake Bay, MD	323	4. Tahlequah–Lake Tenkiller, OK	40
5. LEXINGTON–FAYETTE, KY	302	5. Athens-Cedar Creek Lake, TX	46

A close examination of the retirement locations with the fewest physicians per capita shows that they are small places that have experienced recent, rapid growth. It is likely that the supply of physicians will rise as these places become more established communities.

What about places with the highest concentrations of physicians? Since a great supply of doctors is typically associated with large metro areas, the list may seem surprising. But it should be noted that the three non-metro locations are all affluent communities long known as good retirement spots. Charlottesville, the leader, is a small metro area that is the home of the University of Virginia and its medical school.

The number of hospitals and hospital beds varies tremendously among the retirement places. Although the number of hospital beds is not as valuable an indicator as it once was, before advances in medicine and pharmacology shortened the typical hospital stay, it is still a valid measurement of the relative health-care supply. The nationwide average is about 500 hospital beds per 100,000 residents. Places with fewer than 300 beds for each 100,000 residents could be considered deficient in this respect, and five of the retirement places fall below this average. Carson City, Nevada, has only 75 beds per 100,000; and Houghton Lake, Michigan; Ocean City-Assateague Island, Maryland; Rappahannock, Virginia; and Rockport-Aransas Pass, Texas, all have no hospitals and therefore no hospital beds.

At the other extreme is Kerrville, Texas, which leads the retirement places with 6,961 beds per 100,000 residents; Charlottesville is a ·distant second, with 2,562 beds per 100,000. Many of Kerrville's hospital beds, however, are not available to the general population; they are in specialty institutions, some of which treat long-term specific ailments, such as burns, tuberculosis, or mental cases.

Don't be discouraged by the statistical unavailability of hospital beds if an area appeals to you. There may be good facilities just a short drive away. If you lived in Carson City, for example, only 30 miles would separate you from Reno, which ranks 12th among the retirement places for its health-care facilities. Residents of Ocean City-Assateague Island may have to travel to Baltimore or Washington for sophisticated care, but there are many good small hospitals on the Eastern Shore, places that are more than adequate for routine care. This is not to say that you should not be concerned about a shortage of hospital beds, but you probably can get to a nearby hospital in case of need. You have to decide if the trade-offs of other facilities in your chosen area are worth some compromise. (The book *Places Rated Almanac*, which rates and ranks America's metro areas, would be a good source for checking out health-care facilities in places other than those surveyed here.)

A number of the retirement places, most of them

Health-Care Price Tag: Out of Sight

If the figure $322 billion sounds high enough to be the U.S. gross national product, guess again—it's the total amount Americans paid in 1982 for health care.

The future promises little improvement. By 1990, government forecasts say, the annual cost of national health care will climb to $756 billion. Standard and Poor's estimates are even higher, putting the total at $480 billion by 1985 and $821 billion by 1990.

According to *Consumers Digest*, health costs in 1982 alone rose three times faster than the overall rate of inflation. The main culprit was hospital costs, which have increased five and a half times since 1965. The average hospital stay, for example, skyrocketed from $316 in 1965 to $1,844 in 1980. Consumer costs rose two and a half times during the same period.

This overall increase in health-care costs has prompted the U.S. Bureau of Labor Statistics to advise the retired person who has been spending 6 percent of his or her income on health care to budget at least 9 percent of that income for health care during retirement.

The average daily cost for a semiprivate hospital room in 1982 was $165, with prices generally highest in parts of the West, Midwest, and East, and lowest in the South.

Average Daily Hospital Room Rates: The States Ranked

State and Rank	Average Daily Room Charge	State and Rank	Average Daily Room Charge
1. District of Columbia	$233	26. Indiana	$146
2. Alaska	217	26. Minnesota	146
3. California	215	26. Utah	146
4. Illinois	190	26. Wisconsin	146
5. Pennsylvania	186	30. Arizona	145
		30. Missouri	145
6. Michigan	185	32. Florida	140
7. New York	184	32. Kansas	140
8. Oregon	182	34. Iowa	139
9. Massachusetts	180	35. West Virginia	137
10. Hawaii	177		
		36. Nebraska	133
10. Ohio	177	36. Oklahoma	133
12. Delaware	172	38. Virginia	132
12. Washington	172	39. South Dakota	131
14. New Jersey	171	40. Kentucky	130
15. Nevada	169		
		40. Wyoming	130
16. Vermont	168	42. Alabama	124
17. Colorado	167	43. Georgia	123
17. New Hampshire	167	44. North Dakota	122
19. Rhode Island	166	45. Texas	119
20. Connecticut	162		
		46. Louisiana	116
21. Maine	159	47. Arkansas	114
22. New Mexico	152	48. Tennessee	111
23. Idaho	151	49. North Carolina	110
23. Montana	151	50. South Carolina	108
25. Maryland	148	51. Mississippi	94

Source: Health Insurance Association of America, *Source Book of Health Insurance Data*, annual.

Figures are for 1982 cost to patient for semiprivate room.

metro areas, include medical schools, teaching hospitals, and comprehensive cancer treatment centers among their facilities. These can all be considered indicators of health-care quality as well as health-care capacity.

Medical schools are scarce; there are approximately 125 in America. They attract every type of medical talent: physicians, diagnosticians, psychiatrists, nurses, teachers, and hospital specialists. Furthermore, these schools are integrated with teaching hospitals, where one can obtain medical care supervised by medical school faculty. The interaction between medical school and hospital encourages the development and use of the most recent techniques, equipment, and therapy. Constant review and discussion of cases by faculty and students, a necessary part of the teaching process, helps prevent sloppy or inept care. Only eight retirement places have medical schools, and all are metro areas: Albuquerque; Charlottesville; Lexington-Fayette, Kentucky; Miami; Reno; San Antonio; San Diego; and Tucson. Each of these eight also has the companion institution, the teaching hospital.

Most hospitals have some equipment and staff for the treatment of cancer, but few are so completely equipped that they qualify as comprehensive cancer treatment centers in accordance with the guidelines defined and maintained by the National Cancer Institute. Of the 107 retirement places, only four—Lexington-Fayette, Miami, San Diego, and Tucson—offer this facility.

Community Mental Health Centers

The role of community mental health centers has expanded over the 20 years since they were mandated by the Mental Retardation Facilities and Community Mental Health Centers Construction Act of 1963. The centers were set up to relieve overburdened state and county hospitals by providing local care to those patients who qualified. The idea was timely, and it coincided with accelerated developments in pharmacology. A whole new generation of drugs effective in treating and controlling many forms of mental illness and depression resulted in a massive outflow of patients who previously had had to be confined. The community mental health centers were forced to grow to handle their load, and they now offer a wide range of services, including:

- Screening and follow-up care to patients who have been discharged from mental hospitals
- Specialized services for children and for the elderly
- Alcohol and drug abuse services
- Counseling and treatment on an outpatient basis for all members of the community
- Other appropriate services on inpatient and emergency basis

Community mental health centers are available in 42 of the retirement places. They are particularly valuable in retirement communities, since they are usually skilled in treating depression, a common problem for older people. For persons on fixed incomes or with limited financial means, the centers are especially beneficial.

Hospices

Hospices, or health-care services and facilities for terminally ill patients, originated in Europe and have recently become one of the fastest-growing segments of health care in America. It is estimated that there are some 1,200 hospices across the country; 25 retirement places have at least one.

The term "hospice" means not just a place but a

Think About Your Drinking Water

About half of all Americans drink water from nearly 9,500 fluoridated community systems. What is fluoride? It is the salt form of the element fluorine, which, like gold, iron, or magnesium, can occur naturally in our soil and water. Natural traces of fluoride are found in many foods and in about a third of the nation's water. Most parts of Texas, Illinois, Iowa, Oklahoma, and Ohio have water that is naturally fluoridated.

Fluoride is ingested much like iron, which is beneficial to the blood and may be obtained by eating certain foods, drinking water with traces of iron in it, or by taking pills, capsules, or liquids that contain iron compounds. You may already be aware that fluoridation benefits young people whose teeth are developing, but did you know that it can also be important to retirement-aged people, whose bones need the extra

protection fluoridation offers?

Fluoride has nothing to do with the taste of water or with other qualities such as softness, hardness, acidity, and so on. Some research indicates that some types of "hard" water—water with large amounts of dissolved salts and minerals—may be helpful in preventing certain cardiovascular problems, principally coronary heart disease and stroke. For reasons that are not clear, the dissolved substances (salts of calcium and magnesium, especially carbonates, as well as sulfates and chlorides) seem to protect people from cardiovascular disease. So if you retire to a place with hard water, check with the local or county health department before you install a water purifier or softener. The minerals causing the hard water may actually be good for you.

concept. There are four basic principles that set hospice care apart from conventional life-saving or life-prolonging alternatives offered by most hospitals:

- The terminally ill patient and his or her family, not just the patient, are considered the unit of care.
- An interdisciplinary team (physician, nurse, social worker, clergy, and volunteers) is used to assess the total needs of the patient and family on a continuing basis and to develop a general plan to provide coordinated care.
- Although pain and other symptoms associated with terminal illness and its previous treatments are controlled, no "heroic" efforts are made to cure the patient.
- Bereavement follow-up is provided to the family to help them cope with their suffering.

Hospices may be any of several types: freestanding units within local hospitals, special units or departments within local hospitals, special hospital teams, freestanding autonomous units, or volunteer home-care personnel. In all cases, however, the function of the hospice program and team is the same: to recognize the inevitability of death, the futility of attempting to prolong life painfully when there is no hope of recovery, and the necessity of providing the intense emotional and psychological support that the terminal patient and the family so desperately need.

Additional Health-Care Options

Many of the retirement places offer additional health-care services that are of special concern to older residents.

Cardiac intensive care units are found in many hospitals and are in more than half the retirement places. For the heart-attack victim, fast and comprehensive cardiac care by experts often means the difference between life and death. Since time is so vital, and three out of ten people over 65 succumb to heart attacks, the desirability of having such an intensive-care unit close by is obvious.

Outpatient hemodialysis, available in 34 retirement places, is a bit more specialized but is vital to those with kidney insufficiency. Such patients usually must undergo dialysis weekly and sometimes more frequently.

Outpatient psychiatric services, like community mental health centers, are critical to retirement communities. We have already noted that older people are prone to depression. Lack of activity, feelings of unimportance, fear of becoming burdensome, loss of friends or loved ones, dread of death or prolonged painful illness, excessive use of alcohol or tranquilizers, even medications for pain, hypertension, or other disorders—any of these may bring on or intensify episodes of acute depression. Outpatient psychiatric

services, offered in 34 retirement places, can do a great deal to alleviate these periods.

Home nursing care is a fast-growing service that can be immensely beneficial to many older persons. Despite its increasing popularity, this service is still not available in most places, although 31 retirement locations have it. Home health care may be provided either as an extension of a local hospital or as an affiliate chapter of the National Homecaring Council. In some instances, both versions are available in the same location.

JUDGING SUPPLY OF HEALTH-CARE FACILITIES

In this age of euphemism, "health" means not only health but also its exact opposite, illness. A hospital is not really a health-care institution; its business is to take care of sick people. The truly healthy need little "health care," save for an occasional shot or checkup; the unhealthy need a lot.

The health-care facilities of different places cannot be rated with total fairness. As noted earlier, the quality of care that a patient receives may be largely the luck of the draw. The skill of the doctor and the training, competence, and dedication of the nursing staff can vary, sometimes greatly. But it is possible to compare the places for relative abundance of facilities. For this reason, *Places Rated Retirement Guide* looks at the availability of facilities for "illness care," as well as at an environmental variable that affects health—fluoridation of drinking water—in ranking the retirement places.

Each retirement place starts with a base score of zero, and points are added according to the following indicators:

1. *Physicians per 100,000 residents.* One point is awarded for every physician per 100,000 people living within the retirement place.
2. *Beds per 100,000 residents.* Each hospital bed per 100,000 residents is worth ½ point, up to a maximum total of 500 points per retirement place.
3. *Medical schools and teaching hospitals.* Each medical school and each teaching hospital is valued at 200 points.
4. *Comprehensive cancer treatment centers.* Each facility is awarded 100 points.
5. *Community mental health centers.* A retirement place receives 100 points for each facility.
6. *Hospices.* Each hospice within the retirement place is worth 100 points.
7. *Cardiac intensive care, outpatient hemodialysis, outpatient psychiatric services, and home nursing care.* These health-care options are valued at 100 points apiece.

8. *Fluoridation.* A retirement place receives 200 points if it has fluoridated drinking water, either natural or adjusted.

Sample Comparison: Miami, Florida, and Houghton Lake, Michigan

As we have already seen, the larger metro areas tend to have more health-care facilities and options for retirees than do the small non-metropolitan counties. The place that ranks first among the retirement places for health-care facilities is Miami, a large city long famous as a retirement destination. While Miami certainly has its problems in other areas (most notably crime), there's no denying that in health-care choices and services it offers the most. The place receiving the fewest points for health care is Houghton Lake, Michigan, a resort area near the center of the state.

First let's see how Miami achieved its number-one ranking. To begin with, Miami has 295 physicians for every 100,000 residents; this is well over the national average and is worth 295 points. For its 682 hospital beds per 100,000 residents (in 39 hospitals), Miami receives ½ point apiece, or 341 points. Miami's medical school—the University of Miami School of Medicine—and three teaching hospitals are worth 200 points apiece, for a combined score of 800 points. The metro area also earns 100 points each for its comprehensive cancer treatment center, six community mental health centers, hospice, and all four of the health-care options —cardiac intensive care, outpatient hemodialysis, outpatient psychiatric services, and home nursing care— for an additional 1,200 points. And finally, Miami's drinking water is fluoridated, worth 200 points. The total score for Miami is 2,836, which places it comfortably in the leading slot, almost 700 points ahead of runner-up Tucson.

At the other end of the scale is Houghton Lake, Michigan, ranking 107th. Its ratio of physicians is 62 per 100,000 residents, way below the national average and worth 62 points. And this marks the extent of the medical services for which Houghton Lake can receive points. Houghton Lake has no hospitals and therefore no hospital beds. It has none of the other health-care facilities that receive points in the *Places Rated* scoring system, not even fluoridated drinking water.

This does not mean that Houghton Lake is not a good place to live; it does mean that for most health-care services, residents must go elsewhere. For example, the retirement place that ranks 15th—Traverse City-Grand Traverse Bay, Michigan—is about 65 miles

Health-Care Winners and Losers

When the final ranking list for health care is examined, a definite pattern emerges reflecting place size and availability of health-care services and facilities. Of the top 20 ranked places, for example, only four are non-metro areas. One of these, San Luis Obispo, California, is large enough so that it soon will become one. Two of them—Traverse City–Grand Traverse Bay, and Petoskey–Straits of Mackinac, both in Michigan—are near enough to each other to form a nexus of smaller towns that might also include Charlevoix and Harbor Springs. All of these places have long been noted for the high incomes and educational level of their residents.

At the bottom end of the list (the 20 lowest-scoring places), only one retirement place—Olympia, Washington—is a metro area, illustrating the direct relationship between city size and the abundance of facilities (be they health-care, cultural, educational, recreational, or other) to be found there.

Health-Care Facilities

Best Retirement Places	Places Rated Score	Worst Retirement Places	Places Rated Score
1. MIAMI, FL	2,836	1. Houghton Lake, MI	62
2. TUCSON, AZ	2,142	2. Ocean City–	
3. ALBUQUERQUE, NM	2,110	Assateague Island,	
4. LEXINGTON-		MD	64
FAYETTE, KY	2,102	3. Rappahannock, VA	87
5. SAN DIEGO, CA	2,067	4. Table Rock Lake,	
		MO	93
		5. Canton-Lake	
		Tawakoni, TX	125

Why then should anyone prefer the smaller places? First of all, many smaller places are close to big ones, and their residents can enjoy the benefits of small-town life and—with a reasonable commute—the amenities of a big city. Virginia's Rappahannock River area is within 50 miles of the metro area of Richmond; Rockport–Aransas Pass, on Texas's Gulf Coast, is within 20 miles of Corpus Christi; residents of Clarkesville–Mount Airy, Georgia, lying midway between Asheville, North Carolina, and Atlanta, have the choice of a large metro area or a small one within reasonable driving time.

Remember, too, the disadvantages of big metro areas. Although they almost always do better on facilities, they often fall down on social indicators such as the crime rate. If you look at the crime rates in the various retirement places, you will see a ranking list that is almost the reverse of that in health care: The larger places almost always have more crime.

away. People who opt for Houghton Lake may decide that the inconvenience of an occasional trip to a larger city is outweighed by the beauty and serenity of Roscommon County.

Places Rated: Retirement Places Ranked for Health-Care Facilities

Eight criteria are used to score the supply of health-care facilities in a retirement place: (1) physicians per 100,000 residents; (2) hospital beds per 100,000 residents; (3) medical schools and teaching hospitals; (4) comprehensive cancer treatment centers; (5) community mental health centers; (6) hospices; (7) cardiac intensive care, outpatient hemodialysis, outpatient psychiatric services, and home nursing care; (8) fluoridation of water. Places that receive tie scores are given the same rank and are listed in alphabetical order.

Retirement Places from Best to Worst

Places Rated Rank	Places Rated Score
1. MIAMI, FL	2,836
2. TUCSON, AZ	2,142
3. ALBUQUERQUE, NM	2,110
4. LEXINGTON–FAYETTE, KY	2,102
5. SAN DIEGO, CA	2,067
6. SAN ANTONIO, TX	2,061
7. PHOENIX, AZ	2,057
8. CHARLOTTESVILLE, VA	2,001
9. ASHEVILLE, NC	1,480
10. FORT LAUDERDALE–HOLLYWOOD, FL	1,342
11. ORLANDO, FL	1,313
12. RENO, NV	1,293
13. San Luis Obispo, CA	1,284
14. SARASOTA–BRADENTON, FL	1,279
15. Traverse City–Grand Traverse Bay, MI	1,254
16. Petoskey–Straits of Mackinac, MI	1,225
17. AUSTIN, TX	1,202
18. BOISE CITY, ID	1,196
19. Winchester, VA	1,187
20. WEST PALM BEACH–BOCA RATON, FL	1,154
21. Beaufort–Hilton Head, SC	1,147
22. SPRINGFIELD, MO	1,145
23. ATLANTIC CITY–CAPE MAY, NJ	1,105
24. BILOXI–GULFPORT, MS	1,097
25. Kerrville, TX	1,076
26. COLORADO SPRINGS, CO	1,039
27. Hot Springs–Lake Ouachita, AR	1,037
28. Roswell, NM	1,017
29. MELBOURNE–TITUSVILLE–COCOA, FL	1,015
30. LAKELAND–WINTER HAVEN, FL	1,001
31. Santa Fe, NM	995
32. Grand Junction, CO	974
33. FORT MYERS–CAPE CORAL, FL	950
34. DAYTONA BEACH, FL	935
35. Missoula, MT	902
36. Rhinelander, WI	868

Places Rated Rank	Places Rated Score
37. Gainesville–Lake Sidney Lanier, GA	828
38. Harrison, AR	817
39. LAS VEGAS, NV	805
40. Prescott, AZ	800
41. STATE COLLEGE, PA	794
42. BRUNSWICK–GOLDEN ISLES, GA	784
43. Camden–Penobscot Bay, ME	782
44. Brevard, NC	776
45. North Conway–White Mountains, NH	772
46. Easton–Chesapeake Bay, MD	768
47. SANTA ROSA, CA	758
48. LANCASTER, PA	718
49. Brattleboro, VT	715
49. Paris, TN	715
51. Mountain Home–Norfork Lake, AR	713
52. Bar Harbor–Frenchman Bay, ME	697
53. Bennington, VT	696
54. OCALA, FL	684
55. Eagle River, WI	685
56. Hendersonville, NC	681
57. Rehoboth Bay–Indian River Bay, DE	678
58. Lincoln City–Newport, OR	669
59. Toms River–Barnegat Bay, NJ	651
60. FORT COLLINS, CO	648
61. Cookeville, TN	646
62. Myrtle Beach, SC	630
63. Crossville, TN	628
64. Front Royal, VA	626
65. Bull Shoals, AR	624
66. Maui, HI	601
67. Fairhope–Gulf Shores, AL	600
68. Bend, OR	597
69. Twain Harte–Yosemite, CA	593
70. LAS CRUCES, NM	583
71. Oak Harbor, WA	578
72. Monticello–Liberty, NY	568
73. Cape Cod, MA	564

Places Rated Rank	Places Rated Score
74. Nevada City–Donner, CA	557
75. Tahlequah–Lake Tenkiller, OK	547
76. MEDFORD, OR	544
77. Yuma, AZ	523
78. St. George–Zion, UT	491
79. Coeur d'Alene, ID	487
80. McALLEN–PHARR–EDINBURG, TX	469
81. Laconia–Lake Winnipesaukee, NH	422
82. Fredericksburg, TX	418
83. Red Bluff–Sacramento Valley, CA	396
84. Keene, NH	395
85. Clarkesville–Mount Airy, GA	386
86. Deming, NM	384
87. Delta, CO	372
88. Lake Havasu City–Kingman, AZ	359
89. OLYMPIA, WA	351
90. Benton–Kentucky Lake, KY	346
91. Rockport–Aransas Pass, TX	314
92. Branson–Lake Taneycomo, MO	300
93. Kalispell, MT	289
93. Oscoda–Huron Shore, MI	289
95. Port Angeles–Strait of Juan de Fuca, WA	270
96. Cassville–Roaring River, MO	245
97. Carson City, NV	243
98. Clear Lake, CA	237
99. Big Sandy, TN	224
100. Athens–Cedar Creek Lake, TX	204
101. Hamilton–Bitterroot Valley, MT	195
102. Lake O' The Cherokees, OK	191
103. Canton–Lake Tawakoni, TX	125
104. Table Rock Lake, MO	93
105. Rappahannock, VA	87
106. Ocean City–Assateague Island, MD	64
107. Houghton Lake, MI	62

Retirement Places Listed Alphabetically

Retirement Place	Places Rated Rank	Retirement Place	Places Rated Rank	Retirement Place	Places Rated Rank
ALBUQUERQUE, NM	3	FORT COLLINS, CO	60	OCALA, FL	54
ASHEVILLE, NC	9	FORT LAUDERDALE–HOLLYWOOD, FL	10	Ocean City–Assateague Island, MD	106
Athens–Cedar Creek Lake, TX	100	FORT MYERS–CAPE CORAL, FL	33	OLYMPIA, WA	89
ATLANTIC CITY–CAPE MAY, NJ	23	Fredericksburg, TX	82		
AUSTIN, TX	17			ORLANDO, FL	11
		Front Royal, VA	64	Oscoda–Huron Shore, MI	93
Bar Harbor–Frenchman Bay, ME	52	Gainesville–Lake Sidney Lanier, GA	37	Paris, TN	49
Beaufort–Hilton Head, SC	21	Grand Junction, CO	32	Petoskey–Straits of Mackinac, MI	16
Bend, OR	68	Hamilton–Bitterroot Valley, MT	101	PHOENIX, AZ	7
Bennington, VT	53	Harrison, AR	38		
Benton–Kentucky Lake, KY	90			Port Angeles–Strait of Juan de Fuca, WA	95
		Hendersonville, NC	56	Prescott, AZ	40
Big Sandy, TN	99	Hot Springs–Lake Ouachita, AR	27	Rappahannock, VA	105
BILOXI–GULFPORT, MS	24	Houghton Lake, MI	107	Red Bluff–Sacramento Valley, CA	83
BOISE CITY, ID	18	Kalispell, MT	93	Rehoboth Bay–Indian River Bay, DE	57
Branson–Lake Taneycomo, MO	92	Keene, NH	84		
Brattleboro, VT	49			RENO, NV	12
		Kerrville, TX	25	Rhinelander, WI	36
Brevard, NC	44	Laconia–Lake Winnipesaukee, NH	81	Rockport–Aransas Pass, TX	91
Brunswick–Golden Isles, GA	42	Lake Havasu City–Kingman, AZ	88	Roswell, NM	28
Bull Shoals, AR	65	LAKELAND–WINTER HAVEN, FL	30	St. George–Zion, UT	78
Camden–Penobscot Bay, ME	43	Lake O' The Cherokees, OK	102		
Canton–Lake Tawakoni, TX	103			SAN ANTONIO, TX	6
		LANCASTER, PA	48	SAN DIEGO, CA	5
Cape Cod, MA	73	LAS CRUCES, NM	70	San Luis Obispo, CA	13
Carson City, NV	97	LAS VEGAS, NV	39	Santa Fe, NM	31
Cassville–Roaring River, MO	96	LEXINGTON–FAYETTE, KY	4	SANTA ROSA, CA	47
CHARLOTTESVILLE, VA	8	Lincoln City–Newport, OR	58		
Clarkesville–Mount Airy, GA	85			SARASOTA–BRADENTON, FL	14
		Maui, HI	66	SPRINGFIELD, MO	22
Clear Lake, CA	98	McALLEN–PHARR–EDINBURG, TX	80	STATE COLLEGE, PA	41
Coeur d'Alene, ID	79	MEDFORD, OR	76	Table Rock Lake, MO	104
COLORADO SPRINGS, CO	26	MELBOURNE–TITUSVILLE–COCOA, FL	29	Tahlequah–Lake Tenkiller, OK	75
Cookeville, TN	61	MIAMI, FL	1		
Crossville, TN	63			Toms River–Barnegat Bay, NJ	59
		Missoula, MT	35	Traverse City–Grand Traverse Bay, MI	15
DAYTONA BEACH, FL	34	Monticello–Liberty, NY	72	TUCSON, AZ	2
Delta, CO	87	Mountain Home–Norfork Lake, AR	51	Twain Harte–Yosemite, CA	69
Deming, NM	86	Myrtle Beach, SC	62	WEST PALM BEACH–BOCA RATON, FL	20
Eagle River, WI	55	Nevada City–Donner, CA	74		
Easton–Chesapeake Bay, MD	46			Winchester, VA	19
		North Conway–White Mountains, NH	45	Yuma, AZ	77
Fairhope–Gulf Shores, AL	67	Oak Harbor, WA	71		

Place Profiles: Health-Care Facilities and Related Features of 107 Retirement Places

In the pages that follow, some of the health-care facilities and other features of the 107 retirement places are profiled. In addition to detailing those items that play a part in the *Places Rated* scoring system, the profiles show the number of hospitals in each place and describe water quality in places for which that information is available. When fluoridation occurs within the retirement place, the profile indicates whether it occurs naturally or is adjusted by the addition of fluoride in the ratio of one part per million to the drinking water. Some of the retirement places have teaching hospitals although they have no medical schools; these teaching hospitals are affiliated with

medical schools that are located outside the retirement place.

The information in the profiles is derived from a number of sources: American Hospital Association, *Guide to the Health Care Field*, 1983; Centers for Disease Control, unpublished data, 1983; Ayer, *Editor and Publisher*, 1983; Anthony Kruzas, *Medical and Health Information Directory*, 1981; National Cancer Institute, 1983; National Center for Health Statistics, *County and City Data Book*, 1978; National Homecaring Council, 1983; and U.S. Department of Health and Human Services, *Hospitals: A County and Metropolitan Area Data Book*, 1982.

ALBUQUERQUE, NM
Physicians per 100,000: 220
Hospital Beds per 100,000: 580
Total Number of Hospitals: 14
Medical Schools:
  University of New Mexico School of Medicine
Teaching Hospitals:
  Bernalillo County Medical Center
  Lovelace–Bataan Medical Center
  Veterans Administration Medical Center
Community Mental Health Centers:
  Bernalillo County Mental Health Center
Hospices:
  Hospital Home Health Care–Hospice Program
Additional Health Care Options:
  Cardiac Intensive Care
  Outpatient Hemodialysis
  Outpatient Psychiatric Services
  Home Nursing Care
Fluoridation: Adjusted
Water Quality: Alkaline, hard
Places Rated Score: 2,110
Places Rated Rank: 3

ASHEVILLE, NC
Physicians per 100,000: 180
Hospital Beds per 100,000: 1,361
Total Number of Hospitals: 9
Community Mental Health Centers:
  Blue Ridge Community Mental Health Center
Hospices:
  Mountain Area Hospice–Asheville
Additional Health Care Options:
  Cardiac Intensive Care
  Outpatient Hemodialysis
  Outpatient Psychiatric Services
  Home Nursing Care
Fluoridation: Adjusted
Water Quality: Acidic, very soft
Places Rated Score: 1,480
Places Rated Rank: 9

Athens–Cedar Creek Lake, TX
Physicians per 100,000: 46
Hospital Beds per 100,000: 316
Total Number of Hospitals: 2
Fluoridation: No
Water Quality: Neutral, soft
Places Rated Score: 204
Places Rated Rank: 100

ATLANTIC CITY–CAPE MAY, NJ
Physicians per 100,000: 155
Hospital Beds per 100,000: 900
Total Number of Hospitals: 7
Additional Health Care Options:
  Cardiac Intensive Care
  Outpatient Hemodialysis
  Outpatient Psychiatric Services
Fluoridation: Adjusted
Water Quality: Acidic, soft
Places Rated Score: 1,105
Places Rated Rank: 23

AUSTIN, TX
Physicians per 100,000: 162
Hospital Beds per 100,000: 680

Total Number of Hospitals: 12
Community Mental Health Centers:
  Austin–Travis County Mental Health/Mental Retardation Center
  Austin–Travis County Mental Health/Mental Retardation Center, Southeast Unit
Hospices:
  Girling and Associates–Home Health Services
Additional Health Care Options:
  Cardiac Intensive Care
  Outpatient Psychiatric Services
Fluoridation: Adjusted
Water Quality: Alkaline, soft
Places Rated Score: 1,202
Places Rated Rank: 17

Bar Harbor–Frenchman Bay, ME
Physicians per 100,000: 148
Hospital Beds per 100,000: 498
Total Number of Hospitals: 4
Additional Health Care Options:
  Outpatient Psychiatric Services
Fluoridation: Adjusted
Water Quality: NA
Places Rated Score: 697
Places Rated Rank: 52

Beaufort–Hilton Head, SC
Physicians per 100,000: 120
Hospital Beds per 100,000: 427
Total Number of Hospitals: 2
Community Mental Health Centers:
  Coastal Empire Mental Health Center
Additional Health Care Options:
  Cardiac Intensive Care
  Outpatient Psychiatric Services
Fluoridation: Adjusted
Water Quality: Alkaline, soft
Places Rated Score: 1,147
Places Rated Rank: 21

Bend, OR
Physicians per 100,000: 191
Hospital Beds per 100,000: 412
Total Number of Hospitals: 2
Additional Health Care Options:
  Cardiac Intensive Care
  Home Nursing Care
Fluoridation: No
Water Quality: Alkaline, very soft
Places Rated Score: 597
Places Rated Rank: 68

Bennington, VT
Physicians per 100,000: 204
Hospital Beds per 100,000: 584
Total Number of Hospitals: 1
Community Mental Health Centers:
  United Counseling Service of Bennington County
Hospices:
  Hospice of the Bennington Area
Fluoridation: No
Water Quality: Neutral, soft
Places Rated Score: 696
Places Rated Rank: 53

Benton–Kentucky Lake, KY
Physicians per 100,000: 54

Hospital Beds per 100,000: 183
Total Number of Hospitals: 1
Fluoridation: Adjusted
Water Quality: NA
Places Rated Score: 346
Places Rated Rank: 90

Big Sandy, TN
Physicians per 100,000: 47
Hospital Beds per 100,000: 354
Total Number of Hospitals: 1
Fluoridation: No
Water Quality: NA
Places Rated Score: 224
Places Rated Rank: 99

BILOXI–GULFPORT, MS
Physicians per 100,000: 97
Hospital Beds per 100,000: 1,014
Total Number of Hospitals: 6
Community Mental Health Centers:
  Gulf Coast Mental Health Center
Additional Health Care Options:
  Cardiac Intensive Care
  Outpatient Hemodialysis
  Outpatient Psychiatric Services
  Home Nursing Care
Fluoridation: No
Water Quality: Alkaline, very soft
Places Rated Score: 1,097
Places Rated Rank: 24

BOISE CITY, ID
Physicians per 100,000: 153
Hospital Beds per 100,000: 485
Total Number of Hospitals: 4
Community Mental Health Centers:
  Idaho Department of Health and Welfare Region IV Mental Health Center
Hospices:
  Mountain States Tumor Institute
Additional Health Care Options:
  Cardiac Intensive Care
  Outpatient Hemodialysis
  Outpatient Psychiatric Services
  Home Nursing Care
Fluoridation: No
Water Quality: Alkaline, soft
Places Rated Score: 1,196
Places Rated Rank: 18

Branson–Lake Taneycomo, MO
Physicians per 100,000: 62
Hospital Beds per 100,000: 476
Total Number of Hospitals: 1
Fluoridation: No
Water Quality: NA
Places Rated Score: 300
Places Rated Rank: 92

Brattleboro, VT
Physicians per 100,000: 215
Hospital Beds per 100,000: 1,090
Total Number of Hospitals: 4
Fluoridation: No
Water Quality: Alkaline, very soft
Places Rated Score: 715
Places Rated Rank: 49

Brevard, NC
Physicians per 100,000: 109
Hospital Beds per 100,000: 493
Total Number of Hospitals: 1
Additional Health Care Options:
   Cardiac Intensive Care
   Home Nursing Care
Fluoridation: Adjusted
Water Quality: NA
Places Rated Score: 776
Places Rated Rank: 44

Brunswick–Golden Isles, GA
Physicians per 100,000: 169
Hospital Beds per 100,000: 629
Total Number of Hospitals: 1
Community Mental Health Centers:
   Coastal Area Community Mental Health
   Center
Fluoridation: Adjusted
Water Quality: Alkaline, hard
Places Rated Score: 784
Places Rated Rank: 42

Bull Shoals, AR
Physicians per 100,000: 64
Hospital Beds per 100,000: 719
Total Number of Hospitals: 1
Additional Health Care Options:
   Cardiac Intensive Care
   Home Nursing Care
Fluoridation: No
Water Quality: NA
Places Rated Score: 624
Places Rated Rank: 65

Camden–Penobscot Bay, ME
Physicians per 100,000: 191
Hospital Beds per 100,000: 382
Total Number of Hospitals: 2
Community Mental Health Centers:
   Mid–Coast Mental Health Center
Additional Health Care Options:
   Outpatient Psychiatric Services
Fluoridation: Adjusted
Water Quality: NA
Places Rated Score: 782
Places Rated Rank: 43

Canton–Lake Tawakoni, TX
Physicians per 100,000: 33
Hospital Beds per 100,000: 184
Total Number of Hospitals: 2
Fluoridation: No
Water Quality: NA
Places Rated Score: 125
Places Rated Rank: 103

Cape Cod, MA
Physicians per 100,000: 212
Hospital Beds per 100,000: 303
Total Number of Hospitals: 3
Additional Health Care Options:
   Cardiac Intensive Care
   Home Nursing Care
Fluoridation: No
Water Quality: NA
Places Rated Score: 564
Places Rated Rank: 73

Carson City, NV
Physicians per 100,000: 105
Hospital Beds per 100,000: 75
Total Number of Hospitals: 1
Community Mental Health Centers:
   Rural Clinics Community Mental Health
   Center
Fluoridation: No
Water Quality: Alkaline, soft
Places Rated Score: 243
Places Rated Rank: 97

Cassville–Roaring River, MO
Physicians per 100,000: 60
Hospital Beds per 100,000: 369
Total Number of Hospitals: 2
Fluoridation: No
Water Quality: NA
Places Rated Score: 245
Places Rated Rank: 96

CHARLOTTESVILLE, VA
Physicians per 100,000: 501
Hospital Beds per 100,000: 2,562
Total Number of Hospitals: 5
Medical Schools:
   University of Virginia School of Medicine
Teaching Hospitals:
   University of Virginia Hospitals
Community Mental Health Centers:
   Blue Ridge Comprehensive Community
   Mental Health Center
Additional Health Care Options:
   Cardiac Intensive Care
   Outpatient Hemodialysis
   Outpatient Psychiatric Services
Fluoridation: Adjusted
Water Quality: Very soft
Places Rated Score: 2,001
Places Rated Rank: 8

Clarkesville–Mount Airy, GA
Physicians per 100,000: 65
Hospital Beds per 100,000: 242
Total Number of Hospitals: 1
Fluoridation: Adjusted
Water Quality: NA
Places Rated Score: 386
Places Rated Rank: 85

Clear Lake, CA
Physicians per 100,000: 101
Hospital Beds per 100,000: 272
Total Number of Hospitals: 2
Fluoridation: No
Water Quality: NA
Places Rated Score: 237
Places Rated Rank: 98

Coeur d'Alene, ID
Physicians per 100,000: 103
Hospital Beds per 100,000: 368
Total Number of Hospitals: 1
Community Mental Health Centers:
   Idaho Department of Health and Welfare
   Region I Community Mental Health Cen-
   ter
Additional Health Care Options:
   Cardiac Intensive Care

Fluoridation: No
Water Quality: Alkaline, very soft
Places Rated Score: 487
Places Rated Rank: 79

COLORADO SPRINGS, CO
Physicians per 100,000: 111
Hospital Beds per 100,000: 456
Total Number of Hospitals: 9
Hospices:
   Penrose Hospital Hospice Program
Additional Health Care Options:
   Cardiac Intensive Care
   Outpatient Hemodialysis
   Outpatient Psychiatric Services
   Home Nursing Care
Fluoridation: Natural
Water Quality: Pure, filtered
Places Rated Score: 1,039
Places Rated Rank: 26

Cookeville, TN
Physicians per 100,000: 76
Hospital Beds per 100,000: 340
Total Number of Hospitals: 5
Community Mental Health Centers:
   Plateau Mental Health Center
Additional Health Care Options:
   Outpatient Hemodialysis
Fluoridation: Adjusted
Water Quality: Soft
Places Rated Score: 646
Places Rated Rank: 61

Crossville, TN
Physicians per 100,000: 99
Hospital Beds per 100,000: 658
Total Number of Hospitals: 1
Fluoridation: Adjusted
Water Quality: Hard
Places Rated Score: 628
Places Rated Rank: 63

DAYTONA BEACH, FL
Physicians per 100,000: 146
Hospital Beds per 100,000: 577
Total Number of Hospitals: 8
Community Mental Health Centers:
   Human Resources Center for Mental
   Health
Hospices:
   Hospice of Volusai
Additional Health Care Options:
   Outpatient Hemodialysis
Fluoridation: Adjusted
Water Quality: Alkaline, soft
Places Rated Score: 935
Places Rated Rank: 34

Delta, CO
Physicians per 100,000: 80
Hospital Beds per 100,000: 183
Total Number of Hospitals: 1
Fluoridation: Adjusted
Water Quality: NA
Places Rated Score: 372
Places Rated Rank: 87

Deming, NM
Physicians per 100,000: 28

Hospital Beds per 100,000: 361
Total Number of Hospitals: 1
Fluoridation: Natural
Water Quality: NA
Places Rated Score: 384
Places Rated Rank: 86

Eagle River, WI
Physicians per 100,000: 67
Hospital Beds per 100,000: 436
Total Number of Hospitals: 2
Additional Health Care Options:
    Outpatient Psychiatric Services
    Home Nursing Care
Fluoridation: Adjusted
Water Quality: NA
Places Rated Score: 685
Places Rated Rank: 55

Easton–Chesapeake Bay, MD
Physicians per 100,000: 323
Hospital Beds per 100,000: 890
Total Number of Hospitals: 1
Fluoridation: No
Water Quality: Alkaline, hard
Places Rated Score: 768
Places Rated Rank: 46

Fairhope–Gulf Shores, AL
Physicians per 100,000: 54
Hospital Beds per 100,000: 292
Total Number of Hospitals: 3
Hospices:
    Villa Mercy Hospice
Additional Health Care Options:
    Cardiac Intensive Care
Fluoridation: No
Water Quality: Alkaline, very soft
Places Rated Score: 600
Places Rated Rank: 67

FORT COLLINS, CO
Physicians per 100,000: 122
Hospital Beds per 100,000: 251
Total Number of Hospitals: 4
Community Mental Health Centers:
    Larimer County Community Mental Health
    Center
Hospices:
    Hospice, Inc., of Larimer County
Additional Health Care Options:
    Home Nursing Care
Fluoridation: Adjusted
Water Quality: Acidic, very soft
Places Rated Score: 648
Places Rated Rank: 60

FORT LAUDERDALE–HOLLYWOOD, FL
Physicians per 100,000: 200
Hospital Beds per 100,000: 683
Total Number of Hospitals: 22
Hospices:
    Gold Coast Home Health Services Hos-
    pice Team
    Hospice of Broward
    Hospice of South Florida
Additional Health Care Options:
    Cardiac Intensive Care
    Outpatient Hemodialysis
    Outpatient Psychiatric Services

Fluoridation: Adjusted
Water Quality: Alkaline, very soft
Places Rated Score: 1,342
Places Rated Rank: 10

FORT MYERS–CAPE CORAL, FL
Physicians per 100,000: 182
Hospital Beds per 100,000: 535
Total Number of Hospitals: 3
Community Mental Health Centers:
    Lee County Mental Health Guidance Cen-
    ter, Inc.
Additional Health Care Options:
    Cardiac Intensive Care
    Outpatient Hemodialysis
Fluoridation: Adjusted
Water Quality: Alkaline, soft
Places Rated Score: 950
Places Rated Rank: 33

Fredericksburg, TX
Physicians per 100,000: 97
Hospital Beds per 100,000: 441
Total Number of Hospitals: 1
Hospices:
    Hill Country Hospice
Fluoridation: No
Water Quality: NA
Places Rated Score: 418
Places Rated Rank: 82

Front Royal, VA
Physicians per 100,000: 92
Hospital Beds per 100,000: 667
Total Number of Hospitals: 1
Fluoridation: Adjusted
Water Quality: NA
Places Rated Score: 626
Places Rated Rank: 64

Gainesville–Lake Sidney Lanier, GA
Physicians per 100,000: 122
Hospital Beds per 100,000: 412
Total Number of Hospitals: 2
Community Mental Health Centers:
    North Georgia Mental Health/Mental
    Retardation Center
Additional Health Care Options:
    Cardiac Intensive Care
    Outpatient Hemodialysis
Fluoridation: Adjusted
Water Quality: Neutral, very soft
Places Rated Score: 828
Places Rated Rank: 37

Grand Junction, CO
Physicians per 100,000: 146
Hospital Beds per 100,000: 855
Total Number of Hospitals: 6
Additional Health Care Options:
    Outpatient Hemodialysis
    Home Nursing Care
Fluoridation: Adjusted
Water Quality: Neutral, soft
Places Rated Score: 974
Places Rated Rank: 32

Hamilton–Bitterroot Valley, MT
Physicians per 100,000: 65
Hospital Beds per 100,000: 260

Total Number of Hospitals: 1
Fluoridation: No
Water Quality: Alkaline, hard
Places Rated Score: 195
Places Rated Rank: 101

Harrison, AR
Physicians per 100,000: 136
Hospital Beds per 100,000: 761
Total Number of Hospitals: 1
Additional Health Care Options:
    Cardiac Intensive Care
Fluoridation: Adjusted
Water Quality: Alkaline, hard
Places Rated Score: 817
Places Rated Rank: 38

Hendersonville, NC
Physicians per 100,000: 148
Hospital Beds per 100,000: 666
Total Number of Hospitals: 3
Community Mental Health Centers:
    Trend Community Mental Health Center
Hospices:
    Hospice of Henderson County
Fluoridation: No
Water Quality: Neutral, very soft
Places Rated Score: 681
Places Rated Rank: 56

Hot Springs–Lake Ouachita, AR
Physicians per 100,000: 158
Hospital Beds per 100,000: 758
Total Number of Hospitals: 3
Community Mental Health Centers:
    Ouachita Regional Counseling and Mental
    Health Center
Additional Health Care Options:
    Cardiac Intensive Care
    Home Nursing Care
Fluoridation: Adjusted
Water Quality: Alkaline, very soft
Places Rated Score: 1,037
Places Rated Rank: 27

Houghton Lake, MI
Physicians per 100,000: 62
Hospital Beds per 100,000: None
Total Number of Hospitals: None
Fluoridation: No
Water Quality: NA
Places Rated Score: 62
Places Rated Rank: 107

Kalispell, MT
Physicians per 100,000: 139
Hospital Beds per 100,000: 300
Total Number of Hospitals: 2
Fluoridation: No
Water Quality: Neutral, hard
Places Rated Score: 289
Places Rated Rank: 93

Keene, NH
Physicians per 100,000: 113
Hospital Beds per 100,000: 364
Total Number of Hospitals: 2
Community Mental Health Centers:
    Monadnock Family and Mental Health
    Center

Fluoridation: No
Water Quality: Acidic, very soft
Places Rated Score: 395
Places Rated Rank: 84

Kerrville, TX
Physicians per 100,000: 276
Hospital Beds per 100,000: 6,961
Total Number of Hospitals: 5
Additional Health Care Options:
　Cardiac Intensive Care
Fluoridation: Natural
Water Quality: Alkaline
Places Rated Score: 1,076
Places Rated Rank: 25

Laconia–Lake Winnipesaukee, NH
Physicians per 100,000: 190
Hospital Beds per 100,000: 463
Total Number of Hospitals: 1
Fluoridation: No
Water Quality: Neutral, very soft
Places Rated Score: 422
Places Rated Rank: 81

Lake Havasu City–Kingman, AZ
Physicians per 100,000: 102
Hospital Beds per 100,000: 313
Total Number of Hospitals: 2
Fluoridation: No
Water Quality: Alkaline, hard
Places Rated Score: 359
Places Rated Rank: 88

Lakeland–Winter Haven, FL
Physicians per 100,000: 131
Hospital Beds per 100,000: 539
Total Number of Hospitals: 8
Community Mental Health Centers:
　Winter Haven Hospital Community Mental
　　Health Center
Hospices:
　Good Shepherd Hospice
Additional Health Care Options:
　Cardiac Intensive Care
　Outpatient Psychiatric Services
Fluoridation: Adjusted
Water Quality: Alkaline, very hard
Places Rated Score: 1,001
Places Rated Rank: 30

Lake O' The Cherokees, OK
Physicians per 100,000: 35
Hospital Beds per 100,000: 311
Total Number of Hospitals: 2
Fluoridation: No
Water Quality: NA
Places Rated Score: 191
Places Rated Rank: 102

LANCASTER, PA
Physicians per 100,000: 104
Hospital Beds per 100,000: 427
Total Number of Hospitals: 6
Additional Health Care Options:
　Outpatient Hemodialysis
　Outpatient Psychiatric Services
Fluoridation: Adjusted
Water Quality: Alkaline, hard
Places Rated Score: 718
Places Rated Rank: 48

LAS CRUCES, NM
Physicians per 100,000: 82
Hospital Beds per 100,000: 201
Total Number of Hospitals: 1
Community Mental Health Centers:
　Southwest Mental Health Center
Additional Health Care Options:
　Cardiac Intensive Care
Fluoridation: Natural
Water Quality: Alkaline, hard
Places Rated Score: 583
Places Rated Rank: 70

LAS VEGAS, NV
Physicians per 100,000: 115
Hospital Beds per 100,000: 379
Total Number of Hospitals: 9
Community Mental Health Centers:
　Las Vegas Mental Health Center
Hospices:
　Nathan Adelson Memorial Hospice
Additional Health Care Options:
　Cardiac Intensive Care
　Outpatient Hemodialysis
　Home Nursing Care
Fluoridation: No
Water Quality: Alkaline, hard
Places Rated Score: 805
Places Rated Rank: 39

LEXINGTON–FAYETTE, KY
Physicians per 100,000: 302
Hospital Beds per 100,000: 1,187
Total Number of Hospitals: 13
Medical Schools:
　University of Kentucky College of Medi-
　　cine
Teaching Hospitals:
　Albert B. Chandler Medical Center
　Veterans Administration Medical Center
Comprehensive Cancer Treatment Centers:
　McDowell Cancer Network, Inc.
Hospices:
　Community Hospital of Lexington
　Ephraim McDowell Community Center
　　Hospice
Additional Health Care Options:
　Cardiac Intensive Care
　Outpatient Hemodialysis
Fluoridation: Adjusted
Water Quality: Alkaline, medium
Places Rated Score: 2,102
Places Rated Rank: 4

Lincoln City–Newport, OR
Physicians per 100,000: 125
Hospital Beds per 100,000: 487
Total Number of Hospitals: 3
Additional Health Care Options:
　Cardiac Intensive Care
Fluoridation: Adjusted
Water Quality: NA
Places Rated Score: 669
Places Rated Rank: 58

Maui, HI
Physicians per 100,000: 166
Hospital Beds per 100,000: 669
Total Number of Hospitals: 5
Community Mental Health Centers:
　Maui Community Mental Health Center

Fluoridation: No
Water Quality: Very soft rainwater
Places Rated Score: 601
Places Rated Rank: 66

McALLEN–PHARR–EDINBURG, TX
Physicians per 100,000: 65
Hospital Beds per 100,000: 208
Total Number of Hospitals: 4
Community Mental Health Centers:
　Tropical Texas Center for Mental Health/
　　Mental Retardation
Fluoridation: Natural (Pharr only)
Water Quality: Alkaline, medium–hard
Places Rated Score: 469
Places Rated Rank: 80

MEDFORD, OR
Physicians per 100,000: 146
Hospital Beds per 100,000: 395
Total Number of Hospitals: 4
Additional Health Care Options:
　Cardiac Intensive Care
　Outpatient Psychiatric Services
Fluoridation: No
Water Quality: NA
Places Rated Score: 544
Places Rated Rank: 76

MELBOURNE–TITUSVILLE–COCOA, FL
Physicians per 100,000: 119
Hospital Beds per 100,000: 392
Total Number of Hospitals: 6
Community Mental Health Centers:
　Brevard County Mental Health Center, Inc.
Hospices:
　Hospice of South Brevard
　Hospice of St. Francis
Additional Health Care Options:
　Cardiac Intensive Care
　Outpatient Psychiatric Services
Fluoridation: Adjusted
Water Quality: NA
Places Rated Score: 1,015
Places Rated Rank: 29

MIAMI, FL
Physicians per 100,000: 295
Hospital Beds per 100,000: 682
Total Number of Hospitals: 39
Medical Schools:
　University of Miami School of Medicine
Teaching Hospitals:
　Jackson Memorial Hospital
　Mount Sinai Medical Center
　Veterans Administration Medical Center
Comprehensive Cancer Treatment Centers:
　Comprehensive Cancer Center for the
　　State of Florida
Community Mental Health Centers:
　Area II–F Community Mental Health
　　Center
　Center for Family and Child Enrichment
　Community Health of South Dade
　　Community Mental Health Center
　Jackson Memorial Hospital Community
　　Mental Health Center
　Miami Beach Community Mental Health
　　Center, Inc.
　North Miami Community Health Center

Hospices:
Hospice of Miami
Additional Health Care Options:
Cardiac Intensive Care
Outpatient Hemodialysis
Outpatient Psychiatric Services
Home Nursing Care
Fluoridation: Adjusted
Water Quality: Alkaline, soft
Places Rated Score: 2,836
Places Rated Rank: 1

Missoula, MT
Physicians per 100,000: 211
Hospital Beds per 100,000: 582
Total Number of Hospitals: 3
Community Mental Health Centers:
Western Montana Regional Community
Mental Health Center
Additional Health Care Options:
Cardiac Intensive Care
Outpatient Hemodialysis
Outpatient Psychiatric Services
Fluoridation: No
Water Quality: Neutral, soft
Places Rated Score: 902
Places Rated Rank: 35

Monticello–Liberty, NY
Physicians per 100,000: 101
Hospital Beds per 100,000: 533
Total Number of Hospitals: 3
Fluoridation: Adjusted
Water Quality: NA
Places Rated Score: 568
Places Rated Rank: 72

Mountain Home–Norfork Lake, AR
Physicians per 100,000: 102
Hospital Beds per 100,000: 421
Total Number of Hospitals: 1
Community Mental Health Centers:
Ozark Regional Mental Health Center, Inc.
Hospices:
Hospice of the Ozarks
Fluoridation: Adjusted
Water Quality: NA
Places Rated Score: 713
Places Rated Rank: 51

Myrtle Beach, SC
Physicians per 100,000: 94
Hospital Beds per 100,000: 471
Total Number of Hospitals: 4
Additional Health Care Options:
Cardiac Intensive Care
Fluoridation: No
Water Quality: Alkaline, hard
Places Rated Score: 630
Places Rated Rank: 62

Nevada City–Donner, CA
Physicians per 100,000: 159
Hospital Beds per 100,000: 395
Total Number of Hospitals: 3
Additional Health Care Options:
Cardiac Intensive Care
Home Nursing Care
Fluoridation: No
Water Quality: NA
Places Rated Score: 557
Places Rated Rank: 74

North Conway–White Mountains, NH
Physicians per 100,000: 187
Hospital Beds per 100,000: 570
Total Number of Hospitals: 2
Community Mental Health Centers:
Northern New Hampshire Mental Health
Center, Inc.
Fluoridation: Natural
Water Quality: NA
Places Rated Score: 772
Places Rated Rank: 45

Oak Harbor, WA
Physicians per 100,000: 56
Hospital Beds per 100,000: 244
Total Number of Hospitals: 2
Additional Health Care Options:
Cardiac Intensive Care
Outpatient Psychiatric Services
Fluoridation: Adjusted
Water Quality: NA
Places Rated Score: 578
Places Rated Rank: 71

OCALA, FL
Physicians per 100,000: 96
Hospital Beds per 100,000: 375
Total Number of Hospitals: 3
Community Mental Health Centers:
West Central Florida Human Resources
Center
Additional Health Care Options:
Cardiac Intensive Care
Fluoridation: No
Water Quality: Alkaline, soft
Places Rated Score: 684
Places Rated Rank: 54

Ocean City–Assateague Island, MD
Physicians per 100,000: 64
Hospital Beds per 100,000: None
Total Number of Hospitals: None
Fluoridation: No
Water Quality: NA
Places Rated Score: 64
Places Rated Rank: 106

OLYMPIA, WA
Physicians per 100,000: 153
Hospital Beds per 100,000: 195
Total Number of Hospitals: 1
Additional Health Care Options:
Cardiac Intensive Care
Fluoridation: No
Water Quality: Alkaline, very soft
Places Rated Score: 351
Places Rated Rank: 89

ORLANDO, FL
Physicians per 100,000: 139
Hospital Beds per 100,000: 547
Total Number of Hospitals: 14
Community Mental Health Centers:
Beth Johnson Community Mental Health
Center
Orange Memorial Community Mental
Health Center
Southwest Community Mental Health Center

Additional Health Care Options:
Cardiac Intensive Care
Outpatient Hemodialysis
Outpatient Psychiatric Services
Home Nursing Care
Fluoridation: Adjusted
Water Quality: Alkaline, hard
Places Rated Score: 1,313
Places Rated Rank: 11

Oscoda–Huron Shore, MI
Physicians per 100,000: 43
Hospital Beds per 100,000: 291
Total Number of Hospitals: 2
Additional Health Care Options:
Outpatient Psychiatric Services
Fluoridation: No
Water Quality: NA
Places Rated Score: 289
Places Rated Rank: 93

Paris, TN
Physicians per 100,000: 87
Hospital Beds per 100,000: 655
Total Number of Hospitals: 1
Additional Health Care Options:
Cardiac Intensive Care
Fluoridation: Adjusted
Water Quality: NA
Places Rated Score: 715
Places Rated Rank: 49

**Petoskey–Straits of
Mackinac, MI**
Physicians per 100,000: 325
Hospital Beds per 100,000: 1,287
Total Number of Hospitals: 2
Additional Health Care Options:
Cardiac Intensive Care
Outpatient Hemodialysis
Fluoridation: Adjusted
Water Quality: Alkaline, very hard
Places Rated Score: 1,225
Places Rated Rank: 16

PHOENIX, AZ
Physicians per 100,000: 199
Hospital Beds per 100,000: 516
Total Number of Hospitals: 29
Teaching Hospitals:
Good Samaritan Hospital
Maricopa County General Hospital
St. Joseph's Hospital and Medical Center
Community Mental Health Centers:
Camelback Hospital Mental Health Center
Central Valley Community Mental Health
Center
Phoenix South Community Mental Health
Center
Hospices:
Hospice of the Valley
St. Joseph's Hospital and Medical Center
Samaritan Health Service
Additional Health Care Options:
Cardiac Intensive Care
Outpatient Hemodialysis
Outpatient Psychiatric Services
Home Nursing Care
Fluoridation: No
Water Quality: Alkaline, hard
Places Rated Score: 2,057
Places Rated Rank: 7

Port Angeles–Strait of Juan de Fuca, WA
Physicians per 100,000: 124
Hospital Beds per 100,000: 292
Total Number of Hospitals: 2
Fluoridation: No
Water Quality: Neutral, very soft
Places Rated Score: 270
Places Rated Rank: 95

Prescott, AZ
Physicians per 100,000: 121
Hospital Beds per 100,000: 958
Total Number of Hospitals: 4
Additional Health Care Options:
  Cardiac Intensive Care
  Outpatient Psychiatric Services
Fluoridation: No
Water Quality: Neutral, soft
Places Rated Score: 800
Places Rated Rank: 40

Rappahannock, VA
Physicians per 100,000: 87
Hospital Beds per 100,000: None
Total Number of Hospitals: None
Fluoridation: No
Water Quality: NA
Places Rated Score: 87
Places Rated Rank: 105

Red Bluff–Sacramento Valley, CA
Physicians per 100,000: 71
Hospital Beds per 100,000: 450
Total Number of Hospitals: 3
Additional Health Care Options:
  Home Nursing Care
Fluoridation: No
Water Quality: NA
Places Rated Score: 396
Places Rated Rank: 83

Rehoboth Bay–Indian River Bay, DE
Physicians per 100,000: 126
Hospital Beds per 100,000: 503
Total Number of Hospitals: 3
Community Mental Health Centers:
  Sussex County Community Health Center
Additional Health Care Options:
  Cardiac Intensive Care
  Outpatient Psychiatric Services
Fluoridation: No
Water Quality: NA
Places Rated Score: 678
Places Rated Rank: 57

RENO, NV
Physicians per 100,000: 193
Hospital Beds per 100,000: 1,006
Total Number of Hospitals: 4
Medical Schools:
  University of Nevada School of Medical Sciences
Additional Health Care Options:
  Cardiac Intensive Care
  Outpatient Hemodialysis
  Outpatient Psychiatric Services
  Home Nursing Care
Fluoridation: No

Water Quality: Alkaline, very soft
Places Rated Score: 1,293
Places Rated Rank: 12

Rhinelander, WI
Physicians per 100,000: 173
Hospital Beds per 100,000: 789
Total Number of Hospitals: 2
Additional Health Care Options:
  Outpatient Hemodialysis
Fluoridation: Adjusted
Water Quality: Alkaline, very soft
Places Rated Score: 868
Places Rated Rank: 36

Rockport–Aransas Pass, TX
Physicians per 100,000: 114
Hospital Beds per 100,000: None
Total Number of Hospitals: None
Fluoridation: No
Water Quality: NA
Places Rated Score: 314
Places Rated Rank: 91

Roswell, NM
Physicians per 100,000: 88
Hospital Beds per 100,000: 658
Total Number of Hospitals: 5
Community Mental Health Centers:
  District VI Community Counseling and Resource Center
Additional Health Care Options:
  Cardiac Intensive Care
  Outpatient Hemodialysis
  Outpatient Psychiatric Services
Fluoridation: Natural
Water Quality: Alkaline, very hard
Places Rated Score: 1,017
Places Rated Rank: 28

St. George–Zion, UT
Physicians per 100,000: 83
Hospital Beds per 100,000: 215
Total Number of Hospitals: 1
Additional Health Care Options:
  Cardiac Intensive Care
  Outpatient Psychiatric Services
Fluoridation: No
Water Quality: NA
Places Rated Score: 491
Places Rated Rank: 78

SAN ANTONIO, TX
Physicians per 100,000: 171
Hospital Beds per 100,000: 780
Total Number of Hospitals: 20
Medical Schools:
  University of Texas Medical School at San Antonio
Teaching Hospitals:
  Audie L. Murphy Memorial Veterans Hospital
  Bexar County Hospital District
  Wilford Hall USAF Medical Center
Community Mental Health Centers:
  Bexar County Mental Health/Mental Retardation Center (Southeast)
  Bexar County Mental Health/Mental Retardation Center (Southwest)

  Northwest San Antonio Mental Health Center
Additional Health Care Options:
  Cardiac Intensive Care
  Outpatient Hemodialysis
  Outpatient Psychiatric Services
  Home Nursing Care
Fluoridation: No
Water Quality: Medium–hard
Places Rated Score: 2,061
Places Rated Rank: 6

SAN DIEGO, CA
Physicians per 100,000: 219
Hospital Beds per 100,000: 496
Total Number of Hospitals: 38
Medical Schools:
  University of California (San Diego) School of Medicine
Teaching Hospitals:
  Mercy Hospital and Medical Center
  University Hospital
  Veterans Administration Medical Center
Comprehensive Cancer Treatment Centers:
  University of California (San Diego) Cancer Center
Hospices:
  College Park Hospital Hospice Program
  El Cajon Valley Hospital Hospice Unit
  San Diego County Hospice Corporation
Additional Health Care Options:
  Cardiac Intensive Care
  Outpatient Hemodialysis
  Outpatient Psychiatric Services
  Home Nursing Care
Fluoridation: No
Water Quality: Alkaline, hard
Places Rated Score: 2,067
Places Rated Rank: 5

San Luis Obispo, CA
Physicians per 100,000: 184
Hospital Beds per 100,000: 1,431
Total Number of Hospitals: 9
Community Mental Health Centers:
  San Luis Obispo Community Mental Health Center
Hospices:
  Hospice of San Luis Obispo County, Inc.
Additional Health Care Options:
  Cardiac Intensive Care
  Home Nursing Care
Fluoridation: Adjusted
Water Quality: Alkaline, hard
Places Rated Score: 1,284
Places Rated Rank: 13

Santa Fe, NM
Physicians per 100,000: 202
Hospital Beds per 100,000: 386
Total Number of Hospitals: 2
Community Mental Health Centers:
  Counseling and Resource Center, Inc.
Additional Health Care Options:
  Cardiac Intensive Care
  Outpatient Psychiatric Services
  Home Nursing Care
Fluoridation: Adjusted

Water Quality: Neutral–hard in winter, soft in summer
Places Rated Score: 995
Places Rated Rank: 31

SANTA ROSA, CA
Physicians per 100,000: 187
Hospital Beds per 100,000: 342
Total Number of Hospitals: 10
Hospices:
Home Hospice of Sonoma County
Valley of the Moon Hospice
Additional Health Care Options:
Cardiac Intensive Care
Outpatient Hemodialysis
Outpatient Psychiatric Services
Fluoridation: No
Water Quality: Alkaline, hard
Places Rated Score: 758
Places Rated Rank: 47

SARASOTA–BRADENTON, FL
Physicians per 100,000: 288
Hospital Beds per 100,000: 581
Total Number of Hospitals: 4
Community Mental Health Centers:
Manatee County Community Mental
Health Center
Hospices:
Hospice of Sarasota County
Additional Health Care Options:
Cardiac Intensive Care
Outpatient Hemodialysis
Home Nursing Care
Fluoridation: No
Water Quality: Hard (Sarasota); neutral–soft
(Bradenton)
Places Rated Score: 1,279
Places Rated Rank: 14

SPRINGFIELD, MO
Physicians per 100,000: 145
Hospital Beds per 100,000: 1,105
Total Number of Hospitals: 5
Community Mental Health Centers:
D.E. Burrell Community Mental Health
Center
Hospices:
Hospice of Southwest Missouri
Additional Health Care Options:
Cardiac Intensive Care
Outpatient Hemodialysis
Outpatient Psychiatric Services
Fluoridation: No
Water Quality: Alkaline, hard
Places Rated Score: 1,145
Places Rated Rank: 22

STATE COLLEGE, PA
Physicians per 100,000: 104
Hospital Beds per 100,000: 380
Total Number of Hospitals: 4
Additional Health Care Options:
Cardiac Intensive Care
Outpatient Hemodialysis
Home Nursing Care
Fluoridation: Adjusted

Water Quality: Alkaline. Very soft December
to July; very hard July to December
Places Rated Score: 794
Places Rated Rank: 41

Table Rock Lake, MO
Physicians per 100,000: 93
Hospital Beds per 100,000: None
Total Number of Hospitals: None
Fluoridation: No
Water Quality: NA
Places Rated Score: 93
Places Rated Rank: 104

Tahlequah–Lake Tenkiller, OK
Physicians per 100,000: 40
Hospital Beds per 100,000: 414
Total Number of Hospitals: 2
Additional Health Care Options:
Outpatient Hemodialysis
Fluoridation: Adjusted
Water Quality: Alkaline, soft
Places Rated Score: 547
Places Rated Rank: 75

Toms River–Barnegat Bay, NJ
Physicians per 100,000: 103
Hospital Beds per 100,000: 295
Total Number of Hospitals: 5
Hospices:
Community Memorial Hospital–Hospice
Program
Additional Health Care Options:
Cardiac Intensive Care
Outpatient Hemodialysis
Home Nursing Care
Fluoridation: No
Water Quality: Hard
Places Rated Score: 651
Places Rated Rank: 59

Traverse City–Grand Traverse Bay, MI
Physicians per 100,000: 254
Hospital Beds per 100,000: 2,313
Total Number of Hospitals: 3
Hospices:
Grand Traverse Area Hospice
Additional Health Care Options:
Cardiac Intensive Care
Home Nursing Care
Fluoridation: Adjusted
Water Quality: Alkaline, soft
Places Rated Score: 1,254
Places Rated Rank: 15

TUCSON, AZ
Physicians per 100,000: 266
Hospital Beds per 100,000: 552
Total Number of Hospitals: 13
Medical Schools:
University of Arizona College of Medicine
Teaching Hospitals:
Tucson Medical Center
University of Arizona Health Sciences
Center
Veterans Administration Medical Center
Comprehensive Cancer Treatment Centers:
University of Arizona Cancer Center

Community Mental Health Centers:
Palo Verde Mental Health Services
Tucson Southern Counties Mental Health
Service, Inc.
Hospices:
Hillhaven Hospice
Additional Health Care Options:
Cardiac Intensive Care
Outpatient Hemodialysis
Outpatient Psychiatric Services
Home Nursing Care
Fluoridation: No
Water Quality: Alkaline, very hard
Places Rated Score: 2,142
Places Rated Rank: 2

Twain Harte–Yosemite, CA
Physicians per 100,000: 150
Hospital Beds per 100,000: 685
Total Number of Hospitals: 3
Additional Health Care Options:
Outpatient Psychiatric Services
Fluoridation: No
Water Quality: Neutral, soft
Places Rated Score: 593
Places Rated Rank: 69

WEST PALM BEACH–BOCA RATON, FL
Physicians per 100,000: 205
Hospital Beds per 100,000: 498
Total Number of Hospitals: 12
Community Mental Health Centers:
Palm Beach County Comprehensive Com-
munity Mental Health Center
Hospices:
Hospice of Boca Raton
Hospice of Palm Beach County
Additional Health Care Options:
Cardiac Intensive Care
Outpatient Hemodialysis
Outpatient Psychiatric Services
Home Nursing Care
Fluoridation: No
Water Quality: Neutral, soft
Places Rated Score: 1,154
Places Rated Rank: 20

Winchester, VA
Physicians per 100,000: 387
Hospital Beds per 100,000: 2,073
Total Number of Hospitals: 1
Additional Health Care Options:
Cardiac Intensive Care
Outpatient Hemodialysis
Fluoridation: Adjusted
Water Quality: Alkaline
Places Rated Score: 1,187
Places Rated Rank: 19

Yuma, AZ
Physicians per 100,000: 83
Hospital Beds per 100,000: 280
Total Number of Hospitals: 3
Additional Health Care Options:
Home Nursing Care
Fluoridation: Natural
Water Quality: Neutral, very hard
Places Rated Score: 523
Places Rated Rank: 77

Et Cetera

YOU ARE WHAT YOU EAT, SMOKE, DRINK . . .

Do you subscribe to the when-your-number's-up-it's-up theory of life expectancy? Then you may be surprised to learn that, based on recent trends, experts conclude that it's less likely to be a stray bullet or virus that kills you than the way you lead your life.

The most common causes of death at the turn of the century—typhoid fever, cholera, tuberculosis, smallpox, gastroenteritis, and nephritis—have been practically eliminated by scientific advances and improved sanitation. Today, more than 70 percent of the two million Americans who die each year are victims of heart disease, cancer, stroke, cirrhosis of the liver, bronchitis, asthma, and emphysema—the so-called life-style diseases that may be aggravated by such behavior as overeating, heavy drinking, smoking, and lack of exercise.

Therefore, a few alterations in your life-style could help reduce your risk of disease. The following are some suggestions that can help you stay healthy.

Get regular exercise. Exercise, now seen almost as a miracle drug, can help you maintain proper weight, keep your body in good operating condition, and relieve stress (which contributes to ulcers and high blood pressure). It's also necessary to prevent premature aging and degeneration of muscles and joints. The use-it-or-lose-it maxim definitely applies here.

Walking, jogging, yoga, and swimming all help promote good health; the important thing is to get in some physical activity each day. Any kind of workout that raises your heartbeat and makes you breathe deeply is likely to help.

But too much exercise can be harmful. You should confer with your doctor as to the most suitable type and amount of exercise for your particular case. Don't be surprised if brisk walking is at the top of the list of recommended exercise. This activity burns about 400 calories an hour and increases both cardiovascular and muscular fitness. Swimming is also often suggested for retirement-aged people.

Eat a balanced diet and watch your weight. Diet is coming to be viewed as more and more important to health. Reducing your intake of refined flour and sugar, salt (which in excess contributes to high blood pressure), and saturated fats (which have been implicated as factors in heart disease and stroke) while choosing from a range of meat, poultry, fish, fruits, vegetables, and fiber foods is highly recommended. A balanced diet can also help you to lose extra weight, which puts added stress on the heart and organs, aggravating disease conditions.

Stop smoking and drink only in moderation. Cigarette smokers run twice the risk that nonsmokers do of death from coronary disease. Smoking also contributes to stroke, lung cancer, emphysema, and bronchitis. Likewise, an excess of alcohol can be dangerous, increasing your chances of developing cirrhosis of the liver (this condition is found six times as frequently among alcoholics as among nonalcoholics) and cardiovascular problems. Drinking combined with driving multiplies the risk of dying in an automobile accident; half of such accidents in the United States involve drunk drivers.

Get regular medical care. Be sure to consult your doctor regularly and have whatever checkups or tests he or she recommends, such as a Pap smear, for cervical cancer, or blood-pressure tests.

IF YOU SUFFER FROM HAY FEVER

Hay fever, which affects more than 16 million Americans, is any allergic reaction of the eyes, nose, or throat to certain airborne particles. These particles may be either pollen from seed-bearing trees, grasses, and weeds, or spores from certain molds. Most individuals might assume that once they're well into adulthood, they already know whether or not they have hay fever. But if you were to relocate for retirement, would you suddenly and mysteriously develop a continual running nose and minor sore throat? Remember the caveat by NOAA's Bill Hodge (page 34) that allergy problems aren't always alleviated by relocation. Sometimes a new allergen—absent where you used to live—causes hay fever in your "golden years."

Percent of Population Engaged in Exercise

	Age 45–64		Age 65 and Over	
	Male	Female	Male	Female
Total Percent Exercising Regularly	42.0	44.6	47.3	38.7
Walking	31.4	34.2	39.4	33.0
Calisthenics	10.1	11.4	5.9	6.3
Swimming	8.1	7.8	4.1	1.9
Bicycling	6.7	6.4	4.3	1.8
Jogging	3.8	1.6	2.1	*
All other	5.9	7.1	8.1	6.0

Source: U.S. Bureau of the Census, *Statistical Abstract of the United States: 1982–83,* 1982.

*Less than minimum required for reliability.

Figures are for 1975.

Where Hay Fever Is Found

The incidence of hay fever varies around the world. In the Arctic, for example, it doesn't exist. Because of low temperatures and poor soil, arctic plants are small and primitive. In the tropics and subtropics, there is very little hay fever because the plants are generally flowered and produce pollen that is so heavy it cannot become airborne.

It is in the temperate regions that one finds the greatest amounts of irritating pollen. The worst places in America for hay fever are the middle regions where grasses and trees without flowers predominate. Because farming continually disrupts the soil and therefore encourages the growth of weeds (especially that archvillain of hay fever, ragweed), America's heartland is the most hay fever–ridden area. It extends from the Rockies to the Appalachian chain, and from the Canadian border down to the states of the mid-South.

Yet no area of the country except Alaska and the southern half of Florida is free of hay fever—it's simply a question of degree. The West Coast is almost ragweed-free, although it has other allergenic pollens.

Counting All Those Pollen Grains

The American Academy of Allergy has devised the Ragweed Pollen Index to indicate the local severity of the pollen problem. This index is derived from (1) length of the season, (2) concentration of pollen grains in the air at the season's peak, and (3) total pollen catch throughout the season. The table below lists Ragweed Pollen Index readings for reporting stations at or near *Places Rated* retirement places. The name of the retirement place is given when it differs from or is in addition to the reporting station. The higher the index number, the worse the problem; an index greater than ten means lots of discomfort.

Ragweed Pollen Index for Selected Places

State	Station	Ragweed Pollen Index	Retirement Place
Alabama	Mobile	8.0	Fairhope–Gulf Shores
Arizona	Phoenix	0.2	
	Tucson	2.0	
California	Alpine	3.0	Twain Harte–Yosemite
	San Diego	11.0	
Colorado	Colorado Springs	4.0	
Florida	Bradenton	4.0	SARASOTA–BRADENTON
	Daytona Beach	3.0	
	Fort Lauderdale	9.0	FORT LAUDERDALE–HOLLYWOOD
	Fort Myers	0.2	FORT MYERS–CAPE CORAL
	Melbourne	21.0	MELBOURNE–TITUSVILLE–COCOA
	Miami	2.0	
	Orlando	3.0	
	West Palm Beach	5.0	WEST PALM BEACH–BOCA RATON
Idaho	Boise City	5.0	
Kentucky	Lexington	151.0	LEXINGTON–FAYETTE
Massachusetts	Nantucket	5.0	Cape Cod
Michigan	Charlevoix	21.0	Petoskey–Straits of Mackinac Traverse City–Grand Traverse Bay
Mississippi	Biloxi	7.0	BILOXI–GULFPORT
Montana	Glacier National Park	0.1	Kalispell
Nevada	Reno	0.1	
New Hampshire	Conway	3.0	North Conway–White Mountains
New Jersey	Atlantic City	30.0	ATLANTIC CITY–CAPE MAY
New Mexico	Albuquerque	7.0	
	Roswell	4.0	
North Carolina	Asheville	57.0	
Texas	Brownsville	24.0	MCALLEN–PHARR–EDINBURG
	San Antonio	16.0	
Utah	Zion National Park	0.7	St. George–Zion
Virginia	Charlottesville	35.0	
Wisconsin	Eagle River	13.0	Rhinelander

Source: American Academy of Allergy, 1977.

Some places that were once havens for asthmatics and hay-fever sufferers are now less free of allergens. Examples are many of the retirement spots found in Arizona. Thirty years ago, Tucson was virtually free of ragweed pollen. Its desert location precluded the growth of the weeds, grasses, and trees that cause hay fever. But as more and more people moved into the area, more trees were planted and lawns seeded. The result? A pollen index that's still good but not as good as it used to be.

Maybe It's Not Hay Fever

Making certain what you're allergic to isn't necessarily easy. Don't assume automatically that it's ragweed or other irritating pollen. For example, if you get "hay fever" out of season, or year round, there's a good chance you are allergic to mold spores, not pollen. Although primarily associated with damp, still places —crawl spaces, attics, cellars, and closed-up rooms— molds are practically everywhere: They spoil bread, rot fruit, and mildew cloth. The spores of the mold plants somewhat resemble pollen, and some molds produce spores that are smaller and even more numerous than ragweed pollen.

The season for mold allergies is a long one, even longer than the season for hay fever; in many damp places, the season can last year round. Molds are less abundant in regions that are high and dry. According to the American Academy of Allergy, the best places to go if you are plagued with this allergy are the dry areas of the Southwest, California, and the Northwest. Molds are found to only a slight extent in the eastern, southern, and Rocky Mountain states. The worst states for mold allergy, in descending order, are Nebraska, Missouri, Iowa, Kansas, Illinois, Indiana, Ohio, Wisconsin, and Michigan.

Spending as much time as possible—at different times of the year—in your proposed new retirement spot *before* committing yourself to a permanent move will allow you to discover if there's any new allergen there that might make you miserable.

AIR POLLUTION

The U.S. Environmental Protection Agency (EPA) measures six major air pollutants that can be injurious to human health. These pollutants are sulfur dioxide, carbon monoxide, lead, ozone, nitrogen dioxide, and total suspended particulates. The first five of these are chemical elements or compounds that have destructive effects on living tissue. The last, total suspended particulates, is a broad category of pollutants encompassing all solid particles that float in the air. These particles may be dust, soot, fly ash, asbestos fibers, wheat or grain dust, or fabric fibers.

The EPA measures these pollutants at special air monitoring stations, most of which are located either in heavily populated areas or else in areas suspected of containing one or more sources of pollution. There-

fore, most of the places discussed in *Places Rated Retirement Guide* contain no air monitoring station whatsoever. Does this mean that they're all pollution-free? Don't count on it. Just remember that when pollutants aren't searched for, they're never found. Generally speaking, however, the lack of a monitoring station in a given county is a fairly good indication that air pollution is not a problem there.

Of the places in *Places Rated Retirement Guide* that are monitored by the EPA, a few do have air pollution. Below are listed those locations that exceed the EPA annual geometric mean for certain pollutants.

Place	Exceeds EPA annual mean for
AUSTIN, TX	Total suspended particulates
MIAMI, FL	Carbon monoxide, ozone, total suspended particulates
PHOENIX, AZ	Carbon monoxide, ozone, total suspended particulates
TUCSON, AZ	Total suspended particulates
SAN DIEGO, CA	Ozone, total suspended particulates

DRIVER AGE DISCRIMINATION?

Once you start feeling your age, will insurance companies and state highway safety committees consider you dangerous when you get behind the wheel of your automobile?

On the face of it, older drivers have a better accident record than younger drivers; people over 65 represent one in nine persons in this country yet are involved in only one in 17 of the automobile accidents. According to the National Safety Council, however, people over 65 drive much less than younger people and actually have a poorer accident record in terms of the miles they drive.

At the 1974 Conference on the Aging Driver, the American Medical Association and the American Association of Motor Vehicle Administrators recommended that no driver's license should be placed in jeopardy just because the licensee is older, but added that "it does make sense for the licensing agency to conduct more frequent reexamination of the senior citizen." Accordingly, six states and Washington, D.C., now require special examinations or reexaminations based solely on age.

Illinois	Complete reexamination every 4 years for drivers over 69.
Indiana	Complete reexamination every 2 years for drivers over 75.
Louisiana	Physical examination every 4 years for drivers over 60.
Maine	Vision reexamination at age 40, age 52, and age 65 and over; driving reexamination at 75 and over.
New Hampshire	Complete reexamination for drivers over 75.
North Dakota	Vision examination for drivers over 70.
Washington, D.C.	Vision and reaction examination for drivers over 70; complete reexamination at age 75 and over.

Source: Federal Highway Administration, *Driver License Administration Requirements and Fees,* 1982.

DRIVING DANGER SIGNALS

Older drivers receive a disproportionately high number of tickets for five different traffic violations, according to data gathered from the records of insurance companies and state police agencies by Dr. Leon Pastalan at the University of Michigan. These violations are:

- Rear-end collisions
- Dangerously slow driving
- Failing to yield the right-of-way
- Driving the wrong way on one-way streets
- Making illegal turns

Even though people age at different rates, normal changes that affect hearing, eyesight, and muscle reflexes are major reasons older people are ticketed for these moving violations more often than the rest of the population. According to Dr. Pastalan, an authority on driving problems encountered by older people, simply recognizing your limitations will help you become a better driver.

Hearing. Hearing loss is usually gradual and can go unnoticed for a long time. One in every five persons over 55 has impaired hearing. So does one of every three persons over 65. When you can't hear the ambulance siren, a ticket for failing to yield the right-of-way to an emergency vehicle may be the likely consequence.

You can compensate somewhat for hearing loss by having periodic checkups. When driving, you can also open a window, turn off the radio, keep the air conditioner fan on low, and eliminate unnecessary conversation.

Eyesight. Research shows that we get 90 percent of all sensory input needed to drive a car through our eyes. As vision loses its sharpness, older drivers find rectangular black-and-white road signs hard to read. Night driving is especially hazardous; the older we get, the more illumination we need (an 80-year-old needs three times the light that a 20-year-old needs to read, for example). Other problems include loss of depth perception (a major cause of rear-end collisions) and limited peripheral vision (dangerous when making turns at intersections).

You can adjust to these hazards by not driving at night, having regular eye checkups, wearing gray or green-tinted sunglasses on days with high sun glare, and replacing the standard rear-view mirror with a wide-angle one to aid peripheral vision.

Muscle Reflexes. Chances are you're slowing down as you're getting older. Strength may dwindle, neck and shoulder joints stiffen, and you may tire sooner. Most important to driving, your reflex reaction may slow. All of these symptoms can affect how safely you enter a busy freeway, change lanes to pass a plodding 18-wheel truck, or avoid a rear-end fender bender.

Ask your physician if any of the medication you're taking might dull your alertness and ability to drive defensively. On long road trips, take along a companion to share the driving and break the day's distance into short stretches to reduce fatigue. Avoid being caught on freeways and major arterial streets during morning and evening rush hours.

"MEDISCARE": SUPPLEMENTING YOUR MEDICARE BENEFITS

Last year the average medical bill for every person over 65 was $2,026, more than twice as high as the mean medical bill for people in the broad 19-to-64 age group. Whether or not they are retired, most Americans upon reaching the age of 65 are covered by Medicare, the two-part insurance program—one for hospital benefits, the other for medical benefits—administered by the Social Security Administration.

But Medicare reimburses only a percentage of many hospital and medical costs, and it does not cover any part of prescription medication, dental care, eyeglasses, hearing aids, and so on. In addition, many doctors will not accept Medicare's "reasonable charge" estimate for various medical supplies and services, which means the patient winds up paying the difference. For example, a clinic in Cleveland might charge $1,000 for gallbladder surgery. Medicare guidelines stipulate a fee of $584 for this operation, of which Medicare will pay 80 percent; this will leave a discrepancy of $533 for which the patient is responsible.

It is therefore little wonder that two thirds of all people over 65 have some kind of supplemental health insurance purchased from a private company. Unfortunately, reports the House of Representatives Select Committee on Aging, every year older people spend $1 billion on fraudulent or unnecessary health-insurance policies.

"Mediscare"

Mediscare is the nickname given the health-insurance racket that siphons off hard-earned cash reserves by selling people worthless supplemental insurance. Mediscare plays on the universal fear older people have of prolonged hospitalization and extensive medical care that will empty the family coffers and leave their children broke, even though chances of full recovery are remote. Many supplemental policies sold to retirees are, when the verbiage is stripped away, long on premiums and short on benefits.

Beware of any company that seems to promise too much. Watch out especially for any policy that guarantees coverage no matter what disease you now have or have ever had. Any insurance company that is legitimate and reliable will probably request a detailed medical history, with premiums to vary accordingly. Some unscrupulous insurance agents have been known to falsify medical histories and insurance applications so that their client will be accepted. The applicant is delighted at being accepted, especially at such a low rate, but when he files the first claim he is denied coverage for falsifying his application. In a few instances, the claimant not only suffered the loss of his claim but also was taken to court for the fraud committed by his agent.

Beware also of any company that promises to begin coverage without a waiting period, the amount of time that must pass after the onset of a medical problem before the benefit payments commence. Most waiting periods are between 30 and 90 days. Policies that offer no waiting period, like those that promise to pay benefits regardless of medical history, are suspect.

Don't think that because you're buying many health-insurance policies you are doubling or trebling your protection and benefits. It is most unlikely that you will ever get money from different companies simultaneously for the same medical problem or treatment. Most policies have a coordination-of-benefits clause that prohibits collecting from more than one company at a time.

Some Guidelines for Buying Supplemental Health Insurance.

• If you have not yet retired and have group health-insurance coverage from your employer, see if this group coverage can be continued at a slightly higher rate. Group plans cost less than individual ones and can often fill many Medicare gaps.

• If you decide to buy private supplemental insurance, buy from a reputable local agent who has an office in your town. Make sure he represents legitimate companies. You can check on any insurance agent or company by contacting your state insurance department. All insurance agents must pass special examinations and be licensed by the states they work in; ask to see proof of licensing. A business card or letterhead does not constitute proof. Do not buy insurance from any person who does not have a local office or who calls at your door without an appointment.

• Supplemental health-insurance policies are neither sold nor serviced by state or federal governmental agencies. Do not believe any statements that a policy is part of a government-sponsored program. If anyone tells you that he or she is from the government and later tries to sell you insurance, report the person to your state insurance department immediately.

• Beware of replacing existing coverage. Be suspicious of any suggestion that you give up your present policy and buy a replacement. On the other hand, if careful study reveals a bargain and if the company and agent have proven to be reliable, there is no reason to keep an expensive or inadequate policy simply because you have had it a long time.

• Whenever possible, buy one complete insurance policy rather than several policies with overlapping or duplicate coverages. For comprehensive coverage, consider extending current group plans or enrolling in a Health Maintenance Organization (HMO), which provides medical and "well care" on a fixed monthly-fee basis. Other possible options include catastrophic health insurance or a major medical policy.

• Do not pay cash when buying an insurance policy. Make out a check or bank draft to the insurance *company*, not the salesman. Refuse to do business with any agent who demands cash or a check payable to him.

• The "free look" provision and refund policy are crucial. Most companies give you at least ten days to review your policy. If you decide you don't want it, you may send it back to the agent for a full refund. Also, companies should issue the policy to you within 30 days. If you do not receive the policy within this time, contact the company. If 60 days elapse without receipt of the policy, notify your state insurance department.

An excellent government pamphlet on this subject, entitled "Guide to Health Insurance for People with Medicare," is available free from the Department of Health and Human Services, Health Care Financing Administration, Baltimore, MD 21207.

FINDING A NEW DOCTOR

Chances are good that you'll have to choose a new physician at some point; even if you don't move after retirement, your doctor might. Finding a replacement for the person in whom you've put so much trust isn't always easy.

Give some thought to the kind of doctor you are most comfortable with. Do you want to place utter faith in your physician? Or do you have questions about your treatment? Do you like a cooperative arrangement, in which you and your doctor work as a team? It's very important to most people that they have a doctor who will listen to their complaints, worries, and concerns, rather than one who may make patients feel that they're questioning the doctor's authority.

If you're planning to move, you might ask your present doctor if he or she knows anything about the doctors in the area where you are going. Or you can get names from the nearest hospital at the new location, from friends you make, from medical societies, from new neighbors. The reference rooms in nearly all libraries have directories telling where all doctors certified in the state were trained, when they received their training, what their specialties are, and some personal information, such as their age (you want your doctor to be practicing during the years you are a patient).

When you have decided whom you want to contact, call that doctor's office, saying that you are a prospective patient, and ask to speak to the doctor briefly. You may have to agree to call back. But this is an important step. If you can't arrange this, if the doctor is "too busy," you probably ought to go to the next name on your list. You need a physician who will be accessible.

When you do make contact, tell the doctor enough

about yourself so that he or she has a fairly good idea of who you are and what your problems may be. If the doctor sounds "right" to you, you could ask about fees, house calls (yes, they are still made when necessary), and emergencies. Or you may wish to save some of these questions for a personal visit. It is important to establish through the initial phone call or the initial visit that you and the doctor will be at ease with each other.

Evaluate the doctor's attitude. If he or she does not want to bother with you now, you will probably get that don't-bother-me treatment sooner or later when dealing with specific problems. Make sure you can consult the doctor by phone when and if that is needed; make sure the doctor is interested in and knowledgeable about the problems of older people. Talk with the doctor about the transfer of your medical records. Some doctors like to have them, especially if there is any specific medical problem or chronic condition. Some prefer not to see them, and to develop new records.

Even if you feel fine, arrange to have a physical or at least a quick checkup. This is more for the doctor's benefit than for yours, but it will help you, too. Should an emergency occur, the doctor will have basic information about you and some knowledge of your needs, and you will avoid the stress of trying to work with a doctor who has to learn about you in an emergency situation.

DON'T PUT OFF YOUR WILL

It's human nature to avoid thinking about the need for a will. Seven out of every ten people die without one, and eight of ten who do have a will fail to keep it up-to-date. If you don't have a will when you die, the state where you live in your retirement years will write one for you according to its own statutes, and the assets you may have worked hard to accumulate will be distributed according to its laws.

This is particularly critical for persons who move to new states. Even if your will is legal in your new state (and it may not be), it might not do the best possible job. So when you resettle, see a lawyer in your new area to make certain your will is one your state will recognize. Some states, for example, require that the executor of a will be a resident of the state where the deceased lived.

Don't put off making a will because of imagined costs. A lawyer can tell you the basic fee in advance; it's usually $50 to $100 for a simple document. And it may save your heirs thousands.

Once you have a will, make a note to yourself in your calendar to review it every year. Births, marriages, deaths, hard feelings, the patching-up of hard feelings, plus changes in your finances, in your health, or in federal or state laws—any of these may affect your will. Regular, periodic review helps ensure that you won't forget to make needed adjustments.

If death and taxes are inevitable—as the old saying goes—so are taxes after death. But it isn't all bad. Since 1981, no estate smaller than $175,625 has been subject to any federal tax. State tax exemptions vary greatly (see the state tax profiles on pages 83-91) and often change, another reason for keeping the document up-to-date.

Where should you keep your will? Put it in a safe place, but don't hide it behind a painting or under a rug. If you conceal it too well, a court may rule that you don't have one! Your lawyer should have a signed copy, and the original should be in a logical place, such as a safety-deposit box or your desk. Be sure your spouse, a close relative, or a friend knows where both the copies and the original are.

MUTUAL-SUPPORT GROUPS: PEOPLE HELPING PEOPLE

For many human problems there are no cures and sometimes few answers; some needs cannot be met through formal health-care agencies or facilities. There are, however, alternatives to coping with problems alone. This is particularly true for older persons, who often find the support and help they need by meeting with others who have nearly identical concerns, or who have dealt with similar emotional, psychological, or physical difficulties. These mutual-support groups —people coming together because of a common experience—provide members an opportunity not only to get help but to give it to others.

Worldwide, there are estimated to be nearly 450,000 of these groups, which are of basically three types:

Self-care groups for those suffering physical or men-

Seniors on the Prowl: The Gray Panthers

One of the best-known groups for older persons is the Gray Panthers, founded by Maggie Kuhn, who—prior to forming the group in 1972—served the Presbyterian church for many years as a program executive for social education and action. The Gray Panthers focus on building coalitions for a wide variety of political actions. Maggie Kuhn looks like a sweet little old lady who should be presiding over a church supper rather than meeting with some of the most well-informed political activists of the decade. The Gray Panthers maintain an information and referral service, and conduct seminars and research on age-related issues. When important court cases involving the rights of the elderly come up, the Gray Panthers are involved, providing back-up support and briefs or filing appeals. If you are an activist, you'll love the group.

For information, contact: Gray Panthers, 3635 Chestnut Street, Philadelphia, PA 19104.

tal illness. There are colostomy groups, groups for paraplegics, for people suffering from epilepsy, schizophrenia, and every other major disease known to mankind.

Reform groups for addiction behaviors. The most famous and the oldest of these is Alcoholics Anonymous, founded more than 50 years ago in Akron, Ohio, for people who cannot control their use of alcohol. Alcoholics Anonymous is often considered the prototype support group, and its tenets, practices, and structure have been widely copied by other "anonymous" groups, mainly because of the excellent success it has achieved.

Advocacy groups for certain minorities, such as disabled veterans, the handicapped, or the elderly.

Despite the enormous diversity of problems they address, all such support groups have the same underlying purpose: to provide emotional support and practical help in dealing with a situation or problem common to all members. If you've been bereaved, if you have trouble with alcohol, if your spouse has had a troublesome colostomy, or if you are just lonesome—whatever your need, there is a group willing to help and anxious to have you as a member.

The following are some of the more well known and widespread support groups that may be of special interest to retirement-aged persons. Many have local branches that can be found by consulting your phone book. Or you can find out more by writing the group at the address given.

Alcoholics Anonymous, 468 Park Avenue, New York, NY 10016. The most famous, the oldest, and probably the most successful of all mutual-help groups. There are chapters everywhere, and enough meetings so that a problem drinker tempted to return to drinking may attend several local meetings daily.

American Schizophrenia Association, 1114 First Avenue, New York, NY 10021. For schizophrenics.

The Compassionate Friends, P.O. Box 1347, Oak Brook, IL 60521. For bereaved parents; peer support.

Emotions Anonymous, P.O. Box 4245, St. Paul, MN 55104. For people with emotional problems; a 12-step program, adapted from the Alcoholics Anonymous program.

Epilepsy Foundation, 4351 Garden City Drive, Landover, MD 20785. For epileptics and their families.

Families Anonymous, P.O. Box 344, Torrance, CA 90501. For concerned relatives and friends of young people with a wide variety of behavior problems.

Gamblers Anonymous, P.O. Box 17173, Los Angeles, CA 90017. For those who cannot control or stop gambling.

Heart to Heart, 7320 Greenville Avenue, Dallas, TX 75231. A one-to-one visitation program coordinated by local American Heart Association chapters; persons who have had coronary problems visit those facing them.

Make Today Count, P.O. Box 303, Burlington, IA 52601. For persons with cancer, and their families.

National Alliance for the Mentally Ill, 1234 Massachusetts Avenue, N.W., Washington, D.C. 20005. For the families and friends of the mentally ill; peer support and advocacy.

National Federation of the Blind, 1346 Connecticut Avenue, N.W., Washington, D.C. 20036. For blind persons and their families; peer support and advocacy.

National Gay Task Force, 80 Fifth Avenue, Room 1601, New York, NY 10011. Advocacy group for gay people.

Neurotics Anonymous, 1341 G Street, N.W., Washington, D.C. 20005. For neurotic people.

Overeaters Anonymous, 2190 West 190th Street, Torrance, CA 90504. For overweight people; peer support and programs to combat compulsive overeating.

Reach to Recovery, 777 Third Avenue, New York, NY 10017. For women who have had mastectomies; visitation by peers, peer support; through local cancer societies.

Recovery, 116 South Michigan Avenue, Chicago, IL 60603. For former mental patients; peer support.

Smokenders, 37 North Third Street, Easton, PA 18042. A nine-session, $150 "course" to stop smoking.

Theos Foundation, Penn Hills Mall Office Building, Room 306, Pittsburgh, PA 15235. For the widowed and their families.

Widowed Persons, 1909 K Street, N.W., Washington, D.C. 20049. For widows and widowers; peer support.

Leisure Living:
Making the most of local recreation

You may have heard stories similar to these: A couple, rebounding from a pleasant winter and spring but a hellish summer and fall in South Florida, moved up the Atlantic Coast to Myrtle Beach, South Carolina. "It seemed as if half our waking hours were spent waiting in line," they recalled of Florida. "Wait an hour to tee off at the par-three golf course, wait in line an hour for tickets to the Sergio Franchi concert, wait in our car for the traffic jam on the Palmetto Expressway to unravel. The place was too crowded."

Another couple, after a disappointing two years in a desert retirement community, returned to their hometown in the Northeast. "Forget it," they said. "The climate was wonderful and the cost of living low, but there wasn't anything to do but sit and play bridge, sit and talk, and sit and watch cable TV, with time out for an occasional square dance. Whoopee!"

Many persons find that their long-awaited retirement in a distant paradise can be a thudding letdown. The leisure time they now have in abundance is fleeing less swiftly than it did when they were working. But it flees without including achievable, dreamed-about activities. Is the new location to blame? Not entirely.

The routine and structure that start with your first day of school back in first grade and last through 40 or more years of employment can suddenly stop with retirement. Unless you've developed some specific hobbies and established some leisuretime goals long before bidding good-bye to full-time work, you may be hard put to take advantage of the approaching months and years, no matter where in the country you decide to live.

For those who are joiners, there will always be something to do. In Roswell, New Mexico, the Four "I's" (retired persons hailing from Illinois, Iowa, Indiana, and Idaho) get together regularly; in Hendersonville, North Carolina, the Men's Garden Club spruces up landscaping in public areas; there are Knife & Fork clubs and American Association of Retired Persons chapters everywhere; in Sarasota–Bradenton, Florida, there are clubs for ex-teachers, ex-Seabees, Catholics, and even clubs for people suffering from the same disease.

But some places possess more recreational facilities and cultural opportunities than others, and many of these attractions are doubly important to retired persons who want to make the most of their leisure time—whether they're avid golfers, movie buffs, opera fans, or outdoor sportsmen.

COMMON DENOMINATORS

When it comes to soaring in gliders, certain parts of the country are better suited than others because of their winds and weather. If you want to go scuba diving, the Florida, Hawaii, and California coasts are your best bets. But there are certain kinds of recreation that you can find in every corner of the country: weekday golf, when the greens fees are lower; bowling in the clapping din at a local tenpin center; moviegoing in town or at a suburban shopping mall off the interstate; browsing among the quiet stacks at a public library; or taking in the exhibits and programs of a local museum.

Public Golf Links

According to the Interior Department's latest *Outdoor Recreation Survey*, the portion of persons between 55 and 64 who play golf regularly is greater than that in any other age group.

If you're an avid golfer and you also belong to a private country club with an 18-hole course, you've got one big advantage besides all the other social activities you're paying dues for: You belong to the fortunate 14 percent of golfers who don't have to kill time waiting to tee off at crowded municipal or daily fee courses. The rest of the country's players—12 million men and women—are public-course golfers, and only six out of ten of the nation's nearly 12,000 courses are open to them.

Still, access to public golf links—especially to courses built and operated by municipalities—is an excellent indicator of the supply of leisure-living options in a retirement place.

Access to Public Links

Best Retirement Places	Residents per 18-Hole Course
1. Myrtle Beach, SC	3,272
2. LEXINGTON–FAYETTE, KY	3,361
3. North Conway–White Mountains, NH	4,655
4. Eagle River, WI	4,724
5. Monticello–Liberty, NY	5,012

Source: National Golf Foundation, unpublished administrative records, 1983.

The national average for public golf is 23,177 residents per 18-hole course.

Seven retirement places have no public golf courses: Bull Shoals, AR; Canton–Lake Tawakoni, TX; Deming, NM; Lake O' The Cherokees, OK; Rappahannock, VA; Rockport–Aransas Pass, TX; and Santa Fe, NM.

Bowling

The sound of a hardwood ball striking hardwood pins was sometimes mistaken for the sound of a thunderclap in early nineteenth-century America. The sport has been around a long, long time indeed, and with all its variations—skittles, fivepins, ninepins, tenpins, candlepins, duckpins—is probably played by more people in the world than any other game (with the exception of soccer).

In the United States, the dominant variation is tenpins, and nearly 52 million people take a turn at it once or twice a year. If the 8,500 bowling centers in this country had to depend on this kind of casual participation alone, however, many of them would soon close their doors. The credit for keeping them in business goes to such highly organized competitive associations as the American Bowling Congress, to which 4.7

million men belong, and the Women's International Bowling Congress, with four million women members, which promote frequent tournaments throughout the country.

The sport is highly recommended for older people. Dr. Morris Fishbein, once editor of the *Journal of the American Medical Association*, told *Family Health* magazine that, aside from relieving the postural backache that comes from sitting too long, the physical exercise and the challenges of making the ball knock down all those pins at once "produce better coordination of vision and mind with practically all the muscles of the body."

Another benefit in retirement is the ready-made social contacts that are a big part of formal bowling competition. Whether you're in Kalispell, Keene, or Kerrville, you'll find team bowling. With 1.5 million teams in 140,000 leagues around the country, what better odds can there be for meeting up with the group that's right for you?

Ninety-nine percent of the bowling centers in this country are certified by the American Bowling Congress (ABC) for tournament competition. To rate each of the retirement places for certified bowling, *Places Rated* counts the number of lanes rather than the number of bowling centers to derive a per capita access score. Athens–Cedar Creek Lake, Texas, for example, and Bar Harbor–Frenchman Bay, Maine, each have one ABC certified bowling center. But there are 12 lanes for bowling in the Texas retirement place and only four in the Down East coastal area.

Access to Certified Bowling

Best Retirement Places	Residents per Lane
1. Mountain Home–Norfork Lake, AR	370
2. DAYTONA BEACH, FL	520
3. OCALA, FL	572
4. Traverse City–Grand Traverse Bay, MI	638
5. Rhinelander, WI	709

Source: American Bowling Congress, unpublished data, 1983.

The national average for certified bowling is 1,494 residents per lane.

Ten retirement places have no ABC-certified lanes: Big Sandy, TN; Camden–Penobscot Bay, ME; Canton–Lake Tawakoni, TX; Clarkesville–Mount Airy, GA; Front Royal, VA; Laconia–Lake Winnipesaukee, NH; North Conway–White Mountains, NH; Rappahannock, VA; Rockport–Aransas Pass, TX; and Table Rock Lake, MO.

Movie Theaters

Over the past ten years, the number of people over age 50 who regularly catch a commercial film at a shopping mall or downtown theater has tripled. Perhaps they are recalling younger days when moviegoing was a routine family activity.

Remember 1948, when John Huston won two Academy Awards—best director and best screenplay —for *The Treasure of Sierra Madre?* And his father, Walter, was named best supporting actor for his performance as the old prospector in the same film? Jane

Wyman won an Oscar that year for her role in *Johnny Belinda; Hamlet* was the best picture, and its star, Laurence Olivier, the best actor.

Thirty-five years ago, moviegoing was the American thing to do of an evening, any evening. Spilled popcorn was regularly swept up from the aisles between shows, the next John Wayne or Spencer Tracy film was announced on a large easel in the lobby, usherettes took you to your seat with a red-lensed flashlight, and you always got a MovieTone or Warner-Pathe newsreel with the show. There were 18,631 motion picture theaters back then, most of them small neighborhood movie houses, with a few downtown palaces for "premieres" and first-run screenings. Never again would there be so many. The year 1948 also marked the commercial appearance of television.

Today there are fewer than 8,000 commercial "four-wall" movie theaters in the United States. Paid attendance has declined from $4.1 billion in the late 1940s to $1.1 billion in the last few years (figures have been adjusted to reflect ticket price inflation).

To rate retirement places for access to movies, *Places Rated* divides their population by the number of local commercial screens. Some are at drive-in theaters, others are resort theaters open only during the season. Most, however, are at places of the Bijou, Strand, or Cinema-Six variety that show recent commercial films year round.

Access to Movies

Best Retirement Places	Residents per Screen	Worst Retirement Places	Residents per Screen
1. St. George–Zion, UT	5,213	1. Bull Shoals, AR	*
2. Hamilton–Bitter-root Valley, MT	5,623	1. Deming, NM	*
3. Rhinelander, WI	6,243	1. Rappahannock, VA	*
4. Bennington, VT	6,669	1. Table Rock Lake, MO	*
5. Santa Fe, NM	6,851	5. Beaufort–Hilton Head, SC	65,634

Source: Bureau of the Census, *1977 Census of Selected Service Establishments,* 1981; and unpublished administrative records, 1983.

The national average is 19,174 residents per movie screen.

*These retirement places have no commercial movie theaters.

Museums and Public Libraries

Do you have a curiosity about whale biology, contemporary Gulf Coast seascapes, or the ancient crafts of the Apache? How about nineteenth-century Montana logging tools, Napa-Sonoma-Mendocino wine making, or steam railroads?

If you doubt whether you do, you may really never know until you visit a museum. There are almost 5,000 of them in this country, ranging in size from tiny local history collections often open by appointment only all the way up to the world's largest, New York's American Museum of Natural History, housed in 19 buildings and covering 23 acres of floor space. Seventy-seven of our retirement places have at least one museum.

In Fairhope–Gulf Shores, Alabama, the museum of the Eastern Shore Art Association is the center for art in all of Baldwin County. The place houses a collection of paintings by American artists, particularly those who use the sights of Mobile Bay and the Alabama Gulf Coast as their motifs. The association hosts an annual outdoor show, as well as lectures, films, and workshops at the museum throughout the year. The exhibits are continually changing in the galleries, and art classes are given in the studio-classrooms.

Let's take a look at Missoula, Montana. The Fort Missoula Historical Museum is housed in the quartermaster's brick warehouse in the old fort southwest of downtown. Aside from the regular tour-and-talk activity found in most local historical museums, there are education programs for anyone who wants to enroll. The focus is the military and agricultural history of western Montana, and the collections include mainly tools used by horny-handed farmers on the advancing nineteenth-century frontier.

The Eastern Shore Art Association and the Fort Missoula Historical Museum are good examples of the kind of local cultural storehouses you may encounter in smaller retirement areas. Whether through the collection of artifacts in history museums, the paintings and sculpture in an art museum, or the technologically fascinating displays in a science museum, these institutions allow us to benefit from the accomplishments of others and participate in a cultural life far beyond our own immediate experience.

Top Retirement Places for Museumgoers

Retirement Place	Places Rated Points*	Museums
1. SAN DIEGO, CA	4,000	24
2. TUCSON, AZ	3,500	19
3. PHOENIX, AZ	2,800	20
4. Cape Cod, MA	2,400	24
5. COLORADO SPRINGS, CO	1,600	12
5. MIAMI, FL	1,600	12

*See the section "Judging the Supply of Leisure-Living Assets," below, for an explanation of how *Places Rated* points are calculated.

Thirty retirement places have no museums.

Another kind of cultural resource is the local public library. Libraries are probably the vital center of any place's intellectual life. Besides books, most libraries also have collections of records, slides, filmstrips, magazines, and other items that may be used in the building or borrowed for free. Many have programs for older persons that go far beyond the traditional mission of acquiring books and periodicals and loaning them for a few weeks to cardholders. Older borrowers are a public library's biggest user during the day.

There are more than 8,500 public libraries in the United States, 5,000 of which are branch libraries of a city, county, or regional library system. You would expect libraries to be the most plentiful of leisure-living institutions. They may well be. Unfortunately, more than a few rural counties have no public library at all, although only one retirement place—Mountain Home–Norfork Lake, Arkansas—lacks this amenity.

As might be expected, in absolute terms libraries and library books are concentrated in the metro areas. San Diego leads the retirement places in number of libraries, with 65; Olympia, Washington, is second, with 45. Miami has only 25 libraries but is far and away the leader in number of volumes, with more than three million. But many of the non-metropolitan counties offer an excellent supply of library books relative to their population, including Benton–Kentucky Lake, Kentucky; Cape Cod, Massachusetts; Delta, Colorado; Fredericksburg, Texas; Kalispell, Montana; and Oscoda–Huron Shore, Michigan.

MUSICAL RETIREMENT: LOCAL PERFORMING ARTS SERIES, SYMPHONIES, AND OPERAS

How do you measure the artistic and cultural climate of the place that may be your next home? If you've never missed a symphony performance in the big city will you, after surfacing in a retirement place, be forced to settle for shaded seats at the annual outdoor Country Harmonica Blowoff? Must you say farewell to the grandeur of opening night at the opera, your local quarterly performing arts guild magazine, and your prized matinee seats at the concert hall?

These considerations aren't unimportant to a significant group of people over 65. According to recent Harris polls, of every ten older persons who have access to the symphony, opera, and ongoing performing arts series, four will take advantage of the opportunity on a regular basis.

Performing Arts Series. Where might you expect to find the best access to the performing arts? Only in the big cities, especially those with more than one million people? Wrong.

Is There Any Cultural Life Out There?

Quick, identify the retirement place whose performing arts series billed the following musical events during its 1982–83 season:

October 16–Barney McClure Jazz Trio
November 20–Istvan Nadas, pianist
December 6–Symphony Pops Concert
December 14–Community Chorus and Symphony, Handel's *Messiah*
February 12–Special Concert by the Symphony
March 19–*Carmina Burana*, Community Chorus and the Pacific Northwest Ballet
April 4–Young People's Concert

Answer: Port Angeles–Strait of Juan de Fuca, on the beautiful Olympic Peninsula in northwest Washington State. The town's population is slightly more than 17,000, and all concerts are given in the Port Angeles High School auditorium (capacity 1,205). So much for the theory that performing arts find little appreciation in small towns.

What about a mix of dates for local opera and symphony, plus frequent popular concerts, a touring boys' choir, and a visiting contemporary dance troupe? Subdivided between New York and Los Angeles, with lesser shares for San Francisco, Chicago, Boston, Washington, D.C., and perhaps Atlanta, Dallas, and Philadelphia? Hardly.

If anything, the enormous growth in attendance at arts performances around the country ever since 1970 is due not to turning up the volume and variety of performances in our big cities but to vastly increased popular interest in smaller cities and towns. And a good part of the increased interest comes from older fans. Among the *Places Rated* retirement places, 39 benefit from established performing arts series.

Symphony Orchestras. Orchestras are more common than opera companies. The American Symphony Orchestra League estimates that there are 1,500 in the United States and Canada. Thirty-four of the 107 retirement places have one or more orchestras. Their music can be heard everywhere, from woodsy state parks to high school auditoriums, and from philharmonic halls in impressive new civic arts centers to small-town bandboxes and pavilions. San Antonio and San Diego have "major " symphonies; that is, orchestras with operating income over $2 million.

Opera. Fourteen retirement places have live opera. Biloxi–Gulfport, Brattleboro, and Brevard may not have much else in common but they all belong to this select group. Opera enthusiasts here and elsewhere like to boast that this type of stagecraft may be the most demanding of the performing arts, because of the unique commingling of instruments and voice with theater and dance.

The growing appeal of opera is confirmed by a few numbers: From about 650 performing groups in the 1969–70 season, the number of opera groups swelled to nearly 900 a decade later, and audiences more than doubled to nearly 11 million during the same period.

Most of these opera groups are college and university workshops; others are community clubs and choruses. But some 200 are companies with annual budgets exceeding $25,000. Full-scale opera productions that use professional orchestras and bring the world's leading singers to the stage are a costly business. In 1980, only 16 companies nationwide were "grand operas," meaning their annual budgets were more than $1 million. Two of these grand operas can be found in the retirement places of San Diego and Santa Fe.

OUTDOOR RECREATION ENDOWMENTS

One force drawing people from urban to rural areas is the lure of open spaces for fishing, boating, hiking, picnicking, or for just getting away from it all. As the time for shedding job responsibilities approaches, many prospective retirees turn their thoughts to find-

The Arts: 10 Outstanding Retirement Places

Retirement Place	Places Rated Points*	Performing Arts Series	Symphony Orchestras	Opera Companies
1. PHOENIX, AZ	16,850	3	4	—
2. SAN ANTONIO, TX	10,950	4	1	1
3. SAN DIEGO, CA	8,000	2	2	1
4. MIAMI, FL	7,800	8	3	1
5. ORLANDO, FL	6,100	1	2	1
6. ALBUQUERQUE, NM	4,850	2	2	—
7. AUSTIN, TX	4,450	1	1	—
8. FORT LAUDERDALE–HOLLYWOOD, FL	3,500	2	1	—
9. LEXINGTON–FAYETTE, KY	3,400	2	1	—
9. WEST PALM BEACH–BOCA RATON, FL	3,400	4	1	1

*See the section "Judging the Supply of Leisure-Living Assets," below, for an explanation of how *Places Rated* points are calculated.

The top non-metropolitan retirement places for the arts, in alphabetical order, are: Bennington, VT; Brevard, NC; Cape Cod, MA; Roswell NM; and Santa Fe, NM.

ing a place where the great outdoors will be right outside their doorstep.

The Water Draw

They boast in Oklahoma that the state is so rich with lakes of every size that if you were to tip it to the south a bit, the water would flow out and flood Texas for a good while.

They say in Michigan's Roscommon County that the locals tend to live away from Houghton Lake, the state's biggest inland body of water, while the transplanted retired people who've migrated up from Detroit or Cleveland or Chicago unerringly light near the shoreline like loons there for the duration.

And Maryland crabbers point out to newcomers that the true length of estuarine shore reached by the Chesapeake Bay's tide would total more than 8,000 miles if all the kinks and bends were flattened out.

It has never been pinned down to anyone's satisfaction exactly what it is about a large body of water that attracts people who can live anywhere they want. Just being able to view a mirrorlike surface at sunset, or walk barefoot along a strand of talcum-fine sand, or enjoy cool breezes off the lapping waves when the weather is hot doesn't tell the whole story.

In 1981, several sociologists at the University of Wisconsin tried to isolate certain environmental features that they believed would determine migration among people over 65. One was a mild average temperature for January and for June. Another was the extent of resort development, indicated by the number of people working in the recreation-services sector of the local economy. A third feature was water.

Was there any correlation between the migration of retired people on the one hand and mild temperatures, resort development, and water on the other? Yes and no. Water, whether found in streams, rivers, lakes, or along ocean and Great Lakes coasts, did not play nearly as great a part in attracting people over 65 as did a mild climate and recreation development. Indeed, there were certain Arizona, Nevada, and New Mexico counties that were desert-dry yet drew retired people at a faster rate than "wet" counties in other parts of the country. So water in itself was not a sufficient magnet for migration, the research showed. Without mild weather and commercial development, retired people as a general rule apparently aren't searching for sandy beaches and alpine lakes alone.

Nonetheless, you'll spot bodies of inland water in nine out of ten of the 107 *Places Rated* retirement locations. Aside from being a basic necessity for supporting life, water is regarded by most people as a scenic amenity; many would regard it as a recreation amenity, assuming that there was enough of it to fish in and boat on, or that the temperature wasn't snowmelt-cold so that one could get in a quick swim. Where would Reno be without Lake Tahoe?

Or Olympia without Puget Sound? Four out of five Americans today live within 100 miles of a coastline; by the end of the decade, the Department of the Interior predicts three out of four will live within 50 miles. Not surprisingly, 31 *Places Rated* retirement places have ocean or Great Lakes coastline.

Large Areas of Inland Water

Retirement Place	Inland Water Area	Percent of Total Surface Area
1. Rockport–Aransas Pass, TX	167.3 sq mi	38%
2. MELBOURNE–TITUSVILLE–COCOA, FL	299.0	23
3. FORT MYERS–CAPE CORAL, FL	220.0	22
3. WEST PALM BEACH–BOCA RATON, FL	555.0	22
5. Easton–Chesapeake Bay, MD	70.0	21
6. Camden–Penobscot Bay, ME	87.1	19
6. Bar Harbor–Frenchman Bay, ME	353.0	19
6. Ocean City–Assateague Island, MD	110.0	19
9. Eagle River, WI	150.5	15
9. Toms River–Barnegat Bay, NJ	113.8	15
11. Laconia–Lake Winnipesaukee, NH	66.9	14
12. Cape Cod, MA	56.9	13
13. DAYTONA BEACH, FL	145.0	12
13. Table Rock Lake, MO	59.8	12
15. Benton–Kentucky Lake, KY	36.3	11
15. Brunswick–Golden Isles, GA	52.6	11
15. Gainesville–Lake Sidney Lanier, GA	48.5	11
15. Hot Springs–Lake Ouachita, AR	77.5	11

Source: U.S. Bureau of the Census, *Area Measurements,* Series G–20, 1962–67.

Inland water area includes ponds and lakes of surface area greater than 40 acres; streams, canals, and rivers if width is one-eighth mile or greater; water area along irregular Great Lakes and ocean coastlines if bays, inlets, and estuaries are between one and ten miles wide.

National Forests, Parks, and Wildlife Refuges

Of all the outdoor activities that persons over 65 participate in at least four times a year, the leading ones—driving for pleasure, walking, picnicking, sightseeing, bird watching, nature walking, and fishing—would probably be more enjoyable in the country's splendid system of national forests, parks, and wildlife refuges.

There are 155 national forests and 19 national grasslands on 191 million acres in the United States. Although various parts of the national forests are classified as "wilderness," "primitive," "scenic," "historic," or "recreation," the main purpose of the National Forest System is silviculture: growing wood, harvesting it carefully, and preserving naturally beautiful areas from the depredations of amateur chain saws, burger palaces, miniature golf, and condomania.

In rainy Deschutes National Forest near Bend, Oregon, for example, the crop is Douglas fir; in the various components of Mark Twain National Forest in the Ozarks of southern Missouri, the trees are mainly local hardwoods of blackjack oak and hickory; down in Pisgah National Forest, in western North Carolina, the trees are virgin oak, beech, and black walnut.

Within the forest system are more than a quarter of a million miles of roads, built not just for loggers but for everyone. They lead to a wide variety of recreation outlets: ski resorts, marinas, fishing lakes and streams, hiking trails, and campgrounds.

Large Areas of National Forest Lands

Retirement Place	Portion of Land Area in National Forests	National Forests
1. Hamilton–Bitterroot Valley, MT	73%	Bitterroot, Lolo
2. Kalispell, MT	52	Flathead, Kootenai, Lolo
3. Bend, OR	50	Deschutes
4. Twain Harte–Yosemite, CA	41	Calaveras Bigtree, Stanislaus
5. Missoula, MT	40	Bitterroot, Flathead, Lolo
6. Prescott, AZ	38	Coconino, Kaibab, Prescott, Tonto
7. FORT COLLINS, CO	37	Roosevelt
8. Brevard, NC	36	Nantahala, Pisgah
9. Clear Lake, CA	30	Mendocino
10. Coeur d'Alene, ID	29	Coeur d'Alene, Kaniksu

Source: U.S. Department of Agriculture, *Land Areas of the National Forest System,* 1983.

In contrast to the National Forest System, the National Park System is meant expressly for recreation. This has been its mission ever since Congress established Yellowstone National Park in adjacent western corners of the old Montana and Wyoming territories "as a public park or pleasuring ground for the benefit and enjoyment of the people" back in 1872. Yellowstone's founding marked the beginning of what has become the oldest and largest national park system in the world.

In the United States, there are 334 national parks, preserves, monuments, memorials, battlefields, seashores, riverways, and trails, covering some 79 million acres. Although the system is best known for great scenic parks like Grand Canyon, Yosemite, Glacier, and Yellowstone, most of the individual areas commemorate persons and events that figured importantly in the country's history.

Large Areas of National Parks Lands

Retirement Place	Portion of Land Area in National Park System	National Park Service Areas
1. MIAMI, FL	39%	Big Cypress National Preserve, Biscayne National Park, Everglades National Park
2. Twain Harte–Yosemite, CA	29	Yosemite National Park
3. Port Angeles–Strait of Juan de Fuca, WA	28	Olympic National Park
4. Kalispell, MT	19	Glacier National Park
4. Rappahannock, VA	19	Shenandoah National Park
6. Lake Havasu City–Kingman, AZ	15	Grand Canyon National Park, Lake Mead National Recreation Area, Pipe Spring National Monument
7. LAS VEGAS, NV	11	Lake Mead National Recreation Area

Source: National Park Service, unpublished administrative records, 1983.

Unlike the National Park System, whose main purpose is keeping irreplaceable geographical and historical treasures in the public domain, the national wildlife refuges protect native flora and fauna from people. This mission hasn't changed since the first refuge, Florida's Pelican Island National Wildlife Refuge, was created in 1903 by President Theodore Roosevelt to save mangrove-nesting egrets from human poachers in search of plumage for women's hats. There are now 413 of these remarkable refuges throughout the country, embracing more than 87 million acres.

Most of these refuges are open to the public for a variety of wildlife activities, particularly photography and nature observation from duck blinds and towers. In certain of the refuges and at irregular times, fishing and hunting are permitted, depending on the size of the wild populations in the refuge. Information is available for each of the refuges, and many are staffed by professional managers from the Interior Department's Fish and Wildlife Service.

Although the majority of the nation's wildlife refuges are located in open, sometimes remote country, they aren't exclusively a rural retirement amenity. Several can be found within metropolitan areas, including Nisqually on Puget Sound near Olympia, San Pablo in the California metro area of Santa Rosa, and St. Johns in Melbourne–Titusville–Cocoa, Florida. Within another Florida metro area, Fort Myers–Cape Coral, there are four—Caloosahatchee, J.N. "Ding" Darling, Matlacha Pass, and Pine Island.

One third of the Las Vegas metro area's land area is

Top Retirement Places for Outdoor Recreation Endowments

Retirement Place	Places Rated Points*	Coastline (mi)	Inland Water Area (sq mi)	Acres in National Parks, Forests, Wildlife Refuges
1. MIAMI, FL	4,021	50	67.1	521,113
2. Kalispell, MT	3,736	—	143.2	2,433,192
3. Hamilton–Bitter-root Valley, MT	3,655	—	6.5	1,112,981
4. Twain Harte–Yosemite, CA	3,573	—	19.7	1,038,077
5. Port Angeles–Strait of Juan de Fuca, WA	3,270	90	34.5	519,879
6. Rockport–Aransas Pass, TX	3,076	23	167.3	52,461
7. LAS VEGAS, NV	2,728	—	209.8	1,475,499
8. Bend, OR	2,548	—	29.3	979,237
9. Oscoda–Huron Shore, MI	2,542	40	19.4	141,423
10. FORT COLLINS, CO	2,326	—	29.7	766,984

*See the section "Judging the Supply of Leisure-Living Assets," below, for an explanation of how *Places Rated* points are calculated.

in national wildlife refuges. Rockport–Aransas Pass, Texas, and Yuma, Arizona, are other retirement places with large areas of national wildlife refuge lands (19 percent and 17 percent, respectively).

JUDGING THE SUPPLY OF LEISURE-LIVING ASSETS

If you are an avid golfer, birder, reader, bowler, hiker, and opera lover, will you enjoy yourself more in Lake Havasu City–Kingman, Lancaster, or Las Vegas?

One can argue that ranking retirement places by their collections of leisure-living assets can't be done with total fairness. A Colorado fisherman, impatiently waiting for the Kokanee salmon to get through their spawning, may care nothing for the approaching dates of a local college's performing arts series. Likewise, an older Miami Beach couple may never know the joys of Bitterroot timber cruising; nor would they ever regret the loss.

But even though there are many different preferences when it comes to recreation, it is still possible to measure and compare the supply of selected amenities in retirement places from coast to coast. It's certainly done all the time in chamber of commerce brochures and state tourism promotion kits. Travelers also make their own comparisons in casual conversation. Hearsay may hold that small-town living in the Georgia mountains is as dull today as it was for many who quit the village for the city generations ago, and that there's little in the way of peaceful outdoor recreation in sunbaked Orlando.

Places Rated Retirement Guide attempts a more objective approach. We don't judge the quality of perfor-

mances by local symphonies and opera companies, nor do we critique museum or library holdings. Neither do we push the recreational benefits of the desert over seashore or forest environs. Rather, we simply indicate the presence or absence of amenities that most of us would agree enhance retirement living. For certain facilities, points are awarded on the basis of how available these facilities are to residents of the retirement place. The access to these items is given a rating of AA, A, B, or C (AA indicating the best access and C the worst), and the retirement place is awarded points accordingly: 400 points for an AA rating, 300 points for A, 200 points for B, and 100 points for C.

Each place starts with a base score of zero, to which points are added according to the following criteria:

1. *Public golf courses.*

A retirement place gets a rating of:	If there is one 18-hole course for every:
AA	12,500 or fewer people
A	12,501–25,000 people
B	25,001–50,000 people
C	50,001 or more people

2. *Bowling lanes.*

A retirement place gets a rating of:	If there is one lane for every:
AA	1,300 or fewer people
A	1,301–1,800 people
B	1,801–3,000 people
C	3,001 or more people

3. *Movie theaters.*

A retirement place gets a rating of:	If there is one theater for every:
AA	10,000 or fewer people
A	10,001–16,000 people
B	16,001–23,500 people
C	23,501 or more people

4. *Museums.* Each museum located in a retirement place, based on inclusion in the 1983 *Official Museum Directory*, receives 100 points. In addition, any museum having a minimum of three curators or the equivalent, each in charge of a specified department or field, with a regular publication and a library of at least 5,000 volumes, receives another 400 points.

5. *Public libraries.*

A retirement place gets a rating of:	If there are 1,000 volumes for every:
AA	4,500 or fewer people
A	4,501–7,500 people
B	7,501–13,000 people
C	13,001 or more people

6. *Performing arts series.* Established performing arts series, whether at local college campuses or in public or private auditoriums, receive 100 points. Moreover, each performance date during the 1982–83 season earns an additional 50 points. The Rollins College Concert Series in Orlando, for example, receives 100 points plus 350 points for its seven dates.

7. *Symphony orchestras.* Local symphony orchestras, regardless of budget size, receive 100 points. Each performance during the 1982–83 season earns an additional 50 points. The San Antonio Symphony Orchestra, for instance, receives 100 points plus 9,000 points for its 180 performances.
8. *Opera companies.* Established opera companies, regardless of budget size, receive 100 points. Each production during the 1982–83 season is also awarded 50 points. Accordingly, the San Diego Opera Association receives 100 points plus 400 points for its eight productions.
9. *Coastlines.* Each mile of general coastline, whether on the ocean or on the Great Lakes, gets 10 points. For example, the 21 miles of Atlantic coastline in Brunswick–Golden Isles earn the Georgia retirement place 210 points.
10. *Inland water area.* The percent of a retirement place's total surface area that is classified as inland water is multiplied by 50. In Harrison, Arkansas, 11.1 of the 604 square miles of surface area is inland water. That works out to 1.84 percent inland water, or 92 points.
11. *National Forests, Parks, and Wildlife Refuges.* The percent of a retirement place's total acreage that is classified as national forest, park, or wildlife refuge acreage is multiplied by 50. The retirement place of Bend, Oregon, has 1,958,400 acres, 50 percent of which compose Deschutes National Forest (979,237 acres), giving Bend 2,500 points. And the four wildlife refuges in Yuma, Arizona, make up 17 percent of the retirement area's total acreage. Yuma, therefore, receives 850 points for its wildlife refuges.

Sample Comparison: Kalispell, Montana, and Phoenix, Arizona

To illustrate the scoring system in most other chapters, *Places Rated* compares a low-rated place with a top-rated one. But in the case of leisure living, we compare Kalispell, a small Montana retirement place that ranks 13th, with the number-one retirement place for recreation, metropolitan Phoenix, some 1,000 miles to the south in the Arizona desert.

Kalispell, in achieving its surprising 13th-place finish, scores well in Common Denominators. It earns three AA ratings—the highest possible—for access to bowling, movie theaters, and the size of its public library collection, for 400 points each. Access to public golf courses gets an A rating, for 300 points, and two museums earn Kalispell another 200 points, bringing its total score for this category to 1,700. The Arts category, however, is another story. Kalispell has one

performing arts series—the Flathead Community Concert Association— that gives four performances a year, but it possesses no symphony orchestras or opera companies. Thus its entire score for Arts is only 300. It is in the category of Outdoor Recreation Endowments that Kalispell and surrounding Flathead County really shine. With an inland water area of 143.2 square miles, which includes Flathead and Whitefish lakes and Hungry Horse Reservoir; three national forests (Flathead, Kootenai, and Lolo); Glacier National Park, with more than 600,000 acres of ruggedly beautiful land within the Kalispell retirement area; and one wildlife refuge, the western Montana retirement place earns 3,736 points, making its total score 5,736.

Phoenix, one of the capitals of Sun Belt retirement over the last 20 years, also gets off to a good start in the Common Denominators category. Although its supply of public golf courses, bowling lanes, movie theaters,

---

Leisure Living Winners and Losers

Best Retirement Places	Places Rated Score	Worst Retirement Places	Places Rated Score
1. PHOENIX, AZ	20,887	1. Athens–Cedar Creek Lake, TX	412
2. MIAMI, FL	14,221	2. Deming, NM	500
3. SAN DIEGO, CA	13,930	3. Canton–Lake Tawakoni, TX	527
4. SAN ANTONIO, TX	13,257	4. Paris, TN	874
5. TUCSON, AZ	7,978	5. Kerrville, TX	1,100

Retirement places can take different routes to arrive at their leisure-living rating.

One place may excel in the supply and access to the various attractions *Places Rated* calls Common Denominators: certified bowling lanes, public 18-hole golf courses, movie theaters, museums, and public library holdings. Another may come up short in some of these facilities yet have outstanding performing arts attractions. A third place may be particularly blessed with opportunities for outdoor recreation.

Take a look at the top five retirement places for leisure living: They all are large Sun Belt metro areas. Do ratings in leisure living tend to improve with city size? Yes, they do. And one reason is the contribution the arts make to a place's score. Four fifths of Phoenix's number-one rating is due to its symphony and performing arts series; 83 percent of San Antonio's rating is owed to the same offerings plus its opera. Nonetheless, even if an arbitrary ceiling of 5,000 total points were set for arts amenities (this would slash 11,250 points from Phoenix's score, for example), the overall ranking list would change hardly at all, the only result being a reshuffling of the top nine places: Miami would rank first, followed by San Diego, Phoenix, Tucson, Albuquerque, San Antonio, Cape Cod, Austin, and Orlando. The top-ranked places tend to be well-rounded, scoring well or at least holding their own in each of the three major categories.

What about the lowest-ranked places? Most of them simply have fewer assets: Only one (Kerrville) makes a fairly good showing for Common Denominators, and none has any of the performing arts facilities that are awarded points.

and public libraries earns two B ratings and two C ratings for only 600 points, Phoenix has 20 museums (good for 2,000 points), two of which receive a 400-point bonus. This adds up to 3,400 points for Common Denominators. But the Arizona metro area owes its top ranking in leisure living to its extremely full calendar of arts events. It supports three performing arts series (300 points) that have 181 performance dates altogether (9,050 points), as well as four symphony orchestras (400 points) that give 142 performances

(7,100 points) every year. The impressive total for the Arts is therefore 16,850 points. Because of Phoenix's desert location, it offers little in the way of water recreation, possessing only 14.9 square miles of inland water. Most of its 637 Outdoor Recreation Endowments points come from the acreage of the Tonto National Forest, northeast of suburban Scottsdale. Phoenix's winning score of 20,887, then, is attributable to its man-made assets, whereas Kalispell comes by its high score due to an enviable array of natural assets.

Places Rated: Retirement Places Ranked for Leisure-Living Assets

Eleven criteria are used to determine the score for a retirement place's supply of leisure-living assets: (1) public golf courses, (2) certified lanes for tenpin bowling, (3) movie theaters, (4) museums, (5) public libraries, (6) performing arts series, (7) symphony orchestras, (8) opera companies, (9) miles of ocean or

Great Lakes coastline, (10) percentage of total surface area occupied by inland water, and (11) percentage of total surface area classified as national forest, national park, or national wildlife refuge acreage. Retirement places that receive tie scores are given the same rank and listed alphabetically.

Retirement Places from Best to Worst

Places Rated Rank	Places Rated Score	Places Rated Rank	Places Rated Score	Places Rated Rank	Places Rated Score
1. PHOENIX, AZ	20,887	29. Traverse City–Grand Traverse Bay, MI	3,784	54. BILOXI–GULFPORT, MS	2,669
2. MIAMI, FL	14,221	30. Missoula, MT	3,748	55. Ocean City–Assateague Island, MD	2,641
3. SAN DIEGO, CA	13,930				
4. SAN ANTONIO, TX	13,257	31. Prescott, AZ	3,697	56. Delta, CO	2,618
5. TUCSON, AZ	7,978	32. DAYTONA BEACH, FL	3,568	57. OCALA, FL	2,555
		33. Oscoda–Huron Shore, MI	3,542	58. Roswell, NM	2,534
6. ALBUQUERQUE, NM	7,744	34. Hot Springs–Lake Ouachita, AR	3,513	59. Lake Havasu City–Kingman, AZ	2,527
7. ORLANDO, FL	7,622	35. STATE COLLEGE, PA	3,500	60. Carson City, NV	2,511
8. Cape Cod, MA	7,046				
9. AUSTIN, TX	6,612	36. FORT MYERS–CAPE CORAL, FL	3,489	61. Nevada City–Donner, CA	2,471
10. WEST PALM BEACH–BOCA RATON, FL	6,354	37. Camden–Penobscot Bay, ME	3,360	62. RENO, NV	2,461
		38. Easton–Chesapeake Bay, MD	3,258	63. Eagle River, WI	2,453
11. FORT COLLINS, CO	6,276	39. Bar Harbor–Frenchman Bay, ME	3,179	64. North Conway–White Mountains, NH	2,431
12. FORT LAUDERDALE–HOLLYWOOD, FL	5,856	40. LAKELAND–WINTER HAVEN, FL	3,157	65. ATLANTIC CITY–CAPE MAY, NJ	2,363
13. Kalispell, MT	5,736				
14. Bennington, VT	5,686	41. Toms River–Barnegat Bay, NJ	3,082	66. MEDFORD, OR	2,261
15. LEXINGTON–FAYETTE, KY	5,503	42. CHARLOTTESVILLE, VA	3,054	67. Brattleboro, VT	2,252
		43. St. George–Zion, UT	2,991	68. Mountain Home–Norfork Lake, AR	2,201
16. Port Angeles–Strait of Juan de Fuca, WA	5,420	44. Clear Lake, CA	2,946	69. Rehoboth Bay–Indian River Bay, DE	2,178
17. Twain Harte–Yosemite, CA	4,873	45. Lincoln City–Newport, OR	2,896	70. Petoskey–Straits of Mackinac, MI	2,173
18. Brevard, NC	4,872				
19. Hamilton–Bitterroot Valley, MT	4,655	46. SANTA ROSA, CA	2,863	71. Red Bluff–Sacramento Valley, CA	2,140
20. MELBOURNE–TITUSVILLE–COCOA, FL	4,601	47. LAS CRUCES, NM	2,809	72. Branson–Lake Taneycomo, MO	2,136
		47. San Luis Obispo, CA	2,809	73. Yuma, AZ	2,077
21. Santa Fe, NM	4,589	49. Maui, HI	2,789	74. LANCASTER, PA	2,043
22. COLORADO SPRINGS, CO	4,569	50. ASHEVILLE, NC	2,743	75. Harrison, AR	2,042
23. SARASOTA–BRADENTON, FL	4,500				
24. LAS VEGAS, NV	4,378	51. BOISE CITY, ID	2,722	76. Cassville–Roaring River, MO	2,033
25. SPRINGFIELD, MO	4,182	52. Coeur d'Alene, ID	2,715	77. Fairhope–Gulf Shores, AL	1,953
26. Grand Junction, CO	3,973	53. Brunswick–Golden Isles, GA	2,679		
27. Rockport–Aransas Pass, TX	3,876				
28. Bend, OR	3,848				

Places Rated Rank	Places Rated Score	Places Rated Rank	Places Rated Score	Places Rated Rank	Places Rated Score
78. Clarkesville–Mount Airy, GA	1,923	87. Myrtle Beach, SC	1,650	98. Winchester, VA	1,287
79. Oak Harbor, WA	1,919	88. Front Royal, VA	1,647	99. Gainesville–Lake Sidney Lanier, GA	1,264
80. Rhinelander, WI	1,910	89. Table Rock Lake, MO	1,538	100. Cookeville, TN	1,193
		90. Tahlequah–Lake Tenkiller, OK	1,482		
81. McALLEN–PHARR–EDINBURG, TX	1,859			101. Lake O' The Cherokees, OK	1,160
82. Houghton Lake, MI	1,854	91. Bull Shoals, AR	1,441	102. Big Sandy, TN	1,106
83. OLYMPIA, WA	1,836	92. Keene, NH	1,440	103. Kerrville, TX	1,100
84. Benton–Kentucky Lake, KY	1,735	93. Monticello–Liberty, NY	1,404	104. Paris, TN	874
85. Laconia–Lake Winnipesaukee, NH	1,717	94. Fredericksburg, TX	1,402	105. Canton–Lake Tawakoni, TX	527
		95. Hendersonville, NC	1,368		
86. Beaufort–Hilton Head, SC	1,697	96. Rappahannock, VA	1,339	106. Deming, NM	500
		97. Crossville, TN	1,307	107. Athens–Cedar Creek Lake, TX	412

Retirement Places Listed Alphabetically

Retirement Place	Places Rated Rank	Retirement Place	Places Rated Rank	Retirement Place	Places Rated Rank
ALBUQUERQUE, NM	6	FORT LAUDERDALE–HOLLYWOOD, FL	12	OCALA, FL	57
ASHEVILLE, NC	50	FORT MYERS–CAPE CORAL, FL	36	Ocean City–Assateague Island, MD	55
Athens–Cedar Creek Lake, TX	107	Fredericksburg, TX	94	OLYMPIA, WA	83
ATLANTIC CITY–CAPE MAY, NJ	65				
AUSTIN, TX	9	Front Royal, VA	88	ORLANDO, FL	7
		Gainesville–Lake Sidney Lanier, GA	99	Oscoda–Huron Shore, MI	33
Bar Harbor–Frenchman Bay, ME	39	Grand Junction, CO	26	Paris, TN	104
Beaufort–Hilton Head, SC	86	Hamilton–Bitterroot Valley, MT	19	Petoskey–Straits of Mackinac, MI	70
Bend, OR	28			PHOENIX, AZ	1
Bennington, VT	14	Hendersonville, NC	95		
Benton–Kentucky Lake, KY	84	Hot Springs–Lake Ouachita, AR	34	Port Angeles–Strait of Juan de Fuca, WA	16
		Houghton Lake, MI	82	Prescott, AZ	31
Big Sandy, TN	102	Kalispell, MT	13	Rappahannock, VA	96
BILOXI–GULFPORT, MS	54	Keene, NH	92	Red Bluff–Sacramento Valley, CA	71
BOISE CITY, ID	51			Rehoboth Bay–Indian River Bay, DE	69
Branson–Lake Taneycomo, MO	72	Kerrville, TX	103		
Brattleboro, VT	67	Laconia–Lake Winnipesaukee, NH	85	RENO, NV	62
		Lake Havasu City–Kingman, AZ	59	Rhinelander, WI	80
Brevard, NC	18	LAKELAND–WINTER HAVEN, FL	40	Rockport–Aransas Pass, TX	27
Brunswick–Golden Isles, GA	53	Lake O' The Cherokees, OK	101	Roswell, NM	58
Bull Shoals, AR	91			St. George–Zion, UT	43
Camden–Penobscot Bay, ME	37	LANCASTER, PA	74		
Canton–Lake Tawakoni, TX	105	LAS CRUCES, NM	47	SAN ANTONIO, TX	4
		LAS VEGAS, NV	24	SAN DIEGO, CA	3
Cape Cod, MA	8	LEXINGTON–FAYETTE, KY	15	San Luis Obispo, CA	47
Carson City, NV	60	Lincoln City–Newport, OR	45	Santa Fe, NM	21
Cassville–Roaring River, MO	76			SANTA ROSA, CA	46
CHARLOTTESVILLE, VA	42	Maui, HI	49		
Clarkesville–Mount Airy, GA	78	McALLEN–PHARR–EDINBURG, TX	81	SARASOTA–BRADENTON, FL	23
		MEDFORD, OR	66	SPRINGFIELD, MO	25
Clear Lake, CA	44	MELBOURNE–TITUSVILLE–COCOA, FL	20	STATE COLLEGE, PA	35
Coeur d'Alene, ID	52	MIAMI, FL	2	Table Rock Lake, MO	89
COLORADO SPRINGS, CO	22			Tahlequah–Lake Tenkiller, OK	90
Cookeville, TN	100	Missoula, MT	30		
Crossville, TN	97	Monticello–Liberty, NY	93	Toms River–Barnegat Bay, NJ	41
		Mountain Home–Norfork Lake, AR	68	Traverse City–Grand Traverse Bay, MI	29
DAYTONA BEACH, FL	32	Myrtle Beach, SC	87	TUCSON, AZ	5
Delta, CO	56	Nevada City–Donner, CA	61	Twain Harte–Yosemite, CA	17
Deming, NM	106			WEST PALM BEACH–BOCA RATON, FL	10
Eagle River, WI	63	North Conway–White Mountains, NH	64		
Easton–Chesapeake Bay, MD	38	Oak Harbor, WA	79	Winchester, VA	98
Fairhope–Gulf Shores, AL	76			Yuma, AZ	73
FORT COLLINS, CO	11				

Place Profiles: Leisure-Living Features in 107 Retirement Places

The following profiles are a detailed catalogue of features of leisure life in each retirement place.

The profiles begin with the category of Common Denominators—selected leisuretime options that are commercially available or municipally funded in most places. The number of public golf courses, certified lanes for tenpin bowling, movie theaters, museums, and public libraries are shown, along with their access rating when applicable. Museums listed by name are those qualifying for 400 bonus points, as described in the scoring system above.

The second category, The Arts, lists local established performing arts series, symphony orchestras, and opera companies, along with the number of performance dates and auditorium seating capacity.

The third category, Outdoor Recreation Endowments, details the place's number of miles of ocean or Great Lakes coastline, its square miles of inland water, and the acreage for all national forests, parks, and wildlife refuges located there. The figures on inland water come from a series of U.S. Census Bureau geographic reports from the 1960s (still the best source for measurement of water surface areas in each of the country's counties). Ponds and lakes are counted if their surface areas are 40 acres or more; streams, canals, and rivers are also counted if their width is one eighth of a mile or more. The water area along irregular Great Lakes and ocean coastlines is counted, too, if the bays, inlets, and estuaries are between one and ten miles in width. Lengths of ocean and Great Lakes coastlines are estimated from state totals measured by the NOAA. State forests and parks are also listed,

although retirement places receive no points for them.

The figure in parentheses opposite each category heading represents the number of points awarded to the retirement place for leisure assets in that category.

Information comes from these sources: ABC Leisure Magazines, Inc., *Musical America: International Directory of the Performing Arts*, 1983; American Bowling Congress, unpublished administrative records, 1983; R. R. Bowker, *American Library Directory*, 1983; National Association of Theatre Owners, unpublished regional statistics, 1983; National Golf Foundation, unpublished administrative records, 1983; National Register Publishing Company, *Official Museum Directory*, 1983; Tennessee Valley Authority, unpublished administrative records, 1983; U.S. Department of Agriculture, Forest Service, *Land Areas of the National Forest System*, 1983, and unpublished administrative records, 1983; U.S. Department of Commerce, Bureau of the Census, *County and City Data Book*, 1978, *1977 Census of Selected Service Establishments*, 1981, and *Area Measurements*, Series G–20, 1962–1967; U.S. Department of Commerce, National Oceanic and Atmospheric Administration, *The Coastline of the United States*, 1975; U.S. Department of the Army, Corps of Engineers, unpublished administrative records, 1983; U.S. Department of the Interior, Bureau of Land Management, unpublished administrative records, 1982; U.S. Department of the Interior, Fish and Wildlife Service, unpublished administrative records, 1983; U.S. Department of the Interior, National Park Service, *Index to the National Park System and Related Areas*, 1982, and unpublished administrative records, 1983.

	Subtotal/ Rating
ALBUQUERQUE, NM	
Common Denominators	**(2,400)**
Public Golf Courses: 4.5 municipal; 1 daily fee	C
Bowling Lanes: 264	A
Movie Theaters: 28	A
Museums: 2 art; 2 general; 1 historical; 5 science Albuquerque Museum	
Public Libraries: 11 (783,834 volumes)	A
The Arts	**(4,850)**
Performing Arts Series:	
University of New Mexico Cultural Program 17 dates; 2,094 seats	
University of New Mexico Guest Artist Series 5 dates; 335 seats	
Symphony Orchestras:	
Chamber Orchestra of Albuquerque 10 performances; 626 seats	
New Mexico Symphony Orchestra 57 performances; 2,002 seats	
Outdoor Recreation Endowments	**(494)**
National Forests, Parks, Wildlife Refuges: Cibola National Forest (73,828 acres)	

	Subtotal/ Rating
State Forests and Parks: Coronado State Park	
Places Rated Score: 7,744 Places Rated Rank: 6	
ASHEVILLE, NC	
Common Denominators	**(1,600)**
Public Golf Courses: 2 municipal; 1.5 daily fee	C
Bowling Lanes: 48	C
Movie Theaters: 6	C
Museums: 1 art; 2 general; 3 historical; 1 natural history; 3 science	
Public Libraries: 10 (388,284 volumes)	A
The Arts	**(700)**
Performing Arts Series:	
Asheville Chamber Music Series 4 dates; 600 seats	
Symphony Orchestras:	
Asheville Symphony Orchestra 6 performances; 2,400 seats	
Outdoor Recreation Endowments	**(443)**
Inland Water Area: .8 square miles	

Subtotal/Rating

National Forests, Parks, Wildlife Refuges:
Blue Ridge Parkway (5,411 acres)
Pisgah National Forest (31,390 acres)
Places Rated Score: 2,743   Places Rated Rank: 50

Athens–Cedar Creek Lake, TX
Common Denominators	(400)
Public Golf Courses: .5 daily fee	C
Bowling Lanes: 12	C
Movie Theaters: 1	C
Public Libraries: 2 (36,435 volumes)	C
Outdoor Recreation Endowments	(12)

Inland Water Area: 2.8 square miles
Cedar Creek Lake
Places Rated Score: 412   Places Rated Rank: 107

ATLANTIC CITY–CAPE MAY, NJ
Common Denominators	(1,300)
Public Golf Courses: 10.5 daily fee	B
Bowling Lanes: 90	C
Movie Theaters: 32	AA
Museums: 2 general; 1 historical	
Public Libraries: 8 (419,834 volumes)	A
Outdoor Recreation Endowments	(1,063)

Coastline: 52 miles
Inland Water Area: 67.2 square miles
Great Egg Harbor Bay
National Forests, Parks, Wildlife Refuges:
Brigantine National Wildlife Refuge
(19,826 acres)
State Forests and Parks: Cape May Point
State Recreation Area
Places Rated Score: 2,363   Places Rated Rank: 65

AUSTIN, TX
Common Denominators	(2,100)
Public Golf Courses: 9 municipal; 5.5 daily fee	B
Bowling Lanes: 254	B
Movie Theaters: 20	C
Museums: 2 art; 2 general; 7 historical; 2 science	
Public Libraries: 16 (1,042,949 volumes)	A
The Arts	(4,450)

Performing Arts Series:
University of Texas Performing Arts Series
30 dates; 3,000 seats
Symphony Orchestras:
Austin Symphony Orchestra
55 performances; 3,000 seats
Outdoor Recreation Endowments	(62)·

Inland Water Area: 35.3 square miles
Tom Miller Dam
State Forests and Parks:
Lockhart State Recreation Area
McKinney Falls State Park
Places Rated Score: 6,612   Places Rated Rank: 9

Bar Harbor–Frenchman Bay, ME
Common Denominators	(1,800)
Public Golf Courses: 5.5 daily fee	AA
Bowling Lanes: 4	C
Movie Theaters: 3	A
Museums: 1 ethnic; 3 general; 3 historical; 1 natural history	
Public Libraries: 3 (54,090 volumes)	B
Outdoor Recreation Endowments	(1,379)

Coastline: 30 miles

Subtotal/Rating

Inland Water Area: 353 square miles
Frenchman Bay
National Forests, Parks, Wildlife Refuges:
Acadia National Park (35,362 acres)
State Forests and Parks: Lamoine State
Recreation Area
Places Rated Score: 3,179   Places Rated Rank: 39

Beaufort–Hilton Head, SC
Common Denominators	(1,300)
Public Golf Courses: 12.5 daily fee	AA
Bowling Lanes: 56	AA
Movie Theaters: 1	C
Museums: 1 general; 1 historical	
Public Libraries: 1 (80,250 volumes)	B
Outdoor Recreation Endowments	(397)

Coastline: 36 miles
Inland Water Area: 2.3 square miles
Port Royal Sound
National Forests, Parks, Wildlife Refuges:
Pinkney Island National Wildlife Refuge
(4,053 acres)
State Forests and Parks: Hunting Island
State Park
Places Rated Score: 1,697   Places Rated Rank: 86

Bend, OR
Common Denominators	(1,300)
Public Golf Courses: 6.5 daily fee	A
Bowling Lanes: 42	A
Movie Theaters: 7	AA
Museums: 1 science	
Public Libraries: 3 (60,507 volumes)	B
Outdoor Recreation Endowments	(2,548)

Inland Water Area: 29.3 square miles
Craine Prairie Reservoir
Wickiup Reservoir
National Forests, Parks, Wildlife Refuges:
Deschutes National Forest (979,237 acres)
State Forests and Parks:
LaPine State Recreation Area
Lava River State Recreation Area
Pilot Butte State Recreation Area
Tumalo State Recreation Area
Places Rated Score: 3,848   Places Rated Rank: 28

Bennington, VT
Common Denominators	(2,200)
Public Golf Courses: 2.5 daily fee	A
Bowling Lanes: 28	AA
Movie Theaters: 5	AA
Museums: 2 art; 1 general; 2 historical	
Bennington Museum	
Public Libraries: 1 (33,000 volumes)	B
The Arts	(2,350)

Performing Arts Series:
Park–McCullough House Concert
45 dates; 225 seats
Outdoor Recreation Endowments	(1,136)

Inland Water Area: .8 square miles
National Forests, Parks, Wildlife Refuges:
Appalachian Trail (375 acres)
Green Mountain National Forest (96,965 acres)
State Forests and Parks:
Emerald Lake State Park
Shaftsbury State Park
Woodford State Park
Places Rated Score: 5,686   Places Rated Rank: 14

Subtotal/
Rating

Benton–Kentucky Lake, KY

Common Denominators	**(1,200)**
Public Golf Courses: 1.5 municipal; 1.5 daily fee	**AA**
Bowling Lanes: 16	**A**
Movie Theaters: 1	**C**
Public Libraries: 3 (112,000 volumes)	**AA**
Outdoor Recreation Endowments	**(535)**
Inland Water Area: 36.3 square miles	
Kentucky Lake	
Places Rated Score: 1,735	Places Rated Rank: 84

Big Sandy, TN

Common Denominators	**(600)**
Public Golf Courses: .5 daily fee	**B**
Movie Theaters: 1	**A**
Public Libraries: 1 (7,168 volumes)	**C**
Outdoor Recreation Endowments	**(506)**
Inland Water Area: 44.1 square miles	
Kentucky Lake	
State Forests and Parks: Nathan Bedford	
Forrest State Park	
Places Rated Score: 1,106	Places Rated Rank: 102

BILOXI–GULFPORT, MS

Common Denominators	**(1,400)**
Public Golf Courses: 8.5 daily fee	**A**
Bowling Lanes: 118	**A**
Movie Theaters: 10	**B**
Museums: 2 historical; 1 science	
Public Libraries: 6 (352,385 volumes)	**A**
The Arts	**(500)**
Symphony Orchestras:	
Gulf Coast Symphony Orchestra	
4 performances; 1,000 seats	
Opera Companies:	
Gulf Coast Opera Theater	
2 productions; 3 performances	
Outdoor Recreation Endowments	**(769)**
Coastline: 30 miles	
Inland Water Area: 20 square miles	
Biloxi Bay	
Louis Bay	
National Forests, Parks, Wildlife Refuges:	
De Soto National Forest (101,747 acres)	
Gulf Islands National Seashore (19,997 acres)	
State Forests and Parks:	
Buccaneer State Park	
Gulf Marine State Park	
Places Rated Score: 2,669	Places Rated Rank: 54

BOISE CITY, ID

Common Denominators	**(1,300)**
Public Golf Courses: 1.5 daily fee	**C**
Bowling Lanes: 90	**B**
Movie Theaters: 9	**B**
Museums: 1 art; 1 historical	
Idaho State Historical Museum	
Public Libraries: 1 (206,420 volumes)	**B**
The Arts	**(1,350)**
Symphony Orchestras:	
Boise Philharmonic	
25 performances; 1,172 seats	
Outdoor Recreation Endowments	**(72)**
Inland Water Area: 8.6 square miles	
Lucky Peak Lake	
National Forests, Parks, Wildlife Refuges:	
Boise National Forest (4,211 acres)	

Subtotal/
Rating

State Forests and Parks:	
Lucky Peak State Park	
Veterans Memorial State Recreation Area	
Places Rated Score: 2,722	Places Rated Rank: 51

Branson–Lake Taneycomo, MO

Common Denominators	**(1,100)**
Public Golf Courses: 1.5 daily fee	**A**
Bowling Lanes: 16	**AA**
Movie Theaters: 2	**A**
Public Libraries: 1 (15,000 volumes)	**C**
Outdoor Recreation Endowments	**(1,036)**
Inland Water Area: 43.6 square miles	
Bull Shoals Lake	
Lake Taneycomo	
White River Lake	
National Forests, Parks, Wildlife Refuges:	
Mark Twain National Forest (59,489 acres)	
Places Rated Score: 2,136	Places Rated Rank: 72

Brattleboro, VT

Common Denominators	**(1,500)**
Public Golf Courses: 3.5 daily fee	**AA**
Bowling Lanes: 20	**B**
Movie Theaters: 4	**AA**
Museums: 1 art	
Public Libraries: 3 (108,928 volumes)	**AA**
The Arts	**(500)**
Performing Arts Series:	
Brattleboro Chamber Music Series	
5 dates; 300 seats	
Opera Companies:	
Vermont Opera Theater	
1 production; 6 performances	
Outdoor Recreation Endowments	**(252)**
Inland Water Area: 9.2 square miles	
Harriman Reservoir	
Somerset Reservoir	
National Forests, Parks, Wildlife Refuges:	
Appalachian Trail (5 acres)	
Green Mountain National Forest (19,839 acres)	
State Forests and Parks:	
Dutton Pines State Recreation Area	
Fort Dummer State Recreation Area	
Places Rated Score: 2,252	Places Rated Rank: 67

Brevard, NC

Common Denominators	**(1,300)**
Public Golf Courses: 3.5 daily fee	**AA**
Bowling Lanes: 18	**AA**
Movie Theaters: 1	**A**
Public Libraries: 1 (30,590 volumes)	**B**
The Arts	**(1,750)**
Symphony Orchestras:	
Brevard Music Center Symphony	
25 performances; 1,500 seats	
Opera Companies:	
Brevard Music Center Opera Company	
6 productions; 6 performances	
Outdoor Recreation Endowments	**(1,822)**
Inland Water Area: .2 square miles	
Lake Toxaway	
National Forests, Parks, Wildlife Refuges:	
Blue Ridge Parkway (1,031 acres)	
Nantahala National Forest (5,226 acres)	
Pisgah National Forest (82,736 acres)	
Places Rated Score: 4,872	Places Rated Rank: 18

Subtotal/
Rating

Brunswick–Golden Isles, GA

Common Denominators	(1,900)
Public Golf Courses: 3.5 municipal; 3.5 daily fee	AA
Bowling Lanes: 32	A
Movie Theaters: 4	A
Museums: 2 general; 3 historical	
Public Libraries: 8 (175,294 volumes)	AA
Outdoor Recreation Endowments	(779)
Coastline: 21 miles	
Inland Water Area: 52.6 square miles	
St. Simons Sound	
National Forests, Parks, Wildlife Refuges:	
Fort Frederica National Monument (211 acres)	

Places Rated Score: 2,679   Places Rated Rank: 53

Bull Shoals, AR

Common Denominators	(700)
Bowling Lanes: 12	AA
Public Libraries: 1 (20,000 volumes)	A
Outdoor Recreation Endowments	(741)
Inland Water Area: 53.2 square miles	
Bull Shoals Lake	
National Forests, Parks, Wildlife Refuges:	
Buffalo National River (23,148 acres)	
Ozark National Forest (3,261 acres)	
State Forests and Parks: Bull Shoals State Park	

Places Rated Score: 1,441   Places Rated Rank: 91

Camden–Penobscot Bay, ME

Common Denominators	(1,900)
Public Golf Courses: 3.5 daily fee	AA
Movie Theaters: 3	A
Museums: 1 art; 2 general; 2 historical	
William Farnsworth Art Museum	
Public Libraries: 2 (50,676 volumes)	A
Outdoor Recreation Endowments	(1,460)
Coastline: 45 miles	
Inland Water Area: 87.1 square miles	
Penobscot Bay	
National Forests, Parks, Wildlife Refuges:	
Acadia National Park (3,136 acres)	
Franklin Island National Wildlife Refuge (12 acres)	
Seal Island National Wildlife Refuge (65 acres)	
State Forests and Parks: Camden Hills State Park	

Places Rated Score: 3,360   Places Rated Rank: 37

Canton–Lake Tawakoni, TX

Common Denominators	(500)
Movie Theaters: 2	A
Public Libraries: 2 (34,862 volumes)	B
Outdoor Recreation Endowments	(27)
Inland Water Area: 4.6 square miles	
Lake Tawakoni	

Places Rated Score: 527   Places Rated Rank: 105

Cape Cod, MA

Common Denominators	(3,700)
Public Golf Courses: 3.5 municipal; 13.5 daily fee	AA
Bowling Lanes: 22	C
Movie Theaters: 21	AA
Museums: 2 art; 11 general; 9 historical; 1 natural history; 1 science	
Public Libraries: 40 (569,343 volumes)	AA
	(1,400)

The Arts
Performing Arts Series:
Cape Cod Conservatory of Music
3 dates; 750 seats
Symphony Orchestras:
Cape Cod Symphony Orchestra
10 performances; 853 seats
Opera Companies
College Light Opera Company
9 productions; 54 performances

Outdoor Recreation Endowments	(1,946)
Coastline: 80 miles	
Inland Water Area: 56.9 square miles	
Cape Cod Bay	
Wellfleet Harbor	
National Forests, Parks, Wildlife Refuges:	
Cape Cod National Seashore (26,931 acres)	
Monomoy Island National Wildlife Refuge (2,657 acres)	
State Forests and Parks:	
Scusset Beach State Recreation Area	
Shawme–Crowell State Recreation Area	

Places Rated Score: 7,046   Places Rated Rank: 8

Carson City, NV

Common Denominators	(1,700)
Public Golf Courses: 1 municipal; 3 daily fee	A
Bowling Lanes: 36	A
Movie Theaters: 1	C
Museums: 2 historical	
The Nevada State Museum	
Public Libraries: 3 (111,165 volumes)	AA
Outdoor Recreation Endowments	(811)
Inland Water Area: 39.3 square miles	
Lake Tahoe	
National Forests, Parks, Wildlife Refuges:	
Eldorado National Forest (53 acres)	
Lahontan National Wildlife Refuge (25 acres)	
Toiyabe National Forest (68,640 acres)	
State Forests and Parks: Dayton State Park	

Places Rated Score: 2,511   Places Rated Rank: 60

Cassville–Roaring River, MO

Common Denominators	(1,400)
Public Golf Courses: .5 municipal; 1 daily fee	A
Bowling Lanes: 16	A
Movie Theaters: 3	AA
Museums: 1 historical	
Public Libraries: 1 (35,388 volumes)	A
Outdoor Recreation Endowments	(633)
Inland Water Area: 17.1 square miles	
Table Rock Lake	
National Forests, Parks, Wildlife Refuges:	
Mark Twain National Forest (53,846 acres)	
State Forests and Parks: Roaring River State Park	

Places Rated Score: 2,033   Places Rated Rank: 76

CHARLOTTESVILLE, VA

Common Denominators	(1,400)
Public Golf Courses: 1.5 municipal; 3 daily fee	B
Bowling Lanes: 40	B
Movie Theaters: 8	A
Museums: 1 art; 2 historical	
Public Libraries: 7 (316,870 volumes)	AA

	Subtotal/ Rating
The Arts	**(1,450)**

The Arts **(1,450)**

Performing Arts Series:
  University of Virginia Artist Series
    4 dates; 2,400 seats
  University of Virginia Tuesday Evening Concerts
    7 dates; 1,000 seats
Symphony Orchestras:
  Charlottesville Community Symphony Orchestra
    12 performances; 1,000 seats

Outdoor Recreation Endowments **(204)**
Inland Water Area: .3 square miles
National Forests, Parks, Wildlife Refuges:
  Appalachian Trail (1,046 acres)
  Shenandoah National Park (29,859 acres)
Places Rated Score: 3,054   Places Rated Rank: 42

Clarkesville–Mount Airy, GA
Common Denominators **(800)**
Public Golf Courses: .5 daily fee **C**
Movie Theaters: 2 **A**
Public Libraries: 6 (129,290 volumes) **AA**
Outdoor Recreation Endowments **(1,123)**
Inland Water Area: .7 square miles
National Forests, Parks, Wildlife Refuges:
  Chattahoochee National Forest (40,009 acres)
Places Rated Score: 1,923   Places Rated Rank: 78

Clear Lake, CA
Common Denominators **(1,200)**
Public Golf Courses: 3 daily fee **AA**
Bowling Lanes: 22 **A**
Movie Theaters: 3 **A**
Public Libraries: 4 (48,991 volumes) **B**
Outdoor Recreation Endowments **(1,746)**
Inland Water Area: 67.1 square miles
  Clear Lake
  Indian Valley Reservoir
National Forests, Parks, Wildlife Refuges:
  Mendocino National Forest (252,978 acres)
State Forests and Parks: Clear Lake State Park
Places Rated Score: 2,946   Places Rated Rank: 44

Coeur d'Alene, ID
Common Denominators **(1,000)**
Public Golf Courses: 2.5 daily fee **A**
Bowling Lanes: 44 **A**
Movie Theaters: 1 **C**
Museums: 2 general
Public Libraries: 1 (35,120 volumes) **C**
Outdoor Recreation Endowments **(1,715)**
Inland Water Area: 70 square miles
  Coeur d'Alene Lake
  Hayden Lake
  Spirit Lake
National Forests, Parks, Wildlife Refuges:
  Coeur d'Alene National Forest (241,071 acres)
  Kaniksu National Forest (3,602 acres)
State Forests and Parks: Farragut State Park
Places Rated Score: 2,715   Places Rated Rank: 52

COLORADO SPRINGS, CO
Common Denominators **(2,400)**
Public Golf Courses: 2.5 municipal; 1.5 daily fee **C**
Bowling Lanes: 310 **AA**
Movie Theaters: 16 **B**

Museums: 1 art; 3 general; 5 historical; 1 natural
  history; 2 science
  Colorado Springs Fine Arts Center
Public Libraries: 10 (151,281 volumes) **C**
The Arts **(1,800)**
Performing Arts Series:
  Music for a Sunday Afternoon
    3 dates; 450 seats
Symphony Orchestras:
  Colorado Springs Symphony Orchestra
    26 performances; 1,875 seats
Opera Companies:
  Colorado Opera Festival
    1 production; 5 performances
Outdoor Recreation Endowments **(369)**
Inland Water Area: 2.1 square miles
National Forests, Parks, Wildlife Refuges:
  Pike National Forest (100,706 acres)
Places Rated Score: 4,569   Places Rated Rank: 22

Cookeville, TN
Common Denominators **(800)**
Public Golf Courses: 1.5 daily fee **B**
Bowling Lanes: 24 **B**
Movie Theaters: 3 **A**
Public Libraries: 1 (23,000 volumes) **C**
The Arts **(350)**
Symphony Orchestras:
  Community Symphony Orchestra
    5 performances; 481 seats
Outdoor Recreation Endowments **(43)**
Inland Water Area: 3.5 square miles
State Forests and Parks: Edgar Evins State
  Rustic Park
Places Rated Score: 1,193   Places Rated Rank: 100

Crossville, TN
Common Denominators **(1,300)**
Public Golf Courses: 1.5 daily fee **A**
Bowling Lanes: 16 **A**
Movie Theaters: 2 **A**
Public Libraries: 2 (159,424 volumes) **AA**
Outdoor Recreation Endowments **(7)**
Inland Water Area: .9 square miles
National Forests, Parks, Wildlife Refuges:
  Obed Wild and Scenic River (174 acres)
State Forests and Parks: Cumberland Mountain
  State Park
Places Rated Score: 1,307   Places Rated Rank: 97

DAYTONA BEACH, FL
Common Denominators **(2,000)**
Public Golf Courses: 3 municipal; 9 daily fee **A**
Bowling Lanes: 498 **AA**
Movie Theaters: 16 **A**
Museums: 1 art; 1 historical
  Museum of Art and Science
Public Libraries: 14 (943,537 volumes) **AA**
The Arts **(250)**
Performing Arts Series:
  Concert Showcase
    3 dates; 2,560 seats
Outdoor Recreation Endowments **(1,318)**
Coastline: 49 miles
Inland Water Area: 145 square miles
  Lake Dexter
  Ponce de Leon Inlet

	Subtotal/ Rating
National Forests, Parks, Wildlife Refuges:	
Canaveral National Seashore (16,177 acres)	
Lake Woodruff National Wildlife Refuge	
(18,225 acres)	
State Forests and Parks:	
Blue Springs State Park	
Bulow Plantation State Historical Site	
Flagler Beach State Recreation Area	
Hontoon Island State Park	
New Smyrna Sugar Mill Ruin State Historic	
Park	
Tomoko State Park	

Places Rated Score: 3,568   Places Rated Rank: 32

Delta, CO

Common Denominators	(1,300)
Public Golf Courses: .5 daily fee	B
Bowling Lanes: 12	A
Movie Theaters: 2	A
Museums: 1 historical	
Public Libraries: 5 (51,202 volumes)	AA
Outdoor Recreation Endowments	(1,318)
Inland Water Area: 6.7 square miles	
National Forests, Parks, Wildlife Refuges:	
Grand Mesa National Forest (91,506 acres)	
Gunnison National Forest (100,141 acres)	
Uncompahgre National Forest (2 acres)	
State Forests and Parks:	
Crawford State Recreation Area	
Sweitzer State Recreation Area	

Places Rated Score: 2,618   Places Rated Rank: 56

Deming, NM

Common Denominators	(500)
Bowling Lanes: 8	B
Public Libraries: 1 (38,819 volumes)	A
Outdoor Recreation Endowments	0
State Forests and Parks:	
City of Rocks State Park	
Pancho Villa State Park	
Rock Hound State Park	

Places Rated Score: 500   Places Rated Rank: 106

Eagle River, WI

Common Denominators	(1,300)
Public Golf Courses: .5 municipal; 2 daily fee	AA
Bowling Lanes: 18	AA
Movie Theaters: 2	AA
Public Libraries: 1 (12,961 volumes)	C
Outdoor Recreation Endowments	(1,153)
Inland Water Area: 150.5 square miles	
Plum Lake	
Trout Lake	
Yellow Birch Lake	
National Forests, Parks, Wildlife Refuges:	
Chequamegon National Forest (6,393 acres)	
Nicolet National Forest (47,394 acres)	

Places Rated Score: 2,453   Places Rated Rank: 63

Easton–Chesapeake Bay, MD

Common Denominators	(1,800)
Public Golf Courses: 1 municipal	A
Bowling Lanes: 24	AA
Movie Theaters: 3	AA
Museums: 1 art; 2 historical	
Public Libraries: 1 (80,975 volumes)	AA

	Subtotal/ Rating
Outdoor Recreation Endowments	(1,458)
Coastline: 40 miles	
Inland Water Area: 70 square miles	
Chesapeake Bay	
State Forests and Parks:	
Tuckahoe State Park	
Wye Oak State Park	

Places Rated Score: 3,258   Places Rated Rank: 38

Fairhope–Gulf Shores, AL

Common Denominators	(1,400)
Public Golf Courses: 1 municipal; 1 daily fee	B
Bowling Lanes: 40	B
Movie Theaters: 4	B
Museums: 1 art; 1 historical	
Eastern Shore Art Association	
Public Libraries: 8 (116,589 volumes)	B
Outdoor Recreation Endowments	(553)
Coastline: 27 miles	
Inland Water Area: 90.8 square miles	
Bon Secours Bay	
National Forests, Parks, Wildlife Refuges:	
Bon Secour National Wildlife Refuge (1,317 acres)	
State Forests and Parks:	
Fort Morgan State Recreation Area	
Gulf State Park	

Places Rated Score: 1,953   Places Rated Rank: 77

Fort Collins, CO

Common Denominators	(1,000)
Public Golf Courses: 4 municipal; .5 daily fee	B
Bowling Lanes: 160	AA
Movie Theaters: 9	B
Museums: 1 historical	
Public Libraries: 1 (135,554 volumes)	C
The Arts	(2,950)
Performing Arts Series:	
Colorado State University Fine Arts Series	
10 dates; 1,500 seats	
Colorado State University Productions	
20 dates; 1,500 seats	
Symphony Orchestras:	
Colorado State University Orchestra	
6 performances; 700 seats	
Fort Collins Symphony Orchestra	
15 performances; 1,200 seats	
Outdoor Recreation Endowments	(2,326)
Inland Water Area: 29.7 square miles	
Horse Tooth Reservoir	
National Forests, Parks, Wildlife Refuges:	
Rocky Mountain National Park (144,713 acres)	
Roosevelt National Forest (622,271 acres)	
State Forests and Parks:	
Boyd Lake State Recreation Area	
Lory State Park	

Places Rated Score: 6,276   Places Rated Rank: 11

Fort Lauderdale–Hollywood, FL

Common Denominators	(2,100)
Public Golf Courses: 5.5 municipal; 36 daily fee	A
Bowling Lanes: 802	AA
Movie Theaters: 44	B
Museums: 1 art; 1 general; 2 historical; 3 science	
Museum of Art	
Public Libraries: 17 (735,765 volumes)	C

	Subtotal/ Rating
The Arts	**(3,500)**
Performing Arts Series:	
Broward Community Guest Artist Series	
30 dates; 1,200 seats	
Broward Friends of Chamber Music	
6 dates; 1,200 seats	
Symphony Orchestras:	
Fort Lauderdale Symphony Orchestra	
28 performances; 2,500 seats	
Outdoor Recreation Endowments	**(256)**
Coastline: 25 miles	
Inland Water Area: 1.3 square miles	
State Forests and Parks:	
Hugh Taylor Birch State Recreation Area	
John U. Lloyd Beach State Recreation Area	
Places Rated Score: 5,856	Places Rated Rank: 12

Fort Myers–Cape Coral, FL

	Subtotal/ Rating
Common Denominators	**(1,300)**
Public Golf Courses: 2 municipal; 13 daily fee	A
Bowling Lanes: 266	AA
Movie Theaters: 10	B
Museums: 1 art; 1 historical; 1 natural history	
Public Libraries: 8 (177,513 volumes)	C
The Arts	**(950)**
Symphony Orchestras:	
Southwest Florida Symphony Orchestra	
17 performances; 1,000 seats	
Outdoor Recreation Endowments	**(1,239)**
Coastline: 10 miles	
Inland Water Area: 220 square miles	
Caloosahatchee River Estuary	
Pine Island Sound	
San Carlos Bay	
National Forests, Parks, Wildlife Refuges:	
Caloosahatchee National Wildlife Refuge	
(140 acres)	
J.N. "Ding" Darling National Wildlife Refuge	
(4,960 acres)	
Matlacha Pass National Wildlife Refuge	
(231 acres)	
Pine Island National Wildlife Refuge	
(404 acres)	
State Forests and Parks: Koreshan State Park	
Places Rated Score: 3,489	Places Rated Rank: 36

Fredericksburg, TX

	Subtotal/ Rating
Common Denominators	**(1,400)**
Public Golf Courses: .5 municipal	B
Bowling Lanes: 10	A
Movie Theaters: 1	A
Musems: 2 historical	
Public Libraries: 1 (34,227 volumes)	AA
Outdoor Recreation Endowments	**(2)**
National Forests, Parks, Wildlife Refuges:	
Lyndon B. Johnson National Historical Park	
(196 acres)	
Places Rated Score: 1,402	Places Rated Rank: 94

Front Royal, VA

	Subtotal/ Rating
Common Denominators	**(900)**
Public Golf Courses: .5 daily fee	B
Movie Theaters: 2	A
Museums: 1 historical	
Public Libraries: 1 (33,000 volumes)	A

	Subtotal/ Rating
Outdoor Recreation Endowments	**(747)**
National Forests, Parks, Wildlife Refuges:	
Appalachian Trail (759 acres)	
George Washington National Forest (6,177 acres)	
Shenandoah National Park (14,013 acres)	
Places Rated Score: 1,647	Places Rated Rank: 88

Gainesville–Lake Sidney Lanier, GA

	Subtotal/ Rating
Common Denominators	**(700)**
Public Golf Courses: 1 municipal; .5 daily fee	C
Bowling Lanes: 24	C
Movie Theaters: 2	C
Museums: 1 historical; 1 natural history	
Public Libraries: 5 (89,220 volumes)	B
Outdoor Recreation Endowments	**(564)**
Inland Water Area: 48.5 square miles	
Lake Sidney Lanier	
Places Rated Score: 1,264	Places Rated Rank: 99

Grand Junction, CO

	Subtotal/ Rating
Common Denominators	**(1,900)**
Public Golf Courses: 1.5 municipal	C
Bowling Lanes: 94	AA
Movie Theaters: 6	A
Museums: 1 art; 2 natural history	
Museum of Western Colorado	
Public Libraries: 7 (221,695 volumes)	AA
The Arts	**(700)**
Performing Arts Series:	
Mesa County Concert Association	
5 dates; 1,500 seats	
Symphony Orchestras:	
Grand Junction Symphony Orchestra	
5 performances; 1,553 seats	
Outdoor Recreation Endowments	**(1,373)**
Inland Water Area: 31.3 square miles	
National Forests, Parks, Wildlife Refuges:	
Colorado National Monument (20,454 acres)	
Grand Mesa National Forest (252,592 acres)	
Manti–La Sal National Forest (4,542 acres)	
Uncompahgre National Forest (207,256 acres)	
White River National Forest (81,289 acres)	
State Forests and Parks:	
Highline Lake State Recreation Area	
Island Acres State Recreation Area	
Places Rated Score: 3,973	Places Rated Rank: 26

Hamilton–Bitterroot Valley, MT

	Subtotal/ Rating
Common Denominators	**(1,000)**
Public Golf Courses: 1 municipal	A
Bowling Lanes: 12	B
Movie Theaters: 4	AA
Public Libraries: 1 (13,379 volumes)	C
Outdoor Recreation Endowments	**(3,655)**
Inland Water Area: 6.5 square miles	
National Forests, Parks, Wildlife Refuges:	
Bitterroot National Forest (1,104,598 acres)	
Lolo National Forest (5,687 acres)	
Metcalf National Wildlife Refuge (2,696 acres)	
Places Rated Score: 4,655	Places Rated Rank: 19

	Subtotal/ Rating
Harrison, AR	
Common Denominators	(1,600)
Public Golf Courses: 1 daily fee	A
Bowling Lanes: 20	A
Movie Theaters: 3	AA
Museums: 1 historical; 1 natural history	
Public Libraries: 1 (40,000)	AA
The Arts	(350)
Performing Arts Series:	
North Central Arkansas Concert Association	
5 dates; 2,000 seats	
Outdoor Recreation Endowments	(92)
Inland Water Area: 11.1 square miles	
Bull Shoals Lake	
Places Rated Score: 2,042	Places Rated Rank: 75

Hendersonville, NC	
Common Denominators	(1,000)
Public Golf Courses: 3 daily fee	A
Bowling Lanes: 24	B
Movie Theaters: 1	C
Museums: 1 historical	
Public Libraries: 3 (90,161 volumes)	A
Outdoor Recreation Endowments	(368)
Inland Water Area: .4 square miles	
National Forests, Parks, Wildlife Refuges:	
Carl Sandburg National Historic Site (247 acres)	
Pisgah National Forest (17,296 acres)	
Places Rated Score: 1,368	Places Rated Rank: 95

Hot Springs–Lake Ouachita, AR	
Common Denominators	(1,800)
Public Golf Courses: 5 daily fee	A
Bowling Lanes: 48	A
Movie Theaters: 5	A
Museums: 1 art; 1 general; 1 natural history; 2 science	
Public Libraries: 2 (185,308 volumes)	AA
Outdoor Recreation Endowments	(1,713)
Inland Water Area: 77.5 square miles	
Lake Ouachita	
National Forests, Parks, Wildlife Refuges:	
Hot Springs National Park (4,782 acres)	
Ouachita National Forest (106,865 acres)	
State Forests and Parks: Lake Ouachita State Park	
Places Rated Score: 3,513	Places Rated Rank: 34

Houghton Lake, MI	
Common Denominators	(1,400)
Public Golf Courses: 3.5 daily fee	AA
Bowling Lanes: 20	A
Movie Theaters: 3	AA
Museums: 1 historical; 1 science	
Public Libraries: 1 (13,985 volumes)	C
Outdoor Recreation Endowments	(454)
Inland Water Area: 52 square miles	
Higgins Lake	
Houghton Lake	
Lake St. Helens	
National Forests, Parks, Wildlife Refuges:	
Huron National Forest (40 acres)	
State Forests and Parks:	
North Higgins Lake State Park	
South Higgins Lake State Park	
Places Rated Score: 1,854	Places Rated Rank: 82

	Subtotal/ Rating
Kalispell, MT	
Common Denominators	(1,700)
Public Golf Courses: 2.5 municipal; 1.5 daily fee	A
Bowling Lanes: 54	AA
Movie Theaters: 6	AA
Museums: 1 art; 1 historical	
Public Libraries: 5 (35,388 volumes)	AA
The Arts	(300)
Performing Arts Series:	
Flathead Community Concert Association	
4 dates; 1,100 seats	
Outdoor Recreation Endowments	(3,736)
Inland Water Area: 143.2 square miles	
Flathead Lake	
Hungry Horse Reservoir	
Whitefish Lake	
National Forests, Parks, Wildlife Refuges:	
Flathead National Forest (1,715,168 acres)	
Flathead Wildlife Protected Area (3,910 acres)	
Glacier National Park (642,504 acres)	
Kootenai National Forest (52,903 acres)	
Lolo National Forest (18,707 acres)	
State Forests and Parks:	
Ashley Lake State Recreation Area	
Bitterroot Lake State Recreation Area	
Logan State Recreation Area	
Whitefish State Recreation Area	
Places Rated Score: 5,736	Places Rated Rank: 13

Keene, NH	
Common Denominators	(1,300)
Public Golf Courses: 3.5 daily fee	A
Bowling Lanes: 24	B
Movie Theaters: 3	B
Museums: 1 general; 1 historical	
Public Libraries: 18 (283,053 volumes)	AA
Outdoor Recreation Endowments	(140)
Inland Water Area: 20.6 square miles	
Lake Chesterfield	
Silver Lake	
Places Rated Score: 1,440	Places Rated Rank: 92

Kerrville, TX	
Common Denominators	(1,100)
Public Golf Courses: 1 municipal	C
Bowling Lanes: 16	B
Movie Theaters: 3	AA
Public Libraries: 1 (59,000 volumes)	AA
Outdoor Recreation Endowments	(0)
State Forests and Parks: Kerrville State Recreation Area	
Places Rated Score: 1,100	Places Rated Rank: 103

Laconia–Lake Winnipesaukee, NH	
Common Denominators	(1,000)
Public Golf Courses: 6 daily fee	AA
Movie Theaters: 2	B
Public Libraries: 8 (162,655 volumes)	AA
Outdoor Recreation Endowments	(717)
Inland Water Area: 66.9 square miles	
Lake Winnipesaukee	
Places Rated Score: 1,717	Places Rated Rank: 85

Lake Havasu City–Kingman, AZ	
Common Denominators	(1,100)
Public Golf Courses: .5 municipal; 4 daily fee	AA
Bowling Lanes: 16	C

	Subtotal/Rating
Movie Theaters: 3	**B**
Museums: 1 general; 1 historical	
Public Libraries: 4 (62,737 volumes)	**B**
Outdoor Recreation Endowments	**(1,427)**
Inland Water Area: 175.9 square miles	
Lake Havasu	
Lake Mead	
National Forests, Parks, Wildlife Refuges:	
Grand Canyon National Park (515,659 acres)	
Havasu National Wildlife Refuge (12,908 acres)	
Kaibab National Forest (5,468 acres)	
Lake Mead National Recreation Area (796,566 acres)	
Pipe Spring National Monument (41 acres)	
State Forests and Parks: Lake Havasu State Park	

Places Rated Score: 2,527   Places Rated Rank: 59

LAKELAND–WINTER HAVEN, FL

	Subtotal/Rating
Common Denominators	**(1,000)**
Public Golf Courses: 3.5 municipal; 10 daily fee	**A**
Bowling Lanes: 206	**A**
Movie Theaters: 15	**B**
Museums: 1 art	
Public Libraries: 2 (106,143 volumes)	**C**
The Arts	**(1,700)**
Performing Arts Series:	
Florida Southern College Fine Arts Festival	
12 dates; 1,800 seats	
Lakeland Civic Center Series	
4 dates; 3,000 seats	
Polk Community College Special Performances	
5 dates; 500 seats	
Symphony Orchestras:	
Lakeland Symphony Orchestra	
6 performances; 1,850 seats	
Outdoor Recreation Endowments	**(457)**
Inland Water Area: 187.2 square miles	
Lake Pierce	
Lake Rosalie	
Weohyakapka Lake	
State Forests and Parks:	
Lake Kissimmee	

Places Rated Score: 3,157   Places Rated Rank: 40

Lake O' The Cherokees, OK

	Subtotal/Rating
Common Denominators	**(700)**
Bowling Lanes: 22	**AA**
Movie Theaters: 1	**B**
Public Libraries: 1 (8,000 volumes)	**C**
Outdoor Recreation Endowments	**(460)**
Inland Water Area: 71.7 square miles	
Lake O' The Cherokees	

Places Rated Score: 1,160   Places Rated Rank: 101

LANCASTER, PA

	Subtotal/Rating
Common Denominators	**(1,500)**
Public Golf Courses: 9.5 daily fee	**B**
Bowling Lanes: 284	**AA**
Movie Theaters: 9	**C**
Museums: 2 general; 4 historical	
Public Libraries: 15 (451,559 volumes)	**B**
The Arts	**(400)**
Performing Arts Series:	
Franklin and Marshall College Artists Series	
6 dates; 850 seats	

	Subtotal/Rating
Outdoor Recreation Endowments	**(143)**
Inland Water Area: 27.9 square miles	
Muddy Run Reservoir	

Places Rated Score: 2,043   Places Rated Rank: 74

LAS CRUCES, NM

	Subtotal/Rating
Common Denominators	**(1,000)**
Public Golf Courses: 2 daily fee	**C**
Bowling Lanes: 50	**B**
Movie Theaters: 6	**A**
Museums: 1 art; 1 historical; 1 science	
Public Libraries: 1 (80,514 volumes)	**C**
The Arts	**(1,700)**
Performing Arts Series:	
New Mexico State University	
Performing Arts Series	
22 dates; 5,000 seats	
Symphony Orchestras:	
Las Cruces Symphony Orchestra	
8 performances; 1,000 seats	
Outdoor Recreation Endowments	**(109)**
National Forests, Parks, Wildlife Refuges:	
San Andres National Wildlife Refuge (2 acres)	
White Sands National Monument (53,059 acres)	

Places Rated Score: 2,809   Places Rated Rank: 47

LAS VEGAS, NV

	Subtotal/Rating
Common Denominators	**(1,300)**
Public Golf Courses: 3 municipal;	
7 daily fee	**B**
Bowling Lanes: 368	**AA**
Movie Theaters: 31	**A**
Museums: 2 art; 1 natural history	
Public Libraries: 15 (413,280 volumes)	**C**
The Arts	**(350)**
Performing Arts Series:	
University of Nevada Master Series	
5 dates; 2,000 seats	
Outdoor Recreation Endowments	**(2,728)**
Inland Water Area: 209.8 square miles	
Lake Mead	
National Forests, Parks, Wildlife Refuges:	
Desert National Wildlife Refuge	
(828,755 acres)	
Lake Mead National Recreation Area	
(588,704 acres)	
Toiyabe National Forest	
(58,040 acres)	
State Forests and Parks:	
Floyd Lamb State Park	
Spring Mountain State Park	
Valley of Fire State Park	

Places Rated Score: 4,378   Places Rated Rank: 24

LEXINGTON–FAYETTE, KY

	Subtotal/Rating
Common Denominators	**(2,100)**
Public Golf Courses: 2 municipal; 6 daily fee	**AA**
Bowling Lanes: 132	**B**
Movie Theaters: 16	**B**
Museums: 2 art; 3 general; 3 historical; 2 natural history; 1 science	
Public Libraries: 4 (316,423 volumes)	**B**

	Subtotal/ Rating
The Arts	**(3,400)**
Performing Arts Series:	
Central Kentucky Concert Association	
8 dates; 10,000 seats	
University of Kentucky Student Center Board	
15 dates; 10,000 seats	
Symphony Orchestras:	
Lexington Philharmonic	
39 performances; 1,494 seats	
Outdoor Recreation Endowments	**(3)**
Inland Water Area: .8 square miles	
State Forests and Parks: Kentucky Horse Park	

Places Rated Score: 5,503   Places Rated Rank: 15

Lincoln City–Newport, OR

	Subtotal/ Rating
Common Denominators	**(1,000)**
Public Golf Courses: 3 daily fee	AA
Bowling Lanes: 20	A
Movie Theaters: 1	C
Public Libraries: 2 (38,097 volumes)	B
Outdoor Recreation Endowments	**(1,896)**
Coastline: 50 miles	
Inland Water Area: 11.8 square miles	
Alsea Bay	
Devil's Lake	
Yaquina Bay	
National Forests, Parks, Wildlife Refuges:	
Siuslaw National Forest (170,716 acres)	
State Forests and Parks: Devil's Lake State Park	

Places Rated Score: 2,896   Places Rated Rank: 45

Maui, HI

	Subtotal/ Rating
Common Denominators	**(1,100)**
Public Golf Courses: 1 municipal; 8.5 daily fee	AA
Bowling Lanes: 30	B
Movie Theaters: 4	B
Museums: 1 historical	
Public Libraries: 1 (95,863 volumes)	B
Outdoor Recreation Endowments	**(1,689)**
Coastline: 150 miles	
Inland Water Area: .8 square miles	
National Forests, Parks, Wildlife Refuges:	
Haleakala National Park (27,456 acres)	
Kakahaia National Wildlife Refuge (45 acres)	

Places Rated Score: 2,789   Places Rated Rank: 49

McAllen–Pharr–Edinburg, TX

	Subtotal/ Rating
Common Denominators	**(900)**
Public Golf Courses: 3 municipal; 2.5 daily fee	C
Bowling Lanes: 60	C
Movie Theaters: 13	B
Museums: 1 general; 1 historical	
Public Libraries: 10 (651,910 volumes)	A
The Arts	**(900)**
Performing Arts Series:	
Pan American University Visiting Artists	
8 dates; 1,050 seats	
Symphony Orchestras:	
Valley Symphony Orchestra	
6 performances; 1,050 seats	
Outdoor Recreation Endowments	**(59)**
Inland Water Area: 12.4 square miles	
National Forests, Parks, Wildlife Refuges:	
Lower Rio Grande Valley National	
Wildlife Refuge (118 acres)	
Santa Ana National Wildlife Refuge	
(3,769 acres)	

	Subtotal/ Rating
State Forests and Parks: Bentsen–Rio	
Grande Valley State Park	

Places Rated Score: 1,859   Places Rated Rank: 81

MEDFORD, OR

	Subtotal/ Rating
Common Denominators	**(1,000)**
Public Golf Courses: .5 municipal; 1.5 daily fee	C
Bowling Lanes: 74	A
Movie Theaters: 7	B
Museums: 1 art	
Public Libraries: 13 (263,159 volumes)	A
Outdoor Recreation Endowments	**(1,261)**
Inland Water Area: 9 square miles	
Emigrant Reservoir	
Howard Reservoir	
Hyatt Reservoir	
National Forests, Parks, Wildlife Refuges:	
Crater Lake National Park (1 acre)	
Klamath National Forest (26,334 acres)	
Rogue River National Forest (412,632 acres)	
Umpqua National Forest (10,624 acres)	
State Forests and Parks:	
Casey State Park	
Joseph P. Stewart State Park	
Tou Velle State Park	

Places Rated Score: 2,261   Places Rated Rank: 66

MELBOURNE–TITUSVILLE–COCOA, FL

	Subtotal/ Rating
Common Denominators	**(1,000)**
Public Golf Courses: 4 municipal; 7 daily fee	A
Bowling Lanes: 196	A
Movie Theaters: 16	B
Museums: 1 art	
Public Libraries: 2 (87,500 volumes)	C
The Arts	**(1,550)**
Performing Arts Series:	
Brevard Community College Lyceum	
12 dates; 1,500 seats	
Symphony Orchestras:	
Brevard Symphony Orchestra	
15 performances; 600 seats	
Outdoor Recreation Endowments	**(2,051)**
Coastline: 72 miles	
Inland Water Area: 299 square miles	
Banana River	
Indian River	
Lake Washington	
National Forests, Parks, Wildlife Refuges:	
Canaveral National Seashore	
(25,600 acres)	
St. Johns National Wildlife Refuge	
(6,254 acres)	

Places Rated Score: 4,601   Places Rated Rank: 20

MIAMI, FL

	Subtotal/ Rating
Common Denominators	**(2,400)**
Public Golf Courses: 9.5 municipal;	
17 daily fee	C
Bowling Lanes: 466	C
Movie Theaters: 104	A
Museums: 5 art; 2 historical; 5 science	
Lowe Art Museum	
Public Libraries: 25 (3,044,438 volumes)	A

	Subtotal/ Rating
The Arts	**(7,800)**
Performing Arts Series:	
Florida International University	
Performing Arts Series	
5 dates; 350 seats	
Friends of Chamber Music Miami	
8 dates; 2,500 seats	
Miami Beach Concert Association	
8 dates; 3,000 seats	
Miami Beach Music and Arts League	
5 dates; 2,900 seats	
Miami Civic Music Association	
6 dates; 2,500 seats	
Miami International Series	
24 dates; 2,500 seats	
Temple Beth Shalom Guest Artist Series	
12 dates; 3,000 seats	
University of Miami Guest Artist Series	
6 dates; 600 seats	
Symphony Orchestras:	
Florida International University	
Community Orchestra	
10 performances; 35 seats	
Florida Philharmonic Orchestra	
36 performances; 2,500 seats	
Miami Beach Symphony	
7 performances; 2,900 seats	
Opera Companies:	
Greater Miami Opera Association	
5 productions; 96 performances	
Outdoor Recreation Endowments	**(4,021)**
Coastline: 50 miles	
Inland Water Area: 67.1 square miles	
Biscayne Bay	
National Forests, Parks, Wildlife Refuges:	
Big Cypress National Preserve (10,402 acres)	
Biscayne National Park (95,001 acres)	
Everglades National Park (415,710 acres)	
State Forests and Parks: Chekika State	
Recreation Area	
Places Rated Score: 14,221	Places Rated Rank: 2

Missoula, MT

	Subtotal/ Rating
Common Denominators	**(1,100)**
Public Golf Courses: 1.5 municipal; .5 daily fee	**B**
Bowling Lanes: 10	**C**
Movie Theaters: 9	**AA**
Museums: 1 art; 1 historical	
Public Libraries: 4 (96,250 volumes)	**B**
The Arts	**(400)**
Symphony Orchestras:	
Missoula Civic Symphony Orchestra	
6 performances; 1,300 seats	
Outdoor Recreation Endowments	**(2,248)**
Inland Water Area: 12.2 square miles	
Salmon Lake	
Seeley Lake	
National Forests, Parks, Wildlife Refuges:	
Bitterroot National Forest (10,060 acres)	
Flathead National Forest (167,810 acres)	
Lolo National Forest (498,830 acres)	
Places Rated Score: 3,748	Places Rated Rank: 30

Monticello–Liberty, NY

	Subtotal/ Rating
Common Denominators	**(1,300)**
Public Golf Courses: 2 municipal; 10 daily fee	**AA**
Bowling Lanes: 50	**AA**

	Subtotal/ Rating
Movie Theaters: 9	**AA**
Public Libraries: 2 (27,542 volumes)	**C**
Outdoor Recreation Endowments	**(104)**
Inland Water Area: 20.7 square miles	
Neversink Reservoir	
Swinging Bridge Reservoir	
Places Rated Score: 1,404	Places Rated Rank: 93

Mountain Home–Norfork Lake, AR

	Subtotal/ Rating
Common Denominators	**(1,000)**
Public Golf Courses: 1 daily fee	**B**
Bowling Lanes: 74	**AA**
Movie Theaters: 2	**A**
Museums: 1 historical	
Outdoor Recreation Endowments	**(1,201)**
Inland Water Area: 40.9 square miles	
Norfork Lake	
National Forests, Parks, Wildlife Refuges:	
Buffalo National River (951 acres)	
Ozark National Forest (61,268 acres)	
Places Rated Score: 2,201	Places Rated Rank: 68

Myrtle Beach, SC

	Subtotal/ Rating
Common Denominators	**(900)**
Public Golf Courses: 31 daily fee	**AA**
Bowling Lanes: 24	**C**
Movie Theaters: 9	**A**
Public Libraries: 1 (69,005 volumes)	**C**
Outdoor Recreation Endowments	**(750)**
Coastline: 75 miles	
State Forests and Parks: Myrtle Beach State Park	
Places Rated Score: 1,650	Places Rated Rank: 87

Nevada City–Donner, CA

	Subtotal/ Rating
Common Denominators	**(1,100)**
Public Golf Courses: 2 daily fee	**B**
Bowling Lanes: 22	**B**
Movie Theaters: 2	**C**
Museums: 1 general; 1 historical	
Public Libraries: 4 (48,991 volumes)	**AA**
Outdoor Recreation Endowments	**(1,371)**
Inland Water Area: 11.9 square miles	
Englebright Lake	
Prosser Creek Reservoir	
National Forests, Parks, Wildlife Refuges:	
Tahoe National Forest (161,791 acres)	
State Forests and Parks: Malakoff	
Diggins State Historical Park	
Places Rated Score: 2,471	Places Rated Rank: 61

North Conway–White Mountains, NH

	Subtotal/ Rating
Common Denominators	**(1,200)**
Public Golf Courses: 6 daily fee	**AA**
Movie Theaters: 4	**AA**
Public Libraries: 11 (126,519 volumes)	**AA**
Outdoor Recreation Endowments	**(1,231)**
Inland Water Area: 58.1 square miles	
Lake Winnipesaukee	
Ossipee Lake	
Silver Lake	
National Forests, Parks, Wildlife Refuges:	
White Mountain National Forest (144,687 acres)	
Places Rated Score: 2,431	Places Rated Rank: 64

Subtotal/
Rating

Oak Harbor, WA

Common Denominators (1,100)
Public Golf Courses: 2 daily fee A
Bowling Lanes: 22 B
Movie Theaters: 4 A
Museums: 1 general; 1 historical
Public Libraries: 1 (35,600) C
Outdoor Recreation Endowments (819)
Coastline: 60 miles
Inland Water Area: 13.4 square miles
Saratoga Passage
Skagit Bay
National Forests, Parks, Wildlife Refuges:
Ebey's Landing National Historical
Reserve (293 acres)
San Juan Islands National Wildlife
Refuge (65 acres)
State Forests and Parks:
Deception Pass State Park
Fort Ebey State Park
Places Rated Score: 1,919   Places Rated Rank: 79

Ocala, FL

Common Denominators (1,100)
Public Golf Courses: 1.5 municipal;
3.5 daily fee A
Bowling Lanes: 214 AA
Movie Theaters: 5 B
Public Libraries: 15 (165,000 volumes) B
Outdoor Recreation Endowments (1,455)
Inland Water Area: 52.5 square miles
Lake Bryant
Lake Kerr
Lake Weir
National Forests, Parks, Wildlife Refuges:
Ocala National Forest (274,074 acres)
Places Rated Score: 2,555   Places Rated Rank: 57

Ocean City–Assateague Island, MD

Common Denominators (1,300)
Public Golf Courses: 3.5 daily fee AA
Bowling Lanes: 28 AA
Movie Theaters: 3 A
Public Libraries: 5 (43,113 volumes) B
Outdoor Recreation Endowments (1,341)
Coastline: 31 miles
Inland Water Area: 110 square miles
Chincoteague Bay
Isle of Wight Bay
Sinepuxent Bay
National Forests, Parks, Wildlife Refuges:
Assateague Island National Seashore
(6,900 acres)
Chincoteague National Wildlife Refuge
(418 acres)
State Forests and Parks:
Assateague State Park
Pocomoke River State Forest
Pocomoke River State Park
Places Rated Score: 2,641   Places Rated Rank: 55

Olympia, WA

Common Denominators (1,400)
Public Golf Courses: 4.5 daily fee B
Bowling Lanes: 80 A

Subtotal/
Rating

Movie Theaters: 5 B
Museums: 1 art; 2 historical
Public Libraries: 45 (1,008,282 volumes) AA
Outdoor Recreation Endowments (436)
Coastline: 10 miles
Inland Water Area: 47 square miles
Budd Inlet
Case Inlet
National Forests, Parks, Wildlife Refuges:
Nisqually National Wildlife Refuge
(1,985 acres)
Olympic National Forest (10 acres)
Snoqualmie National Forest (612 acres)
State Forests and Parks:
Millersylvania Memorial State Park
Places Rated Score: 1,836   Places Rated Rank: 83

Orlando, FL

Common Denominators (1,000)
Public Golf Courses: 4 municipal; 45.5 daily fee A
Bowling Lanes: 232 C
Movie Theaters: 26 C
Museums: 1 art; 1 general; 1 historical; 1 science
Public Libraries: 12 (535,141 volumes) C
The Arts (6,100)
Performing Arts Series:
Rollins College Concert Series
7 dates; 366 seats
Symphony Orchestras:
Florida Symphony Orchestra
100 performances; 2,456 seats
University of Central Florida Symphony
Orchestra
4 performances; 650 seats
Opera Companies:
Orlando Opera Company
3 productions; 7 performances
Outdoor Recreation Endowments (522)
Inland Water Area: 297.1 square miles
Lake Apopka
Lake Kissimmee
Tohopekaliga Lake
Places Rated Score: 7,622   Places Rated Rank: 7

Oscoda–Huron Shore, MI

Common Denominators (1,000)
Public Golf Courses: 3.5 daily fee AA
Bowling Lanes: 6 C
Movie Theaters: 1 C
Public Libraries: 8 (118,336 volumes) AA
Outdoor Recreation Endowments (2,542)
Coastline: 40 miles
Inland Water Area: 19.4 square miles
Tawas Lake
National Forests, Parks, Wildlife Refuges
Huron National Forest (141,423 acres)
State Forests and Parks: Tawas Point State Park
Places Rated Score: 3,542   Places Rated Rank: 33

Paris, TN

Common Denominators (600)
Public Golf Courses: 1 municipal B
Bowling Lanes: 12 B
Movie Theaters: 1 C
Public Libraries: 1 (13,805 volumes) C

	Subtotal/ Rating
Outdoor Recreation Endowments	(274)
Inland Water Area: 32.8 square miles	
Kentucky Lake	
State Forests and Parks: Paris Landing State Park	
Places Rated Score: 874 Places Rated Rank: 104	

Petoskey–Straits of Mackinac, MI

	Subtotal/ Rating
Common Denominators	(1,500)
Public Golf Courses: 4 daily fee	AA
Bowling Lanes: 24	AA
Movie Theaters: 2	A
Museums: 1 historical	
Public Libraries: 2 (38,000 volumes)	A
Outdoor Recreation Endowments	(673)
Coastline: 50 miles	
Inland Water Area: 16.5 square miles	
Little Traverse Bay	
Walloon Lake	
State Forests and Parks:	
Petoskey State Park	
Wilderness State Park	
Places Rated Score: 2,173 Places Rated Rank: 70	

PHOENIX, AZ

	Subtotal/ Rating
Common Denominators	(3,400)
Public Golf Courses: 7.5 municipal;	
37.5 daily fee	B
Bowling Lanes: 422	C
Movie Theaters: 63	B
Museums: 3 art; 3 ethnic; 4 general;	
6 historical; 3 natural history; 1 science	
The Heard Museum	
Phoenix Art Museum	
Public Libraries: 27 (1,223,219 volumes)	C
The Arts	(16,850)
Performing Arts Series:	
Arizona State University Critics Choice	
95 dates; 3,029 seats	
Scottsdale Center for the Arts	
80 dates; 790 seats	
Sun City Fine Arts Society	
6 dates; 1,000 seats	
Symphony Orchestras:	
Arizona State University Symphony	
Orchestra	
15 performances; 3,000 seats	
Mesa Symphony Orchestra	
12 performances; 1,200 seats	
Phoenix Symphony Orchestra	
110 performances; 2,490 seats	
Sun City Symphony Orchestra	
5 performances; 7,200 seats	
Outdoor Recreation Endowments	(637)
Inland Water Area: 14.9 square miles	
Apache Lake	
Bartlett Reservoir	
Canyon Lake	
Cave Creek Dam	
National Forests, Parks, Wildlife Refuges:	
Tonto National Forest (658,428 acres)	
State Forests and Parks: Lost Dutchman	
State Park	
Places Rated Score: 20,887 Places Rated Rank: 1	

Port Angeles–Strait of Juan de Fuca, WA

	Subtotal/ Rating
Common Denominators	(1,700)
Public Golf Courses: 2 daily fee	B
Bowling Lanes: 48	AA
Movie Theaters: 2	C
Museums: 1 historical; 1 science	
Public Libraries: 4 (139,107 volumes)	AA
The Arts	(850)
Performing Arts Series:	
Port Angeles Fine Arts Series	
7 dates; 1,205 seats	
Symphony Orchestras:	
Port Angeles Symphony Orchestra	
6 performances; 1,205 seats	
Outdoor Recreation Endowments	(3,270)
Coastline: 90 miles	
Inland Water Area: 34.5 square miles	
Lake Crescent	
Ozette Lake	
National Forests, Parks, Wildlife Refuges:	
Dungeness Spit National Wildlife Refuge	
(245 acres)	
Flattery Rocks National Wildlife Refuge	
(125 acres)	
Olympic National Forest (200,099 acres)	
Olympic National Park (319,410 acres)	
Places Rated Score: 5,420 Places Rated Rank: 16	

Prescott, AZ

	Subtotal/ Rating
Common Denominators	(1,800)
Public Golf Courses: 1 municipal;	
2.5 daily fee	A
Bowling Lanes: 4	B
Movie Theaters: 5	A
Museums: 1 art; 1 ethnic; 2 general;	
2 historical	
Public Libraries: 10 (124,494 volumes)	AA
Outdoor Recreation Endowments	(1,897)
Inland Water Area: 4.2 square miles	
Pleasant Lake	
National Forests, Parks, Wildlife Refuges:	
Coconino National Forest (426,986 acres)	
Kaibab National Forest (25,119 acres)	
Montezuma Castle National Monument	
(841 acres)	
Prescott National Forest (1,193,326 acres)	
Tonto National Forest (316,917 acres)	
Tuzigoot National Monument (58 acres)	
State Forests and Parks:	
Dead Horse Ranch State Park	
Fort Verde State Historical Park	
Jerome State Historical Park	
Places Rated Score: 3,697 Places Rated Rank: 31	

Rappahannock, VA

	Subtotal/ Rating
Common Denominators	(400)
Public Libraries: 1 (14,244 volumes)	AA
Outdoor Recreation Endowments	(939)
National Forests, Parks, Wildlife Refuges:	
Appalachian Trail (300 acres)	
Shenandoah National Park (31,766 acres)	
Places Rated Score: 1,339 Places Rated Rank: 96	

Red Bluff–Sacramento Valley, CA

	Subtotal/ Rating
Common Denominators	(1,100)
Public Golf Courses: .5 daily fee	C
Bowling Lanes: 16	B
Movie Theaters: 4	AA
Museums: 1 historical	
Public Libraries: 8 (76,008 volumes)	A

	Subtotal/ Rating
Outdoor Recreation Endowments	**(1,040)**
Inland Water Area: .7 square miles	
Black Butte Lake	
National Forests, Parks, Wildlife Refuges:	
Lassen National Forest	
(188,903 acres)	
Lassen Volcanic National Park	
(4,206 acres)	
Mendocino National Forest	
(126,978 acres)	
Trinity National Forest	
(76,947 acres)	

Places Rated Score: 2,140   Places Rated Rank: 71

Rehoboth Bay–Indian River Bay, DE

Common Denominators	**(1,200)**
Public Golf Courses: 1.5 daily fee	**C**
Bowling Lanes: 60	**A**
Movie Theaters: 9	**A**
Museums: 1 art; 1 historical	
Public Libraries: 14 (164,923 volumes)	**A**
The Arts	**(250)**
Performing Arts Series:	
Seaford Community Concert Association	
3 dates, 1,200 seats	
Outdoor Recreation Endowments	**(728)**
Coastline: 52 miles	
Inland Water Area: 37.1 square miles	
Indian River Bay	
Rehoboth Bay	
National Forests, Parks, Wildlife Refuges:	
Prime Hook National Wildlife Refuge	
(8,817 acres)	
State Forests and Parks:	
Cape Henelopen State Park	
Craig Pond State Park	
Delaware Seashore State Park	
Gordon Pond Wildlife State Park	
Ingrams Pond	
Trap Pond	

Places Rated Score: 2,178   Places Rated Rank: 69

RENO, NV

Common Denominators	**(1,700)**
Public Golf Courses: 4.5 municipal; 2.5 daily fee	**B**
Bowling Lanes: 150	**AA**
Movie Theaters: 10	**B**
Museums: 2 art; 1 general; 1 historical;	
2 science	
Public Libraries: 5 (448,301 volumes)	**A**
The Arts	**(300)**
Opera Companies:	
Nevada Opera Association	
4 productions; 13 performances	
Outdoor Recreation Endowments	**(461)**
Inland Water Area: 232.9 square miles	
Lake Tahoe	
Pyramid Lake	
Washoe Lake	
National Forests, Parks, Wildlife Refuges:	
Anaho Island (248 acres)	
Sheldon National Wildlife Refuge	
(187,200 acres)	
Toiyabe National Forest (53,692 acres)	
State Forests and Parks: Washoe Lake State Park	

Places Rated Score: 2,461   Places Rated Rank: 62

Rhinelander, WI

Common Denominators	**(1,400)**
Public Golf Courses: 2 daily fee	**A**
Bowling Lanes: 44	**AA**
Movie Theaters: 5	**AA**
Public Libraries: 1 (56,000 volumes)	**A**
Outdoor Recreation Endowments	**(510)**
Inland Water Area: 106.4 square miles	
Lake Tomahawk	
Pelican Lake	
Willow Lake	
National Forests, Parks, Wildlife Refuges:	
Nicolet National Forest (11,274 acres)	

Places Rated Score: 1,910   Places Rated Rank: 80

Rockport–Aransas Pass, TX

Common Denominators	**(800)**
Movie Theaters: 2	**AA**
Public Libraries: 2 (47,209 volumes)	**AA**
Outdoor Recreation Endowments	**(3,076)**
Coastline: 23 miles	
Inland Water Area: 167.3 square miles	
Aransas Bay	
Copano Bay	
National Forests, Parks, Wildlife Refuges:	
Aransas National Wildlife Refuge	
(52,461 acres)	
State Forests and Parks:	
Capano Bay Causeway State Park	
Goose Island State Park	
Mustang Island State Park	

Places Rated Score: 3,876   Places Rated Rank: 27

Roswell, NM

Common Denominators	**(1,400)**
Public Golf Courses: 1 municipal	**C**
Bowling Lanes: 50	**AA**
Movie Theaters: 2	**C**
Museums: 1 art; 1 historical; 1 science	
Roswell Museum and Art Center	
Public Libraries: 1 (37,579 volumes)	**C**
The Arts	**(1,050)**
Performing Arts Series:	
Roswell Community Concerts	
4 dates; 1,500 seats	
Symphony Orchestras:	
Roswell Symphony Orchestra	
13 performances; 1,400 seats	
Outdoor Recreation Endowments	**(84)**
Inland Water Area: 2.9 square miles	
Two River Reservoir	
National Forests, Parks, Wildlife Refuges:	
Bitter Lake National Wildlife Refuge	
(23,350 acres)	
Lincoln National Forest (40,332 acres)	
State Forests and Parks: Bottomless Lake	
State Park	

Places Rated Score: 2,534   Places Rated Rank: 58

St. George–Zion, UT

Common Denominators	**(1,300)**
Public Golf Courses: .5 municipal; 2 daily fee	**AA**
Bowling Lanes: 12	**B**
Movie Theaters: 5	**AA**
Museums: 1 historical	
Public Libraries: 1 (35,000 volumes)	**B**

	Subtotal/Rating
Outdoor Recreation Endowments	**(1,691)**

Inland Water Area: 1.1 square miles
National Forests, Parks, Wildlife Refuges:
  Dixie National Forest (394,572 acres)
  Zion National Park (130,357 acres)
State Forests and Parks:
  Gunlock Lake State Beach
  Snow Canyon State Park
Places Rated Score: 2,991   Places Rated Rank: 43

San Antonio, TX

	Subtotal/Rating
Common Denominators	**(2,300)**
Public Golf Courses: 7 municipal; 4.5 daily fee	C
Bowling Lanes: 660	A
Movie Theaters: 48	B
Museums: 2 art; 4 general; 7 historical; 1 natural history; 1 science	
Public Libraries: 13 (1,149,135 volumes)	B
The Arts	**(10,950)**

Performing Arts Series:
  San Antonio Chamber Music Society
    8 dates; 900 seats
  San Antonio Performing Arts Association
    8 dates; 2,779 seats
  Tuesday Musical Club Artists Series
    4 dates; 1,221 seats
  Trinity University New Entertainment Series
    4 dates; 2,965 seats
Symphony Orchestras:
  San Antonio Symphony Orchestra
    180 performances; 2,780 seats
Opera Companies:
  San Antonio Opera
    3 productions; 8 performances

Outdoor Recreation Endowments	**(7)**

Inland Water Area: 3.7 square miles
  Canyon Lake
  Colavevas Lake
National Forests, Parks, Wildlife Refuges:
  San Antonio Missions National
    Historical Park (6 acres)
Places Rated Score: 13,257   Places Rated Rank: 4

San Diego, CA

	Subtotal/Rating
Common Denominators	**(4,800)**
Public Golf Courses: 6.5 municipal; 41.5 daily fee	B
Bowling Lanes: 748	B
Movie Theaters: 79	B
Museums: 4 art; 1 ethnic; 5 general; 3 historical; 2 natural history; 9 science	
Natural History Museum	
San Diego Museum of Art	
San Diego Museum of Man	
San Diego Wild Animal Park	
Public Libraries: 65 (1,952,372 volumes)	B
The Arts	**(8,000)**

Performing Arts Series:
  Point Loma College Cultural Affairs Series
    6 dates; 3,200 seats
  San Diego State University Cultural Arts Series
    13 dates; 1,100 seats
Symphony Orchestras:
  San Diego State University Philharmonia
    8 performances; 1,000 seats
  San Diego Symphony Orchestra
    115 performances; 2,945 seats

	Subtotal/Rating

Opera Companies:
  San Diego Opera Association
    8 productions; 30 performances

Outdoor Recreation Endowments	**(1,130)**

Coastline: 55 miles
Inland Water Area: 52.2 square miles
  Cuyamaca Reservoir
  El Capitan Lake
  Lake Henshaw
  Lake Hodges
National Forests, Parks, Wildlife Refuges:
  Cabrillo National Monument (144 acres)
  Cleveland National Forest (286,148 acres)
  Tijuana Slough National Wildlife Refuge
    (407 acres)
State Forests and Parks:
  Palomar Mountain State Park
  San Elijo State Park
  South Carlsbad State Beach
Places Rated Score: 13,930   Places Rated Rank: 3

San Luis Obispo, CA

	Subtotal/Rating
Common Denominators	**(1,500)**
Public Golf Courses: 2 municipal; 3.5 daily fee	B
Bowling Lanes: 56	B
Movie Theaters: 7	B
Museums: 4 historical; 1 natural history; 1 science	
Public Libraries: 16 (237,261 volumes)	A
Outdoor Recreation Endowments	**(1,309)**

Coastline: 60 miles
Inland Water Area: 146.2 square miles
  Lake Nacimiento
  Morro Bay
National Forests, Parks, Wildlife Refuges:
  Los Padres National Forest (189,267 acres)
State Forests and Parks:
  Atascadero Beach State Park
  Montana Bay State Park
  Morro Bay State Park
  Morro Strand State Park
  Pismo State Park
Places Rated Score: 2,809   Places Rated Rank: 47

Santa Fe, NM

	Subtotal/Rating
Common Denominators	**(1,600)**
Bowling Lanes: 24	C
Movie Theaters: 11	AA
Museums: 1 ethnic; 3 general; 2 historical	
Public Libraries: 3 (250,000 volumes)	AA
The Arts	**(1,950)**

Performing Arts Series:
  College of Santa Fe Performing Arts Series
    7 dates; 512 seats
  Santa Fe Concert Association
    4 dates; 900 seats
Symphony Orchestras:
  Orchestra of Santa Fe
    15 performances; 750 seats
Opera Companies:
  Santa Fe Opera
    5 productions; 34 performances

Outdoor Recreation Endowments	**(1,039)**

Inland Water Area: 3.9 square miles
  Cochiti Reservoir

	Subtotal/ Rating

National Forests, Parks, Wildlife Refuges:
Bandelier National Monument (826 acres)
Santa Fe National Forest (250,577 acres)
State Forests and Parks:
Hyde Memorial State Park
Santa Fe River State Park
Places Rated Score: 4,589   Places Rated Rank: 21

SANTA ROSA, CA

Common Denominators	**(1,700)**
Public Golf Courses: 3.5 municipal;	
7.5 daily fee	**B**
Bowling Lanes: 40	**C**
Movie Theaters: 13	**B**
Museums: 1 art; 1 ethnic; 3 general;	
3 historical; 1 natural history	
Public Libraries: 13 (622,954 volumes)	**A**
The Arts	**(800)**
Symphony Orchestras:	
Santa Rosa Symphony Orchestra	
14 performances; 1,600 seats	
Outdoor Recreation Endowments	**(363)**

Coastline: 35 miles
Inland Water Area: 4.5 square miles
National Forests, Parks, Wildlife Refuges:
San Pablo National Wildlife Refuge (249 acres)
Places Rated Score: 2,863   Places Rated Rank: 46

SARASOTA–BRADENTON, FL

Common Denominators	**(1,600)**
Public Golf Courses: 3.5 municipal; 30.5 daily fee	**AA**
Bowling Lanes: 192	**B**
Movie Theaters: 20	**B**
Museums: 3 art; 2 historical; 2 science	
Public Libraries: 7 (240,645 volumes)	**C**
The Arts	**(2,100)**
Performing Arts Series:	
Celebrity Series	
5 dates; 1,779 seats	
Sarasota Opera Society Performing Arts Series	
6 dates; 1,779 seats	
Symphony Orchestras:	
Florida West Coast Symphony Orchestra	
19 performances; 1,776 seats	
Opera Companies:	
Asolo Opera Company	
4 productions; 4 performances	
Outdoor Recreation Endowments	**(800)**

Coastline: 52 miles
Inland Water Area: 78.7 square miles
Sarasota Bay
National Forests, Parks, Wildlife Refuges:
De Soto National Memorial (25 acres)
Passage Key National Wildlife Refuge (36 acres)
State Forests and Parks:
Lake Manatee State Park
Manatee Springs State Park
Myakka River State Park
Oscar Scherer State Recreation Area
Places Rated Score: 4,500   Places Rated Rank: 23

SPRINGFIELD, MO

Common Denominators	**(1,000)**
Public Golf Courses: 2.5 municipal; 2 daily fee	**B**
Bowling Lanes: 140	**A**
Movie Theaters: 10	**B**
Public Libraries: 6 (345,095 volumes)	**A**

The Arts	**(2,850)**
Performing Arts Series:	
Drury College Series	
3 dates; 2,000 seats	
Evangel College Performing Arts Series	
8 dates; 2,200 seats	
Southwest Missouri State University	
Convocations	
10 dates; 3,500 seats	
Symphony Orchestras:	
Springfield Symphony Orchestra	
28 performances; 1,480 seats	
Outdoor Recreation Endowments	**(332)**

Inland Water Area: .6 square miles
National Forests, Parks, Wildlife Refuges:
Mark Twain National Forest (50,807 acres)
Wilson's Creek National Battlefield
(1,750 acres)
Places Rated Score: 4,182   Places Rated Rank: 25

STATE COLLEGE, PA

Common Denominators	**(900)**
Public Golf Courses: 3 daily fee	**B**
Bowling Lanes: 55	**B**
Movie Theaters: 2	**C**
Museums: 1 historical	
Public Libraries: 4 (201,797 volumes)	**A**
The Arts	**(2,600)**
Performing Arts Series:	
Pennsylvania State University Artists Series	
50 dates; 2,500 seats	
Outdoor Recreation Endowments	**(0)**

State Forests and Parks:
Black Moshannon State Park
Whipple Dam State Park
Places Rated Score: 3,500   Places Rated Rank: 35

Table Rock Lake, MO

Common Denominators	**(700)**
Public Golf Courses: 1 daily fee	**A**
Public Libraries: 1 (46,900)	**AA**
Outdoor Recreation Endowments	**(838)**

Inland Water Area: 59.8 square miles
Table Rock Lake
National Forests, Parks, Wildlife Refuges:
Mark Twain National Forest (16,325 acres)
Places Rated Score: 1,538   Places Rated Rank: 89

Tahlequah–Lake Tenkiller, OK

Common Denominators	**(1,000)**
Public Golf Courses: 1.5 municipal	**A**
Bowling Lanes: 20	**A**
Movie Theaters: 1	**C**
Museums: 2 ethnic	
Public Libraries: 1 (1,400 volumes)	**C**
The Arts	**(300)**
Performing Arts Series:	
Northeastern Oklahoma Allied Arts Series	
4 dates; 1,475 seats	
Outdoor Recreation Endowments	**(182)**

Inland Water Area: 28.5 square miles
Lake Tenkiller
State Forests and Parks:
Tenkiller State Park
Places Rated Score: 1,482   Places Rated Rank: 90

	Subtotal/ Rating

Toms River–Barnegat Bay, NJ

Common Denominators	**(1,000)**
Public Golf Courses: 1 municipal; 2.5 daily fee	**C**
Bowling Lanes: 142	**B**
Movie Theaters: 15	**B**
Museums: 2 general; 1 historical	
Public Libraries: 3 (340,436 volumes)	**B**
The Arts	**(750)**
Performing Arts Series:	
Ocean County College Fine Arts Series	
6 dates; 609 seats	
Symphony Orchestras:	
Garden State Philharmonic	
5 performances; 1,266 seats	
Outdoor Recreation Endowments	**(1,332)**
Coastline: 50 miles	
Inland Water Area: 113.8 square miles	
Barnegat Bay	
National Forests, Parks, Wildlife Refuges:	
Barnegat National Wildlife Refuge (7,427 acres)	
Brigantine National Wildlife Refuge (256 acres)	

Places Rated Score: 3,082   Places Rated Rank: 41

Traverse City–Grand Traverse Bay, MI

Common Denominators	**(2,000)**
Public Golf Courses: 4.5 daily fee	**AA**
Bowling Lanes: 86	**AA**
Movie Theaters: 5	**A**
Museums: 1 ethnic; 1 general; 1 science	
Great Lakes Area Paleontological Museum	
Public Libraries: 2 (72,465 volumes)	**B**
The Arts	**(750)**
Performing Arts Series:	
Interlochen Arts Academy Concerts	
5 dates; 2,000 seats	
Symphony Orchestras:	
Northwestern Michigan Symphony Orchestra	
6 performances; 1,000 seats	
Outdoor Recreation Endowments	**(1,034)**
Coastline: 75 miles	
Inland Water Area: 27.8 square miles	
Duck Lake	
Grand Traverse Bay	
Long Lake	
National Forests, Parks, Wildlife Refuges:	
Manistee National Forest (2 acres)	
State Forests and Parks:	
Interlochen State Park	
Traverse City State Park	

Places Rated Score: 3,784   Places Rated Rank: 29

Tucson, AZ

Common Denominators	**(4,500)**
Public Golf Courses: 5 municipal; 8 daily fee	**B**
Bowling Lanes: 324	**A**
Movie Theaters: 25	**B**
Museums: 2 art; 1 ethnic; 4 general; 4 historical;	
3 natural history; 5 science	
Arizona Heritage Center	
Arizona Historical Society	
Arizona State Museum	
Tucson Museum of Art	
Public Libraries: 18 (870,410 volumes)	**A**
The Arts	**(2,450)**
Performing Arts Series:	
University of Arizona Artist Series	
7 dates; 2,520 seats	

Symphony Orchestras:	
Tucson Symphony Orchestra	
30 performances; 2,277 seats	
Opera Companies:	
Arizona Opera Company	
6 productions; performances NA	
Outdoor Recreation Endowments	**(1,028)**
Inland Water Area: 1.1 square miles	
National Forests, Parks, Wildlife Refuges:	
Cabeza Prieta National Wildlife Refuge	
(416,210 acres)	
Coronado National Forest	
(382,093 acres)	
Organ Pipe National Monument	
(329,199 acres)	
Saguaro National Monument	
(81,958 acres)	
State Forests and Parks:	
Catalina State Park	
Picacho Peak State Park	

Places Rated Score: 7,978   Places Rated Rank: 5

Twain Harte–Yosemite, CA

Common Denominators	**(1,300)**
Public Golf Courses: 4.5 daily fee	**AA**
Bowling Lanes: 16	**B**
Movie Theaters: 4	**AA**
Museums: 1 historical	
Public Libraries: 1 (46,578 volumes)	**B**
Outdoor Recreation Endowments	**(3,573)**
Inland Water Area: 19.7 square miles	
Beardiley Lake	
Cherry Lake	
Don Pedro Reservoir	
National Forests, Parks, Wildlife Refuges:	
Calaveras Bigtree National Forest (380 acres)	
Stanislaus National Forest (609,093 acres)	
Yosemite National Park (428,604 acres)	

Places Rated Score: 4,873   Places Rated Rank: 17

West Palm Beach–Boca Raton, FL

Common Denominators	**(1,400)**
Public Golf Courses: 7.5 municipal; 34 daily fee	**A**
Bowling Lanes: 420	**A**
Movie Theaters: 18	**C**
Museums: 3 art; 2 historical; 1 science	
Public Libraries: 9 (285,447 volumes)	**C**
The Arts	**(3,400)**
Performing Arts Series:	
Florida Atlantic University Performing Arts Series	
4 dates; 2,400 seats	
Regional Arts Music and Dance	
30 dates; 2,002 seats	
Society of the Four Arts	
4 dates; 718 seats	
Tuesdays with Music	
8 dates; 250 seats	
Symphony Orchestras:	
Greater Palm Beach Symphony	
7 performances; 850 seats	
Opera Companies:	
Palm Beach Opera	
3 productions; 9 performances	
Outdoor Recreation Endowments	**(1,554)**
Coastline: 47 miles	
Inland Water Area: 555 square miles	
Lake Okeechobee	
Palm Beach Harbor	

	Subtotal/ Rating
National Forests, Parks, Wildlife Refuges:	
Loxahatchee National Wildlife Refuge	
(2,550 acres)	
State Forests and Parks: Pahokee State	
Recreation Area	
Places Rated Score: 6,354	Places Rated Rank: 10

Winchester, VA

	Subtotal/ Rating
Common Denominators	(900)
Public Golf Courses: 1 municipal; 1 daily fee	B
Bowling Lanes: 40	A
Movie Theaters: 1	C
Museums: 1 historical	
Public Libraries: 1 (52,368 volumes)	B
The Arts	(300)
Performing Arts Series:	
Shenandoah College Artists Series	
4 dates; 700 seats	
Outdoor Recreation Endowments	(87)
National Forests, Parks, Wildlife Refuges:	
George Washington National Forest	
(4,873 acres)	
Places Rated Score: 1,287	Places Rated Rank: 98

Yuma, AZ

	Subtotal/ Rating
Common Denominators	(1,200)
Public Golf Courses: 1 municipal; 2 daily fee	B
Bowling Lanes: 50	B
Movie Theaters: 5	B
Museums: 1 art; 2 general	
Public Libraries: 6 (199,328 volumes)	A
Outdoor Recreation Endowments	(877)
Inland Water Area: 29.1 square miles	
Imperial Reservoir	
National Forests, Parks, Wildlife Refuges:	
Cabeza Prieta National Wildlife Refuge	
(443,800 acres)	
Cibola National Wildlife Refuge	
(40 acres)	
Havasu National Wildlife Refuge	
(1,942 acres)	
Kofa National Wildlife Refuge	
(660,000 acres)	
State Forests and Parks: Buckskin Mountain	
State Park	
Places Rated Score: 2,077	Places Rated Rank: 73

Et Cetera

GOLDEN AGE PASSPORTS: ANOTHER BREAK AT 62 PLUS

Since 1974, nearly two million Golden Age Passports have been issued to U.S. citizens and permanent residents who are 62 or older. These are free permits to any national park, monument, or recreation area run by the federal government and are valid for the life-time of the holder.

With a Golden Age Passport, friends who accompany you will also be admitted free as long as everyone arrives in the same private vehicle (a car, station wagon, pickup truck, motor home, or motorcycle; busloads don't qualify). If you walk in, the Passport admits you, your spouse, and children.

It isn't necessary to obtain the Passport before trucking off on a combined vacation and retirement-place inspection trip. You can get one at most federally operated recreation areas where they are used and at any National Park Service regional office, National Forest supervisor's office, and most ranger station offices. They aren't available by mail, however; you have to obtain one in person. All you need is proof of age—a driver's license, birth certificate, or signed affidavit attesting to your age.

There are real savings involved if you plan on frequent visits to the national parks, forests, wildlife refuges, and Corps of Engineers waterways. Not only are entrance fees waived (they currently range from $0.50 to $4.00), but the Passport-holder gets an addi-tional 50 percent discount on federal use fees, such as parking, overnight camping, and boat launching. With camping charges approaching $10.00 a night, and with increased parking and boat-ramp fees, 50 percent discounts can add up to a real bargain.

PUBLIC LAND: A GIANT RECREATION RESOURCE

In the United States, 291 million acres of land have been set aside for the public's use and for preservation as national forest, national park, national wildlife refuge, and state park. Aside from the obvious oppor-tunities for hiking, camping, boating, swimming, and fishing, these public lands also offer some unusual activities.

If you're a history buff, for example, you might enjoy poking around Fort Frederica National Monu-ment in Georgia, site of an eighteenth-century British fort built during the Anglo-Spanish struggle for control over the South Atlantic coast of the New World. Or you might want to explore Colorado National Monu-ment, which preserves some 20,000 acres of sandstone country that embrace sheer-walled canyons, bizarre wind and water formations, and the remains of both dinosaurs and prehistoric Indians. These national monuments are part of the National Park System, as are the many national military parks and battlefields around the country that draw Civil War fans.

And the four national parkways, made up of swatches of land along roadways, provide a chance for unhurried driving through areas of scenic interest. The Blue Ridge Parkway, for example, follows the crest of the Blue Ridge Mountains of western Virginia and North Carolina for 469 miles and meanders through several large recreation areas.

The table below shows the amount and kind of public land in each state. Predictably, the states with the most such land are those with the most *total* land; of the eight states with the most public land, six rank

in the top ten for total area. Alaska, the largest state in the nation, also has the most public land—89 million acres of it. Likewise, the least amount of public land is found in the smallest states. Rhode Island, 50th in size, also ranks last in public land, with only 13,205 acres. Delaware (32,900 acres) and Maryland (109,000)—49th and 42nd, respectively, in area—place in the bottom six for public land acreage.

But there are a few surprises. Texas, the second-biggest state in the Union, has only three million acres devoted to public land. And in Washington, 20th in size, there are more than 12 million acres of public land, 16 times the amount in neighboring Oregon.

Public Lands: A State-by-State Summary

State	National Forests	National Park System Units	National Wildlife Refuges	State Parks
Alabama	4 (1,263,000 acres)	3 (2,300 acres)	7 (11,700 acres)	21 (48,000 acres)
Alaska	2 (24,018,000 acres)	16 (54,400,000 acres)	16 (7,535,000 acres)	65 (3,314,000 acres)
Arizona	7 (11,883,000 acres)	22 (1,843,000 acres)	5 (1,533,000 acres)	15 (29,000 acres)
Arkansas	3 (3,488,000 acres)	5 (105,000 acres)	7 (136,400 acres)	42 (42,000 acres)
California	22 (24,112,000 acres)	20 (5,080,000 acres)	25 (125,400 acres)	230 (1,005,000 acres)
Colorado	12 (15,355,000 acres)	11 (650,000 acres)	6 (53,000 acres)	44 (159,000 acres)
Connecticut	—	Appalachian National Scenic Trail	1 (183 acres)	234 (198,000 acres)
Delaware	—	—	2 (23,900 acres)	9 (9,000 acres)
Florida	4 (1,225,000 acres)	10 (2,320,000 acres)	27 (171,000 acres)	115 (286,000 acres)
Georgia	2 (1,832,000 acres)	10 (63,000 acres)	10 (462,300 acres)	55 (52,000 acres)
Hawaii	—	10 (270,000 acres)	5 (3,100 acres)	53 (25,000 acres)
Idaho	15 (21,625,000 acres)	3 (56,000 acres)	10 (23,500 acres)	22 (83,000 acres)
Illinois	1 (715,000 acres)	1 (12 acres)	5 (57,200 acres)	186 (327,000 acres)
Indiana	1 (644,000 acres)	3 (13,000 acres)	2 (7,700 acres)	20 (54,000 acres)
Iowa	—	2 (2,000 acres)	7 (26,400 acres)	82 (52,000 acres)
Kansas	—	2 (700 acres)	1 (21,800 acres)	35 (29,000 acres)
Kentucky	2 (1,415,000 acres)	4 (73,000 acres)	2 (2,100 acres)	45 (41,000 acres)
Louisiana	1 (1,022,000 acres)	1 (20,000 acres)	11 (286,000 acres)	37 (30,000 acres)
Maine	1 (54,000 acres)	3 (91,000 acres)	10 (30,500 acres)	58 (67,000 acres)
Maryland	—	15 (74,000 acres)	6 (26,000 acres)	45 (9,000 acres)
Massachusetts	—	12 (46,000 acres)	8 (11,300 acres)	126 (238,000 acres)
Michigan	4 (4,867,000 acres)	3 (714,000 acres)	6 (106,000 acres)	93 (244,000 acres)

State	National Forests	National Park System Units	National Wildlife Refuges	State Parks
Minnesota	1 (606,000 acres)	5 (140,000 acres)	31 (300,300 acres)	92 (189,000 acres)
Mississippi	6 (2,310,000 acres)	5 (124,000 acres)	9 (109,000 acres)	24 (21,000 acres)
Missouri	—	4 (82,000 acres)	69 (43,000 acres)	58 (96,000 acres)
Montana	11 (19,087,000 acres)	8 (1,137,000 acres)	39 (550,000 acres)	130 (43,000 acres)
Nebraska	2 (346,000 acres)	3 (6,200 acres)	13 (152,000 acres)	92 (131,000 acres)
Nevada	4 (5,424,000 acres)	3 (1,497,000 acres)	8 (2,178,000 acres)	16 (151,000 acres)
New Hampshire	1 (798,000 acres)	2 (149 acres)	3 (1,700 acres)	65 (70,000 acres)
New Jersey	—	7 (6,000 acres)	5 (36,200 acres)	106 (260,000 acres)
New Mexico	10 (236,000 acres)	12 (267,000 acres)	8 (323,000 acres)	33 (72,000 acres)
New York	—	20 (41,000 acres)	10 (23,000 acres)	209 (253,000 acres)
North Carolina	5 (2,953,000 acres)	10 (141,000 acres)	10 (136,000 acres)	34 (117,000 acres)
North Dakota	2 (760,000 acres)	3 (72,000 acres)	73 (19,000 acres)	18 (16,000 acres)
Ohio	1 (833,000 acres)	5 (33,000 acres)	5 (8,000 acres)	124 (188,000 acres)
Oklahoma	1 (413,000 acres)	2 (9,500 acres)	3 (80,000 acres)	74 (95,000 acres)
Oregon	15 (17,302 acres)	4 (175,000 acres)	21 (472,000 acres)	242 (92,000 acres)
Pennsylvania	1 (743,000 acres)	15 (160,000 acres)	4 (9,000 acres)	119 (275,000 acres)
Rhode Island	—	1 (5 acres)	4 (1,200 acres)	85 (12,000 acres)
South Carolina	2 (1,380,000 acres)	5 (21,000 acres)	9 (103,000 acres)	48 (68,000 acres)
South Dakota	1 (1,405,000 acres)	4 (273,000 acres)	52 (130,000 acres)	45 (90,000 acres)
Tennessee	1 (1,204,000 acres)	11 (650,000 acres)	7 (23,000 acres)	83 (131,000 acres)
Texas	4 (1,730,000 acres)	13 (1,042,000 acres)	18 (227,000 acres)	87 (134,000 acres)
Utah	9 (9,973,000 acres)	13 (2,089,000 acres)	4 (92,000 acres)	43 (69,000 acres)
Vermont	1 (629,000 acres)	Appalachian National Scenic Trail	3 (5,700 acres)	41 (157,000 acres)
Virginia	2 (3,224,000 acres)	19 (244,000 acres)	15 (101,000 acres)	37 (53,000 acres)
Washington	9 (10,038,000 acres)	10 (1,930,000 acres)	28 (111,000 acres)	171 (86,000 acres)
West Virginia	3 (1,838,000 acres)	4 (65,000 acres)	3 (300 acres)	33 (149,000 acres)
Wisconsin	2 (2,027,000 acres)	3 (89,000 acres)	23 (122,000 acres)	73 (69,000 acres)
Wyoming	10 (9,120,000 acres)	7 (2,565,000 acres)	8 (44,000 acres)	48 (123,000 acres)

Source: U.S. Bureau of the Census, State and Metropolitan Area Data Book, 1982; and National Park Service, U.S. Fish and Wildlife Service, and U.S. Forest Service, unpublished administrative records, 1983.

A STATE-BY-STATE GUIDE FOR OLDER SPORTSPEOPLE

One out of five Americans fishes and one in ten hunts. There are several breaks for older Americans who pursue these hobbies. Older sportspeople need no fishing licenses in 18 states and no hunting licenses in nine. In 16 other states that require all persons who fish or hunt to be licensed, older sportspeople can apply for free licenses (six of these states require established residency, ranging from 30 years in Alaska to one year in South Carolina). Eight states grant lifetime licenses for a small fee, and eight more give significant discounts.

ALABAMA

Fishing: $6.25 annual resident's license. Channel catfish; bluegill, redear, and longear sunfish; rainbow trout; rock bass; and flier.

Hunting: $10.25 annual resident's license. Deer, turkey, quail, squirrel, wild hog, and fox.

Breaks for Older Sportspeople: Residents over 65 can buy a fishing license or a hunting license for $0.25 each.

ALASKA

Fishing: $10.00 annual resident's license. Arctic char, salmon, Dolly Varden and cutthroat trout, and burbot.

Hunting: $12.00 annual resident's license. Black bear, bison, deer, elk, mountain goat, moose, and small game.

Breaks for Older Sportspeople: Residents over 60 who've lived in the state more than 30 years can obtain free hunting and fishing licenses.

ARIZONA

Fishing: $6.00 annual resident's license. Bass, walleye, char, salmon, and northern pike.

Hunting: $9.00 annual resident's license. Cottontail, quail, partridge, muskrat, raccoon, otter, and upland game birds.

Breaks for Older Sportspeople: Residents over 70 who've lived in the state 25 years can obtain a free Pioneer License for hunting and fishing.

ARKANSAS

Fishing: $7.50 annual resident's license. Trout, bass, bream, catfish, and white amur.

Hunting: $7.50 annual resident's license. Turkey, quail, rabbit, squirrel, rail, woodcock, and crow.

Breaks for Older Sportspeople: Residents over 65 can obtain lifetime fishing and hunting licenses for $3.50 each.

CALIFORNIA

Fishing: $7.00 annual resident's license. Steelhead and other trout, salmon, sargo, striped bass, sturgeon, corbina, and ocean fish.

Hunting: $10.25 annual resident's license. Antelope, wild pig, bobcat, raccoon, mink, beaver, tree squirrel, rabbit, hare, fox, and upland game birds.

Breaks for Older Sportspeople: Veterans with a 70% service disability qualify for free hunting and fishing permits.

COLORADO

Fishing: $7.50 annual resident's license. Trout, grayling, whitefish, Kokanee salmon, bluegill sunfish, drum, catfish, northern pike, and carp.

Hunting: $5.00 annual resident's license. Sage and blue grouse, ptarmigan, chukar, rabbit, snipe, crow, coyote, duck, teal, and goose.

Breaks for Older Sportspeople: Residents over 64 can buy a lifetime license for fishing and small-game hunting for $2.00.

CONNECTICUT

Fishing: $5.00 annual resident's license. Trout, char, Kokanee and Atlantic salmon, calico and other bass, chain pickerel, and eel.

Hunting: $5.00 annual resident's license. Quail, pheasant, partridge, rabbit, hare, fox, opossum, duck, and goose.

Breaks for Older Sportspeople: Residents over 64 are eligible for free hunting and fishing licenses.

DELAWARE

Fishing: $4.20 annual resident's license. Striped bass, trout, white shad, pickerel, perch, bluegill sunfish, and carp.

Hunting: $5.20 annual resident's license. Deer, squirrel, rabbit, bobwhite, raccoon, snipe, crow, and dove.

Breaks for Older Sportspeople: Residents over 65 need no licenses for hunting and fishing.

FLORIDA

Fishing: $6.50 annual resident's license. Black and sunshine bass, chain pickerel, bream, redfinned pike, catfish, and gar.

Hunting: $11.50 annual resident's license. Otter, mink, bobcat, armadillo, beaver, deer, bear, turkey, quail, and dove.

Breaks for Older Sportspeople: Residents over 65 need no licenses for fishing and hunting.

GEORGIA

Fishing: $3.25 annual resident's license. Bream, crappie, white and other bass, redfinned pike, shad, sauger, catfish, and muskie.

Hunting: $4.25 annual resident's license. Bobcat, fox, grouse, rabbit, quail, squirrel, and armadillo.

Breaks for Older Sportspeople: Residents over 65 need no license for fishing, and can obtain an honorary hunting license.

HAWAII

Fishing: $3.75 annual resident's license. Rainbow trout, black bass, bluegill sunfish, channel catfish, tucunaré, oscar, tilapia, and oopuhue.

Hunting: $7.50 annual resident's license. Pheasant, Japanese quail, chukar, francolin, dove, turkey, wild pig, and deer.

Breaks for Older Sportspeople: None.

IDAHO

Fishing: $6.50 annual resident's license. Trout, bass, perch, crappie, bluegill sunfish, and channel catfish.

Hunting: $5.50 annual resident's license. Pheasant, partridge, grouse, rabbit, fox, raccoon, dove, and bobcat.

Breaks for Older Sportspeople: Residents over 70 who've lived in the state more than ten years get free licenses to hunt and fish; residents between 65 and 69 who've lived in the state more than ten years can buy a $1.50 license for fishing and hunting.

ILLINOIS

Fishing: $5.50 annual resident's license. Steelhead and lake trout, salmon, muskie, sauger, bass, catfish, and cisco.

Hunting: $7.50 annual resident's license. Turkey, woodchuck, squirrel, pheasant, quail, rabbit, fox, woodcock, dove, and rail.

Breaks for Older Sportspeople: Residents over 65 need no license to fish or hunt.

INDIANA

Fishing: $6.00 annual resident's license. Bluegill and redear sunfish, rock and other bass, walleye, muskie, sauger, and smelt.

Hunting: $6.00 annual resident's license. Squirrel, rabbit, fox, rail, gallinule, and snipe.

Breaks for Older Sportspeople: Residents over 65 need no license to fish.

IOWA

Fishing: $6.00 annual resident's license. Frog, turtle, largemouth and rock bass, bluegill sunfish, bullhead, catfish, tiger muskie, and trout.

Hunting: $6.00 annual resident's license. Pheasant, quail, ruffed grouse, cottontail, squirrel, opossum, and fox.

Breaks for Older Sportspeople: None.

KANSAS

Fishing: $7.00 annual resident's license. Black bass, channel catfish, sauger, shovelnose sturgeon, trout, eel, and perch.

Hunting: $7.00 annual resident's license. Antelope, deer, turkey, fox, pheasant, quail, prairie chicken, rabbit, and hare.

Breaks for Older Sportspeople: Residents over 65 need no license to hunt and fish.

KENTUCKY

Fishing: $6.50 annual resident's license. Frog, rock and other bass, sauger, northern pike, chain pickerel, and rockfish.

Hunting: $6.50 annual resident's license. Squirrel, rabbit, quail, raccoon, opossum, and woodcock.

Breaks for Older Sportspeople: Residents over 65 need no license to hunt and fish.

LOUISIANA

Fishing: $2.00 annual resident's license. Striped bass, crappie, bream, warmouth, buffalo, and channel catfish.

Hunting: $5.00 annual resident's license. Rabbit, squirrel, raccoon, armadillo, fox, quail, dove, and rail.

Breaks for Older Sportspeople. Residents who've lived in the state two years prior to application can obtain free fishing and hunting licenses.

MAINE

Fishing: $9.50 annual resident's license. Trout, salmon, black bass, pickerel, perch, and crappie.

Hunting: $9.50 annual resident's license. Deer, bear, game birds (pheasant, ruffed grouse, and gallinule), bobcat, and rabbit.

Breaks for Older Sportspeople: Residents over 70 get free fishing and hunting licenses.

MARYLAND

Fishing: $4.50 annual resident's license. Non–tidal-water game fish, including bass and pickerel.

Hunting: $10.00 annual resident's license. Fox, rabbit, raccoon, and migratory waterfowl.

Breaks for Older Sportspeople: Residents over 65 pay $1.00 for an annual fishing license and $1.25 for an annual hunting license.

MASSACHUSETTS

Fishing: $11.25 annual resident's license. Lake and other trout, salmon, smelt, black bass, walleye, and shad.

Hunting: $11.25 annual resident's license. Deer, bear, turkey, quail, fox, and merganser.

Breaks for Older Sportspeople: Residents over 70 get complimentary fishing and hunting licenses; residents between 65 and 69 get 50% discounts on fishing and hunting licenses.

MICHIGAN

Fishing: $6.75 annual resident's license. Brook, brown, rainbow, and lake trout; largemouth and smallmouth bass; muskie; and coho and chinook salmon.

Hunting: $6.25 annual resident's license for small game, including squirrel, rabbit, ring-necked pheasant, and mink, and excluding turkey and deer.

Breaks for Older Sportspeople: Residents over 65 can obtain a $1.00 annual fishing license and a $4.00 annual hunting license.

MINNESOTA

Fishing: $5.50 resident's Angling License. Northern pike, walleye, lake trout, bullhead, and sauger.

Hunting: $9.50 resident's unrestricted small-game license, which includes raccoon, lynx, sora, and various migratory waterfowl.

Breaks for Older Sportspeople: Residents over 65 need no license to fish, and can obtain a 50% discount on a hunting license.

MISSISSIPPI

Fishing: $4.00 annual resident's license. Bream, goggle-eye, crappie, black bass, jack salmon, sauger, blue and tabbie catfish.

Hunting: $6.00 annual resident's small-game license. Rabbit, quail, opossum, crow, and wild turkey.

Breaks for Older Sportspeople: Residents over 65 need no license for fishing or for hunting.

MISSOURI

Fishing: $5.90 annual resident's license. Channel cat and blue catfish, rock bass, chain and grass pickerel, and muskie.

Hunting: $5.90 annual resident's license. Opossum, quail, pheasant, weasel, and gray fox.

Breaks for Older Sportspeople: Residents over 65 need no license for fishing but must pay full fee for a hunting permit.

MONTANA

Fishing: $5.00 annual resident's license. Dolly Varden, brook, brown, rainbow, and cutthroat trout; salmon; bass; walleye; burbot; and northern pike.

Hunting: $35.00 resident sportsman's license includes tags for deer, elk, black bear, game birds, and fishing.

Breaks for Older Sportspeople: Residents 62 or older can obtain a free Conservation License for fishing and for hunting upland game birds (excluding turkeys).

NEBRASKA

Fishing: $7.50 annual resident's license. Brook, brown, and rainbow trout; catfish; perch; bluegill and other sunfish; and drum.

Hunting: $14.00 annual resident's license for small game (including habitat stamp). Pheasant, coot, partridge, bobcat, woodcock, dove, and common snipe.

Breaks for Older Sportspeople: Residents over 70 and resident veterans over 65 can obtain free fishing and hunting permits (big game excluded).

NEVADA

Fishing: $10.00 annual resident's license. Largemouth and smallmouth bass, mackinaw and rainbow trout, and salmon.

Hunting: $10.00 annual resident's license (many stamps extra). Sage, blue, and ruffed grouse; quail; and chukar.

Breaks for Older Sportspeople: Residents over 65 who've lived in the state six months can obtain $2.00 Older Fishing Licenses and $2.00 Older Hunting Licenses.

NEW HAMPSHIRE

Fishing: $9.25 annual resident's license. Trout, coho salmon, largemouth bass, white perch, pickerel, and horned pout.

Hunting: $8.25 annual resident's license. Deer, bear, turkey, squirrel, and quail.

Breaks for Older Sportspeople: Residents over 68 qualify for a free license to fish and hunt.

NEW JERSEY

Fishing: $9.50 annual resident's license. Rock bass, northern pike, tiger muskie, chain pickerel, smallmouth bass, crappie, and catfish.

Hunting: $14.00 annual resident's firearm license. Deer, turkey, ruffed grouse, and migratory waterfowl.

Breaks for Older Sportspeople: Residents over 70 can obtain a free fishing license and a 50% discount on a hunting permit.

NEW MEXICO

Fishing: $15.75 annual resident's trout license. Trout (all kinds), grayling, salmon, catfish, striped bass, and bluegill sunfish.

Hunting: $15.00 annual resident's license. Squirrel, game birds, deer, bear, and fall turkey.

Breaks for Older Sportspeople: Residents over 64 pay $1.25 for a general fishing license and $10.50 for a general hunting license.

NEW YORK

Fishing: $6.25 annual resident's license. Trout (all kinds), coho and chinook salmon, bass, muskie, northern pike, and crappie.

Hunting: $6.25 annual resident's license. Small game, furbearers, and birds.

Breaks for Older Sportspeople: Residents over 70 can obtain free fishing and hunting licenses.

NORTH CAROLINA

Fishing: $9.50 annual resident's license. Black bass, mountain trout, chain pickerel, tiger muskie, bream, Kokanee salmon, and perch.

Hunting and Fishing: The Thrill of the Chase

The call of the wild—and particularly the wild animal—appears to be a potent lure for many Americans. According to a U.S. Fish and Wildlife Service survey, in 1980 there were 59 million hunters and fishermen, representing some 35 percent of the total U.S. population over age 16.

The national survey, conducted by the Census Bureau for the Fish and Wildlife Service, also disclosed the following facts:

- There were 17 million hunters and 42 million fishermen in 1980; together they spent $27 billion on their sports.
- The number of fishermen has increased 101 percent since 1955, with the proportion of the population that fishes rising from 18 percent to 23 percent.
- The number of hunters increased by only 42 percent over the same period, and the proportion of Americans who hunt dropped to 9 percent.
- 89,000 people age 65 or older started fishing for the first time in 1980.
- 24 percent of hunters are 45 or older, compared with 30 percent of fishermen.
- The most popular freshwater fish in 1980 were bass and panfish (more than 18 million fishermen tried to catch them), catfish (13 million), and trout (11 million).
- In the Great Lakes, perch were the most sought-after fish.

Hunting: $9.50 annual resident's license. Deer, wild boar, bear, wild turkey, squirrel, and rabbit.

Breaks for Older Sportspeople: Residents over 70 may buy a lifetime combination fishing-and-hunting license for $10.00.

NORTH DAKOTA

Fishing: $5.00 annual resident's license. Largemouth and smallmouth bass, crappie, and catfish.

Hunting: $5.00 annual resident's license for upland game birds, including turkey, pheasant, coot, and sandhill crane.

Breaks for Older Sportspeople: Residents over 65 can buy a $1.00 fishing license.

OHIO

Fishing: $7.75 annual resident's license. Trout, muskie, salmon, northern pike, buffalo, and bowfin.

Hunting: $7.75 annual resident's license. Weasel, squirrel, woodchuck, and crow (deer and turkey excluded).

Breaks for Older Sportspeople: Residents over 66 need no license to fish, and residents over 64 can obtain a permanent $7.75 hunting license.

OKLAHOMA

Fishing: $5.00 annual resident's license. Bass, crappie, blue and channel catfish, and northern pike.

Hunting: $5.00 annual resident's license. Bobcat, gray fox, raccoon, quail, prairie chicken, badger, mink, otter, and weasel.

Breaks for Older Sportspeople: Residents over 65 need no licenses to fish or hunt.

OREGON

Fishing: $9.00 annual resident's Angling License. Trout, largemouth and smallmouth bass, and catfish.

Hunting: $7.00 annual resident's license. Small game only, excluding bobcat, otter, beaver (unless licensed for fur-bearers), pheasant, quail, and sage grouse.

Breaks for Older Sportspeople: Persons over 70 who've lived in the state five or more years need no license to fish; persons over 65 who've lived in the state at least 50 years are eligible for a $1.00 annual Pioneer Hunting License.

PENNSYLVANIA

Fishing: $9.25 annual resident's license. Herring, pickerel, trout, salmon, and amur pike.

Hunting: $8.25 annual resident's license. Squirrel, ruffed grouse, hare, quail, woodchuck, fox, and crow.

Breaks for Older Sportspeople: Residents over 65 are eligible for a $10.25 lifetime fishing license and a one-third discount on annual hunting licenses.

RHODE ISLAND

Fishing: $6.50 annual resident's license. Northern pike, chain pickerel, pumpkinseed and redbreasted sunfish, black crappie, and chub sucker.

Hunting: $6.50 annual resident's license. Deer, partridge, mourning dove, quail, and raccoon.

Breaks for Older Sportspeople: Residents over 65 can obtain free fishing and hunting licenses.

SOUTH CAROLINA

Fishing: $5.25 annual resident's license. Black bass, trout, pickerel, jack, bream, and stumpknocker warmouth.

Hunting: $6.25 annual resident's license. Bobcat, marsh hen, quail, raccoon, and rabbit.

Breaks for Older Sportspeople: Persons over 65 who've lived in the state at least one year are eligible for free fishing and hunting licenses.

SOUTH DAKOTA

Fishing: $7.00 annual resident's license. Walleye, sauger, northern pike, perch, catfish, bass, trout, and salmon.

Hunting: $6.00 annual small-game stamp. Pheasant, rabbit, quail, squirrel, and snipe.

Breaks for Older Sportspeople: Persons over 65 get a two-thirds discount on fishing licenses only.

TENNESSEE

Fishing: $7.80 annual resident's license for both hunting and fishing. Black and striped bass, muskie, trout, bluegill sunfish, and catfish.

Hunting: $7.80 annual resident's combination license. Small game only, such as squirrel, grouse, rabbit, and quail.

Breaks for Older Sportspeople: No fishing or hunting licenses required for residents over 65.

TEXAS

Fishing: $4.50 annual resident's license. Bass, bream, catfish, Nile perch, and coho salmon.

Hunting: $8.75 combination hunting-and-fishing resident's license. Antelope, black bear, javelina, deer, badger, fox, nutria, civet cat, and various game birds including turkey.

Breaks for Older Sportspeople: No fishing license required for residents over 64; persons over 65 can obtain a $1.25 resident-exempt hunting license.

UTAH

Fishing: $10.50 annual resident's license. Grayling, salmon, trout, Bonneville cisco, and bass.

Hunting: $8.00 resident small-game license. Many predators, grouse, partridge, quail, and coot.

Breaks for Older Sportspeople: Persons over 65 get a three-fourths discount on fishing licenses only.

VERMONT

Fishing: $4.00 annual resident's license. Trout, salmon, wall-eye, and bass.

Hunting: $5.00 resident's annual license. Upland game birds, squirrel, rabbit, deer, bear, and fox.

Breaks for Older Sportspeople: Residents over 65 can buy a $1.75 lifetime fishing-and-hunting license.

VIRGINIA

Fishing: $7.50 annual resident's license. Bass, northern pike, sunfish, perch, and catfish.

Hunting: $7.50 annual resident's license. Small game, including squirrel, rabbit, quail, grouse, pheasant, and bobcat.

Breaks for Older Sportspeople: Residents over 65 can buy a $5.00 lifetime fishing-and-hunting license.

WASHINGTON

Fishing: $8.50 annual resident's license. Salmon, trout, white-fish, freshwater ling, sunfish, walleye, and warmouth bass.

Hunting: $7.50 annual resident's license, with many addition-al tags required. Bobcat, cougar, cottontail, rockchuck, and upland game birds.

Breaks for Older Sportspeople: No fishing license required for residents over 70; no hunting license required for veterans of the Spanish-American War, or for any veteran over 65 who has lived in the state for five years.

WEST VIRGINIA

Fishing: $6.00 annual resident's license. Trout, bass, muskie, chain pickerel, channel catfish, and bullhead.

Hunting: $6.00 annual resident's license. Squirrel, upland game birds, and turkey.

Breaks for Older Sportspeople: No fishing or hunting licenses required for residents over 65.

WISCONSIN

Fishing: $6.50 annual resident's license. Trout, salmon, perch, crappie, and bass.

Hunting: $6.50 annual resident's small-game license. Squir-rel, gray fox, raccoon, quail, pheasant, opossum, and weasel.

Breaks for Older Sportspeople: No fishing license required for residents over 65; older residents can also get a $7.50 lifetime permit for small-game hunting and for admission to state parks and forests.

WYOMING

Fishing: $7.50 annual resident's license. Walleye, sauger, trout, salmon, grayling, and northern pike.

Hunting: $5.00 annual resident small-game license. Rabbit, squirrel, fox, and upland game birds.

Breaks for Older Sportspeople: Persons over 65 who've lived in the state for 30 years prior to application can get a free lifetime Pioneer License for birds and fish.

Source: U.S. Fish and Wildlife Service, unpublished survey, 1981.

HOW DOES YOUR GARDEN GROW?

If you are a dedicated gardener, then you're one of those hardy souls willing to deal with nature's vagaries, ranging from savage winters and sandy soils to slimy snails and slugs, in order to enjoy the splendor of June roses, vine-ripened tomatoes, and a blaze of petunias. You use the winter to read Katherine White's *Onward and Upward in the Garden* and the gardening catalogs, you put humus in the sandy soil, and you set out saucers of flat beer for the slugs. (No, it's not meant as a treat—they are attracted by the odor, climb in, get tipsy, and drown!)

You're also not alone if you love to garden. Forty-seven percent of all homeowners have vegetable and flower gardens. Seventy-two percent of retired homeowners care for their own lawns; 52 percent grow vegetables, with tomatoes, peppers, and cucumbers, in that order, the most popular crops. Impatiens, petunias, and marigolds are the front-runners in annuals among the 49 percent of retired homeowners who grow flowers; roses are far and away the most popular perennials. Forty-eight percent grow shrubs, and 86 percent of those who grow vegetables also grow berries, with strawberries, red raspberries, and blueberries the favorites. Blackberries run a poor fourth. In the Midwest, 65 percent of households grow flowers as well as vegetables; in the East, 46 percent grow both. Nearly half of western households grow both vegetables and flowers, and a surprising 45 percent of western households also grow fruits and berries.

An acre or a pot, a treat for the eye or for the palate—no matter what your aim, gardening affords the delight of seemingly inexhaustible diversity. Years of growing both flowers and food reinforce your sense of change and renewal as well as your curiosity.

But what if you decide to move after retiring? Will the roses in your new garden bloom this year? Will the tomatoes thrive in the heat or the moisture, or the lack of both? Will the beloved tulips of the northern garden do well in the warm climate of the new home? (Probably, if you refrigerate the bulbs for a few months before planting.) Will the charming flowering dogwoods of the East prosper in the wintry blasts around the Great Lakes? (They won't prosper, but they will survive, if placed in a sheltered spot.) You'll never know if the peonies of your last home will do well in the new location unless you try to transplant some of their fleshy roots. And if you try, maybe you can disprove the doomsayers who hold that oriental poppies can never be moved once planted (their long carrotlike root

dislikes being transplanted). One old-timer claims you can't kill them.

As noted in an earlier chapter, the United States offers a dizzying number of variables in climate and terrain, many of which can either throw a sizable wrench into your gardening efforts or guarantee success. There are a few constants, however, that you will find wherever you may decide to move.

Soil

All soil is made up of varying amounts of clay particles, humus, and sand. The mix you have is dependent on where you live and on what others may have done to alter the natural state of the soil. Fortunately, the majority of plants are tolerant and will grow fairly well in most soils. Some can be grown most successfully in what is known as acid soil. Other plants like "sweet," or highly alkaline, soil. The acidity or alkalinity of soil is indicated by its pH number, a figure chemists use to measure the concentration of hydrogen ions (*pH* stands for "potential of hydrogen"). The midpoint in soil chemistry is 7, or neutral, on the pH scale. Less than 7 (down to 0) means acid; more than 7 (up to 14) means alkaline.

If you send a sample of soil to a testing laboratory, you may be told that it has a pH rating of 8.5, which would explain why the clematis looks so good, why you have the best onions and lettuce you've ever grown, and why your lilies and tomatoes are in bad shape. And now you know you'll have to put some alum or sulfur in the tomato patch.

You can test your soil yourself with litmus paper purchased from the drugstore. If the blue paper turns red when placed in moist soil, the soil is acid. If the red paper turns blue or purple, the soil is sweet. If there is no change, the soil is neutral. Or, you can take a representative slice of soil from the top down to about 6 inches, mix it, and send about half a cup to your County Extension Agent for testing.

A word of caution: If your soil is very acid or very sweet, take time to correct it, but change the pH by no more than a point per year.

Garden Pests

Unfortunately, pests are everywhere. If you leave the beetles and gypsy moths of the East for the gardens of California, chances are good that you will have to learn to do battle with snails and slugs, pests that were never a problem before. The cutworm that did damage only in the early part of the growing season in New England may reproduce several times a year in warm climates. One gardener who has lived in the East, on the Pacific Coast, and in the Midwest claims to have learned three distinct sets of gardening rules, so pronounced are the variables of good gardening from area to area. And the ants, beetles, billbugs, borers, grubs, nematodes, and webworms are always with us.

So no matter where you live, you will have to have some kind of pest control. How much pesticide and what kind depends on the local pests, how perfect you want your crop to be, and what kind of growing season you are coping with. Purists who abhor any kind of chemical spray will have to be extra diligent about the varieties of plants they buy, about keeping the gardening area free of any debris and weeds—both of which harbor insects and other pests—and about pruning assiduously.

Length of Growing Season

The number of frost-free days in the United States ranges from a mere eight in frosty Barrow, Alaska, to 365 in San Diego, Los Angeles, Miami, and Key West. The latter group would qualify as superior gardening areas from the standpoint of temperature, since killing frosts occur there less than one year in ten and plants can be grown year round. Below are figures for some of *Places Rated's* 107 retirement places.

Growing Seasons and Killing Frosts

Retirement Place	Growing Season (Days)	Last Spring Frost	First Fall Frost
ALBUQUERQUE, NM	196	Apr. 16	Oct. 29
ASHEVILLE, NC	195	Apr.12	Oct. 24
ATLANTIC CITY–CAPE MAY, NJ	225	Apr. 4	Nov. 15
BEND, OR	62	June 17	Aug. 17
BOISE CITY, ID	171	Apr. 29	Oct. 16
KALISPELL, MT	135	May 12	Sept. 23
LAKELAND–WINTER HAVEN, FL	349	Jan. 10	Dec. 25
LAS VEGAS, NV	245	Mar. 13	Nov. 13
LEXINGTON–FAYETTE, KY	198	Apr. 13	Oct. 28
MEDFORD, OR	178	Apr. 25	Oct. 20
MIAMI, FL	*	*	*
ORLANDO, FL	319	Jan. 31	Dec. 17
PHOENIX, AZ	317	Jan. 27	Dec. 11
Red Bluff-Sacramento Valley, CA	277	Feb. 25	Nov. 29
RENO, NV	141	May 14	Oct. 2
SAN DIEGO, CA	*	*	*
SPRINGFIELD, MO	203	Apr. 10	Oct. 31
TUCSON, AZ	261	Mar. 6	Nov. 23
YUMA, AZ	350	Jan. 11	Dec. 27

Source: National Climatic Center.

*Frosts occur in less than one year in ten.

BECOME A VOLUNTEER

The Me Decade may finally be over. One out of every four Americans over age 14 is involved in some kind of volunteer work, a recent Census Bureau study reported. In fact, the value in dollars of all the time volunteered by Americans adds up to more than $65 billion a year.

Older Americans make up an especially high percentage of volunteers; according to an American Association of Retired Persons (AARP) survey, at least 31 percent of those people between 55 and 64 participated as volunteers in 1981. The activities of AARP volunteers, for example, range from lobbying for legislation to help older people to tax counseling and driver training.

Want some good reasons for becoming a volunteer?

- When you wake up, you've got something different to look forward to
- When you dress up for work, it boosts your morale
- You've got a good reason for getting out of the house
- You come into contact with people
- You've got something to talk about with family and friends
- You can pass on your skills and experience to others
- You can broaden your experience
- If you have a hobby, you can both work at it and teach it
- You earn a sense of accomplishment

The abrupt release from routine that retirement brings is sometimes unwelcome. Volunteering can replace some of the structure you may be missing from your working years, and it does so in an atmosphere free from pressure.

But don't think that your telephone will start ringing with offers of volunteer work. You have to let others know you're available, perhaps by responding to the Volunteer Opportunities column in your local newspaper.

Putting It All Together:

Finding your best
retirement place

Is there an ideal retirement haven in America?

Various chambers of commerce, eager real-estate promoters, and state tourism and economic development agencies may claim the title for their own particular locales. After all, with 21 million persons due to turn 65 during the 1980s, attracting footloose retired people to the Leisure Villages, Palm Shores, and Mountain Homes of this country is seen as a very promising growth industry.

But if we use the criteria of *Places Rated*, the ideal retirement place would have the climate of San Diego, where the balmy Pacific Ocean keeps the temperature close to a mild 65 much of the time. It would have to be a small place if it were to equal the low crime rate of Clarkesville–Mount Airy, Georgia, or the inexpensive housing of Cassville–Roaring River, in the Missouri Ozarks. Yet our ideal spot would also have to be a major metropolitan area to match Miami's full range of health-care facilities, which gives it the top ranking in that category. For variety in recreation, you'd probably choose a place like Phoenix, which not only has a busy calendar of symphony orchestra performances, opera productions, and guest artist dates, but good opportunities for outdoor activities as well. Finally, our ideal place should offer retired persons the low living costs, low taxes, and promising economic future of the McAllen–Pharr–Edinburg metro area, on the banks of the Rio Grande in southernmost Texas.

Obviously, this ideal retirement haven is a fiction. You can explore the geography long and hard but you will never find the single retirement place that combines all of the "bests" according to the *Places Rated* criteria. Moreover, because one person's retirement heaven can often be another's purgatory, and your rural retreat someone else's boondocks, one can argue that there really is no such thing as *the* ideal retirement place.

Because of better health care and increasing longevity, your retirement years can now amount to one quarter of your life span. Choosing where to spend these retirement years isn't an easy task. The best tactic is to focus on *your* own preferences and needs. Having said as much, we can still try to discover which of the 107 places come closest to the ideal.

FINDING THE BETTER ALL-AROUND RETIREMENT PLACES

Our method for determining America's better all-around retirement places is very simple: The ranks of every place for each of the six factors—climate, housing, money matters, personal safety, health, and leisure living—are added together for a cumulative score. Cape Cod, on the south shore of Massachusetts, for example, ranks 13th in climate, 91st in housing, 105th in money matters, 79th in personal safety, 73rd in health, and eighth in leisure living. The total of these ranks—13 + 91 + 105 + 79 + 73 + 8—equals 369, giving Cape Cod a rank of 82 among the 107 retirement places. Because this rating system is based on ranks,

the lower the cumulative score, the better the retirement place is judged to be all-around. The list that follows highlights the places that rise to the top as the better spots for retirement in America.

For the Reader Who Turns to This Chapter First

Those of you who have skipped ahead to learn how each retirement place is finally ranked may be intrigued by the cumulative table on pages 172–174. If you are curious about how the rank in a particular category was calculated, consult the explanation of the scoring system in the appropriate chapter; each uses different criteria and a different method of combining them. Looking at Maui, the Hawaii retirement place composed of four islands, and the fastest-growing of Hawaii's four counties, may help to review how the rankings were arrived at.

Maui's famous paradise climate is certainly free from the temperature extremes of most of the U.S. mainland, owing to the Pacific Ocean's constantly moderating effect. Since *Places Rated* uses mildness as its chief criterion in judging climate, Maui comes out extremely high, with a rank of sixth.

Because the climate is so mild, most Maui homes are neither heated nor air-conditioned. Even with these minimal energy requirements, however, the basic electricity costs for cooking, lighting, and running appliances are high. But the major reason behind Maui's 107th-place ranking in housing is its astronomical land costs and housing prices. Note that *Places Rated*'s standards for housing are strictly economic ones and do not measure construction quality or comfort.

Maui's rank of 100 in money matters is due to very high living costs, reflected in part by high personal incomes and high state income and sales taxes. Like the rest of Hawaii, Maui County depends on the mainland for much of its packaged food and manufactured products, a dependence that contributes to the high cost of consumer goods here.

In personal safety (based on crime rates) and supply of health-care facilities, Maui comes in 82nd and 66th, respectively, among the retirement places.

Such assets as an encircling ocean coastline, Haleakala National Park, Kakahaia National Wildlife Refuge, an excellent supply of public golf courses, above-average marks for the supply of bowling lanes, and the size of the public library give Maui a respectable 49th-place rank in leisure living. However, as in many other posh resorts, there is a weak market for the arts here, given the overwhelming competition from golf, beaches, and tropical terrain.

Taken altogether, Maui's rankings in these six categories of retirement living add up to 410, placing it 99th among the 107 retirement places on the basis of *Places Rated*'s scoring system.

One caveat: Bear in mind that the units of comparison throughout *Places Rated Retirement Guide* are counties.

America's Top 25 Retirement Places

Retirement Place	Cumulative Score
1. Brevard, NC	151
2. ASHEVILLE, NC	187
3. Clarkesville–Mount Airy, GA*	197
4. Crossville, TN*	213
5. LEXINGTON–FAYETTE, KY	217
6. LAS CRUCES, NM	222
7. Harrison, AR	223
8. Roswell, NM	230
9. Camden–Penobscot Bay, ME	231
9. Cookeville, TN*	231
11. Bar Harbor–Frenchman Bay, ME	234
12. STATE COLLEGE, PA	239
13. Bull Shoals, AR*	241
14. BILOXI–GULFPORT, MS*	245
15. Hot Springs–Lake Ouachita, AR*	246
16. ALBUQUERQUE, NM*	254
17. Prescott, AZ	255
18. Mountain Home–Norfork Lake, AR	263
19. Cassville–Roaring River, MO*	266
20. Port Angeles–Strait of Juan de Fuca, WA*	270
21. Lake O' The Cherokees, OK*	271
22. SPRINGFIELD, MO	274
22. St. George–Zion, UT	274
24. Paris, TN*	277
25. SAN ANTONIO, TX*	278

*These retirement places rank in the bottom 25—that is, 82nd or lower out of 107—in one or more of *Places Rated*'s six categories.

The list above may be surprising not so much for which retirement places are on it as for which are *not*. Where, you may be wondering, are the retirement utopias of Florida and California? A review of the scores of Miami and San Diego, both popular and long-established retirement spots, may help explain this apparent discrepancy.

Both metro areas have obvious strengths. San Diego has the mildest climate of the 107 retirement places, and has some of the traditional metro area advantages, ranking very high in health-care facilities (fifth) and leisure living (third). Similarly, Miami finishes first in health care and second in recreation. High humidity and warm weather keep its climate ranking to 22nd.

It is in the remaining three categories—housing, money matters, and crime—that these Sun Belt giants run into trouble. Miami has the worst rates for property and violent crime of all 107 places, and San Diego, at 98th, is not much better. Living costs are high in San Diego, which places 103rd in money matters; in this category Miami finishes at a low but respectable 63rd. But in homeowning costs both places hit the bottom of the scale: San Diego ranks 106th and Miami 95th.

Like San Diego and Miami, the rest of the retirement places in California and Florida have at least one

And the Winner Is . . .

The retirement place of Brevard, North Carolina, which encompasses Transylvania County in the rugged mountains of southwestern North Carolina, finishes at the top of the list of *Places Rated*'s 107 selected places.

How so? It has moderate housing and living costs, a mild and variable climate, a crime rate that's practically nonexistent, above-average health-care facilities, a good mix of recreational and cultural opportunities, and (although this item is not scored), spectacular scenery courtesy of the Blue Ridge Mountains, which surround the town of Brevard. A measure of this place's consistently high marks is the fact that the lowest rank it receives in any of the six categories is a healthy 44th.

But what about the things that can't be scored? What about those intangibles like mood, ambience, friendliness of the residents, and community spirit? Brevard has them all . . . in abundance. Perhaps another name for this profile could be "Yes, Virginia, There Really *Is* a Mayberry."

Most of the readers of this book will remember the television series starring Andy Griffith and Don Knotts set in the small town of Mayberry, where everyone knew each other and the local characters stood out distinctly like bright patches of calico on a crazy quilt. The town of Brevard (pop. 5,323), the seat of Transylvania County, is such a place. If you enter the local pharmacy to buy film or tobacco, you'd better be prepared to stay and shoot the breeze for a few minutes. In the hardware store, where things are even less hurried, the talk may last longer.

Brevard calls itself the Land of Waterfalls. The town sits alongside huge Pisgah National Forest, where the world's first school of forestry was begun in 1898. At an elevation of 2,230 feet, Brevard, like its sister cities of Asheville and Hendersonville, combines a southerly latitude with a fairly high altitude, a combination that spells a winning climate (in "Climate and Terrain" see the Place Profile for Hendersonville, which also represents the weather picture in Brevard and Asheville). As you drive north from Brevard on U.S. Highway 276 and enter Pisgah National Forest, you'll find yourself slowing your car to hear the roars and whispers that come across the highway every few miles. These are the waterfalls and cataracts that give Brevard its nickname. Perhaps the most famous of these is Looking Glass Falls, but there are many others, including Diamond Creek Falls, Pounding Mill Falls, Cove Creek Falls, and Laughing Falls. The forests are impressive stands of pine and hemlock, along with maple, birch, beech, and balsam. Ferns grow thick on the forest floor, and bright green moss covers tree trunks and boulders.

In the center of the forest area is the Pisgah Fish Hatchery, one of the largest trout hatcheries in the East. Visitors are always welcome, although it's a temptation, looking at the hundreds of large browns and rainbows, to bring along a dip net.

The cultural scene in Brevard centers on two institutions: Brevard College, a two-year liberal arts school that sends 90 percent of its graduates on to four-year schools, and the Brevard Music Center, which presents concerts daily from July 1 through August 14 each year. The programs include orchestras, bands, choruses, opera, chamber music, and outstanding guest artists. This is complemented by the Brevard Little Theatre, a performer of popular plays, and the Festival of the Arts, a cultural celebration held during the third week of July that embraces country and western music, gospel singing, clog dancing, and exhibitions of mountain crafts.

The local stores in Brevard are adequate for most everyday needs, but a trip to Hendersonville, Asheville, or Greenville, South Carolina, is recommended for specialized shopping. None of these is more than 45 minutes away by car, and the drive to any of them will be beautiful. The nearest air transportation is provided by the Asheville Municipal Airport, served by two commercial airlines. It's about a half hour's drive from Brevard.

Recreation, especially of the outdoor variety, is ample and diverse. There are more than 200 miles of mountain streams in Transylvania County, and they're kept plentifully stocked by the Pisgah Fish Hatchery. Golf, hiking, hunting, swimming, dancing (both western and mountain style), camping, tennis, archery, and horseback riding are all available.

The principal industry here is lumbering, but some other major industrial plants in the county are those of M-B Industries, Olin Corporation (Fine Paper and Film Group), DuPont Photo Products, and the American Thread Company.

The only drawback to Brevard is its small size, which, of course, is also its strength and charm. If you've spent most of your working life in a big city, it might be a bit too small for you. Not to worry, though, because just 40 minutes north on the scenic Blue Ridge Parkway is Asheville, the major city of western North Carolina. And, as fate would have it, Asheville ranks second behind Brevard in desirability for retirement out of *Places Rated*'s 107 spots.

---

ranking near the bottom of the list. The California retirement spots score very poorly in housing costs; the Florida locales have extremely high crime rates and warm, muggy climates.

In contrast, 17 of our top retirement places are non-metropolitan counties—the "boomdocks," as one demographer dubbed them, noting their open spaces, rural character, and currently rapid growth. Eight of them have at least one very low rating in the health-care and leisure-living categories, reflecting two traditional shortcomings of small places. But they are strong in the areas where metropolitan places are typically deficient: They have low crime rates, low living costs, and affordable housing. Fifteen of these 17 non-metropolitan retirement places rank in the top ten in at least one of these categories. And three places have impressively high ranks in all three: Clarkesville-

Mount Airy, Georgia, is sixth in housing, 13th in money matters, and first in crime; Bull Shoals, Arkansas, is second, eighth, and second in the same categories; and Lake O' The Cherokees, Oklahoma, ranks fifth, second, and 15th, respectively.

Putting It All Together: Cumulative Scores and Overall Ranks of 107 Retirement Places

In the following table, the rank of every retirement place in each of *Places Rated Retirement Guide*'s six categories is given. The sum of these—the retirement place's cumulative score—is also shown, along with its overall rank, on the table's right-hand side. For example, Cape Cod's cumulative score of 369 ranks it 82nd

overall among the 107 retirement places. As in the game of golf, the lower the cumulative score the better. The best possible score is 6, meaning a first-place rank in all six categories. The lowest possible rank a retirement place can receive is 107, so the worst possible cumulative score would be 642.

Retirement Place	Climate and Terrain	Housing	Money Matters	Crime	Health and Health Care	Leisure Living	Cumulative Score	Overall Rank
ALBUQUERQUE, NM	16	77	53	99	3	6	254	16
ASHEVILLE, NC	12	27	57	32	9	50	187	2
Athens–Cedar Creek Lake, TX	86	25	9	18	100	107	345	66
ATLANTIC CITY–CAPE MAY, NJ	26	93	104	103	23	65	414	101
AUSTIN, TX	92	83	50	78	17	9	329	53
Bar Harbor–Frenchman Bay, ME	45	24	43	31	52	39	234	11
Beaufort–Hilton Head, SC	23	92	67	100	21	86	389	96
Bend, OR	46	86	48	50	68	28	326	50
Bennington, VT	82	52	91	37	53	14	329	53
Benton–Kentucky Lake, KY	70	21	17	10	90	84	292	32
Big Sandy, TN	71	4	7	5	99	102	288	27
BILOXI–GULFPORT, MS	40	29	15	83	24	54	245	14
BOISE CITY, ID	37	71	93	74	18	51	344	65
Branson–Lake Taneycomo, MO	62	19	60	41	92	72	346	68
Brattleboro, VT	82	34	69	37	49	67	339	59
Brevard, NC	10	30	40	9	44	18	151	1
Brunswick–Golden Isles, GA	79	44	96	101	42	53	415	102
Bull Shoals, AR	73	2	8	2	65	91	241	13
Camden–Penobscot Bay, ME	65	11	47	28	43	37	231	9
Canton–Lake Tawakoni, TX	86	3	16	12	103	105	325	49
Cape Cod, MA	13	91	105	79	73	8	369	82
Carson City, NV	60	103	37	29	97	60	386	92
Cassville–Roaring River, MO	62	1	25	6	96	76	266	19
CHARLOTTESVILLE, VA	24	78	106	60	8	42	318	45
Clarkesville–Mount Airy, GA	14	6	13	1	85	78	197	3
Clear Lake, CA	66	82	61	95	98	44	446	106

	Climate and Terrain	Housing	Money Matters	Crime	Health and Health Care	Leisure Living	Cumulative Score	Overall Rank
Coeur d'Alene, ID	39	54	102	69	79	52	395	98
COLORADO SPRINGS, CO	67	72	92	85	26	22	364	80
Cookeville, TN	19	26	6	19	61	100	231	9
Crossville, TN	19	14	3	17	63	97	213	4
DAYTONA BEACH, FL	50	47	29	97	34	32	289	29
Delta, CO	73	35	11	45	87	56	307	37
Deming, NM	41	13	18	76	86	106	340	60
Eagle River, WI	106	55	33	16	55	63	328	51
Easton–Chesapeake Bay, MD	25	99	107	63	46	38	378	88
Fairhope–Gulf Shores, AL	91	17	24	39	67	76	314	42
FORT COLLINS, CO	78	90	35	54	60	11	328	51
FORT LAUDERDALE–HOLLYWOOD, FL	44	98	79	102	10	12	345	66
FORT MYERS–CAPE CORAL, FL	105	84	59	71	33	36	388	94
Fredericksburg, TX	96	43	64	8	82	94	387	93
Front Royal, VA	34	40	72	34	64	88	332	57
Gainesville–Lake Sidney Lanier, GA	29	32	56	56	37	99	309	39
Grand Junction, CO	73	79	30	59	32	26	299	34
Hamilton–Bitterroot Valley, MT	81	39	27	14	101	19	281	26
Harrison, AR	59	17	23	11	38	75	223	7
Hendersonville, NC	7	50	69	24	56	95	301	35
Hot Springs–Lake Ouachita, AR	89	12	49	35	27	34	246	15
Houghton Lake, MI	101	15	31	81	107	82	417	103
Kalispell, MT	93	48	71	25	93	13	343	64
Keene, NH	88	38	97	23	84	92	422	104
Kerrville, TX	97	56	68	21	25	103	370	83
Laconia–Lake Winnipesaukee, NH	98	58	84	48	81	85	454	107
Lake Havasu City–Kingman, AZ	50	57	21	84	88	59	359	76
LAKELAND–WINTER HAVEN, FL	103	28	33	95	30	40	329	53
Lake O' The Cherokees, OK	46	5	2	15	102	101	271	21
LANCASTER, PA	49	60	101	22	48	74	354	74
LAS CRUCES, NM	57	33	12	3	70	47	222	6
LAS VEGAS, NV	50	100	28	106	39	24	347	69
LEXINGTON–FAYETTE, KY	21	66	36	75	4	15	217	5
Lincoln City–Newport, OR	2	76	66	68	58	45	315	43
Maui, HI	6	107	100	82	66	49	410	99
McALLEN–PHARR–EDINBURG, TX	100	9	1	51	80	81	322	48
MEDFORD, OR	32	81	51	53	76	66	359	76
MELBOURNE–TITUSVILLE–COCOA, FL	50	75	58	86	29	20	318	45
MIAMI, FL	22	95	63	107	1	2	290	31
Missoula, MT	84	73	78	48	35	30	348	70
Monticello–Liberty, NY	68	36	87	55	72	93	411	100
Mountain Home–Norfork Lake, AR	73	23	41	7	51	68	263	18
Myrtle Beach, SC	17	45	19	88	62	87	318	45

	Climate and Terrain	Housing	Money Matters	Crime	Health and Health Care	Leisure Living	Cumulative Score	Overall Rank
Nevada City–Donner, CA	9	102	82	52	74	61	380	89
North Conway–White Mountains, NH	98	65	80	30	45	64	382	90
Oak Harbor, WA	5	88	55	13	71	79	311	40
Ocala, FL	102	31	20	93	54	57	357	75
Ocean City–Assateague Island, MD	29	53	86	98	106	55	427	105
Olympia, WA	11	69	75	64	89	83	391	97
Orlando, FL	103	63	52	104	11	7	340	60
Oscoda–Huron Shore, MI	80	20	38	47	93	33	311	40
Paris, TN	71	7	10	36	49	104	277	24
Petoskey–Straits of Mackinac, MI	85	62	77	43	16	70	353	72
Phoenix, AZ	54	89	73	92	7	1	316	44
Port Angeles–Strait of Juan de Fuca, WA	4	64	65	26	95	16	270	20
Prescott, AZ	32	67	45	40	40	31	255	17
Rappahannock, VA	17	40	74	4	105	96	336	58
Red Bluff–Sacramento Valley, CA	15	59	39	73	83	71	340	60
Rehoboth Bay–Indian River Bay, DE	41	42	95	67	57	69	371	84
Reno, NV	60	104	54	90	12	62	382	90
Rhinelander, WI	106	37	85	33	36	80	377	87
Rockport–Aransas Pass, TX	90	68	26	61	91	27	363	79
Roswell, NM	31	10	46	57	28	58	230	8
St. George–Zion, UT	55	74	4	20	78	43	274	22
San Antonio, TX	95	49	44	80	6	4	278	25
San Diego, CA	1	106	103	89	5	3	307	37
San Luis Obispo, CA	3	101	83	58	13	47	305	36
Santa Fe, NM	26	97	32	91	31	21	298	33
Santa Rosa, CA	8	105	98	70	47	46	374	85
Sarasota–Bradenton, FL	94	80	76	77	14	23	364	80
Springfield, MO	58	16	81	72	22	25	274	22
State College, PA	43	51	42	27	41	35	239	12
Table Rock Lake, MO	62	22	22	41	104	89	340	60
Tahlequah–Lake Tenkiller, OK	46	8	5	65	75	90	289	29
Toms River–Barnegat Bay, NJ	26	85	88	62	59	41	361	78
Traverse City–Grand Traverse Bay, MI	73	70	99	44	15	29	330	56
Tucson, AZ	38	87	62	94	2	5	288	27
Twain Harte–Yosemite, CA	36	94	93	66	69	17	375	86
West Palm Beach–Boca Raton, FL	68	96	89	105	20	10	388	94
Winchester, VA	34	62	90	46	19	98	349	71
Yuma, AZ	56	47	14	86	77	73	353	72

Choice Places in America's Retirement Regions

When it comes to finding your best place for retirement, you would do well to ignore the shopworn truisms about states and their track records in attracting retired persons. Just saying you're considering Arizona as a destination isn't going far enough. You still can choose from more than a thousand cities, towns, villages, and unincorporated places, from desolate Indian country in the northeast corner of the state all the way down some 390 miles to the desert around Yuma in the southwest corner. People don't retire to states, they retire to specific places.

Having said that, though, it is nonetheless possible to identify among our 107 retirement places a number of retirement *regions*, 15 to be exact. Few of their boundaries match the political borders you'll find in your road atlas; most of them embrace parts of more than one state and, conversely, some states are apportioned among more than one region. Rockport–Aransas Pass, Texas, for example, is grouped with Fairhope–Gulf Shores, Alabama, and the other South Atlantic and Gulf Shore spots because it has more in common with them than with such Texas Interior places as Austin or the Rio Grande area of McAllen–Pharr–Edinburg.

On the following pages *Places Rated* describes the 15 regions into which the 107 retirement places seem to fall. Each region looks, feels, talks, and acts differently from the others, and yet the places within the region have a number of shared characteristics that bind them together. Some have been resort country, on and off, for well over a century. Others are relatively new and heavily promoted. One—the Metropolitan Florida Peninsula—is nationally synonymous with retirement. Still others aren't associated with retirement by anyone but the savvy residents of nearby metropolitan areas. The North Woods country of Michigan and Wisconsin is such a place for Chicagoans, Milwaukeeans, and Detroiters. So are some of the Yankee Belt locations of coastal Maine and rural New Hampshire and Vermont to Bostonians and New Yorkers.

Each regional heading is accompanied by a list of the retirement places in the region, along with their overall ranks. Ten of the regions include one or more of the 25 best all-around retirement places, and these are indicated with a star. For each of these choice locations (except top-ranked Brevard, North Carolina, described on page 171) we offer a capsule description that we hope will pique your interest and also help as you weigh the pros and cons in making plans for your retirement.

Needless to say, whether you decide to move far, far away or end up staying right where you are, *Places Rated* hopes that your retirement years will rank among your best.

YANKEE BELT

★ Bar Harbor–Frenchman Bay, ME (11)
Bennington, VT (53)
Brattleboro, VT (59)
★ Camden–Penobscot Bay, ME (9)
Cape Cod, MA (82)
Keene, NH (104)
Laconia–Lake Winnipesaukee, NH (107)
North Conway–White Mountains, NH (90)

In New England, the preferred retirement places aren't in the heavily urbanized southern states of Connecticut, Massachusetts, or Rhode Island. The one exception is Massachusetts's Barnstable County (Cape Cod), where one in three residents since 1970 was a newcomer and where one in five is now over 65. If it weren't for large numbers of people moving to Cape Cod, the Bay State would have shown a population loss instead of the modest one percent increase it posted between 1970 and 1980.

The most popular Yankee Belt retirement spots are in rural pockets of the northern tier of states, in Maine, New Hampshire, and Vermont. Between 1970 and 1980, Maine's population jumped 13 percent. That may not seem like much until one realizes it was the Pine Tree State's best upsurge in 130 years. Most of the retired newcomers have chosen the rocky Atlantic Coast counties over the depressed farming areas and aging paper- and lumber-mill towns in the interior. Within these counties—especially Hancock, Lincoln, Knox, and York—the places that have drawn the most people are the small, picture-postcard lobster ports and summer resort towns off old U.S. Highway 1.

New Hampshire is the fastest-growing of the eastern states (its population rose 25 percent during the 1970s), largely at the expense of Massachusetts, its heavily taxed next-door neighbor. But rapid growth has often spoiled the piney, bucolic environment with cheap subdivisions and tacky storefronts, particularly around Lake Winnipesaukee. People pay neither personal income nor retail sales taxes here, the only state where this is still possible. Partly as a consequence, if you don't expect much in the way of public services in your retirement, you won't be disappointed in New Hampshire.

Although Vermont's number of inhabitants grew 15 percent in the 1970s, the state remains the most rural in America, according to the Census Bureau. Two of every three Vermonters live outside urban areas. The state still seems part of the nineteenth century of Currier and Ives. Taciturn farmers tap sugar maples; sleek cows graze over green hillsides; white, steepled Congregational churches dominate the town squares; and in early October, the brilliant fall foliage draws busloads of weekenders from Boston and New York. As a general rule, the southern counties draw retired people, and the northern counties draw skiers.

★ Bar Harbor–Frenchman Bay, ME

Early travelers wrote home that Mount Desert Island, off Maine's middle coast, wasn't "pure Norway, it is Norway and Italy combined."

In the late nineteenth and early twentieth centuries, Bar Harbor, the principal town on the island, became an exclusive playground of millionaires, much as Newport down in Rhode Island's Narragansett Bay did. Prominent Philadelphia and Boston families staked out acreage to capture the spectacular ocean views and built summer "cottages" of 20 to 30 rooms with ample servants' quarters.

With the coming of income taxes, World War I, and the Depression, many of the old hotels and summer homes were permanently boarded up. The final blow was the Great Fire of 1947. Today, many of the old mansions that survived have been converted into country inns. The forests have come back, and virtually the only sign of the island's tony past are the old horse and carriage paths, which delight hikers and cyclists. In addition to Bar Harbor, the island also includes the villages of Southwest Harbor, Northeast Harbor, and Seal Harbor.

Off island across a short bridge is Ellsworth (pop. 5,179), county seat and trading center for Hancock County. In its time, Ellsworth was the second-busiest lumber port in the world. Its business district was destroyed by fire in 1933, but has been handsomely rebuilt, contrasting with the old residential streets.

Pluses: Reasonable housing costs off Mount Desert Island; below-average crime rate; above-average leisure-living options, especially for outdoor recreation.

Minuses: Harsh winter climate; middling ratings in living costs and range of health-care facilities.

★ Camden–Penobscot Bay, ME

Camden (pop. 4,584), one of Maine's prettiest coastal towns, lies "under the high mountains of the Penobscot, against whose feet the sea doth beat," Capt. John Smith wrote long ago. It is a well-groomed seaport and home port to several of Maine's famous Windjammer fleet of wooden sailing schooners.

But this retirement place, which encompasses Knox County, offers more than just Camden. A short distance south on U.S. Highway 1 are Rockport (pop. 2,749), home of *Down East* magazine, and Rockland (pop. 7,919). All three seacoast towns are worthy retirement destinations; the return of older vacationers to their former second homes for year-round living proves it.

Although the area is popular with thousands of tourists for its clambake summers and spectacular falls, for many locals the winter is the best season of all. With the departure of tourists, the focus returns to town, family, church, and school. There is a diversified adult education program. The YMCA features indoor swimming, gourmet cooking, weight control,

and art classes. The big topic is local high school basketball. On weekends, skiers and skaters come from miles around to the Camden Snow Bowl. Ice fishermen wait for the lakes and ponds to safely harden, and at Christmas a huge electric star shines down from the top of Mount Battie.

Pluses: Low housing costs away from the coast in the rural townships to the west of U.S. Highway 1; low crime rate; above-average leisure options for such a small place.

Minuses: Harsh winter climate; high taxes; limited range of health-care facilities.

NORTH WOODS

Eagle River, WI (51)
Houghton Lake, MI (103)
Oscoda–Huron Shore, MI (40)
Petoskey–Straits of Mackinac, MI (72)
Rhinelander, WI (87)
Traverse City–Grand Traverse Bay, MI (56)

The northern counties of Michigan's Lower Peninsula and several of the Wisconsin counties in Packer Country north of Green Bay are experiencing a population increase unequaled since waves of Finns, Germans, Czechs, and Poles arrived in the 1890s. On any summer weekend, campers, RVs, and boat-trailing cars crowd the northbound lanes of Interstate Highway 75 out of Detroit and Interstate 94 out of Chicago. They offer a clue to why these formerly depressed North Woods counties, forested with hemlock and Norway pine, have made a dramatic comeback.

This is prime recreation land with a rugged, Paul Bunyan flavor—not just in summer but during the fall deer hunting and winter skiing seasons, too. Most of Michigan's 11,000 and Wisconsin's 15,000 lakes are up here. "In some lakes," the *New York Times* reported in a recent profile of Eagle River and its environs, "the fisherman can see 30 feet down in waters forest green, or black, or blue, depending on the time of day or the perspective, and can retrieve dropped eyeglasses or snagged fishing lures." So strong is the area's pull that many former vacationers from the big industrial cities have decided to retire here and have winterized their rural lakefront or flatwoods second home, taking up year-round residency. Illustrating the area's popularity with retired people is the fact that Roscommon County, where Houghton Lake is the main draw, now has a population with a median age of 41, about 11 years older than the national average. Eagle River and surrounding Vilas County are close behind at 39.

Except for small cities like Rhinelander in Wisconsin and Traverse City and Petoskey in Michigan, don't expect to find much in the way of structured retirement activities or a full range of health-care facilities. Do expect to drive a good deal for retail shopping; this is rough, beautiful, and sparsely settled country.

Pluses: Low living costs and housing prices in the

rural counties; generally low crime rates; excellent natural outdoor recreation.

Minuses: Short springs and summers, long winters; sparse health and social services outside the larger communities.

MID-ATLANTIC METRO BELT

ATLANTIC CITY–CAPE MAY, NJ (101)
CHARLOTTESVILLE, VA (45)
Easton–Chesapeake Bay, MD (88)
LANCASTER, PA (74)
Monticello–Liberty, NY (100)

Ocean City–Assateague Island, MD (105)
Rehoboth Bay–Indian River Bay, DE (84)
★ STATE COLLEGE, PA (12)
Toms River–Barnegat Bay, NJ (78)

The area south from New York City to Washington and through the northern Virginia suburbs to Richmond is the most densely settled in America. Many metro areas in this region—notably Newark, Trenton, Philadelphia, Wilmington, and Baltimore—are saddled with the twin curses of sunset industries and long-term population losses.

In the midst of this stagnation, one can easily forget the pockets of retirement growth not visible from the Amtrak rails or Interstate Highway 95: the Atlantic beach counties, Chesapeake Bay, the Catskills, and smaller metro areas like civilized Lancaster, Pennsylvania; State College, in the Nittany Valley; and Charlottesville, Virginia, south of Washington and northwest of Richmond.

The 130 miles of New Jersey's sandy Atlantic coastline, particularly from the tip of Cape May north to Toms River, is rebounding after years of decline. One in five residents of Ocean County—the Toms River–Barnegat Bay retirement place—is over 65, compared with the U.S. average of one in nine. The retired newcomers among them didn't have to come far; they are often New Yorkers and Philadelphians, some returning after a disappointing stint in Florida. Many planned retirement communities have been built or are being developed here, though people who want less structure can find many small seaside towns, particularly south of Atlantic City (still seedy, in spite of casino gambling and new hotels) and west of the Garden State Parkway.

Farther south, you'll find retirement destinations within hailing distance of Washington and Baltimore on the Delmarva Peninsula and the shores of Chesapeake Bay. Many of the bigger summer resorts resemble Miami Beach rather than the charming, small seaside communities they once were before the opening of the Chesapeake Bay Bridge in 1952. Delaware's Rehoboth Beach, which has a winter population of 1,730 and a summer population of 50,000, calls itself the nation's summer capital since so many federal workers crowd its beaches. Ocean City, just over the border in Maryland, is also a popular resort with Washington and Baltimore residents.

★ STATE COLLEGE, PA

Centre County, the home of State College, is, as its name suggests, close to the geographical center of Pennsylvania, in the heart of this mountain semi-wilderness. Although isolated in a sense in the sylvan seclusion of beautiful Nittany Valley, this retirement place, with a sizable population and a major university (Pennsylvania State University), has ample recreational, cultural, and shopping facilities to please all but the most particular big-city sophisticate.

About 90 percent of the land area in Centre County is forest and farmland, which means that within a very short drive from the Penn State campus or downtown shopping area you can be in the wilderness, fishing for trout, muskie, bass, or pike; or you can be golfing, swimming, or riding the mountain trails on horseback. For hunters there's a wide variety of game, small and large. No fewer than ten major parks and picnic areas are in the immediate vicinity.

Educationally and culturally, State College thrives. Besides continuing adult education offered at various schools, including the university, the Centre County Vocational-Technical School offers night courses to adults as well. Penn State has a performing artist series with 50 dates a year. Another cultural feature is the annual Central Pennsylvania Festival of the Arts, held during the second week of July.

Pluses: Above-average ratings in all six *Places Rated* categories, especially personal safety (27th) and leisure living (35th); varied four-season climate.

Minuses: Stagnant local economy; stiff competition from 35,000 Penn State students for part-time jobs.

NEW APPALACHIA

★ ASHEVILLE, NC (2)
★ Brevard, NC (1)
★ Clarkesville–Mount Airy, GA (3)
Front Royal, VA (57)

Gainesville–Lake Sidney Lanier, GA (39)
Hendersonville, NC (35)
Rappahannock, VA (58)
Winchester, VA (71)

The region *Places Rated* calls New Appalachia stretches along the southern half of the Appalachian Mountain chain from Frederick County in northern Virginia to Hall County in northern Georgia. New Appalachia has become a major destination for retirees, and many of the region's communities can be considered virtually ideal for retirement living, offering a wide range of special services for older residents. It is not simply coincidence that the three top all-around places for retirement—Brevard, Asheville, and Clarkesville–Mount Airy—are in New Appalachia. The Appalachian counties generally combine low costs of living and housing, low crime rates, adequate health-care facilities (in most places), and some of the best mild four-season climates in the world. Not to mention the scenery, which ranges from beautiful to spectacular.

This is the land of rolling hills and craggy peaks, of

rushing streams and thundering waterfalls. In the spring, the hillsides explode with flowering trees and shrubs: rhododendron, azalea, dogwood, and magnolia. There are magnificent stands of pine, beech, poplar, birch, and oak. The mountain vistas, showing row after row of parallel mountain ridges, are awesome. Outdoor recreation abounds here: hunting and fishing, golf and tennis, skiing and sledding, horseback riding and river rafting, hiking and camping . . . or, that favorite outdoor pastime of all in Appalachia, just sitting.

Many people are surprised at the ruggedness and untamed wildness of the southern mountains. Pisgah National Forest and Great Smoky Mountains National Park, for example, are so remote and inaccessible in parts that it's unlikely that humans have regularly traversed more than 10 percent of the topography.

New Appalachia has a lot going for it. It is a rough wilderness area abundant in natural beauty and fish and game. Yet it is located within reach of major eastern population centers, which eliminates the feeling of isolation so often associated with wilderness areas. (But you'll probably need a car to get around comfortably in much of the region.) It is easy on the wallet, has a relatively low crime rate, and purrs along at a relaxed pace, giving retirees plenty of time to "smell the flowers."

★ ASHEVILLE, NC

Asheville, seat of Buncombe County, serves the entire western tip of North Carolina—an area composed of perhaps 20 counties—as headquarters for services, specialized shopping, and transportation. Despite its role as a commercial center, Asheville and the rest of the county conduct business at an easy, quiet pace. People always have time to "set a spell" and catch up on the latest local news and gossip.

One of Asheville's charms is its mountain scenery. Far, far off on every horizon are the spectacular ridges, rises, cliffs, domes, and peaks of the Blue Ridge. West of the city lie the Great Smoky Mountains, once the domain of the Cherokee Nation. Despite the fact that Asheville rests on a broad valley between two tall mountain ranges, the elevation of the city is still about 2 300 feet, which accounts for the year-round clear air and cool nights. You always sleep with a blanket in Asheville, even in August. The mildness of the climate earned this retirement place a 12th-place rank in that category.

But Buncombe County has many more attractions than just scenery and pleasant weather. There's the Folk Arts Center on the Blue Ridge Parkway. Pisgah National Forest (composed of the remnants of George Vanderbilt's immense estate). Several outstanding ski areas. Wonderful and varied architecture. An extension of the University of North Carolina. Three country clubs. A new horse-show pavilion. A civic center and arena that book national acts and big-name enter-

tainment. The Thomas Wolfe Auditorium, which provides symphonies, opera, and ballet. The Asheville Community Theatre. A minor league baseball team.

Asheville has a major shopping mall east of town, where all but the most specialized needs can be easily met. It also has four shopping centers. Additionally, the downtown area is full of boutiques, cafés, and gourmet food shops.

As lovely and special as Buncombe County is, it does have problems. There is some urban blight, and the effects of suburban growth and urban flight (many residents have moved to neighboring smaller towns, such as Hendersonville) are apparent in some sections of Asheville. However, this retirement place remains strong on all counts.

Pluses: Natural beauty; ideal four-season climate; excellent health-care facilities; moderate housing costs.

Minuses: Lacks the cultural and entertainment amenities of large metro areas.

★ Clarkesville–Mount Airy, GA

Habersham County, the site of the Clarkesville–Mount Airy retirement place, has, like other counties in northeastern Georgia, recently begun to attract retirees in substantial numbers. This corner of Georgia has long been a popular resort area, and private cottages, summer hotels, and fishing camps have been built along the shores of its many lakes. Northern Habersham County is famous for Tallulah Gorge. In the valleys, land has been cleared for pastures, truck gardens, and apple and peach orchards.

The principal towns in Habersham County (pop. 25,020) are Clarkesville, Cornelia, and Mount Airy. None of these towns is likely to send the visitor into immediate ecstasy, although they are quiet, peaceful, and charming. The necessities of life are here to be sure, but for the exotic and the exciting, you must venture north to Charlotte or Asheville or west to Atlanta to find the hustle and bustle, the specialty shopping, and that electric "buzz" that only bigger cities can give. Clarkesville–Mount Airy's strength lies in what it doesn't have (crime, high costs, rigorous weather, high taxes, congestion) rather than what it has. But what's wrong with that?

Outdoor recreation is everywhere, from fly-fishing the miles of mountain streams and lazy rivers to mountain skiing, golf, and all the other standard recreational pastimes. Much of Habersham County lies in the beautiful Chattahoochee National Forest, which has excellent hiking and camping facilities.

There is no major airport in Clarkesville–Mount Airy. The nearest commercial service is out of Athens, about 50 miles distant. Your best bet is Atlanta's Hartsfield International, second-busiest airport in the nation and less than two hours away by car.

Pluses: Lowest crime rate of the 107 retirement places; low living costs; beautiful rolling terrain and pleasant climate.

Minuses: Little in the way of cultural recreation; small supply of health-care facilities.

SOUTH ATLANTIC AND GULF COAST SHORE

Beaufort–Hilton Head, SC (96)

★ BILOXI–GULFPORT, MS (14)

Brunswick–Golden Isles, GA (102)

Fairhope–Gulf Shores, AL (42)

Myrtle Beach, SC (45)

Rockport–Aransas Pass, TX (79)

The retirement places in the South Atlantic and Gulf Coast Shore region have a special appeal and flavor. Although this coastline is dotted with many very old cities, such as Charleston, Savannah, Biloxi, and Galveston, it has enjoyed a boom growth only in comparatively recent years.

Most of these resort-retirement areas lie in low, marshy land either on the mainland itself or on nearby barrier islands. Palmetto palms, scrub oak, dune grass, and Spanish moss swaying in the sea breezes impart a languid, relaxed mood. Fishing shanties lie scattered near the piers and docks where shrimpers, crabbers, and trawlers moor. Stately planter-style cottages set back from the narrow streets are almost hidden behind tall hedges and surrounded by massive live oaks. Streets paved with old oyster and clam shells; small gift shops, boutiques, and shops offering seafood, gumbo, and chicory coffee; taverns and inns of all ages and sizes—these are what you'll find in every metro area, town, and village of the coastal islands.

The South Atlantic and Gulf Coast Shore resorts are less crowded and have lower living costs than most comparable places in the Florida peninsula. Furthermore, their summer months, while sometimes uncomfortable, are less rugged than those farther south. You are likely to find newer buildings and younger people here than in some older retirement havens. Many places have numerous activities geared to appeal to senio citizens.

Or the minus side, crime rates are high. Of the six retirement places in this region, only Fairhope–Gulf Shores is above the median in its ranking for safety from crime. Health-care facilities can be inadequate, and while housing costs are generally low for the region, some places (such as Beaufort–Hilton Head) are expensive. Finally, these low-lying oceanside locations are subject to damage from severe tropical storms.

★ BILOXI–GULFPORT, MS

Biloxi–Gulfport, which finishes 14th overall among the retirement places, is a metro area with a population of nearly 200,000 and encompasses three counties.

Biloxi is said to be the oldest European town in the Mississippi Valley. Settled by the French in 1699, the city is confined to the low ridge of a narrow, fingerlike peninsula, with 25 miles of coastline. It has been noted not only as a seaside resort but as a major fishing and shipbuilding center as well. The heaviest concentration of these industries is still to be found on the Point, or the eastern end of the peninsula. Here are the shrimp and oyster packing and canning plants, the fishing fleet, boatyards, and other maritime centers.

For those of you who think that Mardi Gras is celebrated only in and around New Orleans, make note of the fact that it is observed in Biloxi, too, although at a slightly more manageable level of insanity. There is also the annual shrimp festival, held the first Sunday in June, which includes the traditional Catholic blessing of the fleet.

Neighboring Gulfport has many of the attributes of Biloxi but lacks its colorful history and intimate charm. It's a bit more industrialized, with lumber, cotton, seafood canning, and shipbuilding its major industries. However, it also has fine beaches, new housing developments of all types, and a reputation as an established resort area. Gulfport is a fisherman's paradise; the Mississippi Sound and a large number of lakes, rivers, bays, and bayous are within a few minutes' drive of downtown, and there are also excellent facilities for deep-sea fishing.

Like many metro areas, Biloxi–Gulfport has a soberingly high crime rate, ranking 83rd out of 107 in this category. But it is atypical in its low living costs: It earns a 15th-place rank in money matters and 29th place in homeowning prices.

The principal transportation link between Biloxi–Gulfport and nearby larger cities is Interstate Highway 10. The Gulfport–Biloxi Regional Airport is not a large facility, having only one carrier and only four flights daily. Your best bet for long-distance travel is to go to Mobile or, better yet, New Orleans for domestic or international flights.

Pluses: Low living costs; excellent health-care services; mild beach climate.

Minuses: High crime rate.

METROPOLITAN FLORIDA PENINSULA

DAYTONA BEACH, FL (29)

FORT LAUDERDALE–HOLLYWOOD, FL (66)

FORT MYERS–CAPE CORAL, FL (94)

LAKELAND–WINTER HAVEN, FL (53)

MELBOURNE–TITUSVILLE–COCOA, FL (45)

MIAMI, FL (31)

OCALA, FL (75)

ORLANDO, FL (60)

SARASOTA–BRADENTON, FL (80)

WEST PALM BEACH–BOCA RATON, FL (94)

Perhaps because they so recently hailed from other places, few of Florida's residents are aware of the state's long and fascinating history. The land was first claimed by Spain in the sixteenth century, wrested away by the British, taken back by Spain, declared an independent republic by a group of Americans, and finally turned over by Spain to the United States in 1819. Very little happened in this remote, mosquito-infested outpost until the real-estate boom of the 1920s. Then, dream cities sprouted up everywhere as the pitch of the real-estate promoter was heard in the land. Property values increased from hour to hour, and thousands of persons bought unseen acres, many of them under salt water. It took three disasters—the hurricanes of 1926 and 1928, and the crash of 1929—to burst the bubble. But by then, the lure of Florida had been implanted in the American soul.

Today the Florida peninsula constitutes America's tropics. The state's first "tourist," Juan Ponce de León, didn't find his fountain of youth when he stepped ashore near St. Augustine in 1513, but modern-day retired persons, who are moving here at the rate of a thousand per week, are still trying. Whether beside a Fort Lauderdale condominium swimming pool, on a Fort Myers–Cape Coral beach, at a Miami jai alai fronton, or on a St. Petersburg park bench, they look for rejuvenation in a warm climate.

Florida, especially in the "frostproof" counties south of Gainesville and St. Augustine, has been elevated to its so-called mega-state niche by a migration unique in American history. In 1950, the state had two and a half million people; when the 1980 census figures were tallied, the total had climbed to nearly ten million, nearly all of the increase coming from people moving from other states. Three out of ten newcomers are over 60, and most have been drawn to the metro areas on the coasts and in the interior of the flat, 150-mile-wide peninsula.

Pluses: High ratings in leisuretime options; full range of health-care facilities accessible throughout the state.

Minuses: High crime rate; sunny climate marked by excessive number of 90-degree days in summer; high housing and living costs in coastal metro areas.

MID-SOUTH

Benton–Kentucky Lake, KY (32)
Big Sandy, TN (27)
★ Cookeville, TN (9)
★ Crossville, TN (4)
★ Lexington–Fayette, KY (5)
★ Paris, TN (24)

Perhaps a good nickname for this region might be In-Between Country: It's not too far north and not too far south; it's in the eastern half of the country, to be sure, but it's in the center of the east. Basically, what *Places Rated* refers to as the Mid-South is two states: Kentucky and Tennessee.

Middle Tennessee, hemmed in by the looping Tennessee River, is gently rolling bluegrass country: fertile, well watered, and famous for its fine livestock. The heart of the state, it is rich in tradition and history, and its inhabitants cling to the customs of the Old South.

Kentucky encompasses mountains in its sandstone area, deep gorges and caves in its limestone region, and swampy flats and oxbow lagoons in the far western part of the state. This end of Kentucky is called the

Purchase, after the Jackson Purchase, which bought 8,500 square miles in Kentucky and Tennessee from the Chickasaw Indians. Benton and Kentucky Lake are found here.

Although Kentucky always had plenty of navigable rivers, it wasn't until the TVA projects of the thirties and forties that it had a large number of lakes. These impoundments, created by dams on the Tennessee River and its tributaries, have transformed both Kentucky and Tennessee into front-runners for fishing and water recreation.

Why is the Mid-South such an attractive retirement region? For one thing, the region lies directly to the north of older, more established retirement areas of the so-called Sun Belt. Recent demographic research shows that although the Sun Belt still remains a big drawing card for retirees, the "Retirement Belt" seems to be moving inexorably north. People are discovering the benefits of being closer to their former homes (often in the Midwest or Northeast), the desirability of mild, four-season climates as opposed to the monotony of the semitropical varieties, and the great advantages of low costs and low crime rates compared with many retirement areas farther south.

Furthermore, the gently rolling terrain with its pleasant scenery, the unhurried pace of life (far less manic than many parts of Florida), and the outdoor recreational options coupled with the weather to enjoy them fully make the Mid-South a winner. Like neighboring New Appalachia, this region has three retirement places that rank in the top ten overall.

★ Cookeville, TN

Cookeville is one of the Tennessee Twins, a nickname the authors have bestowed on this town of about 20,000 and its sister town of Crossville. Not only are they fairly close together in the same state, but they have a lot in common. Looking at the rankings of both retirement places for the six *Places Rated* categories reveals why they indeed deserve their nickname: Cookeville and Crossville tied in one category (climate), came within three places of each other in four others (money, safety from crime, health, and leisure living), and were separated by only 12 places in housing costs. Consequently, their overall rankings are also very close, with Cookeville finishing only five places behind fourth-ranked Crossville.

Cookeville has a wilderness area nearby, the Edgar Evins State Rustic Park, a 6,000-acre preserve with hiking trails, campsites, and furnished cabins. There is also the Joe Evins Appalachian Center for Crafts, a professional crafts school dedicated to preserving and advancing the many crafts and professions native to the Appalachian region.

For recreation, besides the standard golf, tennis, horseback riding, and swimming, there is the Center Hill Dam and Lake, an impoundment with a shoreline 415 miles long. Boating, water skiing, fishing, hunting, and camping are available all around this sizable lake.

Why did Cookeville score and rank so well for retirement living? In addition to beautiful terrain and a mild climate, the answer lies in its lack of liabilities. Cookeville ranks 19th in personal safety, and as far as living costs are concerned its performance is equally strong: a sixth-place rating in general economic matters and 26th in stretching your housing dollar.

The major drawbacks you'll find in Cookeville are lacks of health services (61st) and leisure options (100th). To retirees, these could be crucial gaps. Also, specialized shopping, whether it be for gourmet foods, fashion clothing, or any other item of a timely nature, will be limited. As might be expected, there is no major airport nearby, although Cookeville, like Crossville, is situated on Interstate Highway 40.

Pluses: Reasonable living and real-estate costs; pleasant scenery and mild climate; freedom from crime; many new housing developments and retirement communities.

Minuses: Limited range of health-care facilities; few recreational choices.

★ Crossville, TN

Crossville, referred to here along with Cookeville as one of the Tennessee Twins, is the seat of Cumberland County. It is also the site of the Cumberland Mountain State Park, a protected wilderness area in the great Cumberland Plateau. This is said to be the largest timbered plateau in America. The park contains cabin accommodations for visitors, a group lodge, restaurant, and hundreds of camping and hiking sites. It covers 1,720 acres and has a 50-acre lake. Also nearby is the Obed Wild and Scenic River.

Crossville's elevation (1,881 feet) and southerly location are the principal reasons for its pleasant climate. Like the other places in the mountain South, Crossville enjoys long springs and falls, mild winters, and summers that are quite warm during the day but cool at night.

The cultural activities and special points of interest are rather limited, due to the county's small size (pop. 20,676). The Cumberland County Playhouse is a major attraction, offering five productions each season. Additionally, the many small and rustic country and general stores add variety and activity to this pretty rural setting.

Crossville's disadvantages, like Cookeville's, are in health care (Crossville ranks 63rd of the retirement places) and recreation (97th). But its showing in the other four *Places Rated* categories is impressive: Its highest place is third, in money matters, and its lowest is only 19th, in climate. In between are a 14th-place finish in homeowner's costs and 17th place in personal safety.

Pluses: Ideal four-season climate; strong finishes in the economic categories; low crime rate.

Minuses: Like the other Tennessee Twin, Crossville has a limited range of health services and leisuretime options.

★ Lexington–Fayette, KY

Lexington–Fayette, a metro area with a third of a million people, lies on a rolling plateau in the very heart of bluegrass country. The golden stallion weather vane atop the Fayette County Courthouse symbolizes Lexington's fame as the home of Thoroughbreds. The metro area's two major industries, horses and tobacco, are everywhere in evidence. Other industries common to the area are whiskey distilling; manufacture of auto parts, electrical machinery, and furniture; meat packing; and rock quarrying.

The terrain of this retirement place, which embraces six counties, is pleasantly rolling, its many pastures and horse farms covered with the famous bluegrass. Stately plantation-type homes sit atop knolls, surrounded by meadows and white rail fences.

One of the metro area's greatest assets is the University of Kentucky, founded during the Civil War. It contributes enormously to the economy and provides many of Lexington–Fayette's cultural, recreational, and health-care benefits.

But who ever said that Lexington was a *retirement* spot? *Places Rated* suggests that the fact that few people think of this place as such may be its strongest advantage. Many of the best-known, popular retirement areas have become crowded, crime-infested, and expensive during the last two or three decades. In contrast, Lexington–Fayette has reasonable living costs

Beware the Change from Big to Small

This book reflects the shifting population patterns of the past decade, which showed an extraordinary change in the preferences of the American public. For the first time since the Civil War, the rural counties of America showed a greater percentile population growth as a whole than did the big cities. This probably means that many people (and most retirees) are fed up with the stress, high crime, pollution, crowding, and high cost of urban living and are choosing to escape to the slower, safer, and perhaps saner lifestyle to be found in small towns and rural counties.

This being the case, we want to issue a warning to those who've lived in big cities most of their lives. If you join the rural march along with your retired friends, you may be unprepared for the sensory, cultural, and recreational "deprivation" associated with some of these charming but isolated spots.

The old saying, "You never miss your water till the well runs dry," applies here. If you're from New York, Chicago, or Los Angeles—or Cedar Rapids, Fort Wayne, or Tulsa—you may find that your new rural home, safe and inexpensive as it may be, seems downright *boring*. If you're a city person who wants to escape it all by settling in a small place, you might be wise to select one that's a reasonable drive or bus ride away from a good-sized city so you can go "back home" when you want to return—if only momentarily —to the big city lights.

(36th place in money matters and 66th in housing) and a crime rate lower than those of most of the Florida retirement places (75th). It also has the fourth-best health-care facilities and the 15th-best mix of recreational options. All these strengths give Lexington–Fayette an overall ranking of fifth.

Pluses: Pleasant four-season climate; beautiful scenery; moderate living and housing costs; excellent health care; above-average opportunities for recreation.

Minuses: Lexington–Fayette's ranking for personal safety, although better than those of many Florida and Texas places, is still below average.

★ Paris, TN

If you ever find yourself close to Land Between the Lakes Country on the Tennessee-Kentucky border during the last week in April, the thing to do is get yourself into Paris for the World's Biggest Fish Fry. The Jaycees string red-white-and-blue bunting across the main street for the carnival, the Consolidated Henry County High School Marching Band gets in its last formal parade of the academic year, and the first potential summer visitors looking for lakeshore rentals start showing up.

Fifteen miles from the world's largest man-made lake, Paris is archetypical small-town America. It is a pleasant place with antebellum homes, some of which were former residences of three governors. It is large enough (pop. 10,728) for in-town retail shopping, yet small enough for a car to be unnecessary much of the time. Within a radius of 35 miles are two state universities and a private college, all with some kind of adult education program. If you require structured retirement community life, however, you won't find it in Paris or surrounding Henry County. Before 1970, this area had no history of drawing older persons. That may have changed as modest numbers of previous summer visitors are returning for a try at inexpensive, safe, year-round living.

Pluses: Low costs of living amid a modestly expanding economy; low housing costs; above-average range of health-care facilities.

Minuses: Excessive number of days when outside temperature climbs above 90 degrees; very low rating in leisure-living options.

OZARKS AND OUACHITAS

Branson–Lake Taneycomo, MO (68)
★ Bull Shoals, AR (13)
★ Cassville–Roaring River, MO (19)
★ Harrison, AR (7)
★ Hot Springs–Lake Ouachita, AR (15)

★ Lake O' The Cherokees, OK (21)
★ Mountain Home–Norfork Lake, AR (18)
★ SPRINGFIELD, MO (22)
Table Rock Lake, MO (60)
Tahlequah–Lake Tenkiller, OK (29)

Like New Appalachia, the Ozarks and Ouachitas of southern Missouri, northern and western Arkansas, and eastern Oklahoma have distinctive highland folk-

ways and geology, and are currently undergoing rapid changes. In both regions, country craft galleries and bluegrass music festivals abound, and the mountain roads that wind through small towns also wind through some of the nation's prettiest countryside. (Here, as in New Appalachia, an automobile is a virtual necessity.) Many Ozark and Ouachita natives can trace their ancestors to New Appalachia. Both regions today are drawing retired persons from all over. No fewer than seven of *Places Rated's* 25 choice retirement places are in this region.

Nearly two million people live in these hilly plateaus (the Ozarks) and ridge-valley mountains (the Ouachitas). Mention this region and you evoke an image of small-scale subsistence farming, chickens roosting in the hickory tree out back, shoeless springs and summers, moonshining, poverty, and isolation. Applied to the rural counties, the image was accurate until the 1960s. However, when the public utilities built hydroelectric dams, they produced a series of large impounded lakes in hardwood forests, which in turn produced resorts and a steady migration of retired people from Des Moines, Omaha, Tulsa, Oklahoma City, Memphis, Kansas City, St. Louis, and especially Chicago.

Many of the newcomers are what demographer Calvin Beale calls the new gentry—professional people with good incomes who buy hobby farms. Others he describes as the new peasantry, back-to-the-land types interested in raising their own food, conservation, rural values, and alternative fuel sources.

Lately, this region is waking up to the problems that come with prosperity. Concerns about the loss of a special way of life are increasingly being voiced; some locals say it may have already passed from the scene, never to be revived, despite local folk culture institutes and craft schools. Outside the metro areas—Fayetteville–Springdale and Fort Smith, Arkansas; and Springfield and Joplin, Missouri—the rural population isn't dense, yet some of the lakes are having pollution problems, and some of the better-known resorts are acquiring a tacky patina of liquor stores, fast food, tourist attractions, palmistry parlors, and diamond-appraisal shops.

★ Bull Shoals, AR

With a population of only 11,334, Marion County, Arkansas, the locale *Places Rated* calls Bull Shoals, is second-smallest of the 107 retirement places. Nonetheless, its desirable features rank it 13th overall among the retirement destinations. Bull Shoals shares the advantages typical of the Ozark country, with low housing and living costs (it ranks second for inexpensive homeowning costs and eighth in money matters), and an extremely low crime rate (second place).

Marion County also has a lovely natural setting and offers good facilities for fishing, hunting, and boating. More than 20 recreation areas and boating docks are located along Bull Shoals Lake, one of the White River group of lakes, which includes Beaver Lake in Arkansas and the Missouri lakes of Table Rock and Taneycomo. A dam completed in 1951 created the huge lake with a surface area of 45,000 acres, a shoreline of some 1,000 miles, and famous lunker largemouth bass fishing. Near the town of Bull Shoals (pop. 1,312) are Bull Shoals Caverns and Mountain Village 1890, a group of storefronts found in old towns in the area and carefully assembled in one place to preserve a genuine nineteenth-century Ozarks settlement. In Bull Shoals and in all of surrounding Marion County, one of five residents is over 65.

This area should appeal to people who yearn for small-town living with true Ozarks flavor, but cultural activities are nil, so city-dwellers who are considering the Ozarks might want to investigate a more populous locale, such as Springfield, Missouri, some 125 miles distant.

Pluses: Extremely low housing and living costs; low crime rate.

Minuses: No cultural amenities; middling range of health-care facilities; climate marked by many 90-degree days.

★ Cassville–Roaring River, MO

You could definitely do without a car much of the time in Cassville (pop. 2,091). The complimentary chamber of commerce map shows that the distance from the Sherwood Forest subdivision on the north side to City Hall on the south side can be walked in 20 minutes via Main Street. Each year, the Rotary Rodeo, the Old Soldiers' and Settlers' Reunion, the Fourth of July fireworks, and the Fall Foliage Festival are regular events. In spite of their small size, Cassville and surrounding Barry County support three local weekly newspapers.

This is one of many pleasant small towns in southwest Missouri. For one brief spell in the fall of 1861, it was the Confederate capital of the state, and the nearby steep terrain and canyonlike gorges became hideouts for Civil War guerrillas. Now it serves as the county seat and trading center of Barry County, one of Missouri's fast-growing Ozark recreation counties on the Arkansas border.

Most older people who migrate to Barry County settle not in Cassville but in the open hilly country bordering the Mark Twain National Forest. The attraction is the outdoors, especially water. Seven miles away from downtown Cassville is Roaring River State Park, Missouri's most popular state park and reputedly its best site for catching trout. A good part of Table Rock Lake falls within Barry County. The lake is the number-one bass lake in the United States, according to *Sports Afield* magazine.

Pluses: Lowest housing costs among *Places Rated*'s 107 retirement places; low costs of living; extremely low crime rate.

Minuses: Humid in summer; sparse health-care facilities; few artistic or cultural amenities.

★ Harrison, AR

If it weren't for edging out nearby Bellefonte for the honor of becoming the seat of Boone County in 1873, Harrison quite likely would have languished for the rest of the nineteenth century and most of the twentieth until it was discovered by retired people from the Midwest.

For a time after Prohibition, it was the beer-barrel-stave capital of the United States. Red cedar and other hardwoods from Ozark forests were milled by several plants working three shifts to meet the demand. Some local old-timers can recall millions of staves being stacked in drying yards on the outskirts of town.

Today, Harrison (pop. 9,567) is a tidy and thriving town. Since the late 1960s, it has become a center for retired people in the Little Chicago section of northwest Arkansas. "You can see the Ozarks better from here," says the city's letterhead.

Harrison is the gateway to a number of popular summer tourist attractions. Driving south of town on Arkansas Highway 7, you will find yourself in the midst of one of the most scenic drives in America. Buffalo River and Dogpatch, U.S.A., are close by. Other attractions are Hurricane River Cave, Diamond Cave, Bryant Art Museum, Ferguson's Country Store, Lost Valley, and Haggard Ford Bridge over Bear Creek, a favorite local swimming hole.

Pluses: Low crime rate; affordable housing; low living costs.

Minuses: Sparse natural outdoor recreation options; few artistic and cultural amenities; middling rating in climatic mildness.

★ Hot Springs–Lake Ouachita, AR

If you're searching for a retirement place that will frequently draw visiting children and grandchildren, consider Hot Springs and the nearby lakes in Arkansas's Ouachita region. Its long history as a popular spa and resort give the colorful town of Hot Springs (pop. 35,781) a wider array of entertainment facilities and a more cosmopolitan atmosphere than one might expect in a place of its size. Hot Springs surrounds portions of the 4,700-acre Hot Springs National Park. Each day, a million gallons of radioactive 143-degree water flow from 47 springs within the park. Since 1832, the springs have been administered by the federal government to prevent the inevitable charlatans and promoters from exploiting persons seeking hydrotherapy.

In the criteria examined by *Places Rated*, Garland County receives above-average ratings in all but climate, due to its long, hot summers. Low homeowner's costs brought a 12th-place rating, and health-care facilities ranked 27th. In the region, only metropolitan Springfield, Missouri, had a higher health-care rating. Hot Springs is home to the Libbey Memorial Physical Medical Center, specializing in hydrotherapy, and a number of other special facilities.

If you are interested in structured retirement community living, you will find more options here than in any other place in the Ozark–Ouachita region. In addition, Hot Springs and surrounding Garland County offer a number of special services for senior citizens and several clubs for retirees.

Pluses: Low housing costs; broad range of health-care facilities and leisure options; moderate crime rate.

Minuses: Hot, humid summers; middling ratings in cost of living; many persons may find it too touristy for year-round residence.

★ Lake O' The Cherokees, OK

You won't get much argument from Sooners that the corner of their state where the Ozark Plateau spills over from Arkansas is the most beautiful part of Oklahoma. In autumn, the area is striking, with stands of oak, ash, and hickory changing colors over the hills and down the deep, narrow valleys. In the spring, dogwood, redbud, and wild plum blossoms splash the woods with color. Since the building of the Fort Gibson, Tenkiller Ferry, and Pensacola dams, the eastern and northeastern parts of the state rank near the top of the nation in total surface area of impounded water.

This region is also home to many Indians. Beginning in the 1830s, their ancestors were forcibly relocated here from the Southwest over the Trail of Tears. Until it was opened up to white settlement in 1889, this part of the state was Indian Territory; the county names today recall some of the Five Civilized Tribes: Cherokee, Choctaw, Creek, and Seminole.

Lake O' The Cherokees (locals call it Grand Lake) is a huge man-made reservoir completed in 1941. It backs up the Neosho River for more than 60 miles, and along its 1,300 miles of shoreline (most of which is in Delaware County) are many resorts and fishing camps. Jay (pop. 2,100) won the special county-seat election of 1908, beating Grove (pop. 3,378), now the largest town on the eastern shore. Both were once trading centers for the local apple and berry farms during the Depression, but their business today is catering to boaters and fishermen. The rest of the area is strictly rural, though with easy access to Tulsa, Oklahoma, and Joplin, Missouri, via Interstate Highway 44.

Pluses: Extremely low housing and living costs; low crime rate; four-season climate with above-average rating for mildness.

Minuses: Low ratings in health-care facilities and man-made recreational options.

★ Mountain Home–Norfork Lake, AR

Like the nearby towns of Harrison, Bull Shoals, and Cotter, Mountain Home gains most of its revenue from one source, a living aquatic creature called *Micropterus salmoides,* or the largemouth bass, and about as important to the local economy as automobiles are to Detroit or furniture to Grand Rapids.

A stroll down the main streets of Mountain Home (pop. 8,066), the largest town in Baxter County, con-

firms this. Besides the usual general and grocery stores, there are taxidermy shops specializing in mounting your trophy bass. Enter almost any store and you can buy plastic worms in any and all colors of the rainbow—purple, gold, red, black, aqua, cream. They come in scents and flavors, too—licorice, strawberry, sassafras—to appeal, supposedly, to even the choosiest old bass. Also for sale are pork rinds, hula poppers, jitterbugs, flatfish, dive-bombers, rubber frogs and crayfish, and hundreds of other kinds of artificial bait, to say nothing of rods, reels, tackle boxes, and bassboats.

On any given day, Norfork Lake, a huge (40 miles long) impoundment on the North Fork of the White River, is dotted with skiffs as anglers try to hook and land a six-pounder. The reservoir is lined with marinas and boat docks. In the wooded hills and high meadows surrounding the lakes are many guest houses and cabins, trailer courts, and private homes.

Mountain Home, situated on a high plateau at an altitude of 800 feet, is less humid and hot than the lowlands in the rest of the state. Nights can be warm in midsummer, but they are usually cool and comfortable most of the year, and the winters are mild. West of town, U.S. Highway 62 winds around the higher hills and rides the tops of the lower ridges as it heads toward Bull Shoals. Patches of hay and potatoes, and occasional stands of cotton alternate with corn and sorghum cane. Land that is too steep and rocky for cultivation is given over to pasture or woods.

Even if you're not "into bass," Mountain Home and Baxter County offer great retirement living. Costs are low, the climate is mild yet variable, crime is practically nonexistent, and the pace of living is relaxed.

Pluses: Low housing costs (23rd) and low crime rate (7th); great recreation for outdoor enthusiasts.

Minuses: Few cultural amenities; middling rating in health-care facilities.

★ SPRINGFIELD, MO

Although it lies north of the heart of the Ozarks, Springfield is considered the capital of the region because of its size and importance. A major railroad junction and agricultural market, the city is the transportation and commercial hub of southwest Missouri and northern Arkansas. The Springfield metro area, embracing Greene and Christian counties, has a population of over 200,000, making it the largest in the Ozark country.

The city is rich in history. Because of its strategic location, it was an important military objective in the Civil War, and was captured by the Confederates in 1861 in what became known as the Battle of Wilson's Creek; the battlefield site is now a national monument.

Springfield is literally surrounded by some of the best fishing and water recreation reservoirs in the nation. To the south are Table Rock Lake, Bull Shoals Lake, and Norfork Lake. To the north lie Stockton and Pomme de Terre lakes and, farther on, the Harry S.

Truman Reservoir and Lake of the Ozarks. Interspersed between these lakes and the charming small towns and farming communities of this rolling country are great expanses of the Mark Twain National Forest. These superlative hardwood forests offer unlimited camping, hiking, and hunting.

Springfield is situated roughly equidistant from St. Louis, Kansas City, Little Rock, and Tulsa, being about a three-and-a-half-hour drive from each. This location enhances Springfield as a retirement spot because you can retire here with all the cultural amenities of a mid-sized city (along with the offerings of Southwest Missouri State University and several small colleges) set amidst rolling farmland, and yet be within a morning's drive of four major cities.

If you are fond of the climate and scenery of the Ozark region and enjoy its rugged hills, gentle pasturelands, folkways, and friendliness, but don't care to spend 90 percent of your leisure hours fishing, you should take a close look at Springfield.

Pluses: Especially attractive combination of affordable housing (16th), good health-care facilities (22nd), and varied leisure options (25th).

Minuses: Below-average ratings in money matters and crime.

TEXAS INTERIOR

Athens–Cedar Creek Lake, TX (66)
Austin, TX (53)
Canton–Lake Tawakoni, TX (49)
Fredericksburg, TX (93)
Kerrville, TX (83)
★ San Antonio, TX (25)

Second largest of all the states, Texas occupies a distinctive place in the American mind. To steal a superlative from the old WPA *Guide to the Lone Star State*, it is *so* large that if it could be folded upward and over, using its northernmost boundary as a hinge, the retirement place of McAllen–Pharr–Edinburg would be a little more than an hour's drive from Canada; if it were folded eastward, El Paso would lie just off the coast of Florida; if folded westward, Port Arthur would lie out in the Pacific Ocean almost 200 miles beyond Baja California. Dalhart, seat of Dallam County, is nearer to the state capitals of Colorado, Kansas, Nebraska, New Mexico, Oklahoma, and Wyoming than it is to the Texas capital at Austin.

Small wonder, then, that there are more internally sharp contrasts here than in any other state. Northeast Texas resembles Arkansas. East Texas is southern in atmosphere; its people, originally from Tennessee, Alabama, Mississippi, and Louisiana, raise such crops as cane, cotton, and rice. Southwest Texas is mainly open-range cattle country. Northwest Texas is dry and mountainous, resembling the Little Texas area of New Mexico.

If you're thinking of retirement inside the state instead of along its Gulf or Rio Grande peripheries, two likely metro areas are Hispanic San Antonio (especially suburban Comal County) and Austin, state capital and home of the University of Texas. For smaller-scale living, the lovely cedar-scented hill country just northwest of San Antonio (especially Fredericksburg and Kerrville) and the rural lake counties east of Dallas are rapidly filling up with retired newcomers, mainly Texans who were formerly city-dwellers.

★ SAN ANTONIO, TX

This retirement place, which spans three counties, has as its heart one of the handful of authentically different cities in America. In San Antonio the South merges with the West, and North American culture blends with Latin. There is no better time to sample San Antonio's distinctive mix than during the Texas Folklife Festival, held each August. Here the multitude of ethnic dancers, food vendors, and craft merchants illustrates the city's rich diversity.

Winding through the heart of downtown is the San Antonio River, modest in size but used to the maximum. Dozens of bridges cross the river, which is lined with restaurants and shops along a tree-shaded walkway.

What does this spot offer retired persons besides atmosphere and charm? Obviously quite a bit, since even conservative estimates put the number of retirees in Greater San Antonio at 15 percent of the population. With four performing arts series, a symphony orchestra, an opera company, and a full slate of outdoor entertainments, the retirement place offers outstanding recreation choices, and ranks fourth in that category. Its health-care services are equally exceptional. There are 18 private, church, or government hospitals here, boosting San Antonio to its sixth-place finish in health care.

The general cost of living is reasonably low, as are homeowner's costs: San Antonio ranks 44th and 49th, respectively, in these categories. Other housing options for older citizens include two new luxury retirement centers.

Shopping is offered in several regional malls as well as in downtown San Antonio. A good network of freeways connects all parts of the city, and three interstate highways link the area to the rest of Texas. For air transportation there's San Antonio International Airport, which offers 87 daily flights.

Pluses: Full range of health-care facilities; big-city calendar of musical events; below-average housing and living costs.

Minuses: Stressfully hot climate; high crime rate.

RIO GRANDE COUNTRY

★ Albuquerque, NM (16)
Deming, NM (60)
★ Las Cruces, NM (6)
McAllen–Pharr–Edinburg, TX (48)
★ Roswell, NM (8)
Santa Fe, NM (33)

The Rio Grande rises in the Rocky Mountains in southwestern Colorado, flows south through the center of New Mexico, west of Santa Fe, through Albuquerque and Las Cruces, and serves as a 1,240-mile boundary between Texas and Mexico before emptying into the Gulf of Mexico some 60 miles downriver from metropolitan McAllen–Pharr–Edinburg.

Like the Delta South, this area has a large ethnic population. Two of every five persons are Mexican-American, and one in ten is American Indian. Like the Delta South, too, Rio Grande Country is distinguished by low incomes, large families, poor housing, joblessness, low levels of education, and other social problems.

Along the river's southward progress are a few pockets of phenomenal retirement growth. Not only Albuquerque, but also the cities of Roswell, Deming, and Las Cruces and the settled areas around them have all seen their number of residents over 65 jump at three or more times the average national rate. This is also where several retirement subdivision promotions, notably Rio Rancho Estates and Cochiti Lake, went sour in the late 1970s.

Even with the well-publicized growth that most of this arid and semiarid region has experienced, there are still fewer than eight persons per square mile. The desert-mesa vastness is imposing, the distances between towns great, and the loneliness outside city limits a little scary to retired persons hailing from large metro areas.

★ ALBUQUERQUE, NM

Bernalillo County is New Mexico's most populous county, and the city of Albuquerque is by far the state's largest, having a population of more than 330,000. Set high in the Rio Grande Valley, this is a place combining the best of Sun Belt retirement with the amenities of big-city living. Outstanding rankings for health-care facilities (third), leisure-living assets (sixth), and climate (16th) help locate Albuquerque among the leading retirement places despite a mediocre rating for homeowner's costs (77th) and a poor one for crime rate (99th).

There's no denying that the rapid growth of Albuquerque (more than 35 percent since 1970) has left scars; some observers have been highly critical of the city's overall appearance. However, you should be pleasantly surprised if you take the time to look beyond surface impressions. First, one must recognize that the beauty of a high (over 5,000 feet), dry, inland setting is a different sort of beauty than that of lowland oases. There is nothing precious or cute here. The delight is in the 50-mile vistas of mountain and desert and the clarity of the mountain air.

Albuquerque does not have the dazzle one associates with cities in Arizona, southern California, or Texas. The values here are more subtle and hidden. Yes, there are some shiny new skyscrapers. But a more typical building is the fine new Albuquerque Museum, tucked discreetly into a back-lot site next to Old Town

so that visitors may walk to it. In the vicinity of the distinctive pueblo-style campus of the University of New Mexico is a hodgepodge of unusual shops and restaurants catering to students and townspeople alike. Two major shopping centers are located adjacent to Interstate Highway 40, near the geographical center of the city.

Behind the busy commercial avenues are miles of neat residential streets. The many small parks are beautifully maintained. Most homeowners take great pride in their property. This caring for the community is reflected in the fact that there are more than 100 active neighborhood associations.

Pluses: Healthful climate (if altitude is not a problem); numerous recreational and cultural offerings; excellent health care.

Minuses: High crime rate; housing can be expensive.

★ LAS CRUCES, NM

With excellent ratings in crime (third) and economic matters (12th) and rankings in housing and leisure living that are well above average, Las Cruces finishes as the top-ranked retirement place in the sunny southwestern quadrant of the country.

A population of just over 45,000 makes the city of Las Cruces small by most standards, but it is the third largest in New Mexico. Only 45 miles from El Paso, Las Cruces is locally thought of as the capital of the Little Texas area of New Mexico. The city and surrounding Dona Ana County became one of the newest metropolitan areas when the 1980 census figures were tallied; its population grew nearly 40 percent between 1970 and 1980, and the number of residents over 65 years of age doubled.

Las Cruces is bounded by mountain ranges on three sides, although the city is most closely identified with the Organ Mountains, which rise 9,119 feet on its eastern limits. This is high desert country, and summers are hot here, with about 100 ninety-degree days per year; nights are generally cool and pleasant. The winters are mild and sunny.

There is more to Dona Ana County than the city of Las Cruces—nearby are the picturesque towns of Mesilla, Dona Ana, Radium Springs, Organ, and Anthony. With its mining ghost towns, extinct volcanoes, frontier forts, and mountains, the area is a good one for exploring by automobile. In fact, a car could be considered a virtual necessity.

In Las Cruces, the campus of New Mexico State University offers a history museum, art gallery, and 18-hole golf course. The university also hosts a variety of cultural activities.

Pluses: Below-average living and housing costs; expanding local economy; extremely low crime rate.

Minuses: Very stiff competition for part-time jobs from 12,500 students at New Mexico State; below-average in health-care facilities; small size may be a drawback to people accustomed to big-city amenities.

★ Roswell, NM

A three-and-a-half-hour drive east of Las Cruces is rapidly growing Chaves County and its seat, Roswell (pop. 39,676). Formerly a cattle town and trading center out on the barren plains, it is now one of the most attractive cities in New Mexico, with fine homes, well-landscaped public buildings and gardens, and wide boulevards shaded by old cottonwoods and willows.

They say in the city of Roswell that there aren't any gray ghettos here. Retired persons, whose number increased nearly 85 percent between 1970 and 1980, live all over town. And although it can't be proved, there would seem to be more organized activities here for older persons than elsewhere in New Mexico.

For openers, the local chapter of the American Association of Retired Persons is the largest in the state. In addition, the Memorial Recreation Center's list of clubs that hold regular meetings is a long one, including Amateur Radio, Armchair Travel, Audubon Society, Barbershop Chorus, Bridge (duplicate and progressive), Canasta, Chaparral Rockhounds, Chess, Cribbage, Diabetics, Four I's (retired persons from Indiana, Illinois, Idaho, and Iowa), Five Staters (retired persons from Wisconsin, Michigan, Minnesota, and the Dakotas), Northeasterners, Pinochle, Retired Teachers, Sertoma, Shuffleboard, Square Dance, Woodmen of the World, and the Writer's Guild. Retirement Services, Incorporated, helps newcomers get settled in the area.

For persons interested in the out-of-doors, hunting, fishing, and nature hiking are available in Bitter Lake National Wildlife Refuge, and there are swimming, camping, and picnicking at Bottomless Lake State Park's six small lakes. Roswell Museum and Art Center includes the early workshop of rocketry pioneer Robert H. Goddard as well as paintings and other works by artists of the Southwest.

Pluses: Outstanding, mild four-season climate; low housing costs and below-average living costs; good ratings in range of health-care facilities.

Minuses: Middling ratings in personal safety and in leisure-living options.

DESERT SOUTHWEST

Lake Havasu City–Kingman, AZ (76)
LAS VEGAS, NV (69)
PHOENIX, AZ (44)
★ Prescott, AZ (17)
★ St. George–Zion, UT (22)
TUCSON, AZ (27)
Yuma, AZ (72)

The Desert Southwest, in the southern end of the Great Basin, lies between the country's two highest mountain ranges, the Rockies to the east and the Sierra Nevada to the west. These two mountain ranges not only add beauty, grandeur, and ruggedness to the region, they also block moist air coming from either the Pacific Ocean or the Gulf of Mexico. Thus the entire region is high, mountainous, and dry, and valleys are dusty, with scant vegetation. The mountains and cliffsides, eroded by wind and sand, are jagged, angular, and knife-sharp.

If it's sun you're after, this is the place—Yuma is the sunniest spot in America. Hot, sunny, cloudless days followed by cool, even chilly nights are the rule here. This means you can enjoy outdoor activities in the daytime and still get a good night's rest . . under a blanket or two.

Relatively low energy costs, moderate living prices, and favorable economic outlook are some of the features that led Chase Econometrics Association to name Utah one of the best states for retirees. In addition, crime rates here are low. Rapidly growing Arizona is the prototypical Sun Belt state. Tucson, which just missed ranking among the 25 choice places, is considered a leading retirement area, offering excellent health-care and recreational facilities. The Phoenix metro area is home to such retirement havens as Sun City, Tempe, and Scottsdale. Many parts of the Desert Southwest, however, suffer from high crime rates and high housing costs (Las Vegas ranks 106th and 100th, respectively, in these categories), and the availability of health-care facilities varies greatly from location to location.

Despite its quick population growth (Arizona, for example, grew 53 percent from 1970 to 1980), this is still thinly settled land. There is so much space here, with such great distances between even small towns, that people who have lived in thickly populated regions like the Upper Midwest or the Northeast might find it difficult to adjust to the occasional feeling of isolation. However, the larger cities have sufficient population and cultural and recreational facilities to offset all but the worst cases of loneliness.

★ Prescott, AZ

Prescott has a true western feeling lacking in many other towns in the Desert Southwest, and the American small-town spirit is alive and well here. The city radiates from a traditional town square containing the classic gray granite courthouse, a bandstand and gazebo, and a bronze equestrian statue of Bucky O'Neill, one of early Arizona's heroes. While a little rough at the edges, the downtown has a solid, settled feeling in refreshing contrast to the instant cities of the lower desert.

Strolling along Mount Vernon Street under the fine old shade trees past well-maintained Victorian houses, you may find it difficult to believe you are in Arizona. Anyone who travels the West with regularity, however, soon learns that contrasts are the norm. Nowhere is this more true than in central Arizona.

Just over a two-hour drive to the north is the ever-inspiring spectacle of Grand Canyon. In the winter there is skiing on 12,000-foot peaks nearby. Excellent fishing and boating are available in Prescott National Forest. To the south it is little more than 90 miles by either of two good roads to the metropolitan shopping and entertainment facilities of Phoenix.

A 50-mile stretch of U.S. Highway 89A to the north and east links Prescott with several delightful small towns in Yavapai County. Sedona, with its setting of soaring red rock formations and green pines, has long been used as the background for major films. This is the glamour spot of the area, with 20 art galleries, elegant boutiques, and fine restaurants. The lush Verde River Valley has been farmed for the past 1,200 years. This is a garden paradise 3,000 feet high with a 200-day growing season. A local cooperative sponsors farmers' markets weekly during harvest season.

If you want a relaxed, casual atmosphere with an Old West flavor but don't want to give up citified pleasures entirely, Yavapai County, Arizona, may be the place for you.

Pluses: Distinct four-season climate, with sparkling springs and autumns, without stifling desert summer heat; above-average health-care facilities (40th); wide range of cultural and recreational facilities.

Minuses: Relatively high housing and living costs; altitude (5,347 feet) could be a problem for some.

★ St. George–Zion, UT

One of the joys of living in southwestern Utah is to experience the "national park feeling" 365 days a year, making it easy to enjoy a spontaneous picnic or a peaceful walk. Most likely the sun will be shining and you'll be comfortable in light clothing here in Utah's Dixie, where the summer is long and the winter is mild.

It wasn't always this relaxed and casual. The first hardy Mormon settlers lived in wagons in long rows on either side of an open ditch. The earliest homes were often only dugouts in the ground. Life was severely trying, but years of suffering and faith eventually brought results: Orchards produced fruit while corn, squash, and melons were raised on farms along the Virgin River. For a while cotton was grown and even mulberry trees in an attempt to produce silk. Completed in 1877, the white Mormon Temple rises above green lawns and is visible for miles.

There is no rail service to St. George or Washington County, so it wasn't until the highway to Salt Lake City brought an outlet for crops and later a steady stream of tourists that the economy stabilized. Interstate Highway 15 is lightly traveled by national standards but provides a link to the bright lights and commerce of Las Vegas, the nearest major city, as well as reaching north to the Salt Lake Valley.

A number of tiny towns stretch eastward from St. George following the Virgin River and its valley to the borders of Zion National Park. Clusters of cabins at Springdale denote the last village. Here, even though your home may be modest, the towering rock backdrop in incredible shadings adds a special dimension of grandeur.

Excellent outdoor recreation is offered at Zion Na-

tional Park, Snow Canyon State Park, and Gunlock Lake State Beach. Shopping facilities at St. George are adequate for day-to-day needs. A medical center there will meet routine requirements, but specialized care must be sought elsewhere. Numerous special services such as meals on wheels, visiting homemakers, and transportation are available for older residents.

Pluses: Spectacular natural setting; excellent economic picture; low crime rate.

Minuses: Mormon tradition may be restrictive to some; health care could be a problem.

ROCKY MOUNTAINS

BOISE CITY, ID (65)
COEUR d'ALENE, ID (98)
COLORADO SPRINGS, CO (80)
DELTA, CO (37)
FORT COLLINS, CO (51)

GRAND JUNCTION, CO (34)
HAMILTON–BITTERROOT VALLEY, MT (26)
KALISPELL, MT (64)
MISSOULA, MT (70)

What does green and rugged Coeur d'Alene in Idaho's panhandle have in common with sun-baked Deming in southwestern New Mexico? Very little. Yet the Census Bureau lumps them together in a region it labels Mountain. By *Places Rated*'s reasoning, Deming, with its desert and Hispanic flavors, more properly belongs in Rio Grande Country. When it comes to certain foothill-and-mountain counties in Colorado, Idaho, and Montana, however, the feel is definitely high-country, definitely Rocky Mountains. In spite of the reservations many older persons have about high altitudes and cold winters, the Rockies are emerging from their "vacation only" status, becoming an area where retirees are moving for year-round living.

In Colorado, one can easily distinguish between the Eastern Slope and Western Slope areas. Large cities like Colorado Springs (in a setting that reminds many of Asheville in the North Carolina mountains) and Fort Collins are Eastern Slope. Smaller places, like Grand Junction and Delta, are Western Slope. The two slopes have different political orientations and different growth rates.

In Idaho, where the population rose by a third in the 1970s, retired newcomers head for the city of Coeur d'Alene, within commuting distance of Spokane, Washington, or they settle near metropolitan Boise. In Montana, the spectacular but sparsely settled western counties—particularly Flathead, Lake, Missoula, and Ravalli—are the ones drawing older newcomers. Only cold weather and a very low health-care rating (101st) kept Hamilton–Bitterroot Valley (Ravalli County) off our list of 25 choice places, for this locale made commendable showings in safety from crime (14th), leisure assets (19th), and money matters (27th).

Pluses: Outstanding outdoor recreation endowments; low crime rates outside metropolitan areas.

Minuses: High housing costs; harsh winter temperatures in the northern part; lack of broad-based health-care facilities in rural areas.

PACIFIC BEACHES

Maui, HI (99)   San Luis Obispo, CA (36)
SAN DIEGO, CA (37)   SANTA ROSA, CA (85)

If there is a single word that most people associate with the region we call Pacific Beaches, that word is probably "paradise." This far-flung region, stretching from the California coast to Hawaii, contains places that have one thing in common: a shoreline on the Pacific Ocean in a climate zone that is so mild and unchanging that *Places Rated* refers to it as the zone of paradise climates. Of the four retirement places in this region, none ranks lower than eighth for climatic mildness. With all this great weather, the abundance of outdoor recreational offerings can be enjoyed year round.

Many California locations have been popular for retirement for years; San Diego is famed as a destination for retired U.S. Navy personnel. Thus, most of these spots provide a wide range of services for senior citizens and boast attractive retirement communities. Good health-care facilities are available, as are transportation services for local and intercity travel.

Nonetheless, the pace of growth in the Pacific retirement areas has slowed in recent years. None of these four retirement places scores well in economic terms—living costs are high and prospects for income growth are generally limited, while tax burdens are high. San Diego ranks 103rd among the 107 retirement places for money matters, for example, and Maui 100th. Housing costs are extremely high as well—Maui ranks dead last in this category, San Diego 106th, Santa Rosa 105th, and San Luis Obispo 101st.

Pacific Beach retirement is great for those who can afford it, but despite the many recreational and cultural amenities and the terrific weather, the costs of living in "paradise" can run extremely high.

Pluses: Extremely mild climate; magnificent scenery; great outdoor leisure choices.

Minuses: Almost prohibitive real-estate and living costs; climate can be monotonous for people used to seasonal change.

TAHOE BASIN AND THE "OTHER" CALIFORNIA

Carson City, NV (92)   Red Bluff–Sacramento
Clear Lake, CA (106)   Valley, CA (60)
Nevada City–Donner, CA   RENO, NV (90)
  (89)   Twain Harte–Yosemite, CA
                              (86)

There is a California the Beach Boys don't sing about. It's Mother Lode Country, the mountain-studded interior, with alpine meadows, blizzard-filled passes, clear lakes, trout streams, and magnificent scenery. On the minus side, several of the retirement places in this region fall short in the amenities associated with more populous areas. So if it's culture you're after, or if you are concerned about the availability of top-notch health care, you should probably look elsewhere.

If there's a more beautiful lake in the world than cobalt-blue Lake Tahoe, nestled high in the Sierra Nevada, we'd like to hear about it. Ringed by snow-capped peaks, the deep lake is surrounded by sloping foothills covered with pine, aspen, and birch. For beautiful resort living, Tahoe cannot be beat . . . but neither can the cost of real estate here. With modest condos overlooking the lake going for half a million dollars, Lake Tahoe is out of reach for all but blue-chip clientele. Nearby Reno and Carson City are somewhat more affordable, though housing costs are still very high (104th and 103rd, respectively). Carson City boasts this retirement region's lowest crime rate (29th) but ranks 97th in health care. Reno, conversely, has excellent health-care facilities (12th) but a very high crime rate (90th). Despite its glittery resort image, Reno has some delightful, quiet residential areas.

West across the ridge of the Sierra Nevada is Nevada County, California, once a mining area and now a tourist haven. Donner Lake, a popular summer beach resort, also doubles as a winter ski area. Even in midsummer, this high mountain lake tends to be on the chilly side. Tuolumne County, roughly a hundred miles to the south, contains spectacular Yosemite National Park, with all of the attendant opportunities for outstanding outdoor recreation. Although the gold rush is over, these areas continue to draw people, with their scenery, mountain climate, and open spaces. But the retirement places of Nevada City–Donner and Twain Harte–Yosemite suffer from high homeowning costs and sluggish economic prospects.

Clear Lake, on the northwest fringe of the Great Interior Valley, is California's largest natural freshwater lake and centerpiece of Lake County's resort area. In addition to excellent fishing, Clear Lake (Bass Capital of the West) offers good boating facilities. Water recreation is also available in nearby Tehama County at Red Bluff, where Diversion Dam spans the Sacramento River. Red Bluff has some splendid Victorian homes. Both these areas have shown substantial population growth in recent years, including a sizable increase due to in-migration of retirement-aged people.

Pluses: Not too crowded; beautiful scenery and excellent outdoor recreation, winter and summer.

Minuses: Generally short of big-city amenities; high housing costs; lack of health-care facilities.

PACIFIC NORTHWEST CLOUD BELT

Bend, OR (50)   Oak Harbor, WA (40)
Lincoln City–Newport, OR   OLYMPIA, WA (97)
  (43)   ★ Port Angeles–Strait of
MEDFORD, OR (76)   Juan de Fuca, WA (20)

No other state has made so clear its desire to discourage in-migration as Oregon did when its former governor Tom McCall urged tourists to give the state a try. "But for heaven's sake," he quickly added, "don't come to live here." This awareness of the harm that rapid population growth can bring to beautiful, pristine land is commonly felt elsewhere in the Pacific Northwest.

Nevertheless, retired city people from California, the Midwest, and even the distant Northeast continue to move here in a quest for clean air, quiet, and uncrowded spaces. Their destinations are most often the two island and four shore counties of Washington's Puget Sound, and the valleys and ocean coast areas of southwest Oregon.

Between 1970 and 1980, Bend and the surrounding forested environs in Deschutes County, Oregon, made up the fastest-growing non-metropolitan county west of Citrus County, Florida. Of more than 300 metro areas, Olympia, Washington's groomed and parklike state capital, ranked in the top ten in rate of growth over the same period, along with the Florida metro areas of Ocala and Fort Myers–Cape Coral. A demographer who has followed American counties for decades as they grow, ebb, and grow again, recently commented that the popularity of this Cloud Belt just goes to show that "'Sun Belt' is a very imperfect synonym for population growth."

★ Port Angeles–Strait of Juan de Fuca, WA

On a mild winter afternoon on the Olympic Peninsula, there is nothing quite like taking your binoculars and driving out to the Coast Guard station at the end of Ediz Hook, a four-mile sandbar curving out from the waterfront of Port Angeles, to watch the distant ship traffic arriving from all points in the Pacific bound for Puget Sound.

A Greek sailor nicknamed Juan de Fuca steered into this strait in 1592. Two hundred years later a Spanish mariner put into the impressive natural harbor on the south shore and named the Indian village he found there Port of Our Lady of the Angels, a name shortened to Port Angeles by early settlers, then changed and rechanged until it stuck in 1890, when it became the seat of Clallam County.

Sitting atop the wild and beautiful Olympic Peninsula, Port Angeles and nearby Joyce and Sequim (locally pronounced "Skwim") have the Olympic Mountains behind them and the beaches along the Strait of Juan de Fuca at their front steps. For such a small place (pop. 17,311), Port Angeles is truly a center of activity. The headquarters of the Olympic National Park are here. In summer, there is heavy ferry traffic to Vancouver Island and to Alaska. Summer and fall, the hikers, berry pickers, clammers, crabbers, beachcombers, and fishermen are everywhere. During the winter, the Port Angeles Symphony puts on six concerts.

There are several structured retirement communities in both Port Angeles and Sequim. Year round, the schedule at the Senior Citizens Drop-In Center on South Lincoln Street is full of Golden Agers, Kitchen Band, Needle Craft, American Association of Retired Persons, and Writers Guild meetings, plus dancing every Tuesday night, exercise programs, craft classes, movies, parties, lectures, and organized tours to other parts of the United States.

Pluses: Mild, marine climate; low crime rate; outstanding leisure-living amenities.

Minuses: Above-average housing and living costs; spotty health-care facilities outside Port Angeles.

Retirement Place Finder

The following listing, organized alphabetically by state, presents the 107 retirement places and selected cities, towns, villages, and Census Designated Places within their boundaries. Population figures are from the 1980 census, updated whenever more recent figures were available.

ALABAMA

Fairhope–Gulf Shores (Baldwin County)

Bay Minette, 7,455
Daphne, 3,406
Fairhope, 7,286
Foley, 4,003
Gulf Shores, 1,349
Lake Forest, 3,489
Loxley, 804
Point Clear, 1,812
Robertsdale, 2,306
Silverhill, 624
Spanish Fort, 3,415

ARIZONA

Lake Havasu City–Kingman (Mohave County)

Bullhead City-Riviera, 10,364
Kingman, 9,257
Lake Havasu City, 15,909

PHOENIX (Maricopa County)

Avondale, 8,168
Buckeye, 3,434
Cashion, 3,014
Cave Creek, 1,589
Chandler, 29,673
Dreamland-Velda Rose, 5,969
El Mirage, 4,307
Fountain Hills, 2,771
Gila Bend, 1,585
Gilbert, 5,717
Glendale, 97,172
Goodyear, 2,747
Guadalupe, 4,506
Litchfield Park, 3,657
Mesa, 152,453
Paradise Valley, 11,085
Peoria, 12,251
Phoenix, 789,704
St. Johns, 3,368
Scottsdale, 88,622
Sun City, 40,505
Sun Lakes, 1,925
Surprise, 3,723
Tempe, 106,743
Tolleson, 4,433
Wickenburg, 3,535
Youngtown, 2,254

Prescott (Yavapai County)

Bagdad, 2,331
Camp Verde, 1,125
Chino Valley, 2,858
Clarkdale, 1,512
Cottonwood, 4,550
Jerome, 420
Prescott, 20,055
Prescott Valley, 2,284
Sedona, 5,368

TUCSON (Pima County)

Ajo, 5,189
Catalina, 2,749
Green Valley, 7,999
Marana, 1,674
Oro Valley, 1,489
Sells, 1,864
South Tucson, 6,554
Tucson, 330,537
Tucson Estates, 2,814

Yuma (Yuma County)

Meadow Brook, 1,300
Parker, 2,542
San Luis, 1,946
Somerton, 5,761
Wellton, 911
Yuma, 42,433

ARKANSAS

Bull Shoals (Marion County)

Bull Shoals, 1,312
Pyatt, 217
Summit, 506
Yellville, 1,044

Harrison (Boone County)

Alpena, 344
Bellefonte, 393
Bergman, 320
Diamond City, 650
Harrison, 9,567
Lead Hill, 247
Valley Springs, 190

Hot Springs–Lake Ouachita (Garland County)

Hot Springs, 35,781
Hot Springs Village, 2,083
Lake Hamilton, 1,054
Mountain Pine, 1,068
Piney, 2,283
Rockwell, 2,675

Mountain Home–Norfork Lake (Baxter County)

Big Flat, 150
Lakeview, 512
Mountain Home, 8,066
Norfork, 399
Salesville, 406

CALIFORNIA

Clear Lake (Lake County)

Clearlake Highlands, 13,300
Clearlake Oaks, 2,000
Kelseyville, 1,567
Lakeport, 3,675
Lower Lake, 1,043
Lucerne, 1,767

Nevada City–Donner (Nevada County)

Alta Hill, 1,229
Alta Sierra, 2,168
Grass Valley, 6,697
Nevada City, 2,431
Penn Valley, 1,032
Truckee, 2,389

Red Bluff–Sacramento Valley (Tehama County)

Corning, 4,745
Los Molinos, 1,241
Red Bluff, 9,490
Tehama, 365

SAN DIEGO (San Diego County)

Alpine, 5,368
Bonita, 6,257
Cardiff-By-The-Sea, 10,054
Carlsbad, 35,490
Casa de Oro-Mount Helix, 19,651
Castle Park-Otay, 21,049
Chula Vista, 83,927
Coronado, 16,859
Del Mar, 5,017
El Cajon, 73,892
Encinitas, 10,796
Escondido, 64,355
Fallbrook, 14,041
Imperial Beach, 22,689
Jamul, 1,826
Lakeside, 23,921
La Mesa, 50,308
Lemon Grove, 20,780
Leucadia, 9,478
National City, 48,772
Oceanside, 76,698
Poway, 32,263
Ramona, 8,173
Rancho Santa Fe, 4,014
San Diego, 875,538
San Marcos, 17,479
Santee, 47,080
Solana Beach, 13,047
Spring Valley, 40,191
Vista, 35,834

San Luis Obispo (San Luis Obispo County)

Arroyo Grande, 11,290
Atascadero, 16,232
Baywood-Los Oscos, 10,933
Cambria, 3,061
Cayucos, 2,301
El Paso de Robles, 9,163
Grover City, 8,827
Morro Bay, 9,064
Nipomo, 5,247
Oceano, 4,478
Pismo Beach, 5,364
San Luis Obispo, 34,252

SANTA ROSA (Sonoma County)

Boyes Hot Springs, 4,177
Cloverdale, 3,989
Cotati, 3,475
El Verano, 2,384
Fetters Hot Springs, 675
Glen Ellen, 1,014
Graton, 1,286
Guerneville, 1,525
Healdsburg, 7,217
Monte Rio, 1,137
Petaluma, 33,834
Rohnert Park, 22,965
Roseland, 7,915
Santa Rosa, 83,320
Sonoma, 6,054

Twain Harte–Yosemite (Tuolumne County)

Jamestown, 2,206
Mono Vista, 1,154
Sonora, 3,247
Tuolumne City, 1,708
Twain Harte, 1,369

COLORADO

COLORADO SPRINGS (El Paso County)

Black Forest, 3,372
Cimarron Hills, 6,597
Colorado Springs, 215,150
Fountain, 8,324
Green Mountain Falls, 607
Manitou Springs, 4,475
Palmer Lake, 1,130
Security, 18,768
Stratmoor, 5,519
Woodmoor, 1,490

Delta (Delta County)

Cedaredge, 1,184
Crawford, 268

Delta, 3,931
Hotchkiss, 849
Orchard City, 1,914
Paonia, 1,425

FORT COLLINS (Larimer County)

Berthoud, 2,362
Estes Park, 2,703
Fort Collins, 65,092
Loveland, 30,244
Wellington, 1,215

Grand Junction (Mesa County)

Clifton, 5,223
Collbran, 344
Fruita, 2,810
Grand Junction, 28,144
Orchard Mesa, 4,876
Palisade, 1,551

DELAWARE

Rehoboth Bay–Indian River Bay (Sussex County)

Bethany Beach, 330
Blades, 664
Bridgeville, 1,238
Delmar, 948
Frankford, 686
Georgetown, 1,710
Greenwood, 578
Laurel, 3,052
Lewes, 2,197
Milford, 5,356
Millsboro, 1,233
Milton, 1,359
Ocean View, 495
Rehoboth Beach, 1,730
Seaford, 5,256
Selbyville, 1,251

FLORIDA

DAYTONA BEACH (Volusia County)

Daytona Beach, 54,176
Daytona Beach Shores, 1,324
De Bary, 4,980
De Land, 15,354
Deland Southwest, 1,481
De Leon Springs, 1,669
Deltona, 15,710
Edgewater, 6,726
Glencoe, 1,640
Lake Helen, 2,047
New Smyrna Beach, 13,557
North Deland, 1,557
Orange City, 2,795
Ormond Beach, 21,378
Ormond By The Sea, 7,665
Port Orange, 18,756
Samsula, 1,971
South Daytona, 11,152
West De Land, 3,055

FORT LAUDERDALE–HOLLYWOOD (Broward County)

Broadview Park, 6,022
Browardale, 7,571
Coconut Creek, 6,288
Collier City, 7,135
Collier Manor, 7,048

Cooper City, 10,140
Coral Springs, 37,349
Dania, 11,811
Davie, 20,877
Deerfield Beach, 39,193
Fort Lauderdale, 153,279
Hallandale, 36,517
Hollywood, 121,323
Kendall Green, 6,768
Lauderdale Lakes, 25,426
Lauderhill, 37,271
Lighthouse Point, 11,488
Margate, 36,044
Melrose Park, 5,725
Miami Gardens, 9,025
Miramar, 32,813
North Andrews Gardens, 8,967
North Lauderdale, 18,479
Oakland Park, 23,035
Pembroke Pines, 35,776
Plantation, 48,501
Pompano Beach, 52,618
Pompano Beach Highlands, 16,154
Riverland, 5,919
Sunrise, 39,681
Tamarac, 29,376
Washington Park, 7,240
Wilton Manors, 12,742

FORT MYERS–CAPE CORAL (Lee County)

Bonita Shores, 2,351
Bonita Springs, 5,435
Cape Coral, 32,103
Cypress Lake, 8,721
Fort Myers, 36,638
Fort Myers Beach, 5,753
Fort Myers Shores, 4,426
Franklin Park, 2,792
Lehigh Acres, 9,604
North Fort Myers, 22,808
San Carlos Park, 3,950
Sanibel, 3,363
Suncoast Estates, 4,399
Tanglewood, 8,229
Tice, 6,645
Villas, 8,724

LAKELAND–WINTER HAVEN (Polk County)

Auburndale, 6,501
Bartow, 14,780
Bradley Junction, 1,108
Combee Settlement, 5,400
Crystal Lake, 6,827
Cypress Gardens, 8,043
Dundee, 2,227
Eagle Lake, 1,678
East Auburndale, 2,402
Eaton Park, 1,385
Eloise, 1,408
Fort Meade, 5,546
Frostproof, 2,995
Gibsonia, 5,001
Gordonville, 2,634
Haines City, 10,799
Highland City, 1,555
Inwood, 6,668
Jan Phyl Village, 2,785
Kathleen, 1,866
Lake Alfred, 3,134
Lake Hamilton, 1,552
Lakeland, 47,406
Lakeland Highlands, 10,426
Lake Wales, 8,466
Medulla, 2,258

Mulberry, 2,932
North Winter Haven, 1,140
Wahneta, 3,329
Willow Creek, 2,115
Winston, 9,315
Winter Haven, 21,119

MELBOURNE–TITUSVILLE–COCOA (Brevard County)

Cape Canaveral, 5,733
Cocoa, 16,096
Cocoa Beach, 10,926
Cocoa West, 6,432
Indialantic, 2,883
Indian Harbour Beach, 5,967
Melbourne, 46,536
Melbourne Village, 1,004
Merritt Island, 30,708
Mims, 7,583
Palm Bay, 18,560
Port St. John, 1,837
Rockledge, 11,877
Sharpes, 4,149
Titusville, 31,910
West Eau Gallie, 2,579
West Melbourne, 5,078

MIAMI (Dade County)

Aventura, 10,162
Bay Harbor Islands, 4,869
Brownsville, 18,058
Coral Gables, 43,241
Coral Terrace, 22,702
Cutler, 15,593
Cutler Ridge, 20,886
Gladeview, 18,919
Glenvar Heights, 13,216
Golden Glades, 23,154
Goulds, 7,078
Hialeah, 145,254
Ives Estates, 12,623
Kendall, 73,758
Key Biscayne, 6,313
Lake Lucerne, 9,762
Leisure City, 17,905
Miami, 346,865
Miami Beach, 96,298
Miami Lakes, 9,809
Miami Springs, 12,350
Naronja-Princeton, 10,381
Norland, 19,471
North Miami, 36,553
North Miami Beach, 36,481
Ojus, 17,344
Olympia Heights, 33,112
Opa-Locka, 14,460
Palmetto Estates, 11,116
Palm Springs North, 5,838
Perrine, 16,129
Pinewood, 16,216
Scott Lake, 14,154
South Miami, 10,944
South Miami Heights, 23,557
Sunny Isles, 12,564
Sunset, 13,531
Sweetwater, 8,251
Tamiami, 17,607
Westchester, 29,272
West Little River, 32,492
Westwood Lakes, 11,478

OCALA (Marion County)

Belleview, 1,913
Dunnellon, 1,427
Ocala, 37,170
Silver Springs, 1,082
Silver Springs Shores, 3,983

ORLANDO (Orange, Osceola, and Seminole counties)

Altamonte Springs, 22,028
Apopka, 6,019
Azalea Park, 8,304
Belle Isle, 2,848
Bithlo, 3,143
Casselberry, 15,247
Conway, 23,940
Fairview Shores, 10,174
Fern Park, 8,890
Forest City, 6,819
Goldenrod, 13,682
Holden Heights, 13,840
Kissimmee, 15,487
Lockhart, 10,571
Longwood, 10,029
Maitland, 8,763
Oak Ridge, 15,477
Ocoee, 7,803
Orlando, 128,291
Orlovista, 6,474
Pine Castle, 9,992
Pine Hills, 35,771
St. Cloud, 7,840
Sanford, 23,176
Sky Lake, 6,692
South Apopka, 5,687
Union Park, 19,175
Wekiva Springs, 13,386
Winter Garden, 6,789
Winter Park, 22,339
Winter Springs, 10,475

SARASOTA–BRADENTON (Manatee and Sarasota counties)

Bayshore Gardens, 14,945
Bee Ridge, 3,313
Bradenton, 30,170
Cortez, 3,821
Englewood, 10,242
Fruitville, 3,070
Gulf Gate Estates, 9,248
Holmes Beach, 4,023
Kensington Park, 2,887
Laurel, 6,368
Longboat Key, 4,843
Memphis, 5,501
Nokomis, 3,018
North Port, 6,205
North Sarasota, 4,997
Oneco, 6,417
Palma Sola, 5,297
Palmetto, 8,637
Phillipi Gardens, 2,525
Ridge Wood Heights, 3,951
Samoset, 5,747
Sarasota, 48,868
Sarasota Springs, 13,860
Siesta Key, 7,010
South Bradenton, 14,297
Southgate, 7,322
South Gate Ridge, 4,259
South Sarasota, 4,267
South Venice, 8,075
Venice, 12,153
Venice Gardens, 6,568
West Bradenton, 4,065
Whitfield Estates, 4,328

WEST PALM BEACH–BOCA RATON (Palm Beach County)

Atlantis, 1,325
Belle Glade, 16,535
Boca Raton, 49,505

Boynton Beach, 35,624
Century Village, 10,619
Delray Beach, 34,325
Greenacres City, 8,843
Haverhill, 1,249
Highland Beach, 2,030
Juno Beach, 1,142
Jupiter, 9,868
Kings Point, 8,724
Lake Clarke Shores, 3,174
Lake Park, 6,909
Lake Worth, 27,048
Lantana, 8,048
Mangonia Park, 1,419
North Palm Beach, 11,344
Pahokee, 6,346
Palm Beach, 9,729
Palm Beach Gardens, 6,102
Palm Springs, 8,166
Riviera Beach, 26,489
Sandalfoot Cove, 5,299
South Bay, 3,886
Tequesta, 3,685
Wellington, 4,622
West Palm Beach, 63,305

GEORGIA

**Brunswick–Golden Isles
(Glynn County)**

Brunswick, 17,605
Dock Junction, 6,189
St. Simons, 6,566

**Clarkesville–Mount Airy
(Habersham County)**

Alto, 618
Baldwin, 1,080
Clarkesville, 1,348
Cornelia, 3,203
Demorest, 1,130
Mount Airy, 670

**Gainesville–Lake Sidney
Lanier (Hall County)**

Clermont, 300
Flowery Branch, 755
Gainesville, 15,280
Gainesville Mills, 1,281
Lula, 857
Oakwood, 723
Westside, 2,769

HAWAII

Maui (Maui County)

Haiku, 619
Haliimaile, 741
Hana, 643
Kahului, 12,978
Kaunakakai, 2,231
Kihei, 5,644
Lahaina, 6,095
Lanai City, 2,092
Lower Paia, 1,500
Makawao, 2,900
Maunaloa, 633
Napili, 2,446
Pukalani, 3,950
Waikapu, 698
Wailea, 1,125
Wailuku, 10,260

IDAHO

BOISE CITY (Ada County)

Boise City, 102,541
Eagle, 2,620
Garden City, 4,571
Kuna, 1,767
Meridian, 6,658

**Coeur d'Alene (Kootenai
County)**

Athol, 312
Coeur d'Alene, 20,054
Dalton Gardens, 1,795
Hauser Lake, 305
Hayden, 2,586
Hayden Lake, 273
Post Falls, 5,736
Rathdrum, 1,369
Spirit Lake, 834

KENTUCKY

**Benton–Kentucky Lake
(Marshall County)**

Benton, 3,700
Calvert City, 2,388
Hardin, 545

**LEXINGTON-FAYETTE (Bourbon,
Clark, Fayette, Jessamine,
Scott, and Woodford
counties)**

Georgetown, 10,972
Lexington, 204,165
Midway, 1,445
Millersburg, 987
Nicholasville, 10,400
North Middletown, 637
Paris, 7,935
Stamping Ground, 562
Versailles, 6,427
Wilmore, 3,787
Winchester, 15,216

MAINE

**Bar Harbor–Frenchman Bay
(Hancock County)**

Bar Harbor, 4,124
Bluehill, 1,644
Bucksport, 4,345
Castine, 1,304
Dedham, 841
Deer Isle, 1,492
Ellsworth, 5,179
Franklin, 979
Gouldsboro, 1,574
Hancock, 1,409
Lamoine, 953
Mount Desert, 2,063
Orland, 1,645
Penobscot, 1,104
Southwest Harbor, 1,855
Stonington, 1,273
Sullivan, 967
Surry, 894
Tremont, 1,222

**Camden–Penobscot Bay
(Knox County)**

Appleton, 818
Camden, 4,584
Cushing, 795
Friendship, 1,000

Hope, 730
Owls Head, 1,633
Rockland, 7,919
Rockport, 2,749
St. George, 1,948
South Thomaston, 1,064
Thomaston, 2,900
Union, 1,569
Vinalhaven, 1,211
Warren, 2,566
Washington, 954

MARYLAND

**Easton–Chesapeake Bay
(Talbot County)**

Easton, 7,536
Oxford, 754
St. Michaels, 1,301
Trappe, 739

**Ocean City–Assateague
Island (Worcester County)**

Berlin, 2,162
Ocean City, 4,946
Pocomoke City, 3,558
Snow Hill, 2,192

MASSACHUSETTS

**Cape Cod (Barnstable
County)**

Barnstable, 30,898
Brewster, 5,226
Buzzards Bay, 3,375
Centerville, 3,640
Chatham, 6,071
Dennis Port, 2,570
East Falmouth, 5,181
Eastham, 3,472
Falmouth, 5,720
Harwich, 8,971
Hyannis, 9,118
Mashpee, 3,700
Orleans, 5,306
Provincetown, 3,536
Sandwich, 8,727
South Yarmouth, 7,525
Wellfleet, 2,209
West Dennis, 2,030
West Yarmouth, 3,882
Woods Hole, 1,080
Yarmouth, 18,449
Yarmouth Port, 2,490

MICHIGAN

**Houghton Lake (Roscommon
County)**

Houghton Lake, 1,500
Houghton Lake Heights, 2,449
Prudenville, 1,000
Roscommon, 834

**Oscoda–Huron Shore (Iosco
County)**

Au Sable, 1,240
East Tawas, 2,584
Oscoda, 2,431
Tawas City, 1,967
Wurtsmith AFB, 5,166

**Petoskey–Straits of Mackinac
(Emmet County)**

Alanson, 508
Harbor Springs, 1,567
Mackinaw City, 820
Pellston, 565
Petoskey, 6,097

**Traverse City–Grand
Traverse Bay
(Grand Traverse County)**

Fife Lake, 402
Kingsley, 664
Traverse City, 15,516

MISSISSIPPI

**BILOXI-GULFPORT (Hancock,
Harrison, and Stone
counties)**

Bay St. Louis, 7,891
Biloxi, 49,311
Diamondhead, 1,011
D'Iberville, 13,369
Gulfport, 39,676
Henderson's Point, 1,114
Long Beach, 7,967
North Gulfport, 6,660
North Long Beach, 7,063
Orange Grove, 13,476
Pass Christian, 5,014
Wiggins, 3,205

MISSOURI

**Branson–Lake Taneycomo
(Taney County)**

Branson, 2,550
Forsyth, 1,010
Hollister, 1,439
Taneyville, 300

**Cassville–Roaring River
(Barry County)**

Cassville, 2,091
Exeter, 588
Monett, 6,148
Purdy, 928
Seligman, 508
Wheaton, 548

**SPRINGFIELD (Christian and
Greene counties)**

Ash Grove, 1,157
Battlefield, 1,227
Billings, 911
Fair Grove, 863
Nixa, 2,662
Ozark, 2,980
Republic, 4,485
Springfield, 133,116
Strafford, 1,121
Willard, 1,799

**Table Rock Lake (Stone
County)**

Crane, 1,185
Galena, 423
Kimberling City, 1,285
Reeds Spring, 461

MONTANA

Hamilton–Bitterroot Valley (Ravalli County)

Darby, 581
Hamilton, 2,661
Stevensville, 1,207

Kalispell (Flathead County)

Bigfork, 1,080
Columbia Falls, 3,112
Evergreen, 3,746
Kalispell, 10,648
Whitefish, 3,703

Missoula (Missoula County)

Bonner, 1,742
East Missoula, 1,707
Lolo, 2,418
Missoula, 33,388
Missoula South, 5,557
Orchard Homes, 10,837
Rattlesnake, 3,474

NEVADA

Carson City (Carson City city and Douglas County)

Carson City, 32,022
Gardnerville Ranchos, 3,542
Kingsbury, 2,695
Minden, 1,300
Zephyr Cove, 1,316

LAS VEGAS (Clark County)

Boulder City, 9,590
East Las Vegas, 6,449
Henderson, 24,363
Indian Springs, 900
Las Vegas, 164,674
Mesquite, 700
North Las Vegas, 42,739
Overton, 1,111
Paradise, 84,818
Sunrise Manor, 44,155
Winchester, 19,728

RENO (Washoe County)

Incline Village, 4,500
New Washoe City, 2,543
Reno, 100,756
Sparks, 40,780
Sun Valley, 8,822

NEW HAMPSHIRE

Keene (Cheshire County)

Alstead, 1,461
Chesterfield, 2,561
Dublin, 1,303
Fitzwilliam, 1,795
Gilsum, 652
Harrisville, 860
Hinsdale, 3,631
Jaffrey, 4,349
Keene, 21,449
Marlborough, 1,846
North Swanzey, 950
North Walpole, 950
Richmond, 518
Rindge, 3,375
Sullivan, 585
Surry, 656
Swanzey, 5 183

Swanzey Center, 700
Troy, 2,131
Walpole, 3,188
Westmoreland, 1,452
West Swanzey, 1,022
Winchester, 3,465

Laconia–Lake Winnipesaukee (Belknap County)

Alton, 2,440
Barnstead, 2,292
Belmont, 4,026
Gilford, 4,841
Gilmanton, 1,941
Laconia, 15,575
Meredith, 1,202
New Hampton, 1,249
Sanbornton, 1,679
Tilton, 3,387

North Conway–White Mountains (Carroll County)

Bartlett, 1,566
Conway, 7,158
Effingham, 599
Madison, 1,051
Moultonborough, 2,206
North Conway, 2,184
Ossipee, 2,465
Sandwich, 905
Tamworth, 1,672
Tuftonboro, 1,500
Wakefield, 2,237
Wolfeboro, 3,968

NEW JERSEY

ATLANTIC CITY-CAPE MAY (Atlantic and Cape May counties)

Absecon, 6,859
Atlantic City, 40,199
Brigantine, 8,318
Cape May, 4,853
Cape May Court House, 3,597
Collings Lakes, 2,093
Egg Harbor City, 4,618
Erma, 1,774
Hammonton, 12,298
Linwood, 6,144
Margate City, 9,179
Mays Landing, 2,054
North Cape May, 4,029
Northfield, 7,795
North Wildwood, 4,714
Ocean City, 13,949
Pleasantville, 13,435
Pomona, 2,358
Rio Grande, 2,016
Sea Isle City, 2,644
Somers Point, 10,330
Ventnor City, 11,704
Villas, 5,909
Wildwood, 4,913

Toms River–Barnegat Bay (Ocean County)

Barnegat, 1,012
Beach Haven West, 3,020
Brick Township, 53,629
Crestwood Village, 7,965
Gilford Park, 6,528
Holiday City, 7,500
Lakewood, 22,863
Mystic Islands, 4,929

New Egypt, 2,111
North Beach Haven, 2,652
Ocean Acres, 4,850
Ocean Beach, 1,629
Silverton, 7,236
Toms River, 7,465

NEW MEXICO

ALBUQUERQUE (Bernalillo County)

Albuquerque, 331,767
Corrales, 2,791
Isleta Pueblo, 1,246
Los Ranchos de Albuquerque, 2,702
North Valley, 13,006
Paradise Hills, 5,096
Sandia, 5,288
South Valley, 38,916

Deming (Luna County)

Columbus, 414
Deming, 9,964

LAS CRUCES (Dona Ana County)

Alameda, 7,800
Anthony, 3,285
Dona Ana, 300
Hatch, 1,028
Las Cruces, 45,086
Meadow Vista, 3,377
Mesilla, 2,029
Organ, 500
Radium Springs, 100
University Park, 4,383
White Sands, 3,120

Roswell (Chaves County)

Dexter, 882
Hagerman, 936
Lake Arthur, 327
Roswell, 39,676

Santa Fe (Santa Fe County)

Chimayo, 1,993
Espanola, 6,803
Nambe, 1,017
Santa Fe, 48,953
Tesuque, 1,014

NEW YORK

Monticello–Liberty (Sullivan County)

Liberty, 4,293
Livingston Manor, 1,522
Monticello, 6,306
South Fallsburg, 1,590
Wurtsboro, 1,128

NORTH CAROLINA

ASHEVILLE (Buncombe County)

Asheville, 53,583
Biltmore Forest, 1,499
Black Mountain, 4,083
Enka, 5,567
Swannanoa, 5,586
Weaverville, 1,495
Woodfin, 3,260

Brevard (Transylvania County)

Brevard, 5,323
Pisgah Forest, 1,899
Rosman, 512

Hendersonville (Henderson County)

Balfour, 1,772
Barker Heights, 1,267
East Flat Rock, 3,365
Hendersonville, 6,862
Mountain Home, 1,381
Valley Hill, 2,396

OKLAHOMA

Lake O' The Cherokees (Delaware County)

Bernice, 318
Colcord, 530
Grove, 3,378
Jay, 2,100
Oaks, 591

Tahlequah–Lake Tenkiller (Cherokee County)

Hulbert, 633
Tahlequah, 9,708

OREGON

Bend (Deschutes County)

Bend, 17,263
Redmond, 6,452
Sisters, 696
Sunriver, 1,095

Lincoln City–Newport (Lincoln County)

Depoe Bay, 723
Lincoln City, 5,469
Newport, 7,519
Siletz, 1,001
Waldport, 1,274

MEDFORD (Jackson County)

Applegate, 800
Ashland, 14,943
Butte Falls, 428
Medford, 39,603

PENNSYLVANIA

LANCASTER (Lancaster County)

Adamstown, 1,119
Akron, 3,471
Christiana, 1,183
Columbia, 10,466
Denver, 2,018
East Petersburg, 3,600
Elizabethtown, 8,233
Ephrata, 11,095
Lancaster, 54,725
Lititz, 7,590
Manheim, 5,015
Marietta, 2,740
Millersville, 7,668
Mount Joy, 5,680
Mountville, 1,505
New Holland, 4,147
Quarryville, 1,558

Rothsville, 1,318
Strasburg, 1,999
Terre Hill, 1,217

STATE COLLEGE (Centre County)

Bellefonte, 6,300
Centre Hall, 1,233
Lemont, 2,547
Milesburg, 1,309
Philipsburg, 3,533
Pine Grove Mills, 900
Pleasant Gap, 1,773
Snow Shoe, 852
State College, 36,130

SOUTH CAROLINA

Beaufort–Hilton Head (Beaufort County)

Beaufort, 8,634
Beaufort Station, 2,165
Burton, 3,619
Hilton Head Island, 11,344
Laurel Bay, 5,238
Parris Island, 7,752
Port Royal, 2,977
Shell Point, 2,475

Myrtle Beach (Horry County)

Briarcliffe Acres, 338
Bucksport, 1,125
Conway, 10,240
Forestbrook, 1,529
Loris, 2,193
Myrtle Beach, 18,446
North Myrtle Beach, 3,960
Surfside Beach, 2,522

TENNESSEE

Big Sandy (Benton County)

Big Sandy, 650
Camden, 3,279

Cookeville (Putnam County)

Algood, 2,406
Baxter, 1,411
Cookeville, 20,535
Monterey, 2,610

Crossville (Cumberland County)

Crab Orchard, 1,065
Crossville, 6,394
Pleasant Hill, 371

Paris (Henry County)

Cottage Grove, 117
Henry, 295
Paris, 10,728
Puryear, 624

TEXAS

Athens–Cedar Creek Lake (Henderson County)

Athens, 10,197
Berryville, 513
Brownsboro 582

Chandler, 1,308
Eustace, 541
Gun Barrel City, 2,118
Malakoff, 2,082
Murchison, 513
Seven Points, 647
Tool, 1,591
Trinidad, 1,130

AUSTIN (Hays, Travis, and Williamson counties)

Austin, 345,496
Bartlett, 1,567
Cedar Park, 3,474
Georgetown, 9,468
Granger, 1,236
Kyle, 2,093
Leander, 2,179
Manor, 1,044
Rollingwood, 1,027
Round Rock, 11,812
San Marcos, 23,420
Taylor, 10,619
West Lake Hills, 2,166

Canton–Lake Tawakoni (Van Zandt County)

Canton, 2,845
Edgewood, 1,413
Fruitvale, 367
Grand Saline, 2,709
Van, 1,881
Wills Point, 2,631

Fredericksburg (Gillespie County)

Doss, 230
Fredericksburg, 6,412
Harper, 400

Kerrville (Kerr County)

Ingram, 1,000
Kerrville, 15,276

McALLEN–PHARR–EDINBURG (Hidalgo County)

Alamo, 5,831
Alton, 2,732
Donna, 9,952
Edcouch, 3,092
Edinburg, 24,075
Elsa, 5,061
Hidalgo, 2,288
La Joya, 2,018
McAllen, 66,281
Mercedes, 11,851
Mission, 22,589
Pharr, 21,381
San Juan, 7,608
Weslaco, 19,331

Rockport–Aransas Pass (Aransas County)

Aransas Pass, 7,173
Fulton, 725
Rockport, 3,686

SAN ANTONIO (Bexar, Comal, and Guadalupe counties)

Alamo Heights, 6,252
Balcones Heights, 2,511
Castle Hills, 4,773
Converse, 4,907

Hollywood Park, 3,231
Kirby, 6,385
Lackland AFB, 14,459
Leon Valley, 8,951
Live Oak, 8,183
New Braunfels, 22,402
Olmos Park, 2,069
San Antonio, 785,410
Schertz, 7,262
Seguin, 17,854
Shavano Park, 1,448
Terrell Hills, 4,644
Universal City, 10,720
Windcrest, 5,332

UTAH

St. George–Zion (Washington County)

Enterprise, 905
Hildale, 1,009
Hurricane, 2,361
Ivins, 600
La Verkin, 1,174
St. George, 11,350
Santa Clara, 1,091
Washington, 3,092

VERMONT

Bennington (Bennington County)

Arlington, 1,309
Bennington, 9,349
Manchester, 563
Manchester Center, 1,719
North Bennington, 1,635
Old Bennington, 353

Brattleboro (Windham County)

Bellows Falls, 3,456
Brattleboro, 8,596
Jacksonville, 252
North Westminster, 310
Saxtons River, 593
West Brattleboro, 2,795
Westminster, 319

VIRGINIA

CHARLOTTESVILLE (Charlottesville city; and Albemarle, Fluvanna, and Greene counties)

Charlottesville, 39,916
Commonwealth, 3,505
Crozet, 1,433
Hessian Hills, 4,103
Rio, 2,851
Scottsville, 250
Stanardsville, 284
University Heights, 6,736

Front Royal (Warren County)

Bentonville, 350
Front Royal, 11,126
Nineveh, 35
Riverton, 350

Rappahannock (Rappahannock County)

Amissville, 150
Chester Gap, 300
Flint Hill, 250
Sperryville, 200
Washington, 247

Winchester (Winchester city and Frederick County)

Brucetown, 200
Middletown, 841
Stephens City, 1,179
Sunnyside, 500
Winchester, 20,217

WASHINGTON

Oak Harbor (Island County)

Ault Field, 2,553
Coupeville, 1,006
Langley, 650
Oak Harbor, 12,271

OLYMPIA (Thurston County)

Lacey, 13,940
Olympia, 27,447
Tanglewilde-Thompson Place, 5,910
Tumwater, 6,705
Union Mills, 4,623
Yelm, 1,294

Port Angeles–Strait of Juan de Fuca (Clallam County)

Forks, 3,060
Port Angeles, 17,311
Port Angeles East, 2,786
Sequim, 3,013

WISCONSIN

Eagle River (Vilas County)

Arbor Vitae, 2,303
Boulder Junction 934
Conover, 826
Eagle River, 1,326
Lac du Flambeau, 2 190
Lincoln, 2,262
Manitowish Waters, 625
Phelps, 1,129
St. Germain, 1,176
Washington, 1,100

Rhinelander (Oneida County)

Cassian, 585
Crescent, 1,702
Hazelhurst, 780
Lake Tomahawk, 738
Minocqua, 3,328
Newbold, 2,171
Nokomis, 883
Pelican, 3,387
Pine Lake, 2,656
Rhinelander, 7,873
Stella, 489
Sugar Camp, 1,337
Three Lakes, 1,864
Woodboro, 547
Woodruff, 1,458

Source: U.S. Bureau of the Census, *1980 Census of Population* and *Rand McNally Commercial Atlas & Marketing Guide,* 1983.

List of Tables and Maps

ABOUT THE AUTHORS

Richard Boyer and David Savageau are authors of the best-selling *Places Rated Almanac.* The book, rating 277 American metropolitan areas for livability, has created much excitement and controversy. The authors have been featured on the *Today* show; they have also appeared on the *David Susskind Show,* the *CBS Evening News,* and *PM Magazine,* as well as numerous local television and radio programs.

Richard Boyer writes both fiction and nonfiction. In addition to co-authoring *Places Rated Almanac* and *Places Rated Retirement Guide,* he is author of three novels, including *Billingsgate Shoal* (awarded the Mystery Writers of America's Edgar award for Best Mystery Novel of 1982) and *The Penny Ferry,* to be published by Houghton Mifflin Company in the spring of 1984. Formerly of Chicago and Boston, Mr. Boyer, upon completion of *Places Rated Almanac,* followed the book's advice for selecting good places to live and now resides in Asheville, North Carolina.

David Savageau, since the publication of *Places Rated Almanac,* has made public appearances throughout the country discussing the inexhaustible topic of quality of life. Mr. Savageau is principal-in-charge of PreLOCATION, a personal relocation consulting firm based in Lynnfield, Massachusetts. Born in Denver, Colorado, a graduate of the University of Notre Dame, he resides in Gloucester, Massachusetts.